COMMUNAL SOCIETIES IN AMERICA
AN AMS REPRINT SERIES

THE REAL MORMONISM

AMS PRESS
NEW YORK

THE REAL MORMONISM

A Candid Analysis of an Interesting but Much Misunderstood Subject in History Life and Thought

BY
ROBERT C. WEBB

"It has always been a cardinal teaching with the Latter-day Saints, that a religion that has not the power to save people temporally and make them prosperous and happy here, cannot be depended upon to save them spiritually, and to exalt them in the life to come."

—Joseph F. Smith.

New York
STURGIS & WALTON
COMPANY
1916

Library of Congress Cataloging in Publication Data

Webb, Robert C.
The real Mormonism.

(Communal societies in America)
Reprint of the 1916 ed. published by Sturgis & Walton Co., New York.
Includes index.
1. Mormons and Mormonism. I. Title.
BX8635.W44 1975 289.3'3 72-2971
ISBN 0-404-10736-2

Reprinted from the edition of 1916, New York
First AMS edition published in 1975
Manufactured in the United States of America

AMS PRESS INC.
NEW YORK, N.Y. 10003

TO THE ILLUSTRIOUS MEMORY OF

JOSEPH SMITH

THE "MORMON PROPHET,"

who, in spite of the evil character and corrupt motives attributed to him by enemies, critics and fault-finders, stands revealed to the candid student of his career as an honest man, a deep thinker, a powerful leader, and a pre-eminent reformer, worthy to be classed with the great men of history, and deserving the respect and attention of honest and intelligent minds

TABLE OF CONTENTS

SECTION I — MORMONISM AND ITS FOUNDER.

CHAPTER I

THE MORMON PROBLEM

CHAPTER II

THE RIDDLE OF JOSEPH SMITH

CHAPTER III

THE COMING-FORTH OF THE BOOK OF MORMON

CHAPTER IV

THE BEGINNINGS OF MORMONISM

CHAPTER V

JOSEPH SMITH AS THE FIRST PROPHET, SEER AND REVELATOR

CHAPTER VI

JOSEPH SMITH AS LAWGIVER AND EXECUTIVE

CHAPTER VII

JOSEPH SMITH AS A STATESMAN AND REFORMER

CHAPTER XI

THE PRACTICAL WORKINGS OF MORMONISM

CHAPTER XII

THE MORAL RECORD OF THE MORMON PEOPLE

SECTION III — THE TEACHINGS OF MORMONISM.

CHAPTER XIII

THE THEOLOGY OF MORMONISM

SECTION V — THE MORMON ORGANIZATION.

CHAPTER XX

THE ORGANIZATION OF THE MORMON CHURCH

CHAPTER XXI

"AUXILIARY ORGANIZATIONS"

SECTION VI — TRUTH. JUSTICE AND MORMONISM.

CHAPTER XXII

ANTI-MORMON ACCUSATIONS

CHAPTER XXIII

THE ALLEGED POLITICAL ACTIVITIES OF THE MORMON AUTHORITIES

CHAPTER XXIV

HOW JUSTICE WAS DONE IN THE MORMON COUNTRY

CHAPTER XXV

A SHELTER FOR THE "ERRING AND OPPRESSED"

SECTION VII — ANTI-MORMON EXPLANATIONS.

CHAPTER XXVI

WAS JOSEPH SMITH AN EPILEPTIC?

CHAPTER XXVII

DID SOLOMON SPAULDING WRITE THE BOOK OF MORMON?

CHAPTER XXVIII

WAS THE BOOK OF MORMON PRODUCED BY "AUTOMATIC WRITING?"

I

MORMONISM AND ITS FOUNDER

"If the reader does not know what to make of Joseph Smith, I cannot help him out of the difficulty. I myself stand helpless before the puzzle."—*Josiah Quincy.*

THE REAL MORMONISM

CHAPTER I

THE MORMON PROBLEM

THE name Mormonism is the popular designation for the system of religious doctrine and practice founded on the teachings of Joseph Smith (1805–1844), who claimed a divinely revealed authority to restore the Gospel of Christ in its original purity, which, as he asserted, had been lost and obscured through centuries of apostasy among Christian people. Although not officially recognized by his disciples — they call their organization the Church of Jesus Christ of Latter-day Saints, in distinction from the "Former-day Saints," or the Church of the time of Christ's apostles — the term has the authority of sufficient good usage to warrant us in retaining it, in preference to the longer title. Hence, following the rooted habit of over three-score years and ten, we will in the present book speak of Mormonism and Mormons, without marks of quotation; remarking, however, that no more disrespect or opprobrium attaches to the use of these words than to that of such analogous epithets as Quakers, Swedenborgians, Wesleyans or Papists.

The title or epithet, Mormon, derives from a prophet and important personage of that name, who, as is claimed, lived anciently on the American Continent, and was largely instrumental in compiling the records of his people — they were known as Nephites — and of God's dealings with them, into the collection of documents, now known as the Book of Mormon. This record, inscribed on "plates resembling gold," was, it is claimed, delivered to Joseph Smith by an angel named Moroni, who during his earth life was the son of Mormon. Translated by Joseph Smith, "through the gift and power of God," it furnishes a recognized inspired scripture for the church founded by him. Hence his disciples were known, first as "Mormonites," later as "Mormons."

Mormonism is a system of large things. It is large in claims, large in efforts, large in results, large in reputation, and very large in importance, if judged by the opposition it has evoked. Like the man through whom it had origin, it possesses an individuality that is intense and vital: it repels and attracts with equal force. One finds difficulty in maintaining a perfectly neutral position in treating of its claims and history.

Like all else in this world, however, both great and small, good or evil, it has its own side of the matters with which it is concerned, and deserves pure, simple justice, if nothing more. But justice it has never received. Anti-Mormon agitators seem to have been literally blinded to the fact that, when not exaggerating weaknesses common to all humanity, they have accused the Mormons of crimes and vices all but preposterous. The average writer on Mormonism and its founder, as if with deliberation, has given the worst possible construction to every fact of its history, teaching and practice; has greedily accepted and aided in the further publicity of all accusations of evil-doing brought against this Church and people by their enemies; has accepted as sufficient authorities on all Mormon teachings and beliefs the statements of persons who, by their own acknowledgment, are violently prejudiced — hence liable to misinterpret or distort opinions and beliefs; and in no case do we find such writers even attempting to understand the Mormon "point of view," in order to criticize and condemn, if at all, on a full show of evidence and with intelligence and righteousness. By such procedures on the part of their self-styled "candid critics" Mormonism has been placed in the anomalous position of a cause suffering, as it is stated, for the sake of conscience, at the hands of those who plead conscience for their violence and injustice; and, in the rôle of a martyr for human liberty, oppressed by the people of a nation, which of all others on earth boasts the most proudly of its liberties and toleration.

From the very moment of its birth, when it had no humanly visible prospect of ever being a "menace," as alleged, to anything, the Mormon Church has been an object of persecution. Its success in making converts was the first occasion against it on the part of various sectarian missionaries and pastors. Even in that day of fierce theological debate these people laid aside their internecine strife to make common cause against this new opponent, who urged large claims and had the courage of conviction. Their pulpit efforts, undoubtedly redolent of things other than "pure theology," persuaded the populace that the Mormons were not only heretics, but also brigands, and the probable perpetrators of all the thefts and murders, so common to the frontier life of the time. Several of these "clergymen," notably a certain Bogart, a certain Sashiel Woods, a certain

Williams, and a certain Brockman, appeared as active inciters and leaders of mobs, which on several occasions inflicted grievous violence on these people, including even the murder of women and children.

We should remember, however, that both mob violence and acrimonious strife were mere commonplaces in the life of the times, and were active against others than Mormons,— notably against Catholics, Abolitionists, alleged "claim-jumpers" and horse-thieves, also against many people innocent of all offense. Had the Mormons escaped, we might have credited their immunity to an actual "miraculous interposition." That they did not escape seems to have been inevitable.

Mormonism, conspicuously suffering from the baleful effects of epidemic hysteria, whether fostered by accredited pulpiteers or mere "wanton gospelers," has been the instrument of demonstrating that, in spite of our boasted culture and advancement, in spite of our intelligence and civilization, the spirit of persecution is not yet dead. That similar conclusions have been reached by prominent and well-informed people is indicated by the following from a speech of Judge Jeremiah S. Black before the Committee on Territories of the United States Senate.

> "By some famous preachers the policy of killing the Mormons by wholesale, unless they leave their property, abandon their homes, and flee beyond the Union, is openly advocated and apparently concurred in with great warmth by congregations supposed to be respectable; and this is accompanied with curses loud and deep upon all who would interpose a constitutional objection to that method of dealing with them. When we read of such things in history, we are apt to think them diabolical. But, approved as they are now and here by popular judgment, and unrebuked even by senatorial wisdom, we must concede, I suppose, that it is very good taste and refined humanity disguised in a new dress.
>
> As a general rule, political piety, wherever it has turned up the whites of its eyes in this country or in Europe, is a sham and a false pretense, but in this exceptional case it would be speaking evil of dignities to call it hypocrisy. The soundness of a religion which slanders a Mormon is not to be questioned. Equally pure is the act of a returning officer who fraudulently certifies the election of an anti-Mormon candidate known to be defeated by a majority of more than fifteen to one, nor will we attribute any sordid motive to those residents of Utah, official and private, who busy themselves here and at home to break down the Territorial government, seize its offices, and grab its money.
>
> Their righteous souls are vexed from day to day by the mere fact that sinful men are allowed to live peaceful and prosperous lives. They are animated solely by disinterested zeal for the advancement of the Lord's Kingdom, which in their judgment would be much obstructed by the further continuance of free goverment in Utah.—*Federal Jurisdiction in the Territories, p.* 5.

Judge Black's statements in this particular may be held to have such weight as can be derived from the careful examination of a subject by a learned and experienced judge and advocate. Since, as he strongly suggests, anti-Mormon agitators have been inconsistent with the traditions of freedom and equal rights, the Mormons, suffering from their onslaughts, have been the real champions of American institutions. Says R. W. Sloan, a Mormon writer:

> "It has been the claim of the Latter-day Saints that in making a defense in their own behalf they have been fighting for liberty in behalf of all men. At first blush this claim seems presumptuous. But if it be examined closely there will be found much to justify the assumption. Not that they have courted the assaults made upon them; but as a peculiarity of their history, no action against them, either by lawless mobs or through legal means, has ever been taken that was not in violation of some principle dear to every liberty-loving heart. Thus, in defending themselves, they have stood manfully for principles that must endure forever, and which, violated even as a temporary expedient, or in response to 'the tyrant's devilish plea'— necessity — bring unerring retribution when turned from their natural purpose. . . .
>
> "It is because of this phase that Mormonism has become known as a 'vexed problem'; because of this also that men possessed of instinctive statesmanship have never touched the problem. But we do find those of vulpine sagacity — madly protesting, despite the experience of all times, temporary evil to be justifiable that worse may not survive, and that such a departure from good will be in the cause of good. . . . It was on this plea — a temporarv evil on behalf of permanent good — that the advocates of this policy urged the adoption of measures against the Mormons by Congress."— *The Great Contest, p.* 1.

It is difficult to believe that the American people and the American Government, pledged as they are to safeguarding the rights of humanity at large, should have wittingly perpetrated such injustices as the Mormons have suffered. Says the Hon. Ambrose B. Carlton:

> "I wish deliberately to record my opinion that the Mormons have been worse misrepresented and lied about than any people I have ever met. Lies about them have been made out of whole cloth; venial faults and weaknesses have been magnified into gross and monstrous offenses, and innocent or indifferent actions have been misinterpreted.
>
> "I have been an eye-witness to transactions, in which the Mormons were cruelly and outrageously abused for conduct that was just and honorable. I have read what purported to be Mormon sermons, that were purely fictitious; one in particular, a very few years ago, a brutal, bloodthirsty, disloyal harangue, alleged to have been delivered by 'Bishop West of Juab,' on a certain day, whereas in truth and in fact no such sermon had been delivered at any time or place, and it was acknowledged afterwards to be a pure and simple fabrication; but not until it had gone abroad as evidence of the disloyalty of the Mormons.
>
> "Every now and then lies are set afloat that the Mormons are about to rise in armed insurrection; when, in truth, I can say after nearly seven years' observation, that there is no community on the civilized globe less liable than the Mormons to take up arms against the government. Polygamy aside, the Mormons have been more sinned against than sinning."
> — *Wonderlands of the Wild West, p.* 151.

Judge Carlton was chairman of the Utah Commission, appointed under the provisions of the Edmunds Law, and sent to Utah in 1882. Although opposed to plural marriage on principle, he was otherwise fair to the Mormons, as will be shown later by other quotations from his writings.

It may be difficult to comprehend the surprising state of affairs set forth in the foregoing quotations. In view, however, of the fact that anti-Mormon persecutions date from the very birth of the Mormon Church, the explanation offered by Charles Ellis, a former clergyman residing in Utah, who wrote considerably in defense of Mormonism, although he never joined the Church, may be accepted tentatively. Says Mr. Ellis:

> "From its appearance, Mormonism has been hated by the evangelical sects as a heresy. The cry against its polygamy, as being a danger to society, and the cry against its priesthood, as being a danger to the government, have never been more than a subterfuge, the object being to detract attention from the real fight, which was to destroy the Mormon heresy. This statement will bear full investigation. . . . Why has Mormonism been so much misunderstood? Simply because the evangelical churches saw in its success their own downfall and they dared not let their own followers know what Mormonism was, lest they should embrace it.
>
> "As compared with the evangelical conception of life here and hereafter, of God and the glories of immortality, Mormonism is as a Rocky-Mountain day in May compared to a New England day in March, when the wind is east and the sun is veiled. Such being the case, it may be readily understood that an investigation of early Mormon history in Utah will reveal a very different spirit from that which has been talked about, and written and preached against in the east for nearly half a century." — *Utah, 1847 to 1870, p. 5.*

A sufficiently large number of the stock allegations urged against the Mormon Church and people will be discussed and analyzed on later pages. It would be, consequently, both unnecessary and unprofitable to give them here. We are concerned most particularly with such an analysis and discussion of the system and its claims as will enable the reader to derive an intelligent idea of an object of so much detestation, and, possibly also, some of the reasons why it has been so much detested.

In the first place, Mormonism claims to be a religious system — furthermore a Christian system of belief and practice — and bases its first and strongest appeal on the profession that it is the true, original Gospel of Christ, perfectly restored on earth after the apostasy of the whole of the "Christian world," because of traditions that have "made God's law of none effect." In making even so radical a claim as this the system is not perfectly unique: its assertion seems to hark back to "reformation" times, indeed, and to savor of a spirit of confidence that has, whether rightly or wrongly, inspired the promulgators and founders of several antecedent sects and systems. Why it is materially worse in Joseph Smith to promulgate a new system of thought and practice, or to interpret the Word of God anew, than the same attempt in John Calvin, Martin Luther, or any other "reformer" or leader, is a question that should logically occur to the candid and unbiassed mind. To answer in the words of his opponents that he was a man of contemptible character, a drunkard, imposter and self-interested exploiter of credulity, also an ignoramus or an "epileptic," is evidently no answer at all; since persons possessing the shortcomings and afflictions in question are not the most likely to accomplish memorable results, even with the best efforts. Furthermore, the most highly esteemed founders of sects and systems in the past — even the vigorous and intrepid Luther, or the gloomy and intellectual Calvin — seem, all of them, to have labored under the handicaps of serious personal faults and failings, oftentimes quite as serious as even the drunkenness and ignorance alleged against Joseph Smith. But, quite apart from all personal considerations, the ideas and beliefs promulgated by any of these men must be judged according to their consistency with reason, Scripture, or other accepted standard of authority, and recommended or rejected accordingly. Since Joseph Smith was also a man, one possessed, presumably, of several of the virtues and failings common to humanity, there can be alleged no sufficient reason for dealing with him by any other method. If the ideas which he originated, or promulgated, or which were originated, as some have alleged, by certain of his associates, are found to be unworthy of serious consideration, we must recognize that he was only another among the host of "guessers," who have confidently announced themselves as "solvers" of the "great problem" of life. If his teachings contain aught that is worthy or excellent, it is no more than just that he should be given credit as a vigorous and independent thinker and leader — even though one may not feel constrained to accept his leadership — and that, quite apart from the failings of character and conduct that he may have manifested at any period of his life. The same candid and honest spirit of investigation has been invoked in dealing with the teachings of all the ancient and "heathen" sages and teachers; nor is there any good reason why the system popularly known as "Mormonism" should be ignored and misrepresented by people otherwise supposed to be intelligent. Even though Smith claimed to have received "revelations" from the Almighty — and many people believe that this is impossible, nowadays at least — it is a highly reasonable act to examine his utterances and history, in order to found a just estimate on his character and influence than merely to dwell on the often ribald accusations of unknown and irresponsible "old neighbors" and "prominent citizens," whose accusations against him and his family form the bulk of the case against Mormonism.

It may be proper to state at this point that, on the basis of an exhaustive and prolonged study of Joseph Smith and of the system founded by him, the writer of the present work is convinced that both deserve better of the world than they have as yet received; that there is an immense amount of the greatest value, to both thought and life, in the teachings of Mormonism, and that, whether an inspired prophet of God, or not, Joseph Smith is entitled to his place, and a conspicuous one at that, among historic thinkers, leaders and reformers. In spite of the dense ignorance and venal character alleged against him, he interpreted the religious life in an entirely new, and decidedly notable light; he dealt with the historic dilemma of "faith and works" in a manner that cannot but excite the admiration of the candid and informed reader; he handled the problems of life in a manner that showed the master-mind; finally, he originated a system of social and community organization that is of the highest significance to sociological theory, as the first of its kind attempting to deal with the "problems" of human life that really seems to solve them rationally, and, at the same time, to possess any of the elements of permanence and efficiency. Surely, the historic originator of all this — whether "inspired" or not, or whether assisted by others or not — deserves earnest and careful attention, and the best efforts of which the investigator is capable, in order to unravel his significance to the world and to the history of thought.

CHAPTER II

THE RIDDLE OF JOSEPH SMITH

THE name of Joseph Smith, founder of Mormonism and professed prophet of God, is destined, doubtless, as was said to him in one of his reported visions, to "be good and evil spoken of among all peoples." Apart from anything that may inspire respect or evoke mistrust, moving one to admire or dislike him, he remains one of the most romantic figures in history, also, perhaps, one of the most problematical. Although born of simple-minded and largely unlettered parents and reared in a wilderness, with only moderate educational advantages, his first appearance before the world is in the rôle of leader and teacher of religion, and the promulgator of a system of doctrine and life that is at once intelligent, logical, practical and persistent. His personality was such that it lent cogency to his teachings, and his teachings have been accepted by thousands, who still hold his name in reverence and endorse his every profession to a divine mission in the world.

Few men have been worse hated, on the one hand, or more thoroughly beloved on the other, in all the world's history. It seems strange, indeed, that a man of inconspicuous origin and defective worldly advantages, "a youth to fortune and to fame unknown," should have appeared so near to our own time to play such a part, and to win such distinguished regard. To the fair-minded student of his career Joseph Smith must appear as a veritable riddle, a character not readily to be estimated at its full value, because evidently so many-sided, so versatile and so forceful. If it is difficult for any of us to understand the "secret of his influence," the reason for the lofty reverence of his followers, it must be equally difficult to comprehend the superlative bitterness of his enemies, particularly if we be asked to countenance or justify the deliberate lies that they have told about him and the savage truculence with which they have opposed him and his followers.

The personality of Joseph Smith, which those who knew him, as friends and sympathizers, describe as wonderfully magnetic and masterful, evidently possessing power and exerting influence, is characterized by others as "uncouth," "awkward," "vulgar" and otherwise disagreeable. Thus, this man who could command the devotion of thousands of sane and normal people, not only in days of calm prosperity, but in the midst of hardship and persecution — yet some people will tell us that many of Smith's disciples were attracted by the prospects of material benefits, not otherwise available to them — is represented to the intelligent public as some sort of buffoon or wholesale "confidence man." Such representations are familiar in the several "testimonies" of anonymous "ladies" and "gentlemen," who seem to vie with the affidaviting "old neighbors" and "prominent citizens," none of whom figure very largely in history — unless, as asserted, a few were "revolutionary soldiers"— in making descriptions which do not describe. Among such is the often-quoted "Girl's Letter from Nauvoo," which contains the following:

> "Joseph Smith is a large, stout man, youthful in his appearance, with light complexion and hair, and blue eyes set far back in the head, and expressing great shrewdness, or I should say, cunning. He has a large head, and phrenologists would unhesitatingly pronounce it a bad one, for the organs situated in the back part are decidedly more prominent. He is also very round shouldered. He had just returned from Springfield, where he had been upon trial for some crime of which he was accused while in Missouri, but he was released by habeas corpus. I, who had expected to be overwhelmed by his eloquence, was never more disappointed than when he commenced his discourse by relating all the incidents of his journey. This he did in a loud voice, and his language and manner were the coarsest possible. His object seemed to be to amuse and excite laughter in his audience. He is evidently a great egotist and boaster, for he frequently remarked that at every place he stopped, going to and from Springfield, people crowded around him, and expressed surprise that he was so 'handsome and good looking.' He also exclaimed at the close of almost every sentence, 'That's the idea!'"

Although the maidenly prejudices and phrenological predilections of this "girl" have evidently led her to discount the abilities of Mr. Smith, it is necessary to remark only that most of his published discourses seem to be of a far different character from the one presumably heard on this occasion. It must be refreshing, however, to the candid reader of the present day to learn that Mr. Smith possessed sufficient sense of humor to appreciate the absurdity of many of the so-called legal proceedings that were brought against him. That he described them in the humorous language suggested in this passage is scarcely remarkable. His critic was evidently deficient in ability to comprehend some situations.

Compared with the common run of estimates and incidents regarding this man's personality and character, we have the famous account written by Josiah Quincy, son of the famous Josiah Quincy, and, himself, at one time, Mayor of Boston, which is competent in evidence to show how Smith affected a really intelligent and experienced mind. It is partly as follows:

"It is by no means improbable that some future text book, for the use of generations yet unborn, will contain a question something like this: What historical American of the nineteenth century has exerted the most powerful influence upon the destinies of his countrymen? And it is by no means impossible that the answer to that interrogatory may be thus written: *Joseph Smith, the Mormon Prophet.* And the reply, absurd as it doubtless seems to most men now living, may be an obvious common-place to their descendants. History deals in surprises and paradoxes quite as startling as this. The man who established a religion in this age of free debate, who was and is to-day accepted by hundreds of thousands as a direct emissary from the Most High — such a rare human being is not to be disposed of by pelting his memory with unsavory epithets. Fanatic, imposter, charlatan, he may have been; but these hard names furnish no solution to the problem he presents to us. Fanatics and imposters are living and dying every day, and their memory is buried with them; but the wonderful influence which this founder of a religion exerted and still exerts throws him into relief before us, *not as a rogue to be criminated, but as a phenomenon to be explained.* The most vital questions Americans are asking each other to-day have to do with this man and what he has left us. . . . A generation other than mine must deal with these questions. Burning questions they are, which must give a prominent place in the history of the country to that sturdy self-asserter whom I visited at Nauvoo."—*Figures of the Past, p.* 367.

Although Mr. Quincy states at another place, that Smith "mingled Utopian fallacies with his shrewd suggestions," many of which he was compelled to endorse in the highest terms, and that "he talked as from a strong mind utterly unenlightened by the teachings of history," he concludes, as follows:

"Born in the lowest ranks of poverty, without book-learning and with the homeliest of all human names, he had made himself at the age of thirty-nine a power upon earth. Of the multitudinous family of Smith, from Adam down (Adam of the *Wealth of Nations,* I mean), none had so won human hearts and shaped human lives as this Joseph. His influence, whether for good or for evil, is potent to-day, and the end is not yet. I have endeavored to give the details of my visit to the Mormon Prophet with absolute accuracy. If the reader does not know just what to make of Joseph Smith, I cannot help him out of the difficulty. I myself stand helpless before the puzzle."

We may be prepared, then, for the statement that a careful study of Smith's life and work, such as would be cheerfully accorded to any other character in history — and even Judas Iscariot has had his defenders — will reveal the surprising fact that, where many writers have found only a vulgar and corrupt charlatan, we shall discern a born leader of men, one possessed of force and intellect, a real reformer along several lines, a thorough student of the Bible, and a teacher of religion, morals, sociology and government with a real message, who evidently attempted to justify his every claim to the intelligence of mankind.

At the very beginning of our study we find a host of alleged "affidavits" embodying the familiar traditional accusations against Joseph Smith and all his family, alleging depravity of several orders, both ordinary and extraordinary, which are "swallowed whole, hair, hide and hoofs," in spite of various inconsistencies and irrelevancies, by the average critic and "student" of Mormonism. Thus, in the words of one Pomeroy Tucker, who has been largely quoted by all subsequent "investigators," we learn that:

> "At this period in the life and career of Joseph Smith, Jr., or Joe Smith, as he was universally named, and the Smith family, they were popularly regarded as an illiterate, whiskey-drinking, shiftless, irreligious race of people — the first named, the chief subject of this biography, being unanimously voted the laziest and most worthless of the generation. From the age of twelve to twenty years he is distinctly remembered as a dull-eyed, flaxen-haired, prevaricating boy — noted only for his indolent and vagabondish character, and his habits of exaggeration and untruthfulness."

Admitting fully the genuineness of the "testimony" upon which these statements are based, its competence is not established — things "unanimously voted" and "distinctly remembered" in this way are not always the justest and most intelligent things that may be said of people. We must remember, also, that, had Smith become a poet, artist or writer of fiction, or even a conspicuous figure in any other walk of life than that which he selected, he would have been remembered as a "dreamy and introspective boy," instead of one possessing an "indolent and vagabondish character." If we may judge from the careers and characters of many of the people noted in these other "walks," we must understand that the variant estimates in the two cases, as explained, indicate differing "animus" in the witnesses, rather than differing conditions in the environments and characters of the subjects. As for the remarks on "illiterate, whiskey-drinking, shiftless" parents, whatever may have been the real facts in the present case, the "cloven foot" of slanderous rural gossip is only too plainly evident. We should have expected to hear that Smith's father had been a notorious housebreaker, highwayman or horse-thief, instead of merely illiterate and shiftless. A man of such a character would, very probably, have been of a grade of intelligence and energy likely to beget a son capable of engineering "hoaxes." To ask the public to believe that a merely worthless and indolent father can account for such a movement as Mormonism is only to insult intelligence, and betray one's own spite, ignorance and credulity. Of very similar value are most of the "affidavits" presented by Howe, Tucker, and others. Of these the following is a good sample:

"We, the undersigned, being personally acquainted with the family of Joseph Smith, Sr., with whom the Gold Bible, so called, originated, state: That they were not only a lazy, indolent set of men, but also intemperate, and their word was not to be depended upon; and that we are truly glad to dispense with their society."

Eleven "prominent citizens of Manchester" apparently swore to this "instrument," thus guaranteeing its truth "to the best of their knowledge and belief," but why any man sufficiently intelligent to write a grammatically-constructed book should consider it worth quoting as authority is very nearly incomprehensible. Without attempting to clear the characters of Joseph Smith, or those of any of his family, we must protest that the futility of such testimony is amply demonstrated in the fact that it never attempts to make really serious criminal charges, and is to be discredited as mere "railing accusation."

Nor, in protesting against this kind of "testimony" can we be justly charged with partiality: we complain only because we hear nothing worse, something colossal, enterprising and really depraved. In view of the results achieved by him, we are bound tc recognize in Joseph Smith a really exceptional man, one worthy to rank far above the average of his associates in point of native abilities. If he was altogether evil, therefore, an "imposter," demagogue and self-seeking scoundrel, he must certainly have been more than merely idle and drunken in his youth. But, here we have no more serious accusations than he himself pleads guilty to, when, as he says in his journal, he fell into "many foolish errors, and displayed the weakness of youth, and the foibles of human nature, offensive in the sight of God." He had the grace, at least, to acknowledge such shortcomings as may have been committed by him: nor does he offer excuses or "explanations."

Apart from the evident reasonableness of such a line of criticism, it is only just to say that the allegations of superlative worthlessness made against the family of Joseph Smith are entirely unproven by any decent show of evidence. The behavior of his parents and brothers in after-life shows no signs of the faults so confidently stated in the affidavits of "old neighbors" and "prominent citizens," who evidently follow the prevalent uncharity of judgment in ascribing poverty and business incapacity to "shiftlessness, whiskey-drinking and general worthlessness of character." Such allegations, however, have played their full part in prejudicing the mind of the public against Mr. Smith, as a man of "humble origin and unfortunate early influences," who has presumed to rise above the level in which he originated. It is curious that such handicaps, which, if present, should rather excite the compassion of generous and informed minds, should become occasions for violent abuse and denunciation from the preachers of religion and the intelligent public in general in a nation, theoretically, at least, emancipated from the sickening traditions of hereditary aristocracy. In Smith's case, this unworthy line of criticism has been carried to a disgusting extreme.

Perfectly similarly, we read in several anti-Smith productions that he himself was so given to over-indulgence in alcoholic drinks that "even his own followers admit" the fault. Careful search among the published statements of his "followers" reveals no such admission, even by implication, except in a remark ascribed to Martin Harris, and his would-be accusers, clerical and literary, have forgotten to give the references. It is quite certain, however, that had Mr. Smith been addicted to the excessive use of alcohol from his youth onward, he would probably have shown its effects in some definite impairment of his energies, and certainly in defective courage to face the truculent assaults of enemies, directed, as they were, by intelligent and relentless leaders.

In the case of Joseph Smith, as may be claimed with some show of reason, there is no element or motive that explains his career quite so well as his sufficient and unfailing belief in the reality of his authority to teach and preach in the name of God. This involves, of course, a sufficient belief in his own mind in the reality of the several visions and revelations which he claims to have had. Nor is it essential to our argument that we determine, theoretically at least, what was, or probably must have been the real nature of the various experiences, which Joseph Smith attributed to direct divine agency. The entire course of his life certainly furnishes an excellent argument for the conclusion that he himself believed implicitly and firmly in their reality and authority. It seems safe, then, to assert with confidence that, whether dreams, delusions or actualities, they played their full part in stimulating a mind whose products have valuably enlightened the world in several important particulars, as will be explained later. If they be held to have been of purely pathological import, as has been suggested by one or two slovenly theorizers, the fact still remains that the consequent productions of the mind of Mr. Smith, stimulated by a conviction of their reality and divine authority, are positively not characterized by any pathological element whatever; being rather admirable and highly practical solutions of sociological, moral and religious difficulties, which have defied the ingenuity of thinkers and religionists of other persuasions to this very day. If, finally, for the mere sake of gratifying sundry critics who talk more than they think or investigate, we assume that Smith's reported visions and revelations were deliberate fictions, we cannot escape the conclusion that, in his speech and actions, he displayed a masterly imitation of real conviction; thus adding excellent histrionic ability to his other talents. It has been said that a falsehood persistently told presently assumes the symptoms of reality in the falsifier's mind. Such alleged fact, however, cannot vitiate the evident conclusion that the several excellent institutions, ecclesiastical and otherwise, devised, or promulgated, by this same person, seem altogether more perfect than anything that should be demanded, in all propriety, to lend mere verisimilitude to an original misrepresentation. We make Mr. Smith work altogether too hard and too well, if we assume merely that all these things were done to uphold the alleged truth of a fable that had been already so eagerly accepted by hundreds of people on his simple word of mouth.

The following passages give the account of Joseph Smith's professed experiences in his own words:

"Some time in the second year after our removal to Manchester, there was in the place where we lived an unusual excitement on the subject of religion. It commenced with the Methodists, but soon became general among all the sects in that region of the country. Indeed, the whole district of country seemed affected by it, and great multitudes united themselves to the different religious parties, which created no small stir and division amongst the people, some crying, 'Lo, here!' and others, 'Lo, there!' Some were contending for the Methodist faith, some for the Presbyterian, and some for the Baptist. For notwithstanding the great love which the converts to these different faiths expressed at the time of their conversion, and the great zeal manifested by the respective clergy, who were active in getting up and promoting this extraordinary scene of religious feeling, in order to have everybody converted, as they were pleased to call it, let them join what sect they pleased—yet when the converts began to file off, some to one party and some to another, it was seen that the seemingly good feelings of both the priests and the converts were more pretended than real; for a scene of great confusion and bad feeling ensued; priest contending against priest, and convert against convert; so that all their good feelings one for another, if they ever had any, were entirely lost in a strife of words and a contest about opinions.

"I was at this time in my fifteenth year. My father's family was proselyted to the Presbyterian faith, and four of them joined that church, namely—my mother Lucy; my brothers Hyrum and Samuel Harrison; and my sister Sophronia. During this time of great excitement, my mind was called up to serious reflection and great uneasiness; but though my feelings were deep and often poignant, still I kept myself aloof from all these parties, though I attended their several meetings as often as occasion would permit. In process of time my mind became somewhat partial to the Methodist sect, and I felt some desire to be united with them; but so great were the confusion and strife among the different denominations, that it was impossible for a person young as I was, and so unacquainted with men and things, to come to any certain conclusion who was right and who was wrong. My mind at times was greatly excited, the cry and tumult were so great and incessant. The Presbyterians were most decided against the Baptists and Methodists, and used all the powers of both reason and sophistry to prove their errors, or, at least, to make the people think they were in error. On the other hand, the Baptists and Methodists in their turn were equally zealous in endeavoring to establish their own tenets and disprove all others,"—*History of the Church, Vol.* I, *pp.* 2-4.

In reading this passage one cannot doubt that it gives a faithful picture of the times (1820), both in the sectarian quarrels and in the mental perturbations likely to occur in young persons of susceptible organization. In fact, we have no reason whatever for doubting that such were the actual experiences of the youthful Smith, and that he records them truthfully. He further records that he determined to put his doubts to the test of Scriptural authority, which was another thing largely done at that period, and that, in the course of his readings, he came upon the passage (James I.5) "If any of you lack wisdom, let him ask of God . . . and it shall be given him." So stirred was he by this admonition, he records, that he determined to put it to the test. The results may be best explained in his own words. In the same narration previously quoted, he proceeds with the following:

"After I had retired to the place where I had previously designed to go, having looked around me, and finding myself alone, I kneeled down and began to offer up the desires of my heart to God. I had scarcely done so, when immediately I was seized upon by some power which entirely overcame me, and had such an astonishing influence over me as to bind my tongue so that I could not speak. Thick darkness gathered around me, and it seemed to me for a time as if I were doomed to sudden destruction. But, exerting all my powers to call upon God to deliver me out of the power of this enemy which had seized upon me, and at the very moment when I was ready to sink into despair and abandon myself to destruction—not to an imaginary ruin, but to the power of some actual being from the unseen world, who had such marvelous power as I had never before felt in any being—just at this moment of great alarm, I saw a pillar of light exactly over my head, above the brightness of the sun, which descended gradually until it fell upon me.

"It no sooner appeared than I found myself delivered from the enemy which held me bound. When the light rested upon me I saw two personages, whose brightness and glory defy all description, standing above me in the air. One of them spake unto me, calling me by name, and said, pointing to the other—'This is my beloved son, hear him.'

"My object in going to inquire of the Lord was to know which of all the sects was right, that I might know which to join. No sooner, therefore, did I get possession of myself, so as to be able to speak, than I asked the personages who stood above me in the light, which of all the sects was right—and which I should join. I was answered that I must join none of them, for they were all wrong, and the personage who addressed me said that all their creeds were an abomination in His sight: that those professors were all corrupt: that 'they draw near to me with their lips, but their hearts are far from me; they teach for doctrines the commandments of men: having a form of godliness, but they deny the power thereof.' He again forbade me to join with any of them: and many other things did he say unto me, which I cannot write at this time. When I came to myself again, I found myself lying on my back, looking up into heaven. When the light had departed, I had no strength; but soon recovering in some degree, I went home."—*Ibid. pp.* 5–6.

As might have been expected, the report of this vision by the youthful seer gained very slight credence, except with the members of his own family. To his neighbors, of course, he could seem to be nothing other than a victim of delusion, and worse than that, of diabolical delusion, or obsession. Nor did it occur to any of them to make mere sport of the young man's professions—a saving sense of humor seems never to have been possessed by any of Smith's detractors—and, as a consequence, their treatment of him partook of a childish brutality that seems in no way less absurd than the most exaggerated claims that he could have ventured to make. Thus, as he records, his narration of his vision to one of the most active of the revivalist Methodist preachers, instead of some pious attempt to exorcise the "delusion," was met with "a great deal of contempt." Smith adds also: "I soon found that my telling the story had excited a great deal of prejudice against me among the professors of religion, and was the cause of great persecution, which continued to increase; and though I was an obscure boy, only between fourteen and fifteen years of age, and my circumstances of life such as to make a boy of no consequence in the world, yet men of standing would take notice sufficient to excite the public mind against me, and create a bitter persecution; and this was common among all sects—all united to persecute me."

However "improbable" such a condition of affairs might seem to the casual reader, one must not forget that it forms an eminently fitting start for the bitter persecutions always visited upon Smith. It is also of a part with the religious persecutions of all ages. Their nature has ever been essentially cowardly, visiting "righteous wrath" upon the weak, the ignorant and the dependent, and reaching to the influential and powerful only exceptionally. As in the reign of "Bloody Mary" of England, as is recorded, it was principally the mean, poor and humble "victims of error" that were selected in the majority of cases for the distinction of martyrdom: very few of the "ringleaders of heresy," comparatively speaking, were "brought to justice." Undoubtedly Smith's report that he had "learned for himself that Presbyterianism is not true," and that all the sects "were all wrong," must have stirred the antagonism of the clergy, particularly, as would seem probable, the youth persisted in telling the story to all who would listen. But it seems strange, indeed, that his narrations should have been received in such a spirit of bitterness, particularly since, as he reminds us, he was "an obscure boy, only between fourteen and fifteen years of age." We seem to have some explanation of the origin of the confidently circulated stories of his youthful worthlessness and depravity, as reproduced by several "authorities": the two parts of the story — his account and the affidavits of "prominent citizens"— seem to belong together.

In the consideration of Smith's reported experience, we must not overlook the readily-verifiable fact that, whether real or unreal, its professed nature and details are quite of a kind with the experiences claimed by numerous others in all ages. Nor need we cite examples of notable and prominent historic personages. The visions of angels, of the departed, of evil spirits, even of the Saviour himself, seem to have been reported and tolerated among the religious, even to this very day. No less a Puritan authority than Increase Mather records numerous cases of "apparitions" in his book, *Remarkable Providences,* and distinctly states that he believed them both possible and frequent. Also in the literature of "wonderful conversions," so popular until within a generation since, we will find numerous cases of such experiences, alleged by persons who were led, seemingly, through such instrumentality, to adopt the Christian life. Now it is an angelic visitant that rebukes the sinner and warns him to repent "ere it is too late"; now, it is a "glorious personage," probably believed to be the Saviour himself, that calls to a special mission for the kingdom of God; again, it is by an "audible voice" that certain eminent Christian people claim to have been called to a "better life." As we may find, also, in the literature of "psychical research," so-called, the numerous and constantly recurring accounts of apparitions, particularly of the deceased, are accepted as evidence of "something not perfectly understood." Whatever may be the explanation of such experiences — since they seem to be sufficiently numerous and sufficiently vivid to avoid the suspicion of either fabrication, on the one hand, or of mere derangement of the senses, on the other — it is quite certain that their acceptance involves no violation of the principles accepted among the pious. The assertion that such visions, as well as other "gifts" and marks of divine favor, are no longer "vouchsafed" seems rather an evidence of growing "scepticism" among the clergy, or of a fear lest the Evil One uses such means to "deceive unwary souls," than the statement of a principle distinctly involved in traditional systems of belief. Such an attitude is distinctly taken by such writers as Increase Mather, as well as by sundry others since his day. Religious writers among Protestants are considerably more "careful" nowadays — fearing, probably, some compromise with the claims of "spiritism," if they should credit such accounts — although, in very many cases, somewhat sceptical, also: but certain reactionaries, the real "conservatives" in theology, do not hesitate to credit the claims of Spiritism, and similar cults, ascribing their "manifestations," one and all, to the Evil One and his angels.

When we consider the fact that visions and supposed visitations of the dead, of angels, also of divine personages, is a part of the common stock of human tradition, accepted among all nations, and to the present day; and, further, that we know of nothing that can warrant us in stating that such experiences are either untrue, or impossible, it is certain that we have a very poor and unreliable "explanation" of Joseph Smith's visions in the theory that he was the victim of some order of pathological delusion. The great trouble is that the allegation of disease in the mind of Mr. Smith involves more or less the same, or a very similar, condition in such a large proportion of the people whose names are notable in religious history. In order to discredit him, therefore, we are asked to believe that religious exaltation partakes of the nature of epilepsy, or some similar form of cerebral affection; also, that its other ill effects are very generally absent, or, at least, quite negligible in their influences.

In one particular this vision of Joseph Smith seems to differ from the majority of recorded experiences of similar character, and this is in the delivery of a message that is (1) strikingly contrary to anything that he might be supposed to have expected, and (2) that forms the real point of departure for the work of his after-life, the foundation of all the strikingly brilliant contributions to sociological and theological sciences, which, as we shall see later, were made by him. As a usual thing the personages, apparently present in a vision, say or do nothing that is of very exceptional interest or value. The subject of the visitation is often told, for example, that he is a sinner, and that he must repent; or that there is a work for him to do, usually in the way of preaching the Gospel or of caring for God's poor. Very often, as we may find by some reading in the scattered sources, visitations or "apparitions," coming in answer to an expressed desire, or to prayer, give answers as enigmatical as the ancient Delphic oracles to any inquiries that may be made. As a general rule, also, Spiritistic messages partake of the mental color and prejudices of the persons engaged in the "inquiry." Why these things are as they are we shall not undertake to determine. It is interesting, however, to consider that the message given to the youthful Smith in his reported vision was scarcely of a character to have originated in the untutored and inexperienced brain of a boy in his surroundings and at his period. To state that it was a conclusion formed in his own mind as the result of anxious cogitation on the discordant claims of the rival sects of his neighborhood — for there were very keen and bitter rivalries among them at this period — is to credit him with considerable power of reasoning, also some alertness of mind to discern the essential incompatibility of bitter rivalries with the Gospel of Love and Good Will to men. Nor is it too much to believe that his recountal of this message to his neighbors, and to the local clergy, must have resulted in precisely the kind of persecution and disfavor which he records. Except for this, his vision would likely have been set down to mere fervid imagination.

During the three succeeding years of Smith's life nothing of great importance seems to have occurred — at least, nothing of the kind is recorded by him or his biographers. In his journal, above quoted, he remarks of this period:

> "During the space of time which intervened between the time I had the vision and the year eighteen hundred and twenty-three — having been forbidden to join any of the religious sects of the day, and being of very tender years, and persecuted by those who ought to have been my friends, and to have treated me kindly, and if they supposed me to be deluded to have endeavored in a proper and affectionate manner to have reclaimed me,— I was left to all kinds of temptations; and mingling with all kinds of society, I frequently fell into many foolish errors, and displayed the weakness of youth, and the foibles of human nature; which, I am sorry to say, led me into divers temptations, offensive in the sight of God. In making this confession, no one need suppose me guilty of any great or malignant sins. A disposition to commit such was never in my nature. But I was guilty of levity, and sometimes associated with jovial company, etc., not consistent with that character which ought to be maintained by one who was called of God as I had been. But this will not seem very strange to any one who recollects my youth, and is acquainted with my native cheery temperament."— *History of the Church, Vol.* I, *pp.* 9–10.

This period must have been that in which Smith's bad reputation was greatly augmented. Nor could it be remarkable that the "levity" of which he makes mention should appear of even graver import, in view of his previously reported vision. It is popularly supposed that he indulged in alcoholic stimulants, also in the fortune-telling and water-witching extravagances, so frequently mentioned by his critics. We need not dwell upon the folly of such lines of behavior, however, since there is no reason to believe them any worse in Smith than in other persons less conspicuous. In a letter to his friend, Oliver Cowdery, written some years later, he comments upon his conduct in the following words:

> "During this time, as is common to most, or all youths, I fell into many vices and follies; but as my accusers are, and have been forward to accuse me of being guilty of gross and outrageous violations of the peace and good order of the community, I take the occasion to remark that, though as I have said above, 'as is common to most, or all youths, I fell into many vices and follies,' I have not, neither can it be sustained, in truth, been guilty of wronging or injuring any man or society of men; and those imperfections to which I allude, and for which I have often had occasion to lament, were a light, and too often, vain mind, exhibiting a foolish and trifling conversation.
>
> "This being all, and the worst, that my accusers can substantiate against my moral character, I wish to add that it is not without a deep feeling of regret that I am thus called upon in answer to my own conscience, to fulfil a duty I owe to myself, as well as to the cause of truth, in making this public confession of my former uncircumspect walk, and trifling conversation and more particularly, as I often acted in violation of those holy precepts which I knew came from God. . . . I only add, that I do not, nor never have, pretended to be any other than a man 'subject to passion,' and liable without the assisting grace of the Savior, to deviate from that perfect path in which all men are commanded to walk."—*Ibid. p.* 10.

In any other man than Smith the last sentence would be quoted as evidence of "manly piety and humility." He makes no attempt to justify or excuse any of the lapses committed by him, whatever these may have been, and states explicitly his complete dependence upon the grace of the Saviour for every good of which he is capable. Nor is there any reason whatever for charging him with "insincerity" or "imposture" in the use of such expressions. His lapses may have been serious, or merely the foolish indiscretions of an immature and irresponsible boy. In either case his maturity need not be charged with them. In some other cases of precisely similar disquietings of conscience we find that the things repented of are matters of no great moment, and that we have to deal rather with a morbid tendency to self-accusation than with anything that is worthy censure, even in the young. His manhood certainly showed no such serious criminality — unless we take account of the stock charge of "imposture"— that we need dwell upon this "confession" as evidence of anything beyond the common failings of human nature. We must remember, also, that St. Augustine, and several others among the "Church Fathers," lived lives by no means exemplary until well into their mature years; but this fact detracts in nothing, in common estimate, from their subsequent contributions to Christian literature and holy living. Like many of them, however, the mind of the youthful Smith was seriously disquieted on the matter of his spiritual standing. Thus we read:

"In consequence of these things, I often felt condemned for my weakness and imperfections; when, on the evening of the above-mentioned twenty-first of September, after I had retired to my bed for the night, I betook myself to prayer and supplication to Almighty God for forgiveness of all my sins and follies, and also for a manifestation to me, that I might know of my state and standing before Him; for I had full confidence in obtaining a divine manifestation, as I previously had done. While I was thus in the act of calling upon God, I discovered a light appearing in my room, which continued to increase until the room was lighter than at noonday, when immediately a personage appeared at my bedside, standing in the air, for his feet did not touch the floor. He had on a loose robe of most exquisite whiteness. It was a whiteness beyond anything earthly I had ever seen; nor do I believe that any earthly thing could be made to appear so exceedingly white and brilliant. His hands were naked and his arms also, a little above the wrist, so, also were his feet naked, as were his legs, a little above the ankles. His head and neck were also bare. I could discover that he had no other clothing on but his robe, as it was open, so that I could see into his bosom. Not only was his robe exceedingly white, but his whole person was glorious beyond description, and his countenance truly like lightning. The room was exceedingly light, but not so very bright as immediately around his person.

"When I first looked upon him, I was afraid; but the fear soon left me. He called me by name, and said unto me that he was a messenger sent from the presence of God to me, and that his name was Moroni; that God had a work for me to do; and that my name should be had for good and evil among all nations, kindreds, and tongues, or that it should be both good and evil spoken of among all people. He said there was a book deposited, written upon gold plates, giving an account of the former inhabitants of this continent, and the course from whence they sprang. He also said that the fulness of the everlasting Gospel was contained in it, as delivered by the Savior to the ancient inhabitants; also, that there were two stones in silver bows — and these stones, fastened to a breastplate, constituted what is called the Urim and Thummim — deposited with the plates; and the possession and use of these stones were what constituted 'Seers' in ancient or former times; and that God had prepared them for the purpose of translating the book."—*Ibid. pp.* 10, 11, 12.

According to the account, the heavenly messenger then quoted and commented on several passages of the Old and New Testaments, and also wrought upon the mind of the youth, so that he was enabled to see the golden plates in their resting-place. The messenger then ascended into heaven, but returned twice again in the same night, repeating his former message, and adding admonitions about the golden plates and similar important matters. On the manner of his ascent into heaven the account has the following:

"After this communication, I saw the light in the room begin to gather immediately around the person of him who had been speaking to me, and it continued to do so, until the room was again left dark, except just around him, when instantly I saw, as it were, a conduit open right up into heaven, and he ascended until he entirely disappeared, and the room was left as it had been before this heavenly light had made its appearance."—*Ibid. p.* 13.

After the third visit of Moroni, the narrator records that "the cock crowed, and I found that day was approaching." He then resumes:

"I shortly after arose from my bed, and, as usual, went to the necessary labors of the day; but, in attempting to work as at other times, I found my strength so exhausted as to render me entirely unable. My father, who was laboring along with me, discovered something to be wrong with me, and told me to go home. I started with the intention of going to the house; but, in attempting to cross the fence out of the field where we were, my strength entirely failed me, and I fell helpless on the ground, and for a time was quite unconscious of anything. The first thing that I can recollect was a voice speaking unto me, calling me by name. I looked up, and beheld the same messenger standing over my head, surrounded by light as before. He then again related unto me all that he had related to me the previous night, and commanded me to go to my father and tell him of the vision and commandments which I had received. I obeyed; I returned to my father in the field, and rehearsed the whole matter to him. He replied to me that it was of God, and told me to go and do as commanded by the messenger. I left the field, and went to the place where the messenger had told me the plates were deposited; and owing to the distinctness of the vision which I had had concerning it, I knew the place the instant that I arrived there."—*Ibid. pp.* 14–15.

CHAPTER III

THE COMING-FORTH OF THE BOOK OF MORMON

WITH the episode commonly known as the "coming-forth of the Book of Mormon" the history of Joseph Smith enters upon a new phase. The production of the alleged "record of the Nephites" introduces him as the preacher of a definite gospel and the arbiter of opinions about God and religion. As in other matters in the history of Smith and his Church, no would-be critic has studied this book with any other motive than to pick flaws and condemn; nor has the reading public ever been informed as to precisely what are its contents, teachings and literary merits. The several theories of its origin, also, are distinguished particularly as masses of bald assumption and plausible possibilities, but without definite and conclusive solutions of the involved matters. Thus, as we shall see, one theory of the origin of this book ascribes its authorship to a certain Solomon Spaulding, a retired Presbyterian preacher of Ohio, whose manuscript had been stolen from a printing office in Pittsburg by a certain Sidney Rigdon, and by him — for some obscure and unsatisfactory reason — delivered to Joseph Smith, to serve as the basis of a movement for restoring the Gospel in an age of doubt and apostasy. As an alternate "explanation," several writers have attempted to demonstrate that this book was the product of "automatic writing," which is another rare, indefinite and imperfectly explained phenomenon, as set forth by certain writers on psychology. And all these improbable, indefensible and undemonstrable theories have been formulated to explain the doings of an arrant and shallow "imposter," as they call Smith, whose claims and assumptions are "their own refutation," and "could be seriously considered by no informed mind!"

In this matter, as in the others, already discussed, the fair and logical procedure is to give Smith's own story of the origin and production of this book, and then discuss, in turn, the several theories devised to fit the facts. Nor can we fail to find out at the end of our discussion that there is positively no complete and final explanation of the matter discoverable to the investigator working on the problem at this late day. That the writing of the Book of Mormon was "no fool's job" must be evident to any unprejudiced reader. Whether or not it be what it professes, a record of God's dealings with certain ancient inhabitants of this continent, it is certainly not the product of an ignorant and diseased brain, bent on perpetrating a hoax—"carrying out the fun," as some critics express it—nor could one readily believe that it had been written originally as a novel. Certain theorists have held that, while the body of the book was written as a novel by Spaulding, the "religious portions" were incorporated by Rigdon, as part of his design for foisting it on the public as a brand-new revelation from God. As may be found on reading the book, Rigdon must have been far more skillful as an editor than was Spaulding as a novelist. The "religious portions," whether appearing in the form of lengthy discourses, or as stray remarks and dialogues, are, so far as the average critic could discern, integral parts of the total work. To omit them, one must seriously mutilate the accounts of various events, as they now stand. It may be asserted, also, that these several discourses and dialogues were evidently uttered, or otherwise promulgated, originally, with no other intention in mind than to enlighten the reader upon the views of Gospel truth therein presented.

Smith's account of the "coming-forth" of this book is as follows: On the morning after the second vision (Sept. 22, 1823), as he records, he visited the hiding place of the plates of Mormon, in company with the angel Moroni. It was on the west side of a "hill of considerable size," now known as Cumorah, and, as Smith says, "owing to the distinctness of the vision which I had had concerning it, I knew the place the instant that I arrived there." He then relates that the golden plates and other objects buried with them were shown him by the angel, who informed him, however, that he would not be allowed to take them away until that date four years thereafter. However, on the anniversary of that day, during the next three years, Smith visited the place, and, finally, on Sept. 22, 1827, was given possession of the plates, the "interpreters" (the prophetic "Urim and Thummim") and other objects concealed with them. Smith's account of this event is thus given in his own words:

"At length the time arrived for obtaining the plates, the Urim and Thummim, and the Breastplate. . . . The same heavenly messenger delivered them up to me with this charge: that I should be responsible for them; that if I should let them go carelessly, or through any neglect of mine, I should be cut off; but that if I would use all my endeavors to preserve them, until he, the messenger, should call for them, they should be protected.

"I soon found out the reason why I had received such strict charges to keep them safe, and why it was that the messenger had said that when I had done what was required at my hand, he would call for them. For no sooner was it known that I had them, than the most strenuous exertions were used to get them from me. Every stratagem that could be invented was resorted to for that purpose. The persecution became more bitter and severe than before, and multitudes were on the alert continually to get them from me if possible. But by the wisdom of God, they remained safe in my hands, until I had accomplished by them what was required at my hand. When, according to arrangements, the messenger called for them, I delivered them up to him; and he has them in his charge until this day.—*History of the Church, Vol.* I, *pp.* 18–19.

The persecutions mentioned became finally so severe that Smith and his wife were obliged to remove from Manchester, New York, to Susquehanna County, Pennsylvania. In his removal he was assisted by the generosity of Martin Harris, a well-to-do farmer of Palmyra, who, although but recently become acquainted with Smith, had given him $50 for his expenses. Later, after Smith had made a "transcript" of some of the characters, said to appear on the plates, Harris took it to New York, and showed it to Dr. Charles Anthon, and Dr. Samuel L. Mitchill, leading scholars and educators of that city. According to the story told by Harris, Prof. Anthon declared that the letters on the transcript "were Egyptian, Chaldaic, Assyriac [Syriac?], and Arabic," and that the purported translations were correct, wherever attached to the professed originals. Anthon subsequently denied Harris' statements, but, whatever may have occurred, the fact remains that Harris returned to Smith convinced of the truth of his claims, and ready to assist in the work of translating the plates, both by personal labor in writing at Smith's dictation and by the contribution of funds. All this may be attributed to "hypnotic influence," but such explanation seems somewhat "far-fetched," particularly in view of the fact that the supposed object of Harris' "investigation" was to discover whether investment of money in the publication of the book would be advisable. However, the story may best be told in the words of the principals. Harris' account, as given by Smith in his journal, is as follows:

"I went to the city of New York, and presented the characters which had been translated, with the translation thereof, to Professor Charles Anthon, a gentleman celebrated for his literary attainments. Professor Anthon stated that the translation was correct, more so than any he had before seen translated from the Egyptian. I then showed him those which were not yet translated, and he said that they were Egyptian, Chaldaic, Assyriac, and Arabic; and he said they were true characters. He gave me a certificate, certifying to the people of Palmyra that they were true characters, and that the translation of such of them as had been translated was also correct. I took the certificate and put it into my pocket, and was just leaving the house, when Mr. Anthon called me back, and asked me how the young man found out that there were gold plates in the place where he found them. I answered that an angel of God had revealed it unto him. He then said to me, 'Let me see that certificate.' I accordingly took it out of my pocket and gave it to him, when he took it and tore it to pieces, saying that there was no such thing now as ministering of angels, and that if I would bring the plates to him, he would translate them."—*Ibid. p.* 20.

In opposition to this statement of Harris', there are two letters ascribed to Prof. Anthon, which give his version of the story. They may be quoted in part as follows:

"The whole story about my pronouncing the Mormon inscription to be reformed Egyptian hieroglyphics is perfectly false. Some years ago, a plain, apparently simple-hearted farmer called on me with a note from Dr. Mitchill, of our city, now dead, requesting me to decipher, if possible, the paper which the farmer would hand me. . . . The paper in question was, in fact, a singular scroll. It consisted of all kinds of singular characters, disposed in columns, and had evidently been prepared by some person who had before him at the time a book containing various alphabets; Greek and Hebrew letters, crosses and flourishes; Roman letters inverted or placed sideways were arranged and placed in perpendicular columns, and the whole ended in a rude delineation of a circle, divided into various compartments, arched with various strange marks, and evidently copied after the Mexican calendar, given by Humboldt, but copied in such a way as not to betray the source whence it was derived."—*Letter to E. D. Howe, Feb.* 17, 1834.

"Many years ago — the precise date I do not now recollect,— a plain-looking countryman called upon me with a letter from Dr. Samuel L. Mitchill, requesting me to examine, and give my opinion upon a certain paper, marked with various characters, which the doctor confessed he could not decipher, and which the bearer of the note was very anxious to have explained. . . . The characters were arranged in columns, like the Chinese mode of writing, and presented the most singular medley that I ever beheld. Greek, Hebrew and all sorts of letters, more or less distorted, either through unskillfulness or from actual design, were intermingled with sundry delineations of half moons, stars, and other natural objects, and the whole ended with a rude representation of the Mexican zodiac. . . . On my telling the bearer of the paper that an attempt had been made to impose on him and defraud him of his property, he requested me to give him my opinion in writing about the paper which he had shown to me. I did so without hesitation, partly for the man's sake, and partly to let the individual 'behind the curtain' [Smith] see that his trick was discovered. The import of what I wrote was, as far as I can now recollect, simply this, that the marks in the paper appeared to be merely an imitation of various alphabetical characters, and had, in my opinion, no meaning at all connected with them."—*Letter to Rev. T. W. Coit (New Rochelle, New York), April* 3, 1841.

These variant accounts have been quoted frequently by writers on both sides of the perennial Mormon "controversy"—the Mormons, on the one hand, usually accepting Harris' version, and their critics, on the other, construing Prof. Anthon's characterizations into a complete "expert condemnation" of the existence of the plates of Mormon and of Smith's honesty in the matter of their professed translation or transcription. As may be reasonably held, however, both conclusions are only partially warranted by the probable facts. Thus, as a careful scholar, it is extremely unlikely that Prof. Anthon remarked definitely that the "translation of such of them as had been translated" was correct; since his knowledge of Egyptian, or "reformed Egyptian"—a term proposed by some writers for Demotic or Hieratic writing—is not known to have been such as would have enabled him to read such texts off-hand. Conversely, also, the remarks in which both the witnesses agree, to the effect that the inscription was a medley of "all sorts of letters," presumably copied, as Anthon suggests, from a "book containing various alphabets," may not be taken as a definite condemnation of the transcription; since, as may be readily verified, a document in Hieratic or Demotic Egyptian script, particularly when copied by one unskilled in, or unaccustomed to, copying such writings, could very easily be made to answer to precisely the description given by Prof. Anthon. Such scripts differ widely from the Hieroglyphic, and so closely resemble archaic forms of several Semitic alphabets that some theorists, notably Isaac Taylor, have suggested that such originated in some earlier forms of the Hieratic style.

Unfortunately, the paper examined by Prof. Anthon has not been preserved for us, but another alleged transcription of the characters on the plates of Mormon has been shown by several writers. While certainly a "screed of indefinite origin," it more closely suggests Egyptian Hieratic than "Greek, Hebrew," or any other script, even "Assyriac." If copied from any book "containing various alphabets," as Prof. Anthon suggests, it is quite reasonable to suppose that some form of Egyptian writing also was included. The identity of this "book" must be somewhat doubtful, since few, if any, available to the general reader at that date (1827), gave very definite information on Egyptian writing, unless, indeed, we except the supplement of the Encyclopedia Britannica, issued in 1819, and containing an article on the Egyptian language by Dr. Thomas Young. It is easier to suggest possible sources of a man's information, however, than to prove that he ever used them. We might assume, also, that such a person as Smith is said to have been—"ignorant," "vagabondish," "dreamy," "epileptic" and "hypnotic"—might have assumed that any scrawl he might be pleased to make would pass for "reformed Egyptian," or anything else he might choose to call it. That such a person would ever think of consulting a "book containing various alphabets" is unlikely.

Whatever may be the real facts regarding the interview of Martin Harris with Prof. Anthon—whether Anthon gave him a written "certificate," as he acknowledges in his letter to Coit and denies in his letter to Howe; or whether, or not, his "warnings" to Harris were of a very definite and emphatic description — the fact remains that, on his return to Harmony, Harris entered upon the work of transcribing the "translation," as dictated by the Prophet. Evidently, he either understood that Anthon had endorsed the translation, as he states, or else, as is equally probable, he was not exactly "overawed" by the personality and opinions even of so great a scholar. After transcribing 116 pages of Smith's dictation, as will be explained later, Harris discontinued his work, and was, for some time, partially estranged from the Prophet. This, however, had no effect on his faith, and we find him later one of the three witnesses to the Book of Mormon, and also mortgaging his farm to defray the cost of its printing.

As to the manner in which, according to various accounts, the translation of the ancient plates was accomplished, there seems to be some variation in details. The story popularly accepted is that Smith sat behind a screen or blanket hung from the ceiling of his room, and dictated the sentences, "as they were given to him," to his amanuensis who sat on the other side of this partition. This gave him the opportunity, as alleged by numerous critics, to read from the manuscript of Spaulding's romance, as edited by Rigdon, thus carrying out the story of the golden plates of Mormon. Why, however, even the most arrant knave, bent on deceiving the people, should have resorted to all this trouble, which occupied months at a time with hard work, it is difficult to understand. Spaulding's edited manuscript, or a transcription of it made by himself, would have served the purpose of printer's copy quite as well as the one laboriously transcribed by his amanuensis. Admitting the truth of any of the accounts which we have, we might seem justified in asserting that there could have been other, and quite as good reasons for the method of "translation" adopted, as any that these hostile critics have suggested. What such "good reasons" may have been may not be perfectly obvious. On this matter Roberts says:

> "The sum of the whole matter, then, concerning the manner of translating the sacred record of the Nephites, according to the testimony of the only witnesses competent to testify in the matter (Smith, Cowdery, Whitmer and Harris) is: With the Nephite record was deposited a curious instrument, consisting of two transparent stones, set in the rim of a bow, somewhat resembling spectacles, but larger, called by the ancient Hebrews 'Urim and Thummim,' but by the Nephites 'Interpreters.' . . . The Nephite characters with the English interpretation appeared in the sacred instrument; the Prophet would pronounce the English translation to his scribe, which, when correctly written, would disappear and the other characters with their interpretation take their place, and so on until the work was completed.

"It should not be supposed, however, that this translation, though accomplished . . . as stated above, was merely a mechanical procedure; that no faith, or mental or spiritual effort was required on the Prophet's part; that the instruments did all, while he who used them did nothing but look and repeat mechanically what he saw there reflected. . . . It required the utmost concentration of mental and spiritual force possessed by the Prophet, in order to exercise the gift of translation through the means of the sacred instruments provided for that work."—*History of the Mormon Church* (*Americana Magazine*," *Oct.*, 1909, *pp.* 808–809).

Of course, the story as accepted by Mormons, involves a distinct element of the supernatural, or, at least, of the superhuman, and this is supposed to constitute its sufficient refutation. It is not too much to claim, however, even in these days of "rationalism" and "naturalism," when the attribute of "omniscience," formerly supposed to belong to God, is unhesitatingly ascribed to man, that any such "refutation" is no refutation at all; and for the very excellent reason that, even now, we know no more about the things outside the realm of our immediate experience than did our remotest ancestors—perhaps, indeed, not quite as much. It is significant, however, that the most confidently urged "explanations" of Smith's performances are in no sense more probable, or even credible, than that offered by himself and his associates. His most "rationalistic" and "scientific" critics have left the matter as much "in the air" as it always was. This we shall see later. Thus, although many of the discussions on this matter of "translation," as given by some of his advocates, partakes of what is often characterized as "sophistical reasoning," the fact remains that there is positively nothing more to be said against their arguments than can be said by the most ignorant doubter of all that is not understood.

Among such curious situations is the condition of Martin Harris' departure as Smith's scribe. According to the story told by all historians of the matter, after Harris had completed the transcription of 116 pages, he importuned the Prophet for the privilege of taking them home to Palmyra and exhibiting them to his wife, his brother, and other members of his immediate family, and the request was finally granted upon the strict agreement that they should be shown to no one beside. Harris broke his promise, however, and, as a result, the pages disappeared, and were never seen again. One supposition has been that they were stolen by enemies of Smith and his "work," although some have asserted that they were burned by Harris' wife, as a protest against his determination to finance the publication of the completed book. Among other penalties visited upon the Prophet, in addition to his mere annoyance at the carelessness and broken faith of his scribe, were the withdrawal by the heavenly messenger of the sacred plates and "interpreters," and the cessation of his own power of receiving revelations from God. As a result of his repentance, however, he was restored to divine favor and privilege, and the work was ordered resumed. On this episode Roberts says:

"All the sacred things were now restored to the Prophet, and upon inquiry of the Lord through Urím and Thummim he received another revelation in which the designs of those who had stolen the manuscript from Martin Harris were made known. Those designs aimed at nothing less than the destruction of the work Joseph Smith had in hand. Having now in their possession so large a part of the ancient record, they would hold it and see if the Prophet in a second translation could reproduce it *verbatim et literatim,* if not, they would say he had no gift for he could not translate the same matter twice alike, therefore he had made false pretensions; he was a false prophet, and his work must be discredited. If, on the other hand, he should reproduce the matter *verbatim et literatim* then they had the manuscript of the first translation in their hands, and could change that and claim that the prophet evidently could not translate the same matter twice alike, hence had not translated by inspiration, hence had no supernatural gift, hence was not a Prophet of God, but an imposter."—*Ibid. p.* 795.

Although the conditions set forth by Roberts have been interpreted by various critics of Smith's claims as proof that the Prophet was seriously embarrassed by the loss of the manuscript, it seems to furnish a very good refutation of the confidently-urged Spaulding authorship theory. If, as alleged, Smith had before him the copy of Spaulding's romance, with Sidney Rigdon's editions, and had dictated it to his amanuensis, what difficulty, beyond the work involved, could there be in the way of reproducing the exact, or approximate wording — for he may have made changes as he read along — of the original? Of course, as has been said, also, he may have destroyed the original, as the work of transcription progressed, and for this reason he could not reproduce it. If, however, we stop to consider all that might have been done, or that one could suppose was done, we have attained no nearer approach to certainty than we had at the very start. Nor is the situation materially improved by the usual line of reflections on this incident. Some Mormon writers have treated the matter of Smith's "translation" in a philosophical manner. Thus, in commenting on the criticisms of Rev. Mr. Lamb, author of *The Gold Bible,* Prof. N. L. Nelson writes:

"In a consideration of this question ['How the Book of Mormon was Translated'] the fundamental proposition — that on which the Mormon and his opponent must alike agree — is the fact that, howsoever he came by his material, Joseph Smith dictated the Book of Mormon, without apparent hesitation, as fast as a scribe could write it in long hand. There is no chance for error on this point. The entire Whitmer family, besides Oliver Cowdery, Martin Harris, and Joseph's wife, sat and listened, or had free access to listen, to the record as it grew day by day during the entire month of June, 1829. . . .

"My idea is, then, that the translation of the Book of Mormon is the joint product of two men — Joseph Smith and most probably the Angel Moroni; that the angel was commissioned by God to act for the dead quite as truly as was the Prophet for the living; that such, in fact, is the meaning of the words spoken to the Three Witnesses, declaring that the record had been translated 'by the gift and power of God.'

"But how, the reader is ready to ask. Nothing could be simpler, as I view it. Moroni, being familiar with the characters on the plates, read them character by character; that is to say, he looked at the symbols and thereby awakened or aroused in his mind the thought corresponding to the symbols — for that is precisely what reading means. The thought so aroused passed by the power of the Spirit directly into the mind of the Prophet, who in turn rendered it into such English symbols as were at his command. Nor did the thought alone so pass: the very image of the character that held the attention of Moroni was flashed into Joseph's mind and visualized before him, just as David Whitmer says. What then would be more natural, than that the English symbols corresponding to the thought in Joseph's mind should also be projected before him as a visual image? This may account for the double line of symbols, ancient and modern, which was seen by the Prophet in the darkness surrounding the Urim and Thummim. . . .

"Fortunately, science has taught us enough concerning the laws of thought communication,— that is to say, concerning the incipient science of telepathy,— that no fact in the above theory need stagger the student. Stranger things are taking place to-day in the laboratories of psychic research. By 'stranger' I mean merely that telepathic communication takes place under circumstances less simple and direct; not that scientific research has yet evolved telepathically — or probably will evolve during the next century — anything to compare with the Book of Mormon either in extent or definiteness. My idea is simply that if man has demonstrated the power of telepathy to exist, then it is surely worthy of faith that God could so shape conditions as to make the communication of the Book of Mormon possible in the manner I have suggested."— *The Mormon Point of View, pp.* 124–130.

However this theory of Prof. Nelson's may affect the general reader, who, in the average, is likely to depreciate all arguments in favor of Mormonism, it is interesting to remark in passing that the latest, and, as considered in many quarters, the "most scientific" theory of the origin of the Book of Mormon — that it was the product of "automatic mental operations" of some kind — involves very nearly a similar line of suppositions. Nor does it seem any better justified on the basis of the common experiences of humanity. Furthermore, both should account very similarly for the phraseology and ideas of the work itself. Thus, continuing from Nelson's work:

"The second question relates to Joseph Smith's mental qualifications. I have suggested that Moroni communicated with him through a medium common alike to the inhabitants of heaven, earth, and hell — the medium of thought divorced from all symbol. His part was consequently to put the thought so received, into English words; and in doing so his personal equation would inevitably be stamped upon the translation, as we have seen that it was. It is important to consider now what that equation was, especially with reference to the use of words.

"In respect of diction, writers are of two extreme types, with all degrees of overlapping. The one extreme is well represented by Henry Ward Beecher, who read or listened with such intensity that he could never quote: the phraseology of others having melted down like slag in the white heat of his mind and yielded up the pure gold of their ideas. When such a man writes, every phrase is coined anew and therefore stamped indelibly with the writer's individuality.

"The other extreme is represented by every beginner in the thought world and, for that matter, by nine-tenths of those who grow old in it. They gather ideas with more or less avidity, both from books and men; but they stow away these ideas without undressing them,—boots and all, so to speak. Consequently, when these try to write, they proceed from phrase to phrase, rather than from word to word; and there is always a certain conventionality or triteness in their style,—a resemblance to others in phraseology which would convict them of plagiarism, should their productions be compared critically with the authors they have read.

"To this latter class belongs, as I have intimated, every tyro in composition, and therefore Joseph Smith; at least this was probably true of him during that early period when he was put to the stress of inventing the style of the Book of Mormon. As long as the thought communicated by Moroni ran along in simple narrative, the experiences of his own life furnished the Prophet with an original diction; but the moment it ascended into abstract realms, he had to draw upon his stock of phrases — upon that part of his vocabulary which, in the language of psychology, had not been apperceived, or melted down in the crucible of individual experience. When we consider that this part of his vocabulary had been stored almost exclusively by contact with ministers of the Gospel, and through reading the King James' version of the Bible, we have an adequate explanation of why scriptural phraseology enters so largely into the style of the Book of Mormon. . . . Had the thought of the Book of Mormon been flashed into a mind like that of Webster or Beecher, it would undoubtedly have been moulded into forms of expression which would have left no chance for the charge of plagiarism. As it was, the thought could do nothing else than take the line of least resistance, and that was the line of expression familiar to the translator through contact with the King James' version of the scriptures.

"As before suggested, from the fact that the witnesses of the mode of translation have nowhere said that Joseph stopped to read passages from the Bible, it is fair to assume that those chapters which occur identical in both books, were received and dictated by the same telepathic communion as the rest of the matter; that is, the Prophet himself did not probably know, at the time of translating, how the result would compare with the English version of the Bible.

"Are we then to assume that the Scriptures as known to the Nephites were identical, in form of expression, with the scriptures in the King James' version? By no means. That the thought was the same we may well believe, since this is God's part of scripture. There is surely no difficulty in holding that Christ would give the Sermon on the Mount in practically the same mental concepts to the Nephites that He did to the Jews. Now, had Joseph never read the English version, he would have been obliged to coin these concepts anew as best he could; in which case his rendering would have differed from Matthew's as much at least as do those of the other three evangelists; but even if we suppose he had read Matthew's only once, we must allow that the thought would take the channel broken in preference to one unbroken, unless the translator strongly willed otherwise.

"As an instance of the truth that probably no impression on the consciousness is ever completely effaced, Mr. Hudson, in his epoch-making book, *The Law of Psychic Phenomena,* relates that a servant-girl, when put into the clairvoyant state, astonished her hearers by reciting perfectly a Greek poem in the original Attic tongue. Theosophists claimed the circumstance as evidence of re-incarnation; but it was finally explained that ten years previous she had been present, dusting a certain library, while a noted scholar had recited the poem to a friend. Psychic research reveals many similar instances. It is not difficult to believe, therefore, that Joseph's mind would without his knowledge retain whole chapters of the Bible, which would spring verbatim unto consciousness when brought into association with the thought that originally inspired them. This view requires that quotations and so-called plagiarisms shall always be from the King James' version — the only Bible probably known to the early life of the Prophet,— and this, as we have seen, was the case."— *Ibid. pp.* 132–137.

Of course, no mind already prejudiced against Mormonism and all that belongs to it can be expected to see in this explanation anything other than an elaborate attempt to justify something confidently classed as a "fraud," but fairness requires that we acknowledge the fact that the conditions outlined by Prof. Nelson — with the sole exception of the alleged activities of an invisible personage, angel or otherwise — are a part of the common stock of phenomena which are receiving serious consideration at the hands of our foremost psychologists at the present day. With any person other than Joseph Smith the explanation would be highly acceptable to our scientific authorities, who would, undoubtedly, admit the activity of the Angel Moroni, in the character of some kind of indefinite "control," presumably, on their theory, a phase of the "subliminal self" or a manifestation of a "second personality." This, at least, would be the method by which they would explain the facts with which Prof. Nelson deals. They would also accept his proffered explanation of the presence of lengthy quoted passages from the Bible, nor would they revert to the theory of "plagiarism" until all the phases of "automatic reproduction of memory records" had been exhausted. Indeed, candidly speaking, there would seem to be some demand for such an explanation of the presence of these passages, because of the fact that, while the Book of Mormon shows no very large or varied vocabulary, there is ample evidence that the writer, or writers, were fully able to express their ideas "in their own words" and forms, and it can be no otherwise than surprising that, in the cases of the lengthy quotations from the prophet Isaiah and the New Testament, the essential ideas are not given in new form, rather than in direct quotation. Nor can we urge Smith's alleged "ignorance," or any other evil quality, which we may assume that he possessed, as a sufficient and final explanation of this fact. The science of psychology must insist that the charge of "fraud" or "plagiarism" be relegated, until all conditions be more fully analyzed.

Although such "scientific attention" as has been accorded the case of Joseph Smith goes very far toward discrediting the theory that his activities may be classed as mere conscious and deliberate fraud, it seems necessary to outline the several explanations, so-called, of the Book of Mormon and its origin. Thus, for example, a certain Lamb, like several other hostile critics, has argued that the book cannot be what it professes, a divine record of God's dealings with the ancient inhabitants of America, because of its defects of style, its "exaggerated miracles" and the essential "improbability" of most of its narrations. These conclusions they profess to argue by comparison with the Bible, which, by their showing, is perfect in literary style, "dignified" in all its accounts of miraculous events — all of which, as they say, were for the definite end of convincing people of the truths of God — and so reasonable and obvious in all its professed historic narrations that no one could doubt. It seems unnecessary to say that all such attempted criticism is essentially and irredeemably unfair and disingenuous, in the mere fact that it applies to the Book of Mormon — no matter what may be the real facts regarding it — the very line of criticisms that have been made against the veracity and credibility of the Bible by the "infidels" of all ages. Thus, we need only compare the amused reflections of Mr. Lamb on the extraordinary rate of increase of the inhabitants of America during the first century, or so, after the arrival of the first colony, about 600 B. C., with the numerous hostile criticisms of the Biblical account of the rapid increase of the Israelites in Egypt from the time of Joseph to that of Moses. It is well to remark that, if the Bible is not to be condemned because of the difficulties of statement and the defects of style repeatedly indicated by hostile critics, it is obviously inadmissable to use the same line of criticism against any other book claiming dignity as a revelation from God, or even as history.

CHAPTER IV

THE BEGINNINGS OF MORMONISM

In entering upon an examination of the alleged supernatural elements in Mormon history, we may quote from Joseph Smith's own words describing the exhibition of the golden plates to the "three witnesses," Oliver Cowdery, David Whitmer, and Martin Harris:

"We four . . . agreed to retire into the woods, and try to obtain, by fervent and humble prayer, the fulfilment of the promises given . . . that they should have a view of the plates. We accordingly made choice of a piece of woods convenient to Mr. Whitmer's house, to which we retired, and having knelt down, we began to pray in much faith to Almighty God to bestow upon us a realization of these promises.

"According to previous arrangement, I commenced by vocal prayer to our Heavenly Father, and was followed by each of the others in succession. We did not at the first trial, however, obtain any answer or manifestation of divine favor in our behalf. We again observed the same order of prayer, each calling on and praying fervently to God in rotation, but with the same result as before.

"Upon this, our second failure, Martin Harris proposed that he should withdraw himself from us, believing, as he expressed himself, that his presence was the cause of our not obtaining what we wished for. He accordingly withdrew from us, and we knelt down again, and had not been many minutes engaged in prayer, when presently we beheld a light above us in the air, of exceeding brightness; and behold, an angel stood before us. In his hands he held the plates which we had been praying for these to have a view of. He turned over the leaves one by one, so that we could see them, and discern the engravings thereon distinctly. He then addressed himself to David Whitmer, and said, 'David, blessed is the Lord, and he that keeps His commandments'; when, immediately afterwards, we heard a voice from out of the bright light above us, saying, 'These plates have been revealed by the power of God, and they have been translated by the power of God. The translation of them which you have seen is correct, and I command you to bear record of what you now see and hear.'

"I now left David and Oliver, and went in pursuit of Martin Harris, whom I found at a considerable distance, fervently engaged in prayer. He soon told me, however, that he had not yet prevailed with the Lord, and earnestly requested me to join him in prayer, that he also might realize the same blessings which we had just received. We accordingly joined in prayer, and ultimately obtained our desires, for before we had yet finished, the same vision was opened to our view, at least it was again opened to me, and I once more beheld and heard the same things;

whilst at the same moment, Martin Harris cried out, apparently in an ecstasy of joy, ''Tis enough; 'tis enough; mine eyes have beheld; mine eyes have beheld'; and jumping up, he shouted 'Hozanna,' blessing God, and otherwise rejoiced exceedingly."—*History of the Church, Vol. I, pp.* 54-55.

As may be noted by any reader who has had the patience to follow us to this point, the account of the appearance of the angelic visitant here given agrees in all substantial particulars with that of the second vision of Joseph Smith in 1823. Although he mentions no physical effects occurring at the time or later, it might be held that, if the former experience is to be explained, as some hold, as a "visual aura of epilepsy," * this one also is in the same category. And such an explanation might be advanced, "for all that it is worth," if the three witnesses could be assumed fictitious personages, or so obscure and unknown that their alleged experiences might be confidently described, without fear of contradiction. As it is, however, they are perfectly well known, from the hour of this visional experience to the day of their deaths. Furthermore, they have testified to the reality of this experience, as they believed it to be, at any rate, and in no equivocal language.

On the publication of the Book of Mormon the famous "Testimony of the Three Witnesses" appeared as a sort of introduction on a page following the title. As may be seen, it substantially endorses the description of the occurrence just given in the words of Joseph Smith. It is as follows:

"Be it known unto all nations, kindreds, tongues, and people unto whom this work shall come, that we, through the grace of God the Father, and our Lord Jesus Christ, have seen the plates which contain this record . . . and we also know that they have been translated by the gift and power of God, for His voice hath declared it unto us; wherefore we know of a surety that the work is true. And we also testify that we have seen the engravings which are upon the plates; and they have been shown unto us by the power of God, and not of man. And we declare with words of soberness, that an angel of God came down from heaven, and he brought and laid before our eyes, that we beheld and saw the plates and the engravings thereon; and we know that it is by the grace of God the Father, and our Lord Jesus Christ, that we beheld and bear record that these things are true; and it is marvelous in our eyes, nevertheless, the voice of the Lord commanded us that we should bear record of it; wherefore, to be obedient unto the commandments of God, we bear testimony of these things."

In dealing with the several visions and theophanies accompanying the founding of Mormonism and the "coming forth of the Book of Mormon," we have a series of situations that fairly challenge the ingenuity of hostile critics to produce a satisfactory rationalistic explanation. It is easy to suppose and assert that the witnesses to this book, together with Sidney

* This theory is discussed in a later chapter.

Rigdon, who has been credited with a large share in its production, were all accomplices of Joseph Smith in the perpetration of an enormous hoax, out of which all hoped "to make money." The fact that most of these people were "ignorant," hence, probably, also "mercenary" has been urged as a good explanation of their complicity in an unworthy scheme. We might readily accept such an explanation as tentative, at least, if these men had continued to be the associates and beneficiaries of Joseph Smith during the remainder of their lives. As a matter of fact, the reverse is the case. The three witnesses and Rigdon — the "arch-conspirators," as alleged — were all cut off from the Mormon Church; two of them, Harris and Cowdery, became bitter and outspoken enemies of Smith, while Rigdon withdrew in surly disaffection. If, then, men of their advertised character and intelligence had thus separated from their leader, whom they knew to be a fraud, what more probable than that they should recant their former "testimony," and denounce him? This would seem to be the most usual procedure for men "bent on revenge"; also, particularly probable, in view of the fact that all of them were more or less severely censured and characterized by the Church authorities, as persons of bad morals and contemptible lives. Other lesser offenders and apostates from this Church — such as Philastus Hurlbutt and John C. Bennett — who, presumably, knew far less about Smith and his history than any of his earlier associates, made strenuous efforts to wreck his work and ruin his reputation. Not one of the three witnesses, however, ever denied the truth of his original testimony: as a matter of fact all reaffirmed it in strong terms years afterward. Even Sidney Rigdon, although himself an ambitious and violent character, never sought to recoup his own position, or to discredit Smith by revealing any part of what he might be supposed to have known about the origin of the Book of Mormon, according to certain popular and highly esteemed theories.

"Respecting the witnesses to whom the Angel Moroni showed the Plates, Mr. Linn [author of *The Story of the Mormons*] has this to say: 'Surely if any three men in the Church should remain steadfast, mighty pillars of support for the Prophet in his future troubles, it should be these chosen witnesses to the actual existence of the Golden Plates. Yet every one of them became an apostate, and every one of them was loaded with all the opprobrium that the Church could pile upon him.' Yet had they remained faithful to the Church, what would have been Mr. Linn's comment? Would he not have said: 'Of course; could you expect anything else from men who consented to remain the tools of an unscrupulous hierarchy? These men have everything to gain and nothing to lose by maintaining their false testimony!' Clearly, so far as the existence of the Plates is concerned, the evidence could not be made stronger than by their turning away from the Church and still remaining true, as they did, to their testimony. The temptation to injure the Church by recanting, must, at a certain period in the life of each, have been very strong; yet the conviction that they had actually seen and handled the plates remained stronger still."—*N. L. Nelson* (*The Mormon Point of View, pp.* 189–190.)

Although, as alleged by one of the multitudinous "affidavits" that seem to be the proper accompaniments of Mormon history — somewhat as "blackfish" accompany a whale — that Oliver Cowdery, after his withdrawal from the Mormon Church in 1838, united with the Methodist Protestant denomination, making a public recantation, in which he "admitted his error and implored forgiveness," it is certain, nevertheless, that he returned to the Mormons in 1848, and a short time before his death publicly affirmed his belief that the Book of Mormon is true, and that "it contains the everlasting Gospel."

Martin Harris also returned to the Church, after years of separation, and died in Utah. According to accounts, he repeatedly reaffirmed the truth of his original story, describing the scene minutely. David Whitmer never reunited with the Church, but, until the day of his death, continued firm in his belief that the vision of the angel was a true one. In an interview with the noted Apostles, Orson Pratt and Joseph F. Smith, at Richmond, Missouri, Sept. 7, 1878, he stated that he saw the plates and the angel at this time, and added:

"The fact is, it was just as though Joseph, Oliver, and I were sitting just here on a log, when we were overshadowed by a light. It was not like the light of the sun nor like that of a fire, but more glorious and beautiful. It extended away around us, I cannot tell how far, but in the midst of this light about as far off as he sits [pointing to John C. Whitmer, sitting a few feet from him], there appeared, as it were, a table with many records or plates upon it, besides the plates of the Book of Mormon, also the sword of Laban, the directors, i.e., the ball which Lehi had, and the interpreters. I saw them just as plain as I saw this bed [striking the bed beside him with his hand], and I heard the voice of the Lord, as distinctly as I ever heard anything in my life, declaring that the records of the plates of the Book of Mormon were translated by the gift and power of God. . . . Our testimony as recorded in the Book of Mormon is strictly and absolutely true, just as it was written." —*Millennial Star, Vol.* XL, *Nos.* 49, 50.

In his discussion of the "three witnesses," Mr. Riley quotes a letter from Whitmer's grandson, George W. Schweich (Sept. 22, 1899), which reads, as follows:

"I have begged him (Whitmer) to unfold the fraud in the case and he had all to gain and nothing to lose but speak the word if he thought so — but he has described the scene to me many times, of his vision about noon time in an open pasture — there is only one explanation barring an actual miracle and that is this — if that vision was not real it was *hypnotism,* it was *real* to grandfather *in fact.*"—*Founder of Mormonism, pp.* 219–220, note.

Mr. Schweich is also quoted as stating that Mr. Whitmer required that there be inscribed on his tombstone the epitaph, "The Record of the Jews and the Record of the Nephites *are one.* Truth is eternal." In addition to these testimonies of Whitmer's unfailing faith in the reality of his vision, we find his published statement, in 1887, one year before his death:

> "It is recorded in the *American Cyclopedia* and the *Encyclopedia Britannica,* that I, David Whitmer, have denied by testimony as one of the Three Witnesses to the divinity of the Book of Mormon; and that the other two Witnesses, Oliver Cowdery and Martin Harris, denied their testimony to that book. I will say once more to all mankind, that I have never at any time denied that testimony or any part thereof. I also testify to the world, that neither Oliver Cowdery nor Martin Harris ever at any time denied their testimony. They both died reaffirming the truth of the divine authenticity of the Book of Mormon."—*David Whitmer* (*Address to all Believers in Christ,* p. 8).

Commenting on the fact that the three witnesses maintained a consistent adherence to their original testimony, B. H. Roberts, writes, as follows:

> "The trying circumstances under which the Witnesses persisted in maintaining the truth of that testimony is also known. Neither separation from Joseph Smith as a companion and associate, nor excommunication from the body religious, brought into existence as a sequence, one may say, of the coming forth of the Nephite Record, affected them as Witnesses. In the Church and while out of it they steadfastly maintained what they first published to the world respecting the Book of Mormon. They never attempted to resolve the appearance of the angel, the exhibition of the plates, or hearing the voice of the Lord into hallucination of the mind; nor did they ever attempt to refer this really great event to some jugglery on the part of Joseph Smith. They never allowed even the possibility of their being mistaken in the matter. They saw; they heard; the splendor of God shone upon them; they felt his presence. They were not deluded. The several incidents making up this great revelation were too palpable to the strongest senses of the mind to admit of any doubt as to their reality. The great revelation was not given in a dream or vision of the night. There was no mysticism about it. Nothing unseemly or occult. It was a simple, straightforward, open fact that had taken place before their eyes. The visitation of the angel as in the broad light of day."—*History of the Mormon Church* (*Americana Magazine, Nov.* 1909, *pp.* 911–912).

While to the general public the testimony of the three witnesses must be judged as a part of the total grand riddle of Joseph Smith, it must be held to embody evidence of some order of unusual influence upon their minds, if not, also, upon their senses. If we assume with Roberts that it recorded an actual divine manifestation, we may concur perfectly in his estimate. If, on the other hand, we seek some "rational" explanation, we have quite as much to explain and justify to the intelligence of the public. Thus on the theory of some writers, the whole affair mentioned in the "testimony" was "set and staged" by

Smith to produce an impression on the minds of his too-confiding friends; but we must credit him with wonderful skill and success as a "stage manager," and could be excused for doubting if any "properties" and "business" could be so arranged, under the conditions, as to deceive even "ignorant farmers." Another theory, as already mentioned, assumes the use of "hypnotism" in the production of this permanent effect upon the minds of the witnesses. This, as we have claimed, is also "supposing a great deal," even though suggested by Whitmer's grandson, as quoted by Riley.

As may be readily found on study of the subject, the hypnotism explanation is no more than an hypothesis, and a very indefinite one at that. To assert that it fits the facts is a plain presumption, even though we have no other explanation to advance in its stead. In the first place, there is no evidence before us that anything like the ordinary procedures of the hypnotist or mesmerist were attempted; and, even if this were the case, as is fairly evident to anyone at all familiar with literature on hypnotism, it is by no means an easy feat to control and suggest to two subjects at a time, unless previous separate hypnotic states have been induced, and definite suggestions for behavior on a given occasion made and acted upon. This supposition involves, of course, a whole array of things and events entirely unmentioned in any accounts we have read on the event. As to the theory that hallucination may be produced in the waking state by strong suggestion we may quote Prof. James, himself a careful investigator of the subject:

> "Some subjects seem almost as obedient to suggestion in the waking state as in sleep, or even more so, according to certain observers. Not only muscular phenomena, but changes of personality and hallucinations are recorded as the result of simple affirmation on the operator's part, without the previous ceremony of 'magnetizing' or putting into the 'mesmeric sleep.' These are all trained subjects, however, so far as I know, and the affirmation must apparently be accompanied by the patient concentrating his attention and gazing, however briefly, into the eyes of the operator. It is probable therefore that an extremely rapidly induced condition of trance is a prerequisite for success in these experiments."—*The Principles of Psychology, Vol.* II. *p.* 615.

Although, as appears in the writings of several of the foremost investigators of hypnotic phenomena, the fact that sensory hallucinations and illusions may be produced by suggestion, as well as a more or less persistent conviction of their reality, there can be no doubt that such delusions, being unreal, or corresponding to no normal experience, cannot, even with the strongest suggestion — or other form of hypnotic influence, if any — be made to assume the permanent semblance of reality. The effects of the influence, whatever its nature, must eventually wear off, and become less vivid, in precisely the same fashion that dreams lose their definite character in the memory, in the course of years. James and others record that the effects of trance suggestion have been manifested after periods more or less remote — " months or even a year, in one case reported by M. Liegeois " — there is no conclusive evidence, even to the present day, that such effects may be permanently registered on the brain, to be constantly referred to and believed in for over fifty years, as in the cases of two of Smith's witnesses. And some such evidence is positively essential to the theory. Whatever may be the truth of the matter, however, the hypnotic explanation involves many difficulties, and cannot be quoted as sufficient and demonstrable. At best, it strongly suggests the general tendency of present-day learning to assume the finality of our knowledge of even doubtful matters, and to label imperfectly reported " cases " as " epilepsy," " hypnotism," etc., on the basis of a few symptoms, which, constituting the sum of our knowledge of the matter, as they do, are quite as compatible with several other explanations.

CHAPTER V

JOSEPH SMITH AS THE FIRST PROPHET, SEER AND REVELATOR

ALTHOUGH the name of Joseph Smith figures largely in literature, and although the work inaugurated by him has been variously discussed, opposed and argued against, it is a curious fact that no systematic account of his career, and no estimate of his character and influence, has appeared, except from the pens of two classes of writers. The first of these, both in time and in the attention secured, are implacable enemies, whose spite and prejudice have blinded them to the fact that Smith is entitled to be considered as any other human being — on the basis of his doings, honestly examined and represented — and have led them into espousing the several silly hypothesis which will be discussed at a later place. The second class of writers is composed of the friends and adherents of the Prophet, whose reverence for his memory has moved them to attribute the highest character and the purest motives to him, and to argue confidently for all the claims made by and for him. Between these two extremes the intelligent mind is left to form its own conclusions, entirely unaided, unless it be by the expenditure of pains and effort involved in examining and studying the records and literature that remain to preserve a first-hand picture of this man and his doings.

There are many things recorded in the history of Smith's career that could scarcely be urged as the strongest and most convincing evidences of his claims, nor even the most probable occurrences. With such matters we are less concerned than with the estimate of his significance to the world. Thus, as the initiatory move in the foundation of his Church, as is recorded, Smith and Cowdery are baptized by order of John the Baptist, now a resurrected personage, and are ordained to the "priesthood of Aaron"; later, also, they are ordained to the "higher priesthood," or, as it is called the "priesthood of Melchisedek," at the hands of the Apostles Peter, James and John, now also "angels," and are given full authority to teach and administer the ordinances of religion in the name of Christ. The first event is thus recorded in the words of Smith himself:

"We still continued the work of translation, when, in the ensuing month (May, 1829), we on a certain day went into the woods to pray and inquire of the Lord respecting baptism for the remission of sins, that we found mentioned in the translation of the plates. While we were thus employed, praying and calling upon the Lord, a messenger from heaven descended in a cloud of light, and having laid his hands upon us, he ordained us, saying:

"Upon you my fellow servants, in the name of Messiah, I confer the Priesthood of Aaron, which holds the keys of the ministering of angels, and of the Gospel of repentance, and of baptism by immersion for the remission of sins; and this shall never be taken again from the earth, until the sons of Levi do offer again an offering unto the Lord in righteousness.

"He said this Aaronic Priesthood had not the power of laying on hands for the gift of the Holy Ghost, but that this should be conferred on us hereafter; and he commanded us to go and be baptized, and gave us directions that I should baptize Oliver Cowdery, and afterwards that he should baptize me. Accordingly we went and were baptized. I baptized him first, and afterwards he baptized me, after which I laid my hands upon his head and ordained him to the Aaronic Priesthood, and afterwards he laid his hands on me and ordained me to the same Priesthood — for so we were commanded.

"The messenger who visited us on this occasion, and conferred this Priesthood upon us, said that his name was John, the same that is called John the Baptist in the New Testament, and that he acted under the direction of Peter, James and John, who held the keys of the Priesthood of Melchisedek, which Priesthood he said would in due time be conferred on us, and that I should be called the first Elder of the Church, and he (Oliver Cowdery) the second. It was on the 15th day of May, 1829, that we were ordained under the hand of this messenger and baptized."—*History of the Church, Vol.* I., *pp.* 30–41.

As may be readily understood, this account involves quite as great an element of the unusual and supernatural as even the reported appearances of the Angel Moroni in Smith's visions of 1823, but without specifying the other extraordinary phenomena that might lead a psychologist to attribute the experience to some subjective derangements of the senses. Moreover, another person, Oliver Cowdery, shares this vision, and makes explicit testimony to its reality many years later. The case with him is precisely the same as that involved in the testimonies of the three witnesses to the Book of Mormon, as already discussed. Commenting on this account, Roberts remarks in a note:

"It may be well at this point to call attention to the singular and important fact that the Prophet, neither in his narrative of the above really great and dramatic event, nor in any of those great visions and revelations which precede or follow it, stops to comment or grow eloquent over the importance of an administration or the grandeur of an occasion. He may never have heard the maxim, 'A true tale speeds best being plainly told,' but had he heard of it and adopted it as his motto, he could not have followed it more closely than unconsciously he has done in his narrative. He seems to have but one object in view, and that is to get on record the plain truth pertaining to the coming forth of the work of God. Oliver Cowdery, however, . . . has left upon record a description of the scene and the impressions it left upon his mind."—*Ibid., p.* 42 *note.*

In a public address delivered on the occasion of his return to the Church, after a separation of eleven years, in 1848, Cowdery expressly reaffirmed his conviction of the reality of this experience. Fourteen years before, however, previous to his defection from the Church, he had written a full and lively description of it, which appeared in the accredited organ of the Church. It is partly as follows:

"The Lord, who is rich in mercy, and ever willing to answer the consistent prayer of the humble, after we had called upon him in a fervent manner, aside from the abodes of men, condescended to manifest to us His will. On a sudden, as from the midst of eternity, the voice of the Redeemer spake peace to us, while the veil was parted and the angel of God came down clothed with glory, and delivered the anxiously looked for message, and the keys of the Gospel of repentance! — What joy! What wonder! What amazement! . . . As in the 'blaze of day'; yes, more — above the glitter of the May sunbeam, which then shed its brilliancy over the face of nature! Then his voice, though mild, pierced to the center, and his words, 'I am thy fellow-servant,' dispelled every fear. We listened, we gazed, we admired! 'Twas the voice of an angel from glory — 'twas a message from the Most High! and as we heard we rejoiced, while His love enkindled upon our souls, and we were rapt in the vision of the Almighty! Where was room for doubt? Nowhere; uncertainty had fled, doubt had sunk, no more to rise, while fiction and deception had fled forever!

"But, dear brother, think, further think for a moment, what joy filled our hearts and with what surprise we must have bowed (for who would not have bowed the knee for such a blessing?), when we received under his hand the Holy Priesthood. . . .

"I shall not attempt to paint to you the feelings of this heart, nor the majestic beauty and glory which surrounded us on this occasion; but you will believe me when I say, that earth, nor men, with the eloquence of time, cannot begin to clothe language in as interesting and sublime a manner as this holy personage. No; nor has this earth power to give the joy, to bestow the peace, or comprehend the wisdom which was contained in each sentence as they were delivered by the power of the Holy Spirit! . . . The assurance that we were in the presence of an angel; the certainty that we heard the voice of Jesus, and the truth unsullied as it flowed from a pure personage, dictated by the will of God, is to me, past description, and I shall ever look upon this expression of the Savior's goodness with wonder and thanksgiving while I am permitted to tarry, and in those mansions where perfection dwells and sin never comes, I hope to adore in that day which shall never cease." — *Messenger and Advocate, Oct.,* 1834, *pp.* 15–16.

It is needless to comment on any such statements. The conviction occurs strongly that its author is either telling the truth, or else deliberately romancing. That it is the result of "hypnotism" or other obscure mental state is by no means evident. Nor could any such theory be easily supported, as we have already seen in another connection. Whatever may be the truth of the matter, however, the fact remains that both Smith and Cowdery behaved, thereafter, as if the experience had been a veritable reality. Immediately after the experience reported above, the baptism of converts began, and within the succeeding eleven months about forty had professed belief in the new teachings. Finally, on April 6, 1830, the Church was formally organized with six members of record, to wit: Joseph Smith, Jr., his brothers, Hyrum and Samuel Harrison Smith, David Whitmer and his brother, Peter Whitmer, Jr., and Oliver Cowdery. On this occasion Cowdery was formally ordained as "second elder," and with Joseph Smith was sustained as an accepted teacher "in the things of the Kingdom of God." Smith records of this meeting:

> "We then laid our hands on each individual member of the Church present, that they might receive the gift of the Holy Ghost, and be confirmed members of the Church of Christ. The Holy Ghost was poured out upon us to a very great degree — some prophesied, whilst we all praised the Lord, and rejoiced exceedingly."—*History of the Church, Vol. I.*, p. 78.

Scarcely had the Church been formally organized, and the work of preaching its message systematically begun, when the conditions characteristic of Mormon history, even to the present day, sprang at once into active existence. Foremost among these was the bitter and persecuting spirit which still survives, and which is popularly supposed to have originated in indignation at teachings advocating "polygamy," and other "immoralities," undreamed of by Mormons, or others, at that period. Nor can any fears of "political menace" be urged in explanation for the violence perpetrated on a few dozen obscure and uninfluential people. Evidently, as previously suggested, the heart and origin of the whole opposition to Mormonism, to-day as well as at the beginning, is that Joseph Smith, a "wanton gospeler," had undertaken to found a new religious body and promulgate teachings out of harmony with those acceptable to the regular Protestant clergy. Had he begun as a recognized preacher of some established sect, or other, the case would have been different, without doubt. The whole character of the proceedings against him evidences this.

The first recorded arrest and trial of Joseph Smith took place in June, 1830, after several days of popular opposition to the attempts of Cowdery to baptize converts to their faith in a stream near the house of a certain Joseph Knight at Colesville, New York. The charge alleged on this occasion is said to have been "disorderly conduct," which seems to have consisted principally in the act of "setting the country in an uproar by preaching the Book of Mormon." Of course, hostile critics of Smith allege that the arrest was caused by even more serious "misdoings" on his part, also that "witnesses were intimidated." In default, however, of any definite and reliable proof to the contrary, it is safe to assume the truth of the accounts given by Smith of this episode, which, as it seems, was as preposterous an example of illegality as could be imagined. An episode from a comic opera, or the trial of the famous cause Bardell *vs.* Pickwick, could scarcely exceed the absurdity manifested in the succeeding trials before local courts. Of the first of these Smith gives the following description:

> "At length the trial commenced amidst a multitude of spectators, who in general evinced a belief that I was guilty of all that had been reported concerning me, and of course were very zealous that I should be punished according to my crimes. Among many witnesses called up against me, was Mr. Josiah Stoal — of whom I have made mention as having worked for him some time — and examined to the following effect:
>
> "'Did not the prisoner, Joseph Smith, have a horse of you?'
>
> "'Yes.'
>
> "'Did not he go to you and tell you that an angel had appeared unto him and authorized him to get the horse from you?'
>
> "'No, he told me no such story.'
>
> "'Well, how had he the horse of you?'
>
> "'He bought him of me as any other man would.'
>
> "'Have you had your pay?'
>
> "'That is not your business.'
>
> "The question being again put, the witness replied:
>
> "'I hold his note for the price of the horse, which I consider as good as the pay; for I am well acquainted with Joseph Smith, Jun., and know him to be an honest man; and if he wishes, I am ready to let him have another horse on the same terms.'
>
> . . . .
>
> "After a few more such attempts, the court was detained for a time, in order that two young women, daughters of Mr. Stoal, with whom I had at times kept company, might be sent for, in order, if possible, to elicit something from them which might be made a pretext against me. The young ladies arrived, and were severally examined touching my character and conduct in general, but particularly as to my behavior towards them, both in public and private; when they both bore such testimony in my favor as left my enemies without pretext on their account."—*History of the Church, Vol.* I., *pp.* 89–91.

At the conclusion of this "trial," which seems to have consisted in a series of vain attempts to force someone or other to assume the rôle of accuser against Joseph Smith on some serious charge, the prisoner was released. Almost immediately, however, he was rearrested on a warrant found in another county, and was hurried thither for trial. Here similar forcical proceedings took place, and he was again set at liberty. Such doings might reasonably be declared impossible, even considering the very irregular methods often followed in rural courts, were it not for the fact, which seems to be admitted on all hands, that the arrest of Smith always followed as a sort of climax to mob violence and disorder. Whatever Smith may have done on any of these occasions, it would seem that he was effectively and ably seconded by the rest of the population, who, in spite of their "righteous indignation," seem to have been able to do no more than fasten upon him the blame for their own acts of violence and disorder in the minds of the already prejudiced public. How far the doings of these mobs may be credited to genuine popular indignation may be judged as the story proceeds. One might reasonably expect that a person so widely accused and so often arrested amid violent manifestations of popular detestation, might at least have been found guilty of some of the grave charges made against him by historians, instead of being repeatedly acquitted, and, when held, detained only under circumstances that permit of a strong suspicion of injustice.

Immediately after his discharge by the courts of Chenango and Broome counties, Smith returned to his interrupted activities for the upbuilding of the church, which, in spite of all unfavorable conditions, seems to have grown steadily. Among the notable movements inaugurated was the first "mission of the Lamanites," or Indians, for whose conversion a number of elders were sent out. Later in the same year, as the result of missionary effort, such prominent and able converts as Parley P. Pratt, Sidney Rigdon, Newel K. Whitney and Edward Partridge were added to the membership. In this same year, also, appeared the distinctive feature of the Mormon system — the doctrine of "gathering"— which has always differentiated it from other sects and bodies professing Christianity.

At the time of the founding of the Church, Joseph Smith was but four months over twenty-four years of age, a very young man, alike in years, in learning and in experience. In view of the surroundings of his birth and education, his prominence, even locally, at this early age is remarkable; whereas the maturity and brilliancy shown in his formulations of the new Church, and in the administrations of its affairs, must seem no otherwise than wonderful to a fair mind. While there is some room for the theory that his ideas on all matters, particularly on the organization of the church, were gradually developed, there is also quite as good reason for considering his claim that the later principles were "revealed" in some manner, as required by the exigencies of external conditions. To have formulated and have attempted to establish the organization of the Church, full-grown and complete, at the very beginning would have seemed remarkable to say the least. Accordingly, we find that the process of development follows consecutive and logical steps, the first of which is to gather the people, the latterly to organize them in the way considered most appropriate and effective. Thus, as we must agree, this doctrine of "gathering" is no less a departure than all that succeeded it, although the primitive first step in the inauguration of the "work." This is expressed by George Q. Cannon, as follows:

"Teaching of the doctrine of the gathering also was a new announcement to the world. The belief common in Christendom was that man was as near to God in one place as another, and He could be worshipped everywhere alike. The idea, therefore, of converts abandoning home, with all its delightful associations and ancestral memories, and going to a new land, remote from kindred and friends, as a religious duty was a startling one and came in contact with all pre-conceived views. Under the inspiration, however, of the Lord, Joseph made it known as a movement required of true believers by the Almighty to prepare them for coming events. It was a bold proclamation, and viewed from a human standpoint, was likely to interfere with successful conversions. But it was from the Lord, and honest seekers after truth were led to look to Him for the evidence of its heavenly origin. The result came in due time, and should have been convincing to every human soul."—*Life of Joseph Smith the Prophet, pp.* 81–82.

The first gathering-place of the Church was at Kirtland, Ohio, although early in 1831 Smith announced a revelation to the effect that Zion, or the final home of the Saints, was to be in Jackson county, Missouri. In this region, as he claimed also, had been enacted many of the important events of antediluvian and early Biblical times — here was located the city of Zion built by Enoch, and which, according to a new version of the old story, now first given to the world, had been taken up to God, along with its founder and ruler — and hither, on Smith's advice, many of the converts to the Church prepared to migrate. Undoubtedly the story of Enoch, as the founder, priest and ruler of a perfect community of people — and in this respect it is not wholly out of accord with the ancient versions of his life and work, as given in the Talmud, and in other Semitic books — played a profoundly significant part in guiding the movements of Joseph Smith. In a revelation dated in March 1832 (*Doctrine and Covenants,* Section lxxviii), in which he is himself addressed as Enoch,* the design was undoubtedly originated in his mind of realizing on earth again the perfection of society said to have been found in the time of the ancient patriarch of the same name. For the achievement of this prodigious ideal, the working-out of the very reforms for which the world is still sadly in need, the gathering of communities of righteous people, devoted to performing the law of God in its fulness, appeared as an essential element of the "Latter-day Gospel." This seems to be expressed in the words of a revelation dated March 7, 1831, as follows:

"I have sent mine everlasting covenant into the world, to be a light

* In several places in the *Doctrine and Covenants* fictitious designations are used for both persons and things. This is explained as due to changes made for the sake of rendering the reference obscure to hostile readers.

to the world, and to be a standard for my people and for the Gentiles to seek to it, and to be a messenger before my face to prepare the way before me; wherefore, come ye unto it, and with him that cometh I will reason as with men in days of old, and I will show unto you my strong reasoning, wherefore hearken ye together and let me show it unto you, even my wisdom — the wisdom of him whom ye say is the God of Enoch, and his brethren, who were separated from the earth, and were received unto myself — a city reserved until a day of righteousness shall come — a day which was sought for by all holy men, and they found it not because of wickedness and abominations; and confessed they were strangers and pilgrims on the earth; but obtained a promise that they should find it and see it in their flesh."— *Doctrine and Covenants, xlv.* 9–14.

The lofty ideal embodied in this and other revelations underlay also the motives involved in the organization of the Order of Enoch, which is discussed at another place. Nor, apart from the confident promise of direct communion with God, on the condition of obedience to the law of righteousness, a distinctly and validly religious consideration, is it evident to the candid student that Smith used any other inducements, such as assurances of the foundation of an earthly Paradise. His appeal gathered around him a company of disciples, evidently sincerely convinced of the truth of his message, and, as events proved, amply ready and willing to brave persecution. Such converts may be acquired, perhaps, by many preachers with a message, but not every such person can hold them together in the face of truculent assaults. Also, as is evident, not every such person can himself endure the brunt of persecution. The successful leader of men must be endowed with firm conviction, courage, and undaunted determination. The possession of these high qualities by Joseph Smith demonstrates that his primary significance to history is in the character of a leader and executive of the highest ability, whose influence, nevertheless, was based in an enthusiasm far greater than either mere personal advantage or the achievement of temporal good ends. Smith has been compared to the Italian insurgent reformer, Rienzi, who in the fourteenth century achieved the liberation of Rome from the clutches of a corrupt oligarchy, and made himself "tribune" by virtue of his high qualities as a popular leader. It is well to note, however, the very essential difference between these two forceful men, in the fact that Rienzi's movement led direct to his own elevation to the seat of government, and that it collapsed with his downfall. Smith, on the other hand, although he carefully reserved for himself the direction of affairs during his own life-time, promulgated the details of a splendidly-conceived organization, which has proved a vital and persistent reality to this very day. Indeed, as stated by himself, his motives in the founding of his church organization had precisely this significance. Thus, under date March 27, 1832, he makes the following entry in his journal:

"We transacted considerable business for the salvation of the Saints, who were settling among a ferocious set of mobbers, like lambs among wolves. It was my endeavor to so organize the Church, that the brethren might eventually be independent of every incumbrance beneath the celestial kingdom, by bonds and covenants of mutual friendship, and mutual love."—*History of the Church, Vol.* I., *p.* 269.

It has been said in way of criticism of Smith's motives that he used his forceful and persuasive powers to induce people to settle in localities in which very many of them were, unfortunately, maltreated, despoiled or killed by "unmanageable mobs"; and this alleged fact is supposed to be very much to his discredit. It is well to note, however, that in every settlement made under his direction, or at his instigation, the people were carefully and stably organized, and in such fashion that, could the violence of mobs have been escaped, such settlements must have continued both prosperous and orderly. The wonderful solidarity of the Mormon people, which is a fact only too evident to admit of denial, is attributed by the Prophet himself to the inculcation and living of "correct principles" of life and truth. In a familiar quotation he is represented as stating this. Thus, "To one who inquired how he governed men so well, he said: 'I do not govern them; I teach them correct principles, and they govern themselves.'" His method is outlined in his own words, as follows:

"The inquiry is frequently made of me, 'Wherein do you differ from others in your religious views?' In reality and essence we do not differ so far in our religious views, but that we could all drink into one principle of love. One of the grand fundamental principles of 'Mormonism' is to receive truth, let it come from whence it may.

". . . If a skillful mechanic, in taking a welding heat, uses borax, alum, etc., and succeeds in welding together iron or steel more perfectly than any other mechanic, is he not deserving of praise? And if by the principles of truth I succeed in uniting men of all denominations in the bonds of love, shall I not have attained a good object?

". . . I will not seek to compel any man to believe as I do, only by the force of reasoning, for truth will cut its own way. Do you believe in Jesus Christ and the Gospel of salvation which He revealed? So do I. Christians should cease wrangling and contending with each other, and cultivate the principles of union and friendship in their midst; and they will do it before the millennium can be ushered in and Christ takes possession of His kingdom."—*History of the Church, Vol.* V., *p.* 499.

It was in Kirtland, Ohio, that the essential social principles of Mormonism were first promulgated. Here several revelations were received requiring such members of the Church as possessed lands to share them with the incoming new arrivals from the east, in order that all might have the means of self-support, until the affairs of the community could be so settled that each could purchase and own his own home. The law of consecrated property and stewardship was also promulgated, and, in several instances, the Saints were urged to hold their surplus at the requisition of the Church authorities, for the benefit of the whole people. Of course, hostile and disingenuous critics have asserted that all these advices and commands were only so many attempts to appropriate the funds of converts for the benefit of certain "ringleaders." The fact remains, however, that although considerable properties were actually assigned to their owners as "stewardships," the only ones mentioned by name in authoritative documents belonged to recognized leaders of the Church. Thus, to Sidney Rigdon is appointed his residence and tannery (*Doctrine and Covenants,* civ. 20–23); to Martin Harris is appointed "a lot of land" (*Ibid.* 24–25); also stewardships are appointed to Frederick G. Williams (*Ibid.* 27), Oliver Cowdrey (*Ibid.* 28–33), John Johnson (*Ibid.* 34–38), and Newel K. Whitney (*Ibid.* 39–42). Furthermore, the surplus of such stewardships, or moneys derived from other ready sources, were largely expended in the benefit of the whole people. It would be difficult, on another supposition, to account for the constantly increasing prosperity of the settlement in and about Kirtland, which, like all others founded by Smith and his associates, was constantly interfered with, and eventually scattered by disorderly mobs. Considerable capital has also been made in the fact that a banking establishment, the Kirtland Safety Society, of which Smith was president for a time and Rigdon cashier, proved a disastrous failure. There is no proof, however, in spite of the bitter denunciations among both outsiders and church members — several of the latter "apostatized" on this account — that either of the leading officers of this concern profited in any way. A certain Warren Parrish, employed in the bank is known to have embezzled a large sum — $30,000 is the amount named — and by this misfortune the concern seems to have been crippled. As failure in a business venture is not classed among crimes in civilized communities — unless, indeed, it results in the poverty of those who fail, if we may judge from the prevailing methods in such cases — the following résumé of this notorious incident is in place:

"The Kirtland 'boom' — as it would now be styled — began in the summer or fall of 1836, and during the following winter and spring went rushing and roaring on toward the whirlpool of financial ruin that soon swallowed it. The all-prevailing desire to amass wealth did not confine itself to mercantile pursuits, real estate dealings, and other branches of business of a legitimate if much inflated character, but was productive of 'wild-cat' schemes of every description, enterprises in every respect fraudulent, designed as traps for the unwary.

"An effort was made by the Prophet, who foresaw the inevitable disaster that awaited, to stem the tide of recklessness and corruption now threatening to sweep everything before it. For this purpose the Kirtland Safety Society was organized, the main object of which was to control the prevailing sentiment and direct it in legitimate channels. The Prophet and some of his staunchest supporters became officers and members of this association.

"The career of the Kirtland Bank was very brief. Unable to collect its loans, victimized by counterfeiters, and robbed by some of its own officials — subordinates having charge of the funds — it soon collapsed. A heroic effort was made to save it. Well-to-do members of the Church beggared themselves to buy up the bank's floating paper and preserve its credit. But in vain. In common with many other banks and business houses throughout the country,— for it was a year of general financial disaster, — it went down in the ruinous crash of 1837.

"Another opportunity was thus given to heap censure upon the Prophet; an opportunity of which his enemies, in and out of the Church, quickly availed themselves. As a matter of fact Joseph had withdrawn from the Society some time before, not being satisfied with the way events were shaping. It mattered not. Someone had done wrong, and someone must be blamed. As usual the most prominent target was the one fired at. Before this, however, so intense had become the feeling against the Prophet at Kirtland, that it was almost as much as one's life was worth to defend him against his accusers."— *Orson F. Whitney, History of Utah, Vol. I., pp.* 132–133.

During the seven years of Mormon residence in Kirtland it seems that a thrifty and prosperous settlement was built up. Farming and other industries were successfully conducted, and large bands of converts and new accessions to the settlement were constantly being received and provided for. The first regular church building, or "temple," was also erected, entirely by the voluntary subscriptions of the Church membership, and the essential laws and regulations of the "new dispensation" were formulated. This building, which still stands, is an especially holy place in the eyes of devout Mormons from the additional reasons that within its walls several important revelations are believed to have been received, and, as testified by Smith, Rigdon and Cowdery, visions of Christ and of several ancient saints and prophets were also manifested. Whatever may have been Smith's failures, or however much he may have excited "intense feeling" against himself, it must seem no less than remarkable that he could so successfully maintain the double office of "prophet, seer and revelator" with that of practical executive and temporal leader. He seems to have been able, not only to inspire a mystical enthusiasm for the "things of the spirit," but also to lead practical men of affairs to combine efficiently for the general good. If, as claimed, he used "hypnotism" to persuade the three witnesses that they had seen an angel, it might be in place to inquire what order of influence he employed to achieve such remarkable results at the very beginning of his career as leader and guide of hundreds and thousands of people.

Nor, in the midst of his other activities, all successful for the general good, did the Prophet omit the consideration of education. Thus, as early as June, 1831, the following revelation is recorded, with specific directions to one William W. Phelps:

> "Behold, thus saith the Lord unto you, my servant William, yea, even the Lord of the whole earth, thou art called and chosen, . . . and again, you shall be ordained to assist my servant Oliver Cowdery to do the work of printing, and of selecting, and writing books for schools in this church, that little children also may receive instruction before me as is pleasing unto me."—*Doctrine and Covenants,* lv. 1–4.

About one year later, in the first number of the *Evening and Morning Star* of Independence, Mo., the following appeared:

> "The disciples should lose no time in preparing schools for their children, that they may be taught as is pleasing unto the Lord, and brought up in the way of holiness. Those appointed to select and prepare books for the use of schools, will attend to that subject, as soon as more weighty matters are finished. But the parents and guardians, in the Church of Christ need not wait—it is all important that children, to become good should be taught so, (good). . . . A word to the wise ought to be sufficient, for children soon become men and women. Yes, they are they that must follow us, and perform the duties which, not only appertain to this world, but to the second coming of the Savior, even preparing for the Sabbath of creation, and for eternity."

In addition to these occasional expressions, it may be safe to state that the enthusiasm for education is an essential part of the Mormon system. Thus, in the authoritative works of the Church occur the following:

> "Whatever principles of intelligence we attain unto in this life, it will rise with us in the resurrection; and if a person gains more knowledge and intelligence in this life through his diligence and obedience than another, he will have so much the advantage in the world to come."—*Doctrine and Covenants,* cxxx. 18–19.

In the public utterances of Joseph Smith perfectly similar ideas are found expressed. Thus:

> "The glory of God is intelligence, or, in other words, light and truth."—*Ibid.,* xciii. 36.

> "A man is saved no faster than he get knowledge, for if he does not get knowledge, he will be brought into captivity by some evil power in the other world, as evil spirits will have more knowledge, and consequently more power than many men who are on the earth. Hence it needs revelation to assist us, and give us knowledge of the things of God."—*History of the Church, Vol.* IV. *p.* 588.

> "The more sure word of prophecy means a man's knowing that he is sealed up unto eternal life by revelation and the spirit of prophecy, through the power of the holy priesthood. It is impossible for a man to be saved in ignorance."—*Ibid., Vol. V. p.* 392.

> "And I give unto you a commandment, that you shall teach one another the doctrine of the kingdom; teach ye diligently and my grace shall at-

tend you, that you may be instructed more perfectly in theory, in principle, in doctrine, in the law of the gospel, in all things that pertain unto the kingdom of God, that are expedient for you to understand; of things both in heaven and in the earth, and under the earth; things which have been, things which are, things which must shortly come to pass; things which are at home, things which are abroad; the wars and the perplexities of the nations, and the judgments which are on the land, and a knowledge also of countries and of kingdoms."—*Doctrine and Covenants,* lxxxiii. 77–79.

Such teachings were undoubtedly understood by many of the Prophet's associates to refer to intellectual training, for which a considerable enthusiasm was manifested at various times. Thus, among other educational institutions founded by the direction of Joseph Smith was a class in Hebrew, under the instruction of a certain Dr. Seixas, a Jewish scholar apparently well equipped to teach the language and literature of his people. Under him Smith himself studied the Hebrew language, which he continued later under another scholar named Piexotto. He evidently believed in his own teachings to this extent, at least. It is also affecting to read that some of his converts, men of force and character, but of defective youthful advantages, eagerly sought to supplement their lack by availing themselves of present opportunities. Thus Wilford Woodruff, subsequently president of the Church, records in his voluminous and carefully kept journal:

"Having returned from my southern mission in the autumn of 1836, in company with Elders A. O. Smoot and Jesse Turpin, I spent the following winter in Kirtland. During this time I received my endowments and attended the school of Professor Haws, who taught Greek, Latin and English grammar. I confined my studies mostly to Latin and English grammar."—*Leaves from my Journal, p.* 25.

What other object could exist in the mind of Mr. Woodruff that should prompt him at the age of thirty years to seek to perfect himself in rudimentary branches, besides a desire to prepare thereby for a more effective ministry? His course, which was adopted by numerous others similarly circumstanced certainly evidences the fact that the influence of Joseph Smith and of his teachings moved men to seek improvement and better equipment. Such facts in themselves are sufficient to discredit the vulgar theory that Smith was merely a semi-insane and venal "hypnotist," and evidence the contention that, whatever his character or motives in any particular respect, he was certainly a wonderful and inspiring leader of men, one also worthy to rank with Napoleon in ability to stimulate enthusiasm for a cause, and devotion to his own person. The Spaulding hypothesis, in which some still profess belief, credits Sidney Rigdon with a phenomenal judgment of human nature, when, as asserted, he chose this man for his "publisher" and "mouthpiece."

However, the influence of Joseph Smith among his followers was by no means confined to matters didactic, educational or communal. It seems veritably to have endowed them with the ability, as mentioned by him, of "governing themselves." While he was residing principally in Kirtland, Ohio, with only an occasional visit to the regions further west, a thriving colony was being built up at Independence, Jackson county, Missouri, on the revealed site of the future Zion. Here, as at Kirtland, within a very few years, a thriving settlement was built up by people who had journeyed from their former homes in New York and Ohio, through a rough and virgin country for most of the distance of between 900 and 1,200 miles. Although settling in a wild and primitive region, whose white inhabitants were mostly of the frontier type of that day, neither enjoying nor desiring any of the benefits of civilization, the Mormons immediately set about introducing the elements of refined living. They laid out and cultivated farms, introduced various industries and mercantile enterprises, and began the publication of a newspaper, *The Upper Missouri Advertiser,* and a monthly periodical, *The Evening and Morning Star.* The printing office then opened by them was, as claimed, farther west by 250 miles than any other then existing in the United States.

Besides building up Independence, the Mormon people established farming settlements in the neighborhood of the Big Blue, immediately southeast of the present location of Kansas City; and within two years nearly 1,200 members of the Church, principally from New York, Ohio, and other northeastern states, had located in the confines of Jackson county. In spite of these, and other, evidences of good citizenship, these people were driven from the county by disorderly mobs in 1833, and were requested to leave Clay county, where they had sought refuge, in 1836. They then migrated to the northern parts of Missouri, then largely unsettled, and became the first inhabitants of the present Caldwell and Daviess counties. During the years 1836, 1837, and 1838 over 12,000 Latter-day Saints settled in this region, principally in Caldwell county, and as the result of their efforts the whole country was transformed from a wild prairie into a flourishing farming country. They also founded the city of Far West in Caldwell county, and the villages of Spring Hill and Adam-ondi-Ahman (later called Diahman) in Daviess county. Nevertheless, their industry and enterprise counted for nothing; for, within three years, they were again driven, this time from the confines of the state, and, migrating eastward, joined their fellow-religionists from Ohio in founding the city of Nauvoo on the Mississippi River in Hancock county, Illinois. Here they were allowed to remain for about eight years, again achieving many things worthy a place in the world's history. Then, because of intolerable persecution, persistently and systematically inflicted, virtually the entire population again migrated, this time to the Rocky Mountain region, in the confines of the present state of Utah, where they still remain.

We have learned already how that the influence of this man, who, as some insist, was a sodden ignoramus, availed to inspire many to seek wider educational advantages, and otherwise to improve themselves. We have also learned that through his leadership several thriving settlements were founded, first in Ohio, later in Missouri, and that, in loyalty to the teachings promulgated by him, the people were kept together, in the face of brutal persecutions. There were defections, of course; many of the Church fell away from their allegiance and professions — nor is this surprising — but the greater body of them held together with a tenacity worthy to rank as heroic. There are several touching incidents in the course of this "Mormon war" in Missouri, which should shed a valuable side-light on the quality of the influence that held them together. Among these is the striking testimony of David W. Patten, one of the apostles, who, in a vain attempt to rescue certain of the Mormons held in captivity by the mob, and threatened with death, was himself shot and mortally wounded. As he lay dying, he remarked simply to his wife, "Whatever you do else, oh, do not deny the faith." It was evidently a faith fit for heroes of which he spoke. In any other connection, as we cannot doubt, such words would be widely quoted among the "dying sayings" of great and good men, and preserved for the edification of posterity. For Patten, at least, the religion preached by Joseph Smith was a great and beautiful reality. Nor do people originate in themselves all the faith and consolations which they profess to find in their religion. There was a reality behind it all, and it was Christian.

In the movement of the Mormons, between twelve and fifteen thousand strong, from the state of Missouri, there was opportunity for the emergence of another colossal figure, whose name survives among the heroes of America — Brigham Young. It was upon his shoulders, as head of the Apostolic body that the duty of conducting the exodus fell, suddenly and unexpectedly, almost like a destiny, through the defection of several of the other officers who had ranked him in the quorum. Immediately, however, he took up his duties, and discharged them with the vigor and directness that characterized all his doings. Brought to the leadership of a band of people, many of whom had been despoiled to the last remnants of fortune, and were reduced to abject misery and dependence, he showed at once how seriously he regarded his title of "apostle." He became the friend and protector of the poor, and exerted himself to enforce the determination that, in accord with the principles of the Gospel, those who had saved anything should share it with all who had been despoiled. Late in September, 1838, he called a meeting of his leaders and proposed the following resolution, which he enforced to the letter, so far as he had influence:

"*Resolved,* That we this day enter into a covenant to stand by and assist each other, to the utmost of our abilities, in removing from this state, and that we will never desert the poor who are worthy, till they shall be out of the reach of the general exterminating order of General Clark, acting for and in the name of the state."

Except for the faithful performance of this resolution by the people and their leaders, it would be difficult to explain how large bodies of refugees could have been guided safely out of Missouri, and into Iowa and Illinois, even in the face of hardships, of the constant danger of defections from their ranks, and the bald uncertainty as to their destination, or as to the future of the very Church itself. At times, indeed, it seemed as though the end of the Mormon Church were at hand, and that its people were to be scattered abroad. Joseph Smith and his brother Hyrum, with Sidney Rigdon, constituting the Presidency, were imprisoned in Missouri, in constant seeming danger of death, but this fact did not discourage Brigham Young, nor any of the stronger men around him, and to their courage and downright faith in something that seemed grand and beautiful to them, is to be awarded a very large part of the credit for bringing this army of helpless refugees out of the reach of their enemies, and to another abiding place.

Of course, as must be acknowledged by all candid minds, such men as Patten, Young, Kimball, and a score of others among the companions and coadjutors of Joseph Smith, were men built on a large scale, men worthy to rank as heroes — if we may judge from the way in which they deported themselves in trying and difficult conditions — but it is truly interesting how large a number of such men Smith actually succeeded in attracting and inspiring. That his message was something real and vital to them — and to all others of his followers, is undoubted, but the highest tributes are paid to his own personality, leadership, ability and courage. That his influence is to be credited to any such devices as "hypnotism," or any other form of chicane pretending, or that he was an ingenious, plausible and indefatigable "imposter," are suggestions altogether too stupid and vulgar to deserve a moment's discussion. Whatever he may be supposed to have done in cases in which, in his presence, wonderful visions and divine manifestations are related by his associates, it is altogether certain that, in the handling of the body of the Church, in dealing with people in the mass — and too many of them were people of strong personality and decided character — he could have had recourse only to the methods and powers of a real leader of men. The following incident is related by George Q. Cannon, and certainly bears out the very qualities which one would logically expect to find manifested by a real leader, not to mention a man who had some quality closely akin to confidence in a Power greater than himself.

"An incident of this period shows that Prophet's calmness and self-command in the face of danger, as well as the influence of his presence even upon sworn enemies.

"He was sitting in his father's house near the edge of the prairie one day, writing letters, when a large party of armed mobocrats called at the place. Lucy Smith, the Prophet's mother, demanded their business, and they replied that they were on the way to kill 'Joseph, the Mormon Prophet.' His mother remonstrated with them; and Joseph, having finished his writing and hearing the threats against himself, walked to the door and stood before them with folded arms, bared head and such a look of majesty in his eyes that they quailed before him. Though they were unacquainted with his identity, they knew they were in the presence of greatness; and when his mother introduced him as the man they sought, they started as if they had seen a spectre.

"The Prophet invited the leaders into the house, and without alluding to their purpose of murder, he talked to them earnestly with regard to the persecutions against the Saints. When he concluded, so deeply had they been impressed, that they insisted upon giving him an escort to protect him to his home. . . .

"It was always so when men would listen to Joseph long enough to let the Spirit which animated him assert itself to their reason."—*Life of Joseph Smith the Prophet, pp.* 249–250.

A similarly striking incident is related by Parley P. Pratt, who states that it occurred on an occasion when he was confined, together with Smith, in a jail at Richmond, Missouri. Here they were confined during several days and nights, awaiting their execution under the orders of a certain Colonel Clark, in command of the state militia.

"In one of those tedious nights," Pratt relates, "we had lain as if in sleep, till the hour of midnight had passed, and our ears and hearts had been pained, while we had listened for hours to the obscene jests, the horrid oaths, the dreadful blasphemies and filthy language of our guards, Colonel Price at their head, as they recounted to each other their deeds of rapine, murder, robbery, etc., which they had committed among the 'Mormons' while at Far West and vicinity. . . .

"I had listened till I became so disgusted, shocked, horrified, and so filled with the spirit of indignant justice that I could scarcely refrain from rising upon my feet and rebuking the guards; but had said nothing to Joseph, or anyone else, although I lay next to him and knew he was awake. On a sudden he arose to his feet, and spoke in a voice of thunder, or as the roaring lion, uttering, as near as I can recollect, the following words:

"'Silence! Ye fiends of the infernal pit! In the name of Jesus Christ I rebuke you, and command you to be still. I will not live another minute and hear such language. Cease such talk, or you or I die this instant!'

"He ceased to speak. He stood erect in terrible majesty. Chained, and without a weapon; calm, unruffled, and dignified as an angel, he looked upon the quailing guards, whose weapons were lowered or dropped to the ground; whose knees smote together, and who, shrinking into a corner, or crouching at his feet, begged his pardon, and remained quiet till a change of guards.

"I have seen the ministers of justices, clothed in magisterial robes, and criminals arraigned before them, while life was suspended on a breath, in the Courts of England; I have witnessed a Congress in solemn session to give laws to nations; I have tried to conceive of kings, of royal courts, of thrones and crowns; and of emperors assembled to decide the fate of kingdoms; but dignity and majesty have I seen but once, and it stood in chains, at midnight, in a dungeon, in an obscure village of Missouri."—*Autobiography of Parley P. Pratt, pp.* 228–230.

Of course, as may be justly objected, both of these heroic incidents are related by devoted disciples of Smith and earnest adherents to his teachings; hence may be somewhat colored by the enthusiasm of their narrators. Although, however, neither of them is justly to be called improbable, nor discounted as altogether exceptional, to say the least, we are less concerned at present in inquiring into their actuality than in presenting excellent examples of the nearly mystical regard in which the Prophet was held by his fellows and disciples. That he was a man of wonderful force, dignity and ability cannot be denied, in view of the influence which he wielded.

Nor is it surprising to find in the writings of Smith's disciples and others accounts of his exercise of "miraculous" powers, as in the healing of the sick, after the manner of the apostles of old. In narrations of some of his earlier doings we find, also, examples of casting out evil spirits, to whose activities he seems to have attributed certain orders of affection, in true New Testament consistency. If, as seems well attested, he possessed and exercised any power whatever to effect the cure of disease, it is unnecessary to inquire into the theories or opinions which he may have held regarding their nature and origin, nor to open discussion with people who would be inclined to regard "demoniacal possession" in all its phases as a "discredited superstition." Scientifically, as we may assert, this matter is an open one, as exampled in the findings of such psychological authorities as Professor William James, and others. In regard to Smith's reputed power to heal disease, we have the following striking testimony from the writings of Wilford Woodruff:

"It was a very sickly time (when the refugees from Missouri first arrived at Commerce, on the site of the future city of Nauvoo) and Joseph had given up his home in Commerce to the sick, and had a tent pitched in his dooryard and was living in that himself. The large number of Saints who had been driven out of Missouri, were flocking into Commerce; but had no homes to go into, and were living in wagons, in tents, and on the ground. Many, therefore, were sick through the exposure they were subjected to. Brother Joseph had waited on the sick, until he was worn out and nearly sick himself.

"On the morning of the 22d of July, 1839, he arose reflecting upon the situation of the Saints of God in their persecutions and afflictions, and he called upon the Lord in prayer, and the power of God rested upon him mightily, and as Jesus healed all the sick around Him in His day, so Joseph, the Prophet of God, healed all around on this occasion. He healed all in his house and dooryard, then, in company with Sidney Rigdon and several of the Twelve, he went through among the sick lying on the bank of the river, and he commanded them in a loud voice, in the name of Jesus Christ, to come up and be made whole, and they were all healed. . . . As they were passing my door, Brother Joseph said: 'Brother Woodruff, follow me.' These were the only words spoken by any of the company . . . till we crossed the public square, and entered Brother Fordham's house. Brother Fordham had been dying for an hour, and we expected each minute would be his last.

"I felt the power of God that was overwhelming His Prophet

"When we entered the house, Brother Joseph walked up to Brother Fordham, and took him by the right hand; in his left hand he held his hat.

"He saw that Brother Fordham's eyes were glazed, and that he was speechless and unconscious.

"After taking hold of his hand, he looked down into the dying man's face and said: 'Brother Fordham, do you not know me?' At first he made no reply; but we could all see the effect of the Spirit of God resting upon him.

"He again said: 'Elijah, do you not know me?'

"With a low whisper, Brother Fordham answered, 'Yes.'

"The Prophet then said, 'Have you not faith to be healed?'

"The answer, which was a little plainer than before, was: 'I am afraid it is too late. If you had come sooner, I think it might have been.'

"He had the appearance of a man awaking from sleep. It was the sleep of death.

"Joseph then said: 'Do you not believe that Jesus is the Christ?'

"'I do, Brother Joseph,' was the response.

"Then the Prophet of God spoke with a loud voice, as in the majesty of the Godhead: 'Elijah, I command you, in the name of Jesus of Nazareth, to arise and be made whole!'

"The words of the Prophet were not like the words of man, but like the voice of God. It seemed to me that the house shook from its foundation.

"Elijah Fordham leaped from his bed like a man raised from the dead. A healthy color came to his face, and life was manifest in every act.

. . . .

"The unbeliever may ask: 'Was there not deception in this?'

"If there is any deception in the mind of the unbeliever, there was certainly none with Elijah Fordham, the dying man, nor with those who were present with him, for in a few minutes more he would have been in the spirit world, had he not been rescued."—*Leaves from My Journal, pp.* 62–64.

Another example of Smith's reported power to heal disease,

"through the gift and power of God," is related in connection with the conversion of Ezra Booth, at one time a Methodist minister, later a Mormon elder, and finally an apostate from Mormonism. The occasion of his defection, as related by Joseph Smith, lay in the fact that he was "disappointed" when he found that he was not granted the "power to smite men and make them believe" (See *History of the Church,* Vol. I. pp 215–216), a very clear evidence of the fact that he was thoroughly convinced of the reality of miraculous powers at the present day. The following account of the miracle which led to the conversion of Booth is given in a publication of the Campbellite denomination:

> "Ezra Booth, of Mantua, a Methodist preacher of much more than ordinary culture, and with strong natural abilities, in company with his wife, Mr. and Mrs. Johnson, and some other citizens of this place (Hiram), visited Smith at his home in Kirtland, in 1831. Mrs. Johnson had been afflicted for some time with a lame arm, and was not at the time of the visit able to lift her hand to her head. The party visited Smith partly out of curiosity, and partly to see for themselves what there might be in the new doctrine. During the interview, the conversation turned on the subject of supernatural gifts, such as were conferred in the days of the apostles. Someone said, 'Here is Mrs. Johnson with a lame arm; has God given any power to men now on the earth to cure her?' A few moments later, when the conversation had turned in another direction, Smith rose, and walking across the room, taking Mrs. Johnson by the hand, said in the most solemn and impressive manner: 'Woman, in the name of the Lord Jesus Christ, I command thee to be whole,' and immediately left the room.
>
> "The company were awe-stricken at the infinite presumption of the man, and the calm assurance with which he spoke. The sudden mental and moral shock — I know not how better to explain the well-attested fact — electrified the rheumatic arm — Mrs. Johnson at once lifted it up with ease, and on her return home the next day she was able to do her washing without difficulty or pain."—*Hayden, History of the Disciples, pp.* 250–251.

Whether, or not, we can agree with the writer of this account that a "sudden mental and moral shock" of this description could avail to "electrify the rheumatic arm," it must be admitted that Smith possessed some power capable of exciting the reverence of his adherents and bringing conviction to the minds of people who had come to visit him "partly out of curiosity."

It is interesting, however, to learn that this man, who could thus impress so many people with a firm belief in his professions as a direct agent of the Almighty, and who evidently believed every word of his own message implicitly, was also by no means a pompous and gloomy "superman," out of touch with the world of mankind, and demanding an exaggerated reverence for his person and opinions. Although a highly successful leader and administrator, he seems to have been a curiously genial and approachable person, one, also, possessed of a redeeming sense of humor that must have added greatly to his influence among the more intelligent people with whom he had to do. A notable instance of this is recorded by Josiah Quincy, who, among other anecdotes of the Prophet, related the substance of a running conversation on religious topics between him and a certain Methodist minister, who was one of the party. The latter gentleman, although freely invited to address the Mormon congregation on the following Sunday, seems to have considered it incumbent on him to controvert all of the Prophet's opinions. Thus, from Quincy:

"As we rode back, there was more dispute between the minister and Smith. 'Come,' said the latter, suddenly slapping his antagonist on the knee, to emphasize the production of a triumphant text, 'if you can't argue better than that, you shall say all you want to say to my people, and I will promise to hold my tongue, for there's not a Mormon among them who would need my assistance to answer you.' Some backthrust was evidently required to pay for this; and the minister, soon after, having occasion to allude to some erroneous doctrine which I forget, suddenly exclaimed, 'Why, I told my congregation the other Sunday that they might as well believe Joe Smith as such theology as that.' 'Did you say Joe Smith in a sermon?' inquired the person to whom the title had been applied. 'Of course I did. Why not?' The Prophet's reply was given with a quiet superiority that was overwhelming: 'Considering only the day and the place, it would have been more respectful to have said Lieutenant-General Joseph Smith.' Clearly the worthy minister was no match for the head of the Mormon Church."—*Figures of the Past, p.* 393.

Although by no means converted to the doctrines preached by Smith, Mr. Quincy seems to have derived a most favorable impression of his personality and influence. Some of his encomiums have already been quoted, and to these he adds the following:

"*A fine-looking man* is what the passer-by would instinctively have murmured upon meeting the remarkable individual who had fashioned the mould which was to shape the feelings of so many thousands of his fellow-mortals. But Smith was more than this, and one could not resist the impression that capacity and resource were natural to his stalwart person. I have already mentioned the resemblance he bore to Elisha R. Potter, of Rhode Island, whom I met in Washington in 1826. . . . Of all men I have met, these two seemed best endowed with that kingly faculty which directs, as by intrinsic right, the feeble or confused souls who are looking for guidance. This it is just to say with emphasis; for the reader will find so much that is puerile and even shocking in my report of the prophet's conversation that he might never suspect the impression of rugged power that was given by the man."—*Ibid., pp.* 381–382.

It is greatly to the credit of a man of Mr. Quincy's instincts and training that he should have derived so favorable and intelligent an opinion of Joseph Smith, in spite of the things which he characterizes as "puerile and even shocking." We must take account of the "personal equation," even with Josiah Quincy. Nor is it strictly just to judge of the significance of a man's work and life to the world of humanity on the basis of the personal traits that repel certain of his acquaintances. Considering the temperament and early environments of Joseph Smith, it is scarcely remarkable that he displayed many traits, and said many things that must have seemed "uncouth" to a "Brahmin" of New England; but, as one might object, etiquette and table manners are not essentials in the curricula of any of the "schools of the prophets." This very element, mentioned by Quincy, is a factor in the grant aggregate of surprises that enter into the career and character of Smith. This man, who, on his first appearance before this scholar from Massachusetts, was "clad in the costume of a journeyman carpenter when about his work," and who showed "a beard of some three days' growth," was not only a leader of men, but, if we really would estimate him justly, a great mystic. He stands for nothing more vividly and emphatically than the belief that, in the true Christian life, both the Church, and each individual member of it, are to be guided by the direct revealed will of God. And his particular revelations, as they are believed to be, embodied in the Book of Doctrine and Covenants, show precisely, with a few notable exceptions, homely and familiar counsels on everyday matters, addressed to various "servants" of God, by God Himself. There are, to be sure, lofty flights, particularly in sections dealing with the blessedness of the future life (See lxxvi. and lxxxviii.), many sayings and directions that are both wise and profound, but, in the majority of passages, God is represented as speaking to his "servants" precisely "as a man speaketh unto his friend." Nor is the Almighty represented as using "university English," elegant diction, "polished literary forms": He comes down, indeed, literally to the level of the persons whom He is represented as addressing. Yet, without desire to prejudice the reader's mind, we must insist that the question of the validity of "possibility" of the authority claimed for these directions and instructions lies primarily with the basic theory of the religious system that embodies them, rather than with any judgment on the matter of "appropriateness" or textual form. If God be assumed to address men thus individually, it may be honestly asked, how otherwise could we expect Him to do it, except in the form of admonitions and commendations on their daily walk? If, in addition, He has seen fit to employ as "mouth" a man uninstructed in literary refinements, could we reasonably expect that He would employ terms and phrases that must necessarily puzzle him, as well as many to whom they are addressed? "Literary form" is not always a "form of godliness."

Whatever may be the true and final answer to all such queries, the fact remains that, with the assistance of such professed revelations as are printed in this book, Joseph Smith succeeded in inspiring the allegiance and devoted enthusiasm of thousands of his personal disciples, and that they still so inspire thousands more, who have lived since his day. It was in the sincere belief, undoubtedly, that God speaks now, in such forms as these, that, as we have learned, the heroic Patten, with his dying breath, whispered, "Oh, do not deny the faith." All such facts really aggravate the riddle of Joseph Smith, as is recognized by truly candid critics. Thus, we may quote again from Quincy, although, perhaps, not wholly with agreement in his conclusions. He remarks, with rather doubtful accuracy:

> "I have quoted enough to show what really good material Smith managed to draw into his net. Were such fish to be caught with Spaulding's tedious romance and a puerile fable of undecipherable gold plates and gigantic spectacles? Not these cheap and wretched properties, but some mastering force of the man who handled them, inspired the devoted missionaries who worked such wonders."—*Ibid., pp.* 395–396.

We cannot insist too often that, as the history of Mormonism amply demonstrates, it was precisely "these cheap and wretched properties," as Mr. Quincy styles them, that appealed most strongly to the imaginations of his foremost converts, and that do still so appeal. Further, whatever may have been the "mastering force of the man," it was evidently combined with a consistent faith in his own professions, even the "gigantic spectacles." As was most truthfully said of him by a writer in *Chambers' Cyclopedia* (Article on "Mormons"), "a mere impostor—i.e. a person who did not, in some sense or other, partly believe in his own mission, but who, on the contrary, felt that he was the liar and cheat that people called him—would have broken down under such a tempest of opposition and hate as Smith's preaching excited." Instead of breaking down under the furious assaults made upon him and his teachings, Smith seems really, like the ancient apostles, to have emerged from each successive trial "rejoicing that [he was] counted worthy to suffer shame" (Acts v. 41). It would be difficult indeed to obliterate the influence of such a man.

In another particular, also, the influence of Joseph Smith manifested great and admirable traits. He was a preeminent leader of men, but also a leader of individuals, an example of the power of personal influence; even as he represented the Divine Being as acting, so he evidently considered that he himself should act. Thus, in the numerous cases of apostacy that occurred in his lifetime, the prevailing sentiment seems to have been a personal antagonism to Smith himself. Thus, were Sidney Rigdon and David Whitmer, who, while adhering to their previous testimonies as to the truth of the Mormon gospel, were disaffected with Smith personally. Furthermore, Smith seems to have entertained for the time being, at least, sore feelings toward several of these persons, particularly against Harris and Cowdery. Small wonder! They had been his friends and confidants, but now they had turned against him. Some of them, also, had denounced him as a "fallen prophet," although fully endorsing his early work, as in the translation of the Book of Mormon. When, however, any of these apostates expressed a desire to return to fellowship, the Prophet, himself, was the first to extend a welcome. Such a spirit was manifested by him in the cases of Orson Hyde and William W. Phelps, who had withdrawn from the Church during the trying times in Missouri. To Phelps he wrote a cordial letter. Some time after, as related, he wrote to Oliver Cowdery, who had withdrawn under charges of misconduct about the same time as Phelps. As Roberts states:

"In a sudden burst of kindness he said to his secretary:

"Write Oliver Cowdery, and ask him if he has not eaten husks long enough; if he is not almost ready to return, be clothed with robes of righteousness, and go up to Jerusalem. Orson Hyde hath need of him.

"A letter was written accordingly, but the Prophet's generous tender of forgiveness and fellowship called forth no response from Oliver Cowdery, once the second Elder of the Church, and the first to make public proclamation of the Gospel to the world. Subsequently, however, he did return, namely in 1848."—*Rise and Fall of Nauvoo, p. 70.*

CHAPTER VI

JOSEPH SMITH AS LAWGIVER AND EXECUTIVE

IN the work of building up the city of Nauvoo, on the site of the little village of Commerce, Smith had the fullest opportunity to manifest his ideas upon governmental and civic matters. With virtually the entire body of the Church collected in one place, he exercised his genius for organization in inaugurating a community and a government that were excellent, in many obvious particulars, as they were novel and original. In the work of organizing the city, it was necessary, first-place, to secure a charter from the state legislature; and such an instrument was drawn up, accordingly, under Smith's direction; giving the city council exceptionally wide powers — virtually in independence, within the limitations of the constitutions, of the state of Illinois and of the United States. It authorized, also, the enlistment and equipment of a military organization, which was subsequently known as the " Nauvoo Legion," and the building of a university. As Smith stated in his journal:

> " The City Charter of Nauvoo is of my own plan and device. I concocted it for the salvation of the Church, and on principles so broad, that every honest man might dwell secure under its protective influence without distinction of sect or party."—*History of the Church, Vol.* IV., *p.* 249.

The charge has frequently been made that the charter of Nauvoo virtually erected the city into an independent state, so far, at least, as an act of legislature could avail to accomplish such a result. This is supposed by critics of Mormonism to indicate the essentially " seditious " character of the procedure, and some have suggested — so far, at least, as any one dares to make such a suggestion in the face of historic facts that are liable to be unearthed by investigators — that the charter was passed by the state legislature under some kind of unlawful pressure, or in an irregular manner. In view of these miserable lies, so widely circulated by disingenuous and slovenly critics, it must be a surprise to the reading public to learn that the first charter of the city of Nauvoo was passed by unanimous vote of both houses of the state legislature in regular session, early in

December, 1840; was signed by Governor Thomas Carlin on the 16th of that month, and was witnessed by Stephen A. Douglas, as Secretary of State, two days later. It will be further interesting to learn that Abraham Lincoln, then a member of the lower house, voted for the charter, and even congratulated the Mormon agent, John C. Bennett, on its successful passage. We may understand, therefore, the calibre of some of the men who "helped perpetrate this enormity," also, how "high up" the alleged "corrupting influence" must have reached. An account of the passage of this measure and of the conditions leading up to it has been given by Thomas Ford, later Governor of the state. If, as he claims, the considerations involved were wholly political, it would seem that no "extraordinary pressure" had been exercised, except by the regular party leaders, who may be assumed to have been moved solely by ambition. Mr. Ford writes, as follows:

"In the State of Missouri, the Mormons had always supported the Democratic party. They had been driven out by a Democratic governor of a Democratic State; and when they appealed to Mr. Van Buren, the Democratic President of the United States, for relief against the Missourians, he refused to recommend it, for want of constitutional power in the United States to coerce a sovereign State in the execution of its domestic polity. This soured and embittered the Mormons against the Democrats. Mr. Clay, as a member of the United States Senate, and John T. Stuart, a member of the House of Representatives in Congress, from Illinois, both Whigs, understood their cause, and introduced and countenanced their memorials against Missouri; so that, when the Mormons came to this State, they attached themselves to the Whig party. In August, 1840, they voted unanimously for the Whig candidates for the Senate and Assembly. In the November following, they voted for the Whig candidate for President; and in August, 1841, they voted for John J. Stuart, the Whig candidate for Congress in their district.

"At the legislature of 1840–41 it became a matter of great interest, with both parties, to conciliate these people. They were already numerous, and were fast increasing by emigration from all parts. It was evident that they were to possess much power in elections. They had already signified their intention of joining neither party, further than they could be supported by that party, but to vote for such persons as had done or were willing to do them most service. And the leaders of both parties believed that the Mormons would soon hold the balance of power, and exerted themselves on both sides, by professions, and kindness and devotion to their interests, to win their support.

"In this state of the case Dr. John C. Bennett presented himself at the seat of government as the agent of the Mormons. This Bennett was probably the greatest scamp in the western country. I have made particular enquiries concerning him, and have traced him in several places in which he had lived before he had joined the Mormons in Ohio, Indiana and Illinois, and he was everywhere accounted the same debauched, unprincipled and profligate character. . . . He flattered both sides with the hope of Mormon favor; and both sides expected to receive their votes. A city charter drawn up to suit the Mormons was presented to the Senate by Mr. Little. It was referred to the judiciary committee, of which Mr.

Snyder, a Democrat, was chairman, who reported it back recommending its passage. The vote was taken, the ayes and noes were not called for, no one opposed it, but all were busy and active in hurrying it through. In like manner it passed the House of Representatives, where it was never read except by its title; the ayes and noes were not called for, and the same universal zeal in its favor was manifested here which had been so conspicuously displayed in the Senate.

"This city charter and other charters passed in the same way by this legislature, incorporated Nauvoo, provided for the election of a Mayor, four Aldermen, and nine Counsellors; gave them power to pass all ordinances necessary for the peace, benefit, good order, regulation, convenience, or cleanliness of the city, and for the protection of property from fire, which were *not repugnant to the Constitution of the United States, or this State.* This seemed to give them power to pass ordinances in violation of the *laws* of the State, and to erect a system of government for themselves. This charter also established a mayor's court with exclusive jurisdiction of all cases arising under the city ordinances, subject to an appeal to the municipal court. It established a municipal court to be composed of the mayor as chief justice, and the four aldermen as his associates; which court was to have jurisdiction of appeals from the mayor or aldermen, subject to an appeal again to the circuit court of the county. The municipal court was also clothed with power to issue writs of habeas corpus in all cases arising under the ordinances of the city.

"This charter also incorporated the militia of Nauvoo into a military legion, to be called the 'Nauvoo Legion.' It was made entirely independent of the military organization of the State, and not subject to the command of any officer of the State militia, except the Governor himself, as commander-in-chief. . . .

"Thus it was proposed to reestablish for the Mormons a government within a government, a legislature with power to pass ordinances at war with the laws of the State; courts to execute them, with but little dependence upon the constitutional judiciary; and a military force at their own command, to be governed by its own by-laws and ordinances, and subject to no State authority but that of the Governor. It must be acknowledged that these charters were unheard-of, and anti-republican in many particulars; and capable of infinite abuse by a people disposed to abuse them. . . . One would have thought that these charters stood a poor chance of passing the legislature of a republican people jealous of their liberties. Nevertheless they did pass unanimously through both houses. Messrs. Little and Douglas managed with great dexterity with their respective parties. Each party was afraid to object to them for fear of losing the Mormon vote, and each believed that it had secured their favor."—*History of Illinois, pp. 262–265.*

In view of the widely repeated charge that the Nauvoo charter had for its primary object some seditious "resistance of organized authority" on the part of Smith and the Mormons, several reflections logically occur at this point. In the first place, it is scarcely remarkable that a lot of people, who had been so outrageously treated in both Ohio and Missouri, should wish to obtain some kind of exceptional powers that should secure them the ordinary rights of human beings, so generously guaranteed in the constitutions of all the states of the union and of the United States. If, however, wittingly, or not, such people sought for and obtained powers "capable of infinite abuse by a people disposed to abuse them," as Ford states, such fact need not be wholly blamed to the Mormons or to Joseph Smith, who "concocted" the charter. The question naturally arises as to whether "republican people jealous of their liberties" need not dread the activities of legislatures who will grant such plenary powers, quite as badly as the persons who ask for them. Whatever may have been Smith's motives in "concocting" such a charter as this, they could scarcely be more incompatible with the "safety of American institutions," as another cant phrase has it, than the kind of lawmakers who will sell their votes for the sake of hoped-for party advantages. The fact remains, however, that there is no distinct evidence that the privileges granted in the Nauvoo charter were abused to any conspicuous degree; also, that the popular uprisings against the Mormons in Illinois were no more in protest against this kind of "favoritism" than were the perfectly similar disorders in both Ohio and Missouri.

In order that the motives of Smith in the founding of Nauvoo may be thoroughly understood, it is necessary to refer to original documents and the testimony of contemporary history. These will furnish a very fair line of evidence that an orderly and stable community was in contemplation, instead of any of the numerous deadly, not to say "preposterous," objects as supposed by various critics. Under date, May 24, 1841, the following proclamation was issued to all the Saints in the stakes outside of Nauvoo, at Kirtland, Ohio, and at Independence, Missouri (the "centre-stake" of Zion):

> "The First Presidency of the Church of Jesus Christ of Latter-day Saints, anxious to promote the prosperity of said Church, feel it their duty to call upon the Saints who reside out of this county [Hancock], to make preparations to come in without delay. This is important, and should be attended to by all who feel an interest in the prosperity of this corner-stone of Zion. Here the Temple must be raised, the University built, and other edifices erected which are necessary for the great work of the last days, and which can only be done by a concentration of energy and enterprise. Let it, therefore, be understood that all the stakes, excepting those in this county, and in Lee County, Iowa, are discontinued, and the Saints instructed to settle in this county as soon as circumstances will permit."—*History of the Church, Vol.* IV., *p.* 362.

Commenting on this announcement and invitation, Orson F. Whitney writes as follows:

> "To this call the Saints responded with alacrity, and came pouring in from all parts outside the two counties mentioned, to engage in the work of building up and beautifying 'the corner stone of Zion.'
>
> "To the followers of the Prophet, as well as to the Prophet himself, this was all that the call really meant. Temple-building, with the Saints, we need scarcely inform the reader, amounts to what might be termed a divine passion; a work done by Time for Eternity. . . . No work in

their estimation is so important,— not even their proselyting labors among the nations. Next to their religious mission of preaching, proselyting, and administering in their temples for the salvation of the living and the dead, is their penchant for founding institutions of learning. This fact Mormon history abundantly verifies, in spite of all that has been said and thought to the contrary. This explains in part that ready obedience,— wrongfully supposed to be a mere servile yielding to the dictum of a despot,— manifested by the Saints to the word and will of their leader. He was simply inviting them to engage in the work most congenial to their souls; and this, as we have said, was all that the call really meant.

"But to the politicians it meant more,— or rather, meant something entirely different. It was construed by them as a shrewd political maneuver, foreshadowing the ultimate domination of Hancock County by the Mormons, and the relegation to the rear, as a hopeless minority, of the combined forces of Whigs, Democrats and whatever else, in spite of all that could be done to hinder. It was believed, in short, to be a 'colonizing' scheme, a trick to increase and render supreme the local Mormon vote. Already jealous of the power wielded by the Saints at the polls, and professing to 'view with alarm' the prospective increase of that power by means of the proposed concentration, some of the politicians now set about organizing in Hancock County a new party, the avowed object of which was to oppose and counteract the political influence of the Mormons in county and in state."— *History of Utah, Vol. I., pp.* 187–188.

The accuracy of this view is borne out by reference to a discourse delivered by Joseph Smith on June 11, 1843. (See *History of the Church, Vol. V.*, p. 423). That he and his associates were primarily far more interested in founding a city that should be a "city of the Saints" in fact, as well as in name, seems to be indicated by the several ordinances early passed by the Council looking toward the maintainance of order, sound morals and human rights. Nor were such ordinances merely verbal declarations, as is amply evidenced by the testimonies of non-Mormon writers. Thus, in his discussion of the chartering and early history of the city, Ford relates:

"The common council passed many ordinances for the punishment of crime. The punishments were generally different from, and vastly more severe, than the punishments provided by the laws of the State."— *History of Illinois, p.* 266.

Some such tendency as this is shown in a debate of the Council held on March 4, 1843, which is reported thus:

"In debate, George A. Smith said imprisonment was better than hanging.

"I (Joseph Smith) replied, I was opposed to hanging, even if a man kill another, I will shoot him, or cut off his head, spill his blood on the ground, and let the smoke thereof ascend up to God; and if ever I have the privilege of making a law on this subject, I will have it so."— *History of the Church, Vol. V.*, p. 296.

This statement was evidently made in harmony with the Old Testament dictum, "By man shall his blood be shed" (Gen. ix.

6), the "blood atonement," so called, which will be discussed at another place. Similarly severe in point of penalties prescribed was the ordinance presented by Smith, Nov. 13, 1841, entitled "Concerning Vagrants and Disorderly Persons." In this act it is prescribed that all vagrants, all drunk or disorderly persons, those guilty of using profane or indecent language, etc., shall "be required to enter into security for good behavior for a reasonable time," or, in default of such security, to suffer imprisonment for not more than six months, or to be fined five hundred dollars, or both, at the discretion of the court. Such provision was undoubtedly intended to discourage the very kind of disorders that had so sorely assailed the people in every other locality. Nevertheless, as seems evident, it contemplated no abridgement of popular rights of assemblage: it could under no circumstances be construed into a "veiled attempt" to curtail individual freedom of conscience. This is true, because, as specifically enacted, on March 1, 1841:

> "Catholics, Presbyterians, Methodists, Baptists, Latter-day Saints, Quakers, Episcopals, Universalists, Unitarians, Mohammedans, and all other religious sects and denominations whatever, shall have free toleration, and equal privileges, in this city; and should any person be guilty of ridiculing, and abusing or otherwise depreciating another in consequence of his religion, or of disturbing or interrupting any religious meeting within the limits of this city, he shall, on conviction thereof before the Mayor or Municipal Court, be considered a disturber of the public peace, and fined in any sum exceeding five hundred dollars, or imprisoned not exceeding six months, or both, at the discretion of said Mayor or Court."—*History of the Church, Vol. IV., p.* 306.

In addition, any municipal officer was required to report any violation of this ordinance to the Mayor, and any officer was authorized to arrest all violators, "either with or without process." Of course, as may be claimed, this ordinance was probably framed with a vivid recollection of the wanton interruptions of Mormon meetings in Missouri, but it must not be forgotten that it proscribes all interruptions of any kind of religious gathering, and protects "all other religious sects and denominations whatever" with equal penalties. Nor has any case of unlawful, or unworthy, discrimination in this matter ever been brought to the attention of the public by any of the enemies of Smith and Mormonism, nor was such discrimination alleged by the mobbers who harried and finally effected the migration of the people of Nauvoo.

That the above, and all similar ordinances, passed by the City Council of Nauvoo, were honestly and deliberately framed for the purpose of maintaining order, decency and the free exercise of individual rights, there can be no doubt in any candid mind. Furthermore, under the leadership of the Prophet himself, the

City Ordinances struck direct at the root of crime and disorder by passing the first effective temperance ordinance in the history of America. With an instinct which, in any other person, would be called truly "statesmanlike," Smith evidently understood that absolute prohibition of the sale of intoxicating liquors would be an abortive measure, as, indeed, it has proved, sadly enough, wherever attempted; and, therefore, sought to reduce the liquor evil to its lowest terms by an ordinance forbidding the sale of alcoholic drinks in small quantities. This measure put a stop to "tippling," which is the principal evil to be combatted, as intelligent reformers will agree. To limit the sales of alcoholic drinks to large quantity lots should, as reflection will show, prove a very effective discouragement to overindulgence. Few persons having a taste for whisky would care to purchase it by the gallon, or not at all; also, the worst form of whisky drinking is not that which is done at home. The following is the Ordinance passed at the instance of Smith, on February 15, 1841:

"AN ORDINANCE IN RELATION TO TEMPERANCE

"Sec. 1. Be it ordained by the City Council of the City of Nauvoo, that all persons and establishments whatever, in this city, are prohibited from vending whisky in a less quantity than a gallon, or other spirituous liquors in a less quantity than a quart, to any person whatever, excepting on the recommendation of a physician, duly accredited in writing, by the Chancellor and Regents of the University of the City of Nauvoo; and any person guilty of any act contrary to the prohibition contained in this ordinance, shall, on conviction thereof before the Mayor or municipal court, be fined in any sum not exceeding twenty-five dollars, at the discretion of said Mayor or municipal court; and any person or persons who shall attempt to evade this ordinance by giving away liquor, or by any other means, shall be considered alike amenable, and fined as aforesaid."—*History of the Church, Vol. IV., p.* 299.

That this ordinance was considered an effective means of curbing the evils of intemperance is evident, since no licensing provision is recorded. Indeed, under date July 12, 1841, Smith records as follows:

"I was in the City Council, and moved that any person in the City of Nauvoo be at liberty to sell vinous liquors in any quantity, subject to the city ordinances."—*History of the Church, Vol. IV., p.* 383.

Previously, on April 6, 1841, he records, in connection with the account of the laying of the corner-stones, of the Temple, at which great crowds of people were present:

"What added greatly to the happiness we experienced on this interesting occasion, is the fact that we heard no obscene or profane language; neither saw we any one intoxicated. Can the same be said of a similar assemblage in any other city in the Union? Thank God that the intoxicating beverage, the bane of humanity in these last days, is becoming a stranger in Nauvoo."—*History of the Church, Vol. IV., pp.* 330–331.

Of course, as may be remarked, "obscene or profane language" and intoxication are not usually expected in persons who gather to a religious service, but it must not be forgotten that the experience of the Mormons had been otherwise. If these testimonies are to be accepted, they seem competent to prove that the "exceptional powers" granted to the City Council of Nauvoo had not been misplaced, but were being used to the advantage of order and decency, in a manner impossible, except by special local legislation. It is interesting to note, that, although the State Legislature afterward "reconsidered," and greatly modified the charter of Nauvoo, that the principle involved, local autonomy within a wide range of power, was not abandoned, even in Illinois; being embodied in the Charter of the great city of Chicago, where local self-government, in such matters, at least, as "option" as to the sale of intoxicants, extends even to the wards of the Municipality. The result, in recent years, has been that prohibition of the liquor traffic has been established in most parts of that city, a result impossible, for example, in New York, where the local government is often hampered by "up-state legislators," as frequently complained. In some points Joseph Smith seems to have had a firm grasp on the principles necessary to conserve popular liberties, and render government effective.

That Smith was intensely alive to the requirements of good government and social order, particularly in matters touching personal morals, seems to be indicated by the following entry in his journal, under date May 14, 1842:

> "I attended city council in the morning, and advocated strongly the necessity of some active measures being taken to suppress houses and acts of infamy in the city; for the protection of the innocent and virtuous, and the good of public morals; showing clearly that there were certain characters in the place, who were disposed to corrupt the morals and chastity of our citizens, and that houses of infamy did exist, upon which a city ordinance concerning brothels and disorderly characters was passed, to prohibit such things. It was published in this day's *Wasp*.
>
> "I also spoke at length for the repeal of the ordinance of the city licensing merchants, hawkers, taverns and ordinaries, desiring that this might be a free people, and enjoy equal rights and privileges, and the ordinances were repealed."—*History of the Church, Vol. V., p.* 8.

From very many points of view it is to be deeply regretted that, at the time of their expulsion from Missouri, the Mormons did not strike westward at once, and, in some unsettled region, build up their own social and governmental institutions, under the direction of Joseph Smith himself. The world might then have had the opportunity of correctly estimating this man and his influence, apart from the disgusting necessity of constantly reviewing the false accusations made by wicked and prejudiced assailants, and describing the doings of scoundrelism masquerading under the disguise of public virtue, with the leadership of alleged righteous men. Had he then attempted to carry out the design attributed to him by various persons of becoming "a second Mohammed," making "one gore of blood from the Rocky Mountains to the Atlantic ocean," and giving the alternatives for peace, "Joseph Smith or the Sword," there would have been ample opportunity and sufficient warrant for dealing with him by the proper use of the accredited guardians of peace and law, without enlisting drunken and disorderly mobs in the militia forces of any state, or in the service of the general government. It would have been interesting, indeed, to have been able to record precisely how far his surprising design of welding government and religion — deriving the powers of government direct from the presumed authority of God — could have been successful and operative. Had he failed utterly, it would have been unnecessary to heap further reproaches upon his head: had he succeeded wonderfully, the alternative would have been no such slogan as "Joseph Smith or the Sword." Despite, then, the wonderful and highly creditable achievements of men inspired by his teachings, who years after his death wrought nobly and well in the deserts of Utah, the world has lost something in the fact that Smith himself, like a modern Moses, was not permitted to enter into even that "land of promise." The following seems to set forth Smith's ideals and purposes, and, if not written by himself, was certainly from the pen of Sidney Rigdon, or some other man close to him. In his journal, under date July 15, 1842, he records this:

"I find an editorial, in the *Times and Seasons,* on the government of God as follows: —

"The Government of God.

"The government of the Almighty has always been very dissimilar to the governments of men, whether we refer to His religious government, or to the government of nations. The government of God has always tended to promote peace, unity, harmony, strength, and happiness; while that of man has been productive of confusion, disorder, weakness, and misery.

"The greatest acts of the mighty men have been to depopulate nations and to overthrow kingdoms; and whilst they have exalted themselves and become glorious, it has been at the expense of the lives of the innocent, the blood of the oppressed, the moans of the widow, and the tears of the orphan.

"Egypt, Babylon, Greece, Persia, Carthage, Rome,— each was raised to dignity amidst the clash of arms and the din of war; and whilst their triumphant leaders led forth their victorious armies to glory and victory, their ears were saluted with the groans of the dying and the misery and distress of the human family; before them the earth was a paradise, and behind them a desolate wilderness; their kingdoms were founded in carnage and bloodshed, and sustained by oppression, tyranny, and despotism. The designs of God, on the other hand, have been to promote the universal good of the universal world; to establish peace and good will among men; to promote the principles of eternal truth; to bring about a state of things that shall unite man to his fellow man; cause the world to 'beat their swords into plowshares, and their spears into pruning hooks,' make the nations of the earth dwell in peace, and to bring about the millennial glory, when 'the earth shall yield its increase, resume its paradisean glory, and become as the garden of the Lord.'

"The great and wise of ancient days have failed in all their attempts to promote eternal power, peace and happiness. Their nations have crumbled to pieces; their thrones have been cast down in their turn, and their cities, and their mightiest works of art have been annihilated; or their dilapidated towers, of time-worn monuments have left us but feeble traces of their former magnificence and ancient grandeur. They proclaim as with a voice of thunder, those imperishable truths — that man's strength is weakness, his wisdom is folly, his glory is his shame.

"Monarchical, aristocratical, and republican governments of their various kinds and grades, have, in their turn, been raised to dignity, and prostrated in the dust. The plans of the greatest politicians, the wisest senators, and the most profound statesmen have been exploded; and the proceedings of the greatest chieftains, the bravest generals, and the wisest kings have fallen to the ground. Nation has succeeded nation, and we have inherited nothing but their folly. History records their puerile plans, their short-lived glory, their feeble intellect and their ignoble deeds.

"Have we increased in knowledge or intelligence? Where is there a man that can step forth and alter the destiny of nations and promote the happiness of the world? Or where is there a kingdom or nation that can promote the universal happiness of its own subjects, or even their general well being? Our nation, which possesses greater resources than any other, is rent, from centre to circumference, with party strife, political intrigues, and sectional interest; our counselors are panic stricken, our legislators are astonished, and our senators are confounded, our merchants are paralyzed, our tradesmen are disheartened, our mechanics out of employ, our farmers distressed, and our poor crying for bread, our banks are broken, our credit ruined, and our states overwhelmed in debt, yet we are, and have been in peace. . . .

"It has been the design of Jehovah, from the commencement of the world, and is His purpose now, to regulate the affairs of the world in his own time, to stand as a head of the universe, and take the reins of government in His own hand. When that is done, judgment will be administered in righteousness; anarchy and confusion will be destroyed, and 'nations will learn war no more.' It is for want of this great governing principle, that all this confusion has existed; 'for it is not in man that walketh, to direct his steps'; this we have fully shown.

"If there was anything great or good in the world, it came from God. The construction of the first vessel was given to Noah, by revelation. The design of the ark (of the Covenant) was given by God, 'a pattern of heavenly things.' The learning of the Egyptians, and their knowledge of astronomy was no doubt taught them by Abraham and Joseph, as their records testify, who received it from the Lord. . . . Wisdom to govern the house of Israel was given to Solomon, and to the judges of Israel; and if he had always been their king, and they subject to his mandate, and obedient to his laws, they would still have been a great and mighty people — the rulers of the universe, and the wonder of the world.

. . . .

"This is the only thing that can bring about the 'restitution of all things spoken of by all the holy Prophets since the world was'—'the dispensation of the fullness of times, when God shall gather together all things in one.' Other attempts to promote universal peace and happiness in the human family have proved abortive; every effort has failed; every plan and design has fallen to the ground; it needs the wisdom of God, the intelligence of God, and the power of God to accomplish this. . . .

"In regard to the building up of Zion, it has to be done by the counsel of Jehovah, by the revelations of heaven; and we should feel to say, 'if the Lord go not with us, carry us not up hence.' We would say to the Saints that come here, we have laid the foundation for the gathering of God's people to this place, and they expect that when the Saints do come, they will be under the counsel that God has appointed. . . . We are trying here to gird up our loins, and purge from our midst the workers of iniquity; and we hope that when our brethren arrive from abroad, they will assist us to roll forth this good work, and to accomplish this great design, that 'Zion may be built up in righteousness; and all nations flock to her standard'; that as God's people, under His direction, and obedient to His law, we may grow up in righteousness and truth; that when His purposes shall be accomplished, we may receive an inheritance among those that are sanctified."—*History of the Church, Vol. V., pp.* 61–66.

Very similar ideas were expressed in a discourse delivered by Sidney Rigdon at the General Conference of the Church in April, 1844. He says in part:

"I will endeavor to show why salvation belongs to us more peculiarly, in contradistinction to all other bodies. Will this be clear enough?

"I discover one thing: Mankind have labored under one universal mistake about this—viz., salvation was distinct from government; *i. e.*, that I can build a Church without government, and that thing have power to save me!

"When God sets up a system of salvation, He sets up a system of government that shall rule over temporal and spiritual affairs.

"Every man is a government of himself, and infringes upon no government. A man is not an honorable man, if he is not above all law and above government.

"I see in our town we have need of government. Some study law only for the purpose of seeing how many feuds, how many broils they can kick up, how much they can disturb the peace of the public without breaking the law, and then say—'I know my rights, and will have them'; 'I did not know it was the marshal, or I would not have done it.'

"He is no gentleman. Gentlemen would not insult a poor man in the street, but would bow to him, as much as those who appear more respectable. No marshal or any one else, should pull me up. We ought to live a great way within the circle of the laws of the land. I would live far above all law.

"The law of God is far more righteous than the laws of the land. The kingdom of God does not interfere with the laws of the land, but keeps itself by its own laws."—*Ibid., Vol. VI., p.* 292.

Although such expressions used by Smith and his coadjutors have often been quoted as evidence of "seditious intent," and the claiming of powers and authority in defiance of the civil law—even to its subversion—it is quite evident that they mean no more than that the law of God is the real source of all authority, and that any one who is animated by a desire to live and act in accord with its principles is "above the law," while, at the same time, "not against the law." Similar teachings have been often propounded throughout Christian centuries, particularly on the authority of St. Paul, and have never been seriously misunderstood. The sole difference in the present case is that the persons here speaking profess the belief that the law of God finds preeminent statement for this age in the mouths of accredited prophets and apostles. Such passages furnish very imperfect grounds for charges of "sedition" or unlawful defiance of authority. At the least, there is no known statement of Joseph Smith, which distinctly voices the sentiments thus ascribed to him by hostile, and, too often also, disingenuous, critics. Nevertheless, in whatever manner such people may distort his words, and refuse to give credit for human sentiments to Smith and his immediate associates, it is altogether evident that most of his followers — those also engaged in work in behalf of the Church — held opinions very different from these, also quite in accord with what we have stated were his actual beliefs and ideals. The following, from the English organ of Mormonism, is significant:

"In the midst of the general distress which prevails in this country [England] on account of want of employment, the high price of provisions, the oppression, priestcraft, and inquity of the land, it is pleasing to the household of faith to contemplate a country reserved by the Almighty as a sure asylum for the poor and oppressed,— a country every way adapted to their wants and conditions — and still more pleasing to think that thousands of the Saints have already made their escape from this country, and all its abuses and distress, and that they have found a home, where, by persevering industry, they may enjoy all the blessings of liberty, peace, and plenty.

"It is not yet two years since the Saints in England, in obedience to the command of their Heavenly Father, commenced a general plan of emigration to the land of Zion.

"They were few in number, generally poor, and had every opposition to encounter, both from a want of means and from the enemies of truth, who circulated every falsehood calculated to hinder or discourage them. Newspapers and tracts were put in circulation, sermons and public speeches were delivered in abundance, to warn the people that Nauvoo was a barren waste on the sea shore — that it was a wild and uninhabited swamp — that it was full of savages, wild beasts and serpents — that all the English Saints who should go there would be immediately sold for slaves by the leaders of the Church — that there was nothing to eat, no water, and no way possible to obtain a living; that all who went there would have their money taken from them, and themselves imprisoned, etc.

"But notwithstanding all these things, thousands have emigrated from this country, and now find themselves comfortably situated, and in the enjoyment of the comforts of life, and in the midst of society where God is worshipped in the spirit of truth and union, and where nearly all are agreed in religious principles. They all find plenty of employment and good wages, while the expense of living is about one-eighth of what it costs in this country. . . .

"Instead of a lonely swamp or dense forest filled with savages, wild beasts, and serpents, large cities and villages are springing up in their midst, with schools, colleges, and temples. The mingled noise of mechanism, the bustle of trade, the song of devotion, are heard in the distance, while thousands of flocks and herds are seen grazing peacefully on the plains, and the fields and gardens smile with plenty, and the wild red men of the forest are only seen as they come on a friendly visit to the Saints, and to learn the way of the Lord. . . .

. . . .

"Who that has a heart to feel, or a soul to rejoice, will not be glad at so glorious a plan of deliverance? Who will not hail the messengers of the Latter-day Saints as the friends of humanity — the benefactors of mankind?

"'Thousands have gone, and millions more must go,
The Gentiles as a stream to Zion flow.'

"Yes, friends, this glorious work has but just commenced; and we now call upon the Saints to come forward with united effort, with persevering exertion, and with union of action, and help yourselves and one another to emigrate to the Land of Promise.

"In this way we shall not only bring about the deliverance of tens of thousands who must otherwise suffer in this country, but we shall add to the strength of Zion, and help to rear her cities and temples —'to make her wilderness like Eden, and her desert like the garden of the Lord,' while the young men and the middle aged will serve to increase her legions — to strengthen her bulwark — that the enemies of law and order who have sought her destruction, may stand afar off and tremble, and her banners become terrible to the wicked.

"Ye children of Zion, once more we say, in the name of Israel's God, arise, break off your shackles, loose yourselves from the bands of your neck, and go forth to inherit the earth, and to build up the waste places of many generations. . . .

"We do not wish to confine the benefit of our emigration plan to the Saints, but are willing to grant all industrious, honest, and well-disposed persons who may apply to us the same information and assistance as emigrants to the western states, there being abundant room for more than a hundred millions of inhabitants."— *Millennial Star,* February, 1842.

This document, which reads like an ultra-sanguine invitation to the "oppressed of every nation" to take up their residence in "this broad country," and enjoy the advantages elsewhere denied them, embodies merely the same kind of golden hopes and promises that have attracted to our shores such myriads of the very class of people, as those to whom it is addressed. If written at the present day, sadly enough, it must misrepresent matters in sundry particulars. It was more nearly true seventy years ago, when it was issued; although, even then, somewhat colored with the high hopes, great ambitions and lively faith of the Prophet's disciples — feelings undoubtedly shared by himself. This man and his followers, in fact, actually hoped to found a "gathering-place for Israel," a nucleus of God's redeemed people on earth, and to prepare the world for the coming of the Lord. At the least, they hoped to provide a refuge for the downtrodden; and in every place where they founded a settlement, they did their best to realize this aim. Of this there can be no doubt whatever. In another aspect, also, this appeal is notable. It was made by the accredited representatives of the most successful agency at work in our midst to-day for the actual welding-together into a type almost tribal or national in character people of diverse origins and instincts, transforming them, as already mentioned, into a "peculiar people" in the highest acceptation of the term. Some such agency at work among us should serve a wonderful use in bringing our armies of immigrants to conform to an "American type," instead of embarrassing us, as at present, to provide for the diverse interests, sentiments and habits of peoples, apparently irreconcilably antagonistic to each other, and to the mass in which they are found. If Smith and his associates went to this length "to make money," as some stupid critics still allege, may we have more such "money-makers" among us. They are the kind of "capitalists" very sorely needed at the present time.

Nevertheless, in spite of all efforts, and in spite of the great faith and courage of the actual workers in the "upbuilding of Zion," there were sore embarrassments encountered in the work. Thus, many of the English converts who gathered at Nauvoo were greatly distressed for lack of work, which matter is mentioned by the Prophet in his journal, under date June 13, 1843, where the following entry occurs:

> "Attended a general council in the lodge room to devise ways and means to furnish the poor with labor. Many of the English Saints have gathered to Nauvoo, most of whom are unacquainted with any kind of labor, except spinning, weaving, etc.; and having no factories in this place, they are troubled to know what to do. Those who have funds have more generally neglected to gather, and left the poor to build up the city and the kingdom of God in these last days."—*History of the Church, Vol. V., p.* 25.

It may be that some critics will find it possible to blame Smith for such conditions, precisely as they blame the Mormons of the present day, for representing the possibilities and advantages of their American settlements altogether too favorably to prospective immigrants. We must not forget, however, that we are considering no "real estate" or colonization enterprises, but, precisely, an order which, in the minds of its directors and agents, has been founded and is being conducted under the direct command of the Almighty. Thus, in such circumstances, as in his explanation of the Missouri persecutions, Smith upbraids the people for their "lack of faith and obedience," which, as he states, are the real occasions for the withdrawal of divine favor and protection. This may seem a severe characterization for people who endured the hardships suffered by the Mormons in Missouri; but it is recorded that there were many examples of defection among them — notably of several of the Apostles, Marsh, Hdye, et al.— and that Smith himself bore the brunt of much of the severest trouble suffered by his people. His experience seems to have agreed with that of other professed advocates of righteousness, in the fact that he found human nature a "refractory material." Thus, four days previous to making the entry above quoted he had delivered an address before the Female Relief Society, which is reported, in part, as follows:

"President Joseph Smith opened the meeting by prayer, and then addressed the congregation on the design of the institution. . . .

"It is one evidence that men are unacquainted with the principles of godliness to behold the contraction of affectionate feelings and lack of charity in the world. The power and glory of godliness is spread out on a broad principle to throw out the mantle of charity. God does not look on sin with allowance, but when men have sinned, there must be allowance made for them.

"All the religious world is boasting of righteousness: it is the doctrine of the devil to retard the human mind, and hinder our progress, by filling us with self-righteousness. The nearer we get to our heavenly Father, the more we are disposed to look with compassion on perishing souls; we feel that we want to take them upon our shoulders, and cast their sins behind our backs. My talk is intended for all this society; if you would have God have mercy on you, have mercy on one another.

"President Smith then referred them to the conduct of the Savior, when He was taken and crucified, etc.

"He then made a promise in the name of the Lord, saying that that soul who has righteousness enough to ask God in the secret place for life, every day of their lives, shall live to three score years and ten. We must walk uprightly all the day long. How glorious are the principles of righteousness! We are full of selfishness; the devil flatters us that we are very righteous, when we are feeding on the faults of others. We can only live by worshipping our God; all must do it for themselves; none can do it for another. How mild the Savior dealt with Peter, saying, 'When thou art converted, strengthen thy brethren.' At another time, He said to him, 'Lovest thou me?' and having received Peter's reply, He said, 'Feed my sheep.' If the sisters loved the Lord, let them feed the sheep, and not destroy them. How oft have wise men and women sought to dictate (to) Brother Joseph by saying, 'O, if I were Brother Joseph, I would do that and that;' but if they were in Brother Joseph's shoes they would find that men or women could not be compelled into the kingdom of God, but must be dealt with in long-suffering, and at last we shall save them. The way to keep all the Saints together, and keep the work rolling, is to wait with all long-suffering, till God shall bring such characters to justice. There should be no license for sin, but mercy should go hand in hand with reproof.

"Sisters of the society, shall there be strife among you? I will not have it. You must repent and get the love of God. Away with self-righteousness. The best measure or principle to bring the poor to repentance is to administer to their wants. The Ladies' Relief Society is not only to relieve the poor, but to save souls.

"President Smith then said that he would give a lot of land to the society by deeding to the treasurer, that the society may build houses for the poor."—*Ibid., pp.* 23-25.

Nor can we doubt that the appeal of the Prophet, here reported in but fragmentary form, met with the ready and generous answer that has been the wont of this worthy organization, founded by him, when, as he remarked, "I will now open the door for woman." It is claimed that, in the foundation of the Woman's Relief Society, as it is now known, was formed the first organization of women for benevolent purposes, in known history. The Prophet was a pioneer here, as in other matters. Strange that it takes a man, so widely and persistently abused as a mere "impostor," to be thus a pioneer in good works! There are several vivid contrasts between Calvin's rule at Geneva—and Calvin was a sort of "prophet"—and Joseph Smith's rule in Nauvoo (the "City Beautiful"); and this is one of them. As we may have guessed, also, there are yet others.

However great may have been Smith's "ignorance"; however halting and ungrammatical may have been his speech; however "uncouth" and "self-assertive" his manner; however much his conversation may have abounded in the "puerile and even shocking" things remarked by Mr. Quincy, the fact remains that he sought to realize the happy consummations for humanity that others have only dreamed of, and called "Utopian"—i.e., "things that happen in Nowhere"—and actually inspired able men and earnest women to help him realize his dreams of justice and righteousness. On several occasions he repeated the statement that God intended His Church to be "a kingdom of priests and kings," and this simple suggestion inspired many of his foremost associates to "take him literally," and really try to manifest priestly and kingly traits. There was something heroic about this. It strongly reminds one of Tullidge's forceful remarks:

"A strange religion indeed, that meant something more than faith and prayers and creeds. An empire-founding religion, as we have said,—this religion of a Latter-day Israel. A religion, in fact, that meant all that the name of 'Latter-day Israel' implies. . . . Out of Egypt the seed of promise, to become a peculiar people, a holy nation, with a distinctive God and a distinctive destiny. Out of modern Babylon, to repeat the same Hebraic drama in the latter age. A Mormon Iliad in every view." —*The Women of Mormondom, p.* 68.

An exhortation worthy to rank—if not in an "Iliad"—in some "epic of faith" is found in the "Epistle of the Twelve to the Saints in America," issued under date, April 12, 1842. It contains the following passages:

"Brethren, the Temple will be built. There are hundreds and thousands who stand ready to sacrifice the last farthing they possess on the earth rather than have the building of the Lord's house delayed, and while this spirit prevails no power beneath the heavens can hinder its progress: but we desire you all to help with the ability which God has given you; that you may all share the blessings which will distil from heaven to earth through this consecrated channel.

"This is not all. It will be in vain for us to build a place where the Son of Man may lay his head, and leave the cries of the widow and the fatherless unheard by us, ascending up to the orphan's God and widow's Friend. It is in vain, we cry Lord, Lord, and do not the things our Lord hath commanded; to visit the widow, the fatherless, the sick, the lame, the blind, the destitute, and minister to their necessities; and it is but reasonable that such cases should be found among a people who have but recently escaped the fury of a relentless mob on the one hand, and gathered from the half-starved population of the scattered nations on the other.

"Neither is this all. It is not sufficient that the poor be fed and clothed, the sick ministered unto, the Temple built — no, when all this is accomplished, there must be a year of Jubilee; there must be a day of rejoicing; there must be a time of release to Zion's sons, or our offerings, our exertions, our hopes, and our prayers will be in vain, and God will not accept of the doings of His people.

"On these days of darkness which overspread our horizon; when the wolf was howling for his prey around the streets of Kirtland; when the burglar was committing his midnight and midday depredations in Jackson County; when the heartless politician was thrusting his envious darts in Clay County — and when the savage war whoop, echoed and reechoed through Far West, and Zion's noblest sons were chained in dungeons, and her defenseless daughters driven by a horde of savages, from their once peaceful homes, to seek a shelter in a far distant land — many of the brethren stepped forward to their rescue, and not only expended all they possessed for the relief of suffering innocence, but gave their notes and bonds to 'obtain more means, with which to help those who could not escape the overwhelming surge of banishment from all that they possessed on earth.'

. . . .

"To accomplish this, the President and Bishops loaned money and such things as could be obtained, and gave their obligations in good faith for the payment of the same; and many of the brethren signed with them at different times and in different places, to strengthen their hands and help them carry out their designs; fully expecting, that, at some future day, they would be enabled to liquidate all such claims, to the satisfaction of all parties.

"Many of these claims have already been settled; many have been given up as cancelled by those who held them, and many yet remain unsettled. The Saints have had many difficulties to encounter since they arrived at this place. In a new country, destitute of houses, food, clothing, and nearly all the necessaries of life, which were rent from them by an unfeeling mob — having to encounter disease and difficulties unnumbered, it is not surprising that the Church has not been able to liquidate all such claims, or that many individuals should yet remain involved, from the foregoing circumstances; and while things remain as they are, and men remain subject to the temptations of evil as they now are, the day of release, and year of jubilee cannot be; and we write you especially at this time, brethren, for the purpose of making a final settlement of all such claims, of brother against brother; of brethren against the Presidency and Bishops, etc.; claims which have originated out of the difficulties and calamities the Church has had to encounter, and which are of long standing, so that when the Temple is completed, there will be nothing from this source to produce jars, and discords, strifes and animosities, so as to prevent the blessings of heaven descending upon us as a people.

"To accomplish this most desirable object, we call on all the brethren who hold such claims, to bring them forward for a final settlement; and also those brethren who have individual claims against each other, of long standing, and the property of the debtor has been wrested from him by violence, or he has been unfortunate, and languished on a bed of sickness till his means are exhausted; and all claims whatsoever between brother and brother, where there is no reasonable prospect of a just and equitable settlement possible, that they also by some means, either by giving up their obligations, or destroying them, see that all such old affairs be adjusted, so that it shall not give occasion for difficulties to arise hereafter. Yes, brethren, bring all such old accounts, notes, bonds, etc., and make a consecration of them to the building of the Temple, and if anything can be obtained on them, it will be obtained; and if nothing can be obtained, when the Temple is completed, we will make a burnt offering of them, even a peace offering, which shall bind the brethren together in the bonds of eternal peace, and love and union; and joy and salvation shall flow forth into your souls, and you shall rejoice and say it is good that we have harkened unto counsel, and set our brethren free, for God hath blessed us.

"How can we prosper while the Church, while the Presidency, while the Bishops, while those who have sacrificed everything but life, in this thing, for our salvation, are thus encumbered? It cannot be. Arise, then, brethren, set them free, and set each other free, and we will all be free together, we will be free indeed."—*History of the Church, Vol. IV., pp.* 591–593.

However, as if to emphasize the "other side" of this matter, in which there might seem to be a danger that injustice might be done, the epistle closes with this paragraph, which effectually absolves its authors from all suspicion of "interested motives" in the premises:

"Let nothing in this epistle be so construed as to destroy the validity of contracts, or give any one license not to pay his debts. The commandment is to pay every man his dues, and no man can get to heaven who justly owes his brother or his neighbor, who has or can get the means and will not pay it; it is dishonest, and no dishonest man can enter where God is."

That the Church also discharged and forgave all indebtedness to it, on the part of its members is altogether probable, although the details of the matter have not been preserved. On the occasion of another "Jubilee," however, thirty-seven years later, when the fiftieth anniversary of the founding of the Church was celebrated in 1880, the Church authorities made the occasion memorable by canceling the entire outstanding indebtedness incurred by numerous immigrants to Utah for expenses paid out of the Perpetual Immigration Fund. The rule was that the prospective emigrant from Europe, or other part, received his expenses of transportation, on signing a contract to "reimburse the same, in labor or otherwise, as soon as their circumstances will admit," making payment in full, "with interest if required."

"That these obligations were never rigorously pressed — some anti-Mormon writers to the contrary notwithstanding — is witnessed by the fact that by the year 1880, the unpaid principal of indebtedness to this fund amounted in the church to the sum of $704,000; and if interest on this outstanding indebtedness (had been charged) during the years it could legitimately have drawn interest at the rate of ten per cent.— the usual rate in the west previous to 1880 — that interest would have amounted to $900,000; making a total of principal and interest of $1,604,-000. Yet instead of oppressively seeking to collect this amount, the Fund Company in the year 1880 — the year known in our annals as the Year of Jubilee, the Church then having been in existence fifty years — one half of this principle and interest was cancelled, being applied on the indebtedness of the worthy poor, they being wholly set free from the obligation of payment."— *B. H. Roberts, History of the Mormon Church, Chap.* lxxvii. (*Americana Magazine, N. Y., Nov.,* 1912.)

Such precepts and performances as are noted above certainly go very far toward establishing the contention that the Mormon Church really represented, on these occasions, at least, a stably-organized and fraternal body of people. In these respects it embodied a realization of high ideals of social and moral reorganization of mankind, which should be the rule among intelligent human beings, instead of the exceptional possession of any one set of people whatsoever. Nor can there be a doubt in any reflecting mind that, although the principles of human brotherhood and mutual helpfulness are a part of the teachings of Christ, which the world has known for eighteen hundred years, they were brought to practical operation in a society of people professing Christianity, solely through the influence of Joseph Smith.

CHAPTER VII

JOSEPH SMITH AS A STATESMAN AND REFORMER

On questions of current political importance Smith's opinions seem to have been both intelligent and statesmanlike, if we are to believe the testimony of contemporaries. He seems to have been particularly interested in discussing slavery, a live topic in his lifetime, and to have shared the opinion of many of the wisest minds that its abolishment was a necessity. His known attitude on this subject, and the opinions of many of his converts, who came largely from the New England and middle states, is alleged by some as the real grounds for much of the violent opposition to the Mormon people in Missouri. While this opinion may be partially correct as applied to that state, it is less valid as explanation of the violent doings in Ohio and Illinois. It is not wholly improbable that a large part of Mr. Quincy's friendly feeling for Smith was due to the latter's anti-slavery opinions. Thus, in the book quoted above, Quincy relates of a conversation with Smith:

"We then went on to talk of politics. Smith recognized the curse and iniquity of slavery, though he opposed the methods of the Abolitionists. His plan was for the nation to pay for the slaves from the sale of the public lands. 'Congress,' he said, 'should be compelled to take this course, by petitions from all parts of the country; but the petitioners must disclaim all alliance with those who would disturb the rights of property recognized by the Constitution and foment insurrection.' It may be worth while to remark that Smith's plan was publicly advocated, eleven years later, by one who has mixed so much practical shrewdness with his lofty philosophy. In 1855, when men's minds had been moved to their depths on the question of slavery, Mr. Ralph Waldo Emerson declared that it should be met in accordance 'with the interest of the South and with the settled conscience of the North. It is not really a great task, a great fight for this country to accomplish, to buy that property of the planter, as the British nation bought the West Indian slaves.' He further says that the 'United States will be brought to give every inch of their public lands for a purpose like this.' We, who can look back upon the terrible cost of the fratricidal war which put an end to slavery, now say that such a solution of the difficulty would have been worthy a Christian statesman. But if the retired scholar was in advance of his time when he advocated this disposition of the public property in 1855, what shall I say of the political and religious leader who had committed himself, in print, as well as in conversation, to the same course in 1844? If the atmosphere of men's opinions was stirred by such a proposition when war-clouds were discernible in the sky, was it not a statesmanlike word eleven years earlier, when the heavens looked tranquil and beneficent?

"General Smith proceeded to unfold still further his views upon politics. He denounced the Missouri Compromise as an unjustifiable concession for the benefit of slavery. It was Henry Clay's bid for the presidency. Dr. Goforth might have spared himself the trouble of coming to Nauvoo to electioneer for a duellist who would fire at John Randolph, but was not brave enough to protect the Saints in their rights as American citizens. Clay had told his people to go to the wilds of Oregon and set up a government of their own. Oh, yes, the Saints might go into the wilderness and obtain justice of the Indians, which imbecile, time-serving politicians would not give them in the land of freedom and equality. The Prophet then talked of the details of government. He thought that the number of members admitted to the Lower House of the National Legislature should be reduced. A crowd only darkened counsel and impeded business. A member to every half million of population would be ample. The powers of the President should be increased. He should have authority to put down rebellion in a state, without waiting for the request of any governor; for it might happen that the governor himself would be the leader of the rebels. It is needless to remark how later events showed the executive weakness that Smith pointed out, —a weakness which cost thousands of valuable lives and millions of treasure; but the man mingled Utopian fallacies with his shrewd suggestions. He talked as from a strong mind utterly unenlightened by the teachings of history. Finally, he told us what he would do, were he President of the United States, and went on to mention that he might one day so hold the balance between parties as to render his election to that office by no means unlikely."—*Figures of the Past, pp.* 397–399.

Apropos of Mr. Quincy's outright comparison of the views of Joseph Smith with those of so able a thinker as Emerson, it seems in place to remark that, with his inevitable mental bias, many of the successful performances, already mentioned, might have been classed among the "Utopian fallacies," as also the apparent over-confidence of himself and his coadjutors, which, in any other people, would undoubtedly be attributed to an all-sufficient "faith." People who believe that they have a mission from God to do any works, great or small, usually exhibit qualities closely suggestive of "over-confidence." In such a category one might reasonably place the famous philanthropist, George Muller, who, if reports are correct, actually fed and clothed several hundred orphans in his asylum on the "answers" given to the prayers of childlike faith. As to whether Smith's mind was "utterly unenlightened by the teachings of history," we must admit, on Quincy's own testimony, that his suggestions, for the most part, seem to have partaken of a larger wisdom than the "teachings of history" would seem to have imparted to those who finally dealt with the question of slavery and its abolishment. Had Smith's suggestions—or Emerson's, if you prefer

— been actually put into practice, the reader of United States history would have been spared the shocking story of the great Civil War, the tedious recountal of the wanton spoliation of the Southern states by government agents and unofficial scoundrels and "carpet-baggers," and the squalid chapter of negro domination in Alabama, and other states, as the result of mere bigotry, self-righteousness and "reforming paranoia," all of which are miserably worse than the largest accusations made against Smith and Mormonism. Although chattel slavery may be an unmitigated evil — and it is not wholly evident that it is abolished, even to-day — the planters of the Southern states purchased their slaves in "good faith," and, on the whole, cared for them far better than many managers of "big enterprises" care for their employes at the present time; and there can be no doubt, from the standpoint of strict justice, that they should have been reimbursed when their "property" was taken from them. This is one of the axiomatic truths recognized only by a mind "utterly unenlightened by the teachings of history."

In another matter, also, Smith's views on the slavery problem showed a degree of wisdom greatly in advance of the agitators of his time. Thus, under date, January 2, 1843, he records:

> "At five went to Mr. Sollars' with Elders Hyde and Richards. Elder Hyde inquired the situation of the negro. I replied, they came into the world slaves, mentally and physically. Change their situation with the whites, and they would be like them. They have souls, and are subjects of salvation. Go into Cincinnati or any city, and find an educated negro, who rides in his carriage, and you will see a man who has risen by the powers of his own mind to his exalted state of respectability. The slaves in Washington are more refined than many in high places, and the black boys will take the shine off many of those they brush and wait on.
>
> "Elder Hyde remarked, 'Put them on the level, and they will rise above me.' I replied, if I raised you to be my equal, and then attempted to oppress you, would you not be indignant and try to rise above me, as did Oliver Cowdery, Peter Whitmer, and many others, who said I was a fallen Prophet, and they were capable of leading the people, although I never attempted to oppress them, but had always been lifting them up? Had I anything to do with the negro, I would confine them by strict law to their own species, and put them on a national equalization."—*History of the Church, Vol. V., pp.* 217–218.

Smith's utterances on the slavery question were, of course, merely expressions of opinion from an intelligent and observant citizen, without further significance, as he himself seems to recognize. The vicissitudes of his own position as leader of his Church and people, and as the constant target of disorderly agitators, and the subject of numerous attempts at prosecution and persecution by an official clique in the State of Missouri, had already forced him into the arena of national politics, in the rôle of petitioner seeking redress for undoubted grievances. He had appealed to Congress and to the President to take some measures to compel the State of Missouri to reimburse the Mormon people for the destruction of their property and the murder of their relatives by drunken and unlawful mobs, who had been whipped into frenzy by wanton agitators, both "religious" and political, but found himself faced by the then popular fetich of "state rights," which, as it seems, was understood to constitute a bar to interference by the Federal Government, even with the most aggravated disorders and insurrections. That this understanding of the matter no longer holds is evidenced by the frequent use, in recent years, of United States troops to put down strike disorders, particularly where interstate commerce was threatened, also, in merely local disorders, such as mining strikes, and the like. That the understanding of the doctrine of "state sovereignty" should extend the privilege to state governors and legislators to connive at such disorders as occurred in Missouri during a term of several years would not be allowed at the present day. Nevertheless, Smith could obtain no redress from the Federal Government, and, as it must seem from the point of view of the present understanding of the matter, he was justly aggrieved.

The whole story of the Mormon sojourn in both Missouri and Illinois is nothing other than a humiliating comment on the kind of governmental efficiency that obtained at the midde of the nineteenth century. Nor is it an answer in any sense to catalogue a lot of alleged acts of treason, violence, disorder, immorality, robbery, etc., against the Mormons themselves. As any reasonable and informed person will admit, such acts, even when proved beyond dispute, as is not the case here, furnish no warrant by which the people can be justified "in taking the matter into their own hands." Even in cases in which atrocious murderers and ravishers are done to death by mobs of "outraged citizens," the public sentiment protests against "lynch law," and regrets that justice is not allowed to take its course. Nor could there be any other verdict in the matter, unless, as ingeniously argued by a certain Southern advocate of this method of "justice," "lynching is the divinely-revealed method of dealing with capital crime since the Bible specifies, 'the people shall stone him with stones.'" It is also a sad comment on the righteousness of partisan politics, so miserably rampant both in this country and in England, that any holder of a public office should hesitate to take measures to put down disorder, merely because, as we must say, after reading the history of the times, he was afraid to jeopardize his own political future by opposing mobbers, lynchers and marauders of any variety. As we shall see later, Governor Thomas Ford attempted by elaborate and specious argument, to "explain" his own conduct in the Mormon disorders in his state; but succeeds very poorly in justifying his failure to "preserve the peace."

As may be understood from the foregoing, it is with very doubtful accuracy or justice, that Smith and his people are variously accused, even to the present time, of seeking "seditiously" to found governments independent of both state and nation. Having been obliged to withdraw from Missouri, and later finding that the same kind of wanton agitation, parading under the disguise of political and social righteousness, even of religion, also, was theatening them in Illinois, the proposed petition to Congress, to make the city of Nauvoo, and its environs, federal territory, must seem reasonable, even if a "forlorn hope." There is at least nothing seditious about it. But the matter never came to anything.

However, as the direct result of failure to obtain justice from accredited authorities and tribunals, and to be protected from the activities of disorderly mobs, the Prophet, as he states, consented to accept nomination for the Presidency of the United States. Several ill-informed writers have attempted to allege this act as evidence of his derangement, but, in all justice and consistency, it must be insisted that his actions and expressions at this time evidence nothing of the kind. Thus, under date, January 29, 1844, he records:

"At ten, A. M., the Twelve Apostles, together with Brother Hyrum and John P. Greene, met at the mayor's office, to take into consideration the proper course for this people to pursue in relation to the coming Presidential election.

"The candidates for the office of President of the United States at present before the people are Martin Van Buren and Henry Clay. It is morally impossible for this people, in justice to themselves, to vote for the re-election of President Van Buren — a man who criminally neglected his duties as chief magistrate in the cold and unblushing manner which he did, when appealed to for aid in the Missouri difficulties. His heartless reply burns like a firebrand in the breast of every true friend of liberty — '*Your cause is just, but I can do nothing for you.*'

"As to Mr. Clay, his sentiments and cool contempt of the people's rights are manifested in his reply — '*You had better go to Oregon for redress,*' which would prohibit any true lover of our constitutional privileges from supporting him at the ballot-box.

"It was therefore moved by Willard Richards, and voted unanimously —

"That we will have an independent electoral ticket, and that Joseph Smith be a candidate for the next Presidency; and that we use all honorable means in our power to secure his election.

"I said—

"If you attempt to accomplish this, you must send every man in the city who is able to speak in public throughout the land to electioneer and make stump speeches, advocate the 'Mormon' religion, purity of elections, and call upon the people to stand by the law and put down mobocracy. . . .

"After the April Conference we will have General Conferences all over the nation, and I will attend as many as convenient. Tell the people we have had Whig and Democratic Presidents long enough: we want a President of the United States. If I ever get into the presidential chair, I will protect the people in their rights and liberties. . . . The Whigs are striving for a king under the garb of Democracy. There is oratory enough in the Church to carry me into the presidential chair the first slide."—*History of the Church, Vol. VI., pp.* 187–188.

One week later, under date, February 8, 1844, he addressed a meeting as follows:

"I would not have suffered my name to have been used by my friends on anywise as President of the United States, or candidate for that office, if I and my friends could have had the privilege of enjoying our religious and civil rights as American citizens, even those rights which the Constitution guarantees unto all her citizens alike. But this as a people we have been denied from the beginning. Persecution has rolled upon our heads from time to time, from portions of the United States, like peals of thunder, because of our religion; and no portion of the Government as yet has stepped forward for our relief. And in view of these things, I feel it to be my right and privilege to obtain what influence and power I can, lawfully, in the United States, for the protection of injured innocence; and if I lose my life in a good cause I am willing to be sacrificed on the altar of virtue, righteousness and truth, in maintaining the laws and Constitution of the United States, if need be, for the general good of mankind."—*Ibid., pp.* 210–211.

In the meantime, Smith had prepared his famous pamphlet, entitled "Views of the Powers and Policy of the Government of the United States," which may be called the "platform," upon which he based his candidacy. After reviewing the principles and practices of the earlier presidents, and deploring the gradual decay and corruption of American ideals, he proceeds to make sundry recommendations, which are interesting historically, if, indeed, no otherwise. In some particulars his recommendations have since been adopted; in some, as already suggested, it is unfortunate that they were not adopted; in others again he was evidently ahead of his times, and, as we may regret, still seems to be so. He recommends partly, as follows:

"Reduce Congress at least two-thirds. Two Senators from a State and two members to a million of population will do more business than the army that now occupy the halls of the national Legislature. Pay them two dollars and their board per diem (except Sundays). That is more than the farmer gets, and he lives honestly. Curtail the officers of Government in pay, number, and power; for the Philistine lords have shorn our nation of its goodly locks in the lap of Delilah. . . .

"Advise your legislators, when they make laws for larceny, burglary, or any felony, to make the penalty applicable to work upon roads, public works, or any place where the culprit can be taught more wisdom and more virtue, and become more enlightened. Rigor and seclusion will never do as much to reform the propensities of men as reason and friendship. Murder only can claim confinement or death. Let the penitentiaries be turned into seminaries of learning, where intelligence, like the angels of heaven, would banish such fragments of barbarism. Imprisonment for debt is a meaner practice than the savage tolerates, with all his ferocity. '*Amor vincit omnia.*'

"Petition, also, ye goodly inhabitants of the slave States, your legislators to abolish slavery by the year 1850, or now, and save the abolitionist from reproach and ruin, infamy and shame.

"Pray Congress to pay every man a reasonable price for his slaves out of the surplus revenue arising from the sale of public lands, and from the deduction of pay from the members of Congress.

". . . Abolish the practice in the army and navy of trying men by court-martial for desertion. If a soldier or marine runs away, send him his wages, with this instruction, that *his country will never trust him again; he has forfeited his honor.*

"Make honor the standard with all men. Be sure that good is rendered for evil in all cases, and the whole nation, like a kingdom of kings and priests, will rise up in righteousness, and be respected as wise and worthy on earth, and as just and holy for heaven, by Jehovah, the author of perfection.

"More economy in the National and State governments would make less taxes among the people; more equality through the cities, towns, and country, would make less distinction among the people; and more honesty and familiarity in societies, would make less hypocrisy and flattery in all branches of the community; and open, frank, candid decorum to all men, in this boasted land of liberty, would beget esteem, confidence, union and love; and the neighbor from any State or from any country, of whatever color, clime or tongue, could rejoice when he put his foot on the sacred soil of freedom, and exclaim, The very name of '*American*' is fraught with *friendship*. . . .

"For the accommodation of the people in every State and Territory, let Congress show their wisdom by granting a national bank, with branches in each State and Territory, where the capital stock shall be held by the nation for the mother bank, and by the States and Territories for the branches; and whose officers and directors shall be elected yearly by the people, with wages at the rate of two dollars per day for services; which several banks shall never issue any more bills than the amount of capital stock in her vaults and the interest.

"The net gain of the mother bank shall be applied to the national revenue, and that of the branches to the States' and Territories' revenues. And the bills shall be par throughout the nation, which will mercifully cure that fatal disorder known in cities as *brokerage,* and leave the people's money in their own pockets.

"Give every man his constitutional freedom and the President full power to send an army to suppress mobs, and the States authority to repeal and impugn that relic of folly which makes it necessary for the Governor of a State to make the demand of the President for troops, in case of invasion or rebellion.

"The Governor himself may be a mobber; and instead of being punished, as he should be, for murder or treason, he may destroy the very lives, rights, and property he should protect. . . .

"As to the contiguous Territories to the United States, wisdom would direct no tangling alliance. Oregon belongs to this Government honorably; and when we have the red man's consent, let the Union spread from the east to the west sea; and if Texas petitions Congress to be adopted among the sons of liberty, give her the right hand of fellowship, and refuse not the same friendly grip to Canada and Mexico. And when the right arm of freemen is stretched out in the character of a navy for the protection of rights, commerce, and honor, let the iron eyes of power watch from Maine to Mexico, and from California to Columbia. . . .

"The Southern people are hospitable and noble. They will help to rid so *free* a country of every vestige of slavery, whenever they are assured of an equivalent for their property. The country will be full of money and confidence when a National Bank of twenty millions, and a State Bank in every State, with a million or more, give a tone to monetary matters, and make a circulating medium as valuable in the purses of a whole community, as in the coffers of a speculating banker or broker. . . .

"In the United States the people are the Government, and their united voice is the only sovereign that should rule, the only power that should be obeyed, and the only gentlemen that should be honored at home and abroad, on the land and on the sea. Wherefore, were I the President of the United States, by the voice of a virtuous people, I would honor the old paths of the venerated fathers of freedom; I would walk in the tracks of the illustrious patriots who carried the ark of the Government upon their shoulders with an eye single to the glory of the people; and when that people petitioned to abolish slavery in the slave States, I would use all honorable means to have their prayers granted, and give liberty to the captive by paying the Southern gentlemen a reasonable equivalent for their property, that the whole nation might be free indeed!

"When the people petitioned for a National Bank, I would use my best endeavors to have their prayers answered, and establish one on national principles to save taxes, and make them the controllers of its ways and means. And when the people petitioned to possess the Territory of Oregon, or any other contiguous Territory, I would lend the influence of a Chief Magistrate to grant so reasonable a request, that they might extend the mighty efforts and enterprise of a free people from the east to the west sea, and make the wilderness blossom as the rose. And when a neighboring realm petitioned to join the union of the sons of liberty, my voice would be, *Come* — yea, come, Texas; come, Mexico; come, Canada; and come, all the world; let us be brethren, . . . and let there be a universal peace.

"Abolish the cruel custom of prisons (except certain cases), penitentiaries, court-martials for desertion; and let reason and friendship reign over the ruins of ignorance and barbarity; yea, I would, as the universal friend of man, open the prisons, open the eyes, open the ears, and open the hearts of all people, to behold and enjoy freedom — unadulterated freedom; and God, who once cleansed the violence of the earth with a flood, whose Son laid down His life for the salvation of all His Father gave him out of the world, and who has promised that He will come and purify the world again with fire in the last days, should be supplicated by me for the good of all people."

On reading this manifesto, the conviction occurs strongly that it must have been read by Josiah Quincy, or, at the least, that its substance must have been imparted to him in conversations by Smith; thus furnishing the real ground for his remarks on "Utopian fallacies," as previously noted. As the candid reader must agree, this document is preëminently the work of an idealist, one whose faith in the principles for which he stood — the imminence of God's providential activities in reorganizing and redeeming human society, as well as all individual men — is constant, consistent and all-sufficient. Thus, he interpolates into a document, which, by all precedents, should be exclusively "political," consideration of matters peculiarly religious, theological and moral. His is the same order of "idealism" as that which wrote into our Declaration of Independence the memorable words:

> "We hold these truths to be self-evident, that all men are created equal, that they are endowed by their Creator with certain inalienable Rights, that among these are Life, Liberty and the pursuit of Happiness. That to secure these rights, Governments are instituted among men, deriving their just powers from the consent of the governed. That whenever any Form of Government becomes destructive of these ends, it is the Right of the People to alter or to abolish it, and to institute new Government, laying its foundation on such principles and organizing its powers in such form, as to them shall seem most likely to effect their Safety and Happiness."

Such sentences could be injected into a political document only because its authors believed that, in some fashion, these "inalienable rights" were through them about to be safeguarded to all mankind — evidently a good case of "Utopian fallacy." It is evident, also, that Smith's protest against governmental corruptions is no more Utopian than Jefferson's Declaration, nor any more fatuous than the expressions found in Jefferson's letter to Thomas Paine, written on the occasion of his own accession to the Presidency.

> "You will, in general," he says, "find us returning to sentiments worthy of former times. In these it will be your glory to have steadily labored, and with as much effect as any man living. That you may live long to continue your useful labors, and reap the reward in the thankfulness of nations, is my sincere prayer."

Jefferson, also, as it seems, held high ambitions to make his own administration ideally fruitful; and, as for Paine, he was an idealist of the most confirmed type. Idealists invariably manifest supreme faith in their ideals, and ever forget the fatal impediment to be encountered in the "inertia" of human depravity, which has acted hitherto to thwart the noblest designs of the greatest minds. Every idealist, also, must seem, like Joseph Smith, "to speak as from a strong mind utterly unenlightened by the teachings of history." These "teachings," indeed, tend to confirm the opinion that between the ideal and the practicable, "there is a great gulf fixed"; although enlightened intelligence indicates, with unwavering certainty, that, before a perfect, or even an efficient, social order can eventuate — before even the most obvious principles of right and justice can be made available — the general average of intelligence and good will among human beings must be raised, and most of the virtues classed as both "ethical" and "moral," must, somehow, be embodied in the behavior of the majority. To men like Paine, who believe that this sublime consummation awaits only the inculcation and acceptance of true and philosophical views of life, and of the mutual relations of man with man, or who, like Smith, anticipate the speedy appearance of the King of kings "to rule the nations with a rod of iron," the ideal seems the more important consideration, although with both the "practical" is ably calculated. Such a document as the above sheds a most important light upon the motives and opinions of Joseph Smith.

However accurate our view of this pamphlet of Smith's may be, the fact remains that the saner portion of the public was content to accept it as a bona-fide declaration of principles, supposing that its "idealism," as we are constrained to call it, was only the flowery rhetoric and enthused oratory, so familiar at that day. Thus, several newspapers commented on Smith's nomination quite as a matter of course, suggesting in no particular that it exhibited "presumption," "insanity," or any of the other defects since "discovered" by unintelligent writers. A Springfield newspaper speaks as follows:

> "It appears by the Nauvoo papers that the Mormon Prophet is actually a candidate for the presidency. He has sent us his pamphlet, containing an extract of his principles, from which it appears that he is up to the hub for a United States bank and a protective tariff. On these points he is much more explicit than Mr. Clay, who will not say that he is for a bank, but talks all the time of restoring a national currency. Nor will Mr. Clay say what kind of a tariff he is for. He says to the south that he has not sufficiently examined the present tariff, but thinks very likely it should be amended.
>
> "General Smith possesses no such fastidious delicacy. He comes right out in favor of a bank and a tariff, taking the true Whig ground, and ought to be regarded as the real Whig candidate for President, until Mr. Clay can so far recover from his shuffling and dodging as to declare his sentiments like a man.
>
> "At present we can form no opinion of Clay's principles, except as they are professed by his friends in these parts.
>
> "Clay himself has adopted the notion which was once entertained by an eminent grammarian, who denied that language was intended as a means to express one's ideas, but insisted that it was invented on purpose to aid us in concealing them."—*Illinois Springfield Register*, 1844.

Another contemporary newspaper comments with equal favor on the candidacy of the Prophet, in the following words:

"We see from the *Nauvoo Neighbor* that General Joseph Smith, the great Mormon Prophet, has become a candidate for the next presidency. We do not know whether he intends to submit his claims to the National Convention, or not; but judging from the language of his own organ, we conclude that he considers himself a full team for all of them.

"All that we can say on this point is, that if superior talent, genius, and intelligence, combined with virtue, integrity, and enlarged views, are any guarantee of General Smith's being elected, we think that he will be a 'full team of himself.'

"The *Missouri Republican* believes that it will be death to Van Buren, and all agree that it must be injurious to the Democratic ranks, inasmuch as it will throw the Mormon vote out of the field."—*Iowa Democrat,* 1844.

This latter newspaper also quotes *in extenso* a letter from a person signing himself "A Traveler," which had formerly been published in the Mormon magazine, *Times and Seasons,* as follows:

"I have been conversant with the great men of the age; and, last of all I feel that I have met with the greatest, in the presence of your esteemed Prophet, General Joseph Smith. From many reports, I had reason to believe him a bigoted religionist, as ignorant of politics as the savages; but, to my utter astonishment, on the short acquaintance, I have found him as familiar in the cabinet of nations as with his Bible, and in the knowledge of that book I have not met with his equal in Europe or America. Although I should beg leave to differ with him in some items of faith, his nobleness of soul will not permit him to take offense at me. No, sir; I find him open, frank, and generous,—as willing others should enjoy their opinions as to enjoy his own.

"The General appears perfectly at home on every subject, and his familiarity with many languages affords him ample means to become informed concerning all nations and principles, which with his familiar and dignified deportment towards all must secure to his interest the affections of every intelligent and virtuous man that may chance to fall in his way, and I am astonished that so little is known abroad concerning him.

". . . I have no reason to doubt but General Smith's integrity is equal to any other individual; and I am satisfied he cannot easily be made the plant tool of any political party. I take him to be a man who stands far aloof from little caucus quibblings and squabblings, while nations, governments, and realms are wielded in his hand as familiarly as the top and hoop in the hands of their little masters.

"Free from all bigotry and superstition, he dives into every subject, and it seems as though the world was not large enough to satisfy his capacious soul, and from his conversation one might suppose him as well acquainted with other worlds as this.

"So far as I can discover, General Smith is the nation's man, and the man who will exalt the nation, if the people will give him the opportunity; and all parties will find a friend in him so far as right is concerned.

"General Smith's movements are perfectly anomalous in the estimation of the public. All other men have been considered wise in drawing around them wise men; but I have frequently heard the General called a fool because he has gathered the wisest of men to his cabinet, who direct his movements; but this subject is too ridiculous to dwell upon. Suffice it to say, so far as I have seen, he has wise men at his side — superlatively wise, and more capable of managing the affairs of a State than most men now engaged therein, which I consider much to his credit, though I would by no means speak diminutively of my old friend.

"From my brief acquaintance, I consider General Smith (independent of his religious views, in which by-the-by, I have discovered neither vanity nor folly), the *sine qua non* of the age to our nation's prosperity. He has learned the all-important lesson 'to profit by the experience of those who have gone before'; so that, in short, General Smith begins where other men leave off. I am aware this will appear a bold assertion to some; but I would say to such, call, and form your acquaintance, as I have done; then judge."

In default of information as to the identity of this "Traveler," it is impossible, of course, to refute the probable accusation that his statements must have been inspired by some pro-Smith agency. It is interesting to consider, however, that he describes precisely the kind of man who would seem most capable of founding such a movement as Mormonism, which, as we shall see later, has operated wonderfully for the benefit, both temporal and moral, of the people adhering to its principles; such a man, also, as would likely express such sentiments as appear in the above-quoted pamphlet; and who, in all probability, would be the object of nearly prostrate devotion, on the one hand, and of an altogether exceptional hatred and detestation, on the other. All of these elements are found in the history of Joseph Smith, and best explain his doings, on the theory that both Quincy and "A Traveler," who saw him in his later days, have furnished a truer picture of his personality and habits than those "second-hand authorities" and vengeful apostates, who confidently accuse him of being "an infamous and villainous deceiver and scoundrel," or else hold that "he was, at times, actually demented."

CHAPTER VIII

JOSEPH SMITH IN HIS PERSONAL ASSOCIATIONS

In completing our study of Smith's character and influence, we are compelled to notice another phase of his personality that seems to have had but scant attention from any of the various writers who have attempted to estimate him. This is his apparently unfailing ability to make enemies. It might be possible to assert with confidence that this quality indicated an "unfathomable depth of turpitude," which was bound to revolt many of his associates, and cause them to apostatize, were it not for the fact that a large and representative percentage of these people, bitter and implacable enemies all, have been of a character not so far removed from the commission of the very iniquities charged against them by Smith and the Church authorities, as to be "revolted at" the things alleged by themselves in turn. Among such may be mentioned the notorious John C. Bennett, who was transformed from the agent who secured the passage of the Nauvoo charters — he was also the first mayor of the city — into one of the bitterest enemies that Smith and Mormonism ever had; but, as noted in a previous quotation, even Governor Ford, who was no advocate of Smith's, testifies to the rascality of Bennett. Similarly, Philastus Hurlburt, the father of the Spaulding hypothesis, who added to his other vices his false pretensions as a qualified physician — a mere "quack," in short — seems an incompetent witness against the promulgators of false assumptions, unless we admit, in the words of a certain noted journalist, that "he was such a sham himself that he was well qualified to detect sham in others," on the classic principle of "setting a thief to catch a thief." Some of the charges made by other apostates are so utterly vile as to seem their own best refutation, since, if true, they are of such a character as to revolt any one possessed of a spark of decency. It is surprising, on the hypothesis that they are true, that persons claiming ordinary decency of character should connive at them for so long a time, as must have been the case, if we accept their testimony that such things are well known. On the other hand, the situation is embarrassed by the fact that so goodly a proportion of clean, able and excellent people have never apostatized from their connection with this Church and its founder, although in positions to know of all the "abominations" alleged by others, if such be assumed to exist at all.

Where superlative wickedness, secretly practiced, is alleged against any man, or against any set of people, it is difficult, of course, to deny its existence with any degree of confidence. It is fair in such cases, however, to consider the character of those who make the accusations, and their reputations for veracity, in order to form a judgment for or against the probability of the conditions alleged by them. Thus only can we discriminate wanton and wicked slander from anything worthy to rank as credible.

In the case of Joseph Smith, as may be safely asserted on any hypothesis regarding him, a greater part of the antagonism displayed by apostates, as well as by outsiders, was undoubtedly personal in character. Like all men capable of accomplishing large results, he was evidently a person of strong will and great determination — people of other varieties are incapable of the greatest influence in the world. Such people must frequently demand implicit obedience from their associates and assistants, and are liable, under frequently-recurring conditions, to excite bitter antagonism in the minds of even their closest associates, even in those whose fortunes they have made, in a literal sense. Thus, apart from the resentment at the vigorous denunciations of their own alleged wrong doings, on the part of Smith and the Church authorities, may be explained much of the bitterness manifested by Oliver Cowdery, Wilson Law, John C. Bennett, and other former advisers and confidants of Smith. He seems to have described the situation accurately in a quotation formerly given, saying:

> "If I raised you to be my equal, and then attempted to oppress you, would you not be indignant and try to rise above me, as did Oliver Cowdery, Peter Whitmer, and many others, who said I was a fallen prophet, . . . although I never attempted to oppress them, but had always been lifting them up?"

No one acquainted with the states of mind, and the variety of expressions, likely to be found in a strong minded person, who believes that he has been grievously oppressed by some associate of his, can derive a vivid conception of the relations of Smith and several of his dissatisfied coadjutors. Nor, in making such a comparison, need we be actuated by any motive favorable to Smith or his claims: we need desire merely to derive an intelligent conception of the personality and influence of this man, about whom so much of an unfavorable character has been alleged, and whose real significance to history is still a puzzle. While with the "Traveler," as above quoted, we may reasonably be "astonished that so little is known abroad concerning him," the temptation is strong to attempt explaining him as a man possessed of ordinary good character and actuated, in the main, by reasonable motives, rather than to believe him so nearly impossibly wicked as many have foolishly sought to represent him to have been. We may claim, at least, that the following affidavit of Thomas B. Marsh, once president of the Twelve apostles, strongly suggests the kind of disaffection and antagonism that arises from some exaggerated sense of injustice suffered. He states:

> "They have among them a company, considered true Mormons, called the Danites, who have taken an oath to support the heads of the Church in all things that they say or do, *whether right or wrong*. Many, however, of this band are much dissatisfied with this oath, as being against moral and religious principles. . . . The Prophet inculcates the notion, and it is believed by every true Mormon, that Smith's prophesies are superior to the laws of the land. I have heard the Prophet say that he would yet tread down his enemies, and walk over their dead bodies; and if he was not let alone, he would be a second Mohammed to this generation, and that he would make one gore of blood from the Rocky Mountains to the Atlantic ocean; that like Mohammed, whose motto in treating for peace was, 'the Alcoran or the sword.' So should it be eventually with us 'Joseph Smith or the Sword.' These last statements were made during the last summer."

This document also alleges that there had been formed a "Destruction Company," whose duty it was to burn several towns, if attacked by the regularly accredited Missouri mobs; thus, of course, perpetrating acts of a distinctly "seditious" character. These statements were also supplemented by the sworn testimony of Orson Hyde, who alleged:

> "The most of the statements in the foregoing disclosure I know to be true; the remainder I believe to be true."

Whatever truth may be contained in any of the allegations made by these deponents, who swore at Richmond, Mo., under date, October 24, 1838, the conclusion is also inevitable that they were actuated by some feelings of excessive bitterness against Smith, rather than by any desire to "right wrongs" or to make "reparation" of any description. It seems clear, also, that the very bitterness of their accusations against Smith was grounded in some hope that he might be, in some way, speedily silenced through the agency of a "posse of indignant citizens." Such a conclusion seems well demonstrated when we consider the conditions under which the accusations were recorded. Here were two men who had occupied prominent positions in a body of people, at that time in the midst of serious hardships, involving the constant jeopardy of property and life to numbers of their former friends and associates, together with their wives and children. Yet, for some consideration, evidently quite other than simple "qualms of conscience," they utter an affidavit that, as they must have understood, would inflame the disorderly elements still further against their former coreligionists, even though Smith himself might have been destroyed in the meantime. It is interesting to note that the incident previously quoted from George Q. Cannon's book, in which Smith withstood certain mobbers dispatched to kill him, occurred at about the same period in which Messrs. Marsh and Hyde thus vented their spleen, to the evident endangering of hundreds of defenseless women and children. It is safe to assert that men who will allow their personal grievances, be they real or fancied, to carry them to any such brutal length, are capable, also, of lying and perjury.

Nevertheless, numerous careless and prejudiced writers, utterly ignorant, apparently, of these conditions, have quoted this iniquitous document, for the purpose of achieving some advantage against the Mormons, either political or sectarian. Notable among these was the late Schuyler Colfax, who, in 1870, inaugurated an anti-Mormon movement of his own, and quoted copiously from this and similar documents.

In this affidavit, as it seems, Messrs. Hyde and Marsh were the originators of the Danite story, which is so vigorously denied *in toto* by Mormon writers, and has been so persistently repeated and exaggerated by their opponents and detractors. We may pause here to remark that there may have been a society among Mormons,* or anti-Mormons, at this period, which was called or known by this name. There is no respectable evidence, however, that any order or society so called ever entertained the bloody and violent designs attributed to them. If they did so organize and act, it must be admitted, in view of the facts of Mormon history, that they were an extremely ineffective crowd of people, also that, as a "menace" of any description, their significance was certainly negligible. The truth of the matter might reasonably be assumed to be that Marsh and Hyde had come to regard themselves as Smith's tools, in a sense distasteful to themselves, and hence, on refusal to obey orders, under some certain condition, they had withdrawn from the Church — the Twelve Apostles, and the other close associates of the President, are then represented under the new title of "Danites,"— people sworn to "support the heads of the Church . . . right or wrong"; and the members of the "band" who are said to be "dissatis-

* For explanation of the persistent stories of "Danites," or destroying angels, which are circulated by opponents of the Mormon Church and system, see Appendix I at the back of the present volume.

fied with this oath," are composed, at the time of speaking, principally of the two deponents. Such, at least, would be the verdict on many persons, presumably situated as were these gentlemen. It was merely one of numerous examples in which Smith's enemies attempted to injure him in any available manner. It is notable, however, that, within two years, Hyde, who swore thus half-heartedly to Marsh's allegations, returned to the Church asking forgiveness, forgetful, apparently, of "iniquitous Danite oaths" and neo-Islamic boasts. The conditions were not entirely intolerable to him, at least, nor entirely "against [his] moral and religious principles." Marsh also renewed his membership in the Church in July, 1857, and, removing to Ogden, Utah, died there a few years later, apparently fearless of "Danites." The whole affair was concerned solely with personal animosity at the start, with a reconciliation at the close.

Even the brief and cursory study of the character and career of Joseph Smith, for which there is space in such a book as the present one, must be sufficient to convince the candid reader that there is no one word that can justly describe him. In his writings he appears as an honest and straightforward man of large affairs and considerable responsibilities, who is fully occupied in carrying out his chosen mission, although harassed constantly by inability to bring his designs to perfection, by the defection of trusted friends, and the unflagging assaults of his constantly increasing enemies. Viewing his life record from the standpoint of the unprejudiced observer, who asks only that he may know the real truth of all matters involved, Smith is no less a surprise. His ability to influence his associates is prodigious, while his success in imparting the spirit of his own convictions to other minds, so that they remain of vital and peculiar import, even to the present day, seventy years after his death, betrays an actual inspiration or genius that cannot but excite reverence. The number of particulars also, in which he seems to have actually grappled and solved the problems of society, rank him as a thinker and teacher of importance to the world, who cannot be discredited by the slanders and misrepresentations of his almost unparalleled enemies. In the interest of simple intelligence, the name of Joseph Smith should be rescued from its position as a synonym for all that is disreputable, since it is quite certain that by unjust and preposterous misrepresentation nearly the most interesting American of the nineteenth century has been obscured to the view of all thinkers and students outside the limit of his own disciples. That he is destined to receive justice at last is certain, and that late award may involve nothing other than according him a high place among thinkers, leaders and reformers — one also who brings a distinct and well-needed message to the world of human endeavor — if, indeed, his own claims to a special mission on earth from a Higher Power be not widely accepted, to the advantage, perhaps, of many who are now suffering in oppression and ignorance, or staggering into the quagmire of infidelity.

The following stanzas by Orson F. Whitney give a fair example of the inspiration derived by his disciples from the record, memory and teachings of Joseph Smith.

"Then was he of the Mighty — one of those
Descended from the Empire of the Sun,
Adown the glowing stairway of the stars?

. . . .

"I saw in vision such a one descend,
And garb him in a guise of common clay;
His glory veiling from the gaze of all,
Who wist not that a great one walked with men;
Nor knew it then the soul incarnate there,
Betwixt the temporal and spirit spheres
So dense forgetfulness doth intervene;
Yet learned his truth betimes by angel tongues,
By voice of God, by heavenly whisperings.

. . . .

"A living prophet unto dying time,
Heralding the Dispensation of the End,
When Christ once more His vineyard comes to prune,
When potent weak confound the puny strong,
Threshing the nations by the Spirit's power,
Rending the kingdoms with a word of flame;
That here the Father's work may crown the Son's,
And earth be joined a holy bride to heaven,
A queen 'mid queens, crowned, throned, and glorified.

"Wherefore came down this angel of the dawn,
In strength divine, a stirring rôle to play
In time's tense tragedy, whose acts are seven.
His part to fell the false, replant the true,
To clear away the wreckage of the past,
The ashes of its dead and dying creeds,
And kindle newly on earth's ancient shrine
The Light that points to Life unerringly;
Crowning what has been with what now must be;
A mighty still bespeaking mightier."

— *Elias: an Epic of the Ages, pp.* 38–40.

II

THE FRUITS OF MORMONISM

"If ye are not equal in earthly things, ye cannot be equal in obtaining heavenly things; for if ye will that I give unto you a place in the celestial world, you must prepare yourselves by doing the things which I have commanded you and required of you."—*Doctrine and Covenants.*

CHAPTER IX

MORMONISM THE EXPONENT OF EQUALITY AND FRATERNITY

In any permanent and complete scheme for the rescue of mankind from the miseries and shortcomings of current social conditions, there must be a strong and permanent organization on a basis distinctly religious in character. The failure to recognize this fact has been the primary source of weakness in virtually all proposed systems of betterment hitherto promulgated. Indeed, it is the greatest element of weakness in Socialism, and other radical movements of the present day, that while righteously protesting against the unjust and abominable system, now in vogue, they attempt to found a vital sense of the inherent and "inalienable rights" of mankind—"life, liberty and the pursuit of happiness"—upon a virtual ignoring of the religious instinct, which is nearly the strongest instinct and propension in human nature.

When we consider the fact that the persistence of real morality depends upon a vital and well-presented religious influence, which shall embody the element of a "superrational sanction for conduct," if we may use a term familiar among certain sociological thinkers, the validity of the appeal for consideration of an organization capable of embodying these desirable qualities is self-evident. The earnestness of conviction and consecration of purpose evidently manifested among adherents of the most futile sects among us are good, so far as they go, but experience has shown that they are sterile of vital and permanent influence, unless coupled with an organism capable of carrying out good intentions and promulgating and conserving excellent principles. This is the reason that Christian influence, with all that has been claimed for it in past centuries, has never been able to neutralize any of the evils of human society, and that these have been mollified solely by the growth of intelligence. But even intelligence is not sufficient to reorganize society, and create prosperity and happiness, where have always been poverty and misery. The crying need is for a practical coordination of all individual wills into a concerted effort for achieving the ends of common good.

When we consider the fact that Christianity, as stated by Christ himself, evidently contemplates the regeneration of society and the establishment of "justice, mercy and truth," quite as much and as certainly as the achievement of "salvation" in the world to come, we begin to realize that, as the Saviour said, religious teachers are to be known "by their fruits." The Roman Church has always emphasized the blessings to be earned in the next world by suffering in this. If we admit that this is the real aim of Christianity, as it is with Buddhism, whose influence has probably been very great on the development of historic theologies, through the imported tendencies embodied in Manicheanism, and other old-time "heresies," we must admit that the Catholic Church has the only organization on earth capable of saving mankind from the "world, the flesh and the devil." The organization of its priesthood and of the numerous orders of "religious," is an admirable system for "overcoming the world" by "scourging the flesh for the spirit's good." Indeed, in this aspect, and in the states of mind that sympathize with this theory of the aim and functions of religion, it makes an appeal to the imagination in the same fashion as the heathen Buddhism, when glorified by the poet's skill.

The trouble, however, with Catholicism, or, indeed, any system holding self-immolation as its supreme ideal, and advocating the suppression of the "carnal self" as the highest duty of religion, is that its message to the world at large, including, as it does, very many people who lack enthusiasm in these directions, must necessarily be a compromise, very ineffective in achieving an order of righteousness that shall be able to do away with the shortcomings and evils of society. Such a system must take the world about as it is, and be satisfied with the "allegiance" of those classes of people who may not be brought to attempt the achievement of its highest ideals of human duty. The result was that the Catholic Church divided its membership into two classes, clergy and laity — which is to say those devoted to the interests of religion and those continuing to live the life of humanity in the world. Thus, even the persons who are devoted to the religious life are divided into two classes, the "religious," who belong to the "orders" and whose occupation consists in fulfilling the higher obligations of the faith, and the "secular," whose duty it is to administer to the needs of those in the world life. The greatest trouble is that the religious life has been too greatly separated from the life of the world, with the result that much "worldliness," such as vanity, cruelty, selfishness, etc., has been tolerated as inevitable, which should have been made clearly and definitely inconsistent with Christian profession of any degree.

The "reformers" of mediæval Europe, in the professed behalf of an improved order of righteousness, produced the systems included under the general term Protestantism. Undoubtedly, the aim in most cases was to bring righteousness down to the basis of every-day life, producing a statement of the Gospel suited to the needs of people in the world, and thus "saving" mankind more evidently and effectively than could be possible with a system holding an ideal of "overcoming" that was not possible, or not acceptable, to all. In spite, however, of the stern ideals of "domestic asceticism," the puritanism and separatism, introduced by some of the foremost of the "reformers" these leaders committed the inexcusable blunder of promulgating the noxious doctrine of "salvation by faith"—which to say, assent,—which, although a mere corollary of scholastic theology, has always been a futile compromise with antinomian tendencies, and has done immense harm in rendering practical and social righteousness inoperative. Protestantism, quite as surely as Catholicism, contrives to make a very real and very unfortunate compromise between the demands of the Gospel and the natural "disabilities" of the human soul in the state of worldly existence.

In the case of the Catholic Church a splendidly conceived organization is devoted solely to the end of "overcoming" the world, rather than subjecting it to the good of God's people: in the case of Protestantism, organization is largely ignored, and practical righteousness largely neutralized by theories of the most indefensible variety.

In the meantime, at the end of eighteen centuries of Christian domination, we have social and moral "problems" that should never have emerged in a world, dominated, in any sense, by intelligence, and our traditional sects have no answers and no solutions. Indeed, the majority of people who are attempting to grapple with these conditions are outside of all sects, often outside of religion in any conscious or professing sense. It is evident, therefore, that there is room for some system of religion that shall follow Catholicism in an effective organization, and shall follow Protestantism in emphasizing the need of salvation for the individual living in the natural conditions of life; which, in short, shall gauge the efficiency of religious influence by its ability to save mankind in the flesh, socially, as well as individually.

One might be excused for believing that some such ideal existed in the mind of the founder of Mormonism. One might also claim toleration for the opinion that the ultimate effective reorganization of religion and society will be a system so closely like Mormonism that the student of history could be excused for suspecting some relation between the two. It is certain that the majority of the Mormon principles of organization are destined to permanance and wide acceptation. In one point, however, there can be no doubt of the ultimate validity of the Mormon theory of religious organization — and in this it is the only valid antithesis of Catholicism — and this is in the principle that the priesthood should be held by all worthy men of mature years. This theory makes religion the immediate concern of every individual, who, in the closely compacted society based upon his religion, owes his standing and significance solely to his religious activity. On such a theory, society cannot fail to achieve some very real order of regeneration in the fact that it is, in the words of the ancient Apostle, a kingdom of "priests unto God." This theory is, in fact, the only one that can be reasonably expected to bring religion into immediate relation with the affairs of everyday life, enabling it to persist as an affair of daily living, rather than an occupation for Sundays and holy days, quite incidental to the business of the world of ordinary existence.

From the point of view of common helpfulness and efficiency, also, this arrangement possesses inestimable value to the community, as the most convenient means ever devised for keeping life in touch with religion and keeping religion in touch with life. The difficulty hitherto has been that any such synthesis has been impossible in by far the greater majority of cases, particularly in Protestant churches, which maintain the absurd tradition, a fragment of the rejected Catholic institutions, of having separate professional ministers or preachers. These men, who are neither priests in the sacerdotalist sense, nor any longer "clergy," or dispensers of learning, nor yet practical participants in the life of the community, form a class by themselves, with their peculiarly biased and defective views of life, and the inevitable shortcomings of character always found in them, serving no end more effectively than to divorce religious interest and effort from the sympathy and participation of the large majority of really manly men. With the elimination of the type of person, which, like the Protestant preacher, has well been described as of a "third sex," it is fairly evident that religion is freed from one of its most harmful impediments. The followers of George Fox, forming the Society of Friends, or Quakers, adhered to this excellent first step in abolishing artificial classes, which is one of the most aggravated evils of human society, whether expressed in the distinction between "clergy" (so called) and laity, or between aristocrats and commoners. The Mormons are not, therefore, the first body of people to recognize and protest against the evils and incumbrances of usual religious and social organizations. They deserve credit, however, for contriving in a thoroughly practical manner to achieve some degree of real equality in human society by first place making all men members of the ministerial body, and affording means for their training in the practical duties required of those who shall be devoted to the life of religion and brotherhood.

In an additional sense the Mormon Church organization is of the utmost significance sociologically. It is the first and only entirely practical mechanism yet devised for reorganizing society on the basis of that equality and brotherhood, which have been the dreams of sociologists, moralists and the saner class of religious thinkers for over a century. That the attainment of these ends was the deliberate aim of the founder of Mormonism there can be no doubt. That their perpetuation has been nearly the foremost interest of his followers is equally clear. The following is a fair sample of the enthusiasm with which this ideal is held among them:

> "One great lesson that has been set before intelligent men and women of today is that of corelation of economics. Moreover, to cooperate in all matters affecting economic and social life is the demand of the ages; if we have learned anything from the pages of history, it is that there should be no classes and masses, no capital and labor in the ideal life, no sex divisions in civil and social affairs. It is true that there are varying grades of capacity in men, and this will always lead to a division or classification. . . . But the statesman who looks toward the altruism of the future will teach the strong that their strength is given its highest expression in protecting the weak; and that superiority of intellect is a menace to civilization, unless it carries with it the compelling force to use all superior advantages for the uplifting of the inferior and ignorant."—*Susa Young Gates,* (*History of the Y. L. M. I. A., p.* 220).

Nor did the Mormon prophet and his associates confine their efforts to achieve the noble ends recommended above to any vain preachments, without vital interest to back them, which have been only too sadly familiar throughout Christian history. He provided the organization for the realization of his ideals, and gave precise and unmistakable directions for its practical operation.

> "One of the first steps taken by the Prophet, after the establishment of headquarters at Kirtland, was the institution of what Latter-day Saints call the 'United Order,' a religio-social system, communal in its character, designed to abolish poverty, monopoly, and kindred evils, and to bring about unity and equality in temporal and spiritual things. It required the consecration to the Church, by its members, of all their properties, and the subsequent distribution to those members, by the Church, of what were termed 'stewardships.' Each holder of a stewardship—which might be the same farm, workshop, store, or factory that this same

person had 'consecrated'— was expected to manage it thereafter in the interest of the whole community; all his gains reverting to the common fund, from which he would derive a sufficient support for himself and those dependent upon him. The Bishops, being the temporal officers of the Church, received the consecration of those properties, and also assigned the stewardships. . . .

"The United Order, the Prophet declared, was the same ancient system that sanctified the City of Enoch; the same also that the Apostles set up at Jerusalem (Acts 4:32–35); and that the Nephites instituted upon this land, according to the Book of Mormon (IV, Nephi, 1:3). The purpose in view, by the Latter-day Saints, was the building up of Zion, the New Jerusalem; an event to be preceded by the gathering of scattered Israel, and preparatory to the second coming of the Saviour and the advent of the Millennium.

"I need not weary the reader with a recital of details as to how the Church grew and prospered along the lines laid down by the United Order, which was established at Kirtland, Ohio, and at Independence, Missouri, during the year 1831. Suffice it, that under the auspices of this beneficent system the Gospel was preached on both hemispheres and the gathering of Latter-day Israel begun. Lands were purchased in both the States named; and in Jackson County, Missouri, the foundations of the City of Zion were laid. A Temple was reared at Kirtland, schools were opened, mercantile and publishing houses instituted, and industrial enterprises of various kinds conducted by the Church; the object being to build up Zion spiritually and temporally, and prepare for the literal coming of the King of Kings to reign upon the earth a thousand years. In this cause, the Apostles as well as the Bishops performed a variety of labors, not only preaching the Gospel and administering its sacred ordinances, but also traveling to collect money and other means for the erection of the Kirtland Temple and the purchase of lands in Missouri.

"The United Order was not perpetuated at that time, and the reason was two-fold. Primarily it was due to the innate selfishness of human nature, which prevented the Saints, as a whole, from entering into the work of 'redeeming Zion' with sufficient zeal and singleness of purpose. But another cause, equally cogent, was the cruel mobbings and drivings of our people, by those who did not comprehend their real motives, or maliciously made evil out of their pure and philanthropic designs. The 'Mormon' colony which settled in Jackson County, Missouri, was violently expelled from that part in the autumn of 1833; and in 1837–39 the main body of the Church was compelled to leave Ohio, and migrated to Missouri."—*Joseph F. Smith, "The Truth about Mormonism"* (*Out West, Sept.*, 1905, *pp.* 244–245.)

That the United Order, or Order of Enoch, was a real order, in the accepted sense of the term, involving a consecration of life and effort, as well as of property, and that, also, a religious consecration in the best and highest sense, is amply shown by the rules of the order, which are still to be seen in Mormon households. The following rules governed the life of all members of this order:

RULES FOR MEMBERS OF THE UNITED ORDER.

"We will not take the name of the Deity in vain, nor speak lightly of His character or of sacred things.

"We will pray with our families morning and evening, and also attend to secret prayer.

"We will observe and keep the Word of Wisdom according to the spirit and meaning thereof.

"We will treat our families with due kindness and affection, and set before them an example worthy of imitation. In our families and intercourse with all persons, we will refrain from being contentious or quarrelsome, and we will cease to speak evil of each other, and will cultivate a spirit of charity towards all. We consider it our duty to keep from acting selfishly or from covetous motives, and will seek the interest of each other and the salvation of all mankind.

"We will observe personal cleanliness and preserve ourselves in all chastity by refraining from adultery, whoredom and lust. We will also discountenance and refrain from all vulgar and obscene language or conduct.

"We will observe the Sabbath day to keep it holy, in accordance with the Revelations.

"That which is committed to our care we will not appropriate to our own use.

"That which we borrow we will return according to promise, and that which we find we will not appropriate to our own use, but seek to return it to its proper owner.

"We will, as soon as possible, cancel all individual indebtedness contracted prior to our uniting with the Order, and, when once fully identified with said Order, will contract no debts contrary to the wishes of the Board of Directors.

"We will patronize our brethren who are in the Order.

"In our apparel and deportment we will not pattern after nor encourage foolish and extravagant fashions, and will cease to import or buy from abroad any article which can be reasonably dispensed with, or which can be produced by combination of home labor. We will foster and encourage the producing and manufacturing of all articles needful for our consumption as fast as our circumstances will permit.

"We will be simple in our dress and manner of living, using proper economy and prudence in the management of all intrusted to our care.

"We will combine our labor for mutual benefit, sustain without faith, prayers, and works those whom we have elected to take the management of the different departments of the Order, and be subject to them in their official capacity, refraining from a spirit of fault-finding.

"We will honestly and diligently labor and devote ourselves and all we have to the Order and to the building up of the Kingdom of God."

The authoritative revelations setting forth the principles of the United Order contain the following significant passages:

"And you are to be equal, or in other words, you are to have equal claims on the properties, for the benefit of managing the concerns of your stewardships, every man according to his wants and his needs, inasmuch as his wants are just; and all this for the benefit of the Church of the living God, that every man may improve upon his talent, that every man may gain other talents, yea, even an hundred fold, to be cast into the Lord's storehouse, to become the common property of the whole church, every man seeking the interest of his neighbor, and doing all things with an eye single to the glory of God. This order I have appointed to be an everlasting order unto you, and unto your successors, inasmuch as ye sin not."—*Doctrine and Covenants,* lxxxii. 17–20.

"Listen to the counsel of him who has ordained you from on high, who shall speak in your ears the words of wisdom, that salvation may be unto you in that thing which you have presented before me, saith the Lord

God; For verily I say unto you, the time has come, and is now at hand; and behold, and lo, it must needs be that there be an organization of my people, in regulating and establishing the affairs of the storehouse for the poor of my people, both in this place (Hiram, Ohio) and in the land of Zion, . . . for a permanent and everlasting establishment and order unto my church, to advance the cause, which ye have espoused to the salvation of man, and to the glory of your Father who is in heaven, that you may be equal in the bands of heavenly things; yea, and earthly things also, for the obtaining of heavenly things; *for if ye are not equal in earthly things, ye cannot be equal in obtaining heavenly things; for if you will that I give unto you a place in the celestial world, you must prepare yourselves by doing the things which I have commanded you and required of you.*

"And now, verily thus saith the Lord, it is expedient that all things be done unto my glory, by you who are joined together in this order; . . . wherefore a commandment I give unto you, to prepare and organize yourselves by a bond or everlasting covenant that cannot be broken. And he who breaketh it shall lose his office and standing in the church, and shall be delivered over to the buffetings of Satan until the day of redemption. Behold, this is the preparation wherewith I prepare you, and the foundation, and the ensample which I give unto you, whereby you may accomplish the commandments which are given you, that through my providence, notwithstanding the tribulation which shall descend upon you, that the church may stand independent above all other creatures beneath the celestial world.—*Ibid.*, lxxviii. 1–3, 4–8, 11–14.

"Verily I say unto you, my friends, I give unto you counsel, and a commandment, concerning all the properties which belong to the order which I commanded to be organized and established, to be an united order, and an everlasting order for the benefit of my church, and for the salvation of men until I come, with promise immutable and unchangeable, that inasmuch as those whom I commanded were faithful they should be blessed with a multiplicity of blessings. . . . I, the Lord, stretched out the heavens, and built the earth as a very handy work, and all things therein are mine: and it is my purpose to provide for my saints, for all things are mine; but it must needs be done in mine own way; and behold this is the way that I, the Lord, have decreed to provide for my saints, that the poor shall be exalted, in that the rich are made low — for the earth is full, and there is enough and to spare; yea, I prepared all things, and have given unto the children of men to be agents unto themselves. Therefore, if any man shall take of the abundance which I have made, and impart not his portion, according to the law of my gospel, unto the poor and the needy, he shall, with the wicked, lift up his eyes in hell, being in torment. (Here follow specifications of various properties, to which certain persons, such as Rigdon, Martin Harris, Frederick G. Williams, Oliver Cowdery, and others, are appointed by name as stewards.) . . . And again, a commandment I give unto you concerning your stewardship which I have appointed unto you. Behold, all these properties are mine, or less your faith is vain, . . . and if the properties are mine, then ye are stewards, otherwise ye are no stewards. But, verily I say unto you, I have appointed unto you to be stewards over mine house, even stewards indeed. . . . For the purpose of building up my church and kingdom on earth, and to prepare my people for the time when I shall dwell with them, which is nigh at hand. And ye shall prepare for yourselves a treasury, and consecrate it unto my name; and ye shall appoint one among you to keep the treasury, and he shall be ordained unto this blessing; and there shall be a seal upon the treasury, and all the sacred things shall be delivered into the treasury, and no man among you shall call it his own, or any part of it, for it shall belong to you all with one accord; and I give it unto you from this very hour: and now see to it, that ye go to and make use of the stewardship which I have appointed unto you. . . . And again, there shall be another treasury prepared, and a treasurer appointed to keep the treasury, and a seal shall be placed upon it; and all moneys that you receive in your stewardships, by improving upon the properties which I have appointed unto you, in houses, or in lands, or in cattle, . . . shall be cast into the treasury as you receive moneys, . . . and let not any man among you say that it is his own, for it shall not be called his, nor any part of it; and there shall not any part of it be used, or taken out of the treasury, only by the voice and common consent of the order. And this shall be the voice and common consent of the order; that any man among you, say unto the treasurer, I have need of this to help me in my stewardship; if it be five talents (dollars), or, if it be ten talents (dollars), or twenty, or fifty, or an hundred, the treasurer shall give unto him the sum which he requires, to help him in his stewardship, until he be found a transgressor, and it is manifest before the council of the order plainly, that he is an unfaithful and an unwise steward; but so long as he is in full fellowship, and is faithful, and wise in his stewardship, this shall be his token unto the treasurer, that the treasurer shall not withhold. But in case of transgression, the treasurer shall be subject unto the council and voice of the order. . . . I give you this privilege, this once, and behold, if you proceed to do the things which I have laid before you, according to my commandments, all these things are mine, and ye are my stewards, and the master will not suffer his house to be broken up. Even so. Amen.—*Ibid.*, civ. 1–2, 14–18, 54–63, 67, 68, 70–76, 86.

The wording of these revelations is significant of the actual objects for which the United Order was originally founded; and they embody a distinct lesson and example to all theoretical sociologists, who are earnestly desirous of achieving the lasting good of their fellow-men. The abolition of poverty is not merely a benevolent aim, but a high religious duty, since "if ye are not equal in earthly things, ye cannot be equal in obtaining heavenly things." Nor can a candid mind fail to discern the fact a high and noble ideal of the responsibility and duty of wealth is actually presented. Our so-called "benevolence" and voluntary "charity" are to be discountenanced as unacceptable to God, just as they are ineffective in permanently benefitting humanity: a man's duties in this respect are precisely defined — if he "impart not his portion, according to the law of my gospel, unto the poor and the needy," his portion shall be that of Dives in Christ's parable. The commands of Christ are to be accepted literally.

The discontinuance of the United Order as a practical reality was not an abrogation, nor yet a substitution of a less stringent law of consecration. It will, as the Mormons confidently believe, be restored again on earth at the coming of Christ and the setting-up of Zion, and remain thereafter as an everlasting covenant. The law of tithing, or consecration of the tenth of the increase for the support of the Church and the care of the poor is now the accepted practice. The revelation establishing it reads as follows:

"Verily, thus saith the Lord, I require all their [the people's] surplus property to be put into the hands of the bishop of my church of Zion, for the building of mine house, and for the laying of the foundation of Zion and for the Priesthood, and for the debts of the Presidency of my church; and this shall be the beginning of the tithing of my people; and after that, those who have thus been tithed, shall pay one-tenth of all their interest annually; and this shall be a standing law unto them for ever, for my holy Priesthood, saith the Lord. Verily I say unto you, it shall come to pass that all those who gather unto the land of Zion shall be tithed of their surplus properties, and shall observe this law, or they shall not be found worthy to abide among you. And I say unto you, if my people observe not this law, to keep it holy, and by this law sanctify the land of Zion unto me, that my statutes and my judgments may be kept thereon, that it may be most holy, behold, verily I say unto you, it shall not be a land of Zion unto you; and this shall be an ensample unto all the Stakes of Zion."—*Doctrine and Covenants,* cxix. 1–7.

On the basis of this command, the practice of tithing has always been faithfully upheld among the Mormons, and has provided the most important source of income for their Church and its activities. Of course, the practice has drawn the criticism of enemies of the Church, who have indulged their spleen in various false representations to the effect that the custom is maintained by forced levies, extortion and threats of various orders. The disingenuousness of such accusations must be evident on honest investigation of the matter; since, whether one agrees with the teachings of the Mormon Church, or not, there is positively no reason for the assumption that there are not very many people who do not heartily and intelligently endorse them all. Furthermore, only a moment's reflection is necessary to demonstrate the fact that wholesale extortion practiced on a body of people, who are in all other matters quite independent and highly individualized, is by no means the easy and cheerful task that our would-be informants would have to suppose.

The practice of tithing is an ancient one, having been enjoined in the Law of Israel (Lev. xxvii:30; Num. xviii:21; Deut. xiv:23, 28; Neh. x:37–38); practiced by the ancient patriarchs (Gen. xiv:20; Heb. vii:5–6; Gen. xxviii:22), and mentioned as an institution in both Old and New Testaments (Prov. iii. 9; Mal. iii:8; II Chron. xxxi:5; Amos lv:4; Matt. xxiii:23; Luke xviii:12). On several occasions the practice has been attempted as a means for raising funds for the support of Christian churches, exampled, notably, by the forced levies formerly in vogue in Great Britain for the support of the established church. Latterly, some of our larger sects, such as the Methodists, have carefully considered a restoration of the practice, if possible, in order to replenish the coffers, none too well filled by offerings, voluntary as to amount as well as to production. The fact remains, however, that the Latter-day Saints, alone among all bodies professing the Christian heritage, have been able to maintain the institution with even approximate success. It is scarcely remarkable, although by no means conclusive, that opponents of this Church should allege oppression and extortion: their own experiences and capabilities in this matter have not been of the most reassuring description. It is very probable, however, that no other body whatever could possibly duplicate the Mormon record, since this, like other things achieved by this Church, seems to be a real corollary to their splendid and vital organization, which, if it does nothing else, begets a strong sense of solidarity among its people.

But the Latter-day Saints obey a broader law of tithing and consecration than applies even to the tithing of their material increase. As if to demonstrate the superior quality of their enthusiasm and devotion at every point, these people dedicate their time, labors and talents to the service of their Church, very often with no hope or expectation of remuneration, or with only meagre returns in any material sense. As already noted, none of their officers receive salaries for their services to the Church, except in the event that their entire time is devoted to the work. The ward bishops are entitled to a small percentage of the tithes and other funds collected by them, and very frequently forego even this consideration. Perhaps nearly the most conspicuous example of devoted time and services is to be found in the missionary work, usually done by the younger men of the Church, who pay their own way to their mission fields, be they at home or abroad, and depend upon the voluntary assistance of friends in the field, or, upon the assistance of their families or friends at home. The Church funds pay only their return fares homeward. It is, indeed, a strong evidence of the vitality of this form of faith that young men from every walk of life should thus cheerfully devote several years of their time, usually in their growing years, to a work devoid of promise or possibility of material returns. While all other Christian bodies, with the sole exception of the Roman Catholic, suffer from a dearth either of funds or of volunteers for missionary work, and are obliged to guarantee the livelihoods of their missionaries, both at home and abroad, the spread of the Mormon gospel is entirely in the hands of people who go out, literally without "purse or scrip."

Voluntary and unremunerated work, however, is by no means confined to the mission field. It is regularly and cheerfully given, whenever required, as, for example, in the building of

Church edifices. The splendid Temple in Salt Lake City, which is one of the most substantial edifices in the entire United States, was built largely by the voluntary labor of the Mormon people, as were also the three other large temples at St. George, Manti, and Logan in Utah, the older temples at Kirtland, Ohio, and Nauvoo, Illinois, and all of the ward chapels throughout Mormondom. Such a record as this shows a degree of enthusiasm, also of genuine community sentiment that is rare, if not entirely unparalleled. In these days of sociological theorizing, when the present order, bad as it is, is menaced by the advocates of sentimental and radical schemes, which have failed wherever attempted on a practical scale, it is remarkable that the success of Mormonism should not be taken as an object lesson on the unescapable necessity of reorganizing society on a basis distinctly religious, instead of being met by lies, slanders and deliberate misrepresentations from the lips of people professing to be teachers of righteousness. If this unworthy and un-Christian attitude evidences nothing else, it is certainly competent in establishing the truth of the Socialist allegation that religion, as it is known among us, cannot be depended on to assist in social betterment to the minutest extent. That the Mormon record argues to a contrary conclusion is good evidence that it is of a different order and origin from many of the familiar sects among us, whether, as it claims, based on direct divine authority, or not.

CHAPTER X

MORMONISM AS THE INSTRUMENT OF TEMPORAL SALVATION

THE unchallenged superiority of the Mormon Church as a successful exponent of social regeneration, of "worldly salvation," in fact, of the order evidently contemplated by Christ Himself, if His words have the plain meaning, which have been so generally and so adroitly ignored by His professed and pretended followers in all ages, is well exampled in the following passage from the experience of John Taylor, third President of the Church. When the Mormons had left Nauvoo, Illinois, in the early part of 1846, the city fell into the hands of a band of Fourierite colonists, under the direction of a certain Etienne Cabet, and proceeded, under the most favorable conditions imaginable, to put their Utopian plans into operation. As with all similar experiments, this was an utter failure — and for the familiar reason that Fourierism, like other forms of Socialism, attempts to grow the flower of altruism and unselfishness in the soil of misery, and without the help of anything vital in the line of a religious influence. While engaged in a mission in Paris, France, Elder Taylor met a certain Fourierite journalist named Krolokoski, with whom he held a conversation touching the merits of their respective "gospels." Thus:

"Mr. K.—'Mr. Taylor, do you propose no other plan to ameliorate the condition of mankind than that of baptism for the remission of sins?'

"Elder T.—'This is all I propose about the matter.'

"Mr. K.—'Well, I wish you every success; but I am afraid you will not succeed.'

"Elder T.—'Monsieur Krolokoski, you sent Monsieur Cabet to Nauvoo, some time ago. He was considered your leader — the most talented man you had. He went to Nauvoo shortly after we had deserted it. Houses and lands could be obtained at a mere nominal sum. Rich farms were deserted, and thousands of us had left our houses and furniture in them, and almost everything calculated to promote the happiness of man was there. Never could a person go to a place under more happy circumstances. Besides all the advantages of having everything made ready to his hand, M. Cabet had a select company of colonists. He and his company went to Nauvoo — what is the result? I read in all your reports from there — published in your own paper here, in Paris, a continued cry for help. The cry is money, money! We want money to help us carry out our designs. While your colony in Nauvoo with all the advantages of our deserted fields and homes — that they had only to move into — have been dragging out a miserable existence, the Latter-day Saints, though stripped of their all and banished from civilized society into the valleys of the Rocky Mountains, to seek their protection among savages . . . which Christian civilization denied us — there our people have built houses, enclosed lands, cultivated gardens, built school-houses, and have organized a government and are prospering in all the blessings of civilized life. Not only this, but they have sent thousands and thousands of dollars over to Europe to assist the suffering poor to go to America, where they might find an asylum.

"The society I represent, M. Krolokoski, comes with the fear of God — the worship of the great Elohim; we offer the simple plan ordained of God, viz. repentance, baptism for the remission of sins, and the laying-on of hands for the gift of the Holy Ghost. . . . Now, which is the better, our religion, or your philosophy?'

"Mr. K.—'Well, Mr. Taylor, I can say nothing.'"—*Life of John Taylor* (*B. H. Roberts*), pp. 226–227.

No more striking contrast exists in literature, and no greater antithesis of human experience can be found in history. That the comparisons made by Elder Taylor are true to the life is evident on careful study of the records of both communities mentioned. The Icarian colony (so called) continued at Nauvoo, with more or less success, from 1849 until 1857. It began then to show the inevitable signs of fatal malady in the spirit of anarchism and discontent that nearly invariably affects such experiments sooner or later. In 1857 the property of the community passed into the hands of a receiver, to be administered for the benefit of its creditors, and, beginning with this year, the colonists gradually removed to another Icarian settlement in Adams county, Iowa. Here, also, the community life continued, with fair prosperity, until 1878, when there was another division, followed by an extended law suit. Finally, in 1895, the community life was abandoned by unanimous vote of the surviving members, and the property was divided among them. Some years before this final catastrophe, M. Cabet (or Cabot) had died near St. Louis, Missouri, heartbroken at the evident failure of his life work.

The unhappy conclusion of the Icarian experiment, and the downfall of poor Cabet, who had, undoubtedly, held high hopes of permanently benefitting his fellow-men, is merely typical of the fate that must inevitably overtake any sociological experiment, that is founded firstplace on mere reaction on the present social order, without sufficient planning to neutralize present evils by rational substitutes. The mere substitution of an ideal of communism is no offset to a régime of individualism, for the simple reason that individualism is, in fundamental principle, natural, whereas communism can subsist only on a community of interest, as when many people combine for national defense, or to save themselves, each one as well as all, from the untoward effects of a natural catastrophe. The prime fault with socialism, and all other current schemes of social reorganization, is that it has not yet outlived the state of reactionism, which, while rebelling against "tyranny," would give the slave his chance in the rôle of tyrant. This tendency has been ably condemned and deplored by Herbert Spencer in his essay, "The Coming Slavery." Speaking of the possible establishment of a socialistic state, he says:

> "The final result would be a revival of despotism. A disciplined army of civil officials, like an army of military officials, gives supreme power to its head — a power which often led to usurpation, as in mediæval Europe and more recently in Japan — nay, has thus so led among our neighbors, within our own times. The recent confessions of M. de Maupas has shown how readily a constitutional head, elected and trusted by the whole people, may, with the aid of a few unscrupulous confederates, paralyze the representative body and make himself autocrat. That those who rose to power in a socialistic organization would not scruple to carry out their aims at all costs, we have good reason for concluding. When we find that shareholders who, sometimes gaining but often losing, have made that railway system by which national prosperity has been so greatly increased, are spoken of by the council of the Democratic Federation as having 'laid hands' on the means of communication, we may infer that those who directed a socialistic administration might interpret with extreme perversity the claims of individuals and classes under their control. And when, further, we find members of this same council urging that the State should take possession of the railways, 'with or without compensation,' we may suspect that the heads of the ideal society desired, would be but little deterred by considerations of equity from pursuing whatever policy they thought needful; a policy which would always be one identified with their own supremacy. It would need but war with an adjacent society, or some internal discontent demanding forcible suppression, to at once transform a socialistic administration into a grinding tyranny like that of ancient Peru; under which the mass of the people, controlled by grades of officials, and leading lives that were inspected out-of-doors and in-doors, labored for the support of the organization which regulated them, and were left with but a bare subsistence for themselves. And then would be completely revived, under a different form, that *régime* of status — that system of compulsory cooperation, the decaying tradition of which is represented by the old Toryism, and towards which the new Toryism is carrying us back."— *The Coming Slavery, pp.* 17–18.

While it is probably true that, with human nature as at present developed, the results indicated by Mr. Spencer would follow sooner or later on the establishment of a Socialist régime, it is safe to say that, on the basis of actual experience, Socialism would probably fail before the stage of autocracy had been reached. The defect may be in human nature, which has never, hitherto, been able to subsist on humanitarian enthusiasm alone, and this bases our objections to Socialism on the ground that it assumes a degree of "goodness" in man, which is not native to his character. It does him an injustice by idealizing him, forgetting that the defects of society, against which it protests, are the outworkings of human nature, quite as much as the usual failures of Socialism, when put to the practical test. This cause of Socialist failure is well set forth in a recent work, which outlines the history of Socialist experiments made by certain Australian and British enthusiasts in Paraguay. These colonists settled at places called by them New Australia and Cosme, and, after battling long to live the principles of their creed, finally yielded to the "logic of events," and abandoned them. The story goes on to relate that the result of discontinuing the Socialist experiment was the incoming of a previously unrealized prosperity. Although the writer of this book is evidently bitterly anti-Socialist, his account seems to be accurate, and his inferences sound. He concludes his account of the ventures in the following words:

"The stalwarts who remained after the collapse of William Lane's wild venture have made a gallant fight back to prosperity, and have disproved the allegation that it was the nature of the country, rather than the evils inseparable from Socialism, which caused the original failure. At the present day the prosperity of those who remain in the New Australia colony is steadily increasing, and a number of the Utopians who were repatriated have found their way back to Paraguay, to share in the great advantages which the settlement offers to Anglo-Saxons with agricultural experience. . . . At the present day, New Australia is neither a Utopian Eden nor a 'hell upon earth.' It is an average community of sane, sober, hard-working, self-respecting farmers, living at peace with one another and taking for their motto: 'What we have we hold!' . . . Cosme for many years made no such progress. Till 1904 it endeavored to keep itself afloat by the publication of its journal of far-fetched articles describing the happiness of its people, which induced other credulous souls to join them in the expectation of experiencing impossible bliss. Cheated by false hopes, these newcomers quickly fell into the growing quagmire of discontent and misery. Things became worse every year; the original glamor faded, and men's hearts hardened as they had done at New Australia. The feeling of bitterness against those who were sick and unable to work, and against widows, and people with large families parasitically dependent upon the exertions of the adult able-bodied, was the saddest feature of the place. It often happened that a man, who was seriously ill, would stagger to his work when he should have been lying up, for fear of the boycotting which came to be systematically practised towards any who failed to do their allotted day's task. Rather than work for the benefit of 'all' any longer, many of the bachelors withdrew to Sapucay, and obtained employment at the engineering works of the Paraguay Central Railway. Married men with families of young children, remained tied to the spot, hopelessly striving to make headway against the dead-weight of debt — for everything was mortgaged — which bore them down.

"Eventually, as at New Australia, the Government stepped in, withdrew the original grant, and divided the Cosme settlement up, on the usual colonization terms, each family being allotted so much agricultural and so much grazing land. 'The Cosme Colony has now definitely thrown its dreams overboard,' wrote a correspondent to an Australian journal. 'For several years before it abandoned the original principles, it was an open secret (scarcely even concealed by the interested parties) that the few remaining members were held together only by the expectation of the final break-up, when the property would be divided, and the fewer that remained the greater individual share would accrue to each.'"— Stewart Grahame (*Where Socialism Failed, pp.* 225–228.)

There is little to be gained by enlarging upon the failure of experiments in Socialism, or in any other system honestly devised for the good of mankind and the betterment of social conditions. Such examples of failure are, however, so many cases in point to uphold the contention that there is in such schemes "one thing lacking." That this is a deliberate recognition of the religious instinct is the conclusion of numerous thinkers, great and small, and the real explanation of the fact that the advocates of even inefficient religious sects are able to wage effective warfare against the most promising schemes of social reform. The fact that, as recognized by sociological theorizers, the religious instinct has been largely perverted throughout historic time, and that it is often associated with the grossest orders of superstition, is no argument against its ultimate validity, nor any sufficient excuse for the theory that it will eventually be outgrown, sloughed off, and may for this reason, be ignored as an element in schemes intended to achieve the perfection of humanity. Such a conclusion is ably set forth in the following paragraphs by a popular writer on sociology:

"Professor Huxley, some time ago, in a severe criticism of the 'Religion of Humanity' advocated by the followers of Comte, asserted, in accents which always come naturally to the individual when he looks at the drama of human life from his own standpoint, that he would as soon worship 'a wilderness of apes' as the Positivist's rationalized conception of humanity. But the comparison with which he concluded, in which he referred to the considerable progress made by Mormonism as contrasted with Positivism, has its explanation when viewed in the light of the foregoing conclusions. Mormonism may be a monstrous form of belief, . . . yet it is seen that we cannot deny to it the characteristics of a religion. Although, on the other hand, the 'Religion of Humanity' advocated by Comte may be, and is, a most exemplary set of principles, we perceive it to be without those characteristics. It is not, apparently, a religion at all. It is, like other forms of belief which do not provide a super-rational sanction for conduct, but which call themselves religions, incapable, from the nature of the conditions, of exercising the functions of a religion in the evolution of society.

"In the religious beliefs of mankind we have not simply a class of phenomena peculiar to the childhood of the race. We have therein the characteristic feature of our social evolution. These beliefs constitute, in short, the natural and inevitable complement of our reason; and so far from being threatened with eventual dissolution they are apparently destined to continue to grow with the growth and to develop with the development of society, while always preserving intact and unchangeable the one essential feature they all have in common in the ultra-rational sanction they provide for conduct. And lastly, as we understand how an ultra-rational sanction for the sacrifice of the interests of the individual to those of the social organism has been a feature common to all religions we see, also, the conception of sacrifice has occupied such a central place in nearly all beliefs, and why the tendency of religion has ever been to surround this principle with the most impressive and stupendous of sanctions."—*Benjamin Kidd* (*"Social Evolution," pp.* 123–125.)

This passage expresses the matured judgment of a sociologist who recognizes the obvious fact that a really scientific solution of the troubles of society must take into consideration all of the factors in human nature, the good and evil alike. Nor is a proposed system properly to be called "scientific" because it deals in terms and principles borrowed from the hypothesis of evolution, or any other systematization of facts and observations of specialists in some branch or other of human knowledge. The popular zoological sociology, formulated as it is by people who are neither zoologists nor scientists in any sense, attempts to make the inner workings of the human being conform to principles presumably derived from an external study of the lower animals, of whose actual psychology we have very defective data, and then we are surprised that our schemes do not work out under life conditions. Most benevolent theorists, being devoid of the scientific sense, are mere reactionists, and, because of the evils experienced under one extreme of social development, assume, inevitably, that the only offset is to be found under an order that emphasizes the opposite extreme. They fail to discern the fact that evil social conditions are the development of human traits, in certain definite environments, and that the ideal and normal is not to be found in revising the constitution of the social order, but in dealing direct with the fountain head of motivation. The difference between the two methods is entirely analogous to the difference between attempting to cure a disease in the physical body by treating the superficial symptoms, the skin eruptions, etc., and ignoring the systemic infection that is the ultimate source of such symptoms, and the saner method, which follows the theory that the superficial symptoms, painful and annoying as they may be, can be eradicated only by removing the infection in the blood.

Nor are we to understand by the theory postulating the supremacy of "religion"—which, in a very real and sufficient aspect, may be defined as the sense possessed by the essential self of some real and organic relationship with and dependence on a source of motive and a standard of thinking, which seems to be, and properly should be, ultimate in character—necessarily involves wholesale toleration for, or a complacent attitude toward any and every form of influence professing to be religious, or even Christian. The ultimate judgment of "truth," as applied to religious systems, must be that of practical efficiency. All considerations of "historical authority" and logical accuracy are totally irrelevant, by the side of the consideration of practical operability. Such a rule enforced, as should be, would class very many of our sects and systems among superstitions and encumberances. Mormonism, however, is justified in the fact that it is evidently an extremely practical form of faith, dealing direct with the most fundamental instincts of the human soul, and dealing so strongly and vividly as to produce, very nearly, a distinct type of mankind, a type almost tribal or national in its strongly marked characteristics. It stands almost, if not quite, unique in the evident power of transforming and unifying people of diverse races to common standards of thought, feeling and behavior. In this particular, it is demonstrated a truly vital religious influence. It is not alone its splendid organization that effects this result, but some very real and organic imperative behind even its organization. Nor is this, as far as appears, wholly the influence of its leaders, able and astute as they may be, nor yet the shadow of its founder's colossal personality. There can be no doubt that it is validly and genuinely religious in its character; since there is positively no influence other than religion known to man — not even patriotism — which is capable of such results.

The logical results of the Mormon influence and organization are, as would be expected, found in the persistent instinct of cooperation and mutual helpfulness, and in the practical brotherhood of Mormons. The discontinuance of their first effort, the United Order, is clearly traceable, as their own writers claim, to the fact that the world and human nature were, and are, not yet ready for such a scheme of reorganization, any more than for the various schemes of communism and socialism that have been tried unsuccessfully by numerous non-religious sociologists. That it is an excellent ideal for the future, as discerned by the leaders of both movements, is probable. One great difference in the experience of the Mormons, as compared with that of experimenters in "communism," is that the spirit and impulse of the system still persists among the Mormons in a very vivid sense, and has not been lost to sight as an ideal for the future. The fact is well outlined in the following quotation from a leading Mormon writer and historian:

"The United Order was not permanently established, nor did its original workings long continue. Human selfishness within, inhuman persecution without, were the twofold cause. . . . The system, therefore, went into abeyance, and the work of organizing Stakes of Zion, preparatory to the founding of Zion proper, has since engrossed the attention of the Church. But the great event has only been postponed. The realization of the ideal is still in prospect. The United Order, with all that it implies, will yet be established — must be, for Zion cannot be built up without it.

"Meanwhile the spirit and genius of that Order has remained with the Church, and has influenced its people, more or less, in all the moves that they have made, in all the enterprises that they have undertaken. The spirit of brotherhood, of cooperation, of mutual helpfulness, has characterized them in all their proselyting, colonizing, commercial, industrial, and educational activities.

"The Pioneers of Utah and the Immigrants who followed in their wake and helped them to found the earliest settlement in the Rocky Mountain region, were actuated by such feelings. Those who came first into these mountain solitudes, these unoccupied valleys, could have made great 'land grabs' if they had felt so disposed, and enriched themselves at the expense of their fellows who came later. But this was not their disposition, nor their desire. . . . Under the leadership and counsel of men imbued with the genius of the United Order, and who set the example themselves, and asked the people to follow it, those early settlers contented themselves with moderate possessions. The real estate was distributed among all the members of the community, each one getting a share. Many of those first upon the ground gave to others who arrived in after years. There was no monopoly of land or water in the Pioneer colony, nor in any of the colonies that sprang from it. Small holdings were the rule. It was a maxim in the community that a man should own no more land than he could cultivate. . . .

"The altruistic spirit of the 'Mormon' community was strikingly shown during certain periods following the original occupancy of Salt Lake Valley, when drought, frost, and the ravages of crickets and grasshoppers brought scarcity and threatened famine to the struggling people. . . . All were not alike destitute. Some, foreseeing the straitness, provided against it, and their bins and barns were full, while others were empty. Those who had, gave to those who had not, the full larders and storehouses being drawn upon to supply the needy and prevent suffering. More than one provident, well-to-do citizen stood as a Joseph in Egypt to the hungry multitude. They took no advantage of their neighbors. Where they did not give outright, as was often the case, they sold at moderate prices their beef and bread-stuffs to those able to reimburse them. When flour commanded as high as a dollar a pound, these big-souled men, who were generally leading authorities of the Church, would not accept more than six cents a pound; nor would they sell at all except to those in need, refusing to speculate, or encourage others to speculate, out of the necessities of the poor. This splendid philanthropy was due to the spirit of the Gospel, the spirit of the United Order, the spirit that will yet redeem Zion and prepare a people for that era of brotherhood, righteousness and peace that is synonymous with the coming of the Kingdom of God."— *Orson F. Whitney* (*"Mormon Activities," pp.* 12–14.)

After the settlement of the Mormon pioneers in the valleys of Utah, there was a well-defined movement to restore the United Order, on the part of Brigham Young and other influential spirits. The scheme was abandoned, however, or, rather, not perfected; very largely, as we may surmise, because of considerations of a more or less practical character. Undoubtedly, such a plan would have been acceptable to a large number of the people, whose resources were none too large, and whose labors in redeeming the desert might have been attractively lightened by a common fund to draw upon for support. Had President Young, and his immediate advisers, been of the venal and unworthy character many informants would have us believe, the scheme of a United Order might have appealed strongly as a convenient means for securing control of the funds and property of the whole of their people. Thus:

> "Had Brigham Young persevered in his predecessor's [Joseph Smith's] project, it is almost certain that he would have established a gigantic 'company' that would have controlled all the temporal interests of the territory, and eventually comprised the whole Mormon population. It is just possible that he himself foresaw that such success would be ruin; that the foundations of the Order would sink under such a prodigious superstructure, for he diverted his attention from the main to subsidiary schemes. Instead of one central organization sending out colonies on all sides of it, he advised the establishment of branch communities, which might eventually be gathered together under a single headquarters' control. The two projects were the same as to results; they differed only as to the means; and the second was the more judicious."—*Phil Robinson* ("*Sinners and Saints,*" *pp.* 223).

Although Mr. Robinson's information and inferences are not always entirely reliable, his explanation of the reasons for not reestablishing the Order in Utah seems reasonable, in view of the actual developments under the administration of President Young and his immediate successors. The foremost thought in the minds of these leaders was, apparently, cooperation, as a reasonable method of providing employment for many of the Saints, and of upbuilding home industries. But the policy consistently followed by President Young in the development of Utah was conspicuous throughout the journeyings of the Mormon people from Nauvoo to the Rocky Mountains. On several occasions temporary settlements were made, and crops planted in the spring for the benefit of journeying "Saints," who should reach these localities in the summer and autumn. All able-bodied men were then called upon to contribute their labor for the common good, and did so cheerfully. During this terrible journey, also, President Young first enunciated the famous "land law of Modern Israel," which demanded that "no man is to hold more land than he can cultivate." It was the principle upon which apportionments of land were made on the arrival in the Salt Lake Valley. The law of cooperation in all temporal matters was also set forth in the Epistle issued by the Apostles at Winter Quarters (now Florence), Nebraska, December 23, 1846, in the following striking sentence:

"It is the duty of the rich saints everywhere, to assist the poor, according to their ability, to gather; and if choose, with a covenant and promise that the poor thus helped, shall repay as soon as they are able. It is also the duty of the rich, those who have the intelligence and the means, to come home forthwith, and establish factories, and all kinds of machinery, that will tend to give employment to the poor, and produce those articles which are necessary for the comfort, convenience, health and happiness of the people; and no one need to be at a loss concerning his duty in these matters, if he will walk so humbly before God as to keep the small still whisperings of the Holy Ghost within continually."

The excellent principles enunciated in this epistle were adhered to as closely as possible in the settlement and up-building of Utah. Indeed, as reflection will reveal, this must have been the case, since, otherwise, it would be difficult to conceive how that stable and prosperous colonies could be made up of all sorts and conditions of people, from all parts of the civilized world. Brigham Young was undoubtedly a great leader, sometimes, perhaps, arbitrary and dictatorial, but, on the whole, a person consistently benevolent and solicitous for the well-being of the people in his charge. Moreover, as is evident to the candid historian, the responsibility largely devolved upon him to carry out the excellent principles of the Mormon Gospel for the temporal benefit of mankind. That he nobly discharged his mission is evident. Indeed, Young's constant activity in all movements for the temporal benefit of the people furnished the occasion seized by certain malcontents, notably Messrs. Godbe, Harrison, Stenhouse, Tullidge, and others, to inaugurate a movement in protest against his activity in temporal affairs, particularly in the matter of founding and conducting large stores and manufacturing enterprises, to the disadvantage, as alleged, of spiritual concerns. This "protest" had, as was evidently desired, a truly pious flavor, but Brigham Young's policy was doubtless nearer to the sort of religious and "spiritual" influence that the world is beginning to demand very insistently, and is amply ready to appreciate. In the words of Joseph F. Smith, as quoted on page 212, "a religion which has not the power to save people temporally and make them prosperous and happy here, cannot be depended upon to save them spiritually, to exalt them in the life to come." This is, in fact, the "law and the prophets" of Mormonism; it is also the alpha and the omega of common sense. We can readily understand, in view of the puny humanitarian achievements of the last eighteen centuries, and the dreadful social order, which we are asked to call "civilized" and "Christian," why Mormonism is regarded as such a " menace " in some quarters: although its spread would mean the end of multitudes of sociological difficulties, traditional religious sects would suffer in the comparison.

"From the first 'home industry' has been a watchword in Utah, and among the first lessons taught to the Mormon people by Brigham Young, after their migration to Utah, was to supply as far as possible their wants by manufactures from raw materials in the surrounding region. It was the plan of Brigham Young to build up an independent sovereignty and to make his people as free as possible from appeal to the outside world. Disposition and need, therefore, early induced the manufacture of many articles in Utah, and thus were revealed many of the resources of Utah and developed the self-supplying faculties of the people. Many of the manufactures they then produced in a primitive way have since been refined upon and expanded, until the quality and quantity of goods manufactured in Utah are by no means insignificant."—"*Utah: Resources, Population, Industries, etc.*" (*U. P. R. R. guide book*) p. 78.

The part played by the Mormon Church in the development of Utah must be apparent to any intelligent and unbiased mind in considering the history of that region from the beginning. It may be safe to assert that no band of pilgrims, of equal size, with a different religious history and character, possibly, also, with a different leadership, would have attempted, in the first half of the nineteenth century, to make a settlement in the valleys of Utah. Not even the understandable, not to say, excusable, desire to escape from the American people, with their generous and liberal professions and their curiously intolerant behavior, could have explained, in other conditions, the Mormon settlement in and subsequent conquest of the wilderness. Unless the interest of their leaders in the temporal welfare of the people, in their "temporal salvation," had been more than a verbal profession of faith, Utah would have been the scene of their dispersal, the point at which the curtain should be rung down on the drama of Mormonism. But Brigham Young, full of faith in his mission, as leader of these people, and possessed of good and well-reasoned plans for transforming the desert into a garden site, was nothing deterred by the challenges of the scout, James Bridger, " I will give you $1,000 for the first ear of corn ripened in that valley." Doubtless, in view of the enormous difficulties to be overcome, the Mormons would consider that the determination to settle in this unpromising region was both predetermined and providential. Many less reasonable calls have been made on providence.

Having brought his people to a place which seemed far from promising, not alone to James Bridger, his work was barely begun. The people must be led and guided in the work of irrigating the waste, and encouraged and held together until the work was well in progress. It is fortunate for the Mormon People that Young was not interested solely in "spiritual concerns," but also in matters temporal and commercial. To him and to his faith are to be credited the successful accomplishment of this mighty work.

"When Brigham Young assumed the awful responsibility of moving his followers to the desert valleys of the Rocky Mountains, he did it upon faith that irrigation, one of the oldest arts of the Old World, could be successfully applied to the lands he proposed to settle, and before the close of the day of his arrival in Salt Lake Valley, he began the building of the first irrigation canal. That his faith was not misplaced is manifested by the great areas now covered by canals and laterals. The first canal was obliterated in a few years by the streets and structures of a city which sprang up because of it; but by that time other canals were in operation and irrigation was well established in the western country. What an important factor that first canal became in the growth of the West! The system it originated has extended in every direction, until now scores of runaway streams have been seized and almost every valley from California to Kansas is filled with the homes of husbandmen. It is stated with confidence that although irrigation has been employed in Spain and elsewhere in the Old World for centuries, in no place has it been brought to greater perfection than in Utah. . . . As long as any of the waters of Utah's streams and lakes remained unappropriated, the building of irrigation systems continued in Utah, and many fertile valleys were brought under the plow. Under the Mormon system the utmost fairness has always prevailed in the distribution of water, and for that reason Utah's reclaimed areas are much larger than they might have been had selfishness prevailed and prior appropriators been disposed to abuse their rights. There has been almost an entire absence of water litigation in Utah, and never a claim of wanton waste. Many of the systems were put in upon the cooperative plan, and the waters have always been distributed with great impartiality — farmers only taking water at stated times and using no more than the needed amount. In this way the waters have been carried over large areas now thickly populated and wonderfully productive."— *Ibid. p.* 60.

In this quotation, which is amply justified by the facts to be drawn from other sources, it is made evident that the influence of the Mormon religion and its leaders has been efficient, not alone in indicating lines of work to be followed, and assisting in them, in any convenient manner, but also in instilling the spirit of coöperation and fellowship, a sense of the unity of human society realized in practice, not merely held as an ideal for some indefinite future, which is sufficiently unusual to excite comment.

Irrigation, which was started on the arrival of the pioneers in Great Salt Lake Valley in 1847, was, in fact, the most important consideration in the founding of all the settlements in the arid regions of the west. In scores of instances the Church has come to the assistance of the settlers in the work of constructing dams and canals, and has also purchased great tracts of land in

Mexico, New Mexico, Nevada, and Canada, for colonization purposes, in order to give the poor an opportunity to obtain cheap lands. Among the greater undertakings of this kind by the Church may be mentioned the Hurricane irrigation project in southern Utah, by which the waters of the Rio Virgen were diverted from their natural channel to a tract of rich bench land lying to the south, and opposite Saint George, Washington County. Another colonization scheme known as the Enterprise colony in southern Utah was backed by Church money. Among the settlements specially founded by the assistance of the Church may be mentioned those on the San Juan river, in southeastern Utah and northwestern New Mexico, where the Church extended material aid and made it possible for those distant settlements to come into existence and thrive. The settlements of Lund and Preston, in Nevada, founded a few years ago, were also the result of purchases made by the Church, with a view to making it possible for members in search of new homes to obtain them on terms within their reach. The colonies of Diaz, Dublan, Juarez, Pacheco, Chuichupa, Garcia, Oaxaca, and Morelos, in Mexico, were all built on lands originally purchased, in whole or in part, with Church capital, with a view to providing homes for any Church members who might desire to settle in the fertile valleys of Mexico.

The introduction of improved breeds of cattle in some of the settlements is another enterprise which has been backed by the Church, and by this means the cattle in different localities have been generally improved to the great advantage of the settlers. As early as 1859 the Church inaugurated the first effort to raise cotton in southern Utah, and made stronger efforts in the same direction in 1861 and 1862.

One of the most important industries of the Far West, the production of beet sugar, was made possible, indeed actually originated and fostered by the Church authorities, with the declared purpose of providing a hopeful source of labor and income for the people of the region. The original experiments, conducted under the immediate direction of President Young, looked toward the perfection of the sorghum sugar industry in Utah, but, after this attempt had proved unsuccessful, the production of beet sugar was undertaken instead, and is now one of the largest industries of the mountain region. The starting of the beet sugar industry at the time of its first inauguration, and under all the conditions then existing, would have been utterly impossible, if the Church had not assisted with its means.

Machinery for the manufacture of sugar from sorghum cane was imported from Europe in 1852, and was hauled across the plains to Salt Lake City on a train of forty-five wagons, each of which was drawn by four yoke of oxen. The first sorghum sugar factory was opened in what is now known as the Sugar House Ward of Salt Lake City in 1855, and, as a mere matter of history, all the vast expense involved was assumed by the Church. The buildings erected for sugar manufacture at this time were, in 1861, remodeled to serve the purposes of a paper manufacturing plant, and at this place paper was manufactured for a number of years to supply local demands. This also was an enterprise inaugurated by the Church. Later, an extensive plant for the manufacture of paper was erected at the mouth of Big Cottonwood Canyon, near Salt Lake City, which for many years helped to supply the demands for paper in the territory of Utah and gave employment to a large number of people. The plant was finally destroyed by fire.

The first beet sugar factory in Utah was built at Lehi, in 1891, and there are now seven establishments engaged in this industry in Utah and Idaho, all under one management. They are situated in Lehi, Elsinore, Payson and Garland, in Utah, and Idaho Falls, Sugar City and Blackfoot, in Idaho. At the present time the sugar industry in Utah and Idaho represents a capital of $11,000,000 and employs about 1,500 people in the busy season, irrespective of those engaged in raising beets on the farms.

This industry has since grown to large proportions in Utah, very largely through the encouragement of the Church authorities, both by leading in the organization of companies, and by the investment of funds, for the assistance of the farmers of the territory and state. This action has, of course, been largely misinterpreted and misrepresented by the ever-active enemies of the Church, who have ascribed all sorts of evil motives to the act, and emphasized the accusation that, because the Mormon Church had helped its people in upbuilding an industry convenient to them, it was really an active accomplice of the so-called Sugar Trust, which is one of the agencies represented to be engaged in "grinding the faces of the poor."

The Church authorities have made able efforts also to assist in attempts to acclimate the silkworm, and materially contributed to establishing the silk industry, which for a time bid fair to become one of the permanent industries of Utah. They were also active in encouraging such necessary industries as cloth and carpet weaving, and other forms of manufacture. Woolen mills were erected, partly by Church means, on Canyon Creek (Salt Lake Co.), in Provo, Beaver, Washington, Ogden, Brigham City, and other places, which have given employment to hundreds of people. Under the guidance of Brigham Young and Lorenzo Snow, Brigham City, in northern Utah, was turned into a centre for home industry. Tanneries were built in considerable numbers in the early days, and vast quantities of so-called Valley Tan leather made. Shoe factories were also founded, prominent among which is the Z. C. M. I. Shoe Factory, which in 1912 turned out 66,000 pairs of men's, boys' and youths' boots and knock about school shoes. This output is valued at $170,000 and the wages amount to $36,000. As another branch of home industry may be mentioned the Z. C. M. I. Overalls Factory, which turns out overalls at the rate of 40 dozen per day, or about 12,500 dozen a year.

One of the main industries inaugurated under the guidance of the Church was the founding of co-operative stores in nearly all the settlements of the saints. Thus in 1869 the great Zion's Co-operative Mercantile Institution was founded in Salt Lake City, and for many years it was known as the parent store, supplying scores of co-operative stores established in the different settlements in the Rocky Mountains. Up to 1868 private parties had become wealthy by importing goods from the States and selling them in Salt Lake City and the other settlements in the mountains at fabulous profits. By the establishment of co-operative stores, the people were taught the principle of self-protection, and that it was far more desirable and profitable to trade in their own interests than to fill the coffers of merchants who generally look too much to their own interests. Until the early eighties money was exceedingly scarce in Utah, and farm and mountain products were taken by merchants in exchange for their goods, and between man and man also the products of the farm and the mountains (in the shape of wood and lumber) were the common articles of exchange.

The Zion's Cooperative Mercantile Institution was, in fact, the pioneer in the movement for the cooperative selling of local products, now so largely followed throughout the country. It was also the first mercantile establishment in the Far West to adopt the department store plan. In 1870 its shoe factory, still in operation, was first opened, and in 1878, its factory for the manufacture of cotton clothing. It is also the accredited sales agent for numerous independent Utah manufacturers of clothing, food stuffs, carpets and general articles of domestic use. According to authoritative figures, its annual business transactions have for many years averaged over $3,000,000, and are at the present time over $6,000,000. Although not cooperative in the sense that its profits are divided with the public, it is a noble example of the fact that a large and productive enterprise may be built up on the principle of assisting home industries and employing home labor. In this sense, it is cooperative as including the entire local public in the advantages of its operations. It was for the distinct and definite purpose of thus benefitting the people and local industries, that Brigham Young founded the institution and influenced the needed capital in its behalf.

In 1849 the so-called Perpetual Immigrating Fund Company was organized for the purpose of helping converts to Mormonism in Europe and the United States who had not the means to come to Utah; and hundreds of thousands of dollars of Church money were expended at an early day to bring immigrants across the oceans, plains and mountains. From 1860 to 1868 wagons were annually sent to the Missouri river after the poor. Each wagon, as a rule, was hauled by four yoke of cattle, or from two to four span of horses or mules. About 50 such teams were sent out in 1860; upwards of 200 wagons, with four yoke of cattle to each, carrying 150,000 lbs. of flour, were sent in 1861; 262 wagons, 293 men, 2,880 oxen, and 143,315 lbs. of flour were forwarded in 1862; 284 wagons, 488 men, 3,604 oxen, taking 335,969 lbs. of flour, were sent in 1863; about 170 wagons were sent in 1864; 397 wagons, 10 captains, 456 teamsters, 49 mounted guards, 89 horses, 134 mules, and 3,042 oxen were sent in 1866; besides these, 62 wagons, 50 oxen and 61 mules were purchased by the Church in the States that year to assist the emigration across the plains. About five hundred teams, partly mule teams and partly ox teams, were sent by the Church to the terminus of the Union Pacific Railroad up to 1868 to help the poor migrating saints to the valleys of Utah.

In early days, when the settlers of Utah were troubled with Indian depredations, the Church came to the front most liberally with its means to protect them and, in some instances, to reimburse them for the losses sustained during the Indian wars. This was particularly the case in the so-called Walker Wars in 1853, the Tintic War in 1856, and the Black Hawk War in 1865–1872.

In 1867 President Brigham Young took a contract to build 90 miles of grade on the Union Pacific Railroad, in order to give employment to the people of Utah whose crops had been destroyed by grasshoppers. President Young relet the grading to smaller contractors who in turn employed thousands of men from the different settlements of the saints in the mountains. This enabled the people to buy breadstuffs from the States, and thus the famine that threatened on account of the devastations of the grasshoppers was averted.

The opening of the transcontinental railroad brought non-

Mormon settlers and traders in large numbers, and brought about serious conditions of competition with home industries, which, as already stated, created the need for local self-protection, and led to the founding of the Z. C. M. I.

There are at the present time 615 cities, towns, villages and neighborhoods (or 706 regularly organized wards) in the United States, Canada, and Mexico, which have been founded and built up principally by the frugality, industry and unison of the Mormon people, directed by the authorities of the Church. Of these settlements 333 are situated in Utah, 166 in Idaho, 31 in Arizona, 6 in Colorado, 10 in Nevada, 27 in Wyoming, 7 in Oregon, 5 in New Mexico, 22 in Alberta, Canada, and 8 in Old Mexico.

The grand results accomplished by the splendid organization of the Latter-day Saints, the actual sense of fellowship that exists among them, and the creditable faithfulness of their officers, are only too evident for denial or depreciation. That they have a significance to the sociologist and moralist, as well as to the statesman and religionist, is evident. Even anti-Mormons are bound to acknowledge these facts. Thus:

"The Dry Gulch District, of which Roosevelt is the centre, is the 'Mormon' part of the reservation, and that explains why it has made more progress than the rest of the country. The wonderful organization of the Mormon Church enforces a spirit of cooperation unknown in Gentile communities. Under these leaders in six years (for settlement did not really begin until 1906) the Latter-day Saints have constructed 223 miles of irrigating canals and lateral ditches at a cost of $300,000. Possibly the Gentile settlers secured better lands than the Mormons, but in their most promising sections they were unable to agree as to methods, and having spent on living expenses most of the money they brought into the country with them, are now in a precarious condition, existing on the hope that some day they will get water on their lands.

"In the Church of Jesus Christ of Latter-day Saints, 90 per cent. of the men are officers. The presidents and bishops are the leading business men. They are able to back up their business judgment as to the course to be taken with the influence they have as heads of the Church. They are well known to the higher authorities in Salt Lake, who are also both religious and financial leaders, and are so able to borrow from the bank on fair terms the needed capital."—*Bishop F. S. Spalding* ("*Spirit of Missions*," *December*, 1912.)

The inestimable value of cooperation is well exampled in such a passage as this. It is the kind of thing that has been advocated by the wisest and best of mankind in both ancient and modern times, but never realized, even with the best-intentioned and most cleverly contrived schemes of social reformation. It is the order that must prevail eventually, if, indeed, the human race is to continue its progress to rational civilization. But this dream of the wise and the good has been made a reality only by the hated Mormons. In spite of all this, we are still told, in the words of Christ, "by their fruits ye shall know them." Further details of the Mormon plan are brought out in the following from another non-Mormon writer:

"The bond of religion is greater than all others, for it is the bond of love, and the Mormon people have proven that whatever difficulties may arise among them or between them, there is something higher and better than mere will power, that will adjust the trouble and adjust it amicably. Perhaps few peoples in all the earth have so typified that . . . allegory which teaches that 'the more the wolves of adversity howl, the closer will the sheep get together in the fold.'

"The Church of Jesus Christ of Latter-day Saints is not aggressively seeking out promising regions where irrigation and arid farming may be exploited, and thus make new communities possible here and there throughout the country, but it is holding a much more paternal attitude toward those of its followers who have gone forth to subdue the desert; and it is always ready to lend an assisting hand wherever expedient, to prevent the disintegration of an established community, or to assist in the upbuilding, or exploiting, of a new one that seems to be in need of help. Especially is this the case where, through some unfortunate circumstance, the people are about to lose heavily, and thus be sorely crippled in their work.

"The Mormon people have always assumed the honest attitude that 'all we want is a chance to help ourselves,' and the Church has always assumed the attitude that 'our temporal interest in our people is to help them to help themselves.' Even where outside help must be taken into a region to build the irrigation system, capital is usually very glad to step in, for it has learned that the Mormon farmer is a good investment. The Church steps in only where some special work is desired, or where it does so for the sole purpose of assisting those who are in trouble; whose canal companies are about to go into bankruptcy, or whose dams are broken, or whose fields have been inundated, or whose crops have failed, or who are rendered helpless by any dire circumstances. These the Church helps with no expectation of an equitable monetary return.

"The colonization work during the past few years has perhaps been most important and most extensive in eastern Wasatch county, in the ecclesiastical district known as the Duchesne Stake of Zion. . . . President Smart, who was transferred from the Heber (Wasatch) Stake at the opening of the reservation six years ago, has spent most of his time on questions of colonisation, encouraging the settlers, assisting in the promotion of the many canal systems, and in locating the various townsites, postoffices and business corporations and companies. . . . The Mormon people have been the organizers and mainstays of most of the canal systems, holding most of the important positions in them. Nearly all these companies are incorporated, and they have been, or are being, constructed under the Mormon cooperation plan, by which the homesteaders build the canal, and when it is completed they own it."—*J. Cecil Alter ("Latter-day Colonizing by Latter-day Saints," Desert Evening News, Dec.* 16, 1911, *p.* 94).

This interesting article then proceeds to example and describe several typical instances of Church assistance given to struggling colonists, all of which typify the consistent policy of the authorities of assisting, without beggaring or humiliating its beneficiaries, and keeping always in view that the truest, indeed the only real, benevolence is that which "helps people to help themselves." Happy the people among whom such a theory of benevolence is practicable and operative! It is immeasurably ahead of the so-called "scientific" charity, now in vogue in most Christian communities and which is, apparently, most useful in furnishing excuses for not giving. From another point of view, also, the Mormon Church method of assisting, financially or otherwise, deals largely with concerns, which, among other people, are not recognized matters for benevolence in any sense. If, for example, a community in any part of the country is afflicted by a flood, an earthquake, a fire, or any other natural calamity, the assistance of the public is readily forthcoming. The benevolently minded, as well as those who "give their alms to be seen of men," discover a laudable activity. If, however, the prosperity of such a community is merely threatened, and no more spectacular ill fortune is imminent than mere business embarrassment, the so-called Christian public sees here no call for benevolent assistance. People in such straits are invariably referred to the "business men," who view the situation wholly from the point of view of investment possibilities, and, if they assist at all, it is only on the basis of owing outright, or lending with prospects of ample returns, on good collateral. The wealthy charity-monger, who endows colleges and builds libraries, sees no field in helping people to live, or even in forwarding enterprises not regularly represented by underwritten securities. We must credit the Mormons, therefore, with the discovery, as well as, to date, the virtual monopoly, of a new, a worthy, and, as it will soon seem, a highly necessary order of practical well-doing. If their method of benevolence could be made to appeal to the general public, which vaunts itself possessed of the "only true Christianity," there would be far fewer social problems among us, also far less socialism, reactionism and discontent. However, our keen sense of "stewardship," which is a term invented to cloak our essential stinginess and real indifference, prevents the spread of any such real charity among us. It is quite evident that we need a slight tincture of the sentiment of practical humanity. The Mormon method is outlined as follows:

"The greatest percentage of increase in population during the past 10 years in Utah was shown by San Juan County, the increase being 132.4 per cent. The Bluff precinct, made up mostly of Mormon settlers and ranchers, showed an increase in population of nearly 500 per cent. Some difficulty had been experienced by the Saints here, as their dams have given way and, were it not for the fact that their appeal to the First Presidency was quite substantially answered, part of this section might have been abandoned. The Church did not invest its money, but simply gave it to them for repairing their canals and dams. The Hammond Irrigation Company was substantially assisted by the Church, and so was the Red Mesa Company, and the Bluff Ward dam. As a prominent Church official puts it: 'It is the Church policy to assist all its people, and where dams wash out and ditches get ruined by floods, the Church steps in and prevents the wrecking of the community; it sustains its people in the work they have attempted.'"—*Ibid.*

We may see from instances such as this that the Mormon Church proposes, not only to preach the Gospel, as it believes that it has received it, but also to act as the representative of God, in a very real and righteous sense. It attempts, honestly and consistently, to embody divine providence to struggling humanity. Therefore, this Church must be credited with another excellent revision of the theory and practice of religion: it holds that God has appointed it, not only to herald his will to mankind, as a real and vital law, but has also established it as a medium on earth, whereby the prayer of need and trouble may be answered. If the Mormon authorities do not believe that in giving money thus to help their struggling people, they are acting for God, and that God is the real Giver of it all, they are merely wasting their funds: these they could readily retain, and yet do as much as other bodies professing the Christian name. In another point such transactions are significant. They show the real disposition of a good part of the monies received for tithing and other donations, which so grievously excites the anxiety of non-Mormon agitators for "right and justice" who are afraid that the Mormons are being "imposed upon."

The wholly unique character of the cooperation of the Mormon Church in the life-affairs of its people is acknowledged, by force of simple honesty of character, by Episcopal Bishop F. S. Spalding in the article previously quoted. In continuing his account of colonizing in the Uintah Basin, he says:

"Practically the system produces this good result: the leading Mormon officers are compelled to take a more helpful interest in the worldly prosperity of their poor brethren than is taken by the wealthy and influential members of the other societies which profess and call themselves Christians. No doubt their Church influence gives them a chance to become rich themselves, but so far, in the Uintah Basin, the leaders in this system of ecclesiastical finance seem to have earned their reward."

If, as the Bishop assumes, the authorities are "compelled" to take this "more helpful interest," it might seem that the compulsion came in the line of trying, in a way, at least, to "live up to" a somewhat higher ideal of service than is instilled into the minds of the "wealthy and influential members of the other societies." Living up to ideals is often arduous, but the fact that these authorities yield so gracefully and uncomplainingly to this "compulsion" is certainly creditable. It may be, in spite of the Bishop's confident statement, that these authorities really believe that this "helpful interest" is an essential part of their duties.

Mr. Alter continues his interesting discussion of Mormon colonization projects with the following, selected from a number mentioned by him:

> "At Teasdale, Wayne county, a large tract of land was slowly but surely slipping away from the Mormon settlers there, and the Church authorities stepped in and bought the land — the Mansfield ranch — and sold it back to the settlers at practically their own terms. This move was purely philanthropic on the part of the Church. . . . An irrigation project, and a thrifty Mormon community was made possible in the fertile Star valley, Wyoming, just north of Afton, by reason of the fact that the irrigation bonds were bought by the Church at a reasonable figure. An irrigation company at Oneida, Idaho, was embarrassed, and the Church aided it, and made possible the continuance of the homes of a great many settlers there by redeeming the irrigation bonds. The Church bought the receiver's bonds of the Hammond canal near Collinston, and thus saved a large community from ruin or disintegration."

In spite of the fact that the Church authorities seem constantly willing to assist struggling settlers in their efforts to keep their homes, whether this assistance comes by "compulsion" or some other motive, it is a real pleasure to find that the people do not always seek this help, so long as they can help themselves by their own efforts. Whatever may be the motives of the leaders, they certainly succeed in fostering and maintaining a spirit of cooperation among their followers that is worthy all acceptation. If they do, or have done, nothing else under the sun, they have inestimably benefitted the world by demonstrating that the social problems of the day are not insoluble, and that, in one corner of the world, at least, they have been really solved. Our sociological theorists have clearly discerned the fact that cooperation is the real solution of the evils of society, but Mormonism has shown a way in which cooperation may be rationally achieved, without vain attempts to revise human nature, by laws or "scientific" preachments, or by attacking and attempting to remodel social institutions. The world may yet be thankful that someone "compelled" the Mormon authorities to follow their chosen course of action in this matter.

In discussing this aspect of the case, Mr. Alter gives the following instance, which is only typical of Mormon life and methods:

> "The community system of the Mormons in revising the old adage about everybody's business being nobody's business, and making it 'everybody's business is everybody's business,' has saved the town of

Kanab many thousands of dollars and many hundreds of settlers. The irrigation dam went out there recently and the community worked to a man in replacing it, without pay, and instead of losing two crops and having to abandon their homes, they lost only part of one crop, and kept each other so well encouraged that not one deserted."

The climax of Mr. Alter's discussion is reached in the following, which merely states facts familiar in all Utah:

"Perhaps the most successful individual colonization proposition that has been attempted by the Mormon people in the United States is the Hawaiian colony at Iosepa (the Hawaiian pronunciation of Joseph) in Tooele county. It is located almost on the border of what the older maps show as the great American desert, and yet if ever there was a place that is truly typical of the desert blossoming as the rose, it is Iosepa — the old hunter's ranch and trader's camp known as the John T. Rich ranch, in the desolate barrenness of Skull Valley.

"There are 1,120 acres practically all in use, and half as much more that is being brought under the magic wand of the Hawaiian irrigator. However, the history of this place does not give the credit to the Hawaiians — it gives them the opportunity, instead. Several years ago, a few wholesouled, honest fellows, among them Will G. Farrell, Henry P. Richards, W. W. Cluff, and H. H. Cluff, both of whom had done missionary work in the Hawaiian Islands, noticed with some regret that many Hawaiian converts were being knocked about the towns of the state, losing money and often their manhood by being thrown into circumstances which they didn't apparently know how to control. These returned missionaries had a little money, and knew how to get more, and were farmers at heart, so they laid a proposition before the First Presidency to colonize the Hawaiians in Skull Valley. Needless to say, it was done. Every Hawaiian in the United States who had come here to be nearer the Mormon people was given the opportunity to go there and move into a house that was built for him, and his family, and work on the ranch at good wages, and have, besides, a large garden patch for his own use.

"The story of Iosepa is a story in itself. Suffice it to say that to-day the several hundred folks there have water in their houses just the same as we have in Salt Lake City, and a power plant will sometime give them their electric lights. Their schools and meetinghouses are as good as the best, . . . and since they grow their own food and raise their own animals, they are far better off than many farmers who have lived in this country all their lives. The Mormon people conceived the plan for them, and the Church made its perfection possible.

"At a recent annual celebration there by the Hawaiians, when President Joseph F. Smith, Gov. William Spry, and other men of prominence attended, Lorenzo D. Creel, a government Indian official from Washington, who was studying the Indians in Tooele county at the time, rose before the great Hawaiian, uniformed audience, after having been shown all over the place, and, with much feeling, said:

"'My friends, if this is a sample of the Mormon colonization work, the best thing the government of the United States could do, would be to assist them in every way possible.'"

The facts set forth in the foregoing passages suggest strongly that the truth involved in the vast and successful colonizing activities of the Latter-day Saints is merely a necessary corollary to their wonderful and nearly unique solidarity, which impels them to form communities and conduct them in accordance with their own principles, rather than the result in any sense of musterings, under direction of recognized authorities for purposes political or otherwise. While it is unnecessary to discuss the charges to this effect made by stupid and prejudiced writers, it is eminently to the point to indicate the fact that colonizing by Mormons, and the successful founding of settlements by them was carried on, long before the suspicion of political significance could have been urged; also that many settlements made by them have since grown into thriving cities under other auspices. The following outline of Mormon colonizing activities was compiled from authoritative historical sources, expressly for use in the present volume.

"Besides building up Independence, Missouri, the Mormon people established farming settlements in the neighborhood of the Big Blue, immediately southeast of the present location of Kansas City; and in the course of a couple of years nearly 1,200 members of the Church from New York, Ohio, and other states, had located in Jackson County, Missouri.

"After their expulsion by mobs from their homes in Jackson County in 1833 and Clay County in 1836, the Saints migrated into an uninhabited part of upper Missouri, which was subsequently organized into Caldwell and Daviess counties. In the first named county the people founded Far West, which grew to contain nearly two thousand inhabitants, and a number of smaller settlements; in Daviess County, at a place called Spring Hill they founded the short-lived city of Adam-ondi-Ahman. Altogether about 12,000 Latter-day Saints settled in upper Missouri, principally in Caldwell County, during the years 1836, 1837, and 1838; and nearly the whole region was transformed from a naked prairie into flourishing farms.

"While these colonization schemes were being carried on in Missouri, the Church authorities were busy founding another flourishing settlement in Geauga County, Ohio; where they built a little city which grew so rapidly from 1831 to 1838 that at the later date it contained over two thousand inhabitants. Here a number of industries were started to give employment to the people. Another printing office was established and an imposing house of worship, known as the Kirtland Temple, was erected.

"Under pressure of persecution the saints were compelled to leave their Ohio possessions in 1838, and those in Missouri in 1839. Under the trying circumstances which surrounded the Mormon people at the time of their expulsion from Missouri, the spirit of brotherly love and mutual helpfulness was manifested in a most practicable way; and in the absence of the head of the Church, the Prophet Joseph Smith, who at that time was unlawfully incarcerated in Liberty Jail, Brigham Young at that time President of the Council of the Twelve Apostles, entered into a covenant with other leading men of the Church in Missouri to extend aid to each other and to the community as a whole until, if they found it necessary, they had spent the last farthing they owned in assisting their co-religionists out of the State of Missouri. By this united effort all of the saints who came under the ban of Governor Bogg's exterminating order left the State.

"After the expulsion of the Mormon people from the State of

Missouri, the greater part of the Church membership gathered on the east bank of the Mississippi River in Hancock County, Illinois, where they founded the beautiful City of Nauvoo. When the saints moved into that locality in 1839 there were but few settlers in the county, and some of these had established themselves in a village called Commerce. The saints bought out the claims of most of these people and transformed the unthrifty village into the City of Nauvoo. This was in 1840; by 1846 Nauvoo contained about 15,000 inhabitants. By this time immigration had brought many members of the Church from most of the states of the Union, as also from Great Britain. In the building up of a city of the dimensions of Nauvoo, many industrial undertakings were of necessity started; among these industries may be mentioned the opening of a splendid stone quarry (from which the stone for the Nauvoo Temple and other public, as well as for many private buildings in Nauvoo, was quarried); the founding of a pottery, carpenter and cabinet shops, blacksmith shops, etc., especially may be mentioned also a number of flour mills which were built in Illinois and Iowa by Fred Kesler, a prominent Mormon, and others.

"With the expulsion of the Church from Nauvoo in 1846 the saints were forced into all experiences incident to pioneer life in the course of which they established many settlements in the wilderness. Thus in 1846 they located what soon became a prosperous town, Garden Grove, Decatur County, Iowa; this stands to-day as a town of importance. They founded also Mount Pisgah, in Union County, and Council Bluffs (originally called Kainesville by the Mormons), in Pottawattamie County, besides a great number of smaller settlements in the county last named. In speaking of the exodus from Nauvoo and the founding of temporary settlements of Garden Grove and Mount Pisgah, the fact may be here emphasized that the leaders of the Church planned these two settlements in the spring of 1846 from the labors of the advanced companies traveling westward; and with these companies sowed and planted several hundred acres of land and then left their fields to be harvested by the companies that followed later in the season. Such action, prompted by brother love, was continuously manifested by the exiled saints toward one another throughout all their experiences in the wilderness and long after their location in the valleys of the Rocky Mountains.

"On the west side of the Missouri River in what is now Douglas County, Nebraska, the saints founded a temporary settlement in 1846; this they called Winter Quarters. This settlement grew until it became the present city of Florence, situated about six miles northerly from Omaha. In these settlements between the years 1846 and 1852 inclusive, industries of different kinds besides the general occupation of farming were introduced among the people by the leaders of the Church; by this means employment was given to thousands.

"While on this march of exile through Iowa, and locating themselves temporarily on the banks of the Missouri, the Mormons responded to a call from the United States government for 500 men, to participate in the war with Mexico; and while the famous march to California by this battalion of men can not consistently be classed as a Mormon industry, yet these 500 men made a march unequaled in the history of modern military travel and made a new road a great portion of the way between Fort Leavenworth and San Diego, California.

"Again, while the bulk of the saints were leaving Nauvoo and dwelling temporarily in the wilderness, a company of Mormons numbering upwards of 200 souls sailed from New York in the historic ship

Brooklyn, doubled Cape Horn and landed July 31, 1846, at the little Spanish village, Yerba Buena. Having brought with them all kinds of implements, machinery, etc., for the purpose of founding a new colony, they soon changed the little insignificant village of Yerba Buena to an American town which was called San Francisco and here was published the first paper of any importance ever issued in California in the English language. It was called the *California Star* and edited by Samuel Brannan, a Mormon Elder. It is not generally known that the Mormons to the extent here mentioned practically were the founders of the great city San Francisco. The saints who came in the *Brooklyn* also located a flourishing settlement on the San Joaquin River, near where the town of San Jose now stands.

"In the meantime the migration of the bulk of the Mormon people westward from their temporary locations on the Missouri river, took place and the consequence was the founding of Salt Lake City, in 1847; the founding of Ogden in 1848, the founding of Provo and Manti in 1849, the founding of Parowan in 1851, and the founding of hundreds of other settlements during the years following. The founding of these early settlements of Utah without money as a means of exchange again suggests true communism in its broadest sense. Labor was in the beginning the only medium used to determine value between man and man. Afterwards the products of the farm came into use as the basis of barter and trade. There was no compulsion in the community, thus to labor in unison, but the people of their own free will and choice united under a common leadership to construct dams and ditches, build school houses and churches, etc., and in this manner the foundation was laid for the commonwealth now extending its influence and industries throughout the whole length and breadth of the intermountain region. As early as 1851 settlements were also founded by the Mormons in Carson Valley, Nevada. In 1853 they founded their first settlement in a tract of country now included in the State of Wyoming. In 1855 in what subsequently has become Lemhi Co., Idaho, they founded the famous Ft. Limhi, on the Salmon river, a tributary of the Columbia. This was the beginning of the numerous cities and towns founded by the Mormons in the great Snake River Valley and other localities in Idaho.

"In 1875 the Mormons commenced to colonize Arizona by locating a settlement in Salt River, and the following year (1876) they located four towns on the Little Colorado River.

"The settlement of San Bernardino, in California, which in a few years grew to be a flourishing town and is now a noted city of southern California was founded by the Mormons in 1851.

"Settlements have also been founded by the saints in New Mexico, Texas, Oregon, and Montana. The policy of the Church leaders from the beginning has been to make the Latter-day Saints an industrious and self-sustaining people. This policy was particularly put to its practical test by the late Pres. Brigham Young who ranks as one of the greatest pioneers that western America has ever known. His watchword was home-industry and he discouraged idleness and pauperism, in all its phases."—*Manuscript Article from the Church Historian.*

In way of correctly representing the situation, encouraging as it may appear on any terms, it must be stated that this colonizing policy is no mere side issue with the Mormon Church—something to which it has been urged by the conditions entailed by the task of settling and subduing a desert country—but an essential and primary part of its message and assumed function in the world. This is ably set forth in the following from a recent address in the great Tabernacle in Salt Lake City, during a conference of the Church:

"The individual Latter-day Saint is the unit in the Church; and in every organization the good or evil of the whole is but the algebraic sum of the good or evil represented by the several units. I remember, years ago, I was very much impressed on a visit to the markets of Paris. . . . I noticed with interest the splendid display of garden vegetables offered for sale, . . . and I was particularly impressed with the fact that every plant that was there brought to market seemed to be in a measure practically perfect; at least, it was good, if it was not excellent. Every head of lettuce that was there offered for sale was a splendid one. I thought all the garden plants — lettuces, radishes, onions, turnips and potatoes, must have been sorted out. I saw no inferior ones at all. And I was so much interested in it that I went out to the gardens where these things were grown, the market gardens of Paris, and I talked with some of the gardeners and watched them at their work. I found there were many peculiarities about their work. They do not talk about having a half acre of lettuce, a half acre of radishes, but they tell you just how many lettuce plants they have, and just how many radish plants they have and just how many turnips they have in their gardens. . . . And I learned that they gave to each one their personal and individual attention. If the gardener found that this particular lettuce head did not seem to develop as well as its neighbor, he looked about to find the cause, and discovered, perhaps, that the shade of yonder gable, or that tree, fell upon the plant during the greater part of the morning, and shut away from it the sunlight; and he straightway transplanted the plant and put it a few feet farther out into the sunlight, where it could receive the kind of energizing influences of which it stood in need. I believe there should be a little more of the individual and intensive cultivation of souls here in the great garden of the Lord. It is all right to farm on the wholesale plan, but it is not always the best kind of farming; and the Lord has provided that, in his garden, there shall be an attendant for every plant — not for every patch, not for every acre, but for every plant, and it shall be tended and watched and guarded and properly cultivated. . . . The spirit of the Gospel is the spirit of individual development, the spirit of mutual help, the spirit of association; and as has been said already in this conference the world, into which we shall pass through the portals of death, will be a real world in which there will be an organization; and that organization . . . we shall find to be on the same plan and pattern as the organization under which we live here, but it may be in a measure more perfect, perhaps more perfectly adapted than ours is here to the conditions and circumstances of the place and of the time."—*J. E. Talmage* (*"Salvation of the Individual, the Aim of the Gospel," Desert Evening News, June* 28, 1913).

CHAPTER XI

THE PRACTICAL WORKINGS OF MORMONISM

As has already been explained in the discussion of the organization of the Mormon Church, the interests of each individual are by no means sacrificed to those of the mass. Each one has his place in the ranks, holding some grade of the priesthood, or belonging to some quorum, in addition to his regular membership in the ward and stake organizations. The whole force of the Mormon organization is exerted to maintain constant association of individual members, and such an arrangement could not fail to promote personal benefit and mutual helpfulness; at least so we would be informed, if the discussion were concerned with any other organization, religious or social.

"As a people the Saints are thriving and prosperous, and are continually extending their settlements throughout the inter-mountain region from the Province of Alberta, Canada, in the North, to the northern states of Old Mexico. They have 20,000 farms, 18,000 of which are free from mortgages and encumbrances; and ninety per cent. of the whole Church membership own their own homes, while the average number of people who own their homes in the United States is something like five per cent. It has ever been the policy of the Church leaders to beget in their people an ambition to own their homes and the lands they cultivate, and avoid debt; the wisdom of which policy is unquestionably vindicated in the above showing."—*B. H. Roberts* ("*Mormonism: its Origin and History,*" *pp.* 65–66).

The interest of the Church in the individual member does not end, however, with the benefits accruing to him as the member of a ward, quorum or community. He is followed up in the midst of his troubles, as well as in the days of his prosperity and strength. As already indicated, it is an essential part of the duties of the ward bishop to inform himself as to the temporal condition of all persons and families in his ward. If a case of need is brought to his notice through the ministrations of the teachers or of the Relief Society, it is his duty to investigate further and give such relief as may be needed. It is the duty of the bishop, moreover, to dispense such charity as may be needed in individual cases, whether the applicant be a member of the Church, or not. Indeed, such is the liberality of

Mormon well-doing that very many outsiders are assisted in their need, particularly those who have no friends or connections in the state.

Accurate accounts of all disbursements for charity are rendered by the ward bishops to the Presiding Bishop. It is customary for the bishops to make regular allowances to the indigent aged and feeble, also, to widows, wherever necessary. Many persons are assisted temporarily, as to tide over a hard winter, or when unable to obtain employment. Very frequently the assistance so rendered is gladly returned, as soon as possible, although no condition ever attaches to any such advances made by the Church authorities.

As represented by authoritative statements, the bulk of the expenditures for beneficence go to the aged, the infirm and the widows, also, as needed, to those out of work and in reduced circumstances. The inestimable advantage to persons of this class to be derived by membership in such an organization as the Mormon Church may thus be understood. But, as if to make good its claim that our present order must be supplanted by some other offering greater justice and opportunity to the individual, the Presiding Bishop is authorized, not only to relieve temporary embarrassment, but also to maintain a regular bureau for soliciting employment for persons out of work. In the operation of this bureau, whose services may be commanded without charge of any kind, the Bishop's office regularly sends out forms of inquiry to all the bishops, asking what opportunities are to be obtained by unemployed men in their wards. Every sixty days, as a rule, answers to such inquiries are received, and unemployed persons directed to places where employment may be had. If necessary, they are assisted to places designated. The regular forms periodically circulated by the Church authorities are given herewith:

Bishop ....
...................Ward.

Dear Brother:

Will you please advise us if there are any opportunities in your vicinity for employment; such as farm work, janitor service, ordinary day labor, work in factories, mills or other similar employment?

Enclosed is a blank form upon which we shall be pleased to receive a report from you within the next 15 days, and if you think it would help in this good work, read this letter at your next ward priesthood meeting.

Many of our brethren are out of work, and we have more applications here at our Employment Bureau than we can fill. Besides this, many Latter-day Saints are arriving from foreign lands, and we feel it a special duty to render them all possible assistance, so that they can obtain a livelihood among our people.

Thanking you for the help you may be able to render us in this good cause, we are

Your brethren in the Gospel,

....

.... Presiding Bishopric.

....

The blank form enclosed with such letters is as follows:

.... Ward

.... Stake

....................19..

LABOR REPORT

Bishop C. W. Nibley & Counselors,
Salt Lake City, Utah.

Dear Brethren:

We can furnish work in our ward as follows:

Class of Work and Wages

....

....

(Here follows a ruled blank for appropriate entries)

....

Respectfully yours,

.... Bishop.

Of course, as may be readily understood, opportunities for securing suitable employment may not always be found for the asking, and, as it sometimes happens, a man may be supported from the Church funds for some time before finding a position that he can fill to satisfaction. He is greatly advantaged, however, in having available to his needs so well organized an "employment bureau" as is conducted by the Presiding Bishop's office, which makes a constant and systematic canvass of all the wards of the Church for the very kind of situations that newcomers may require. In special cases such letters as the following are sent out to the ward bishops. These letters are actual transcripts from letters mailed by the Presiding Bishop.

SPECIAL APPEAL FOR NEWLY ARRIVED FAMILIES: UNEMPLOYED.

.... 191...

Bishop ....
.... Ward.

Dear Brother:

It has been deemed advisable to extend our efforts in the matter of assisting our people along the line of their industrial activities. It is desirable that our brethren and sisters, who come to us from the mission fields, should be properly located and begin their new homes in an environment and under conditions that will be conducive of their best temporal and spiritual welfare. Besides this, there are many families now residing in the crowded centers of population, who would be far better off in every way if they could locate in the country districts.

We have thought of your locality as a likely place for such people to settle, and we shall be glad to have you advise us just what the situation is in your ward. Can you assist one or more families to get started, who might come to you with nothing more than a willingness to work and determination to succeed? If so, please give us the specific conditions on which such a family could begin, as for instance, "we have in this ward a farm of 20 acres, with a fairly good three room house, barn, etc., which a family might take on shares, with an option to purchase, etc."

If there is no such opening, what is the possibility for a family with a very limited capital?

The spirit back of our efforts is the same that has prompted our people from the beginning of the history of the Church. We feel that it is the duty of each member to help his brother as far as possible. In the earlier days, when a new brother came to reside among us, one neighbor gave him a chicken, another gave him a pig, and possibly some more prosperous brother gave him a cow. Occasionally the neighbors helped him to plow his first ten acres, and a general interest was taken in him until he got well started and then he in turn was able to assist some one else. Many of our people have to thank this interest taken in them upon their arrival for their present success and temporal prosperity.

To obtain the successful results hoped for in this movement it will be necessary to have the cooperation of the presiding brethren and the saints as a whole in the wards where new comers locate. We feel confident that this movement meets a long felt need among our people and, therefore, will have your hearty support.

Your brethren in the Gospel,

THE PRESIDING BISHOPRIC.

By ....

SPECIAL LETTER TO MISSION PRESIDENTS IN BEHALF OF YOUNG MISSIONARIES ABOUT TO RETURN FROM THEIR FIELDS OF LABOR.

..............................191...

President ....

..........................Mission.

Dear Brother:

It has been deemed advisable to extend our efforts in the matter of assisting our people along the line of their industrial activities. It is especially desirable that our brethren and sisters who come from the mission fields should be properly located, and begin their new homes in an environment and under conditions that will be conducive of their best temporal and spiritual welfare. The department, having this matter in charge, is under the direction of Elder Roscoe W. Eardley, late President of the Netherlands Mission.

It will be our endeavor to assist returned missionaries, where necessary, to secure suitable employment or take up their work where they laid it down to enter the missionary service. We will also enlist the services of elders who are returning from their missions abroad, and who are in a position to assist those who have emigrated from the fields in which they have labored, by asking them to take a fatherly interest in such immigrants until they have established themselves in the stakes of Zion.

To attain the best results in these matters, it will be necessary that we have the co-operation of the presiding brethren in all the mission fields, and to facilitate this matter, we are sending under separate cover forms to be filled in and forwarded to this office, prior to the departure of the missionary or immigrant from the field. These reports are confidential.

Will you please ask all returning missionaries to call at this office upon their arrival in Salt Lake City, and enquire for Brother Eardley?

We feel confident that this movement meets a long felt need among our people, and therefore will have your hearty support.

Your brethren in the Gospel.

THE PRESIDING BISHOPRIC.

By..................

The practice of circulating such appeals to the Church authorities, also of advertising in the public prints, as is also done on occasions, indicates a laudable benevolent activity, and may be held to signify no more than a practical application on a systematic scale of the very spirit that inspires all intending benefactors of their fellow-men. We must not lose sight of one essential feature, however, and this is that the Mormon Church, unlike other religious bodies, does not leave this highly important branch of practical benevolence to unassociated good intentions, nor yet to auxiliary organizations, as is the current practice elsewhere. It gains an immense prestige among its followers by meeting them and providing to supply their needs at the very times and at the very crises in their several careers, when help and encouragement, temporal and material, as well as spiritual, is most sorely needed. If the mechanism of this Church's organization is kept running, as it was intended by its founders that it should run; if, in other words, the accredited officers are faithful in the performance of their appointed and designated duties, there need be no just charge of unanswered prayers of need and distress. If such officers do not perform their proper duties — and it must be said to their credit that the average of faithfulness is high among them — the fault is in them, and in the failings common to humanity, and not in the organization. In any case, the organization is there, but, like every other machine, designed for practical work in the world, it must be kept well oiled and in running order.

As previously suggested, the Church itself frequently provides, not only temporary relief for the distressed and for those out of employment, but also, in many cases, has created work for the sake of employing those among its poor who had not been located otherwise. This, as previously stated, was Brigham Young's object in taking the contracts for the building of the Union Pacific and Central Pacific railroads in 1868–69. He also projected and built, entirely with home capital and home labor, the Deseret Telegraph line in Utah, which was later operated in connection with the great transcontinental system. Other more local enterprises were undertaken in precisely the same spirit. Thus, to give employment to the unemployed he caused a high wall to be erected around the Temple Block, and another high wall, built of cobble stones and concrete, around the tithing office and his own premises. A wall intended to encompass the city, which, while intended as a protection against Indians, was undertaken with a view to create labor.

The building of Saltair as a great bathing resort on the Great Salt Lake is another enterprise which has given employment to many people, and it could not have come into existence at the time it did if the Church with its means and credit had not backed the enterprise. This famous resort was built in 1893.

In view of the facts mentioned above, even the smallest, as last given, it would take no very great insight to discern the fact that the Mormon Church has set itself to the very laudable task of actually abolishing poverty, or, at the least helpless indigence. That this is a very desirable end in our present civilization cannot be denied; that it is, also, quite in the line of what Christ evidently had in view, no matter how much his pretended followers may have ignored and neutralized his teachings, is too evident to need discussion of any kind. Apart, however, from consideration of the teachings of Christ, or of the claims of any organization whatsoever, it is clear that poverty and indigence, as well as the vices causing them — extravagance, indifference, hypocrisy, on the one hand, and intemperance, shiftlessness and ignorance, on the other — must be done away with, if civilization is to continue. That the Mormon Church recognizes this fact, and acts accordingly, while all other professed religious bodies have stupidly and culpably ignored it, is decidedly to the credit of its founders and leaders, and a rebuke to its opponents, who, while busying themselves with criticisms and fault-seeking, have contrived no effectual rivalry to its practical methods, leaving really humanitarian souls no alternatives other than socialism, or some other schemes of so-called sociology or economics, which are both non-religious and non-Christian.

CHAPTER XII

THE MORAL RECORD OF THE MORMON PEOPLE

In the discussion of any other social and religious system, similarly well organized, the moral and ethical benefits of close association would be cheerfully admitted, and appreciatively discussed. In the case of the Mormon Church, however, the wall of prejudice is so high and the clouds of downright misrepresentation so thick, that it will be necessary to give figures and examples to demonstrate the fact that, in this case of close association, also, the rule operates normally.

In our study of the institution of plural marriage, which has so terribly inflamed our preacher-folk, in spite of the fact that it was a recognized institution among God's people of ancient times, and was not forbidden or condemned by Christ in any unmistakable terms, we shall find that the women of Mormondom, while highly independent, individual and self-reliant, as a rule, are, at the same time, nobly womanly, holding the begetting and rearing of offspring as their highest prerogative. While the much-mooted right of female suffrage was first granted under Mormon rule, and the equality of the sexes first openly advocated by Joseph Smith, there was never a "woman movement" among these people, nor any of the degenerate spirit of "sex-antagonism," so disgustingly rampant in England, and, to a great extent, in America. Any person informed in sociology, let alone morals, cannot help but recognize that, in this particular, at least, the Mormon influence has been wholly on the side of right, decency, justice and of intelligent and normal sentiment. If the Christian public in England and America can view the exasperated reaction, known as the "woman movement," as a "phase of evolutionary development," or as an "incident" in the life of nations, it is a sad comment on the sufficiency of the ideals and spiritual influences under which they have been reared. Whatever they may think of their own case, they have no just ground of criticism of a people who have accomplished grand results with none of these grievous and pathological "labor pains."

Nearly the most important and typical phase of public morality lies in the matter of temperance; which is usually understood to connote moderation in the use of alcoholic drinks. The

Mormons claim considerable immunity from the ravages of this social disease of "gin-guzzling," because of their belief in the Word of Wisdom, an accepted revelation condemning the practice, along with the use of tobacco, tea, and coffee, and gluttony in meat eating. This claim by itself is, of course, no argument in favor of their practical consistency; since the world has seen a sufficiency of high professions and low practices, and is inclined to discount the former, except in the case of itself and friends. There is one good reason, however, for assuming the probability, at least, of the consistency of Mormon claims in this particular: this is, again, the fact of the strong and close association of the members of the Church. Among the loosely organized sects of Protestantism, or in the other-worldly Catholic Church, hypocrisy and inconsistency in religious and moral professions may be long maintained, without fear of detection — as a matter of experience, this is evidently true — but where people are constantly associated in their religion, social life, amusements and business employments, as are the Mormons, there is always a liability to discovery and condemnation. No one can deny that some of these people, at least, are sincerely consistent in their professions: and such are always liable to "run amuck" and really denounce hypocrisy. We may understand, therefore, that the principle of strong and close organization is undoubtedly justified as a moral safeguard, as well as an effective engine for social and religious benefits to the people included in its "quorums."

In the matter of indulgence in alcoholic drinks, which all agree is undesirable, and all are allowed to condemn seriously, except Mormons, the following from a seasoned traveler and keen observer is significant:

> "The Mormons drunken! Now what, for instance, can be the conclusion of any honest thinker from *this* fact — that though I mixed constantly with Mormons, all of them anxious to show me every hospitality and courtesy, I was never at any time asked to take a glass of strong drink? If I wanted a horse to ride or to drive I had a choice at once offered me. If I wanted someone to go with me to some point of interest, his time was mine. Yet it never occurred to them to show a courtesy by suggesting 'a drink.'
>
> "Then, seriously, how can any one have respect for the literature or the men who, without knowing anything of the lives of Mormons, stigmatize them as profane, adulterous, and *drunken?* As a community I know them, from personal advantages of observation such as no non-Mormon writer has ever previously possessed, to be at any rate exceptionally careful in maintaining the appearance of piety and sobriety; and I leave it to my readers to judge whether such solid hypocrisy as this, that tries to abolish all swearing and all strong drink both by precept from the pulpit and example in the household, is not, after all, nearly as admirable as the real thing itself.
>
> "This, at all events, is beyond doubt — that the Mormons have al-

ways struggled hard to prevent the sale of liquors in Salt Lake City, except under strict regulations and supervision. But the fight has gone against them. The courts uphold the right of publicans to sell when and what they choose; and the Mormons, who could at one time boast — and visitors without number have borne evidence to the fact — that a drunkard was never to be seen, an oath never to be heard, in the streets of their city, have now to confess that, thanks to the example of Gentiles, they have both drunkards and profane men among them. But the general attitude of the Church toward these delinquents, and the sorrow that their weakness causes in the family circle, are in themselves proofs of the sincerity in sobriety which distinguishes the Mormons. Nor is it any secret that if the Mormons had the power they would to-morrow close all the saloons and bars, except those under Church regulation, and then, they say, 'we might hope to see the old days back when we never thought of locking our doors at night, and when our wives and girls, let them be out ever so late, needed no escort in the streets.'"— Phil Robinson (*Sinners and Saints, pp.* 239–240).

At another page, Mr. Robinson gives figures to bolster up such contentions as are made above. Speaking of the results of a canvass made in the year of his visit to Utah (1882), he says:

"Last winter there was a census taken of the Utah Penitentiary and the Salt Lake City and county prisons with the following result: — In Salt Lake City there are about 75 Mormons to 25 non-Mormons: in Salt Lake County there are about 80 Mormons to 20 non-Mormons. Yet in the city prison there were 29 convicts, all non-Mormons; in the county prison there were 6 convicts, all non-Mormons. The jailer stated that the county convicts for the five years past were all anti-Mormons except *three!*

"In Utah the proportion of Mormons to all others is as 83 to 17. In the Utah Penitentiary at the date of the census there were 51 prisoners, only 5 of whom were Mormons, and 2 of the 5 were in prison for polygamy, so that the 17 per cent. 'outsiders' had 46 convicts in the penitentiary, while the 83 per cent. Mormons had but 5!

"Out of the 200 saloon, billiard, bowling alley and pool-table keepers not over a dozen even profess to be Mormons. All of the bagnios and other disreputable concerns in the territory are run and sustained by non-Mormons. Ninety-eight per cent. of the gamblers in Utah are of the same element. Ninety-five per cent. of the Utah lawyers are Gentiles, and 98 per cent. of all the litigation there is of outside growth and promotion. Of the 250 towns and villages in Utah, over 200 have no 'gaudy sepulchre of departed virtue,' and these two hundred and odd towns are almost exclusively Mormon in population. Of the suicides committed in Utah ninety odd per cent. are non-Mormon, and of the Utah homicides and infanticides over 80 per cent. are perpetrated by the 17 per cent. of 'outsiders.'— *Ibid., p.* 72.

Mr. Robinson's testimony is quotable; first, because he was a careful and unprejudiced observer, as keen to notice the defects of Mormon character as its excellencies — this anyone may understand from reading his book; second, because he quotes correctly figures gathered authoritatively, and to be found in other printed records of the times. Assuming, for the sake of argument, that the Mormon professions of opposition to the traffic in intoxicants is perfectly sincere, the consequences, as noted by Robinson, are precisely those one would expect to find. Beyond doubt, the greater proportion of crimes flows from indulgence in alcohol, which degrades the physical system and weakens the sense of right and wrong, along with the strength of will to resist temptation. It is also a well recognized fact that the initial step in the path of drunkenness, and eventual ruin and disgrace, is to be traced to bad influences in youth, or to no effective influences at all. If, therefore, one is brought up in an atmosphere in which moral influences repel, rather than excite respect, and allow the notion to grow in the mind that carelessness in speech and act, and indulgence, to any extent in forbidden pastimes, is either "manly" or "smart," the fault is quite as certainly to be found in the method of presenting moral teachings, as in the native depravity of the delinquent himself. If, on the other hand, one is reared and educated in a society, in which he is brought into constant association with men who make a public boast that they eschew all the vices, against which youth are warned, and lead such lives as excite respect and emulation, instead of half-hearted and womanish attitudes toward the world, the result cannot fail to keep a large percentage of young men in the strait way, until they are old enough, at least, to be wicked clandestinely, as we are informed. This is, in brief, the antithesis between the impracticable, other-worldly attitude of current influences, and the well-organized, practical, "this-world" attitude, as embodied in the Mormon Church.

So far as concerns the influence of this organization on the moral of its young men, the record of the Deseret Gymnasium, in Salt Lake City, is significant. Of 1,100 applicants for admission, examined in three years, the physical director, William R. Day, reports a clean record so far as any evidence of personal immoralities are concerned. The attitude of the people toward the liquor traffic is even more satisfactory. The table on following page shows the number of liquor saloons in the regularly organized stakes of the Church, during two record years.

As is explained in place, a stake is a section of territory, either in the country or in a city, analogous to the diocese or see of a bishop of the Roman Catholic Church. As such, it is merely an ecclesiastical jurisdiction, without reference to the religious or racial affiliations of the inhabitants included in its confines. Thus, there are four stakes in the city limits of Salt Lake City, which, at the present time, are known as the Salt Lake, Ensign, Liberty, and Pioneer stakes. As in this city in 1910, the Mormons numbered about 40,000 out of a total population of about 93,000, they cannot be blamed either for the existence of all the 130 saloons, nor for the failure to close them. The figures

LIQUOR SALOONS IN MORMON STAKES

Stake.	*1909*	*1910*	*Inc.*	*Dec.*	*Stake.*	*1909*	*1910*	*Inc.*	*Dec.*
Alberta	..	3	3	..	North Sanpete	4	2	..	2
Alpine	8	1	..	7	North Weber	4	4	..	..
Bannock	5	..	..	5	Ogden	3	3	..	..
Bear Lake	7	2	..	5	Oneida	..	..	..	..
Bear River	2	2	..	..	Panquitch	..	..	..	..
Beaver	7	7	..	..	Parowan	..	..	..	..
Benson	2	2	..	..	Pioneer	7	6	..	1
Big Horn	2	..	..	2	Pocatello	..	..	..	..
Bingham	3	..	..	3	Rigby	2	..	..	2
Blackfoot	10	8	..	2	Salt Lake	67	75	8	..
Box Elder	2	2	..	..	St. George	2	..	..	2
Cache	5	1	..	4	St. Johns	1	1	..	..
Carbon	..	24	24	..	St. Joseph	94	38	..	56
Cassia	11	..	..	11	San Juan	..	..	..	..
Davis	4	3	..	1	San Luis	..	..	..	..
Duchesne	..	..	..	..	Sevier	7	8	1	..
Emery	17	2	..	15	Snowflake	1	1	..	..
Ensign	48	42	..	6	South Sanpete	2	2	..	..
Fremont	2	..	..	2	Star Valley	..	1	1	..
Granite	14	12	..	2	Summit	22	23	1	..
Hyrum	..	..	..	..	Taylor	6	6	..	..
Jordan	40	40	..	..	Teton	1	1	..	..
Juab	3	..	..	3	Tooele	21	12	..	9
Juarez	..	..	..	..	Uintah	4	4	..	..
Kanab	..	..	..	..	Union	14	14	..	..
Liberty	9	11	2	..	Utah	13	20	7	..
Malad	..	..	..	..	Wasatch	..	..	..	..
Maricopa	4	4	..	..	Wayne	..	..	..	..
Millard	4	..	..	4	Weber	47	47	..	..
Morgan	..	..	..	..	Woodruff	77	77	..	..
Nebo	25	18	..	7	Yellowstone	5	2	..	3

Totals—

Number of saloons open in 1909	624
Number of saloons open in 1910	512
Local Increases, as shown in 1910	47
Local Decreases, as shown in 1910	154
Total decrease from 1909 to 1910	112
Stakes without saloons in 1909	17
Stakes without saloons in 1910	23
Stakes without saloons in both years	14

given in the above table, however, show a general trend toward improvement in the matter of liquor selling resorts. Thus, while an increase of such places occurs in 8 cases, there is a decrease in 23, and this represents the closing of 112 saloons and beer shops. It is also notable that the number of stakes having no saloons rose from 17 to 23 in one year, with 14 having none in both years. Also, the several local increases totaled less than one-third of the total decreases in the same period.

It has been the claim of the Mormon Church authorities that the Stakes of Zion have always been virtually free of saloons, on the general ground that, as there was no business for these resorts, they could not maintain themselves. This allegation has been frequently substantiated by the reports of travelers of all classes of sympathy, who have remarked on the order and sobriety to be found in Mormon towns. Of course, with the introduction of outside elements, largely of the adventurous classes, the liquor traffic grew, and is now strongest in the sections of the state having the largest percentage of non-Mormon population.

The attitude of the people toward the liquor traffic was even better demonstrated in 1911, when the popular vote was taken under the new local option law. According to the official figures for 103 towns and cities, as given by the state statistician, there were 40,780 votes cast against licensing the liquor traffic, and 31,504 in favor of the traffic. The no license measure was carried in 86 towns and cities by a total vote of 26,358 against 6,691; while in the remaining 17 places the license was established by a vote of 22,594 against 13,898. Furthermore, out of this total of favorable votes, 18,710 were cast in Salt Lake and Ogden, where "gentiles" outnumber Mormons by the ratios of 53 to 40 and 24 to 10, respectively, leaving a total in the remaining 15 places of 3,884 votes for and 1,681 against license. According to the figures furnished by the federal excise office, there were 599 places, saloons, beer shops and drug stores, in these 17 "wet" towns, doing a retail business in alcoholic liquors, out of which 410 were in Salt Lake and Ogden, leaving a total of 189 in the remaining 15 towns and villages.

In the meantime, the 86 "dry" towns and villages contained, according to the federal records, 135 shops and drug stores licensed to retail liquors, distributed through 51 of these towns, 35 of which had contained no such licensed places before the election.

Of the 17 towns voting "wet," 9 were in the mining counties of Carbon (3), Juab (2), Summit (1), and Tooele (3); 6 were in the Salt Lake and Weber counties, populous in non-Mormons, and the remaining 2, in Beaver and Emery counties, were on the lines of the railroads. Such data very effectively divide any responsibility that one may attempt to lay at the doors of Mormon voters. The fact is, however, that the votes of this election show conclusively that the Mormons have made good on their profession of opposition to the liquor traffic, and that the responsibility of keeping it among them lies, almost, if not entirely, on the shoulders of the "gentile" voters in the state.

According to the returns of this election, it will be impossible for any really honest and candid person to deny that Mormonism has done its best to oppose the liquor traffic, which is the most prolific source of crime and vice among us, and has, so far, made good on its claims to propagating a superior order of morality among its people. Leaving out of account the hypocritical rant about "polygamy"—and even this may be preferable to the orders of immorality, which our traditional sects have never succeeded in neutralizing—statistics show that Mormon communities certainly average far higher in other virtues than communities under other auspices. If the aim of religion is, in any sense, to benefit the public, and to overcome the grosser forms of evil, at least, it must be acknowledged that Mormonism certainly ranks near the top as a beneficial religious influence. These matters, however, can be determined only by statistics, since the bare assertion of travelers and other observers, who wish to be just to their fellow-men, are habitually contradicted by such a mass of sectarian misrepresentation that it is impossible to make the public believe even the plainest facts.

In several books and periodicals we find statistics, apparently authoritative, to the general effect that the larger proportion of the crimes ever brought to the attention of the authorities in his territory and state, has been committed by the minority of "gentiles" there resident or sojourning. This contention seems to derive some element of probability, in view of the facts on the liquor traffic already noted.

A considerable amount of such statistical matter was contributed to Utah newspapers in the early "eighties" by a writer using the nom-de-plume of Historicus. His findings deserve some attention because they have been widely quoted, both by such writers as Phil Robinson, and several Mormon compilers. The figures given at this time are significant from another point of view, also, since the Territory was then less populous than at present, and the Mormons were rather largely in the majority in most centres. This statistician furnishes the data tabulated on the following page on the crime record of Ogden to the *Deseret Evening News* of Sept. 18, 1884. He says:

> "To fully appreciate the magnitude of non-Mormon lawlessness over that of the Mormons who reside in Utah's second city, it must be borne in mind that in a total population of 7,000 souls, the Mormon and non-Mormon elements are as 7 to 3, or 71 Mormons to 29 non-Mormons. Here is a delectable repast, which no doubt will appetize the local regenerators, and reassure them that they are succeeding admirably in reforming the Mormons, whom they persistently stigmatize as being 'uncivilized,' 'semi-barbarous,' 'brutal,' 'lustful,' 'lawless,' etc., etc., etc."

In addition to the practical accomplishments mentioned in the following list, which shows the immense superiority (1 to none) of "gentiles" over Mormons in the matter of "cruelty

MORMON CRIMES
(During the year ending December 31, 1883.)

Crime	*Mormons*	*Non-Mormons*
Assault	2	5
Assault and Battery	6	27
Drunk	17	97
Drunk and Disorderly	3	37
Disturbing the Peace	25	79
Petit Larceny	9	36
Indecent Conduct	2	6
Lewd Conduct	5	40
Vagrancy	1	64
Fast Driving	3	4
Cruelty to Animals	1	..
Totals	74	395

to animals," the author proceeds to name 17 other crimes committed among 68 offenders, all non-Mormons:

Burglary	1
Grand Larceny	2
Keeping Brothels	3
Gambling	23
Keeping Gambling Houses	3
Illegal Liquor Selling	11
Other Police Offenses	25

Of inmates of brothels, employés of breweries, saloons and billiard rooms, arrested for various disorders, in addition to those named above, the report specified 5 Mormons (none in the brothels) and 52 non-Mormons. Historicus then concludes, as follows:

"Now, if the 29 per cent. non-Mormons of Ogden City had respected and upheld the laws of that municipality with the same fidelity as the 71 per cent. Mormons have been doing, their arrest product would have been but 21, and not 463, as shown in the list. And again, if the 71 per cent. Mormons had last year been as lawless as the 29 per cent. non-Mormons, 1,621 arrests of their class would have been recorded, instead of the comparatively small number of 74, as the same exhibit shows."

In treating of such a matter as this from the public records, it must be distinctly borne in mind that it is by no means easy to make such bold comparisons on the delinquency of members of different religious faiths. In many cases the arrested person, particularly when accused of a grave crime, will falsify on the matter of his religious connection and other personal concerns. For this reason, it has been the habit in many prisons to make no record of religion, except in rare occasions. This objection did not apply so easily in the early days of Utah, when the religious affiliations of most people were easy to discover. Nor is it so great an objection in that state at present, when a large proportion of the inhabitants are Mormons. Average figures may indicate fairly well, therefore, the moral character of the inhabitants.

If by no other method, or by no other testimony, the character and moral status of a community, or state, may be judged from the police and prison records. Unless we expect to find angelic perfection, however, we must not make too much of the former; but convictions for felonies are real indicators, and these are to be found recorded in the reports of state prisons. Accordingly, the following table has been compiled from the annual reports of the state penitentiary of Utah for the first sixteen years of statehood.

Convictions for Felonies, 1896–1911

County	96	97	98	99	00	01	02	03	04	05	06	07	08	09	10	11	Tot.
Beaver	..	1	..	..	1	1	..	2	..	2	..	3	1	1	2	1	15
Box Elder	7	3	3	4	8	8	6	3	9	7	1	3	9	13	3	9	96
Cache	4	5	8	5	..	2	6	1	3	5	1	5	1	5	4	8	63
Carbon	..	3	..	4	..	3	2	6	6	9	4	4	8	2	7	15	73
Davis	2	3	2	3	9	3	2	..	3	1	3	5	1	2	5	8	52
Emery	1	4	5	1	2	6	..	3	..	2	2	9	2	6	6	1	50
Garfield	2	..	3	5	1	..	..	1	..	2	..	..	..	..	..	..	14
Grand	..	1	..	..	..	2	1	..	2	..	2	1	2	1	..	4	16
Iron	..	1	1	2	3	..	..	1	..	..	1	..	..	1	..	..	10
Juab	3	1	2	1	1	..	2	1	..	..	1	1	..	6	3	3	25
Kane	..	1	4	2	..	..	..	..	1	1	1	..	..	..	..	..	10
Millard	..	3	1	1	1	1	..	2	1	2	1	1	1	1	..	1	17
Morgan	..	..	..	..	1	1	..	2	2	..	2	1	1	1	..	2	13
Piute	..	3	1	1	..	2	..	1	..	1	1	..	..	..	..	..	10
Rich	..	4	..	..	..	..	1	..	1	..	..	..	..	2	..	..	8
Salt Lake	19	29	32	35	31	34	25	24	29	52	51	56	74	61	75	79	706
San Juan	..	..	1	1	..	..	2	..	..	..	2	2	..	1	2	..	11
Sanpete	1	4	2	3	2	7	3	8	2	2	1	1	2	..	1	3	42
Sevier	2	2	..	1	3	2	2	..	2	..	..	..	1	2	1	3	21
Summit	2	2	..	3	1	1	5	1	1	3	1	3	..	3	..	1	27
Tooele	..	2	..	1	..	1	5	2	..	1	1	1	..	4	3	6	27
Uintah	2	1	5	..	2	1	..	1	3	2	1	1	9	3	2	..	33
Utah	10	21	14	12	8	14	5	4	11	13	3	5	5	12	8	4	149
Wasatch	..	2	1	2	3	1	1	1	2	3	1	2	2	3	2	1	27
Washington	2	..	1	1	..	..	1	..	..	1	..	1	..	..	..	1	8
Wayne	..	2	..	2	1	1	..	1	..	..	1	..	..	..	..	..	8
Weber	23	14	4	10	18	11	24	50	32	25	22	20	31	34	26	11	355
U. S. Ct.	4	4	9	..	3	..	2	6	5	..	1	3	..	..	..	..	37
Various	..	..	..	..	..	..	1	10	..	..	4	6	7	2	5	..	35
Residents of Utah	12	25	30	33	17	21	17	24	24	26	21	22	26	26	29	24	377
Non-Residents of Utah	72	91	69	67	82	81	79	107	91	108	88	112	131	140	126	137	1581
Totals	84	116	99	100	99	102	96	131	115	134	109	134	157	166	155	161	1958

The analysis of this table is most interesting, as an indicator of the law-abiding character of the people of Utah. Apparently, we have, in the first 16 years of statehood, a total of 1958 commitments to the State Penitentiary; out of which but 377 were of residents of the State of Utah, or about 19.25% of the whole. Taking the average population, as given in the last three censuses (1890, 1900, 1910), as about 286,000, we find that the 377 commitments of residents represent about 1.32% of the total average population during the entire period. Furthermore, according to the representations of the authorities, the greater number of commitments in any year come from places near railway centres, or from mining regions, or localities in which large numbers of outsiders are likely to be employed. The large numbers of commitments from Salt Lake, Utah and Weber counties, 1,210 in all, or a little less than ⅔ of the total, shows the results of the influx of outsiders, who are particularly numerous in these counties. It is also interesting to notice that the figures already given, combined with those for Carbon and Juab counties, now prevailingly "gentile" in population, give a total of 1308, or over ⅔ of the entire number of commitments, although the population figures in the last three censuses are only slightly over one-half of the figures for the entire territory or state.

According to the reports of the state bureau of statistics, the total number of convictions in the state courts for all classes of offenses are as follows: 339 in 1900; 431 in 1902; 506 in 1903; 459 in 1904; 520 in 1905; 195 in 1909; 222 in 1910. The most serious of these offenses, numerically speaking, are given in the following table compiled from the records of the bureau of statistics:

Crimes and Misdemeanors Commonest in Utah in Seven Years of Record

Offense	1900	1902	1903	1904	1905	1909	1910	Totals	Pop. Centres
Assault	16	23	21	26	13	5	10	114	51
Battery	10	14	19	32	3	5	3	86	30
Burglary	21	30	19	29	57	75	60	291	199
Disturbing Peace	58	56	81	62	21	2	..	280	101
House-breaking	12	19	21	11	8	..	..	71	31
Gd. Larceny	14	14	23	19	19	22	34	145	75
Pt. Larceny	57	75	81	45	64	3	4	329	205
Mal. Mischief	23	7	11	6	5	..	..	52	24
Unclassified	58	115	162	130	193	10	..	668	482
Totals	269	353	438	360	383	122	111	2036	1198
Total for Year	339	431	506	459	520	195	222	2672	1745

This table exhibits the fact that, in the seven years of record, there analyzed, 2,036 convictions out of a grand total of 2,672 were had for eight crimes and misdemeanors of varying degrees of gravity, and a number of others, here bunched together under the head of "unclassified." Moreover, 1,198 of these were committed in the centres of population, Salt Lake, Utah and Weber counties, which, as shown by the preceding table, gave, also, the greater number of commitments to the state penitentiary in the first 16 years of statehood. Out of the grand total of convictions for every class of crime, as just given, 1,745 were had in these same three counties, leaving a remainder of 927 convictions in seven years of record to be distributed over the entire remainder of the state of Utah. We also see that, with the eight offenses specified, and the "unclassified," 1,198 were committed in these centres of population, leaving a total of 838 for evil-doers in the remainder of the state.

When we consider that the state of Utah is largely Mormon, with the exception of Carbon, Juab and Salt Lake counties, and sections of Utah and Weber counties, where there are large settlements of people of other persuasions, it is fairly clear that Mormonism is effective in reducing the crime average to some intelligible extent. It may be objected that the larger percentage of all offenses have been committed in or near the great centres of population, as in all states, but the penitentiary records, as above quoted, show only 377 actual residents of Utah, in a total of 1,958 convictions, of which 1,210 were recorded from Salt Lake, Utah and Weber counties.

The state statistics of the state of Utah give us, also, significant data on the classes of crimes most often charged against Mormons, by their traducers — impurity and homicide. We will, therefore, analyze the returns in these matters also. Taking the figures covering the offenses of adultery, bigamy, fornication, unlawful cohabitation, rape, criminal conversation, homicide, and, also, abortion, during the seven years already analyzed, we have the results shown in the following table.

Crimes of Impurity and Violence in Seven Years of Record in Utah

Offense	1901	1902	1903	1904	1905	1909	1910	Totals	Pop. Centres
Adultery, etc.	18	8	7	14	15	12	17	91	38
Abortion	..	..	..	1	1	1	..	3	..
Rape	4	2	2	..	..	..	..	8	5
Crim. Con.	2	2	6	4	9	3	6	32	15
Homicide	3	3	5	..	4	3	2	20	9
Totals	27	15	20	19	29	19	25	154	67

This table shows that of crimes of lewdness 58 out of 131 were committed in the centres of population, as would be the case in any other state; 9 out of the twenty homicides occurred in the same region. It is significant that no evidence of florid excess exists in the records. Although, in default of data touching the religious or national affiliation of any of the persons convicted of crimes and misdemeanors, it must be admitted that the State of Utah shows a very clean record, so far as its regular residents are concerned. We find, at least, no figures condemning Mormonism.

The accusations of evil behavior have been absurdly overdone by the enemies of Mormonism. The following homely verses sum the virtues claimed by Mormons as the consequence of their faith. They are worthy attention as being from the pen of a non-member of the Church.

"Where courts, rumshops, brothels are naught,
Except where Gentiles their customs brought.
Where water instead of wine is sent
To administer the sacrament!
Where thieves and blacklegs never go,
And tramps and bummers have no show!
Where idle fellows all dislike,
And where the workmen never strike!
Where bad diseases are not known,
And Restelism has never grown!
Where every workman has house and barn,
And every farmer owns his farm!
Where all the children go to school,
And where you cannot find a fool!
Where banks don't break and Ring intrigues
Are not as thick as Union Leagues!
Where women as well as men are sent
When Mormons elect their President!
Where no drunkard murders his bride,
And ends his life by suicide!
Where reform don't mean a prison,
The flag that floats is Mormonism!"

—*The Agitator* (Buffalo, N. Y.), Oct., 1877.

III

THE TEACHINGS OF MORMONISM

"It is the first principle of the Gospel to know for a certainty the character of God, and to know that we may converse with Him as one man converses with another."

—*Joseph Smith.*

CHAPTER XIII

THE THEOLOGY OF MORMONISM

THE theology of Mormonism is a consistent body of doctrine, in which all parts belong together as elements of a logical system, also, in a very real sense, a definite and intelligent attempt to forestall the numerous questions, and to settle the many problems that have arisen in traditional systems of thought. Whether or not, as claimed, its doctrines are based upon a new series of divine revelations, it is perfectly evident to the informed and unprejudiced mind that these new doctrines and interpretations were first formulated by a mind keenly and intelligently alive to the current difficulties and contradictions of theological thinking, also thoroughly convinced of the ultimate and sufficient authority of Scripture. Careful and conscientious study will reveal no trace of the "illogicality" and "irrationality" so confidently attributed to it by numerous critics; nor, in view of the hideous absurdities and perversions in several representative systems, do these accusations come with any very good grace.

Mormon theology is based flatly upon a thorough and consistent belief in divine revelation, and, if it is to be criticized at all, it may be said to be somewhat more "literal" in its interpretation of Scripture than many authorities might consider necessary. It holds a position, however, which may be called "rational" and "consistent" in a very superior sense, since, as seems evident, it holds to two reasonable principles: (1) that the Author of revelation was competent to express His thoughts in comprehensible language; (2) that revelation is intended to *reveal,* to furnish the mind with actual information on matters spiritual, and not to puzzle it with evident contradictions and manufactured "mysteries," which, although indicating nothing more forcibly than the essential limitations in the minds of theological speculators of the past, are impudently recommended as matters for the "exercise of faith," since so evidently baffling to the reason. Thus, while asserting its belief in the almightiness of God, it avoids curious questionings in regard to His ultimate "nature," which represent His being as hopelessly contradictory to the "unassisted reason" and, in the last analysis, composed of a "substance" so utterly foreign to anything evidently real to human thought, that it seems to be equivalent to nothingness. This system of doctrine is, therefore, both logical in thought and practical in applicability to life; avoiding the wretched refinements and speculations of all schools of traditional scholasticism, and propounding principles capable of meeting the human mind on its own ground. These qualities inhere in no other system whatever, as is amply evidenced by the fact that most of the sects of Protestantism — each of them founded originally on the groundwork of somebody's findings and opinions on God, sin, etc.— are at the present day rapidly retreating from the old-time theological standards and accepting such "infidel" hypotheses as the so-called "higher criticism" and "evolution theologies," along with various sentimental and half-fledged formulations on various bases of compromise, all of which are mere transitions "from bad to worse." If a system of theology is such in any real sense, a "God-science," it would not be necessary to accord a secondary consideration to "mere doctrines," and to make feeble and ineffective attempts to emphasize "righteousness" and the various long-neglected "social and moral virtues."

The fundamental tenet of Mormonism is that the system of doctrine and practice embodied in its theology and church organization represents a full and complete restoration of pure, primitive Christianity, as preached by Christ and his apostles, but, supposedly lost and obscured through the general apostasy of all professing Christian bodies and systems throughout the succeeding centuries. In this position, of course, it makes no unfamiliar claims or charges, since accusations of "apostasy" and claims to "restoration" abound in Christian history. Without considering all the eccentric and local movements of the first fifteen centuries of our era, each of which professed more or less definitely to be the true Christianity restored, the conditions are all fulfilled in the great disturbance of the sixteenth century, known as the Protestant "reformation." At this time, in the bitter denunciation of the Catholic Church, and of all that belongs to it, the accusation of apostasy, also the vital need of a "restoration" of the Gospel, were abundantly expressed. In opposition to the Roman claim of a centralized and permanent authority, located in the Pope, the reformers emphasized the doctrine of the "sufficiency of Scripture," which each man was urged to read and digest for himself. They evidently relied less upon Scripture, however, than upon their own interpretations of its teachings. Hence, they separated and quarrelled among themselves on hair-splitting points of mere metaphysics, and repelled all well-intentioned efforts after unity. They neglected, also, the valuable element of strong organization among their followers, and were not moved to attempt any such achievement, even as a simple means of combatting the strongly-knitted forces of Catholicism. It may be seen, therefore, that they launched a regime of individualism and self-assertion, rather than an era of restored truth of any variety. Thus, there has followed, as an inevitable result, the heresy-building and sect-launching activities of the last four centuries, which have weakened the influence of Protestantism as a movement, and absurdly divided the forces supposedly assembled to combat evil. They have also acted most effectively to obscure many vital points of Scripture teaching, without which, as may be considered evident, full obedience to the commands of Christ are difficult or impossible.

It may be logical to hold, therefore, that the work which the founders of Protestantism rashly undertook still remains to be accomplished, and that there is still a demand for real reformation and a genuine restoration of the Gospel — if, indeed, it be any longer rational to consider the Gospel as something fundamental, essential and permanent, rather than a " consummation " of the " best efforts " of the " rationalistic " dreamers of the present or of the future. The discernment and statement of this fact by Joseph Smith, or by any other person, is not unmistakable evidence of evil qualities or intentions — it may even be held to be an evidence of clear discernment and real spiritual vitality, either with or without a valid call from God. The consequent attempt to supply the world's crying need of numerous neglected and dishonored truths and virtues must be judged as proper or abortive, solely on the basis of the principles which it embodies and the performances which it renders possible. Whatever one may see fit to say about the origin, character and motives of Joseph Smith, it cannot be denied that he deserves credit for accurately gauging the needs of the world, as regards the ethical duties recommended by Christ and so completely neglected by his professed followers, and for contriving, or promulgating, means and methods which have succeeded, in a great measure, where others have failed sadly. That a " restoration " or " revival " of the pure, primitive Christianity is a great desideratum of our religious, moral and social life has been acknowledged by numerous representative thinkers and preachers, who have not hesitated to state that our past performances promise ill enough in the way of preparing the world for a reign of truth and righteousness.

The professions of Mormonism as the actual restoration of New Testament Christianity derive a considerable show of plausability in the fact that, in a very real and vivid sense, it proposes to follow the Bible implicitly. Thus, in its primary teaching, it postulates the actual restoration of revelation, which is to say, the direct communication of the will and counsel of God to mankind. With very consistent adherence to many strong suggestions in Scripture, it may be credited with holding that, just as the person of the man Christ brought the presence and power of God down to this world, so the Church, founded to continue his work and incarnation, must perpetuate the personal presence and communion of God, precisely as they were enjoyed by those living in the days of Christ's earth life. Whether or not, as may be questioned by some, such an attitude be authorized or Christianly proper, it may be held consistently that it represents a very normal and vital phase of religious development. Even in this day of "material progress" and crude intellectual resolutions of the "religious consciousness," which have already eliminated for many minds all ideals not "rationally consistent" with the hypotheses of experimental scientists, one must be touched often and truly by that "childlike outlook," which, with Abraham, looks to find God "at the door of the tent," or hopes, like Moses, to talk with God, "as a man speaketh unto his friend." There is certainly much in the New Testament that strongly suggests a belief in the constant direct communion of the believing soul and its God, as a means of individual divine guidance, an element sorely missed among us, also for imparting the various blessings and endowments, known as the "gifts of the Spirit." A perfectly restored Christianity should certainly give some other account of these matters than to deny merely that they are of operative importance at the present time, or to assert that they were reserved solely for the "formative period" of the Christian era, the days of Christ's apostles, neither of which statements is warranted in authority, or even intelligent.

This point was touched in a sermon preached by Joseph Smith, June 11, 1843, in which he defends his claim to be the instrument of revelation from God in the following words:

> "Many of the sects cry out, 'Oh, I have the testimony of Jesus; I have the Spirit of God: but away with Joe Smith; he says he is a prophet; but there are to be no prophets or revelators in the last days.' Stop, sir! The Revelator (John) says that the testimony of Jesus is the spirit of prophecy; so by your own mouth you are condemned."—*History of the Church, Vol. V., p.* 427.

Some six months previously he had made an entry in his journal to the same effect, as follows:

"If any person should ask me if I were a prophet, I should not deny it, as that would give me the lie; for, according to John, the testimony of Jesus is the spirit of prophecy; therefore, if I profess to be a witness or teacher, and have not the spirit of prophecy, which is the testimony of Jesus, I must be a false witness; but if I be a true teacher and witness, I must possess the spirit of prophecy, and that constitutes a prophet; and any man who says he is a teacher or preacher of righteousness, and denies the spirit of prophecy, is a liar, and the truth is not in him; and by this key false teachers and imposters may be detected."—*History of the Church, Vol. V., pp.* 215–216.

About ten years previously, however, on April 13, 1833, he had written a letter to one Jared Carter, in which occurs the following explanation of the recognized limitation in respect to receiving revelations, entailed by the constitution of the Church government and constitution. He says:

"Respecting the vision you speak of we do not consider ourselves bound to receive any revelation from any one man or woman without his being legally constituted and ordained to that authority, and giving sufficient proof of it.

"I will inform you that it is contrary to the economy of God for any member of the Church, or any one, to receive instructions for those in authority, higher than themselves; therefore you will see the impropriety of giving heed to them; but if any person have a vision or a visitation from a heavenly messenger, it must be for his own benefit and instruction; for the fundamental principles, government and doctrine of the Church are vested in the keys of the kingdom."—*Ibid., Vol. I.,* p. 338.

As the doctrine of restored revelation is the fundamental teaching of Mormon theology, so also is it the sufficient explanation of the absurd and abominable persecutions visited upon Smith and his people, since the very beginning of their career. The claim that these acts of violence were originated in resistance to actual "impurities" and other forms of evil-doing are mere pretences, without sufficient warrant. The fact is that Joseph Smith, being an accredited minister or preacher of no sect whatever, had dared to "usurp the functions and prerogatives" of the preacher class, or profession, who, in current estimation, should have been the proper channels for any further revelations that God might be pleased to give to the world. He was, in this matter, precisely what the Puritan hierarchy of New England denominated a "wanton gospeler," which is to say, an unauthorized preacher, and his influence had the same significance in the minds of the Protestant clergy as has an "unethical" or "quack" physician to the medical profession. That he claimed to have received revelations, in spite of the current understanding of Revelation xxii. 18, as applying to all presumed or alleged revelations in addition to the Scriptures of the Old and New Testaments, may have excited the opposition of some minds. The bulk of the arguments used against him, however, have been devoted to proving, by fair means or foul, that he was not at all the kind of person who could be considered worthy to commune with God on any terms — worse than the repentant thief on the cross, worse, also, than Saul on the way to Damascus.

Although the leading examples of revelation claimed by the Mormons are to be found in the inspired utterances and commandments in the Book known as *Doctrine and Covenants,* promulgated by Joseph Smith, the accepted teaching is that revelation is continuous and constantly augmenting. Thus, the higher officers of the Church are the regular and accredited channels of revelations on all matters pertaining to government and faith. This constitutes the reality of the theocratic rule, so widely advertised and condemned by anti-Mormon writers and agitators. If unfounded, however, it is merely a very devout and human belief that has never been notably misrequited by the accredited authorities of the Church.

Such inspiration, however, by no means totals the possibilities of association and communication between God and man. The Mormons live literally, as they devoutly believe, in constant communion with God. They hold that the true believer becomes in a literal sense, and in this life, a "joint heir with Christ," and is to be endowed, therefore, with "spiritual gifts," as promised in the Scriptures, in addition to the continuous "testimony" of the truth of the Gospel, following on the "gift of the Holy Ghost." Indeed, if we may judge from published statements and from the genius of the entire system, religion is not merely a totality of beliefs and duties, additional to and apart from the affairs of every-day life, but, in a very real sense, the proper sum and center of life's activities. That is, at least, the design apparently followed in conceiving and carrying out the details of the wonderful organization of the Church. Thus, because religion is properly to be regarded as life itself, we find the often-repeated claim that, so far as the doctrines of religion are concerned, their truth is not merely accepted "on faith," not merely believed, but known and understood, sure and certain.

With Mormonism, therefore, theology is the God-science, *par excellence,* and its characteristics are thus summarized by Parley P. Pratt:

> "First. Theology is the science of communication, or of correspondence, between God, angels, spirits, and men, by means of visions, dreams, interpretations, conversations, inspirations, or the spirit of prophecy and revelation.
>
> "Second. It is the science by which worlds are organized, sustained and directed, and the elements controlled.
>
> "Third. It is the science of knowledge, and the key and power thereof, by which the heavens are opened, and lawful access is obtained

to the treasures of wisdom and intelligence — inexhaustible, infinite, embracing the past, the present, and the future.

"Fourth. It is the science of life, endless and eternal, by which the living are changed or translated, and the dead raised.

"Fifth. It is the science of *faith,* reformation, and remission of sins, whereby a fallen race of mortals may be justified, cleansed, and restored to the communion and fellowship of that Holy Spirit which is the light of the world, and of every intelligence therein.

"Sixth. It is the science of spiritual gifts, by which the blind see, the deaf hear, the lame walk, the sick are healed, and demons are expelled from the human system.

"Seventh. It is the science of all other sciences and useful arts, being, in fact, the very fountain from which they emanate. It includes philosophy, astronomy, history, mathematics, geography, languages, the science of letters, and blends the knowledge of all matters of fact, in every branch of art, or of research. It includes, also, all the scientific discoveries and inventions, agriculture, the mechanical arts, architecture, ship-building, the properties and applications of the mariner's compass, navigation, and music. All that is useful, great and good, all that is calculated to sustain, comfort, instruct, edify, purify, refine or exalt intelligences, originated by this science, and this science alone, all other sciences being but branches growing out of *this,* the root."— *Key to Theology, pp.* 15–16.

Elder Pratt then proceeds to justify his claim that theology includes and originates all other sciences, by a series of examples from Scripture, showing that God originated the various arts and industries before man ever practiced them, and that at the beginning, at least, they resulted from man's communion with the Deity.

It may be readily understood from this passage that the Gospel of the Latter-day Saints is at bottom a very typical example of theosophic mysticism, which is to say, a system postulating the essential congruity of Divine and human spirits, their proper constant association, and the possibility of their complete harmony, present as well as ultimate. In this particular it makes a strong appeal to the normal religious instinct, since the mystical tendency is always effective in imparting a sense of reality to religious experience and authority. Undoubtedly, this essential mysticism was the secret of the wonderful growth of the church in the early days of its history. In the midst of the seething unrest in religious circles at the time, there were very many who passionately desired something more vital than the conventional creedalisms of the traditional sects, and whose minds were prepared to believe that God must speak again to show the true way of life. Hence, the announcement of the claim that he had actually spoken, to restore the Gospel and give new directions for human guidance, was welcomed in many quarters. Furthermore, the Mormon insistence that the "spiritual gifts" mentioned in the Gospels, and in the writings of Christ's apostles, are to be expected,— nay, actually exist — as a consequence of conforming to the requirements and ordinances of the faith, is another very essential point of advantage over the sectarian quibble that such gifts were intended only for the early days of Christianity. In this belief Mormonism antedated by many years the belief, now growing in our midst, and early emphasized by Edward Irving, that healing, prophecy, and other "miraculous powers," are the proper endowments of believers. This matter is well explained by Elder James E. Talmage, as follows:

> "All men who would officiate with propriety in the ordinances of the Gospel must be commissioned for their exalted duties by the power and authority of heaven. When so divinely invested, these servants of the Lord will not be lacking in proofs of the Master's favor; for it has ever been characteristic of the dealings of God with his people, to manifest his power by the bestowal of a variety of ennobling graces, which are properly called gifts of the Spirit. These are oft-times exhibited in a manner so diverse from the usual order of things as to be called miraculous and supernatural. . . . We may safely regard the existence of these spiritual powers as one of the essential characteristics of the true Church; where they are not, the priesthood of God does not operate.
>
> "Mormon solemnly declares that the days of miracles will not pass from the Church, as long as there shall be a man upon earth to be saved; 'For,' says he, 'it is by faith that miracles are wrought: and it is by faith that angels appear and minister unto men; wherefore if these things have ceased, wo be unto the children of men, for it is because of unbelief, and all is vain.' . . .
>
> "The gifts here spoken of are essentially endowments of power and authority, through which the purposes of God are accomplished, sometimes with accompanying conditions that appear to be supernatural. By such the sick may be healed, malignant influences overcome, spirits of darkness subdued, the Saints, humble and weak, may proclaim their testimonies and otherwise utter praises unto God in new and strange tongues, and others may interpret these words; the feeble human intellect may be invigorated by the heavenly touch of spiritual vision and blessed dreams, to see and comprehend things ordinarily withheld from mortal senses; direct communication with the fountain of all wisdom may be established, and the revelations of the Divine will may be obtained. . . .
>
> "The Latter-day Saints claim to possess within the Church all the sign-gifts promised as the heritage of the believer. They point to the unimpeached testimonies of thousands who have been blessed with direct and personal manifestations of heavenly power; to the once blind, and dumb, halt, and weak in body, who have been freed from their infirmities through their faith and by the ministrations of the priesthood; to a multitude who have voiced their testimony in tongues with which they were naturally unfamiliar; or who have demonstrated their possession of the gift by a phenomenal mastery of foreign languages, when such was necessary to the discharge of their duties as preachers of the word of God; to many who have enjoyed communion with heavenly beings; to others who have prophesied in words that have found their speedy vindication in literal fulfillment; and to the Church itself, whose growth has been guided by the voice of its Divine Leader, made known through the gift of revelation."— *The Articles of Faith, pp.* 219–221, 236–237.

Writing to a very similar purpose, Brigham H. Roberts, the voluminous historian and apologist of Mormonism, has the following:

> "Protestant writers insist that the age of miracles closed with the fourth or fifth century, and that after that the extraordinary gifts of the Holy Ghost must not be looked for. Catholic writers, on the other hand, insist that the power to perform miracles has always continued in the Church. . . . Nor is there anything in the Scriptures or in reason that would lead one to believe that they were to be discontinued. Still this plea is made by modern Christians — explaining the absence of these spiritual powers among them — that the extraordinary gifts of the Holy Ghost were only intended to accompany the proclamation of the Gospel during the first few centuries, until the church was able to make its way without them, and then they were to be done away. It is sufficient to remark upon this that it is assumption pure and simple, and stands without warrant either of scripture or right reason; and proves that men had so far changed the religion of Jesus Christ that it became a form of godliness without the power thereof."—*Outlines of Ecclesiastical History, Part* II. *pp.* 161–162.

It must be evident, therefore, that Mormonism has an immense advantage over its traditional opponents in its insistence that the statments of Scripture are to be literally received, also that there are no time limits to God's promises. Such an insistence must make a strong appeal, particularly to simple minds — these are often the normal minds — and is altogether more consistent. Its teachings, accordingly, tolerate no evasions based on "typical," "symbolical," or "figurative" wrestings of passages "hard" even for the "faith of believers," but insists on such interpretations as the language of Scripture suggests. Of course, this method has drawn the criticism of "dead literalism," the "letter that killeth," "sodden materialism," etc., from the advocates of systems open to even graver characterizations. If, however, the acceptance of Scripture as it stands argues to a *reductio ad absurdum,* it is well to understand that fact, and encouraging to learn it from the statements of alleged "believers."

It is distinctly unprofitable, however, to dwell upon criticisms, originated primarily as mere bickerings aimed at the efforts of a "non-professional theologian," or, yet, to enlarge upon the superior claims, as alleged, of other systems, whose assumptions, in the last analysis, are unintelligible, even to the learned. Nor would any informed mind suspect undue prejudice at the basis of the statement that the "subtleties" of traditional theology are derived far more directly from the theories of speculative metaphysicians than from the statements of Scripture, or any of the reported words of Christ or his apostles. As a matter of fact, it is no more than logical that a system of religious teachings "hidden from the wise and prudent and revealed unto babes" (in learning), also so clear and simple that "a wayfaring man, though uninstructed, should not err therein," should be presented in terms that would admit of literal acceptation. Even the attempt, found in all traditional systems of theology, to read immense metaphysical refinements into the Epistles of Paul is not justified by the results. As a matter of fact, the plain and simple statements of Scripture, addressed in the first instance to simple and unlearned people, outlining the duties of man to God and to his neighbor, also setting forth the merciful provisions of God for the benefit of man, have been lost to sight, contemptuously neglected, and actually rendered largely inoperative, by the perverse habit of placing the greater emphasis upon mere speculative intellectualisms, which have been obtruded as the real objects of faith. The only antidote for this intellectual fetichism is to accept literally, or else to reject as unintelligible the principles upon which the Gospel is supposedly based. It is a desirable achievement, indeed, to rescue religious thought from the toils of so-called philosophy, which, starting out to explain things as they are, has always ended by inventing even more puzzling and unintelligible situations, which have been "improved" only by substituting others of precisely similar character. It is scarcely remarkable, therefore, that we hear the familiar Protestant statement of the present day that "theology is not religion," and witness frantic and largely ineffective attempts to achieve a practical moral and social reform in the sectarian presentation of Christianity. The attitude of Mormonism on this matter is well set forth in the following words of Judge A. B. Carlton, a close observer of this system and its adherents:

> "One trouble about the Mormons is that they are too primitive. They have gone back to the infancy of the Christian faith and organization, and fanatically hold on to a literal interpretation of what the Christians generally treat as 'figurative,' or, as having gone into 'innocuous desuetude.' . . . With each remove from the Catholic Church — first, 'the Reformation'— and then the successive branches, off-shoots, schisms, and sects, the zealous propagandist of each new faith devoutly maintains that there is nothing new about it — it is only a restoration of primitive Christianity. So the Mormons claim that they have the genuine article of religion; that they are the true Church of Jesus Christ, and are the Saints in these latter days."— *Wonderlands of the Wild West, p.* 122.

This much-condemned "literalism" involves, apparently, the line of thinking usually characterized as "materialism," which, by habitual connotation, involves all that is the reverse of "spiritual," and, as some pretend to argue, also the notion that for God we must substitute some sort of blind and impersonal "force" or "law." The truth is otherwise, however, even upon the terms of speculative philosophy, since the assumption that all reality is to be understood by the mind as analogous to the order of experiences derived from the world of "material existence" may be credited as a distinct and laudable attempt to render things "unseen and eternal" in some sense intelligible. This object is perfectly apparent in the following statement of Joseph Smith:

> "It is impossible for a man to be saved in ignorance. There is no such thing as immaterial matter. All spirit is matter, but it is more fine and pure, and can only be discerned by purer eyes. We cannot see it; but when our bodies are purified, we shall see that it is all matter."—*Doctrine and Covenants,* cxxxi. 6–8.

This teaching is explained by Prof. John A. Widtsoe, a man of no mean learning, in the following words:

> "Mormonism has frequently been charged with accepting the doctrine of materialism. In one sense, the followers of Joseph Smith plead yes to this charge. In Mormon theology there is no place for immaterialism; i.e. for a God, spirits and angels that are not material. Spirit is only a refined form of matter. It is beyond the mind of man to conceive of an immaterial thing. On the other hand, Joseph Smith did not teach that the kind of tangible matter, which impresses our mental senses, is the kind of matter which is associated with heavenly beings. The distinction between the matter known to man and the spirit matter is very great; but no greater than is the difference between the matter of the known elements and that of the universal ether which forms one of the accepted dogmas of science."—*Joseph Smith as Scientist, p.* 12–13.

Mormon "materialism" has also been extensively explained and defended by Orson Pratt in his well-known work, *The Absurdities of Immaterialism.* Of course, the whole matter has been ridiculed and travestied by anti-Mormon writers, who have effectually revealed their own ignorance in such statements as that Smith represented God as a man "grossly material in character," and that the kingdom of heaven is understood to be made of earth, stones, coal, and still other varieties of substance of even lesser dignity and beauty. None of these critics seem able to apprehend the philosophical bearings of the matter, which argue to conclusions far different in effect. According to the data of the religious consciousness, the things of God are realities in a preeminent sense. According to life experience, all realities are to be variously perceived, or "sensed": in other words, "matter is the constant basis (or possibility) of perceptive experience." Consequently, spiritual things, being also perceptible, "when our bodies are purified"—since "spiritual things are spiritually discerned," however we may understand this statement—are in this sense directly analogous to things understood under the term "material." Nor, in the last analysis, is the mind capable of comprehending any other alternative, however well reasoned it may appear in the writings of speculative thinkers. Even though the mind be so biassed that the idea of

God is inadmissible, we find as a very general rule that the idea thus rejected is that of a perfectly personal and anthropomorphic First Cause which experimental science is supposed to have ruled out of the universe, or relegated to the domains of the hopelessly indefinite and unknowable. And this attitude is assumed, not because the idea of God is unintelligible, but rather because, as supposed, there is no evidence that it corresponds to a reality. In the famous phrase, so often quoted from the astronomer Laplace, "The telescope sweeps the heavens without finding God": therefore, as some conclude, He is not there. The moment, however, that we admit the existence of a God, in any sense "personal," that moment we visualize a being in human form, visible to the eyes, audible to the ears, and, supposedly, tangible also.

Nor is the disagreement on this point other than a merely verbal difference. It is a controversy over words and terms, rather than over ideas. It involves an excellent example of "distinction without difference." Even in the most "spiritual" speculations about the divine nature, there is an involved recognition of the fact that "spirit," so-called, and "matter," so-called, are to be dealt with in the same terms. Thus, in the famous Athanasian controversy, touching the divine dignities of Christ, the final issue with the Arians reached the point of opposing the statement that He is "of the same substance with the Father," rather than "of like substance" merely, in Greek phrase, *homo-ousia* against *homoi-ousia*. Nor did the "spiritual substances" herein discriminated correspond to any of the "four varieties of negation," mentioned by the German philosopher Hegel.

The point of view from which the "materialistic" conception of the universe is attacked is evidently founded in a very prevalent confusion between findings based on an "objective" consideration of the being and attributes of God and spirit, as in the Athanasian controversy, and the purely "subjective" considerations treated by others, in the attempt to systematize the universe of thought-experience. Thus, as given in the famous formulations of Descartes, we find "two substances," discriminated by their "attributes," which are "extension and thought." Matter, we are told, is "extended, but has no thought"; whereas spirit has "thought, but no extension." However, according to Descartes, these "two substances" find their sole point of union in the organ of the brain known to anatomists as the "pineal gland"; here the "unextended" meets the "extended." Now, that which such philosophers describe as "spirit" is not the same thing as appears in theological literature. All that Descartes accomplished, in effect, was to discriminate the experiences ("attributes") of subjective and objective, as may be understood by an example. Thus, in deep thought or meditation, a man knows himself subjectively, as, in the words of Prof. William James, a "stream of consciousness." When, however, he turns to other activities than those of mere thinking, he recognizes that he is also a something extended in space, or "extension," which is not involved in "thought." Nor does Spinoza, in resolving the "two substances" into "two attributes" of the one "substance absolutely infinite," which he calls "God," accomplish any other intelligible result. He separates the subjective and the objective. Just as a man thinks, so also God thinks — howbeit "the thought of God differs from the thought of man as the Dog-star from the dog." Just as a man knows himself as existing in a limited "extension," so God knows himself as existing in all extended space. This expresses Spinoza's solution of the universe.

Other thinkers attempting similarly to wrestle with the situation have postulated a universe composed entirely of "spirit," in which all things material are but the effects of its proper activity. Thus, we have the idealism of Bishop Berkeley and others, which postulates essential "spirit," whose attribute is "to perceive" (*percipere*), and its antithesis, "matter," whose sole attribute is "to be perceived" (*percipi*), and which ceases to exist when out of thought. The uniformity of experiences were explained, of course, by the influence of the divine mind upon the human; thus, apparently, constituting "thought" the constant and eternal medium of creation. From the general tendencies embodied in Berkeley's system arose the "absolute idealism," or "solipsism," of Fichte and others, whose logic argues the complete identity of all minds with the One Self as effectively as the Adwaita philosophies of India. While these and similar conclusions seem to follow on the logic of very many writers — and by "proper handling," indeed, nearly any conclusion may be reached by a well-conceived line of reasoning — the critic of the history of thought is able to discern in the tendency toward "idealism" a series of intellectual inventions or contrivances to enable avoidance of the perfectly evident conclusion that to call spirit "immaterial" involves for the average mind that we call it nothingness. Nor is there any real avenue of escape from the dilemma, but to acknowledge, in the words above quoted, that "all spirit — i.e. the substance of which 'spiritual' beings consist — is matter, but it is more fine and pure." To say that matter exists only as it is "perceived," or thought, in the mind of God and of man is merely a verbal subterfuge, based upon the assumption that, because "thought (or thinking) is immaterial"—and, like electricity, magnetism and gravity, having no "consistency," such as is found in stone, metal, etc.—therefore all that exists for it and in it must be, in essence, some kind of nothingness, known under another name. Nor could we sharply discriminate the concept of an "immaterial human spirit" from the *karma* of Buddhism—"all that total of a soul, which is the things it did, the thought it had, the 'Self'"—a mere vortex, echo, or numerically conceivable valency, capable of producing activity in favorable concrete conditions; just as a bell of given tone answers the vibrations of another of the same tone, thus reproducing and continuing the activities of the first bell.

The real situation involved in the type of "materialism" under discussion is to provide an intelligible answer to the very reasonable question as to the real constitution of the human spirit, when disembodied at death, and supposedly residing in the "world of spirits," also to justify to the thinking mind the assertion that God is personal, and not a mere central "force or law," acting upon the material universe. The traditional antithesis between "matter" and "spirit," except in the sense of "object" and "subject," "extension" and "thought," is really meaningless. Nor has it a direct bearing on the religious consciousness, as exalting the idea of God above the comprehension of the human mind. The notion of immaterial "spirit" merely confuses the devout mind, while attracting—and, in a great measure, justifying—the ridicule of the skeptic. The scholastic teaching about God, calling Him "formless, passionless and immaterial"—for the actual concepts of no Christian people correspond to any such notion, even could it be "visualized"—a "being having his centre nowhere and his circumference everywhere," is merely a philosophical whimsey, unwarranted in sound reason, devoid of authority in Scripture, and of no religious significance. The God revealed in Scripture, whatever more may be said of His being, powers or attributes, is personal and anthropomorphic, and thus He remains for the religious consciousness to this very day,—"I hope to see my Pilot face to face, when I have crossed the bar"—in spite of the impudent "subtleties" propounded by theological dreamers, which amount, in reality, to formal atheism. Such a conclusion was ably asserted by Orson Pratt, in the following passage:

"There are two classes of atheists in the world. One class denies the existence of God in the most positive language; the other denies his existence in duration or space. One says 'There is no God'; the other says 'God is not *here* or *there*, any more than he exists *now* and *then*.' The infidel says 'God does not exist anywhere.' The immaterialist says 'He exists *nowhere.*' The infidel says 'There is no such substance as God.' The immaterialist says 'There is such a substance as God, but it is *without parts.*' The atheist says 'There is no such substance as *spirit.*' The immaterialist says 'A spirit, though he lives and acts, occupies no room, and fills no space in the same way and in the same manner as matter, not even so much as the minutest grain of sand.' The atheist does not hide his infidelity; but the immaterialist, whose declared belief amounts to the same thing as the atheist's, endeavors to hide his infidelity under the shallow covering of a few words. . . . The immaterialist is a religious atheist; he only differs from the other class of atheists by clothing an indivisible, unextended *nothing* with the powers of a God. One class believes in no God; the other believes that *Nothing* is God and worships it as such."—*Absurdities of Immaterialism, p.* 11.

CHAPTER XIV

THE MORMON DOCTRINE OF GOD

THE "materialistic" conception of God, which is to say the conception that is humanly intelligible, is thus explained in the words of Parley P. Pratt:

> "The idea of a God without 'body, parts or passions' is not more absurd or inconsistent than that modern popular doctrine, that all things were created from nonentity, or, in other words, that something originated from nothing.
>
> "It is a self-evident truth, which will not admit of argument, that nothing remains nothing. Nonentity is the negative of all existence. This negative possesses no property or element upon which the energies of creative power can operate.
>
> . . . .
>
> "To speak more philosophically, all the elements are spiritual, all are physical, all are material, tangible realities. Spirit is matter, and matter is full of spirit. Because all things which do exist are eternal realities, in their elementary existence. . . . In the capacity of mortals, however, some of the elements are tangible, or visible, and others invisible. Those which are tangible to our senses, we call physical; those which are more subtle and refined, we call spiritual."—*Key to Theology, pp.* 49–51; 43–45.

On the basis of this characteristic "literalism," Mormon writers and teachers insist that the Biblical mentions of hands, face, feet, arms, heart, and other physical parts, in reference to God, are to be understood literally, although "figurative" and "symbolical" uses of these words are often found; furthermore, that the primeval suggestion, "Let us make man in our image," was no rhetorical figure. Nor is there any advantage to be found in criticizing and characterizing this teaching, as some have done,— so long, at least, as the Bible remains the recognized standard of authority — since the opposing concept is entirely extra-Biblical. God is represented as appearing in human form to Adam, Abraham, and other patriarchs. Moses, desiring to see His "glory," is warned that he cannot see His face, but that, standing "in a clift of the rock," God would cover him with His hand, while He passed by, allowing him to see only His "back parts." (Exod. xxxiii. 18–23.) Stephen, the martyr, declared that he had a vision of the "Son of man standing on the right hand of God" (Acts vii. 5 God, by prophets, by Chri implicit references to ar should be sufficient for actual authority of the evidently attempted t statements from the ric could God reveal to then

Much of the logical de God by Mormon writers the advocates of other syst in this matter, as cannot be to ment whatever can safely claim ex There is certainly nothing of contrary in the wordy speculations of metaphysical theo or nothing that can be credited with permanent v world of living humanity. The crudest concept that strates consistency with authority, and expresses faith in its finality, is preferable to much else that is based upon some man's intellectual ingenuity, rather than upon consistency with the terms used in Scriptures believed to be "given by inspiration of God." For example, by what Scriptural argument could one oppose the following statement given by Joseph Smith?

> "The Father has a body of flesh and bones as tangible as man's; the Son also; but the Holy Ghost has not a body of flesh and bones, but is a personage of Spirit."—*Doctrine and Covenants,* cxxx. 22.

This statement is explained and defended by Mormon apologists by an analysis of Scripture passages. Thus, Christ, after his resurrection, had a body of flesh and bones, which ascended also into heaven—"for a spirit hath not flesh and bones, as ye see me have" (Luke xxiv. 39). So also, they assert, the same must be said of God the Father, since, in the words of the Epistle to the Hebrews, Christ is called the "express image of his person" (Heb. i. 3), indicating the idea that "his person" is visible and tangible, after the manner of a body of "flesh and bones." Nor can it be said in criticism of this teaching that it is either "crude," "materialistic," or "literalistic," because it is precisely the logical development of the doctrine explicitly stated by all the great confessions of faith. Thus in the Articles of Faith of the Church of England, the following is to be found:

> "The Son, which is the Word of the Father, begotten from everlasting of the Father, the very and eternal God, and of one substance with the Father, took Man's nature in the womb of the Blessed Virgin, of her substance: so that two whole and perfect Natures, that is to say, the Godhead and Manhood, were joined together in one Person, never to be divided, whereof is one Christ, very God, and very Man."—*Article* II.

ruly rise again from death, and took again his body, nes, and all things appertaining to the perfection of ; wherewith he ascended into Heaven, and there sitteth, urn to judge all Men at the last day."—*Article* IV.

stminster Confession expresses the same teaching in similar terms. Thus:

e Son of God, the second person in the Trinity, being very and al God, of one substance, and equal with the Father, did, when fullness of time was come, take upon him man's nature, with all e essential properties and common infirmities thereof, yet without in: being conceived by the power of the Holy Ghost, in the womb of the Virgin Mary, of her substance. So that two whole, perfect, and distinct natures, the Godhead and the manhood, were inseparably joined together in one person, without conversion, composition, or confusion. Which person is very God and very man, yet one Christ, the only Mediator between God and man."—*Chapter* VIII, *Section* ii.

"On the third day he arose from the dead, with the same body in which he suffered; with which also he ascended into heaven, and there sitteth at the right hand of his Father, making intercession; and shall return to judge men and angels, at the end of the world."—*Chapter* VIII, *Section* iv.

Answering the familiar caviling criticism that the Mormon conception of God postulates only a "very large and powerful man"—for so certain writers have chosen to travesty the real statement—B. H. Roberts speaks as follows:

"Mark what is said here of Jesus. You say that 'the Godhead and manhood' in Jesus 'were joined together in one person,' that is, his spirit and his body are united, never to be severed or disunited. Now I put to you this question: Is the Lord Jesus Christ God? Yes, you must answer. Then is not God an exalted man according to your creed? . . . According to this statement of the matter, Jesus has not been dissolved into some spiritual, immaterial essence, and widely diffused throughout the universe as some spiritual presence. No; he is a substantial, resurrected personage, a united spirit and body; . . . 'never to be divided.' . . . This, of course, scarcely meets the description of the first paragraph of the creed used here, where God is declared to be not matter, that is 'without body, parts or passions.' . . . It is enough that I call your attention to the fact that the second part of your creed leads you closely to the 'Mormon' doctrine that God is an exalted, perfected man, since Jesus, according to your creed, is God, and yet a resurrected man sitting in heaven until his return to judge all men at the last day.

"And now as to there being more Gods than one. We believe the Scripture which says that Jesus was the brightness of God's glory, 'and the express image of his person' (Heb. i, 3). And as we know what kind of a person the Christ is, who 'possessed all the fullness of the Godhead bodily'; and who, when he declared that all power in heaven and in earth had been given unto him, and he was in the act of sending his disciples into all the world to teach and baptize in the authority of the Father, Son, and Holy Spirit—was a resurrected, immortal man, of spirit, flesh and bone. And since, I say, the scripture teaches that the Son was the express image of the Father's person, we conclude that the Father must be a personage of spirit, flesh and bone, just as the Son, Jesus, is. Indeed your Athanasian creed says 'that such as the Father is, such is the Son'; and, of course, it follows that, such as the Son is, such is the Father; that is, the Father is a personage of spirit, flesh and bone, united in one person, 'very God and very man,' just as Jesus is."—*Answer to the Ministerial Association Review, pp.* 16–17.

The foregoing explanations and parallels seem to bring us logically to the discussion of some other points of Mormon teaching, which, although very widely quoted, are very imperfectly understood by the average critic of the system. These points are involved in the familiar quotations from the sermons of Joseph Smith, which are evidently intended to set forth (1) the essential and eternal deity of Christ, and (2) the proper divine heritage of mankind. The equality of Christ with God the Father, and the various authoritative passages evidently setting forth correspondences in their respective persons and characters, have evidently appealed strongly to the imagination of the Prophet, who does not hesitate to postulate a "human element" in the Supreme Being, as well as an essential divine element in the human. It is difficult sometimes to discern whether the Prophet is speaking of God the Father, or of Christ, but, recognizing the deity of the latter, such discrimination is often not important. The following passage, bold in its statements, evidently refers primarily to Christ, who is called, therefore, "the Great God who holds this world in its orbit":

"God himself was once as we are now, and is an exalted Man, and sits enthroned in yonder heavens! That is the great secret. If the vail was rent to-day, and the Great God who holds this world in its orbit, and who upholds all worlds and all things by his power, was to make himself visible,—I say, if you were to see him to-day, you would see him like a man in form—like yourselves in all the person, image, and very form as a man; for Adam was created in the very fashion, image, and likeness of God, and received instruction from, and walked, talked, and conversed with him, as one man talks and communes with another."—*Compendium of the Doctrines of the Gospel, p.* 190.

The following passage, quoted from an evidently fragmentary discourse by Joseph Smith, presents the doctrine of God's body in another aspect, with a strong suggestion of speculation of higher and hidden mysteries:

"As the Father hath power in Himself, so hath the Son power in Himself, to lay down His life and take it again, so He has a body of His own. The Son doeth what He hath seen the Father do: then the Father hath some day laid down His life and taken it again; so He has a body of His own; each one will be in His own body; and yet the sectarian world believe the body of the Son is identical with the Father's."—*History of the Church, Vol. V., p.* 426.

Both these passages suggest an idea, more definitely expressed by some other writers, that the drama of redemption, as carried out in this world, is a necessary and eternally significant procedure, which has been duplicated in other worlds and universes from eternity, and always involving that a divine personage should assume the full nature of man, should lay down his life and take it again, and, thereby, provide a means by which the souls of all true believers should be exalted to become "partakers in the divine nature" (II Peter i, 4). Thus, in the same discourse, Joseph Smith speaks further, as follows:

> "The Scriptures say that there are Gods many and Lords many, but to us there is but one living and true God, and the heaven of heavens could not contain Him; for He took the liberty to go into other heavens. . . .
>
> "Peter and Stephen testify that they saw the Son of Man standing on the right hand of God. Any person that had seen the heavens opened knows that there are three personages in the heavens who hold the keys of power, and one presides over all. . . .
>
> "Gods have an ascendency over the angels, who are ministering servants. In the resurrection, some are raised to be angels; others are raised to become Gods."—*Ibid. pp.* 426–427.

Immediately following the passage just quoted, we find the statement, "These things are revealed in the most holy place in a Temple prepared for that purpose." Also, some four years previously, while confined in Liberty jail, Clay county, Missouri, he had written as follows:

> "God shall give unto you (the saints) knowledge by his Holy Spirit, yea by the unspeakable gift of the Holy Ghost, that has not been revealed since the world was until now; which our forefathers have waited with anxious expectation to be revealed in the last times, which their minds were pointed to, by the angels, as held in reserve for the fulness of their glory: a time to come in which nothing shall be withheld, whether there be one God or many Gods, they shall be manifest; all thrones and dominions, principalities and powers, shall be revealed and set forth upon all who have endured valiantly for the gospel of Jesus Christ . . . according to that which was ordained in the midst of the Council of the Eternal God of all other Gods, before this world was, that should be reserved unto the finishing and the end thereof, when every man shall enter into his eternal presence, and into his immortal rest."—*Doctrine and Covenants,* cxxi. 26–29, 32.

It is noticeable that, while emphasizing in all these passages, the teachings of the "humanity of God" and the divinity of man, the Prophet expressly declares his belief in the "one living and true God" and the "Eternal God of all other Gods." Whether we understand that the word "Gods" refers sometimes to an order of supernal beings, not included in the Godhead nor classed as angels, or whether we understand it as confined to a designation of the "spirits of just men made perfect," it is equally certain that we have good scriptural authority for the usage. Nor does the presence of this word in the teachings of Joseph Smith indicate that he held to a belief in "polytheism," or the plurality of gods, either as an actuality or a possibility, any further than must any careful student of the text of Scripture, who is determined to interpret faithfully the expressions which it evidently contains. It is probable, however, that he understood this word to indicate preeminently the proper dignity of the blessed dead, as will be explained in our discussion of the "Celestial glory." According to the suggestions involved in his utterances on this point, one might be led to suppose that the exalted and glorified saints of other worlds than ours, or, at least, of ages long past, already exist in the Celestial Kingdom among those whom, in Scriptural phrase, it is proper to term "gods."

In this connection we may understand somewhat the meaning intended to be expressed in Lorenzo Snow's famous couplet on God and man, which has been widely quoted as the authoritative statement of the Mormon doctrine of the Deity. Elder Snow thus explains its origin:

> "Early in the spring of 1840, . . . I was at the house of Elder H. G. Sherwood; he was endeavoring to explain the parable of our Savior, when speaking of the husbandman who hired servants and sent them forth at different hours of the day to labor in his vineyard.
>
> "While attentively listening to his explanation, the Spirit of the Lord rested mightily upon me—the eyes of my understanding were opened, and I saw as clear as the sun at noonday, with wonder and astonishment, the pathway of God and man. I formed the following couplet which expresses the revelation, as it was shown me, and explains Father Smith's dark saying to me at the blessing meeting in the Kirtland Temple, prior to my baptism, as previously mentioned in my first interview with the Patriarch:
>
> 'As man now is, God once was;
> As God now is, man may be.'"
>
> —*Autobiography and Family Record of Lorenzo Snow* (*by Eliza R. Snow*), *p.* 46.

Although Elder Snow esteemed this conception very highly, and along with very many others of his Church, seems to have accepted it as the truth of the matter in some very vital sense, it is not, as is usually represented, an authoritative utterance of Mormon teaching. Like the foregoing quotation from Joseph Smith's discourse, it evidently sets forth the idea of the necessary incarnation of God and the consequent exaltation of man, and may be held to refer primarily to Christ. The participation of exalted humanity in the divine nature is thus set forth by Smith in the same discourse as previously quoted:

> "The teachers of the day say that the Father is God, the Son is God, and the Holy Ghost is God, and they are all in one body and one God. Jesus prayed that those that the Father had given him out of the world might be made one in them, as they were one; (one in spirit, in mind, in purpose)."—*History of the Church, Vol. V., p.* 426.

The bridge across the gulf separating the human and divine,

the finite and the infinite, is found in the functions and activities of the Holy Spirit, and this, also, with stricter scriptural consistency than is observed in some other systems of theology. Thus, while in most traditional systems the Holy Spirit is represented as a definite and personal entity, and a proper object of worship, along with the Father and the Son, with whom He is mystically identified, the teachings of Joseph Smith rather emphasize His activities in the work of redemption; in a very real sense seemingly making Him appear preeminently as the medium and evidence of God's creative and redemptive activities. All this is perfectly scriptural, since, in whatever actual or mystical manner we may conceive that the Holy Spirit is properly personal, it is evident that His significance to the life of mankind is rather that of an emanation of God's power, life and activity. Thus, while called in the Greek original by a term properly translatable as the "Holy Breath," which is to say, perhaps, the Divine Life or Presence, He is represented as "promised," "sent," "given," "received," "quenched," "dwelling in" human lives, "filling" the souls of men; also, "proceeding," etc., but always and primarily as an active presence, only once (at the baptism of Christ) represented as visible. It is thus possible to hold that, although, perhaps, possessing a proper personal life in Himself, the Holy Spirit is preeminently the community of "spirit, mind, purpose," etc., between the Father and the Son, to be shared also by exalted and believing humanity. We may thus understand why the sin of "blasphemy against the Holy Spirit" is the supreme offense against God, being the act of rejecting Him, vitally and evidently present, as a factor in the life of the individual man, not merely as a distant and unknown Creator and Governor of the universe. This immediate and immanent presence and activity of the Divine Life, which is called the Holy Spirit, also, as set forth in Scripture, determines the individual man as a partaker in the divine nature, because the unity with God's life which its activity begets is of the same character and description as the unity among the Persons of the Godhead. (John xvii. 21.) The description of the Divine Nature given by Joseph Smith, and his immediate disciples is, if nothing more, according to the claims of his followers, certainly a careful and faithful rendering of apparent Scriptural meanings.

The following passage from the Lectures on Faith, regularly included in the same volume with the Doctrine and Covenants, sets forth a view of the function and significance of the Holy Spirit very closely in accord with that just discussed. Thus, with apparent contradiction, the writer states in the first sentence that "two personages" only "constitute" the Godhead, but, developing the theme, he indicates that the unity of these two personages consists in the common possession of the "same mind," and that this mind is the Holy Spirit. He then proceeds to state that "these three" constitute the Godhead. The reconciliation lies in the fact that, in the first instance he is speaking of the functions and significance of the Spirit, in which He does not appear as primarily of personal significance, and that, in the second instance, he recognizes that this mystical element of the Godhead is really and properly personal. Thus:

> "There are two personages who constitute the great, matchless, governing, and supreme power over all things, by whom all things were created and made, that are created and made, whether visible or invisible, whether in heaven, on earth, or in the earth, under the earth, or throughout the immensity of space. They are the Father and the Son — the Father being a personage of spirit, glory, and power, possessing all perfection and fullness, the Son, who was in the bosom of the Father, a personage of tabernacle, made or fashioned like unto man, or being in the form and likeness of man, or rather man was formed after his likeness and in his image; he is also the express image and likeness of the personage of the Father, possessing all the fullness of the Father, or the same fullness with the Father; being begotten of him, and ordained from before the foundation of the world to be a propitiation for the sins of all those who should believe on his name, and is called the Son because of the flesh. . . . And he being the Only Begotten of the Father, full of grace and truth, and having overcome, received a fullness of the glory of the Father, possessing the same mind with the Father, which mind is the Holy Spirit, that bears record of the Father and the Son, and these three are one; or, in other words, these three constitute the great, matchless, governing and supreme, power over all things; by whom all things were created and made that were created and made, and these three constitute the Godhead, and are one; the Father and the Son possessing the same mind, the same wisdom, glory, power, and fullness — filling all in all; the Son being filled with the fullness of the mind, glory, and power; or, in other words, the spirit, glory, and power, of the Father, possessing all knowledge and glory, and the same kingdom, sitting at the right hand of power, in the express image and likeness of the Father, mediator for man, being filled with the fullness of the mind of the Father; or, in other words, the Spirit of the Father, which Spirit is shed forth upon all who believe on his name and keep his commandments; and all those who keep his commandments shall grow up from grace to grace, and become heirs of the heavenly kingdom, and joint heirs with Jesus Christ; possessing the same mind, being transformed into the same image or likeness, even the express image of him who fills all in all; being filled with the fullness of his glory, and become one in him, even as the Father, Son and Holy Spirit are one."— *Lectures on Faith, V.* (*Doctrine and Covenants, pp.* 54–55).

As may be seen in this quotation, the doctrine of the Godhead, as presented in Mormon theology, differs in little from the general lines of belief held to be orthodox, except in the fact that it carefully avoids the evident contradiction involved in the assumption of a God "without body, parts or passions," in immediate coordination with the teaching that one "person" of the Godhead possesses a "body, with flesh, bones, and all things appertaining to the perfection of man's nature, wherewith he ascended into heaven," and whose Godhead and manhood are "never to be divided." Instead of the utterly baffling, and really meaningless, formulation of the doctrine of the Trinity, as found, for example, in the Athanasian Creed, we find here an intelligible effort to make the essential truths of that doctrine clear to the human mind — and this should be the function of a real revelation — by postulating an identity of mind and spirit, and the common possession of the "same fullness," as between two personages, who are not to be "confounded." It may be said, also, that it demonstrates some sort of approach to a higher authority in the matter in the fact that it attempts, evidently, to further clarify the situation by asserting that the same community of spirit, life, and mind, is to be possessed by true "believers" in common with the persons of the Godhead, as constitutes the unity of the Godhead; and this is the Scriptural position in the matter. The Biblical authorities for the doctrine are to be found particularly in John xvii. 20–21, Rom. viii. 29, I Cor. xv. 49, II Cor. iii. 18, etc. It seems preferable, indeed, to appeal to the statements of Scripture, the sole authorities we have in this matter, rather than to the speculations of the best-equipped metaphysicians of ancient or modern times. It is safe to say that we have in this statement all that is humanly intelligible in the accepted doctrine of the Trinity, since, however much it may be condemned for failure to accord with traditional standards of doctrine, it is in complete accord with Scripture in regarding the Father as the One God *par excellence,* and postulating Christ's participation in the Godhead in Biblical terms.

It may be admissible to assert, therefore, that the doctrine of the Godhead found in the theology of the Mormon Church is, purely and simply, the doctrine to be derived from Scripture teachings, when unmingled with philosophical speculations. As the advocates of this Church would doubtless claim, it is the revealed doctrine, untouched by human ingenuity. On this point B. H. Roberts writes:

"Against the dogma that God was an incorporeal, immaterial, passionless being, the Prophet [Joseph Smith] announced the splendid doctrine of anthropomorphism — God in the human form, and possessed of human qualities, but sanctified and perfected. In the first great revelation which opened this last dispensation our Prophet beheld Father and Son as separate persons, distinct from each other; persons in the form of men, but more glorious and more splendid, of course, than words could describe them to be. All through the revelation received, and all through his discourses, the Prophet reaffirms the old doctrine of the Scriptures, the doctrine of all the prophets, asserting that man indeed was created in the image of God, and that God possessed human qualities, consciousness, will, love, mercy, justice; together with power and glory — in a word, a Man 'exalted and perfected.'"— *Joseph Smith, the Prophet-Teacher, pp.* 22–23.

In another work, Roberts commenting on the statement that man was created "in the image of God," writes as follows:

"Now, if that were untouched by 'philosophy,' I think it would not be difficult to understand. Man was created in the image and likeness of God. What idea does this language convey to the mind of man, except that man, when his creation was completed, stood forth the counterpart of God in form? But our philosophers have not been willing to let it stand so. . . . They tell us that this plain, simple, straightforward language of Moses, which says that man was created in the image of God — and which everybody can understand — means, not the 'full-length' image of God, but God's 'moral image'! Man was created in the 'moral image' of God, they say.

"The meaning of this language from the 26th. and 27th. verse of the first chapter of Genesis, where it is written, is made perfectly clear when compared with the third verse of the fifth chapter of Genesis, where it is written; 'And Adam lived an hundred and thirty years, and begat a son in his own likeness, after his image; and called his name Seth.' What do these words imply, but that Seth was like his father in features, and also, doubtless, in intellect and moral qualities? And if, when it is said Adam begat a son in his 'own likeness, after his image,' it simply means that Seth, in form and features, and intellectual and moral qualities, was like his father — then there can be no other conclusion formed upon the passage that says God created man in his own image and likeness, than that man, in a general way, in form and feature, and intellectual and moral qualities, was like God."— *The Doctrine of Deity, pp.* 176–177.

CHAPTER XV

THE DOCTRINES OF MAN, OF THE FALL, AND OF THE CHARACTER OF EVIL

THE doctrine that God made man "in His own image" is confined neither to his physical body, nor yet to his origin in the Garden of Eden. Just as the proper destiny of the human race is to attain to union with the divine nature, so, with equal propriety, essential divinity is believed to have been its origin. Man partakes of God's image and likeness also in possessing the proper attributes of God; intelligence — which is the "glory of God" (*D. and C.*, Sec. xciii. 36) — and eternity, both past and future. This teaching involves, of course, that the spirit of man is self-existent, uncreated (although "begotten," being less than God), and that it had an actual and, in a very real sense, a conscious preexistence. This doctrine is an essential part of the teachings of Mormon scriptures, especially the Book of Abraham and the *Doctrine and Covenants*. In the latter book the following passages occur:

> "And now, verily I say unto you, I (Jesus Christ) was in the beginning with the Father, and am the first-born. . . . Ye were also in the beginning with the Father; that which is spirit, even the Spirit of truth. . . . Man was also in the beginning with God. Intelligence, or the light of truth, was not created or made, neither indeed can be." — *Section* xciii, 21, 23, 29.

The same idea is still further developed in the following extract from an address delivered by Joseph Smith in July, 1839:

> "The spirit of man is not a created being; it existed from eternity, and will exist to eternity. Anything created cannot be eternal; and earth, water, etc., had their existence in an elementary state, from eternity. Our Savior speaks of children and says, Their angels always stand before my Father. The Father called all spirits before Him at the creation of man, and organized them. He (Adam, as mentioned in the preceding paragraph) is the head, and was told to multiply. The keys were first given to him, and by him to others. He will have to give an account of his stewardship, and they to him." — *History of the Church, Vol.* III. *p.* 387.

Of the condition of the spirits of mankind previous to their incarnation, and of the significance of the doctrine of preexistence to the body of the theological system of this Church, the following is an excellent explanation:

"From the little knowledge we have on this subject (need of an earthly probation) we reach the following conclusions: That at the time of the creation of the earth, all who were to become its inhabitants were living in the spirit with God. There we communed with Him, partook of His kindness and mercy, received His counsel and instruction, and enjoyed, as fully as we were capable of enjoying, His glory. But happy and free from care and temptation though we doubtless were, safe from the snares, and dangers, and toils, and pains, and sins that beset us now, we were not perfectly contented. This because we were well aware that we had attained to the highest possible point of excellence — the greatest degree of advancement of which we were capable in the spiritual state. True, we were in heaven, sons and daughters of God, enjoying, no doubt, His fatherly care and protection; but we knew that that was not the highest and greatest destiny the Father had in mind for us. He desired that we should be fathers and mothers, as well as sons and daughters; rulers, as well as subjects; Gods, as well as children of God. This great, expanding, exalted destiny was closed to us, as long as we remained in the spiritual condition.

"We fully knew that we must, first, obtain bodies; second, endure the tests of a temporary separation from our Father; third, form the relationships of husband and wife, parent and child, etc.; fourth, prove ourselves worthy in these relationships, in the midst of sorrow, sin, and suffering. Without these varied experiences, away from our heavenly home, and forgetful of our spiritual life with God, we knew that this higher exaltation would be impossible."— *Anon., "Principles of the Gospel," Part* I., *pp.* 33–34. (*Y. M. M. I. A. Manual.* 1901–02.)

As explained in the foregoing passage, the doctrine of an "earthy probation" for the spirits — or "souls"— of mankind involves that the experiences of life on earth are in some manner necessary for their "perfecting." Why this is true has always been a very real problem to earnest thinkers, quite as insistent, in fact, as the similar query as to why a good God has allowed evil. Whatever may be said in way of criticism or "confutation," however, no one can deny that the explanation here given is both intelligible and plausible. The following passages contain the official explanation of the doctrine.

"Man is spirit. The elements are eternal, and spirit and element, inseparably connected, receiveth a fullness of joy; and when separated, man cannot receive a fullness of joy."— *D. & C.*, xciii. 33–34.

"The spirit and the body is the soul of man. And the resurrection from the dead is the redemption of the soul."— *Ibid.* lxxxviii. 15–16.

Separated from its particular methods of expression, the sense of these passages may be held to be that the spirit of man cannot by any means attain to its proper perfection until incarnated. But this is no new teaching: it is merely a restatement of a belief that has been common to humanity from remote ages: that the spirit and the body shall, at the resurrection, be reunited, and shall continue in association to eternity. This is the Christian doctrine of the resurrection, as well as the Egyptian. Mormonism merely expresses what other teachings have always implied, that this eternal union of the spirit and the body is a necessary and essential condition of blessedness, rather than one merely accidental (so far, at least, as we can derive an intelligible explanation). It also enables us to understand, on these terms, why it is that God, embracing in Himself the sum of all perfections, should logically be regarded as possessed of a proper body.

The doctrine of preexistence coupled with this teaching, however, is of importance in yet another phase of the situation. Briefly expressed, it is capable of explaining in humanly intelligible form the numerous passages of Scripture which have been held to teach the doctrine of foreordination. Indeed, with the acceptance of these passages as literal, not merely "figurative," expressions, we are able, with a belief in eternal preexistence, to justify the "justice of God" to our own minds, without abrogating the freedom of the individual will, which has been a great problem among theologians for many centuries. Coupled with the Mormon doctrine of the "fall" of Adam and the operation of the atonement of Christ, it avoids the further troublesome dilemma of a foreknowing and foreordaining God, who is not also the actual author of sin and evil.

The corollary of this teaching is that the spirits of mankind, gathered, as it were, in a "great council," acquiesced perfectly in all the conditions of earth life; accepting at that time the parts they were to play in the drama of time, in accordance with the purposes of God in inaugurating the plan. Forthwith, Adam was chosen by divine decree to become the progenitor and "patriarch" of the human race; being then appointed to play his part, which, by the terms of this system, also made possible the procreation of the human species. Thus, we may glean the outlines of an idea of the significance of the "fall" of man to the divine economy of the universe. The "fall" was foreseen of God as a part of the plan of "redemption"— which also becomes a necessary, not merely an "accidental," manifestation of divine power — and was participated by Adam, by free choice, and in obedience to the decrees of the "great council" of spirits, although in a very real sense a "transgression," as indicating, in effect, the assertion of the will of a finite intelligence, in opposition to the expressed commands of the Supreme Intelligence. Thus, whether "foreknown," and, in a sense, "sanctioned" by God, or not, it is evident that this act of Adam's involved a very real "new order," in which, contrary to what should be, the human spirit no longer depends upon the divine will and law for its guidance, but rather upon itself. But, as all systems of theology argue in some way, God used the sin of Adam as the starting point of the work of redemption. Here, however, His foreknowledge is not associated with alleged "divine decrees" by which, as the Westminster Confession asserts, "some men and angels are . . . foreordained to everlasting death," but, surprisingly enough, a means, literally, of a higher and completer blessing, as will be explained presently.

Most of the passages of Scripture supposed to teach the doctrine of foreordination may with equal propriety be held to involve the idea of preexistence also, and by no very wide departure from established canons of interpretation. Thus, we read:

> "Before I formed thee in the belly I knew thee; and before thou camest forth out of the womb I sanctified thee, *and* I ordained thee a prophet unto the nations."—*Jer.* i, 5.
>
> "For whom he did foreknow, he also did predestinate *to be* conformed to the image of his Son, that he might be the firstborn among many brethren. Moreover whom he did predestinate, them he also called: and whom he called, them he also justified: and whom he justified, them he also glorified."—*Rom.* viii, 29–30.

In this connection it is needless to argue, on philosophical grounds, that, for God, who "inhabits eternity," foreknowing is knowing, and that what He foresees already exists for Him. On this view, however, the fact that, as stated in Acts xv. 18, "known unto God are all his works from the beginning of the world," involves for the philosopher that they preexisted in a preeminently real sense, as existing for the mind and contemplation of the Almighty: that which exists in time for finite minds exists in eternity for God. If, then, in the words of Christ (Mark xii. 27), "He is not the God of the dead, but the God of the living," involving that Abraham, Isaac, and Jacob still live, even though dead, it is no immense stretching of the sense of this passage to hold that those whom He "foreknew, predestinated, called, justified and glorified," may with propriety be covered by the same statement, even though, at the period mentioned, as yet unborn into the world of time.

As exhibiting the method by which individual freedom of choice is represented as combining with the decisions of God, in establishing the things to be accomplished in earth life, the following from one of the leading scriptures of the Mormon Church, may be quoted as illustration:

> "That Satan, whom thou hast commanded in the name of mine Only Begotten, is the same which was from the beginning, and he came before me, saying — Behold, here am I, send me, I will be thy son, and I will redeem all mankind, that one soul shall not be lost, and surely I will do it; wherefore give me thine honor. But, behold, my Beloved Son, which was my Beloved and Chosen from the beginning, said unto me — Father, thy will be done, and the glory be thine forever. Wherefore, because that Satan rebelled against me, and sought

to destroy the agency of man, which I, the Lord God, had given him, and also, that I should give unto him mine own power; by the power of mine Only Begotten, I caused that he should be cast down; and he became Satan, yea, even the devil, the father of all lies, to deceive and to blind men, and to lead them captive at his will, even as many as would not hearken unto my voice."—*Moses* iv. 1–4.

As may be understood, this passage refers primarily to the "origin of evil" by postulating a "war in heaven," or the "rebellion" of a great archangel, known as Lucifer, the Son of the morning. As embodied in various oriental literatures, and introduced at a comparatively late period into the Bible—although this fact is no argument against its antiquity—the account has varied in differing degrees from the postulation of an eternal "dualism" [as between Ahura-Mazda, the good Creator, and Angro-Manyu, the evil creator, in the system of Zoroaster] to a vague and general belief in the existence of an evil influence in the spiritual world, potent over mankind, but inferior to, and permitted to exist by, God, for some "mysterious reasons." The explanation offered by Joseph Smith, curiously enough, contains the suggestion of a wonderfully clear solution of this problem. We learn here that all spirits, being eternal and uncreated, are in a very real sense "divine." We learn, also, that there are grades and degrees of dignity in the eternal world, as found in certain beings called archangels, seraphim, etc., who, as in the case of Gabriel, "stand in the presence of God" (Luke i. 19). We learn also that the freedom of the will consists in the really ultimate and uncaused character of all spirit life. With these postulates, we may understand much more readily how that Satan, or Lucifer, was a prototvpe in the eternal world of Korah and his company (Num. xvi. 3), who, with his followers, "gathered themselves together against [God] and against [the Eternal Son], and said, Ye take too much upon you, seeing all the congregation are holy, every one of them." Of course, the failure of this eternal spirit to recognize the infinite exaltation of God the Father above him—because accustomed to "stand in his presence"—is of the same description of "blindness" as that in which the traducers of the Eternal Son brought about his crucifixion. This sin explains why it was that Satan fell "as lightning from heaven" (Luke x. 18), also why it was that Judas, the betrayer, "went and hanged himself" (Matt. xxvii. 5).

A very similar solution of the vexed problem of "free will," placing the scene of its operation in a preexistent state of some order, is presented by several philosophers. Thus Prof. Josiah Royce, although basing his argument on a quite different concept of the universe, concludes as follows:

"The limits of a relatively untechnical discussion permit . . . only this dim suggestion of one of the deepest insights of modern philosophy. If it is right, your acts are at once from the temporal point of view absolutely bound, and from the eternal point of view absolutely free. For you enter into the divine order of two ways. In this world you are a fact in time, . . . a creature with just this brain, doomed for countless ages to precisely this conduct. But the whole temporal order is for the absolute Self, of whom you are a part, only one way of looking at truth. All eternity is before him at a glance. He has chosen not temporally, but in an act above all time, yet an act in which you yourself share, to conceive this world which contains you. He has chosen this world for the sake of its worth. And in the estimate that eternally chooses, your will, your time-transcending personality, your consciousness has its part also. You are not morally free to change laws in *this* world. But you are moral and free because you are in the eternal sense a part of the eternal World-Creator, who never made the world at any moment of time, but whose choice of this describable world of time in its wholeness is what constitutes the world of appreciation, which is the world of truth."—*Spirit of Modern Philosophy, pp.* 433–434.

The theologian and the philosopher, despite the wide divergence of their terminologies, are arguing to the same conclusions, and very momentous they are. We may see that both grapple with the problem of a transcendental and eternal essence—term it soul, spirit, or otherwise—involved in the limitations of time and causation. Having found them thus associated, the problem of unraveling the limitation easily appears as very real and consistent. It is not impossible, therefore, to conceive how that the eternal soul of man, associated with worldly limitations by the operation of natural generation, whereby, in some unexplained fashion, he inherits and transmits to his offspring the habit of subservience to these limitations, should require the operation of another order of "generation" to regain his primeval spiritual harmony with God, with a transcendence of all that is involved in sin and death. This, as we shall see, is the very situation to be unraveled in the grand doctrine of salvation.

The following extract from a discourse by Joseph Smith, delivered in 1843, continues the line of explanation already undertaken:

"Salvation is nothing more nor less than to triumph over all our enemies and put them under our feet. And when we have power to put all enemies under our feet in this world, and a knowledge to triumph over all evil spirits in the world to come, then we are saved, as is the case of Jesus, who was to reign until He had put all enemies under His feet, and the last enemy was death.

"Perhaps there are principles here that few men have thought of. *No person can have this salvation except through a tabernacle.*

"Now, in this world, mankind are naturally selfish, ambitious and striving to excel one above another; yet some are willing to build up others as well as themselves. So in the other world there are a variety of spirits. Some seek to excel. And this was the case with

Lucifer when he fell. He sought for things which were unlawful. Hence he was sent down, and it is said he drew many away with him; and the greatness of his punishment is that he shall not have a tabernacle. This is his punishment. So the devil, thinking to thwart the decree of God, by going up and down in the earth, seeking whom he may destroy — any person that he can find that will yield to him, he will bind him, and take possession of the body and reign there, glorying in it mightily, not caring that he had got merely a stolen body; and by-and-by some one having authority will come along and cast him out and restore the tabernacle to its rightful owner. The devil steals a tabernacle because he has not one of his own; but if he steals one, he is always liable to be turned out of doors."— *History of the Church, Vol. V, pp.* 387–388.

It is perhaps unnecessary to call the reader's attention to the fact that herein we have merely an explanation, in the words of Joseph Smith, for the cases of "demoniacal possession," so familiar in Scripture, and so often discussed by Christ Himself. In one case, as will be remembered, the "demons" cast out of a maniac, were allowed to possess the bodies of a herd of swine, as the best available substitute for a human "tabernacle."

As regards the significance of the "fall" of man, it is sufficient to say that we find it represented here, as in other formulations of theology, as a predestined and necessary event; with the notable exception that, in foreordaining it, God had in mind only the larger blessings of the race. Just as the sins and evils, incident on the flesh, appear to be in a very real sense the inevitable accompaniments of life in this world, and as salvation is "nothing more nor less than to Triumph over all our (spiritual) enemies," and, because of this fact, "it is impossible for a man to be saved in ignorance" (*D. and C.* cxxxi. 6), so the transition of the human spirit into an environment in which this order of knowledge is necessary and obtainable, is really the first step in the way of a "higher progression." Thus may we understand the meaning of the Book of Mormon principle, "Adam fell that men might be; and men are, that they might have joy." (II Nephi ii. 25.) The explanation of this principle is given, as follows:

"It has become a common practice with mankind to heap reproaches upon the progenitors of the family, and to picture the supposedly blessed state in which we would be living but for the Fall; whereas our first parents are entitled to our deepest gratitude for their legacy to posterity,— the means of winning glory, exaltation, and eternal lives, on the battlefield of mortality. But for the opportunity thus given, the spirits of God's offspring would have remained forever in a state of innocent childhood; sinless through no effort of their own; negatively saved, not from sin, but from the opportunity of meeting sin; incapable of winning the honors of victory because prevented from taking part in the battle. As it is, they are heirs to the birthright of Adam's descendants,— mortality, with its immeasurable possibilities and its God-given freedom of action. From Father Adam we have inherited all the ills to which flesh is heir; but such are necessarily incident to the knowledge of good and evil, by the proper use of which knowledge man may become even as the Gods."—*James E. Talmage* (*The Articles of Faith, p.* 73).

Roberts develops the same idea as follows:

"To bring to pass these conditions essential to man's earth-experiences, on which is to be builded future progress, the 'fall' must be; which is only another way of saying that the transition from heaven conditions to earth must be made. In no way else could this earth department of God's great university for Intelligences be established. May it not, however, from some points of view be regarded as a misnomer, this 'fall'? certainly it is but an incident in the process of rising to greater heights. It is but the crouch for the spring; the steps backward in order to gain momentum for the rush forward; a descending below all things only that there might be a rising above all things. Such the benefits to arise from the fall; at least to some, and doubtless to the benefit ultimately, of most of the Intelligences that participate in earth-life, though there will be real losses in the adventure. The fall is to eventuate in the advantage of God's children, then, in the main."—*The Seventy's Course in Theology, Fourth Year, pp.* 38–39.

The teachings developed in these passages are stated in the Book of Mormon, as follows:

"If Adam had not transgressed, he would not have fallen; but he would have remained in the Garden of Eden. And all things which were created, must have remained in the same state which they were, after they were created; and they must have remained for ever, and had no end . . . wherefore they would have remained in a state of innocence, . . . doing no good, for they knew no sin. But behold, all things have been done in the wisdom of him who knoweth all things."—II Nephi ii. 22–24.

The view of the "fall" of man, as set forth in these passages involves in a very logical sense that, in this matter at least, Adam was the delegate of God in the consummation of an important part of the grand scheme of salvation, by taking the first step essential to the incarnation, hence, also, to the ultimate "exultation" of the spirits of mankind. Therefore, although recognizing the sad consequences of the "fall" in many particulars, in the origination of sin and evil in the world, and emphasizing the involved necessity of redemption, the person of Adam has been accorded an exalted place in the world of mankind. According to the authoritative literature of the Mormon Church, Adam is identified with the Archangel Michael, also with the Ancient of Days mentioned in the seventh chapter of Daniel. Joseph Smith writes thus about him:

"The Priesthood was first given to Adam; he obtained the First Presidency, and held the keys of it from generation to generation. He obtained it in the Creation, before the world was formed, as in Gen. i. 26, 27, 28. He had dominion given him over every living creature. He is Michael the Archangel, spoken of in the Scriptures. . . . The Priesthood is an everlasting principle, and existed with God from eternity, and will to eternity, without beginning of days or end of years. The keys have to be brought from heaven whenever the Gospel is sent. When they are revealed from heaven it is by Adam's authority.

"Daniel in his seventh chapter speaks of the Ancient of Days; he means the oldest man, our Father Adam, Michael, he will call his children together and hold a council with them to prepare them for the coming of the Son of Man. He (Adam) is the father of the human family, and presides over the spirits of all men, and all that have had the keys must stand before him in this grand council. This may take place before some of us leave this stage of action. The Son of Man stands before him, and there is given him glory and dominion. Adam delivers up his stewardship to Christ, that which was delivered to him as holding the keys of the universe, but retains his standing as head of the human family."—*History of the Church, Vol. III. pp.* 385–387.

As developed in other connections, it is recorded that Adam, as the first holder of the Priesthood among mankind, is appointed the "patriarch" of the human race under the direction of God, precisely, as is held, he played so important a part in the origination of the world in which the spirits of mankind should have opportunity to attain to their proper exaltation. On his installation in Eden, he was given two commands — to "increase and multiply," and to forbear eating of the Tree of Knowledge. Nor is Mormon theology the first connection in which we find the doctrine that these two commands were, in a very real sense, alternatives of action, impossible of performance by the same individual. Neither is it the first connection in which we encounter the situation that God must have given the prohibition against eating of the Tree of Knowledge with full understanding that He would not be obeyed. It is not unreasonable to insist that the command was given as the condition of maintaining his state of primeval innocence, in which the performance of the other command would have been impossible, supposedly. However, it is needless to reason upon alternative explanations. The text of Scripture asserts boldly that by eating of the Tree, thus disobeying God, man became "as gods knowing good and evil" which may be held to be the first step toward the very perfection postulated as the ultimate proper destiny of mankind in this system of theological teaching. The interpretation here given has the advantage over all others whatever in the fact that it gives humanly intelligible explanations of the counsel and predestination of God, which is to say explanations that do not impugn His love, His mercy, and His justice, in the mind and conscience of any rational man.

In the further consideration of the exalted position ascribed to Adam in Mormon theology, we cannot but take notice of the bold comparisons made between him and Christ. The Saviour is called the "Second Adam" (I Cor. xv. 22, 45, 47); Adam is called "the figure of him that was to come" (Rom. v. 14). Thus the "federal headship" of Adam, if we may use a term recognized in theological systematizations long previous to the rise of the Latter-day Gospel, and supposed to explain the fact that all mankind are justly involved in the guilt of Adam's transgression, even before their birth, attains a new emphasis, and rather a better one, since in this case Adam is represented as God's agent in the work of redemption, as well as in achieving the "fall" of man, already foreknown by God. Indeed, the justification for the view that Adam is the actual "Prince" and "Patriarch" of the human race, as well as its "federal Head," as a means merely of proving all mankind guilty of his sin, as set forth by others, is presented in Joseph Smith's explanation of the obscure passages in Daniel vii, describing the throned personage, known as the "Ancient of Days." This passage is interesting in this connection, since, although there is no clear clue to the identity of this personage in the text, it has usually been held that God Himself is referred to. However, the interpretation making him Adam, or some other vicegerent, may be held to be justified in part by the reference to "one like the Son of Man," who came to him. Thus:

> "I saw in the night visions, and, behold, *one* like the Son of man came with the clouds of heaven, and came to the ancient of days, and they brought him near before him. And there was given him dominion, and glory, and a kingdom, that all people, nations, and languages, should serve him: his dominion is an everlasting dominion, which shall not pass away, and his kingdom *that* which shall not be destroyed. . . . and judgment was given to the saints of the Most High; and the time came that the saints possessed the kingdom. . . . And the kingdom and dominion . . . shall be given to the people of the saints of the Most High, whose kingdom is an everlasting kingdom, and all dominions shall serve and obey him."—*Dan.* vii. 13, 14, 22, 27.

It seems evident that the "dominion and glory" are given up to the Son of man by the Ancient of days, which, instead of a delegation of power from God, becomes—and with equal propriety, according to the text—a yielding of authority to a Higher Power by one who had held it as vicegerent. It is evident that, in this view, the passages in Daniel vii. bear some sort of analogy in idea to that contained in I Cor. xv. 24–28; the two being, in fact, consecutive. In the second it is said Christ himself "delivered up the kingdom to God, even the Father."

The belief that some such "vicegerency was actually awarded to Adam by divine decree is set forth in the following passage:

> "Three years previous to the death of Adam, he called Seth, Enos, Cainan, Mahaleel, Jared, Enoch, and Methuselah, who were all High Priests, with the residue of his posterity who were righteous, into the valley of Adam-ondi-Ahman, and there bestowed upon them his last

blessing. And the Lord appeared unto them, and they rose up and blessed Adam, and called him Michael, the Prince, the Archangel. And the Lord administered comfort unto Adam, and said unto him, I have set thee to be at the head — a multitude of nations shall come of thee, and thou art a prince over them for ever. And Adam stood up in the midst of the congregation, and notwithstanding he was bowed down with age, being full of the Holy Ghost, predicted whatsoever should befall his posterity unto the latest generation. These things are all written in the book of Enoch, and are to be testified of in due time."— *Doctrine and Covenants,* cvii. 53–57.

The peculiar regard for Adam manifested in Mormon theology, coupled with the terms in which he has been mentioned by some of their authorities, has given rise to the popular idea that Adam is really identified with God. Thus, as frequently urged by hostile critics, President Young once said that Adam is "our father and our God," also, "the only God with whom we have to do." Whether or not Young actually intended to convey the ideas that his words suggest, or merely did not realize the possible connotation of his words, it is altogether certain that the Mormon Church holds to no doctrine by which Adam is represented as anyone other than a being eternally inferior to God the Father. Undoubtedly this alleged doctrine of Mormonism, which mean minds have ruthlessly advertised, without any investigation whatever, is, like other "obnoxious doctrines," ascribed to this system, more properly a matter of words than of ideas. As we shall see later, this identical situation is involved in the use of the word "gods" in this theology; thus giving the wanton enemies of this Church the opportunity to accuse it of teaching polytheism, which is very far from the truth of the matter, as must be acknowledged in the simple cause of justice, truth-telling, and intelligence. It is an excellent thing to investigate sufficiently to discover what a man really says, or a system really teaches, before proceeding to condemn it for "harmful errors." The allegation in regard to the alleged "Adam-God doctrine" is thus discussed in a letter, under date Feb. 20, 1912, addressed by the First Presidency of the Church to one of its missionaries, who, as it seems, had been reproached with this doctrine by opponents:

"You speak of the 'assertion made by Brigham Young that Jesus was begotten of the Father in the flesh by our father Adam, and that Adam is the father of Jesus Christ and not the Holy Ghost,' and you say that Elders are challenged by certain critics to prove this.

"If you will carefully examine the sermon to which you refer, in the Journal of Discourses, Vol. I., you will discover that, while President Young denied that Jesus was 'begotten by the Holy Ghost,' he did not affirm, in so many words, that 'Adam is the father of Jesus Christ in the flesh.' He said, 'Jesus, our elder brother, was begotten in the flesh by the same character that was in the Garden of Eden and who is our Father in Heaven.' Who is our 'Father in Heaven'? Here is what

President Young said about him: 'Our Father in Heaven begat all the spirits that ever were or ever will be upon this earth, and they were born spirits in the eternal world. Then the Lord by his power and wisdom organized the mortal tabernacle of man.' Was He in the Garden of Eden? Surely He gave commandments to Adam and Eve; He was their Father in Heaven; they worshipped Him, and taught their children after the fall to worship and obey Him, in the name of the Son who was to come.

"But President Young went on to show that our father Adam,—that is, our earthly father,—the progenitor of the race of men, stands at our head, being 'Michael the Archangel, the Ancient of Days,' and that he was not fashioned from earth like an adobe, but begotten by his Father in Heaven. Adam is called in the Bible 'the Son of God' (Luke iii. 38). It was our Father in Heaven who begat the spirit of him who was 'the Firstborn' of all the spirits that come to this earth, and who was also his Father by the Virgin Mary, making him the 'Only Begotten in the flesh.' Read Luke i. 26–35. Where is Jesus called the 'Only Begotten of the Holy Ghost'? He is always singled out as the 'Only Begotten of the Father.' . . . The Holy Ghost came upon Mary, and her conception was under that influence, even of the spirit of life; our Father in Heaven was the Father of the Son of Mary, to whom the Savior prayed, as did our earthly father Adam.

"When President Young asked, 'Who is the Father'? he was speaking of Adam as the father of our earthly bodies, who is at our head, as revealed in Doctrine and Covenants, Section cvii, verses 53–56. In that sense he is one of the gods referred to in numerous scriptures, and particularly by Christ (John x, 34–36). He is the great Patriarch, the Ancient of Days, who will stand in his place as 'a Prince over us forever,' and with whom we shall 'have to do,' as each family will have to do with its head, according to the holy patriarchal order. Our father Adam, perfected and glorified as a god, will be the being who will carry out the behests of the great Elohim in relation to his posterity (Daniel vii. 9-14).

"While, as Paul puts it, 'there be gods many and lords many (whether in heaven or in earth), unto us there is but one God the Father, of whom are all things, and one Lord Jesus Christ by whom are all things.' The Church of Jesus Christ of Latter-day Saints worships Him, and Him alone, who is the Father of Jesus Christ, whom He worshipped, whom Adam worshipped, and who is God the Eternal Father of us all."

Although, as must be admitted in all honesty, this statement is a perfectly candid and straightforward presentation of the Mormon position on this much discussed issue, it is, nevertheless, difficult to make the matter entirely clear to a non-Mormon mind. It must be said, therefore, that the position of Adam, even as stated in Brigham Young's much-discussed remark, is merely a corollary, and a very logical one, of the exalted idea of the sacredness of organization held among the Mormons, rather than of any tendency to deify a man. It is their belief that the organization of their Church is merely a duplicate of the organization of the universe of spirits. Thus, in discussing the doctrine of the Godhead, it is not uncommon to hear mention of the "Great Presidency in Heaven," which, like the Presidency of the Church on earth, is composed of Three Personages. The "federal headship" of Adam, therefore, involves that he is a factor in a great organization, which is composed of all the spirits of mankind, who exist on earth, or who have already existed. In this capacity, he discharges his functions as the first and foremost holder of the Priesthood on earth. Since, also, "when the keys of Gospel ordinances are revealed from heaven, it is by Adam's authority," there is an involved suggestion that the holders of priestly authority are, in a sense, personally under his direction. B. H. Roberts explains the matter as follows:

"The Scriptures represent in many places the existence of a plurality of divine personages, how many we do not know, and it does not matter. But we hear of God saying, 'Let us make man in our image'; 'the man has become as one of us, knowing good and evil'; 'God standeth in the congregation of the Mighty, he judgeth among the Gods' . . . 'I have said Ye are Gods, and all of you are children of the most High.' The last a passage of the Psalms, quoted and defended by the Savior as a justification of his own claim to sonship with God. And now, if the great archangel, Michael, or Adam, is among that number of exalted, divine souls, what more fitting than that the father of the human race shall become the great presiding patriarch of our earth and its redeemed inhabitants; and the one with whom our race would most immediately have to do? What sacrilege is there in this thought? Is it not reasonable that it should be so?"—*Answer to the Ministerial Association Review, p.* 17.

In accord with the "patriarchal" concept of the government of the universe, the "fall" of man, as already seen, was an integral part of the divine plan for man's exaltation. Thus, the view that it was a distinct benefit reaches its height in the following passage from the Pearl of Great Price:

"And in that day Adam blessed God and was filled, and began to prophesy concerning all the families of the earth, saying: Blessed be the name of God, for because of my transgression my eyes are opened, and in this life I shall have joy, and again in the flesh I shall see God.

"And Eve, his wife, heard all these things and was glad, saying: Were it not for our transgressions we never should have had seed, and never should have known good and evil, and the joy of our redemption, and the eternal life which God giveth unto all the obedient."—*Moses* v. 10–11.

The expressions so far given very closely suggest that this accepted teaching on the "fall" is quite in harmony with the findings of current optimism in theology and life. This is not wholly true, however, since the fact of Adam's sin and the need of an atonement are in no sense lost to sight.

Continuing the discussion of the atonement given in a former quotation, Roberts proceeds as follows:

"But Adam did sin. He did break the law, which is sin, and violation of law involves the violator in its penalties, as surely as effect follows cause. Upon this principle depends the dignity and majesty of law. Take this fact away from moral government and your moral laws become mere nullities. Therefore, notwithstanding Adam fell that men might be, and that in his transgression there was at bottom a really exalted motive — a motive that contemplated nothing less than bringing to pass the highly necessary purposes of God with respect to man's existence in the earth — yet his transgression of law was real; he did brave the conditions that would be brought into existence by his sin; it was followed by certain moral effects in the nature of men and in the world. The harmony of things was broken; discord ruled; changed relations between God and men took place; moral and intellectual darkness, sin and death — death, the wages of sin — stalked through the world, and made necessary the Atonement for man, and his redemption." —"*The Atonement*," (*The Seventy's Course in Theology, p.* 39).

"Not only must the sin of Adam be atoned, but satisfaction must be made for the sins of every man, if the integrity of the moral government of the world is to be preserved.

"Man is just as helpless with reference to his own, individual sins, as Adam was with reference to his sin. Man when he sins by breaking the laws of God, sins of course against divine law; commits a crime against the majesty of God, and thereby dishonors him. And man is just as helpless to make adequate satisfaction to God, I repeat, as Adam was for his sin in Eden; and is just as hopelessly in the grasp of inexorable law as Adam and his race were after the first transgression. For individual man from the beginning was as much in duty bound to keep the law of God as Adam was; and if now, in the present and for the future he observes the law of God and remains righteous, he is doing no more than he ought to have done from the beginning; and doing his duty now and for the future can not free him from the consequences of his past violations of God's law. The individual man, then, is just as much in need of a satisfaction being made to the justice of God for his individual transgression of divine law, for his violence to the honor of God, for his insult to the majesty of God, as was Adam for his sin."— *Ibid. pp.* 98–99.

In the reading of these passages the informed reader must recognize their consistency with commonly-received opinions on the subject of Christ's atonement, although with the obvious difference that the Mormon Articles of Faith distinctly aver the belief "that men will be punished for their own sins, and not for Adam's transgression." (Article 2.)

CHAPTER XVI

THE DOCTRINES OF ATONEMENT, RELIGIOUS DUTY, AND PERSONAL RIGHTEOUSNESS

THE doctrine of the atonement, as explained by Mormon preachers and writers, is eminently reasonable and beautiful. Its operation also is set forth in no uncertain terms. Thus, in the words of Brigham Young:

"There never was, and never will be, a world created and redeemed except by the shedding of the blood of the Saviour of that world. I know why the blood of Jesus was shed. . . . It is all to answer a purpose. Adam subjected himself to the conditions of this world, as did our Lord and Master, that redemption and exaltation might come to man. Without descending below all things, we cannot rise above all things. The gospel of salvation will never change. It is the same in all ages of the world and will be through all the ages of eternity."—"*Wilford Woodruff*," (*Cowley*) *pp.* 447–448.

The operation of Christ's atoning power is thus explained by Roberts:

"To bring to pass the redemption of man from the Fall—the effect of which was to subject the race to the power of death and the bond of sin—a Redeemer was provided in the person of Jesus Christ, the second personage of the God-head; who, being possessed of the power of the resurrection in his own person, broke the bands of death and released man from the power thereof, by bringing to pass the resurrection from the dead, a reality in which all men born into the world will ultimately participate. Jesus Christ also released men from the bondage of their own sins on condition of their acceptance of the principles of His Gospel, and obedience to the laws and ordinances thereof."—*Mormonism, its Origin and History, pp.* 36–37.

President John Taylor gives the following:

"In some mysterious, incomprehensible way, Jesus assumed the responsibility which naturally would have devolved upon Adam; but which could only be accomplished through the mediation of Himself, and by taking upon Himself their sorrows, assuming their responsibilities, and bearing their transgressions or sins. In a manner to us incomprehensible and inexplicable, He bore the weight of the sins of the whole world; not only of Adam, but of his posterity; and in doing that, opened the Kingdom of Heaven, not only to all believers and all who obeyed the law of God, but to more than one half of the human family who die before they come to years of maturity, as well as to the heathen, who, having died without law, will, through His mediation, be resurrected without law, and be judged without law, and thus participate, according to their capacity, works, and worth, in the blessings of his atonement." —"*Mediation and Atonement*," *pp.* 148–149.

The following explanation occurs in the writings of the Prophet Joseph Smith:

"The Son . . . ordained from before the foundation of the world to be a propitiation for the sins of all those who should believe on his name . . . descended in suffering below that which man can suffer; or, in other words, suffered greater sufferings, and was exposed to more powerful contradictions than any man can be. But, notwithstanding all this, he kept the law of God, and remained without sin, showing thereby that it is in the power of man to keep the law and remain also without sin; and also, that by him a righteous judgment might come upon all flesh."—*Lectures on Faith*, V.

"For, behold, the Lord your Redeemer suffered death in the flesh; wherefore he suffered the pain of all men, that all men might repent and come unto him. And he hath risen again from the dead, that he might bring all men unto him, on conditions of repentance."—*Doctrine and Covenants, Section* 18, 11–12.

Through all of these explanations of this august doctrine a distinct logical consistency is manifest. The souls of mankind, subjected to the limiting conditions of material earth-life, which inevitably involve the existence of sin and death, because of the vividness of sense experience, etc., gradually tend to forget God and the "glory which [they] had with him before the world was." And this is the sum total of all that is sin. They become blinded and incapable in respect to spiritual things through the domination in their minds of considerations gross and sensuous. It is obviously impossible, therefore, that they could, by and through their own efforts, transcend the limitations into which they have been born.

The logical consequence is that an "intervention" must take place. Thus it is that the Son of God himself becomes a man, "in all points tempted as are we," emptying himself, as the Apostle Paul informs us, of all his dignities and powers, and becoming poor for our sakes. Yet, because he was, even as man, also a perfected man he alone could achieve the mastery of conditions common to humanity, and rising above them, even above a death of torture and ignominy, demonstrate to man and God alike the possibilities of God-assisted humanity. Therefore, as a consequence of his "atonement," which is to say, his reconciliation, the sin and "fall" of Adam ceases to appear in the eyes of God as an obstacle or barrier to man's restoration to spiritual life on a plane of higher development, and is thus said to have been "forgiven" through Christ. In other words, the achievements of Christ have brought to a demonstration the truth that man's nature was not irretrievably ruined by the "fall," and that God's "experiment" is not a failure. Human nature in the person of Christ has stood the uttermost test and remained faithful to the heavenly vision. And this same test is possible to, even if not required of, all men whose hearts are set into harmony with God's will, and whose trust is in Him.

There are many figures that might be used to symbolize the atoning act of Christ; but the following from Professor John A. Widtsoe will excellently suffice:

"Conditions that may be likened to the atonement are found in science. Suppose an electrical current, supplying a whole city with power and light, is passing through a wire. If for any reason the wire is cut the city becomes dark and all machines driven by the current cease their motion. If a person, in his anxiety to restore the city to its normal conditions, seizes the ends of the wire with his bare hands, and unites them, he probably will receive the full charge of the current in his body. Yet, as a result, the light and power will return to the city; and one man by his action, has succeeded in doing the work for many." —*Science and the Gospel, p.* 119.

Mormon theology, however, discriminates the action of the atonement into two distinct and separate channels of application, which may be described as the general and the particular. In accordance with the analysis of the doctrine, as given above, the general application is concerned with God's view of the matter, and consists in virtually neutralizing the effects of Adam's sin, which, from henceforth and forever, is done away, blotted out and forgotten by God. The human race has been reborn according to the generation of the "Second Adam, the Lord from heaven."

Thus, by Christ's act in restoring the broken circuit between God and man, all humanity stands before Him in the same relation, perfectly restored, as that occupied by Adam before the fall, with the exception, however, that every man must "work out his own salvation" by obedience to the law and ordinances of the Gospel. And here comes in the personal, or special, application.

From the foregoing we may see the force of the article in the Articles of Faith announcing that "men shall be punished for their own sins, and not for Adam's transgression." Furthermore, by these two lines of application there is struck a surprisingly beautiful balance, avoiding the extremes alike of the doctrine of universal salvation, as formulated by the New England reaction against Calvinism, and the traditional teaching that mankind are doubly burdened with their own and Adam's sins.

Explaining the universal application of Christ's atoning power, Professor Orson Pratt writes, as follows:

"We believe that through the sufferings, death, and atonement of Jesus Christ, all mankind, without exception, are to be completely and fully redeemed, body and spirit, from the endless banishment and curse to which they were consigned by Adam's transgression; and that this universal salvation and redemption of the whole human family from the endless penalty of the original sin, is effected without any conditions, whatever, on their part; that is, they are not required to repent, or be baptized, or do anything else, in order to be redeemed from that penalty; for whether they believe or disbelieve; whether they repent or remain impenitent; whether they are baptized or unbaptized; whether they keep the commandments or break them; whether they are righteous or unrighteous, it will make no difference in relation to their redemption, both soul and body, from the penalty of Adam's transgression. The most righteous man that ever lived on the earth, and the most wicked wretch of the whole human family, were both placed under the same curse without any transgression or agency of their own, and they both alike will be redeemed from that curse without any agency or conditions on their part."

Because Christ, through His death and resurrection, "brought life and immortality to light," on the plane of earth experience, which is the plane of intelligent comprehension, He made available to mankind the means of finding God, each man for himself, in the world of earth experience, and through association with Him in the appointed ways of achieving a complete restoration of spiritual harmony with the Father. These appointed ways are (a) compliance with the "ordinances of the Gospel," and (b) the fulfilling of the law of righteousness.

In the teachings upon the matter of fulfilling the law of righteousness we find a healthy consistency with the conclusions of life experience and sound reason; avoiding the extremes of several systems of theology, which seem to have set an exaggerated estimate upon the divine requirements in this particular. It is noticeable, however, that the common line of teachings on "human disability," "total depravity," and the like, which assert man's impotence to do God's will, or to obey the positive commands given by him, have acted in many instances to discount the value of even the commonest social virtues and to encourage, in effect, their actual neglect. Thus, in the commonly-received Protestant doctrine of "salvation by faith" (assent) the supreme virtue is made to consist in the mere act of believing a given line of teachings, which is supposed to insure salvation, even with the commission of mean and unethical sins, which are only too common among all peoples to require designation. It is a sad comment on the logical sense of most formulators of traditional systems that they have neglected to follow the plain Scriptural teaching that in the God-led Christian life a man is to be endowed with power to fulfill the moral and ethical law to a sufficient extent to please God, who knows his limitations, and that when he fails notably in this matter it is because he is more devoted to the world and its concerns than to the commands of God, as he professes.

We must consider, therefore, that the teaching of religion should emphasize righteousness as a duty, equal at least with the act of believing, and as the test of the reality of belief, or "faith," rather than an incidental — too often, also, a negligible — quantity. This is true because, in ultimate constitution, both the individual and the social order presuppose, for their normal continuance, the fulfilment of the very duties most emphasized by Christ and most often neglected in Christian performance. Nor are these only the line of virtues usually classed as "moral," those relating to "purity," "temperance," and the like, but those usually classed as "ethical" also, the "weightier matters of the law"—"justice, mercy and truth"— the avoidance of the sins of pride, covetousness, self-aggrandisement, the amassing of useless wealth, and the development of a spirit of indifference to the sufferings of humanity, which latter is a notable mark of what is usually labeled "aristocratic." Had the clever formulations of the Calvins, and others of similar tendencies, been sufficiently logical to recognize the true Scriptural teaching in this matter, we should have had a nearer approach to Christ's advocated standards of right living and fewer serious "social problems" to confront us at the present day, with the long train of "solutions" of an utterly unreligious character.

The simple truth is, in this matter, that a "perfect man" in the eyes of God's law is not of necessity an archangel, any more than a perfect animal of any species — according to the standard that may be adopted in any given case — approximates at all to characteristics usually classed as "human." Whether or not, therefore, good works can merit salvation, as is denied by the traditional "confessions" and creeds, it remains true that they are enjoined upon man as emphatically as is faith itself. The question of their intrinsic worth is not to enter into the discussion; since, whether as mere promises of payment, without "collateral," or coin current at full face value, God has declared that they are acceptable to Him as duties done and demands performed, which are to be requited by Him, according to the faith and devotion which they demonstrate ("show," as in James ii, 17–18).

James E. Talmage, writing of faith as a consequence of accepting the teachings and work of Christ, has this:

"Inasmuch as salvation is attainable only through the mediation and atonement of Christ, and since this is made applicable to individual sin only in the cases of those who obey the laws of righteousness, faith in Jesus Christ is indispensable to salvation. . . . As is fitting for so priceless a pearl, it is given to those only who show by their sincerity that they are worthy of it, and who give promise of abiding by its dictates. Although faith is called the first principle of the Gospel of Christ, though it be in fact the foundation of all religion, yet even faith is preceded by sincerity of disposition and humility of soul, whereby the word of God may make an impression upon the heart. . . . Faith is a passive sense, that is achieve as mere belief, is inefficient as a means of salvation. This truth was clearly set forth by Christ and the apostles, and the vigor with which it was declared may be an indication of the early development of a most pernicious doctrine — that of justification by belief alone. The Saviour taught that works were essential to the validity of profession and the efficacy of faith."—*Articles of Faith, pp.* 110–111.

Dr. Talmage then proceeds to justify his contention by quoting such passages of Scripture as Matt. vii, 21; John xiv, 21; James ii, 14–18; I John ii, 3–5, and concludes:

"Yet in spite of the plain word of God, sectarian dogmas have been promulgated to the effect that by faith alone man may achieve salvation, and that a mere profession of belief shall open the doors of heaven to the sinner. The Scriptures cited and man's inherent sense of justice furnish a sufficient refutation of these false teachings."—*Ibid. p.* 112.

According to Mormon teachings, the acceptance of the truth of the Gospel must be followed by repentance, which involves a sense of sin and the desire for forgiveness. This latter end is achieved in the rite of baptism, which, as with John the Baptist, is held to be "for the remission of sins." This act, however, does not sanctify or blanket subsequent ill-doings, nor furnish excuse or palliation for persistence in evil practices. But, as faith is declared to be a "gift of God," so also is the ability to fulfil the law of righteousness a gift of the Spirit, as a consequence of faith. At this point we may understand how that belief in the reality of "spiritual gifts" is highly logical and practical. Roberts writes thus:

"But after forgiveness of past sins the human weakness still remains, human inclination to sin still drives man on toward error, and his imperfect judgment is not sufficient to guide him aright; his human strength alone is not sufficient to make him equal to the task of living in harmony with the divine law. God knew this would be the condition of man, and hence provided in His gospel the baptism of the Holy Ghost through the ordinance of laying-on of hands, by which this baptism is effected. By this baptism of the Spirit man's life is brought in touch with the spirit life of God, and some of God's strength imparted to him, by reason of which he may hope to overcome the world, the flesh and the devil. He receives in the companionship of the Holy Ghost, and the privilege of perpetually walking within the circle of His influence, an unction from the Holy One, by which he may know all things, an anointing which, if it abide upon him, will teach him all things. Under this companionship and its influence man begins the work of character-building, which at the last shall prepare him to dwell with God."—*Mormonism, its Origin and History, p.* 38.

While it is true that the Mormon Church, quite as much as any other, would be inclined to discount the Godward value of "works done by unregenerate men"—emphasizing as it does the need of performing the divinely-ordained ordinances, particularly baptism, which it declares necessary to salvation, or admission to the higher glories of the Kingdom of God — it makes the most elaborate provisions for ensuring the end of righteous living, in all that the expression connotes, among its people. Indeed, in its familiar phrases, "salvation of the earth," "salvation of the total man," "salvation of society," it expresses a wider and completer idea of salvation than that of the individual soul merely. That it is essentially a social system is demonstrated in its "hierarchic" organization, which, in effect, reorganizes human society on a religious basis, doing as much as seems humanly or terrestrially possible to enable the living of a righteous life by all its members. Thus, as is explained in the section dealing with this organization, the element of close and constant association of each member of the Church, with all others, first with the members of his own quorum, and through it with all other quorums, to the very highest, makes him a factor in a strongly organized machine; giving him such assistance, spiritual, moral and temporal, as he may require, also moving him to form the habit of helpfulness to others, as a part of his religious duties. This element of strong organization and close association undoubtedly begets a sense of fellow-feeling among men — the very thing most needed in these days of social perplexities. The claim is that this very organization was revealed for the purpose of achieving the development of superior personal and social righteousness, impossible without some such device. Indeed, the failure of traditional systems to counteract social and moral difficulties, as well as the familiar derogation of formal righteousness, are held to be notable evidences of their "apostasy" — they have ignored the divine institutions of society, and have thus lost the power of the "priesthood." It would seem reasonable, indeed, that God, requiring the development of social virtues, and allowing such sad perversions to result from their neglect — and we see enough of this sort of thing nowadays — should have provided a mechanism in His Church that should be capable of assisting materially in the work of fulfilling His commands. Nor is the claim that a stable and vital organization, when working to achieve such ends, directly evidences its own divine authority and origin by any means absurd. Christ put the "duty to the neighbor" — "Thou shalt love thy neighbor as thyself" — second only to the "duty toward God"; but he talked about it very much oftener, and frequently came near to identifying the two (I John iv. 20–21). If, then, as is claimed, he founded his Church, with authority to preach his Gospel and administer the ordinances of religion, for the glory of God and the salvation of mankind, it would seem nearly inevitable that he should endow it with the proper means of fulfilling his constantly urged commands regarding the ethical duties, which should redeem society from its "problems" and perplexities. It is a sad thing that we must record that this evident truth was lost to sight for eighteen hundred years, and that, as we must confess, no one, reformer or otherwise, thought of it as a necessary element in Gospel administration, until the day of Joseph Smith.

Because the Mormon gospel stands upon this evident New Testament basis of emphasizing temporal and social well-being, and the virtues upon which these depend, nearly the first act of Joseph Smith, after the foundation of his church, was to inaugurate the United Order, or Order of Enoch, whose object was to realize practical cooperation for the common good. This Order, which attempted to carry out on a consistent scale the community of goods practiced by the ancient saints at Jerusalem, was one of the most interesting and significant sociological movements of modern times. Its discontinuance as a practical reality by no means eliminated the ideals which it embodied, and its restoration, as the highest type of divine righteousness in human society, is confidently expected. Indeed, while making no attempt to remodel the customs of society, the whole organization of the Church still maintains loyalty to this noble ideal.

It would be difficult to see how the organization of the "hierarchy" could operate otherwise than to the temporal and moral advantage of all concerned. Indeed, it supplies an excellent model for such a reorganization of society on a religious basis as shall insure the happiness and well-being of a goodly majority, as against the present absurd and brutal social order which speciously harbors, on the one hand, complacent self-righteousness, fatly thriving on worldly advantage and solaced with the alleged "blessed assurances" of a debased "Christianity," and, on the other, black despair, filthy vice and degrading poverty, so that neither interferes with the other. Traditional religion leaves society utterly unorganized, and offers no encouragement, except for those who may be

> "Lured by hope of some diviner drink
> To fill the cup that's crumbled into dust."

In broad contrast with these performances, or lack of performances, Mormonism has always had a very important "temporal side," which has drawn railing accusations from its critics, who violently denounce any public, social and industrial activities in a professedly religious body, simply because their own sects have demonstrated their complete futility in their impotence before the great moral and sociological complications of the times. In this one particular, as will be explained later, the Mormon gospel contains a real and valid message and example to the whole world in these days of social and moral unrest. On this point President Joseph F. Smith writes as follows:

> "No sacred system of government, having in view the salvation of the bodies as well as the spirits of men, can successfully accomplish its mission without being temporal as well as spiritual in character. It was the doctrine of Joseph Smith, the original revelator of 'Mormonism,' that the spirit and the body constitute the soul of man. It has always been a cardinal teaching with the Latter-day Saints, that a religion which has not the power to save people temporally and make them prosperous and happy here, cannot be depended upon to save them spiritually, and exalt them in the life to come."—*The Truth about Mormonism, Out West*, Sept., 1905, *p.* 242.

The Mormon Church is thus the first body claiming to be the true Church which has promulgated the theory that this claim must be made good, according to the New Testament standard, that a tree is to be judged as good or evil, according to its fruits. Says Charles Ellis:

> "I do not care for these cries of fraud against Smith and Mormonism any more than I do for the same cries that have rung down the centuries against Jesus and His religion. The only question is—what have these alleged frauds done for the good of mankind? 'Christianity' has shed more blood than all other systems and powers on earth, and civilization has come in spite of it. What has 'Mormonism' done, what is it doing? Christianity has given martyrs to its cause—so has Mormonism, and Mormonism has given help, home and happiness to many thousands of Christians who would have known neither without its helping hand. Very early in the career of the Mormon Church the principle of cooperation was set up as the line along which the Church should work for 'the brotherhood of man,' and while it has never been realized as anticipated, several attempts have been made that have been at least partially successful, even against bitter opposition by government officials and anti-Mormons in general. . . . Owing to the many adversities against which the Church and people have had to struggle the principle of cooperation may be said to be yet largely latent, but it is deeply rooted in the minds of the people that the time is sure to come when cooperation will exist wherever it can be made practicable among Mormons. . . . Below it is the theological belief that this world, practically as it is now, is to be the home of the people who lived upon it in mortal life, through that endless life upon which they will enter 'in the resurrection,' and cooperation will then be the rule. . . . Brigham Young, all admit, was a wonderful colonizer. Yet his work was all done to carry out this Mormon idea of an eternal life on this very world. His policy has been followed. The Mormon leaders have bought land for the Church in most of these mountain states and territories, as well as in Mexico and Canada. Why? Because they, for their people, could buy vastly more advantageously than individuals could. But that land the Church sells on easy terms to its immigrants, and so welcomes them by cooperation and brotherhood.
>
> "Whether Mormonism is right or wrong, its this-world-religion of cooperation and brotherhood-of-man seems to have been and to continue to be good for the Mormon people,—and why should we not all admit

the fact? Mormonism is a practical every-day religion of this life and this world looking upon the advancement of its people here as the best preparation for that eternal life they expect to live on this same world 'in the resurrection.' All peoples have equal right to form and hold their opinions as to the meaning and purpose of this life and that which is to come, and, therefore, it strikes me that among religious sects Mormonism has achieved sufficient success to give it a pull strong enough to withstand all ministerial and political misrepresentation and abuse. If I were a Mormon I should not be uneasy as to the result."—*Christian and Mormon Doctrines, pp.* 32–35.

In the study of the Mormon system, in spite of the partial explanations given by most authorities, and the evident crudities of style and expression found in the writings of some of its prominent exponents in the past, one catches, every now and then, sure glimpses, apparently, of a grand and admirable philosophy, behind and beneath all its principles. Thus, strange as it may seem to the casual reader, this "materialism" of which we hear so much, this "this-world religion" of practical ideals and standards, appears as an essential element in a consistent and far-reaching scheme of salvation that is to include, not only the spirits and bodies of mankind, but also the earth itself, which, according also to very many Bible commentators other than Mormons, is to be the eternal home of the blessed.

Furthermore, as it seems, this salvation, or redemption, of the earth from the "curse" need not wait wholly upon the miraculous interposition of God: man himself is the appointed instrument of its achievement. He is to figure forth the divine life in his own person, and is to make the earth the habitation of a redeemed race, which, upon the return of the Lord Jesus Christ and the resurrection of the righteous, shall be transformed, so as to eliminate all traces of the strife and stress under which it has suffered hitherto. It will be, in short, a fitting habitation for the sons and daughters of God, a material world, but a world of refined, perfected, purified material, in which, as in the form of a crystal, is to be found the most perfect equilibrium of natural forces in matter. This grand idea is expressed among some "important items of instruction," given by Joseph Smith, as follows:

"The angels do not reside on a planet like this earth. But they reside in the presence of God, on a globe like a sea of glass and fire, where all things for their glory are manifest—past, present, and future, and are continually before the Lord. The place where God resides is a great Urim and Thummim.

"This earth, in its sanctified and immortal state, will be made like unto crystal and will be a Urim and Thummim to the inhabitants who dwell thereon, whereby all things pertaining to an inferior kingdom, or all kingdoms of a lower order, will be manifest to those who dwell on it; and this earth will be Christ's."—*Doctrine and Covenants, Sec.* cxxx. 6–9.

"The spirit and the body is the soul of man. And the resurrection from the dead is the redemption of the soul; and the redemption of the soul is through him who quickeneth all things, in whose bosom it is decreed that the poor and the meek of the earth shall inherit it. Therefore it must needs be sanctified from all unrighteousness, that it may be prepared for the celestial glory; for after it hath filled the measure of its creation, it shall be crowned with glory, even with the presence of God the Father; that bodies who are of the celestial kingdom may possess it forever and ever; for, for this intent was it made and created, and for this intent are they sanctified."—*Ibid. Sec.* lxxxviii. 15-20.

In contemplating this noble ideal of the earth's destiny, we gain a new insight into the essential relation between righteousness and the service of God. Mankind are not merely God's beneficiaries, but, literally, His coadjutors, His instruments in perfecting the work of creation. And this work must occupy all their time and efforts. The virtues commanded by the law of God are included in the law not because God chose to call one thing good and another unlawful, but because, in an order such as the present one, certain acts are consistent elements in the grand perspective of human and terrestrial perfection and redemption, and others are inconsistent. Thus, as in every harmony, each separate instrument, each particular note, must be perfectly attuned to its part in the total effect—otherwise, the harmony is imperfect—so each human element in God's grand symphony of redemption must take its part perfectly, and in complete harmony with all others. We may see, also, that, while the importance of the moral virtues, purity, temperance, etc., as very real forms of piety—our bodies being "temples of the Holy Ghost"—cannot be too highly estimated, it remains true, nevertheless, that those which express the "duty to man," justice, mutual helpfulness, brotherly kindness, and the like, traditionally neglected to so large an extent, are of no lesser importance or significance. It is a real revelation to the world, this proclamation that man must be perfected socially, as well as personally: it had been almost altogether forgotten.

In view of the principles just explained, it seems reasonable to assert that we find in this system an idea of the essential nature of the Church of God which contains notable elements of improvement on the one existing in popular acceptation, or understanding. We cannot deny that there has been, hitherto, altogether too much of a tendency to picture the Church somewhat under the similitude of a lifeboat filled with the salvage of a shipwreck, its passengers receiving their seats and titles to safety through "grace" or favoritism, and having as their greatest obligation to feel a gratefulness to the Author of their rescue. Thus, it is, that, in current estimation, a man "joins the Church" for the sole purpose of "saving his soul." It is needless to state that the Biblical authority for this view is extremely imperfect; the actual theory of the Church, as found in Scripture, being that of a "peculiar people," chosen by God for a special work and mission in the world — precisely as He chose the descendants of Abraham — and to be favored with special instructions for their guidance, and endowed with peculiar gifts and capacities for fulfilling the duties specified in this law. In other words, instead of a crowd of cowering refugees or survivors from some calamitous happening, the Church should be considered rather, as in the words of John the Revelator, an order of "kings and priests unto God." Nor should it be only, considered in this light, in the estimation of its members and advocates — it should not be so called, merely, just as one race is called Mongols and another Kaffirs, and to be distinguished from one another by no evident moral or spiritual orders of superiority, apart from their mental and physical attributes — but should evidently embody reasonable and effective means for rendering them actually capable of embodying, in some measure, the qualities involved in kingly and priestly dignities.

With evident apprehension of some such idea, Mormonism postulates directly that the preparation of the individual soul to discharge the functions of a true son of God must consist in literal exercise of the spiritual endowments specified in Scripture. Thus, in the ordinance of the laying-on of hands of the Higher Priesthood, a man is believed to receive directly the gift of the Holy Ghost, which involves that the divine life is imparted to him, henceforth to dwell in him, and that actually, not formally or by imputation merely, he becomes a "new creature" and a "partaker in the divine nature." The awful responsibility involved in this new creation of his being must be expressed inevitably in the discharge of the duties and obligation specified in the commands of Christ, and foreshadowed in the law of Moses. Nor does this indwelling of the Holy Ghost involve merely an unconscious formative influence at work in his inward parts, resulting in the refined susceptibilities and the "lofty sentiments," which are so habitually associated with the word "spirituality" in the deliverances of the average religionist. As a man is a conscious and rational being, as Christ spoke in plain and comprehensible terms, and as it is "impossible to be saved in ignorance"— or through any merely "unconscious" and "chemicalizing" action or influence — it follows that the principles of the Gospel must be consciously learned, assimilated and observed, in order that each child of God may be "conformed to the image of His Son." Thus, after all that has been said, the true and vital Theology is the "God-science, the formal presentation of the truths of life and of religion. And it is an essential part of religious life. This explains the meaning of Parley P. Pratt, as above quoted, in calling theology the science of (1) God-communication, (2) of creation, (3) of knowledge, (4) of life, (5) of faith, (6) of spiritual gifts, and (7) "of all other sciences and useful arts," which are piously regarded as originated and imparted through the communion of divine and human spirits.

For the purpose of effecting this grand result, as is claimed, all the institutions of the Church were organized and are maintained. As a special help, however, we find the ceremony of "endowment" is prescribed. This is regularly administered in the temples, which are built for this purpose, in addition to the special ordinances for the living and the dead, as will be explained at a later place. Of the "endowment" ordinances, James E. Talmage writes, as follows:

> "The Temple Endowment, as administered in modern temples, comprises instruction relating to the significance and sequence of past dispensations, and the importance of the present as the greatest and grandest era in human history. This course of instruction includes a recital of the most prominent events of the creative period, the condition of our first parents in the Garden of Eden, their disobedience and consequent expulsion from that blissful abode, their condition in the lone and dreary world when doomed to live by labor and sweat, the plan of redemption by which the great transgression may be atoned, the period of the great apostasy, the restoration of the Gospel with all its ancient powers and privileges, the absolute and indispensable condition of personal purity and devotion to the right in present life, and a strict compliance with Gospel requirements.
>
> ". . . the temples erected by the Latter-day Saints provide for the giving of these instructions in separate rooms, each devoted to a particular part of the course; and by this provision it is possible to have several classes under instruction at one time.
>
> "The ordinances of the endowment embody certain obligations on the part of the individual, such as covenant and promise to observe the law of strict virtue and chastity, to be charitable, benevolent, tolerant and pure; to devote both talent and material means to the spread of truth and the uplifting of the race; to maintain devotion to the cause of truth; and to seek in every way to contribute to the great preparation that the earth may be made ready to receive her King,—the Lord Jesus Christ. With the taking of each covenant and the assuming of each obligation a promised blessing is pronounced, contingent upon the faithful observance of the conditions.
>
> ". . . In every detail the endowment ceremony contributes to covenants of morality of life, consecration of person to high ideals, devotion to truth, patriotism to nation, and allegiance to God. The blessings of the House of the Lord are restricted to no privileged class; every member of the Church may have admission to the Temple with the right to participate in the ordinances thereof, if he comes duly accredited as of worthy life and conduct."—*The House of the Lord, pp.* 99–101.

In addition to the covenants and blessings of the endowments, all men are expected to enter the priesthood, thus effectually identifying themselves with the Church and its interests, and engaging to live in accordance with the requirements of the Gospel. As provided by the regular grading of offices and functions, from the lowest in the Aaronic order to the High Priesthood of the Melchisedek order, as will be explained in place, this "official" service of God may begin, as is the rule, with a boy of twelve or thirteen years of age, and be continued by regular successive ordinations to higher and higher functions, until the highest office in the gift of the Church may be attained. This excellent arrangement, which, if nothing beside, achieves a most desirable *esprit de corps,* cannot fail to give a reality to all religious teachings and encouragement in the performance of prescribed duties. It literally brings religion into intimate touch with everyday life, as is desirable, and is thus, in reality, a most effective means for transforming life, society, and, at last, the world itself. The "hierarchy" of the Mormon Church is the masterpiece of the ages.

As acknowledged by all unbiased observers, the Mormon people are most serious and earnest in following the law of righteousness. In no connection is this more evident than in the matter of purity, temperance and the social virtues. Drunkenness, prostitution, and similar pestilent concomitants of civilization, are virtually unknown in communities controlled by them. Nor is this anything other than a distinct evidence of the reality of their faith to these people, and an argument for the proposition that the commands of Christ are capable of being obeyed to the letter. Of course, the institution of plural marriage, or polygamy, will be mentioned as an example of something quite different, but as it is fully discussed and explained in another place, it will be needless to do more here than to remark that the institution is nowhere unmistakably condemned or forbidden in either the Old or the New Testament, and may be shown to have been recognized by Christ himself in his discussion of marriage and divorce by perfectly evident consistency with the Mosaic law.*

The most valued and oftenest mentioned revelation among the Mormons is the so-called "Word of Wisdom," which expresses, if not remarkable scientific foresight, as some argue, at least a high ideal of temperance and abstinence, particularly in the matters of using artificial stimulants and in the excessive eating of meat foods, both very desirable in civilized communities. It is as follows:

"Not by commandment or constraint, but by revelation and the word of wisdom, showing forth the order and will of God in the temporal

* See Note 2 at the end of this volume.

salvation of all saints in the last days. Given for a principle with promise, adapted to the capacity of the weak and the weakest of all saints, who are or can be called saints.

"Behold, verily, thus saith the Lord unto you, consequence of evils and designs which do and will exist in the hearts of conspiring men in the last days, I have warned you, and forewarn you, by giving unto you this word of wisdom by revelation, that inasmuch as any man drinketh wine or strong drink among you, behold it is not good, neither meet in the sight of your Father, only in assembling yourselves together to offer up your sacraments before him. . . . And, again, strong drinks are not for the belly, but for the washing of your bodies. And, again, tobacco is not for the body, neither for the belly, and is not good for man, but is an herb for bruises and all sick cattle, to be used with judgment and skill. And, again, hot drinks (tea or coffee) are not for the body or belly. And, again, verily I say unto you, all wholesome herbs God hath ordained for the constitution, nature, and use of man. Every herb in the season thereof, and every fruit in the season thereof; all these to be used with prudence and thanksgiving. Yea, flesh also of beasts and of fowls of the air, I, the Lord, have ordained for the use of man with thanksgiving; nevertheless they are to be used sparingly; and it is pleasing unto me that they should not be used only in times of winter, or of cold, or famine. . . . And all saints who remember to keep and do these sayings, walking in obedience to the commandments, shall receive health in their navel, and marrow to their bones, . . . and shall run and not be weary, and shall walk and not faint; and I, the Lord, give unto them a promise, that the destroying angel shall pass by them, as the Children of Israel, and not slay them. Amen."—*Doctrine and Covenants, Section* lxxxix. 2–5, 7–13, 18–21.

In the matter of formal righteousness it seems evident that the Mormon polity contemplates a literal obedience to the moral law, as formulated by Moses, but which it is the duty of the follower of Christ to understand in its true relation to the everlasting Gospel. According to the claim, therefore, that the truth of God has been the same in all "dispensations," it is held that the essentials of the Mosaic legislation have been specifically reenacted in the Church of to-day. This is exampled in the fact that, unlike many other people who claim the name of Christian, the Mormons believe that the severe penalties prescribed for certain offences under the Mosaic law should, in justice and righteousness, still be administered, since, as is frequently stated in their literature, such laws and retributions have "never been repealed." In a certain very real sense, the Mormon Church bears a singular analogy to the Mosaic commonwealth, since in both the severest penalties are advocated for the gravest offences, but — and this point must be borne in mind — this follows only after the utmost provision has been made to cultivate righteousness of life and to render its exercise easy and "natural" to all. In both cases the theory is that heinous offences against God and the social order must be severely requited, because "bereft of all just excuse."

Thus it is that, while preaching a doctrine as nearly like "universal salvation" as would be possible in consistence with reason and Scripture — and the claim is that the "Gospel is a message of salvation, not of condemnation"— the strongest denunciations have been launched against the "unpardonable sin," which must literally doom its perpetrator to endless banishment from the presence of God, among the "sons of Perdition." These accursed ones represent, of course, all those whose wickedness is irredeemable in all ages of the world, those who have "sinned against the Holy Spirit," after having received His blessings and presence into their lives. For, as is argued with good consistency, it is obviously impossible to sin against the Holy Ghost, unless He has been already received, or imparted. Under other conditions, even the gravest sin is to be compared with the guilt of this offence, only because in violence to the fundamental laws of being and of human society. In writing of the "sons of Perdition," Talmage has the following:

> "These are they who, having learned the power of God, afterward renounce it; those who sin wilfully, in the light of knowledge; those who open their hearts to the Holy Spirit, and then put the Lord to a mockery and a shame by denying it; and those who commit murder, wherein they shed innocent blood; these are they of whom the Savior has declared that it would be better for them had they never been born." — *The Articles of the Faith, p.* 62.

The matter is also explained in the authoritative scriptures:

> "Thus saith the Lord, concerning all those who know my power, and have been made partakers thereof, and suffered themselves, through the power of the devil, to be overcome, and to deny the truth and defy my power . . . they are vessels of wrath, doomed to suffer the wrath of God, with the devil and his angels in eternity; concerning whom I have said there is no forgiveness in this world nor in the world to come, having denied the Holy Spirit after having received it, and having denied the Only Begotten Son of the Father — having crucified him unto themselves, and put him to an open shame. These are they who shall go away into the lake of fire and brimstone, with the devil and his angels, and the only ones on whom the second death shall have any power; yea, verily, the only ones who shall not be redeemed in the due time of the Lord, after the sufferings of his wrath."— *Doctrine and Covenants,* lxxvi. 31–38.

But because, as we may assume, the Church is regarded as the visible body and representative of God on earth, and because, for that very reason various sins and crimes in its members must appear all the more heinous, it is definitely held that such defilements of the person and of society as adultery and harlotry, as well as murder, should be punished with death, even as the law of Moses prescribes. Although for offences of lesser gravity than murder — offences in which restitution can be made, apparently — there is distinct provision for forgiveness, even after several commissions, the belief that "there is a sin unto death" is consistently maintained. Nor may such sin be forgiven or atoned, even after repentance, or apparent repentance, except as God's law specifies. In this connection emerges the doctrine, which, under the title of "blood atonement," has been wilfully and wantonly misrepresented, and made the occasion for monstrous and unprovable charges against the Mormon Church, by persons professing acquaintance with the Bible, also a love of truth and justice. If represented as a teaching justifying murder and bloodshed, as has been done too often, it may be stated without hesitation that there is no such doctrine. If represented as a part of Scripture interpretation, a fresh example of "ultra-literalism," possibly, it may be explained and justified from authoritative sources.

Expressed in a few words, the teaching is that, as the Bible states, this "sin unto death" may not be included under the benefits of Christ's atonement. In it, as it were, a man repeats in his own person, and for himself the very sin of Adam — even after it had been blotted out by Christ's atonement — that sin which entailed banishment of every real sort from the presence and favor of God, thus neutralizing Christ's work and contemning his love. Hence, according to the standards set up in Scripture, the sole hope of forgiveness for such a man lies in the shedding of his own blood as a "sin offering" to God. This teaching has been expressed several times in the sermons of Brigham Young and President Jedediah M. Grant, occasionally in picturesque and pointed sentences, which have been widely quoted, also garbled and mutilated, for the purpose of evidencing false charges against the Mormon Church and its teachings. The following is the teaching in the words of President Young:

"There are sins that men commit for which they cannot receive forgiveness in this world, or in that which is to come, and if they had their eyes open to see their true condition, they would be perfectly willing to have their blood spilt upon the ground, that the smoke thereof might ascend to heaven as an offering for their sins; and the smoking incense would atone for their sins, whereas if such is not the case, they (the sins) will stick to them and remain upon them in the spirit world. . . .

"And furthermore I know that there are transgressors, who, if they knew themselves, and the only condition upon which they can obtain forgiveness, would beg of their brethren to shed their blood, that the smoke thereof might ascend to God as an offering to appease the wrath that is kindled against them, and that the law might have its course. I will say further I have had men come to me and offer their lives to atone for their sins.

"It is true that the blood of the Son of God was shed for sin through the fall and those committed by men, yet men can commit sins which it can never remit." — *Journal of Discourses, Vol.* IV, *p.* 53–54.

Were it not for the prodigious mass of misrepresentation of this doctrine at the hands of avowed enemies of Mormonism, it would be necessary, merely, to mention and explain it among the teachings of this system, and pass on to the next subject item. Under present conditions, however, it is necessary to go further, and demonstrate that, so far as the formal statement is concerned, this doctrine is entirely scriptural, being evidently derived from faithful and literal interpretation of the text of the Bible, and being in no sense, whatever, "read into" any passage. If there is any consistency whatever in the Bible upon the matter of sin and transgression, there is nothing more evident than the teaching that all transgression of the law of God entails, justly and normally, the penalty of death. This is involved in the first great commandment to Adam, the penalty for its transgression being expressed in the words, "In the day that thou eatest thereof thou shalt surely die" (Gen. ii. 17). According to the same sentence, as developed in the Mosaic law, also, even, in the sacrificial cults of "heathen" religions, the practice and teaching of vicarious sacrifice was established, and the blood of an animal victim was shed to atone for the sins of the repentant transgressor. According to traditional Christian teaching, also, the efficacy of this law of sacrifice is fully recognized, although, as taught, abrogated and fulfilled in the atonement of Christ, which is held to have been typified by the previous slaughter of animal victims, under the Jewish law. The theory in both cases is precisely the same as expressed in Leviticus xvii. 11, "for the life of the flesh is in the blood; and I have given it to you upon the altar to make an atonement for your souls: for it is the blood that maketh an atonement for the soul." Commenting on the foregoing, we find the following from Charles W. Penrose, now one of the First Presidency of the Mormon Church:

"Here you see the doctrine of blood atonement laid down, and the reason for it. 'The life of the flesh is in the blood,' and it requires the shedding of blood to make 'atonement for the soul.' But, . . . the blood of every individual man and woman is not required, because of the atonement wrought out by Jesus Christ. Here is the cardinal principle of the law of God — that without shedding of blood there is no remission of sins. Therefore, if Christ's blood had not been shed, each individual would have had to have his blood shed, according to Bible doctrine. This may sound very horrifying to some people; but it is Bible doctrine all the same. It is the doctrine of the Old Testament, it is the doctrine of the New Testament; atonement or sacrifice was based on this, and this doctrine was practised by the people before the law of Moses was given. . . .

"All those sacrifices which were offered up before Jesus Christ, our Redeemer, came into the world were typical of the atonement that He was to work out. It was not the shedding of the blood of goats, sheep and bullocks upon the altar that made the atonement; but this was typical of the atonement of Jesus Christ in the future, just as we, when we partake of the Lord's Supper, have a piece of bread and a cup of water, or wine, as the case may be, to represent the atonement wrought out in the past. . . .

"But there are persons who, after having been washed and made clean through the blood of Christ, and made members of His Church, again commit sin. What about them? Why, if they truly repent, and make all the restitution that lays in their power, they may be forgiven, they may be cleansed again. But there are some sins that can be committed from which they cannot be cleansed by the blood of Christ. After receiving the Gospel and entering into sacred covenants with God Almighty, after having been enlightened by the spirit of truth, having tasted of the good word of God and the power of the world to come; if they commit certain sins they cannot gain the remission of those sins through the blood of Jesus Christ. That may be a new doctrine to many people of the world, but it is an old doctrine to the Latter-day Saints, and you can find it laid down distinctly and clearly in the Bible."—*Blood Atonement, pp.* 13, 14, 16–17.

As explained by Elder Penrose, there is a complete chain of Biblical teachings to uphold the allegations here made. He quotes the following passages:

"For it is impossible for those who were once enlightened, and have tasted of the heavenly gift, and were made partakers of the Holy Ghost, and have tasted the good word of God, and the powers of the world to come, if they shall fall away, to renew them again unto repentance; seeing they crucify to themselves the Son of God afresh, and put him to an open shame" (*Heb.* vi. 4–6). "For if we sin wilfully after that we have received the knowledge of the truth, there remaineth no more sacrifice for sins. . . . He that despised Moses' law died without mercy under two or three witnesses: of how much sorer punishment, suppose ye, shall he be thought worthy, who hath trodden under foot the Son of God, and hath counted the blood of the covenant, wherewith he was sanctified, an unholy thing, and hath done despite unto the Spirit of Grace?" (*Heb.* x. 26, 28–29). "No murderer hath eternal life abiding in him" (*I John* iii. 15). "If any man see his brother sin a sin which is not unto death, he shall ask, and he shall give him life for them that sin not unto death. There is a sin unto death: I do not say that he shall pray for it. All unrighteousness is sin: and there is a sin not unto death." (*I John* v. 16–17.)

Although, as some may argue, the "sin unto death" mentioned in these several connections may indicate such "moral sin," as involves the eternal wrath of God, and which, even in the Catholic Church, which claims the power to forgive all sins, involves the infliction of the severest penances, if there is to be any forgiveness whatever, they do not necessarily involve the death penalty. It is well to reflect, however, that, judging by the words, "they crucify . . . the Son of God afresh," etc., many commentators have concluded that "heresy" and apostasy were specifically referred to—and there is room for some such interpretation—and have made these offenses capital crimes. This explains the persecutions of the Middle Ages, the massacres of

Anabaptists, Huguenots, etc., the Inquisition, John Calvin's destruction of his friend Servetus, and other truculent doings. There have been suggestions also, although not definitely promulgated doctrines, that the "martyrdom" of the "heretic" might mitigate his sin in the eyes of God. Some have even stated that the real object of destroying heretics was to "save their souls." Although such an interpretation of Scripture may seem "fantastic," it is not inadmissable to argue that any fulfilment of the law of God, even in the matter of dealing with murderers, and other criminals, involves an opportunity for divine mercy to act in the world to come, even though there can be only "justice" here. This is the teaching of Mormon commentators, as will be seen in the following from Elder Penrose's pamphlet:

"In the ancient church of Christ some apostatized, and those who came into that church and afterwards fell away, became much worse than people who had never tasted of the word of God, nor of the power of the world to come. The Apostle Paul writes (*I Cor.* v. 3, 5) about a gross sin that I need not mention, but he says:

"'For I verily, as absent in body, but present in spirit, have judged already, as though I were present, concerning him that hath done this deed,

"'To deliver such an one unto Satan for the destruction of the flesh, that the spirit may be saved in the day of the Lord Jesus.'

"I wonder how much our modern Christian friends understand of that doctrine. Paul understood it, the Corinthian saints understood it. Here was a man who came into the church, received the Holy Ghost, was made partaker of the heavenly gift, had rejoiced in the truth, and then, through temptation and wickedness, he went into corruption, violated the covenants he had made to be true and faithful to God by ceasing from sin, and committed a gross transgression for which he could not have forgiveness — such a one was to be delivered unto Satan for the destruction of the flesh, that the spirit might be saved in the day of the Lord Jesus. Now, it seems, according to this doctrine of the Apostle Paul, that if that man was destroyed in the flesh there would be some chance for him to be saved in the day of the Lord Jesus. Why? Because he had made as much atonement as he possibly could for his sin. He had given his life. What is life? The life of the flesh is the blood. So the scriptures say. He was delivered over to the buffetings of Satan that he might be saved in the day of the Lord Jesus. This is the same as the doctrine taught by the Saviour. Brigham Young understood it perfectly. He says there are some sins men may commit for which they cannot get forgiveness, for which they will have to suffer the penalty in the world to come, but if their blood is shed as an offering for their sin, their spirits might be saved in the day of the Lord Jesus; just exactly as the Apostle Paul teaches here, in the text I have read to you.

. . . .

"But I want to carry this subject a little further. Suppose we grant the position that a murderer is worthy of death, and that he is particularly worthy of death if he has been enlightened by the power of God and knows the full extent of that great transgression — supposing we admit that for the sake of argument — the next question that arises is, Who is to inflict the penalty? What do our Church laws say on this subject. I will refer you to section xlii of the Book of *Doctrine and Covenants,* and the eighteenth verse:

"'And now, behold, I speak unto the Church. Thou shalt not kill; and he that kills shall not have forgiveness in this world, nor in the world to come.

"'And, again, I say, Thou shalt not kill; but he that killeth shall die.'

"Here is the law of God to the Church. You know it is represented abroad that the Latter-day Saints believe in killing in a great many different directions. But here is the law of God to the Church by revelation. This is the word of God Almighty to the Saints. This law is given to people who have been baptized, who have received the Holy Ghost, who have been made partakers of the heavenly gift—'Thou shalt not kill; but he that killeth shall die.' But that does not answer the question, Who is to inflict the penalty? I will refer you to a passage a little further on in the same revelation—section xlii, verse 79:

"'It shall come to pass, that if any persons among you shall kill, they shall be delivered up and dealt with according to the laws of the land; for remember that he hath no forgiveness, and it shall be proven according to the laws of the land.'"—*Blood Atonement, pp.* 22–23, 29–30.

That the foregoing correctly represents the position of Brigham Young upon the matter, in spite of the garbled quotations from his sermons, and the wild and unfounded charges of bloodshed and murder instigated by him, we may understand on reading the whole of the sermons referred to. Then, we shall understand that he was stating what should be done, if God's law, as he understood it to be, were in force, rather than what he intended to do himself, or, indeed, had done. Thus he deplores the fact that the laws of the nations at the present day prevent the fulfillment of the righteous laws of God, which were framed quite as truly in mercy, as we have seen already, as in justice, or in way of inflicting vengeance on the sinner. He says:

"The time has been in Israel under the law of God, the celestial law, or that which pertains to the celestial law, for it is one of the laws of the kingdom where our father dwells, that if a man was found guilty of adultery, he must have his blood shed. . . .

"I could refer you to plenty of instances where men have been righteously slain, in order to atone for their sins. I have seen scores and hundreds of people for whom there would have been a chance (in the last resurrection there will be) if their lives had been taken and their blood spilled on the ground as a smoking incense to the Almighty, but who are now angels to the devil until our Elder Brother Jesus Christ raises them up—conquers death, hell, and the grave. . . . The wickedness and ignorance of the nations forbid this principle's being in full force, but the time will come when the law of God will be in full force."—*Journal of Discourses, Vol* IV. *pp.* 219, 220.

CHAPTER XVII

THE DOCTRINES OF RESTORATION, RESURRECTION AND SALVATION

ALTHOUGH, in some aspects of the matter, the strenuous insistence on the Mosaic law of retributive justice might seem needlessly severe, it remains true that, in dealing with human nature, a law that is all "love" and no severity is no law at all. "Love" and leniency are often confused with laxity and complacence, with the result that the standards of right and truth come to be less seriously considered. We can understand some of this insistence, when we remember that the Mormon Church represents a serious attempt to found an order of social righteousness and equity. It is also the only one of all so-called Christian bodies that includes this social ideal as an essential element of its creed. Various persons in other bodies at the present time are doubtless attempting to retrieve the historic neglect of this branch of effort, and much good work has been begun in various quarters, also there is, so we are told, a "general awakening of the social conscience," etc. It will be interesting information for people working along these lines of effort to learn that the Mormon Prophet anticipated their movement by over three-quarters of a century, and that, whatever their future success, he was probably the first man of modern times to found a stable and equable social order on a religious basis.

With the Mormons, however, the restoration of the Law is only a part of their grand doctrine of the unity of the Gospel throughout all time. As a corollary of this doctrine, they divide history into seven separate periods, known as "dispensations": (a) the Adamic; (b) the Enochian; (c) the Noachian; (d) the Abrahamic; (e) the Mosaic; (f) the Dispensation of the Meridian of Time, beginning with the ministry of John the Baptist and continued in the work of Christ and His Apostles; (g) the Dispensation of the Fulness of Times, consisting in the work of the Gospel restored by revelation to Joseph Smith, and to continue until the end of the world.

The Dispensation of the Fulness of Times is characterized by a complete restoration of the Gospel after a universal apostasy of the church; and, as such, is, in effect, a means of preparing the world for the return of Christ as visible judge and ruler, and for the events preceding the "last times." The Mormons are taught that, like the ancient Israelites, they are a "peculiar people," called to a lofty and wonderful mission in the world. This inspiring belief, like most of their tenets, is no figure of speech, but is accepted as a literal and an essential fact. They hold that it is no strain upon revealed truth to believe that the blood of the "dispersion of Israel," the "lost tribes of Joseph," is demonstrated in those who accept the "fulness of the Gospel," as revealed on earth in these "latter days." This is explained by Orson F. Whitney, as follows:

> "It must be borne in mind, as a basic fact, upon which to found all further argument or theory in relation to the Saints (Mormons) and their religion, that they sincerely believe themselves to be literally of the blood of Israel; children of Abraham, Isaac and Jacob,—mostly of Joseph through the lineage of Ephraim. The loss of their tribal identity, and their scattered state among the nations — whence the Gospel, they say, has begun to gather them,— is explained to them by the Scriptures, which declare that Ephraim 'hath mixed himself with the people'; that is, with other nations, presumably from the days of the Assyrian captivity. They believe, moreover, that in this age, 'The Dispensation of the Fulness of Times,'— a figurative spiritual ocean, into which all past dispensations of divine power and authority like rills and rivers run,— it is the purpose of Jehovah, the God of Israel, to gather His scattered people from their long dispersion among the nations, and weld in one vast chain the broken links of the fated house of Abraham. . . . This gathering of Israel, they claim, is a step preparatory to the 'gathering together in one' of 'all things in Christ,' both in heaven and on earth, as spoken of by Paul the Apostle.
>
> . . . .
>
> "Israel's gathering in the 'last days,'— the closing period of our planet's mortal probation,— is a cardinal doctrine of the Latter-day Saints, accounting, as it does for their world-wide proselytism, the wanderings abroad of their Apostles and Elders in quest of the seed of Ephraim, their fellows, and their migrations from the ends of the earth to the American Continent, believed by them to be the land of Zion. Upon this land, which they hold to be the inheritance of Joseph, — given him by the Almighty in the blessings of Jacob and Moses (Gen. xlix. 22–26; Deut. xxxiii. 13–17), and occupied for ages by his descendants, the Nephites and Lamanites (as recorded in the Book of Mormon),— is to arise the latter-day Zion, New Jerusalem, concerning which so many of the prophet-poets of antiquity have sung. It was for this purpose, say the Saints, that the land was held in reserve, hidden for ages behind Atlantic's waves — the wall of waters over which, in Lehi and his colony, climbed Joseph's 'fruitful bough.' Next came the Gentiles, with Columbus in their van, to unveil the hidden hemisphere; then a Washington, a Jefferson and other heaven-inspired patriots to win and maintain the liberty of the land,— a land destined to be 'free from bondage.' And all this that Zion might here be established, and the Lord's latter-day work founded and fostered on Columbia's chosen soil. Yes, these Latter-day Saints,— false and fa-

natical as the view may seem to most,— actually believe that the greatest and most liberal of earthly governments, that of the United States, was founded for the express purpose of favoring the growth of what the world terms Mormonism. . . .

"But the gathering of Israel is to include the whole house of Jacob; not merely the half-tribes of Ephraim and Manasseh. It involves the restoration of the Jews and the rebuilding of old Jerusalem, prior to the acceptance by Judah of the Gospel and mission of the crucified Messiah; also the return of the lost Ten Tribes from the 'north country.'"—*History of Utah, Vol.* I, *pp.* 66–69.

This, like other Mormon doctrines, is significant as being a wonderfully ingenious, even if not a true and authoritative, solution of the question as to how the promises of God to Abraham and his seed are apparently fulfilled, instead, for the advantage of "gentiles," or non-Israelites, who have ever "despitefully used and persecuted" the Chosen Nation, which, meantime, seems to have been literally "cut off." To hold that all who accept the Gospel in its fulness are actually of the blood of Abraham, "after the flesh," through the "dispersion" of the "lost Tribes," is both inspiring and illuminating. It follows, then, that the "Chosen People of God" are, after all, the first care with Him, and ever the real heralds of His will and law. Thus, the extensive and persistent missionary activities of this people are found to be only movements to assist in the gathering of the Lord's chosen from all parts of the world.

But the missionary duty entailed upon believers in the Latter-day Gospel does not stop with the "dispersion of Israel," nor yet with the nations of the world. It achieves yet other heights and depths in the stupendous doctrine of *salvation for the dead.* This merciful and comforting doctrine offsets effectually the hopelessness of the situation of those who have died unrepentant or unconverted. Nor does it seem presumptuous to hold that it actually illustrates the "loving-kindness" of God, and justifies to human reason, at least the statement that "God is love." The special application of this doctrine is to two classes, (a) those who lived when the Gospel "was not in the earth," and (b) those who failed to hear it truly preached in their life-time.

"From a remark made in the writings of the Apostle Peter we learn that after the Messiah was put to death in the flesh 'he went and preached unto the spirits in prison, which sometime were disobedient, when once the long-suffering of God waited in the days of Noah.' (I Pet. iii. 18, 21.) During the three days, then, that the Messiah's body lay in the tomb at Jerusalem, His spirit was in the world of spirits preaching to those who had rejected the teaching of righteous Noah. The Christian traditions, no less than the scriptures, hold that Christ went into hell and preached to those there held in ward. Not only is the mere fact of Messiah's going to the spirits in prison stated in the scriptures, but the purpose of His going there is learned from the same source. 'For this cause was the gospel preached also to them that are dead, that they might be judged according to men in the flesh, but live according to God in the spirit.' (I Pet. iv. 6.) This manifestly means that the spirits who had once rejected the counsels of God against themselves had the gospel again presented to them and had the privilege of living according to its precepts in the spirit life; and of being judged according to men in the flesh, or as men in the flesh will be judged; that is, according to the degree of their faithfulness to the precepts of the gospel. It should be observed from the foregoing scripture that even to those who have rejected the gospel in the days of Noah it was again presented by the ministry of the Lord Jesus Christ; upon which consideration the following reflection forces itself upon the mind: viz. If the gospel is preached again to those who have once rejected it, how much sooner will it be presented to those who never heard it — who lived in those generations when neither the gospel nor the authority to administer its ordinances were in the earth. Seeing that those who had rejected it had it again preached to them (after paying the penalty for their disobedience), surely those who lived when it was not upon the earth or who, when it was upon the earth perished in ignorance of it, will much sooner come to salvation.

"The manner in which the ordinances of the gospel may be administered to those who have died without having received them is plainly stated by Paul. Writing to the Corinthians on the subject of the resurrection — correcting those who said there was no resurrection — he asks: 'Else what shall they do which are baptized for the dead, if the dead rise not at all? Why are they then baptized for the dead?' In this the apostle manifestly refers to the practice which existed among the Christian saints of the living being baptized for the dead; and argues from the existence of that practice that the dead must rise, or why the necessity of being baptized for them. This passage of the scripture of itself is sufficient to establish the fact that such an ordinance as baptism for the dead was known among the ancient saints."— *B. H. Roberts* (*Mormonism, etc.*, 50–52).

The practice of this doctrine which claims the same authority as the Catholic doctrine of Purgatory, involves that some living believer shall be baptized as proxy for some one of the dead, either for one from among his or her own ancestors, or for any other person who died without knowledge of the Gospel in its fulness. This is explained by Elder Talmage, as follows:

"The redemption of the dead will be effected in strict accordance with the law of God, which is written in justice and framed in mercy. It is alike impossible for any spirit, in the flesh or disembodied, to obtain even the promise of eternal glory, except on condition of obedience to the laws and ordinances of the gospel. And, as baptism is essential to the salvation of the living, it is likewise indispensable to the redemption of the dead. . . . The necessity of vicarious work is here shown,— the living laboring in behalf of the dead; the children doing for their progenitors what is beyond the power of the latter to do for themselves. . . .

"The plan of God provides that neither the children nor the fathers can alone be made perfect; and the necessary union is effected through baptism and associated ordinances for the dead. The manner in which the hearts of the children and those of the fathers are turned toward one another is made plain through these scriptures. As the children learn that without the aid of their progenitors they cannot attain perfection, assuredly will their hearts be opened, their faith will be kindled, and good works will be attempted, for the redemption of their dead; and the departed, learning from the ministers of the gospel laboring among them, that they must depend upon their children as vicarious saviours, will seek to sustain their still mortal representatives with faith and prayer for the perfecting of those labors of love. . . .

"The results of such labors are to be left with God. It is not to be supposed that by these ordinances (baptism, laying-on of hands and the 'higher endowments') the departed are in any way compelled to accept the obligation, nor that they are in the least hindered in the exercise of their free agency. They will accept or reject, according to their condition of humility or hostility in respect to things divine; but the work so done for them on earth will be of avail when wholesome argument and reason have shown them their true position."— —*Articles of Faith, pp.* 152–156.

The ordinances for the dead are performed in the temples maintained by the Latter-day Saints, and are frequently attended to by persons known as "temple-workers," who are regularly "set apart" for this form of service, although any members of the Church in good standing may enter the Temple and fulfil the ordinances for his deceased ancestors and other relatives. The work of vicarious baptism is always superintended by some elder, who administers the rite, and complete records are kept of all ceremonies, with the names, or identities, of all departed beneficiaries.

Roberts, concluding a brief summary of the doctrine of salvation for the dead, remarks:

"There must be a sealing and binding together of all the generations of men until the family of God shall be perfectly joined in holiest bonds and ties of mutual affections. These ordinances attended to on earth by the living, and accepted in the spirit world by those for whom they are performed, will make them a potent means of salvation to the dead, and of exaltation to the living, since the latter become in very deed 'saviors upon Mount Zion.' This work that can be done for the dead enlarges one's views of the gospel of Jesus Christ. One begins to see indeed that it is the 'everlasting gospel'; for it runs parallel with man's existence both in this life and in that which is to come."—*Mormonism, p.* 53.

Speaking of the twofold character of this work, both in this world and in the world of spirits, Talmage writes:

"How often do we behold friends and loved ones, whom we count among earth's fairest and best, stricken down by the shafts of death, seemingly in spite of the power of faith and the ministrations of the priesthood of God! Yet who of us can tell but that the spirits so called away are needed in labor of redemption beyond, preaching perhaps the gospel to the spirits of their forefathers, while others of the same family are officiating in a similar behalf on earth?"—*Articles of Faith, p.* 156.

When one considers the absurd and ignorant criticisms made

on this doctrine by persons professing a knowledge of Scripture, it will seem surprising, doubtless, that it is a teaching of the greatest vitality, held in the very highest esteem among the Latter-day Saints. It is to them a veritable sacrament of grace, the "sign of a divine and spiritual grace." Thus, instead of the threats of hopeless perdition for those who have not heard the Gospel in this world, we find that "the hearts of the children are turned to the fathers" in a very real and inspiring sense. The following examples of the vital character of this belief are significant:

"Let me ask those who look upon Joseph Smith as an imposter, why should an imposter bother himself with such a work as the salvation of the dead? Let the world cite an instance of an imposter engaging in such a work. No, if Joseph Smith had been an imposter he would have devoted his time and attention to the living. But the redemption of the dead was one of the most important parts of Joseph Smith's mission. He urged it strongly upon the Saints, declaring that they without their dead could not be made perfect. The Church has not for a single day lost sight of this work. Temples have been erected at enormous cost and sacrifice in which the ordinances necessary for the redemption of the dead have been and are being performed, and tens of thousands of dollars and years of precious time have been spent by the Saints in searching for the genealogies of their deceased relatives, in order that they might become their saviors.

"One day while in England I met an old gentleman who told me he had traveled over seven thousand miles in the hope that he might obtain the genealogies of his deceased relatives, so that he could perform the work for them in the temple. For years this old man had lived the life of a sheep herder, out on the desert in all kinds of weather, for days alone, with not a human being to speak to him. All this time his thoughts were upon one thing — the redemption of his kindred dead. The loneliness he endured, the hardships he suffered, were swallowed up in the joy he felt as he looked forward to the day when he would have sufficient means to enable him to go back to the land of his forefathers to gather genealogies. His faithful labors were rewarded. He obtained hundreds of names, and since his return to Utah has been working in one of the temples, officiating in behalf of his departed kindred.

"Another case comes to my remembrance. It is that of a young woman and her mother who embraced the gospel in Switzerland and came to Utah a number of years ago. For over two years these faithful souls lived almost on bread and water in order to save means to send back to their native land to pay for genealogical work. They were rewarded with a record of a thousand names.

"Many similar instances could be cited. It is the testimony of thousands who have embraced the Gospel of Christ revealed through Joseph Smith, that just as soon as they accepted the Gospel, and began to partake of its spirit and blessings, just so soon did their hearts turn to their fathers who had died without having heard of the restoration of the gospel. And in many instances this was the case before the converts had heard of such a thing as salvation for the dead.

"Who was it, I ask, that put this spirit into the hearts of the Latter-day Saints? Who was it that has performed this wonderful work — the turning of the hearts of the fathers to the children, and the hearts of the children to the fathers? Was it Joseph Smith? No, it would have been impossible for Joseph Smith or any other man to have done such a thing. It is the Lord who has done it. It was He who devised the glorious plan of salvation for the dead. It was He who sent Elijah the prophet to Joseph Smith with the keys of this blessed dispensation. Therefore, let His name be praised, and at the same time let the name of the Prophet Joseph Smith be glorified."—*William A. Morton* (*Young Woman's Journal, September,* 1913, *pp.* 553–554).

This doctrine, coupled with that of the "eternity of the marriage covenant," cannot fail to render belief in a future life unusually real and certain. It involves that, not only shall those at present alive, if faithful to the Gospel, attain eternal life, but also that their family relations shall be perpetuated — the fathers and mothers with their children to all eternity, and the descendants with their remote ancestors, also; great families in the Everlasting Kingdom. Whatever objections one may urge against this belief, or against the authority which bases it, there can be no doubt that it represents as true and inevitable, under the conditions specified, precisely the sort of immortality that most people of really human sentiments sincerely hope may be theirs. Because, however, the rite of eternal marriage may be celebrated only in the temple, and at the hands of the priesthood of God, it follows that those ancestors who have been made partakers in the benefits of Christ's atonement through proxy baptism, must also be sealed by proxy in eternal marriage, and have their children sealed to them also. There can be no doubt that all this vastly enforces belief in the reality of a future life, as well as of the Church's divine mission and authority in this.

The doctrine of the condition of the blessed in the eternal life, as held in the Latter-day theology is an elaborate and inspiring one: moreover, as with very many of the other "Mormon" doctrines, it seems to be founded on the same implicit belief in the literal truth of Scripture statements, without either evasion or qualification. Briefly characterized, it may be said to teach universal salvation, without encountering the difficulties of "Universalism," and to teach the eternal punishment of the finally reprobate, without imposing statements of doctrine, difficult or impossible to reconcile with humanly intelligible notions of divine love and justice.

As a prelude to the final conditions of all mankind, it is taught that there are three separate resurrections of the dead. One widely accepted teaching on this matter is thus set forth in the words of Parley P. Pratt, who, contrary to the opinion expressed by some other writers, believes that the first resurrection is already past.

"The first general resurrection took place in connection with the resurrection of Jesus Christ. This included the Saints and Prophets of both hemispheres, from Adam down to John the Baptist; or, in other words, all those who died in Christ before His resurrection.

"The second will take place in a few years from the present time, and will be immediately succeeded by the coming of Jesus Christ, in power and great glory, with all His Saints and angels. This resurrection will include the Former and Latter-day Saints, all those who have received the Gospel since the former resurrection.

"The third and last resurrection will take place more than a thousand years afterwards, and will embrace all the human family not included in the former resurrection or translations. . . .

"In the resurrection which now approaches, and in connection with the glorious coming of Jesus Christ, the earth will undergo a change in its physical features, climate, soil, productions, and in its political, moral and spiritual government.

"Its mountains will be leveled, its valleys exalted, its swamps and sickly places will be drained and become healthy, while its burning deserts and its frigid polar regions will be redeemed and become temperate and fruitful.

"Kingcraft and priestcraft, tyranny, oppression and idolatry will be at an end, darkness and ignorance will pass away, war will cease, and the rule of sin and sorrow and death will give place to the reign of peace and truth and righteousness.

"For this reason, and to fulfill certain promises made to the fathers, the Former and Latter-day Saints included in the two resurrections, and all those translated, will then receive an inheritance on the earth, and will build upon and improve the same for a thousand years."—*Key to Theology, pp.* 138–140.

According to the position of individual souls in one or another of the resurrections here specified, the last of which takes place at the end of the world and the beginning of eternity, their condition is determined in the kingdom of God. Here, also, as indicated in I Corinthians xv. 40–42, there are grades of glory and degrees of salvation, which are designated in Pauline phrase as (1) the Celestial Glory; (2) the Terrestrial Glory; (3) the Telestial Glory, the last term indicating Paul's reference to the "glory of the stars"—the word, "telestial" being derived, evidently, from the Greek word, *telos,* meaning "fleet," "flock," etc., referring to the vast number of stars.

The Celestial Kingdom is, of course, the highest of all, including all those of whom it is said they shall be "partakers in the Divine Nature" (II Peter i. 4); "partakers of His holiness" (Hebrews xii. 10); who shall "see Him as He is" (II John iii. 2); to whom it is granted to sit with Christ upon His throne (Revelation iii. 21); and who have been made one with the Godhead, even as Christ and the Father are one (John xvii. 21–23). These are called, accordingly, "gods," after the authority of Christ's words in John x. 34–36. The conditions requisite for an inheritance in this "kingdom" are as follows:

"And again we bear record, for we saw and heard, and this is the testimony of the gospel of Christ concerning them who come forth in the resurrection of the just; they are they who received the testimony of Jesus, and believed on his name and were baptized after the manner of his burial, being buried in the water in his name, and this according to the commandment which he has given, that by keeping the commandments they might be washed and cleansed from all their sins, and receive the Holy Spirit by the laying-on of hands of him who is ordained and sealed unto this power, and who overcome by faith, and are sealed by the Holy Spirit of promise, which the Father sheds forth upon all who are just and true. They are they who are the church of the first born. They are they into whose hands the Father has given all things — they are they who are Priests and Kings, who have received of his fullness, and of his glory, and are Priests of the Most High, after the order of Melchisedek, which was after the order of Enoch, which was after the order of the Only Begotten Son; wherefore, as it is written, they are Gods, even the sons of God — wherefore all things are theirs, whether life or death, or things present, or things to come, all are theirs and they are Christ's and Christ is God's. And they shall overcome all things; wherefore let no man glory in man, but rather let him glory in God, who shall subdue all enemies under his feet — these shall dwell in the presence of God and his Christ for ever and ever. These are they whom he shall bring with him, when he shall come in the clouds of heaven, to reign on the earth over his people. These are they who shall have part in the first resurrection. These are they who shall come forth in the resurrection of the just. These are they who are come unto Mount Zion, and unto the city of the living God, the heavenly place, the holiest of all. These are they who have come to an innumerable company of angels, to the general assembly and church of Enoch, and of the first born. These are they whose names are written in heaven, where Christ and God are the judge of all. These are they who are just men made perfect through Jesus the mediator of the new covenant, who wrought out this perfect atonement through the shedding of his own blood. These are they whose bodies are celestial, whose glory is that of the sun, even the glory of God, the highest of all."—*Doctrine and Covenants,* lxxvi. 51–70.

The highest glories and exaltations are all reserved for those counted worthy to inherit the Celestial glory. It is the Heaven of the Blessed *par excellence,* and here all the powers and capacities of the human spirit shall receive the greatest development of which it is capable.

The Terrestrial Glory, which, according to the understanding of Paul's words in I Corinthians xv., corresponds to the "glory of the moon," is inherited by those who have lived righteously without the law of God and by those who have not earned the fullest blessing by hearing the highest testimony under Law and Gospel conditions, as explained in the following from the same revelation as quoted above:

"And again, we saw the terrestrial world, and behold and lo, these are they who are of the terrestrial, whose glory differs from that of the church of the first born, who have received the fullness of the Father, even as that of the moon differs from the sun in the firmament. Behold, these are they who died without law, and also those who are the spirits of men kept in prison, whom the Son visited, and preached the gospel unto them, that they might be judged according to men in the flesh, who received not the testimony of Jesus in the flesh, but afterwards received it. These are they who are honorable men of the earth, who were blinded by the craftiness of men. These are they who receive of his glory, but not of his fullness. These are they who receive of the presence of the Son, but not of the fullness of the Father; wherefore they are bodies terrestrial, and not bodies celestial, and differ in glory as the moon differs from the sun. These are they who are not valiant in the testimony of Jesus; wherefore they obtain not the crown over the kingdom of our God."—*Ibid.* 71–79.

The Telestial Glory is inherited by those who have committed sins and crimes, not of an unpardonable description, and who have suffered the wrath and just punishment of God, "until the resurrection," as is explained in the same revelation as is quoted above, in the following words:

"And again, we saw the glory of the telestial, which glory is that of the lesser, even as the glory of the stars differs from that of the glory of the moon in the firmament. These are they who received not the gospel of Christ, neither the testimony of Jesus. These are they who deny not the Holy Spirit. These are they who are thrust down to hell. These are they who shall not be redeemed from the devil, until the last resurrection, until the Lord, even Christ the Lamb shall have finished his work. These are they who receive not of his fullness in the eternal world, but of the Holy Spirit through the ministration of the terrestrial; and the terrestrial through the ministration of the celestial; and also the telestial receive it of the administering of angels who are appointed to minister for them, or who are appointed to be ministering spirits for them, for they shall be heirs of salvation. . . . These all are they who will not be gathered with the saints, to be caught up into the church of the first born, and received into the cloud. These are they who are liars, and sorcerers, and adulterers, and whoremongers, and whosoever loves and makes a lie. These are they who suffer the wrath of God on earth. These are they who suffer the vengeance of eternal fire. These are they who are cast down to hell and suffer the wrath of Almighty God, until the fullness of times when Christ shall have subdued all enemies under his feet, and shall have perfected his work, when he shall deliver up the kingdom, and present it unto the Father spotless, saying—I have overcome and have trodden the wine-press alone, even the wine-press of the fierceness of the wrath of Almighty God.—*Ibid.* 81–88, 102–107.

In all these states which are designated as "kingdoms" or "glories," it is understood that the inhabitants shall reside in a state of blessedness and happiness to eternity, the divine element in each soul being realized in life as far as the conditions in which he has lived on earth will permit. In other words, the doctrine of salvation as here developed, is that all mankind shall receive of God "as they are able." Howbeit, only in the Celestial Kingdom is the direct presence and glory of God to be enjoyed, and it is confidently expected that all who desire to live to please Him shall strive to earn this exaltation. In the other kingdoms, while the inhabitants enjoy evidences of the love and mercy of God, through the "ministering of angels," they are not admitted to His Presence, nor do they see Him. Their happiness is, therefore, of a lesser quality than that of the Celestial Kingdom, and not at all that which the pious soul is naturally moved to desire — the presence and favor of God. The Telestial world, composed of those, as explained, who have committed grievous sins, "not unto death," is comparable to the somewhat merciful concession of mediæval theologians, the *levissima damnatio,* the "easiest room in hell." Because, however, as specified, Christ's Gospel is a message of Salvation, not of condemnation, the "lightest degree of damnation" of mediæval theologians, appears here as the "lowest grade of salvation." From the point of view of the most ideal piety, the distinction is one of terms, rather than of ideas, since the soul is shut out from sight of God, except for the fact that all men in the Latter-day theology are considered to be proper sons of God, and heirs of life, unless irredeemably rebellious and guilty of the sin which "hath no forgiveness, neither in this world, neither in the world to come."

According to this theology, also, there is a hell, and a very real one, reserved for the unpardonable, irredeemable and incorrigible. (Cf. Jude, 11–13.) These are the ones described and specified in the great revelation above quoted, in the following words:

> "And this we saw also, and bear record, that an angel of God who was in authority in the presence of God, who rebelled against the Only Begotten Son, whom the Father loved, and who was in the bosom of the Father — was thrust down from the presence of God and the Son, and was called Perdition, for the heavens wept over him — he was Lucifer a son of the morning. And we beheld, and lo, he is fallen! is fallen! even a son of the morning. . . . Wherefore he maketh war with the saints of God, and encompasses them round about. And we saw a vision of the sufferings of those with whom he made war and overcame, for thus came the voice of the Lord unto us. Thus saith the Lord, concerning all those who know my power, and have been made partakers thereof, and suffered themselves through the power of the devil, to be overcome, and to deny the truth and defy my power — they are they who are the sons of perdition, of whom I say that it had been better for them never to have been born, for they are vessels of wrath, doomed to suffer the wrath of God, with the devil and his angels in eternity; concerning whom I have said there is no forgiveness in this world nor in the world to come, having denied the Holy Spirit after having received it, and having denied the Only Begotten Son of the Father — having crucified him unto themselves, and put him to an open shame. These are they who shall go away into the lake of fire and brimstone, with the devil and his angels, and the only ones on whom the second death shall have any power; yea, verily, the only ones who shall not be redeemed in the due time of the Lord, after the sufferings of his wrath; for all the rest shall be brought forth by the resurrection of

the dead, through the triumph and the glory of the Lamb, who was slain, who was in the bosom of the Father before the worlds were made.

"And this is the gospel, the glad tidings which the voice out of the heavens bore record unto us, that he came into the world, even Jesus, to be crucified for the world, and to cleanse it from all unrighteousness; that through him all might be saved whom the Father had put into his power and made by him, . . .; wherefore, he saves all except them: they shall go away into everlasting punishment, which is eternal punishment, to reign with the devil and his angels in eternity, where their worm dieth not, and the fire is not quenched, which is their torment; and the end thereof, neither the place thereof, nor their torment no man knows, neither was it revealed, neither is, neither will be revealed unto man, except to them who are made partakers thereof: . . . wherefore the end, the width, the height, the depth, and the misery thereof, they understand not, neither any man except them who are ordained unto this condemnation."—*Ibid.* 25–27, 29–42, 44–46, 48.

IV

MORMON MARRIAGE INSTITUTIONS

"The great problem of humanity . . . the development of each individuality to its highest possibility. . . . That polygamy, wisely and faithfully practiced, will be a grand factor in bringing to pass this millennium of usefulness and happiness, I sincerely believe."— *Susa Young Gates.*

CHAPTER XVIII

PLURAL MARRIAGE AND THE POSITION OF WOMEN AMONG THE MORMONS

THE Mormon institution of polygyny, or, as it is preferably termed, "plural marriage," was, as we are told, founded in obedience to the commands of a divine revelation to the Prophet Joseph Smith about 1832. Although this revelation was not committed to writing until over ten years later, its principles were imparted to several of the Prophet's close associates before that date, and its provisions were actually being obeyed by many leaders of the Church many years before its formal promulgation in Utah in 1852.

Undoubtedly, this institution is, and always has been, the sorest occasion of opposition and criticism of the Mormon Church and its members. Except for it, the task of appealing for justice for them at the bar of conscience would have been unspeakably easier: their many excellent traits would undoubtedly have compelled the respect of fair and candid minds long before this date. It remains, however, for the world in general precisely what, as history records, it was, in the beginning, to the "Saints" themselves, a veritable "stone of stumbling and rock of offence." Indeed, if the doctrine and practice of this "principle" were not believed to be of divine origin, its establishment must have seemed to be the worst possible tactical blunder in the leaders of a people, who had already suffered as much persecution as could be possible in Nineteenth Century America.

However, we find that devout Mormons, women as well as men, speak of plural marriage as a "holy order," an eminent means of blessing, both personal and social; something, in fact, closely analogous to the several sacraments of traditional Christianity. This fact cannot fail to be a surprise to the general reader. We know that there are, and have been, very many systems of religious teaching, as well as many systems of civil law, that have not only "allowed" the practice of polygyny, or polygamy, but have provided distinctly for its maintenance. But there is a difference between merely asserting that it is right for a man to have a plurality of wives and the apparent attribution of a very real form of blessedness to such as take them, even with the authority of the Priesthood of God. The truth of the matter is that the Mormon estimate of this institution makes it an actual means of grace, an eminent instrument for the salvation of souls. Just as they hold most strenuously to the doctrine of salvation of the dead by means of proxy baptism, just so, with the belief in preexistence, as already explained, they consider it an act of eminent piety to provide for the birth of a human soul under the fullness of Gospel influences. That the birth of as many souls as possible under such conditions will hasten the redemption of humanity, and of the world, is an evident corollary to the high importance attached to life on earth in the teachings of the Mormon system. In this aspect of the matter, it is easy to see how that parenthood could be made to assume the aspect of a high virtue, involving that a person who had brought many souls into life was entitled to honor, as an instrument in God's hands in the grand work of populating the world with a race, whose leading attribute is the possession of the divine Spirit. Because, however, the child-bearing capacity of the average woman is limited, it is evident that the only available means by which a worthy man could multiply his offspring would be by taking to himself a plurality of wives. Nor, with this aim in view, is the usual cavilling charge of "sensuality" in such a relation at all well taken.

The doctrine of plural marriage among the Mormons is also a part or incident of a really grand and impressive concept, the eternity of the marriage relation for all such as are joined and "sealed" by the authority of God's priesthood. Not only does this doctrine involve implicit belief in the promise that "whatsoever thou shalt bind on earth shall be bound in heaven" (Matt. xvi. 19), as applied to the supreme authority of the Church, but also that those so married for eternity shall become the progenitors of multitudinous blessed offspring in the world to come. They partake, therefore, in the creative function of Deity. There is much in such a teaching to appeal strongly to the imagination and the sentiments of normal minds.

The revelation embodying the doctrine of "Celestial Marriage," or marriage for eternity, is to be found in the Book of *Doctrine and Covenants,* Section cxxxii, bearing date July 12, 1843. The crucial passages of this document are as follows:

"And verily I say unto you, that the conditions of this law are these: — All covenants, contracts, bonds, obligations, . . . that are not made, and entered into, and sealed, by the Holy Spirit of promise, of him who is anointed, both as well for time and for all eternity, . . . whom I have appointed on the earth to hold this power (and I have appointed unto my servant Joseph to hold this power in the last days, and there is never but one on the earth at a time, on whom this power and the keys of this priesthood are conferred), are of no efficacy, virtue or force, in and after the resurrection from the dead; for all contracts that are not made unto this end, have an end when men are dead. . . . Therefore, if a man marry him a wife in the world, and he marry her not by me, nor by my word; and he covenant with her so long as he is in the world, and she with him, their covenant and marriage are not of force when they are dead, and when they are out of the world; therefore, they are not bound by any law when they are out of the world; therefore, when they are out of the world, they neither marry, nor are given in marriage; but are appointed angels in heaven, which angels are ministering servants, to minister for those who are worthy of a far more, and an exceeding, and an eternal weight of glory; for these angels did not abide my law, therefore they cannot be enlarged, but remain separately and singly, without exaltation, in their saved condition, to all eternity, and from henceforth are not gods, but are angels of God, for ever and ever. . . . And again, verily I say unto you, if a man marry a wife by my word, which is my law, and by the new and everlasting covenant, and it is sealed unto them by the Holy Spirit of promise, by him who is anointed, unto whom I have appointed this power, and the keys of this Priesthood; and it shall be said unto them, ye shall come forth in the first resurrection; and if it be after the first resurrection, in the next resurrection; and shall inherit thrones, kingdoms, principalities, and powers, dominions, all heights and depths . . . it shall be done unto them in all things whatsoever my servant hath put upon them, in time, and through all eternity, and shall be of full force when they are out of the world; and they shall pass by the angels, and the Gods, which are set there, to their exaltation and glory in all things, as hath been sealed upon their heads, which glory shall be a fullness and a continuation of the seeds forever and ever. Then shall they be Gods, because they have no end; therefore shall they be from everlasting to everlasting, because they continue; then shall they be above all, because all things are subject unto them. . . .

. . . .

"Abraham received promises concerning his seed, and of the fruit of his loins,— from whose loins ye are, namely, my servant Joseph,— which were to continue so long as they were in the world; and as touching Abraham and his seed, out of the world they should continue; both in the world and out of the world should they continue as innumerable as the stars; or, if ye were to count the sand upon the sea shore, ye could not number them. This promise is yours, also, because ye are of Abraham, and the promise was made unto Abraham; and by this law are the continuation of the works of my Father, wherein he glorifieth himself. Go ye, therefore, and do the works of Abraham; enter ye into my law, and ye shall be saved. But if ye enter not into my law ye cannot receive the promise of my Father, which he made unto Abraham. . . .

"David's wives and concubines were given unto him, of me, by the hand of Nathan, my servant, and others of the prophets who had the keys of this power; and in none of these things did he sin against me, save in the case of Uriah and his wife; and, therefore he hath fallen from his exaltation, and received his portion; and he shall not inherit them out of the world; for I gave them unto another, saith the Lord. . . .

"And verily, verily I say unto you, that whatsoever you seal on earth, shall be sealed in heaven; and whatsoever you bind on earth, in my name, and by my word, saith the Lord, it shall be eternally bound in the heavens; . . . and whosesoever sins you retain on earth, shall be retained in heaven. . . .

"And again, as pertaining to the law of the Priesthood: If any man espouse a virgin, and desire to espouse another, and the first give her consent; and if he espouse the second, and they are virgins, and have vowed to no other man, then is he justified; he cannot commit adultery, for they are given unto him; for he cannot commit adultery with that that belongeth unto him and to no one else; and if he have ten virgins given unto him by this law, he cannot commit adultery, for they belong to him, and they are given unto him, therefore is he justified."

It is evident that the leading points set forth in these passages are: (1) that a contract of marriage "for time and for all eternity" can be ratified only by the authority of God's priesthood, which has been restored in and through Joseph Smith; (2) that such authority and promise was given to the ancient patriarchs, specifically to Abraham; (3) that the priestly authority, vested in the ancients, and restored in Joseph Smith, can permit a restoration of polygynous marriages, also, as among the patriarchs of old time; (4) that the promise to Abraham, "concerning his seed . . . as innumerable as the stars, . . . is yours, also, because ye are of Abraham." Holding, as it did, that the highest evidence of God's blessing on earth lies in obeying the primeval command to Adam, and begetting a numerous and godly offspring, which, also, should continue to increase in eternity, this teaching formed the basis of a very real religious impulse.

Quite apart from the religious or moral significance of this "principle," there can be no doubt that it is a "social phase" of eminent interest. For, unless all indications are misleading, it furnished a good working solution of the so-called "sex problem," which is a serious consideration in all rational humanitarian minds not dominated by unreasoning dogmatic traditions. Such candid minds know perfectly well that the many grave questions involved in the relations of the sexes must one day be met and grappled; also, that traditional notions have not evidently contributed to any permanent solution of the involved difficulties. The Mormon solution presented several conspicuous advantages which will be appreciated by the sociologist. Among these were specified:

"The right and privilege of every honorable woman to be a wife and mother, which in monogamy, under existing conditions, preponderance of women over men, disinclination of men to marry, etc., was virtually denied: the extirpation of the social evil; the production of a healthier posterity, and the physical, mental and moral improvement of the race. These were among the temporal or tangible reasons put forth."— *O. F. Whitney* (*History of Utah, Vol.* I, *p.* 212.)

That polygyny, as practiced by the Mormons, actually embodied these very desirable advantages is a fact to which competent observers bear testimony. That these advantages are of a real and universally intelligible character, whether or not secured by polygynous relations, can be denied by no sociologist whatever. The assertion of the right of every good woman to the hallowed joys of wifehood and maternity is alone inestimable. The virtual abrogation of this right under prevailing social institutions has worked unmixed misery to multitudes of good women, and is rapidly becoming a matter of prime gravity to society as a whole. Both the physiologist and the sociologist know perfectly well that with the normal woman the supreme demand is for maternity, also that a woman devoid of maternal instinct is a sad and pitiable being. The constantly increasing number of unmarried women, particularly in America, indicates a condition by no means healthy or desirable. Such women, often driven to seek unnatural substitutes for the normal occupations of life, expend their energies in the various feminist movements of the day, which, apart from any good sought or achieved, nurture the common vice of asserting the "cause" of woman against man, thus merely complicating the sorrows and difficulties of an already unstable social order by antagonism to nature's arrangements, which is both preposterous and deplorable. The outlook for the race, whose mothers are maturing under such an influence, filled with the false ideas of life, inevitably derived from those who have not properly experienced it, must be dubious indeed. It is interesting to note, however, that, while, under Mormon influences, women first received the right to vote, also, the first impulse to combine in distinctively feminine organizations for charity, mutual improvement, and other activities, there never was a "woman movement" among these people, nor any agitation for the "rights" of the sex, otherwise, supposedly, to be withheld by the "selfishness of men," as the perverse expression has it. Not only do the women of this people average high in all qualities classed as "womanly," but they are, and always have been the strongest advocates of the "plural order." Also, while, as a rule, trained and educated to independence and self-reliance, they have maintained a nearly uniform enthusiasm for home duties and the training and rearing of children that might well be advertised as "worthy of all acceptation." Mormonism has achieved the virtue of mutual confidence and cooperation between the sexes, and has provided to avoid the monstrous perversity, commonly known as "sex-consciousness" among wanton agitators.

As an illustration of the grounds on which Bishop Whitney and others claim that the practice of plural marriage operated to "extirpate the social evil" the following quotation is eminently suggestive. In the *Mormon,* published in New York City, March

24, 1855, this may be found under the caption "Mormonism Revised":

"The Boston *Herald* of the 15th inst., under the above heading has the following: 'On Tuesday morning last, Henrietta Podafew, a very little woman, was brought before Judge Spooner, in Cincinnati, charged with having attempted to force herself into a permanent residence at the houses of four different married gentlemen. It appears that she had been the extra wife of each of these gentlemen for some time, and has two children belonging to the quartette, and thinking it her right, she sought to establish her home in the house of either one of them; the four wives made a common cause of it, and united in a complaint against Henrietta, who was sent to the county residence, provided by law for offenders.'

"The writer must be wofully ignorant of Mormonism, or being himself a monogamist, of the kind specified in this article, shrinks from the responsibility of his darling institution by making Mormonism his scapegoat. I would say to him, 'Don't take the advantage, Mr. Herald, of Mormon liberality, and ride to death the free "Pegasus."' To show the writer his mistake we will compare his notes with Mormonism, under the legal restriction of Monogamy.

"One woman clandestinely becomes the dishonored wife of four dishonorable men. Mormonism unclandestinely makes four women the honored wives of one honorable man.

"Monogamy keeps one wife in the house, and turns the rest out of doors to suffer unsheltered and unprotected: Mormonism provides for them all, and treats them kindly and impartially.

"Monogamy floods society with illegitimate children having no ostensible father, unprotected, uneducated, and unprovided for: Mormonism requires that every man shall provide for his own offspring, in everything that shall qualify them to become honorable men and women in society.

"Monogamy puts a Henrietta in the county jail, for claiming the support of her children, at the hands of their father, and allows the father freedom to continue his clandestine operations: Mormonism allows the right to a mother to claim the support of her children at the hands of their father.

"Monogamy, owing to its narrow, contracted matrimonial relations, on the one hand, throws the mantle of charity over adultery, with great magnanimity: on the other hand, Mormonism, liberal in its matrimonial relation, holds the adulterer, or adulteress, to be worthy of death (according to the laws of God), but owing to the prejudices of the age, they are cut off from Mormonism, and permitted to depart immediately to those countries, where the results of monogamic laws make their cause more tolerable.

"If this brief contrast meets the eye of the writer in the *Herald,* he will no doubt see his mistake, and, if honest, will head his next article of like character, 'Monogamy Illustrated,' instead of 'Mormonism Revised.'"

President John Taylor is quoted as speaking to precisely similar effect, as follows:

"You acknowledge one wife and her children; what of your other associations unacknowledged? We acknowledge all of our wives and all of our children: we don't keep a few only and turn the others out as outcasts, to be provided for by orphan asylums, or to turn out vagabonds on the street to help increase the fearfully growing evil. Our actions are all honest, open and above board. We have no gambling hells, no drunkenness, no infanticides, no houses of assignation, no prostitutes. Our wives are not afraid of our intrigues and debauchery, nor are our wives and daughters corrupted by designing and unprincipled villains. We believe in the chastity and virtue of woman, and maintain them. There is not to-day in the wide world a place where female honor, virtue and chastity are so well protected as in Utah."—*Quoted in Utah and its People, by a Gentile,* (1882).

This claim that plural marriage operates to neutralize the social evil, which seems to have been more or less borne out by the testimony of numerous observers, requires some further explanation. The thought most immediately occurring to the candid mind is that this good result followed from Mormonism's frank recognition of the facts of life, which is only another way of saying that polygny — even if not polygamy — is a general practice among civilized and Christian, as well as among uncivilized and heathen peoples, and that the sanest and wisest policy is to recognize and justify it, rather than to manufacture sin and crime by foolishly attempting to ignore nature. In this particular the assumed revelation to Joseph Smith is dignified by its analogy to the consistent policy of the Mosaic Law, which made every concession to human frailties and propensities before decreeing punishments that often seem unduly severe. It may be objected to this line of reasoning that the wayward tendencies, often found in the male human, should be discouraged and reprobated, rather than considered in any dignified light. An evident answer to this must be that, first, the facts of life demand attention, rather than any theory as to what should exist, and, second, that the evils of society quite as frequently result from attempts to achieve artificial virtues as from any real native depravity of human nature itself. If society, with assumed consistency to a lofty ideal of right, chooses to decree that the inborn tendency of the individual to beget his kind, instead of being guided in proper and normal channels, by observance of nature's decrees, shall be allowed to involve conditions that end in social ostracism, misery, disease and death, we must blame the stupid short-sightedness of society for the result, which all right-minded people cannot help but deplore. The inevitable conclusion must be that prostitution and other orders of perversity are recognized and established institutions of society, also that the most wicked and abandoned individual cannot be blamed for all the evil which he or she commits. It cannot be rationally denied that the wisest policy is to contrive for some method of maintaining natural tendencies on the lines in which the Creator evidently intended that they should be expressed, thus avoiding the sad results of misuse. Some such idea as this is developed in the following passage, quoted by Mrs. Helen Mar

Whitney, a Mormon writer, from a work entitled, *History and Philosophy of Marriage:*

"'A woman's instincts revolt against the thought of a plurality of husbands, and judging his feelings by her own, she cannot see how a man can want, or at least can love a plurality of wives. But, as this point involves a constitutional difference of sex, it is one in which we must be aware that our feelings cannot guide us. A man can never know the infinite tenderness and the infinite patience of a mother's love, except imperfectly, by reason and observation. His experience does not teach him. His paternal love does not resemble it. So a woman can never know the purity and sincerity of a man's conjugal love for a plurality of wives, except by similar observation and reason. Her conjugal love is unlike it. Her love for one man exhausts and absorbs her whole conjugal nature: there is no room for more. And if she receives the truth that his nature is capable of a plural love, she must attain it by the use of her reason, or admit it upon the testimony of honest men.'

"This is correct reasoning (says Mrs. Whitney) but I confess that it has been a very great puzzle to me; and only by using my reasoning faculties and by the testimony of my husband and other honest men could I bring myself to admit it. But if my life depended upon giving a true testimony concerning my belief and practice in the order of plural marriage, I could not now contradict these statements, but must still acknowledge the truth of them.

"'Great men are always polygamists (continues the quotation), . . . no matter under what social system they may live, . . . even though they transgress the laws of ordinary social life, . . . and it is a shame and a pity that our social laws cannot be so amended, and brought into harmony with those of God and nature, that our noblest men would yield them the most prompt obedience. And is it not a sad pity, a burning shame, and a fearful wrong that our laws are such that men cannot acknowledge their mistresses, and avow their children? The wrongs of these women and children are crying to God from the ground, and he will hear and judge. These great men are brave; but they are not brave enough. They have no just right to practice their polygamy in in the dark. Let us have either an honest monogamy or an avowed polygamy. Hence it is that I am called by the justice of God and the sufferings of humanity to appeal to every honorable sentiment in mankind in behalf of a greater freedom to marry, and a greater purity in the marriage relation. Let us have such marriage laws, that whatever relations any honorable man shall determine to form with the opposite sex can be honorably formed and honorably maintained.'"— *Why We Practice Plural Marriage, pp.* 50–52.

Such a line of reasoning will undoubtedly be met with grave and displeased objections by a very large number of readers. There is no use, however, in concealing facts, for the sake of upholding even the most attractive theory, and, whatever may be one's prejudices or predilections, there can be no doubt in any honest mind that an institution, ensuring the happiness and well-being of as many women and children as possible, even if that institution be plural marriage itself, is unspeakably superior to any other whatsoever, which does not always contrive to protect such persons from misery and death, as the result of supposed wrongdoing. When we consider further that the Bible contains not one unmistakable word in condemnation of plural marriage, it is evident that "scriptural consistency" cannot be urged as a valid argument against it.

It is a sad and sickening comment on our alleged sense of right that any intelligent person can accept the unspeakable conditions of our present social order, as inevitable, and displays the impudence to declare unrighteous and intolerable any institution that gives any promise of neutralizing these. Whether, or not, sins against the august nature of the procreative instinct, including the dreadful crimes of infanticide and fœticide, are damnable in all their phases, and whether, or not, they manifest solely in detestable types of individuals, the fact remains that they continue to be committed, and that they form already a menace to the life of civilization itself. This fact is ably set forth in the following quotation from W. E. H. Lecky, the English historian:

> "There are two ends which a moralist . . . will especially regard—the natural duty of every man doing something for the support of the child he has called into existence, and the preservation of the domestic circle unassailed and unpolluted. The family is the center and the archetype of the state, and the happiness and goodness of society are always in very great degree dependent upon the purity of domestic life. The essentially exclusive nature of marital affection, and the natural desire of every man to be certain of the paternity of the child he supports, render incursions of irregular passions within the domestic circle a cause of extreme suffering. Yet it would appear as if the excessive force of these passions would render such incursions both frequent and inevitable.
>
> "Under these circumstances, there has arisen in society a figure which is certainly the most mournful, and in some respects the most awful, upon which the eye of the moralist can dwell: That unhappy being whose very name is a shame to speak; who counterfeits with a cold heart the transports of affection, and submits herself as the passive instrument of lust; who is scorned and insulted as the vilest of her sex, and doomed, for the most part, to disease and abject wretchedness and an early death, appears in every age as the perpetual symbol of the degradation and the sinfulness of man. Herself the supreme type of vice, she is ultimately the most efficient guardian of virtue. But for her, the unchallenged purity of countless homes would be polluted, and not a few who, in pride of their untempted chastity, think of her with an indignant shudder, would have known the agony of remorse and despair. On that one degraded and ignoble form are concentrated the passions that might have filled the world with shame. She remains, while creeds and civilizations rise and fall, the eternal priestess of humanity, blasted for the sins of the people."—*History of European Morals, Vol. II, pp.* 284–285.

If the fact that a nominally Christian writer can thus enlarge upon any condition existing in a social order also nominally Christian, is tolerable to any person possessing one spark of human sentiment, there is no more to be said. What are we to say of persons, who, finding such results involved in Christian society, conceive no suspicion that there is something radically wrong with our standards of right and justice? In the discussion of such a matter as the present one, however, we rapidly outride the limits of Mormonism or anti-Mormonism, and emerge upon a basis of fact in which the rights of mankind and the stability of the social order are the paramount considerations. In this connection, therefore, it is proper to affirm that true civilization must inevitably achieve the heights of intelligence and sanity in which one form of plural marriage, polygamy or polygyny — call it what one may — shall be established and enforced: this is that the father of any child that may be proved to be his shall be compelled to acknowledge and provide for it and its mother, according to the righteous statute of the Mosaic Law, "He shall surely endow her to be his wife, and shall not put her away all his days."

The claim that Mormon plural marriage was conducive to "the production of a healthier posterity, and the physical, mental and moral improvement of the race" is partially elucidated in the following passage quoted from a capable and unbiassed observer of the workings of the Mormon system:

"The literalism with which the Mormons have interpreted Scripture has led them directly to polygamy. The texts promising to Abraham a progeny numerous as the stars above or the sands below, and that "in his seed (a polygamist) all the families of the earth shall be blessed," induce them, his descendants, to seek a similar blessing. The theory announcing that 'the man is not without the woman, nor the woman without the man,' is by them interpreted into an absolute command that both sexes shall marry, and that a woman cannot enter the heavenly kingdom without a husband to introduce her. . . . The 'chaste and plural marriage,' being once legalized, finds a multitude of supporters. The anti-Mormons declare that it is at once fornication and adultery—a sin which absorbs all others. The Mormons point triumphantly to the austere morals of their community, their superior freedom from maladive influences, and the absence of that uncleanness and licentiousness which distinguish the cities of the civilized world. They boast that, if it be an evil, they have at least chosen the lesser evil; that they practice openly as a virtue what others do secretly as a sin — how full is society of these latent Mormons! — that their plurality has abolished the necessity of concubinage, cryptogamy, contubernium, celibacy, *marriages du treizieme arrondissement,* with their terrible consequences, infanticide, and so forth; that they have removed their ways from those 'whose end is bitter as wormwood, and sharp as a two-edged sword.'

"There are rules and regulations of Mormonism — I can not say whether they date from before or after the heavenly command to pluralize — which disprove the popular statement that such marriages are made to gratify licentiousness, and which render polygamy a positive necessity. All sensuality in the married state is strictly forbidden beyond the requisite for insuring progeny — the practice, in fact, of Adam and Abraham. During the gestation and nursing of children, the strictest continence on the part of the mother is required — rather for a hygienic than for a religious reason. The same custom is practiced in part by the Jews, and in whole by some of the noblest tribes of savages; the splendid physical development of the Kaffir race in South Africa is attributed by some authors to a rule of continence like that of the Mormons, and to a lactation prolonged for two years. The anomaly of such a practice in the midst of civilization is worthy of a place in Balzac's great repertory of morbid anatomy: it is only to be equaled by the exceptional nature of the Mormon's position, his past fate and his future prospects. Spartanlike, the Faith wants a race of warriors, and it adopts the best means to obtain them."—*Richard F. Burton* (*City of the Saints, pp.* 427–429).

To precisely similar import is the following passage from another observer, equally candid, unprejudiced and careful. He writes:

"Physically, Mormon plurality appears to me to promise much of the success which Plato dreamed of, and Utah about the best nursery for his soldiers that he could have found. Look at the urchins that go clattering about the roads, perched two together on the bare backs of horses, and only a bit of rope by way of bridle. Look at the rosy, demure little girls that will be their wives some day. Take note of their fathers' daily lives, healthy outdoor work. Go into their homes and see the mothers at *their* work. . . . And then as you walk home through one of their rural towns along the tree-shaded streets, with water purling along beside you as you walk, and the clear breeze from the hills blowing the perfume of flowers across your path in gusts, with the cottage homes, half smothered in blossoming fruit-trees, on either hand, and a perpetual succession of gardens,— then, I say, come back and sit down, if you can, to call this people 'licentious,' 'impure,' 'degraded.'"—*Phil Robinson* (*Sinners and Saints*), *p.* 97.

The sociologist can feel no emotion other than real joy in learning that any sect, or body of people, claiming a standing as Christians, has departed so far from the discredited and footless principle of "other-worldliness," as actually to profess a vital interest in the improvement of the human race — not only socially and morally, by strong organization and cooperation and a consistent advocacy of lofty principles of righteousness, but even physically, also — by advocating, and enforcing, so far as is possible, so sane and hygienic an order of continence as that mentioned by Mr. Burton. That this line of conduct is, and always has been, preached and advocated by Mormon teachers and authorities, and followed to the letter by the best among them, is a truth which can not be denied by any candid and unprejudiced investigator.

CHAPTER XIX

WOMAN UNDER PLURAL MARRIAGE

As is familiar to anyone who has read the current literature on Mormonism or the "Mormon problem," so-called, an immense amount of unsolicited sympathy has been lavished upon the presumed sufferings of Mormon plural wives. The women of America, deceived by the false opinions circulated by biassed observers and professional anti-Mormons, have frequently united in petitions to Congress, and in movements, intended to be benevolent, with the sole intent to deliver their "downtrodden sisters" from the thraldom of an institution, popularly classed with slavery as the "twin relic" of barbarism. However, the "downtrodden sisters" of Mormondom, far from welcoming, or even secretly conniving at, any of these well-intentioned meddlings, on their behalf, have invariably protested as emphatically as could be possible, bearing impassioned and eloquent testimony to what, as they assert, are the positive benefits of the institution to womankind. Nor were these protests against the efforts of would-be saviors uttered by women of the so-called "lower classes," they whose ignorance of life and general dependent condition would render them convenient tools of an "ambitious and tyrannical priesthood." Few, if any, of these humble souls have emerged from their lowly surroundings to "root" for their "priests." On the other hand, the strongest utterances of the kind have come from the women of prominent families, who in a discouragingly large percentage of cases have been of the highly-educated and finely-sensitive stock of the "best families of New England."

All this argues very definitely to several evident conclusions: first, that the presumed religious basis, upon which rests the institution of plural marriage, is really and vitally religious; second, that the institution evidently involves actual and valuable advantages for womankind — whatever may be the disadvantages — being in no sense rooted in the selfishness and self-indulgence of man, as variously alleged; third, that, as shown by the testimonies of its women, the claims of Mormonism to restoring woman to her proper place in the social order have some elements of justification.

Among other reflections that force themselves upon the candid mind is that it is, with the most doubtful propriety imaginable, that the male portion of a community could be credited with any intelligible worldly advantage from the inauguration of such an institution as plural marriage. From the point of view of the ordinary man, few prospects could be less attractive, or more fraught with the certainty of vexation, than the effort — unceasing and resultless, if one may judge from the sentiments of the average woman — to adjust and reconcile the conflicting claims and inevitable quarrels of several openly-acknowledged wives. Should the public relations of any man of ordinary calibre with several women be primarily other than normal and righteous, such interfeminine disagreements must be seriously aggravated by his own present feelings of preference or distaste in any given case. Thus, the polygynous household must quickly disintegrate through satiety, mutual quarrels, and defections. That such unhappy consequences were rare among Mormons constitutes a very strong and definite evidence that their claims to religious consistency and pure, normal sentiment in these unions are amply justified.

Touching the mutual relations of husband and wives in these polygynous unions, the following from an article by Mrs. Susa Young Gates, a daughter of Brigham Young, is significant:

"The statement that polygamy will make a god of a man argues nothing to me. My frank opinion is that men will necessarily be god-like who enter heaven, where will dwell woman, the purer and better part of humanity. The care of a large family naturally increases a man's anxieties and capabilities; and it is these very forces which unite to ennoble and elevate any man who accepts them cheerfully and fulfills them faithfully.

"What woman's respect would not deepen for the man she saw guarding her own feelings tenderly while still gentle and kind to the young wife recently taken beneath his roof; who would measure every act, weigh every word, that no heart given into his keeping might unnecessarily suffer? Would she not reverence the man who sought to soothe every heartache and bind up every wound made by this new order of things? She might, she certainly would, suffer in giving up a share of that time and attention that had been all her own, but her love and esteem would deepen for him who had asked and obtained her willing consent, and who then helped her to gradually rise from under Mother Eve's curse, and find that life had also problems, aims, and paths for her in which to awaken and develop the gifts and talents given her by a wise Father. He, also — would he not find his loving devotion deepened every hour for the noble woman who had consented to this thing that they might be spiritually blessed thereby — seeing her kindness, her forbearance, her growing affection for the young wife, who, in her turn was sinking selfishness in this struggle for the highest and the best — would he not feel that God had blessed him above his expectations?

"Nowhere on the face of this wide earth is the love of husbands for their wives and wives for their husbands so intense, so thrilling, and so divine as it is here in Utah. Men go by hundreds into prisons, by thousands into willing exile, rather than sacrifice the hearts of their beloved companions. Women cheer them in this determination, separating for this life in the glad hope of an eternal reunion, which no law, no court of public opinion, can ever deny them. To be true in this life through trial and separation is preferred by these faithful people to the breaking of solemn covenants.

"In connection with this idea of the undue exaltation of the husband, and consequent debasement of the wives, let me offer an illustration. When a body of American people unite as a State and elect a Governor, they choose a man because of his honor, integrity and superior intelligence. In the same way Mormon women select a husband. The affections of the people twine around their chosen head, if he is worthy, and his presence is welcomed and courted everywhere. It is so with Mormon husbands."—*Family Life Among the Mormons,* (*North American Review, March,* 1890, *p.* 348.)

While it is necessary to a complete understanding of the institution of plural marriage to explain the religious basis upon which it was professedly founded, this is by no means the most interesting phase of the matter to the average reader. The point of greatest interest, undoubtedly, to such a one is the effect of the practice upon the women involved, and their opinions of its operation, together with such data on their intelligence and experience, as would give a clue to the competency of their testimony, either for or against the facts alleged. In the course of such an inquiry we shall discover frank acknowledgments of the fact that the practice of the institution, at the start at least, was a "burden grievous to be borne," but nearly uniformly the testimony follows that, having taken up this cross, from a strong sense of right and duty, the ultimate consequence was a compensation of greater joy and peace than had seemed, otherwise, possible. This allegation follows, of course, upon the consistently religious regard for the institution, which alone served to vitalize it. The Mormon wife was willing, for the sake of her religion, to undergo the inevitable sorrow of sharing the husband, whom she loved, with yet other women, and to battle with the impulses of jealousy and resentment, even of an intrusion fully permitted and connived at. Whether such a sacrifice was necessary in them, or in any other women is immaterial: it demonstrated the power of religion to strengthen the human spirit for patient suffering, also, to compensate, with greater blessings, for the things shared and the sentiments sacrificed. It is scarcely remarkable, therefore, that we hear the familiar tribute to Mormon wives—"the world never saw such women before"—quite as though their characters, "made perfect through suffering," displayed the glory of womanhood at its highest reach.

This must be to non-Mormon readers nearly the strangest thing about the whole matter. Some of them will undoubtedly balk at the story of sorrow and crosses, and forget the story of the "higher compensations" achieved through these. But we must not forget that any effort to "live religion" inevitably involves sacrifice and suffering. Even with the abolishment of polygyny, or of any other social custom, for that matter, this law is not abrogated. If from this institution arose the only crosses ever laid upon the back of woman, we might well condemn it, but the case is far otherwise. The reality of religious conviction is demonstrated solely in its power, under any or all circumstances, to lend the ability to suffer and achieve. Certainly, the Mormon wives and mothers suffered no more under the regime of polygyny than at the hands of their sectarian persecutors, long before such an institution was dreamed of among them.

As a notable example of the nearly mystical exaltation in which some of the earlier Mormon wives entered into this "order," the testimony of Mrs. Bathsheba W. Smith is significant. She writes:

> "Immediately after my marriage, my husband, as one of the apostles of the Church, started on a mission to some of the Eastern States. . . . He returned in the fall; soon after which we were blessed by receiving our endowments, and were sealed under the law of celestial marriage. I heard the prophet Joseph charge the twelve with the duty and responsibility of administering the ordinances of endowments and sealing for the living and the dead. . . . I heard the prophet give instructions concerning plural marriage; he counseled the sisters not to trouble themselves in consequence of it, that it would be all right, and the result would be for their glory and exaltation. . . . Being thoroughly convinced, as well as my husband, that the doctrine of a plurality of wives was from God, and having a fixed determination to attain to celestial glory, I felt to embrace the whole Gospel, and believing that it was for my husband's exaltation that he should obey the revelation on celestial marriage, that he might attain to kingdoms, thrones, principalities and powers, firmly believing that I should participate with him in all his blessings, glory and honor; accordingly, within the last year, like Sarah of old, I had given to my husband five wives, good, virtuous, honorable young women. They all had their home with us; I being proud of my husband, and loving him very much, knowing him to be a man of God, and believing he would not love them less because he loved me more for doing this. I had joy in having a testimony that what I had done was acceptable to my Father in Heaven."—*The Women of Mormondom*, (*Tullidge*), *pp.* 319–321.

The testimony of Mrs. Smith, who was, if we may judge from her record, as noble and thoroughly Christian soul as ever lived, introduces wifely devotion in a new and strange light. Whatever may have been her pangs when, "like Sarah of old," she gave her husband "five wives, good, virtuous, honorable young women," she has nothing to say about them. Evidently, the doctrine of eternal marriage afforded her some valuable consolations, as regards the next world and its glories, as a partial compensation, at least, for her sorrows and sacrifices — if she so viewed them — in this.

Quite as affecting is the fervid testimony of Phœbe Carter Woodruff, the first wife of President Wilford Woodruff, who also accepted the plural "order," and gave her husband several other wives. She is quoted as follows:

> "When the principle of polygamy was first taught I thought it the most wicked thing I ever heard of; consequently I opposed it to the best of my ability, until I became ill and wretched. As soon, however, as I became convinced that it originated as a revelation from God through Joseph, and knowing him to be a prophet, I wrestled with my Heavenly Father in fervent prayer, to be guided aright at that all-important moment of my life. The answer came. Peace was given to my mind. I knew it was the will of God; and from that time to the present I have faithfully sought to honor the patriarchal law.
>
> "Of Joseph my testimony is that he was one of the greatest prophets the Lord ever called; that he lived for the redemption of mankind, and died a martyr for the truth. The love of the Saints for him will never die. . . . Of my husband I can truly say, I have found him a worthy man, with scarcely his equal on earth. . . . He has been faithful to God and his family every day of his life. My respect for him has increased with our years, and my desire for an eternal union with him will be the last wish of my mortal life."—*Ibid., pp.* 413–414.

No one could possibly believe that such a tribute to a husband, as closes this quotation, could have been made by a noble and intelligent woman, unless their relations, in the plural order, had been in all particulars, both inspiring and exemplary. It is evident that this Mormon institution is valuable in teaching us some new and surprising facts about human nature and its capabilities. Nor were Mrs. Woodruff's expressions of devotion confined to the mystical anticipations of bliss in the life to come. In 1870, on the occasion of a mass meeting of women, called to protest against the proposed provisions of the Cullom bill, she spoke as follows:

> "Whatever may be the final result of the action of Congress in passing or enforcing oppressive laws, for the sake of our religion, upon the noble men who have subdued these deserts, it is our duty to stand by them and support them by our faith, prayers and works, through every dark hour, unto the end, and trust in the God of Abraham, Isaac and Jacob to defend us and all who are called to suffer for keeping the commandments of God. Shall we, as wives and mothers, sit still and see our husbands and sons, whom we know are obeying the highest behest of heaven, suffer for their religion, without exerting ourselves to the extent of our power for their deliverance? No; verily no! God has revealed unto us the law of the patriarchal order of marriage, and commanded us to obey it. We are sealed to our husbands for time and eternity, that we may dwell with them and our children in the world to come; which guarantees unto us the greatest blessings for which we were created. If the rulers of this nation will so far depart from the spirit and letter of our glorious constitution as to deprive our prophets, apostles and leaders of

citizenship, and imprison them for obeying this law, let them grant this, our last request, to make their prisons large enough to hold their wives, for where they go we will go also."—*Ibid., p.* 400.

On the same occasion, Mrs. Hannah T. King, also speaking of the proposed provisions of the Cullom bill, spoke as follows:

"Who, or what, is the creature who framed this incomparable document? . . . What isolated land produced him? What ideas he must have of women! Had he ever a mother, a wife, or a sister? In what academy was he tutored, or to what school does he belong, that he so coolly and systematically commands the women of this people to turn traitors to their husbands, their brothers and their sons? . . . Let us, the women of this people—the sisterhood of Utah—rise *en masse,* and tell this non-descript to defer 'the bill' until he has studied the character of woman, such as God intended she should be; then he will discover that devotion, veneration and faithfulness are her peculiar attributes; that God is her refuge, and his servants her oracles; and that, especially, the women of Utah have paid too high for their present position, their present light and knowledge, and their noble future, to succumb to so mean and foul a thing as Baskin, Cullom & Co's bill. Let him learn that they are one in heart, hand and brain, with the brotherhood of Utah—that God is their father and their friend—that into his hand they commit their cause."—*Ibid., pp.* 398–399.

Among further accounts of the personal experiences of Mormon wives under the regime of plural marriage, the testimony of Mrs. Mary A. Freeze bears unmistakable evidence of true conviction. She writes:

"In the spring of 1871, my husband, a faithful man, desirous of keeping all the commandments of God, saw fit, with my full consent, to take to himself another of the daughters of Eve, a good and worthy girl, Jane Granter by name. It tried my spirit to the utmost endurance, but I always believed the principle to be true, and felt that it was time we obey that sacred order. The Lord knew my heart and desires, and was with me to overcome the selfishness and jealousy of my nature. With his help, added to the great kindness of my husband, who has ever stood at the head of his family as a wise and just man, I soon obtained peace. . . .

"My husband has since taken two other wives, and I praise the Lord that I have so far overcome, that instead of feeling it to be a trial, it has been a source of joy and pride that we were counted worthy to have such noble girls enter our family. The two last were my counselors in the Young Ladies' Mutual Improvement Association of our ward. I have loved the wives of my husband as I would have my own sisters, realizing that the power of the Holy Priesthood that has bound us together for time and eternity is stronger than kindred ties. Sophia lived with me nearly seven years; she died December, 1879, which was one of the greatest trials of my life. I could as willingly have parted with one of my own daughters. She left me a beautiful boy who seems as near to me as my own. I wish to bear testimony to my descendants, and to all who may read this sketch, that I know by the power of the Holy Ghost which bears testimony to my spirit, that the Patriarchal Order of Marriage is from God, and was revealed for the exaltation of the human family, also that I have had peace, joy and satisfaction in living in that Order such as I had never known before; and have had many proofs that God will pour out his blessings upon those who keep his laws, seeking him with full purpose of heart, for he will be sought after by his children.—*Representative Women of Deseret, (Augusta Joyce Crocheron), p.* 54.

In similar vein we find the testimony of Mrs. Louis Felt, who has been for many years president of the Primary Associations of the Mormon Church. She writes:

"I became a member of the Young Ladies' Mutual Improvement Association, and thereby received a better understanding of my religion, which brought me peace and happiness, such as I had never known before. I also became thoroughly convinced of the truth of the principle of celestial marriage, and having no children of my own was very desirous that my husband should take other wives that he might have a posterity to do him honor, and after he took another wife and had children born to him, the Lord gave me a mother's love for them; they seemed as if they were indeed my own, and they seem to have the same love for me that they do for their own mother."—*Ibid., p.* 58.

To this testimony Mrs. Crocheron adds the following comment, which seems worthy repetition:

"I have seen the real mother in this family rocking her babe to sleep, and the other mother—Louie—would sit beside her and hold one little hand, or lay her own upon its little head, and it would quietly resign itself to sleep, so closely were all these three true hearts united in love."

Mrs. Felt's experience, which must seem nearly unique to the non-Mormon reader, is undoubtedly true and certainly adds materially to the evidence already cited, that polygynous marriage may present opportunities for valuable unsuspected consolations, also for the propagation of unfamiliar and noble forms of virtue. When we consider that every one of the women giving these testimonies belongs to the intelligent and self-respecting class, and are, one and all, persons of the highest character, each of them a recognized leader among her fellows, the conclusion is inevitable that we have here records of actual experiences and honest convictions. In considering the sorrows and trials, to which they confess, it must be carefully remembered that such experiences are by no means peculiar to a polygynous order of marriage, also, that the real issue is precisely on the question as to how far institutions claiming religious authority should be allowed to control human behavior and to neutralize the selfishness and other shortcomings of the "natural man," for the sake, either, of real advantages to humanity at large, or the attainment, as believed, of higher blessings in the world to come. We hear a great deal of talk about the virtue of self-denial, but when we see an eminent example of it, we complain and condemn. So, we do not want self-denial, after all.

The peaceful, even loving, cohabitation and association of plural wives was an experience sufficiently common to be called "the rule." Many tales of this are told, both by the wives themselves, and also by first-hand observers. The following quotation from the account written by Mrs. Sarah A. Peterson, is unusually interesting in this connection:

"In the fall of 1857 my husband added another wife to his family; but I can truly say that he did not do so without my consent, nor with any other motive than to serve his God. I felt it our duty to obey the commandment revealed through the prophet Joseph, hence, although I felt it to be quite a sacrifice, I encouraged him in so doing. Although not so very well supplied with house-room, the second wife and I lived together in harmony and peace. I felt it a pleasure to be in her company, and even to nurse and take care of her children, and she felt the same way toward me and my children. A few years afterwards my husband married another wife, but also with the consent and encouragement of his family. This did not disturb the peaceful relations of our home, but the same kind feelings were entertained by each member of the family to one another. We have now lived in polygamy twenty years, have eaten at the same table and raised our children together, and have never been separated, nor have we ever wished to be."—*Women of Mormondom,* p. 467.

Mrs. Elizabeth Birch writes with similar conviction and effect:

"In 1858, my husband having become convinced that the doctrine of celestial marriage and the plurality of wives was true, instructed me in regard to it; and becoming entirely convinced that the principle is not only true, but that it is commanded, I gave my consent to his taking another wife, by whom he had one daughter; and again in 1860 I consented to his taking another one, by whom he had a large family of children. These children we have raised together, and I love them as if they were my own. Our husband has been dead two years, but we still live together in peace, and each contributes to the utmost for the support of the family."—*Ibid., pp.* 470–471.

In addition to these accounts of personal experiences, we find that the women of Mormondom were completely convinced that the institution of plural marriage was an eminent means of begetting a noble posterity. Nor can there be the slightest doubt that the basis of this judgment was the sane and exemplary continence mentioned by Mr. Burton. In reading these testimonies the conclusion is inevitable that in them we have to do with pure and noble women, whose highest worldly aspiration was to become the mothers of a perfected humanity. In these days, after the "righteous wrath" of the American people has succeeded in suppressing plural marriage as an institution of society, it is a familiar experience to hear the lament, "Why could they not have left us alone? We were hoping to beget the noblest and best race of people that ever lived on earth." In harmony with these convictions we find the testimony of Mrs. Zina D. Young, a wife of President Brigham Young, and one of the reputed widows of the Prophet Joseph Smith. On the occasion of one of the several mass meetings of women, held in Salt Lake City, Nov. 16, 1878, she spoke as follows:

"The principle of our religion that is assailed is one that lies deep in my heart. Could I ask the heavens to listen; could I beseech the earth to be still, and the brave men who possess the spirit of a Washington to hear what I am about to say. . . . Would that . . . the Congress of the United States, the lawmakers of our nation could produce a balm for the many evils which exist in our land through the abuse of virtue, or could so legislate that virtue could be protected and cherished as the life which heaven has given us. We, in common with many women throughout our broad land, would hail with joy the approach of such deliverance, for such is the deliverance that woman needs. The principle of plural marriage is honorable; it is a principle of the Gods; it is heaven born. God revealed it to us as a saving principle; we have accepted it as such, and we know that it is of him, for the fruits of it are holy. . . . We are proud of the principle, because we know its true worth, and we want our children to practice it, that through us a race of men and women may grow up possessing sound minds and bodies, who shall live to the age of a tree."

In similar vein the noted poetess, Eliza R. Snow, known as Mormonism's "high priestess," and another of the Prophet's plural wives, defends the institution, as follows:

"I believe in the principle of plural marriage just as sacredly as I believe in any other institution which God has revealed. I believe it to be necessary for the redemption of mankind from the low state of corruption into which it has sunken. . . . Virtue is the foundation of the prosperity of any nation; and this sacred principle of plural marriage tends to virtue, purity and holiness."

The strangest thing about the whole doctrine and practice of plural marriage will probably seem the fact that it is seriously recommended as the best means, ever made available, for the complete elevation of woman. This claim is set forth by Mrs. Gates, in the article already quoted:

"Statistics will bear me out in saying that there are fewer paupers, fewer criminals, fewer insane among polygamous than among monogamous families. It is a well-known fact here in Utah that there are fewer physical defects and greater intelligence in plural homes than in the same grade or class of monogamy.

. . . .

"The Mormon women are working grandly on the sex problem of the nineteenth century. They are beginning to move out on independent lines of business, of art, and of the professions. Their marital relations make this an easy matter. The woman will always be the head and genius of the home, but whether it is a corollary that she shall forever wash dishes and scrub floors has become a grave question. The rapid progress of the age finds ready disciples in Mormon wives, who feel the natural craving for home life and children satisfied, yet withal have ample time for the development and cultivation of every faculty within them.

"Content in knowing herself beloved, and wedded to a man whose purity of mind and body is equal to her own, while his intelligence is one degree higher, his wisdom a rock upon which to lean in every emergency, the plural wife may, from her own threshold, look out into the broad world and choose such enterprise as she feels herself adapted to, the twenty years of her middle life spent in the care and rearing of her children the while she is quietly studying and preparing herself for that further mission. At the end of her child-bearing period she may, while aiding her own and her husband's family with her wisdom and experience, launch out into her chosen vocation, ready to add the mite of her experience to the great problem of humanity. That problem is the development of each individuality to its highest possibility, the wise care and rearing of dependent childhood, and the peace, happiness, and well-being of all God's children. That polygamy, wisely and faithfully practiced, will be a grand factor in bringing to pass this millennium of usefulness and happiness, I sincerely believe."—*Family Life Among the Mormons* (*North American Review, pp.* 347, 349, March, 1890).

Phil Robinson dwells on this matter at even greater length, throwing further valuable light upon this curious phase of the subject. He writes:

"But the 'woman's rights' aspect of polygamy is one that has never been theorized on at all. It deserves, however, special consideration by those who think that they are 'elevating' Mormon women by trying to suppress polygamy. It possesses also a general interest for all. For the plural wives of Salt Lake City are not by any means 'waiting for salvation' at the hands of the men and women of the East. Unconscious of having fetters on, they evince no enthusiasm for their noisy deliverers.

"On the contrary, they consider their interference as a slur upon their own intelligence, and an encroachment upon those very rights about which monogamist females are making so much clamor. They look upon themselves as the *leaders* in a movement for the emancipation of their sex, and how, then, can they be expected to accept emancipation at the hands of those whom they are trying to elevate? Thinking themselves in the van of freedom, are they to be grateful for the guidance of stragglers in the rear? They laugh at such sympathy, just as a brave man would laugh at encouragement from a coward, or wealthy landowners at a pauper's exposition of the responsibilities of property. Can the deaf, they ask, tell musicians anything of the beauty of sounds, or need the artist care for the blind man's theory of color?

"Indeed, it has been in contemplation to evangelize the Eastern States, on this very subject of woman's rights! To send out from Utah exponents of the proper place of women in society, and to teach the women of monogamy their duties to themselves and each other! 'Woman's true status'—I am quoting from their organ—'is that of companion to man, but so protected by law that she can act in an independent sphere if he abuse his position, and render union unendurable.' They not only, therefore, claim all that women elsewhere claim, but they consider marriage the universal birthright of every female. First of all, they say, *be married,* and then in the case of accidents have all other rights as well. But to start with, every woman must have a husband. She is hardly worth calling a woman if she is single. Other privileges ought to be hers lest marriage should prove disastrous. But in the first instance she should claim her right to be a wife. And everybody else should insist on that claim being recognized. The rest is very important to fall back upon, but union with man is her first step towards her proper sphere.

"Now, could any position be imagined more ludicrous for the would-be saviors of Utah womanhood than this, that the slaves whom they talk of rescuing from their degradation should be striving to bring others *up* to their own standards? When Stanley was in Central Africa, he was often amused and sometimes not a little disgusted to find that instead of *his* discovering the Central Africans, the Central Africans insisted on 'discovering' him. . . . Something very like this will be the fate of those who come to Utah thinking that they will be received as shining lights from a better world. They will not find the women of Utah waiting with outstretched arms to grasp the hand that saves them. There will be no stampede of downtrodden females. On the contrary, the clarion of woman's rights will be sounded, and the intruding 'champions' of that cause will find themselves attacked with their own weapons, and hoisted with their own petards. 'With the sceptre of woman's rights the daughters of Zion will go down as apostles to evangelize the nation. "Who is she that looketh forth as the morning, fair as the moon, clear as the sun, and terrible as an army with banners?" The daughter of Zion!'

"Mormon wives, then, are emphatically 'woman's rights women,' a title which is everywhere recognized as indicating independence of character and an elevated sense of the claims of the sex, and as inferring exceptional freedom in action. And I venture to hold the opinion that it is only women who are conscious of freedom that can institute such movements as this in Utah, and only those who are enthusiastic in the cause, that can carry them on with the courage and industry so conspicuous in this community.

"A Governor once went there specially instructed to release the women of Utah from their bondage, but he found none willing to be 'released.' The franchise was then clamored for, in order to let the women of Utah 'fight their oppressors at the polls,' and the Mormon 'tyrants' took the hint to give their wives votes, and the first use these misguided victims of plurality made of their new possession was to protest, 20,000 victims together, against the calumnies heaped upon the men of Utah 'whom they honored and loved.' To-day it is an act of Congress that is to set free these worse-than-Indian-suttee-devotees, and whether they like it or not they are to be compelled to leave their husbands or take the alternative of sending their husbands to jail. . . .

"Monogamist reformers, having twice failed to persuade the wives of Utah to abandon their husbands by giving them the facilities for doing so, are now going to take their husbands from them by the force of the law. 'Sua si bona norint' is the excuse of the reformers to themselves for their philanthropy, and, like the old Inquisitors who burnt their victims to save them from heresy, they are going to make women wretched in order to make them happy. Says the *Woman's Exponent:* 'If the women of Utah are slaves, their bonds are loving ones and dearly prized. They are to-day in the free and unrestricted exercise of more political and social rights than are the women of any other part of the United States. But they do not choose as a body to court the follies and vices which adorn the civilization of other cities, nor to barter principles of tried worth for the tinsel of sentimentality or the gratification of passion.'

"It is of no use for 'Mormon-eaters' to say that this is written 'under direction,' and that the women who write in this way are prompted by authority. Nor would they say it if they knew personally the women who write thus. Moreover, Mormon-eaters are perpetually denouncing the 'scandalous freedom' and 'independence' extended to Mormon women and girls. And the two charges of excessive freedom and abject slavery seem to me totally incompatible. . . .

"This aspect of the polygamy problem deserves, then, I think, considerable attention. An Act has been passed to compel some 20,000 women to leave their husbands, and the world looks upon these women as slaves about to be freed from tyrants. Yet they have said and done all that could possibly be expected of them, and even more than could have been expected, to assure the world that they have neither need nor desire of emancipation, as they honor their husbands, and prefer polygamy, with all its conditions, to monogamy which brings with it infidelity at home and prostitution abroad. Again and again they have protested, in petitions to individuals and petitions to Congress, that 'their bonds are loving ones and dearly prized.' But the enthusiasm of reformers takes no heed of their protests. They are constantly declaring in public speeches and by public votes, in books and in newspapers — above all, in their daily conduct — that they consider themselves free and happy women, but the zeal of philanthropy will not be gainsaid, and so the women of Utah are, all else failing, to be saved from themselves. The 'foul blot' of a servitude which the serfs aver does not exist is to be wiped out by declaring 20,000 wives mistresses, their households illegal, and their future children bastards!"—*Sinners and Saints, pp.* 103-109.

In connection with Mr. Robinson's explanation of the position of women in Mormon communities, there are numerous testimonies available from the pens of prominent and able women, which argue very closely to the conclusion that only in such communities do women have the slightest promise of real "elevation." The following from Mrs. Emmeline B. Wells, President of the Women's National Relief Society, and for over thirty years editor of the *Woman's Exponent,* a paper filled with aspirations for the elevation of the sex, is interesting:

"We believe in redemption from the curse placed upon woman. If you ask why, we will tell you it is a part of our religion, and we are working to bring it to pass. . . . Woman will be redeemed from that curse, as sure as the sun shines or the Lord lives. And the man and the woman will be equal, except there must necessarily always be a first, and the man is first.

"In the Church termed 'Mormon,' women have always voted in all Church assemblies, on all questions relating to temporal or spiritual matters, just as freely as men, therefore it was not strange that equal suffrage should be accorded to our women at an early period. In fact, woman suffrage is in keeping with the institutions of Mormonism and in harmony therewith. Brigham Young was one of the most progressive men of the age, and the moment woman suffrage was talked of, he favored it. The legislature then in session in the winter of 1869 and 1870, passed a bill giving women equal suffrage, and the Hon. Abraham O. Smoot (father of Senator Reed Smoot) was the man who introduced the bill, which passed, as you doubtless know, and was signed by the Secretary of State, the Hon. S. A. Mann, then Acting Governor in the absence of the Governor. . . .

"How can one help thinking woman will have some vital part in the great work of redeeming her own sex, the daughters of Eve, when she has played so conspicuous a part, first in the Garden of Eden; and as in the great drama of the world woman is and has been a vital, active force, so it will be at the close of the most sublime drama ever introduced upon any stage, woman in her purity and magnanimity will rise victorious, having finished the part assigned her and made restitution. Redeemed from the curse, her triumph, her song of victory will be greater and loftier far than Miriam's or Deborah's of old. . . .

"Mormon women are the happiest women in the world, taken as a whole. I know them intimately, in their homes, in their organizations, in politics, in religion. We have more actual freedom than most other women, we are a very independent body of women; we vote, we attend political primaries and conventions and take part in them, we have helped to make this country, (some of us were a sort of pioneers,) and we feel as if it belonged to us, we believe in homes, we are home-makers, we are some of us colonizers, our young people marry and go out into new lands, north and south, and build up new settlements somewhat as we did when we came here, only they are better supplied with what is needed."—"*Why a Woman Should Desire to be a Mormon.*" (*Woman's Exponent, December* 1907—*January* 1908.)

In a public speech before one of the numerous meetings of women, called to protest against unjust federal laws aimed at settling the so-called "Mormon problem," Mrs. Phœbe C. Woodruff is quoted, as follows:

"The cry has ever been the 'down-trodden women of Utah.' ... They would have the world believe us the most degraded and neglected beings of all God's creation. Now, *we know* this is not so; we enjoy full as much liberty as they do, and a great deal more, with all their boasted civilization. We enjoy all the rights that are accorded to our sex anywhere, and know as well how to use them as any of our compeers in the eastern cities would. Indeed, we enjoyed more before they kindly introduced so much of their vaunted civilization into our midst. The day has been when one could walk the streets of Salt Lake City at any hour of the day or night, if necessary, without fear of insult, for every man we met would be a brother and a friend."—*Quoted in Utah and Its People by a Gentile* (*D. D. Lum*).

Another prominent woman, Mrs. Isabella Horne, argued in precisely similar strain before the same meeting, as follows:

"You say that you would like to know how the Mormon women do feel. I will tell you. They all know that they are honored wives and mothers, acknowledged in society with their children, and are happy in knowing that their husbands are true to their marriage covenants, whether they have one wife or more. The Lord, seeing the wickedness and corruption on the earth, in his Wisdom has revealed the principle of Plural Marriage, to purify society and elevate woman from the degradation in which man has placed her; and woe will be unto the man that degrades woman, for she is a gift from God. And I can positively assert that in no place on earth are chastity and virtue in women more honored and protected than among the people called 'Mormons.'"—*Ibid.*

Probably the strongest protest ever uttered by the Mormon women was in the mass meeting at Salt Lake City, March 6, 1886, when the judicial injustices perpetrated under the provisions of the Edmunds Law were under discussion. This occasion was conspicuous, not only for the fervid eloquence of the speakers, but also for their high average of intelligence. Indeed, the strongest protests were uttered by several women physicians, who must be credited with a degree of education and intelligence above the dead level of the common schools. Nor, do the deliverances of these ladies betray any such fact as that they were merely desirous of maintaining their prestige with their patients and the public generally. Something closely akin to real conviction is evident in their remarks. On this occasion, Dr. Romania B. Pratt spoke as follows:

"A true marriage cannot be productive of evil, for it is the perfect union of heart and soul, sanctified by mutual consent and sealed by God's holy ordinance. The 'Mormon' marriage covenant is as binding on the man as the woman, for any departure from the marriage law is a deadly sin and is punished with us by excommunication from the Church, which we regard as spiritual death. And it is dependent upon the covenants the sinner has made whether he can ever be readmitted as a member again. The Latter-day Saints regard plural marriage as an extension of all the privileges and good results arising from single marriage. Has not every woman the undeniable right to be an honorable wife and mother — of fulfilling the end of her creation, and do not the circumstances of life and statistics prove this to be impossible under the monogamic system? And were this the acknowledged law of the land, would it not lay the ax at the root of the greatest evil that has ever cursed the land?

"If the same ceremony seals each wife to her husband, may not each family be a realization of the beautiful picture of one father and one mother, each the equal of the other in that family, happy in the consciousness of mutual and eternal affection? . . . The rearing of an intelligent and God-fearing family is the very essence of the reason for the revelation of celestial marriage, for God has said 'He will raise up unto himself a righteous seed.' Can the children of men who daily pollute themselves in the society of abandoned women be a righteous seed? Can wives love, honor and be faithful to husbands they absolutely know are faithless to them? Thank God that by virtue of woman's inherent goodness, wives in the monogamy of the world are more faithful a thousand to one than the husbands.

"And a pertinent question arises in speaking of abandoned women. If it had been possible for them to become loving and beloved wives, would there be so many abandoned? The fidelity, the hallowed sacredness and dignity of each wife's family hearthstone can be abundantly verified among this people. The marriage covenant is eternal, and is equal to each wife in all its blessings, powers and privileges, as each is equally faithful and worthy. The union for all eternity is the keystone sentence of the ceremony. The bonds, then, of these plural families are true, virtuous, eternal; welded by power given of heaven, and what 'God hath joined together let no man put asunder.'

. . . .

"Our faith and confidence in the chastity and pure motives of our husbands, fathers, mothers and sons are such that we challenge the production of a better system of marriage and the records of more moral or purer lives. Hand in hand with celestial marriage is the elevation of woman. In Church she votes equally with men, and politically she has the suffrage raising her from the old common-law monogamic serfdom, to political equality with men. Rights of property are given her so that she, as a married woman, can hold property in her own individual right. Women are not thrown off in old age as has been most untruthfully and shamefully asserted.

There is nothing in our plural marriage system that countenances any such thing. The very nature of the covenant forbids it. . . . Instances of wrong-doing may be found in families of plural households, but the exceptions are not the rule; the weight of good results of the *majority* should be the standard of judgment. It cannot be true, as asserted, that plural marriage is entered into as a rule from sensual motives. It is self-evident that it is not the case with the women, and it is unreasonable to suppose that men would bring upon themselves the responsibilities, cares and expenses of a plural family, when they could avoid all this, yet revel in sin, and, in the language of a distinguished man of the world, 'be like the rest of us.'"—*Mormon Women's Protest, pp.* 29–31.

Another woman physician, Dr. Ellis R. Shipp, spoke on the same occasion with equal emphasis and effect, as follows:

"And this is our grievous offense. A certain tenet of our religious faith our opponents cannot countenance, because so contrary to their own sinful practices. The evil results of these practices we have personally observed, particularly in the hospitals of the world, where fallen women seek the shelter they cannot obtain from those who should have protected them instead of throwing them and their offspring upon the mercies of a cold, unfeeling world. By consulting the national statistics, we find New York with thirty thousand women leading lives of prostitution; Chicago twenty thousand; Boston and Cincinnati each ten thousand, and other cities with a like ratio according to the number of inhabitants.

"Unfortunately, a record of the opposite sex is not kept.

"We are accused of being down-trodden and oppressed. *We deny the charge* for we know there cannot be found a class of women upon the earth who occupy a more elevated position in the hearts of their husbands, or whose most delicate and refined feelings are so respected as here in Utah.

"True we practice plural marriage, not, however, because we are compelled to, but because we are convinced that it is a divine revelation, and we find in this principle satisfaction, contentment and more happiness than we could obtain in any other relationship.

"Let our works speak for us. We are a temperate, God-fearing, law-abiding people. We consider virtue and chastity the crowning ornaments of a woman's character. Our ladies are educated and refined, and their lives are constantly characterized by acts of nobility, fortitude, and usefulness. . . .

"How strange that the rulers of this nation should overlook the glaring and palpable evils that so thickly beset themselves and traverse thousands of miles, in order to stigmatize a small handful of inoffensive people called 'Mormons,' who have already been driven to a desert land where it was supposed they would soon perish and die from starvation and exposure!"—*Ibid. pp.* 37–38.

Although American "philanthropy," usually so "busy elsewhere" when real evils are to be corrected with no opportunity for notoriety and a chance to obtain huge credits for sanctified generosity, has decreed, and succeeded in enforcing the decision that the women of Mormondon must be "saved from themselves," the protests of these same "victims" are always on file for the information of the intelligent reader. There is one last argument against this "principle" that is still used with an evident intent to justify our previous injustice to these people. That is that the Mormon plural wife, in spite of her statements to the contrary, could not possibly be happy. Even Phil Robinson discriminates carefully between happiness and "content," and concludes, because according to his understanding, the former was not available in plural marriage; therefore, "polygamy" is an evil in itself. Presently, however, he proceeds to enlarge upon another "singular feature" of the matter, as follows:

"The advocates of woman's rights are a very strong party in Utah; and their publications use the very same arguments that strong-minded women have made so terrible to newspaper editors in Europe, and members of Parliament. Thus the *Woman's Exponent* — with 'the Rights of the Women of all Nations' for its motto — publishes continually signed letters in which plural wives affirm their contentment with their lot, and in one of its issues . . . 'Hints on Marriage,' signed 'Lillie Freeze.' But for a sentence or two it might be an article by a Gentile in a Gentile 'lady's paper,' for it speaks of 'courtship' and 'lovers,' and has the quotation, 'two souls with but a single thought, two hearts that beat as one,' and all the other orthodox pretty things, about true love and married bliss. Yet the writer is speaking of polygamy! In the middle of this article written 'for love's sweet sake,' and as womanly and pure as ever words written by woman, comes this paragraph: —

"'In proportion as the power of evil increases, a disregard for the sacred institution of marriage also increases among the married until this most sacred relationship will be overwhelmed by disunion and strife, and only among the despised Latter-day Saints will the true foundation of social happiness and prosperity be found upon the earth; but in order to realize that state we must be guided by principles more perfect than those which have wrought such dissolution. God has revealed a plan for establishing a new order of society which will elevate and benefit all mankind who embrace. The nations that fight against it are working out their own destruction, for their house is built upon the sand, and one of the cornerstones is already loosened through their disregard and dishonor of the institution of marriage.'

"Now what is to be done with women who not only declare they are happy in polygamy, but persist in trying to improve their monogamous sisters? How is the missionary going to begin, for instance, with Lillie Freeze?" — *Sinners and Saints, pp.* 98–100.

The question of the attitude of woman toward this "principle" could be no better concluded than by the quotation of the following verses, written by Mrs. Emmeline B. Wells, whose experience of love and marriage was confined entirely to the plural "order." Mrs. Wells has always been a leader in movements for the elevation of her sex, and is widely known as an advocate of "equal suffrage." She is also one of the most graceful poets among her people, having published several volumes of verse, highly esteemed for sentiment and imagery, as well as for elegance of diction. Her husband was Daniel H. Wells, one of the First Presidency.

"THE WIFE TO HER HUSBAND

"It seems to me that should I die,
And this poor body cold and lifeless lie,
And thou shouldst touch my lips with thy warm breath,
The life-blood, quickened in each sep'rate vein,
Would wildly, madly rushing back again,
Bring the glad spirit from the isle of death.

It seems to me that were I dead,
And thou in sympathy should'st o'er me shed
Some tears of sorrow, or of sad regret,
That every pearly drop that fell in grief,
Would bud or blossom, bursting into leaf,
To prove immortal love could not forget.

I do believe that round my grave,
When the cool fragrant evening zephyrs wave,
Should'st thou in friendship linger near the spot,
And breathe some tender words in memory,
That this poor heart in grateful constancy,
Would softly whisper back some loving thought.

I do believe that should I pass
Into the unknown land of happiness,
And thou should'st wish to see my face once more,
That in my earnest longing after thee,
I would come forth in joyful ecstasy,
And once again gaze on thee as before.

I do believe my faith in thee,
Stronger than life, an anchor firm to be;
Planted in thine integrity and worth,
A perfect trust implicit and secure;
That will all trials and all grief endure,
And bless and comfort me, while here on earth.

I do believe who love hath known,
Or sublime friendship's purest, highest tone,
Hath tasted of the cup of ripest bliss,
And drunk the choicest wine life hath to give,
Hath known the truest joy it is to live;
What blessing rich or great compared to this?

I do believe true love to be
An element that in its tendency
Is elevating to the human mind,
An intuition which we recognize
As foretaste of immortal paradise,
Through which the soul will be refined.

—*Musings and Memories.*

V

THE MORMON ORGANIZATION

"And he gave some, apostles; and some, prophets; and some, evangelists; and some, pastors and teachers; for the perfecting of the saints, for the work of the ministry, for the edifying of the body of Christ: till we all come into the unity of the faith, and of the knowledge of the Son of God."— Ephesians v. 11–13.

CHAPTER XX

THE ORGANIZATION OF THE MORMON CHURCH

PROBABLY the best known fact about the Mormon Church is that it embodies a singularly efficient organization, which permits it to achieve results impossible to virtually all other religious bodies, and binds its people into a wonderfully close solidarity. This organization has been compared to that of the Society of Jesus, the Jesuit Order, whose organization is essentially military; also, to army organizations of the most efficient type. It differs from all such, however, in the fact that it is a curious blending of perfect democracy with a very distinct recognition of a strong centre of authority. The latter supplies a purely theocratic element. That the organization of the Mormon Church is a very real and very remarkable masterpiece cannot be denied. That it is also a wonderfully efficient engine for achieving grand results, both social and moral, must be evident after examination of the facts. That it is, furthermore, the model and prototype, upon which the ultimate and perfectly effective religious influence must be organized, is a postulate liable to be suspected somewhere toward the close of a thorough study.

As a matter of fact, the Mormon organization accords well with what is, after all, the obvious conclusion in regard to the ultimate solution of the troublesome problems of civilization: that our problems may be met and solved only when society is organized on a basis distinctly religious, and when religion shall be expressed in an organization, giving full and complete recognition to matters distinctively social and human. The fact that the Mormon Church actually embodies these requirements, and in this respect, harmonizes these apparent contradictions, furnishes an explanation, alike, of its vitality and of the grand results, evidently approximated, even if not fully realized, in its operation. In fine, the organization of the Church furnishes consideration of the utmost significance to sociology, ethics and religion alike. Nevertheless, that it could be copied or adapted to any other system of religion, even one professing the same interest in human and visible concerns of life, is highly doubtful; it seems to be an institution inevitable to the peculiar genius of Mormonism, and inseparable from it.

Beyond doubt, the entire edifice of the Mormon "hierarchy," so-called, was erected in the day and through the agency of the Prophet Joseph Smith. To the unprejudiced non-Mormon it is a noble monument to his superlative genius as an organizer; to his disciples, and to himself, if we may judge from his statements, it is merely the restoration of the Church as founded by Christ Himself, and was formed on the type let down from God.

The sixth of the thirteen "Articles of Faith" of the Mormon Church states:

> "We believe in the same organization that existed in the Primitive Church, viz.: apostles, prophets, pastors, teachers, evangelists, etc."

Several historic sects have postulated similarly, notably the disciples of Edward Irving, who organized the so-called Catholic Apostolic Church, with numerous scriptural dignities and offices unfamiliar in Christian history. In fact, the organization of this body presents several interesting points of correspondence with Mormonism, particularly in starting with a body of twelve apostles. The Irvingites, however, do not regard the Twelve as a self-perpetuating council, and allowed it to lapse with the deaths of their original apostles. The Mormon Church, on the other hand, has maintained its apostolic "quorum" as a permanent institution, always filling vacancies created by death, or other causes, as speedily as possible.

The organization of the Mormon Church includes two orders of priesthood, called respectively, the Melchisedek, or "Higher Priesthood," and the Aaronic, or "Lesser Priesthood." Thus two orders, although distinct, in point of functions and dignities, interact with perfect harmony. Nor is this discrimination of two priesthoods without warrant in Scripture. The authority commonly quoted is in the following passage from the Epistle to the Hebrews:

> "For every high priest taken from among men is ordained for men in things *pertaining* to God, that he may offer both gifts and sacrifices for sins. . . . And no man taketh this honor unto himself, but he that is called of God, as was Aaron. So also Christ glorified not himself to be made an high priest; but he that said unto him, Thou art my son, to-day have I begotten thee. As he saith also in another *place,* Thou *art* a priest for ever after the order of Melchisedec. . . . For this Melchisedec, King of Salem, priest of the most high God, who met Abraham returning from the slaughter of the kings, and blessed him; to whom also Abraham gave a tenth part of all; first being by interpretation King of righteousness, and after that also King of Salem, which is *King of peace;* without father, without mother, without descent, having neither beginning of days, nor end of life but made like unto the Son of God, abideth a priest continually. Now consider how great this man *was,* unto whom even the patriarch

Abraham gave a tenth of the spoils. And verily they that are of the sons of Levi, who receive the office of the priesthood, have a commandment to take tithes of the people according to the law, that is, of their brethren, though they come out of the loins of Abraham: but he whose descent is not counted from them, received tithes of Abraham, and blessed him that had the promises. . . . If therefore perfection were by the Levitical priesthood, (for under it the people received the law,) what further need *was there* that another priest should rise after the order of Melchisedec, and not be called after the order of Aaron? For the priesthood being changed, there is made of necessity a change also of the law. For he of whom these things are spoken pertaineth to another tribe, of which no man gave attendance at the altar. For it is evident that our Lord sprang out of Juda; of which tribe Moses spake nothing concerning priesthood. And it is yet far more evident; for that after the similitude of Melchisidec there ariseth another priest, who is made, not after the law of a carnal commandment, but after the power of an endless life."— Heb. v. 1, 4-7; vii, 1-7, 11-16.

According to the interpretation here offered, the Levitical, or Aaronic, priesthood, belonging properly to the children of Aaron, but restored in modern times through the instrumentality of John the Baptist in the persons of Joseph Smith and Oliver Cowdery, is, as it were, a step toward the higher and complete priesthood, "after the order of the Son of God," although many persons ordained into it rise no higher. The Melchisedek priesthood, it is believed, was restored in modern times in the same persons, through the instrumentality of the Apostles Peter, James and John, and was by them transmitted to others in the Church. These matters have authoritative statement as follows:

"There are, in the church, two Priesthoods, namely, the Melchisidek, and Aaronic, including the Levitical Priesthood. Why the first is called the Melchisedek Priesthood, is because Melchisedek was such a great High Priest. Before his day it was called *the Holy Priesthood, after the order of the Son of God;* but out of respect or reverence to the name of Supreme Being, to avoid the too frequent repetition of his name, they, the church, in ancient days, called that Priesthood after Melchisedek, or the Melchisedek Priesthood. All other authorities or officers in the church are appendages to this Priesthood; but there are two divisions or grand heads — one is the Melchisedek Priesthood, and the other is the Aaronic, or Levitical priesthood."— *Doctrine and Covenants,* cvii. 1-6.

"Abraham received the Priesthood from Melchisedek, who received it through the lineage of his father, even till Noah. . . . Which Priesthood continueth in the church of God in all generations, and is without beginning of days or end of years. And the Lord confirmed a priesthood also upon Aaron and his seed, throughout all their generations — which priesthood also continueth and abideth forever with the Priesthood, which is after the holiest order of God. And this greater Priesthood administereth the gospel and holdeth the key of the mysteries of the kingdom, even the key of the knowledge of God. Therefore, in the ordinances thereof, the power of godliness is manifest; and without the ordinances thereof, and the authority of the Priesthood, the power of godliness is not manifest unto men in the flesh; for without this no man can see the face of God, even the Father, and live. Now this Moses plainly taught to the children of Israel in the wilderness, and sought diligently to sanctify his people that they might behold the face of God; but they hardened their hearts and could not endure his presence, therefore the Lord in his wrath (for his anger was kindled against them) swore that they should not enter into his rest while in the wilderness, which rest is the fulness of his glory. Therefore he took Moses out of their midst, and the Holy Priesthood also; and the lesser priesthood continued, which priesthood holdeth the keys of the ministering of angels and the preparatory gospel."—*Ibid.* lxxxiv. 14, 17–26.

"The power and authority of the Higher or Melchisedek Priesthood, is to hold the keys of all the spiritual blessings of the church—to have the privilege of receiving the mysteries of the kingdom of heaven—to have the heavens opened unto them—to commune with the general assembly and church of the first born, and to enjoy the communion and presence of God the Father, and Jesus the Mediator of the new covenant. The power and authority of the lesser, or Aaronic priesthood, is to hold the keys of the ministering of angels, and to administer in outward ordinances, the letter of the gospel—the baptism of repentance for the remission of sins, agreeable to the covenants and commandments."—*Ibid.* cvii. 18–20.

Although, in the Mormon Church, there is no distinct, or professional, class holding the priesthood or ministry, as in other bodies, the general understanding of the duties and privileges of the priestly office is quite similar to that postulated elsewhere. A man holding any degree of priesthood among the Mormons may occupy any position in the community, or make his livelihood by any trade, occupation or profession, and yet possess, by virtue of his ordination, or "setting-apart," a distinct religious significance and dignity. In addition to his regular secular calling, he is an authorized and accredited minister of religion, and, in very many cases, works for the Church and its interests quite as hard and as long as for himself. According to the established rule, moreover, no priest, whether also an officer in any Church organization or not, receives remuneration for his services to religion, unless they are of such a nature as to demand his entire time and attention—in that case he is paid a salary proportionate to the needs of his family. Theoretically, every male member of the Church becomes a priest in some degree: practically, about 90 per cent. of the men hold the priesthood. While women are not regularly ordained, each one partakes of the dignity of her husband, and, as a matter of fact, in temple ordinances, etc., they discharge some of the most important functions of religion.

The accepted definition of priesthood is given in the following passage in one of the accredited text-books of the Church:

"Priesthood is power and authority given to men to act in the name of the Lord. It is a right conferred on men to officiate in the ordinances of the Gospel; and to advocate the principles thereof. In other words, Priesthood is Divine Authority by which men perform acts for the benefit of their fellow men under the law of the Gospel; and God acknowledges such acts as if they were His own. In a large sense, Priesthood signifies 'the holy order of the Son of God,' which He holds in connection with heavenly beings. It is that which places man in a condition to receive the ministration of angels, and to enjoy the presence of God the Father, and His Son Jesus Christ."—Joseph B. Keeler (*The Lesser Priesthood, etc., pp.* 1–2).

According to the best understanding of established modes of expression, the term Priesthood — and it is here preferably spelled with a capital — indicates the dignity of the higher, or Melchisedek, order; the lesser, or Aaronic, order seeming to be somewhat in the nature of a preparation for the dignities of the higher. This is suggested in the revelation previously quoted. Because the children of Israel "hardened their hearts and could not endure his (God's) presence, therefore the Lord in his wrath . . . took Moses out of their midst, and the Holy Priesthood also," leaving them only the lesser priesthood, which "holdeth the key of the ministering of angels and the preparatory Gospel." However, the term applies in usage with equal propriety to all the varying degrees and dignities in which the service of religion is expressed; the lesser priesthood being considered an "appendage" to the Higher. In usage the word "priesthood" may designate the dignity of any person holding an ordination to office, although the word "priest" is properly used to designate only one holding the rank in the Aaronic order. In the Melchisedek order, those ordained to office are called "elders" and "high priests"— the former term being usual in address — but never "priests."

"The second priesthood is called the priesthood of Aaron, because it was conferred upon Aaron and his seed, throughout all their generations. Why it is called the lesser priesthood, is because it is an appendage to the greater or the Melchisedek Priesthood, and has power in administering outward ordinances."—*Doctrine and Covenants*, cvii. 13–14.

In order to explain the matter as clearly as possible, it will be necessary, at the start, to specify the fact that both orders of the priesthood may be divided in two ways: first, as to specific offices, involving certain definite duties and functions; second, as to degree, or dignities, according to successive ordinations, from the lowest to the highest. Occasionally, it is difficult to discriminate the two perfectly, since in many cases a man, in being ordained regularly to some specific grade or dignity, is set apart to some particular office or "quorum," which may rank him above others of his grade in point of authority or dignity. However, for the sake of clearness, the following classifications may be given.

The Higher Priesthood contains three distinct degrees or dignities: (1) high priests; (2) seventies; (3) elders — howbeit, the latter term applies in general usage to any person holding this Priesthood. As to offices, the Higher Priesthood contains, or involves eligibility to: (1) the first presidency; (2) the apostleship; (3) the patriarchship; (4) stake presidencies and high councils; (5) the bishopric. In point of definite functions, the eldership proper and the bishopric are considered as "appendages" to the High Priesthood; the former as "standing ministers of the Church," the latter as involving the "presidency of the lesser priesthood."

The lesser priesthood, with which the bishop is evidently associated and identified, involves three proper degrees of its own: (1) priests; (2) teachers; (3) deacons, each class with its proper duties and quorums. The grades of teacher and deacon are called "necessary appendages belonging to the lesser priesthood" (*Doctrine and Covenants,* lxxxiv. 30), being, according to New Testament analogy, regular assistants to the higher grade, particularly in temporal or outward matters, properly local, as distinguished from the traveling duties of members of the Higher Priesthood. Accordingly, the deacon is set apart (1) to care for the poor; (2) to collect money and supplies for the poor from private sources, also, for building and maintaining houses of worship; (3) to care for, clean and repair such houses and their grounds; (4) to render such general services as may be required by those above him in office or authority.

A man holding the grade of teacher may exercise (1) any of the functions of a deacon; (2) the duties of a standing minister, "to watch over the Church always," exerting himself to be of personal assistance to any of its members, particularly in urging them to attend services and to remain faithful to their religious duties; (3) to act as "policeman of the Church," in searching out and discouraging "iniquity" in all its forms; (4) to act as peacemaker between members of the Church who have disagreed on any matters, and to admonish such, and all others who may lapse from the straight way of righteousness; (5) "to warn, expound, exhort and teach, and invite all to come to Christ." Neither the teacher nor the deacon may officiate in any of the ordinances of religion, not even in the initiatory rite of baptism, but either of them may ordain candidates, who have been properly qualified and elected, to his own grade, but, properly enough, to none above his own.

The next higher grade is the priest, who holds the Aaronic order, the fulness of which was invested in John the Baptist. His duties are authoritatively set forth in the following passage:

"The priest's duty is to preach, teach, expound, exhort, and baptize, and administer the sacrament, and visit the house of each member, and exhort them to pray vocally and in secret, and attend to all family duties; and he may also ordain other priests, teachers, and deacons. And he is to take the lead of meetings when there is no elder present; but when there is an elder present, he is only to preach, teach, expound, exhort, and baptize, and visit the house of each member, exhorting them to pray vocally and in secret, and attend to all family duties. In all these duties the priest is to assist the elder if occasion requires."—*Doctrine and Covenants,* xx. 46–52.

In addition to the strict rule that he shall discharge all the functions of his office as assistant to an elder, when such a person is present in any case, the priest may act as a teacher or as a deacon. He may not, however, confirm new members by the "laying-on of hands for the gift of the Holy Ghost," since this is a right belonging exclusively to the higher priesthood.

The scriptural consistency of the latter regulation is obvious, when we consider that the Aaronic priesthood, although here incorporated in the Christian Church and discharging duties peculiar to it, rather than the duties prescribed under the Mosaic Law, represents an order prior, historically, to the manifestation of the fulness of the Gospel of Christ. Hence, it cannot contain the power of imparting the gift of the Holy Ghost. Again, this sharp discrimination between the two priesthoods, in point of authority and powers, illustrates the statement of Christ regarding John the Baptist, who represented the culmination of the "Old Order," according to scripture, that "he who is least in the kingdom of heaven is greater than he." John baptized, hence baptism is a rite proper to the priesthood to which he belonged; but he himself testified that "one cometh after me, who shall baptize with the Holy Ghost and with fire." Hence, the "baptism of the Holy Ghost" belongs exclusively to the Son of God, and to those who follow after His "order," His Apostles and other authorized servants, sharing with him the "higher priesthood." Similarly, also, the lesser priesthood ministers in the "outward things of religion" and in temporal affairs, as distinguished from the higher rites and mysteries of religion, peculiarly reserved for the participation of the Higher Priesthood.

The office and dignity of a bishop forms a true connecting link between the two priesthoods; since the bishopric is at once the presiding authority over the lesser priesthood, and an "appendage" to the Higher Priesthood. The bishop, however, is not chosen from the ranks of the lesser priesthood, as might be expected, but is invariably a high priest of the Melchisedek Order. However, there are two distinct ranks of bishop: The Presiding Bishop, who has direct control of the temporal affairs and of the lesser priesthood in the whole Church, and the numerous ward bishops, whose function in the several wards,—parishes, as they would be called in other connections—is to combine the duties of pastor and administrator. While most of the striking provisions of the *Doctrine and Covenants* apply most directly to the former officer, or to his prototype in the early days, the general bishop, the rule that each man holding the bishopric, local or general, shall be a priest of the Higher Order, is invariable. The authoritative law relating to bishops is as follows:

> "They shall be High Priests who are worthy, and they shall be appointed by the First Presidency of the Melchisedek priesthood, except they be literal descendants of Aaron, and if they be literal descendants of Aaron, they have a legal right to the bishopric, if they are the firstborn among the sons of Aaron; for the firstborn holds the right of the presidency over this priesthood, and the keys or authority of the same. No man has a legal right to this office to hold the keys of this priesthood, except he be a literal descendant and the firstborn of Aaron; but as a High Priest of the Melchisedek Priesthood has authority to officiate in all the lesser offices, he may officiate in the office of bishop when no literal descendant of Aaron can be found, provided he is called, and set apart and ordained unto this power under the hands of the First Presidency of the Melchisedek Priesthood. And a literal descendant of Aaron, also, must be designated by this Presidency, and found worthy, and anointed, and ordained under the hands of this Presidency, otherwise they are not legally authorized to officiate in their priesthood; but by virtue of the decree concerning their right of the priesthood descending from father to son, they may claim their anointing, if at any time they can prove their lineage, or do ascertain it by revelation from the Lord under the hands of the above named Presidency."—*Doctrine and Covenants,* lxviii. 15–21.

In another passage (Sec. cvii. 76) it is specified that a "literal descendant of Aaron," when filling the office of bishop, may, contrary to the general rule, as will be seen later, act without the usual two counselors, "except in a case where a President of the high priesthood, after the order of Melchisedek, is tried, to sit as a judge in Israel." Such rules are, however, inoperative, since no descendant of Aaron has ever claimed the bishopric.

Since, as specified in the *Doctrine and Covenants,* "a literal descendant and the firstborn of Aaron" is the only person having "a legal right to this office" of Presiding Bishop, and, as "the firstborn holds the right of Presidency over this (the lesser) Priesthood," in line of heredity from father to son, it is quite evident that, in this office we have, in a very actual sense, the restoration and continuation of the Jewish High Priest, the dignity first awarded to Aaron, and transmitted by descent to his sons.

The specified duties of the Presiding Bishopric include: (1) the presidency of the whole body of the lesser priesthood, with the superintendence over all business and ordinances within its sphere; (2) the receiving and caring for all the property of the Church, including the building and care of houses of worship; (3) necessary money disbursements for the relief of the poor; (4) the superintendence of all Church enterprises for the purchase of lands and the building-up of settlements upon them. He may also act as special judge, even in cases involving members of the Higher Priesthood. In virtually all matters, however, he acts in council with, and under the direction of the First Presidency of the Church.

The duties of the ward bishop are concerned with (1) maintaining the ward meeting-house, or chapel; (2) conducting regular services; (3) collecting the tithes and other offerings of the people; (4) inquiring into the needs and conditions of the people, and distributing such aid as may be required; (5) presiding over all priest's quorums in his ward. He is also judge of the ward court, sitting with his two counselors, who, like himself, are High Priests of the Melchisedek order, specifically set apart, to decide disputes between persons under his charge, or to try causes based upon accusations against any persons in his ward. This court has the power to excommunicate any lay member or any holder of the lesser priesthood, when convicted of grave offences, but may only disfellowship a member of the High Priesthood, when similarly convicted of grave offences.

The theory and constitution of the High Priesthood, as representing the consummation and inclusion of all that is contained in the lower order, precisely as the Gospel is held to relate similarly to the Mosaic Dispensation, involves implicit harmony with what may be held to be the real sense of Scripture. This Priesthood is not hereditary, even in theory, as should be the highest office, at least, in the lesser priesthood, the bishopric — which should properly be held by a "lineal descendant of Aaron" (cf. *Doctrine and Covenants,* lxviii, 16 *and* cvii. 70)— but is imparted by the direct authority of God. Although, as specified in passages already quoted, this priesthood was taken away from the Children of Israel, because of unbelief, the sense of authoritative utterances seems to be that it was imparted to, and held by, some of the various prophets of Israel, who evidently exercised some authority, as direct agents of God, which was recognized as superior to the official priests, also to the kings of Israel, even from the earliest times. (Cf. *Doctrine and Covenants,* cxxxii. 39.) It seems reasonable, therefore, on the assumption that the Dispensation of the Fulness of Times should include all previous dispensations, that an order should be recognized, whose members "have the privilege of receiving the mysteries of the kingdom of heaven, . . . and to enjoy the communion and presence of God"; in other words, to fill the place of the prophets recognized in all older dispensations.

However, although, as distinctly specified, the Melchisedek Priesthood entitles one holding it to fill any office in the Church, even the most exalted, provided he be "called and sustained" in prescribed fashion, there are certain powers and dignities which belong exclusively to the offices, and may not be exercised by any elder or high priest, unless he hold some such office. This right or authority to exercise special powers or functions in the Church comes by virtue of certain "keys," or official gifts or dignities, by which, as it were, the doors of divine favor may be opened. This is explained, as follows:

> "Jesus said to Peter: 'I will give unto thee the keys of the kingdom of heaven.' (Matt. xvi. 19.) And he said to Joseph in a revelation: 'Unto you I have given the keys of the kingdom.' *(Doc. and Cov., Sec.* lxxxi. 2). And in many instances and at divers times has the Lord given his servants the keys for special purposes. The meaning of this term is better explained by illustration. Every High Priest, for instance, is eligible to presidency, either as bishop or stake president, or any other presiding office in the Priesthood; and he has all the general authority he needs to act in any of the positions named. But no High Priest acts in a presiding capacity until he is called and inducted into office. (*Doc. and Cov.,* Sec. xxvii. 5–13.)
>
> "The Priesthood gives a man general authority to act in the name of the Lord; the *keys* of the Priesthood give him the special authority to act or administer in any particular office or calling. It will be remembered that none of the keys of the Priesthood are exercised except through office."—*Joseph B. Keeler* (*The Lesser Priesthood, etc., p.* 74).

The respective duties of the High Priest and the elder are set forth in the *Doctrine and Covenants,* as follows:

> "High Priests after the order of the Melchisedek Priesthood, have a right to officiate in their own standing, under the direction of the Presidency, in administering spiritual things; and also in the office of an elder, priest, (of the Levitical order,) teacher, deacon, and member. An elder has a right to officiate in his stead when the High Priest is not present. The High Priest and elder are to administer in spiritual things, agreeable to the covenants and commandments of the church; and they have a right to officiate in all these offices of the church when there are no higher authorities present."—*Section* cvii. 10–12.
>
> "The High Priests should travel, and also the elders, and also the lesser priests; but the deacons and teachers should be appointed to watch over the church, to be standing ministers unto the church."—*Section* lxxxiv. 111.
>
> "The elders are to conduct the meetings as they are led by the Holy Ghost, according to the commandments and revelations of God." —*Sec.* xx. 45.

The several grades or degrees of priestly or ecclesiastical dignity having been thus outlined and described, we understand the several varieties of material — if such metaphor be proper — which may be arranged and correlated to constitute the organism of the Church. For, as must be evident, even a gradation of dignities or degrees, from top to bottom of the scale, can constitute no stable unity, unless individuals are properly associated and classified in permanent fashion. Consequently, we find, as a primary unit of association, that every holder of ecclesiastical dignity, high or low, is related to others of his own grade, also to the Church as a whole, in the fact that he is also a member of some particular "quorum." As understood in the Mormon Church, this is a class or company of a specified number of members for each grade — except in the case of the High Priests' quorums — having a definite individual designation, local or numerical, each with its own officers and members, and its own specific functions. The word, "quorum," as here used, refers to the whole membership in any given case, and not, as by usual understanding, to a voting majority.

Classifying all ordained members of the Church by quorums, we have several orders of such bodies. Thus, quorums may be official and administrative, or primarily associative or educational. Also, there may be general quorums, affecting the whole Church, and local quorums, belonging to some ward or stake organization. The matter may be best explained by outlining the organization of all such quorums, beginning, as before, at the bottom of the scale.

Thus, twelve deacons form a quorum of deacons; one of them being chosen president, "to sit in council with them, and teach them their duty — edifying one another, as it is given according to the Covenants." (*Doc. and Cov.* cvii. 85.) The president is to be assisted by two counselors, also chosen from the twelve, the three composing the presidency of the quorum. Another member is elected clerk, or secretary. The object of this association, as above specified, is to promote mutual agreement and cooperation in the performance of the duties of deacons. Consequently, all activities of the quorum are under the superintendency of the bishop of the ward, who is the responsible and real authoritative head.

All quorums in the Church, except the several councils of the Seventies, are presided over in similar fashion, by a president and two counselors; also all Church societies and associations, outside of the priesthood organizations proper. This arrangement is a wise one, serving to divide responsibility, in great measure; also, in assisting the presiding officer with constant advice and counsel from perfectly sympathetic persons, acquainted with all situations involved in given cases.

The quorum of teachers consists of twenty-four members, from the number of whom are chosen, in precisely similar fashion, a president, two counselors and a clerk. The teachers' quorum has as its object to promote cooperation among those holding this grade of the ministry, and to discuss methods of performing their duties. It is also subject to the direction and superintendence of the ward bishop.

The next higher quorum, that of the priests of the Levitical order, consists of forty-eight members, but, unlike the others, chooses no president and counselors from its number; the bishop himself being its presiding officer in his capacity of "president over the priesthood of Aaron."

Each quorum of ninety-six elders has its own president with two counselors and a clerk, chosen from their number. Such quorums are regularly organized by the stake presidency in any district, in which ninety-six elders (or a few more or less) have their residence. However, the elders resident in a given ward, when at home, usually associate, more or less informally, for the furtherance of local Church affairs, under the general supervision of the bishop.

Above the elders' quorums are those of the High Priests, whose membership is not limited, but may include as few or as many men holding this dignity as reside in a given stake or district. Like all other quorums in the Church, these organizations have a president with two counselors and a secretary. There are also local or ward divisions, organized for convenience, but these are in no sense independent of the stake or district quorum. The object of the High Priests' quorum is "self-culture, discipline, and such other spiritual development as shall prepare them in every way for the ministry of their holy calling." (Keeler.) From these quorums, also, the stake and ward officers, presidents and bishops, are regularly selected and appointed.

All the quorums thus far described are composed of persons whose duties, religious or administrative, keep them at home, or of persons not engaged in work abroad. The quorums of deacons, teachers, priests and elders include, as already stated, "the standing ministry of the Church" and their assistants. There is, however, another rank of elders, whose calling includes the duty of preaching the Gospel abroad, as well as at home, and this is known as the Seventy. The term "Seventy" indicates the fundamental principle of organization holding in this rank or office. Its quorum consists of seventy members, and is presided over by a presidency of seven presidents, selected from the members, among whom the president first ordained or chosen to the office is the presiding officer at all meetings or deliberations. The Seventy is, however, a general, as opposed to a merely local, or district, body, and acts through its own presidency, under the immediate supervision of the Council of the Twelve Apostles of the Church.

The organization of the Seventy was first formed in the Mormon Church in harmony with the act of Christ (Luke x) in appointing seventy of His disciples to go "two and two before His face into every city and place, whither He himself would come," to herald the Kingdom of God. Although many scriptural commentators believe that the seventy disciples thus sent out did not constitute a permanent body, some others, such as Eusebius in his *Ecclesiastical History* (Chap. xii) argue to a contrary conclusion. In the Mormon Church it has always proved an efficient and valuable institution. The outline of its institution is thus set forth:

> "The seventy are . . . called to preach the gospel, and to be especial witnesses unto the Gentiles and in all the world. . . . The seventy are to act in the name of the Lord, under the direction of the Twelve or the traveling High Council, in building up the Church and regulating all the affairs of the same in all nations — first unto the Gentiles and then to the Jews. . . . And it is according to the vision, showing the order of the seventy, that they should have seven presidents to preside over them, chosen out of the number of the seventy; and the seventh president of these presidents is to preside over the six; and these seven presidents are to choose other seventy besides the first seventy, to whom they belong, and are to preside over them; and also other seventy, until seven times seventy, if the labor in the vineyard of necessity requires it. And these seventy are to be traveling ministers unto the Gentiles first, and also unto the Jews."— *Doctrine and Covenants,* cvii. 25, 34, 93–97.

The presidency of the first quorum of Seventy, having the power of appointing other seventies, as required, is the supreme council in the order. The rule that the increase may be "until seven times seventy" seems to have been modified by later authority, by which it was almost indefinitely extended. Thus, according to Joseph Smith's record, we read, under date May 2, 1835, as follows:

> "If the first Seventy are all employed, and there is a call for more laborers, it will be the duty of the seven presidents of the first Seventy to call and ordain other Seventy and send them forth to labor in the vineyard, until, if needs be, they set apart seven times seventy, and even until there are one hundred and forty-four thousand thus set apart for the ministry."— *History of the Church, Vol.* ii. p. 221.

The authority of the first quorum of the Seventy is even more exalted, since, by special law, it is equal in authority to the Council of the Twelve Apostles, in all matters pertaining to their work and office. This is specified, as follows:

"And they (the Seventy) form a quorum equal in authority to that of the Twelve special witnesses or apostles."—*Doctrine and Covenants*, cvii. 26.

"And in case that any decision of these quorums is made in unrighteousness, it may be brought before a general assembly of the several quorums, which constitute the spiritual authorities of the church, otherwise there can be no appeal from their decision."—*Ibid.* cvii. 32.

The duties of the Seventy, however, are primarily evangelical. They are preachers and witnesses, rather than administrators in any proper sense. Consequently, their part in the organism of the Church is largely auxiliary to the more nearly executive functions of the Apostolic quorum. They are the soldiers in the field rather than the governors and commanders, having the supreme authority in directing campaigns, as well as special movements.

In the organization of the two highest quorums of the Church we arrive at the point where authority in both religious and temporal, or outward, affairs of the Church is centered. This double authority is vested to a certain extent in the Council of the Twelve Apostles, and completely in the First Presidency. These two quorums act together in a very large number of instances, although the First Presidency has such wide powers that the cooperation of the Apostolic Quorum is virtually never obligatory, except in certain judicial sessions, in which, as specified by law, the Presidency shall act in council with a jury of twelve high priests as advisers.

In their quorum of the Twelve Apostles the Latter-day Saints maintain, as a permanent institution, another primitive order, which traditional bodies have supposed to be merely temporary, and of significance only for the early Church. The Mormon claim that, on the contrary, this "quorum," as originally established by Christ, was intended to persist, gains some probability from the act of the eleven survivors in electing Matthias as successor to Judas Iscariot; also, from the fact that St. Paul maintains the unchallenged claim to apostleship, thus suggesting his election to fill some other vacancy. On the theory that this body was to be permanent and self-perpetuating, its restoration, with the restored Church, seems logical, if not inevitable.

The word apostle is used several times in authoritative Mormon documents before the formal establishment, or reestablishment, as they claim, of the Twelve. Thus, in a revelation dated in June, 1829, Oliver Cowdery is addressed in the following words:

"I speak unto you, even as unto Paul mine apostle, for you are called even with that same calling with which he was called."—*Doctrine and Covenants*, xviii. 9.

Similarly, in a revelation dated in April, 1830, and referring to the "will and commandments of God," in regard to the organization of the Church, the following passages occur:

> "Which commandments were given to Joseph Smith, jun., who was called of God, and ordained an apostle of Jesus Christ, to be the first elder of this Church; and to Oliver Cowdery, who was also called of God, an apostle of Jesus Christ, to be the second elder of this church."—*Doctrine and Covenants,* xx. 2–3.

The following formal command to organize the quorum of the Twelve Apostles was given in June, 1829, although the organization did not take place until February, 1836.

> "And now, behold, there are others who are called to declare my gospel, both unto Gentile and unto Jew; yea, even Twelve, and the Twelve shall be my disciples, and they shall take upon them my name; and the Twelve are they who shall desire to take upon them my name with full purpose of heart; and if they desire to take upon them my name with full purpose of heart, they are called to go into all the world to preach my gospel unto every creature; and they are they who are ordained of me to baptize in my name, according to that which is written. . . . And now I speak unto you the Twelve—Behold, my grace is sufficient for you: you must walk uprightly before me and sin not. And, behold, you are they who are ordained of me to ordain priests and teachers; to declare my gospel, according to the power of the Holy Ghost which is in you, and according to the callings and gifts of God unto men. . . . And now, behold, I give unto you Oliver Cowdery, and also unto David Whitmer, that you shall search out the Twelve, who shall have the desires of which I have spoken; and by their desires and their works you shall know them; and when you have found them you shall show these things unto them."—*Doctrine and Covenants,* xviii. 26–29, 31, 32, 37–39.

The duties of the Apostles are also fully explained in several passages, as follows:

> "An apostle is an elder, and it is his calling to baptize, . . . and to administer bread and wine—the emblems of the flesh and blood of Christ—and to confirm those who are baptized into the church, by the laying on of hands for the baptism of fire and the Holy Ghost, according to the scriptures; and to teach, expound, exhort, baptize, and watch over the church; and to confirm the church by the laying on of the hands, and the giving of the Holy Ghost, and to take the head of all meetings."—*Doctrine and Covenants,* xx. 38–44.
>
> "The Twelve traveling counselors are called to be the Twelve apostles, or special witnesses of the name of Christ in all the world; thus differing from other officers in the church in the duties of their calling. And they form a quorum, equal in authority and power to the three Presidents. . . . The Twelve are a traveling presiding High Council, to officiate in the name of the Lord, under the direction of the Presidency of the church, agreeable to the institution of heaven; to build up the church, and regulate all the affairs of the same in all nations; first unto the Gentiles, and secondly unto the Jews. . . . The Twelve being sent out, holding the keys, to open the door by the proclamation of the gospel of Jesus Christ—and first unto the Gentiles and then unto the Jews. . . . It is the duty of the traveling High Council to call upon the Seventy, when they need assistance, to fill the

several calls for preaching and administering the gospel, instead of any others. . . . It is the duty of the Twelve also to ordain and set in order all the other officers of the church. . . . Whosoever ye shall send in my name, by the voice of your brethren, the Twelve, duly recommended and authorized by you, shall have power to open the door of my kingdom unto any nation whithersoever ye shall send them."—*Ibid.* cvii. 23–24, 33, 35, 38, 58; cxii. 21.

Although, as stated above, the Twelve Apostles "form a quorum, equal in authority and power to the three Presidents," their activities are always directed by the Presidency, except when, as the Traveling High Council, they are abroad. In this case there is no appeal from their decisions, except upon allegation and proof of "unrighteousness" (*Doc. and Cov.* cii. 30–33). It may seem a strange fact that, in so stable and well-working an organization as that of the Mormon Church, there should be several quorums with specified equal authority. A question would logically occur to any mind, as to how the First Quorum of the Seventy could be equal in authority to the Quorum of the Apostles, and, that, in turn, to the Quorum of the First Presidency, and, yet, that the three bodies should interact with good harmony. The matter is still further aggravated by the law regarding the stake high councils, which, as we shall see later, are in the several divisions what the Apostles are to the whole Church. Thus:

"The standing High Councils, at the Stakes of Zion, form a quorum equal in authority, in the affairs of the church, in all their decisions, to the quorum of the Presidency, or to the traveling High Council. The High Council in Zion, form a quorum equal in authority, in the affairs of the church, in all their decisions, to the Councils of the Twelve at the Stakes of Zion."—*Doctrine and Covenants,* cvii. 36–37.

Instead of being contradictory, however, the matter is really surprisingly logical, and also exhibits most effectively the real genius of the Mormon Church. The explanation of the matter lies in the fact that peculiar duties and dignities attach to the several offices, as already suggested, and that, although certain other quorums, under certain definite conditions and within just limits of authority, may be equal to those ranked above them, the higher quorums hold "keys" to powers and dignities, not shared by those beneath them in the scale. Consequently, the rulings and decisions of the higher quorums are respected and accepted from the fact that, as is the accepted belief, they partake of a measure of divine authority proportionate to the dignity of the quorum from which they emanate. Thus, with nearly uniform regularity, nominations for offices originate in or are approved by the First Presidency, which is the recognized medium of divine authority. All such nominations, however, are voted upon, and, from time to time, regularly "sustained" by the people of the Church.

Numerous critics of the Mormon system, evidently moved by a desire to find fault rather than to represent matters truthfully, have argued that this curious cooperation of theocratic authority and democratic autonomy is nothing other than centralized absolutism with a pretence of popular government. They assert, in short, that the general vote to establish or "sustain" any man in an exalted office is obtained by "fear" (of ostracism, at least), and is, in no sense, freely accorded. Such a criticism could be based only upon utter ignorance of this system, or else upon deliberate misrepresentation. It also overlooks the fact, evident upon proper examination, that the belief in the divine authority of the "keys" of office in the Church is perfectly sincere and vitally real in the minds of these people. Leaving this out of account, a study of the organization of the Church shows most definitely that the theoretical equality of the several governing quorums must, under any other conditions, furnish a ready source of disagreement and partisan politics. In short, without the belief in the divine authority back of the higher quorums, the system could not work at all. The people vote together, with such singular unanimity, because they have full confidence in the wisdom and righteousness of those set above them officially; also, because they recognize that the faithful discharge of official duties is a matter of greater importance than the consideration of preferring one person, rather than another, in any given dignity. However, the accusation of unrighteousness, as shown by indulgence in any sin or crime, is always recognized as a sufficient reason for reconsidering any nomination, or for withholding a vote to sustain any one already in an office, even the First Presidency of the whole Church. This principle is set forth, as follows, in an address by President Anthon H. Lund, at the organization of the Liberty Stake of Zion, February 26, 1904:

> "In voting, you are free to vote as you choose. Some have accused us of all voting the one way, and that voting of the 'Mormons' was a sham. Well, you know better than this, my brethren and sisters. The order of the Church is that the Priesthood has the right to nominate; but, . . . everything is done by common consent. It is your right to vote for or against the person or persons presented. If you do not know of any crime or sin against the men, be careful not to oppose them. But if you know of transgression, it is not only your right but your duty to vote against them. Let not personal feeling move you to oppose any presented before you to-night, or in any of our conferences."—*Deseret Evening News,* February 27, 1904.

From another point of view, also, the equality in authority of the several governing quorums is a wise provision — the offices of the Church could always be completely filled, in the extraordinary event that some catastrophe should eliminate the First Presidency and the Apostles. As a matter of fact, this is precisely the contingency distinctly provided for in the organization of a new First Presidency. Upon the death of the President, the First Presidency is dissolved, the two counselors of the President taking their places in the Quorum of the Twelve Apostles, if they had been Apostles, or, if not, in their proper High Priests' quorums. The Twelve then become the governing body in the Church, assuming its equality of authority with the First Presidency, and proceeds, as soon as possible, to form a new Presidency. After the death of President Young, the Apostles ruled the Church for three years; after the death of President Taylor, for two years. In both cases the choice of the successor was by the exercise of the power of receiving revelations, then transferred to the Apostolic Quorum, but the choice, thus determined, was ratified by the entire body of the Church membership, voting in public meetings. In the event that a new President is chosen and sustained by general vote, he succeeds to the "keys" and powers inherent in the office, and these are, accordingly, withdrawn from the Twelve.

The supreme authority in the Church is vested in the President, who, with his counselors, accordingly, holds the presidency over both priesthoods and of all quorums in the Church, and is recognized as the directing head of all activities, both spiritual and temporal. His dignities include, therefore, that of "prophet, seer, revelator and translator," the authorized medium for imparting the will and counsels of God to the Church; the "Presiding High Priest over the High Priesthood of the Church," holding all the "keys" of all the "sealing ordinances"; Trustee-in-Trust of the Church, holding title to all general Church property, and authorizing all disbursements. Officially and personally, he may act in the capacity of lawgiver, executive and judge, and may officiate in any and all functions of either priesthood, should he so desire. His relation, in short, to the Church as a whole is that of Moses to the Israelites.

The President, however, although the bearer of such great and numerous dignities and authorities, regularly acts with two counselors, like any other President of any organization or quorum of the Church; habitually, also, with the Council of the Twelve Apostles. His counselors, chosen by himself from the number of the Apostles or High Priests, are also known by the title of president, the three forming the First Presidency of the Church. These counselors participate in the authority and dignity of the President only through official association with him. They are not properly vice-presidents, except in the temporary absence of the President, when they may discharge some of his administrative functions, nor do they continue in office after his decease.

The President, also, in a very real sense, holds his office "during good behaviour," since, in spite of the exalted character of his dignities, his conduct must always be above all reproach. The definite and extended provisions, made to meet the contingency of his failure in this respect, sufficiently exemplify the fact that the Mormon idea of theocracy involves no notion of monarchic absolutism. It also exhibits to a marked degree the actual influence of the rank and file in matters governmental and administrative. The curious blending of theocracy and democracy in the government of the Church achieves its most surprising climax in the provisions that the regularly appointed agent of divine authority may be displaced on the proof of charges based on merely human testimony, against his character and behaviour. It examples the fact that all believers partake of the divine authority of their highest officers, imparted with the gift of the Holy Ghost and other endowments.

Thus, as already specified, the Council of the Twelve Apostles in their decisions are equal to the First Presidency, and the same is true of the decisions of the first quorum of the Seventy. The proviso is made, however, that

> "every member in each quorum must be agreed to its decisions, in order to make their decisions of the same power or validity one with the other. (A majority may form a quorum, when circumstances render it impossible to be otherwise.) Unless this is the case, their decisions are not entitled to the same blessing which the decisions of a quorum of three Presidents were anciently, who are ordained after the order of Melchisedek, and were righteous and holy men. The decisions of these quorums, or either of them, are to be made in all righteousness, in holiness, and lowliness of heart, meekness and long-suffering, and in faith, and virtue, and knowledge, temperance, patience, godliness, brotherly kindness and charity; because the promise is, if these things abound in them, they shall not be unfruitful in the knowledge of the Lord. And in case that any decision of these quorums is made in unrighteousness, it may be brought before a general assembly of the several quorums, which constitute the spiritual authorities of the church, otherwise there can be no appeal from their decision."—*Doctrine and Covenants,* cvii. 27–32.

That the unanimous decision of either, or both, these quorums should suffice to constitute a case against the Quorum of the First Presidency, or any member of it, is evident. However, the matter is definitely treated in the following laws:

> "And inasmuch as a President of the High Priesthood shall transgress, he shall be had in remembrance before the common council of the church,

who shall be assisted by twelve counselors of the High Priesthood; and their decision upon his head shall be an end of controversy concerning him. Thus, none shall be exempted from the justice and the laws of God, that all things may be done in order and in solemnity before him, according to truth and righteousness. . . . He that is slothful shall not be counted worthy to stand, and he that learns not his duty and shows himself not approved, shall not be counted worthy to stand."—*Ibid.*, cvii. 82–84, 100.

The procedure to be followed in such an extraordinary case is outlined as follows:

"It will be observed here that even a President of the Church may be impeached or tried for transgression. The law has been made to reach all — officers and members alike. Three counselors to President Joseph Smith were rejected by the Church and afterward tried and excommunicated on the charge of apostasy and treachery: namely, Frederick G. Williams, March 17, 1839; William Law, April 18, 1844; and Sidney Rigdon, Sept. 8, 1844.

"The law and order of the Church is, that when a President of the High Priesthood, who is also President of the Church, is tried, it shall be before a 'common council'— that is, a council or court of twelve High Priests. A High Council, or a common council, organized for this purpose is presided over by the Presiding Bishop of the Church. (D. & C. sec. 107, 76.) The trial of Sidney Rigdon, for example, was held before Bishop Whitney, a Presidency of the Nauvoo Stake of Zion, nine High Councillors of that Stake, and three other High Priests.

"If condemned by such a court, the extreme penalty would be severance from the Church; and a less penalty might be the withdrawal of the keys, rights, and powers of the Presidency."—*Joseph B. Keeler, (The Lesser Priesthood, etc., pp.* 97–98.)

The general officers of the Church exercise their authority and leadership through the several orders of district and local executives, each of whom has definite powers and responsibilities. Thus, directly beneath the First Presidency are the Presidency and High Council of each separate stake, and beneath these, again, as far as concerns spiritual and general administrative affairs, are the ward presidencies, composed of the bishops and their counselors. The bishops owe a double allegiance to superior authorities, consisting, however, in the fact that they fill a double capacity in relation to the people in their charges. So far as concerns outward and temporal affairs, the ward bishop, as local president of the lesser priesthood, is directly responsible to the Presiding Bishop of the whole Church, to whom he must render regular accounts of his stewardship in business matters. In such concerns the bishop, however, reports through the stake Presidency. But in the spiritual matters of the ward the stake President, with his council, directs the actions of the ward president, or bishop, and also in general matters, to the extent, at least, that the affairs of one ward bear relation to others in the stake.

The district subdivision of Church government, known as the

"stake," is in many particulars analogous to one of the separate states of the American republic. Just as each state has its governor, corresponding, within his limits of authority, to the President of the United States; and, just as each state has its legislature of two houses, corresponding to the Federal Congress, so each separate stake of the Mormon Church has its presidency, consisting of the President and his two counselors, and the High Council of twelve High Priests, corresponding, respectively, to the First Presidency of the whole Church, and the Council of the Twelve Apostles. Indeed, as has been often remarked, the stake is the "Church in miniature."

The use of the word, "stake," to indicate a subdivision of territory, is peculiar to the terminology of the Mormon Church, and is based on a metaphor found several times in the Old Testament scriptures. Just as a tent is held up by cords attached to stakes driven in the ground, so a separate centre of power and authority is represented by this word, as indicating a source of strength and stability to the total structure of the Church. This is explained as follows:

> "Isaiah uses it (stakes) as a figure of speech in which he makes Jerusalem a tent with its stakes and cords stretching out the curtains, and the stakes marking off the boundary of space the tent occupies. "Look upon Zion, the city of our solemnities; thine eyes shall see Jerusalem a quiet habitation, a tabernacle that shall not be taken down; not one of the *stakes* thereof shall ever be removed, neither shall any of the cords thereof be broken." (Isa. xxxiii: 20). Again, prophesying of Israel when in the latter times they would need more room, he says: 'Enlarge the *place* of thy tent, and let them stretch forth the curtains of thine habitations: spare not, lengthen thy cords, and strengthen thy stakes.' (Isa. liv. 2). The implied comparison in this metaphor is that the stakes and cords mark off or broaden the boundary of their habitation. The Lord uses similar language in a revelation: 'For Zion must increase in beauty, and in holiness: her borders must be enlarged, her *stakes* must be strengthened.' (*Doc. and Cov.* lxxxii: 14). 'Until the day cometh when there shall be found no more room for them; and then I have other places which I will appoint unto them, and they shall be called *Stakes for the curtains* or for the strength of Zion.' (*Ibid.*, ci: 21)."—*J. B. Keeler*, (*The Lesser Priesthood, etc., pp.* 62–63.)

The stake President and his two counselors, as well as the high council of twelve members, are nominated by the First Presidency of the Church, and then voted upon by the people of the stake in their stated conferences. The choice of the First Presidency is made, of course, upon mature consideration of the character and fitness of the candidates, and may be vetoed by the vote of the people, upon allegation and proof of charges sufficiently grave to constitute definite disqualification. These officers, when once properly elected by popular vote, have, as already specified, a judicial authority within their own district equal to that of the general authorities of the Church. (*Doc. and Cov.* cvii:36–37.)

The stake Presidency has authority over the spiritual and educational affairs of the district, including the recommendation of missionaries for foreign work, the selection of home missionaries within the stake, and the direction of the latter, also, all matters relating to the moral, spiritual and temporal welfare of the people. They act somewhat as the bishops of prelatical churches in the scope of their powers, also in their relationships to the ward presidents, or bishops, who correspond to the parish priests of such bodies. The stake Presidency also exercises direct regular supervision over all stake quorums, such as those of the High Priests and elders; these being regularly organized under stake auspices, and belonging to the stake, rather than to the ward, although, as occasionally happens, one or more quorums, as of elders, may exist within the limits of a ward.

Apart from general administrative affairs, the stake Presidency regularly presides at the monthly priesthood meeting and at the quarterly conferences of stake membership, both of which are important functions in the religious and community life of the district. At the priesthood meeting, which is a sort of stake senate, the reports of the bishops and communications from the First Presidency, and other general authorities, are received and read, and matters of doctrine and stake administration are discussed and acted upon. While distinctly a deliberative, and, to a considerable extent, also, a legislative body, the monthly meeting is of primary importance in promoting mutual understanding and cooperation among persons holding the priesthood in the stake, who thus enjoy the advantages of association with others outside of their own wards and quorums. In short, it is one of the most effective means for promoting mutual understanding and maintaining a spirit of unity among members of the priesthood.

Of scarcely less importance, and of somewhat greater interest to the general public is the quarterly conference of the entire membership of the stake. At such meetings the people of the stake, men and women, priesthood and laity, exercise the right of voting upon all matters in discussion, that affect them spiritually or temporally. Among such matters are the elections of general and stake officers, who, as previously explained, are regularly nominated by the First Presidency, and then submitted to the votes of the people in conference. General and stake officers already in office are also regularly "sustained" in these conferences, their names being presented, as if for original election, and voted upon by the entire membership.

Such opportunities to "sustain," or reject, any officer whatever, occurring four times in a year, give clear indication of the feelings of the people, also of the continued faithfulness of the officers. Undoubtedly many people in the Church have strong personal objections to some of those set over them in office; however, the rule is strictly observed that only proved unworthiness or unfaithfulness in an officer is sufficient ground for impeachment, or even of failure to sustain him formally. There can be no doubt but what such disaffection as would lead to non-election of an officer, or the failure to sustain him in any given stake, would be made the subject of serious investigation and earnest efforts at reconciliation, in case of non-proof of charges made. Nor, in other points of view, is the voting of the Mormon people in any sense perfunctory, or an unmeaning performance. To be sure, the right of nomination is not vested in the ranks, which ratify, rather than initiate in this matter, but this appears in some real senses a distinct contribution to stable and effective government, and in no way really undemocratic. That this is true must be obvious, when we consider that the moral end of government is proper administration of public affairs, and not the gratification of personal or party ambitions. Thus, in France, for example, the President is elected by the Senate, rather than by popular vote, and this procedure has resulted in no conspicuous miscarriages of judgment. Also, as contemplated by the United States Constitution, the President is chosen by the College of Electors, which, in turn, is chosen by popular vote. Originally, the members of this College had complete freedom of choice, as the delegates or representatives of the people, who left the matter entirely to their judgment. But, with the growth of partisan politics, not wholly an improvement on the original plan, their functions gradually became merely formal. At present, unofficial cliques and "machines" largely engineer the nomination and election of public officers, and the people have no choice but to ratify or reject their candidates at the polls. Our party government scheme is too often tainted with considerations quite foreign to real statesmanship; and this is the penalty that we must pay for the doubtful privilege of choosing our executive officers more or less directly. Furthermore, we have no right of voting periodically to "sustain" or displace any unfaithful or unworthy officials; the impeachment or removal of such an one in a high office being a difficult and tedious process. We may judge, therefore, whether the "Mormon" system, which certainly works very far toward the end of incurring faithful and competent officers in important positions, is so very undemocratic, after all.

At the quarterly conferences of the stake membership, also, many matters relating to the life and welfare of the people are regularly introduced and voted upon. Such matters may be introduced by any member, if submitted in the prescribed manner, and through the recognized channels. This, also, is an excellent plan, in no sense abrogatory of personal rights — unless the most conspicuous element in such is the precipitation of discussion, often useless and acrimonious — but it is rather a contribution toward efficiency, according to the often-recommended principle of " doing all things decently and in order."

Beneath the stake authorities, and, in matters spiritual and ecclesiastical, directly responsible to them, come the authorities of the several wards. The ward is, in fact, the ecclesiastical unit of the stake, to which it is related precisely as are the separate stakes to the general authorities of the Church. Moreover, it is the organization that most intimately affects the individual; being closer to his personal life and interests than either the stake or general authorities.

Each ward, as previously explained, is presided over by a bishop, who, with two counselors, constitutes its presidency. Under the immediate supervision of this presidency, or bishopric, are, as already explained, the several quorums of the lesser priesthood; also, the ward branches of the official Church societies and organizations. These latter are the Women's Relief Society; the Young Men's and the Young Ladies' Mutual Improvement Associations; the Primary Association; also, a ward Religion Class, and the Sunday School organization. Such ward associations, while under the supervision of the ward bishopric, are regularly formed and accredited branches of general bodies, whose activities affect the whole Church. They are efficient helpers to the bishopric, both in dispensing relief to the needy, and in promoting the moral, religious and intellectual welfare of the people. They will be treated and discussed in the proper place.

In addition to these numerous responsibilities, the bishop exercises the general functions of pastor; superintending all religious rites and offices in his ward; issuing recommendations for persons wishing to enter any of the temples, or to remove to other wards; receiving the tithes and other offerings of the people, and rendering such advice and assistance as may be required by any in his charge. Under the direction of the stake Presidency, the bishop also convenes the periodical ward conferences, and, in the absence of a higher authority, who frequently assumes the chair by courtesy, presides over its deliberations.

At these ward conferences all officers, both general, stake and ward, are elected or "sustained"; ward business is transacted, and reports from local organizations and quorums are received. It is to the ward, in short, what the quarterly conference is to the stake, and the general conference to the whole Church. Although, of course, effective only in transacting ward business and defining the local attitude toward general Church and community affairs, it is an efficient instrument for promoting local action among the people, and bringing them into close association, as a sort of "committee of the whole," in addition to their organization and quorum work.

The system of Church courts is closely related to the general organization of its government. These courts, while convened usually to try and decide causes based upon charges against the character or conduct of members of the Church, and empowered to disfellowship or excommunicate the guilty, also take cognizance of matters in dispute between such members in good standing, which cannot be reconciled by the offices of the teachers and others representing Church authority. In no case have such courts attempted to review or reverse the decisions of civil courts, either in matters criminal or general. It is the rule, however, to formally try a member accused of public crime, and to administer to such the rebukes and disabilities available to Church authority, if guilty.

There are three regularly organized courts and as many special tribunals, usually convened to try exceptional causes, and under exceptional conditions. The three former are: the ward bishop's court, the stake high council, and the Council of the First Presidency. The three latter are: the Presiding Bishop's Court, convened specifically to try charges against a "presiding high priest," the Council of High Priests Abroad, convened usually to decide important difficulties arising outside the organized stakes of Zion; and the Traveling High Council of the Twelve Apostles.

The ward court consists of the Bishop of the Ward and his two counselors, or, in event of the absence or disability of either of the counselors, with any High Priest selected by him, and acceptable to the litigating parties; in the event of the absence or disability of both counselors, with two High Priests, similarly chosen. The trial of any cause before this court proceeds in recognized fashion, by the taking of testimony and the argument of the case on both sides. The decision is rendered in writing, and represents the majority opinion of the three judges; the Bishop having the "casting vote," in case of disagreement between his counselors. Thus, a decision agreed on by the Bishop and one of his counselors is valid; but in case both counselors disagree with the Bishop, there is no decision, and the case must be retried, or be appealed to the High Council of the stake.

The Stake High Council, sitting as a court, consists of the twelve High Councillors, or any one or several of their six "alternates" filling vacancies, and is presided over by the Stake Presidency. This body may sit as a court of original jurisdiction, and so does in all stake matters, or as an appellate court, for the review of cases already tried in any of the ward courts. The High Council may review any case already tried by a ward court, whether the testimony be objected to or not, and may reverse, modify or confirm the decision of the Bishop. In case of appeal, based on objections, or "exceptions," the Council may try the case over from the start, as if at original hearing. On the ground of irregularities or of new evidence, the High Council may direct a new trial by the Bishop's Court. The Council of the Twelve Apostles, sitting as a High Council, may also hear causes, but the practice of so doing is concerned wholly with considerations on the importance of the given case, such as would warrant this General Authority in assuming the function prescribed for the ward or stake authorities.

Above all other Church courts, either regular or special, stands the First Presidency, when sitting as a Council. It has both original and appellate jurisdiction, and may sit as a court of original jurisdiction, or as an appellate body reviewing the evidence and decisions of any lower court. Although, as distinctly specified (*Doc. and Cov.* cvii:36), the authority of the stake high councils is such that its decisions admit of no appeal, the Council of the First Presidency may order a retrial on the ground of irregularities, or, as specified, of "unrighteousness." In the hearing of any cause, either in the first instance or on appeal, the First Presidency may act alone (i.e. the First President and his two counselors) or with the assistance of twelve High Priests. (*Doc. and Cov.* cvii:79.) This Council is not inclined, however, to interfere in cases, except where considerations of general importance emerge, or where there has been evident irregularity in the original trial. It has exercised its prerogative most often on matters affecting claims in dispute, as on property rights, etc., between the authorities of separate stakes. In such matters it does not infringe on the jurisdiction of the civil courts, since it is concerned only with disputes and causes arising between members and organizations of the Church. None of the Church courts will take cognizance of cases involving disputes between members and non-members of the Church.

The quorums of the Church organization, erroneously called

the "hierarchy," includes, according to general estimates, about 90 per cent. of the total male membership, beginning with boys of twelve or thirteen, who are regularly inducted into the grade of deacons. In 1914, the official figures for the quorum memberships were as follows:

Quorums of High Priests	11,450
Quorums of Seventies	11,112
Quorums of Elders	27,382
Total Melchisedek Priesthood	49,944
Quorums of Aaronic Priests	8,830
Quorums of Teachers	10,607
Quorums of Deacons	22,722
Total Aaronic Priesthood	42,159
Total Quorum Membership	92,103

CHAPTER XXI

"AUXILIARY ORGANIZATIONS"

In addition to the priesthood quorum organizations of the Mormon Church, there are several associations and societies, called collectively "auxiliary organizations." Like the several quorums of the Priesthood proper, as for example, the Seventy, these organizations have their separate and individual governing and administrative bodies, which operate under the immediate supervision of the Church authorities. Indeed, so intimately are these auxiliary bodies associated with the religious and community life of the Mormon people that it is perfectly correct to include them in an exhaustive account of the Church proper. They example notably the Mormon tendency to organize and cooperate for mutual advantage.

The earliest, also, the best known of these auxiliary organizations is the Women's Relief Society, now an organization of national scope and associated with the National Council of Women. While organized by, and consisting almost entirely of Mormon members, it distributes benevolent assistance with an exemplary impartiality. Indeed, in any great calamity its name has always been conspicuous among generous dispensers of relief for the needy and impoverished. This society was founded by Joseph Smith at Nauvoo, Ill., March 17, 1842. It was the first regular organization of women in the world, and also, as is believed, the first association for the systematic distribution of beneficence. During the earlier years of Mormon occupancy of Utah the work of relief was largely in the hands of ward organizations, the relations between these branches being merely associative, and the connection with a general headship being rather loose and undefined. In 1877, however, stake societies were founded, which assumed control of work in the several wards, and in 1880 a general presidency was established. The advantage of the last step in the development was that the work of benevolence could be pursued in obedience to a systematic directorate, which, in turn, could be in close touch with the central authorities of the Church.

Each ward branch, presided over, in the usual fashion, by a president and two counselors, assisted by a clerk and treasurer, regularly enlist the services of several teachers, who visit the people of the ward, and ascertain their needs. Relief is then dispensed through the ward bishop. The ward officers regularly report their work to the stake authorities, who, in turn, report to the central presidency, which is thus kept in close and constant touch with the entire mechanism of the organization. Precisely as in the organization of the Church in general, the stake officers of the Relief Society regularly visit the wards under their direction, and the central presidency similarly visit the stake organizations. There are now over 700 ward societies included in 64 stakes, and about 100 Relief Society organizations maintained in connection with the important missions of the Church throughout the world. All of these together represent a membership of over 40,000. While by systematic work in ferreting out cases of need and reporting such to the bishops for prompt relief, financial or otherwise, the Relief Society is instrumental in distributing about $200,000 annually, it has also figured on generous scale in contributing to the relief of the sufferers by the San Francisco fire, and other calamities, that have ranked it among the most practical agencies of benevolence in the world.

In addition to the practical relief distributed by this society, it is a valuable adjunct to the practical work of the Church in affording a center for the sympathetic association of women in the practical activities of the community. The members of the branches meet constantly in sewing circles, in which clothing, carpets, quilts, etc., are made for use in Church buildings and in the homes of the poor. They also hold fairs, and unite in entertainments of other varieties to raise funds for charitable purposes. Certain of the women are regularly set apart to serve in the capacity of workers, and these do noble and unselfish work in caring for the sick, assisting the bereaved, and caring for the dead. They also distribute clothing, food, and medicines.

Next to the Relief Society, both in point of age and also in importance in the life of the Church and of the community, come the Mutual Improvement Associations, known, respectively as the Young Men's and the Young Ladies' associations. These organizations are largely educational in character, being intended to form centres for personal training in matters pertaining primarily to the conduct of life and the principles of religion. The reason for the foundation of these organizations lay in the conviction of the authorities that there was an actual "necessity for a general organization of the young people into societies for their mutual improvement — associations that should be separate from the priesthood, and yet so organized that they should be under its guidance, and for its strength." In the case of both organizations the original impulse came from the local societies formed for the purposes specified, which were gathered into stake and general associations with a strong central authority to direct all proceedings. The fact that local societies, more or less widely distributed throughout the Church wards, formed the real origins of the general body in each case examples the Mormon instinct for organization, also, the general desire of the people for advancement and improvement on educational and practical lines. That the idea of the authorities was to found organizations "separate from the priesthood" shows an intelligent comprehension of the fact that religion, while pervading all the affairs of everyday life, as it does among the Mormons, should have an individual application, as well as one essentially official and organic.

The development of the Young Men's Mutual Improvement Association is thus outlined by its former general secretary:

> "In 1873 it became the rule in some of the more thickly populated settlements of the Saints for the young people to form associations for entertainments and improvement. These were called night schools, literary societies, debating clubs, young men's clubs, or any other name that indicated the object of the gathering. Frequently they were solely for amusement, and, taking pattern after the early efforts in Salt Lake City, were formed to instruct the people by theatrical exhibitions and dramatic performances. In Weber county, about a dozen young men met, at the invitation of Apostle F. D. Richards, in his home, on the 20th day of April, 1873, to consider the importance of organizing themselves into a society for mutual improvement. . . . Meetings were thereafter held weekly, simple rules being adopted to govern the same, and a small mutual assessment was levied on the members to cover the expenses. The numbers grew until in a short time the association was compelled to move into the City Hall to accommodate the membership. . . . This association was not discontinued, but when the general movement was inaugurated, it was divided into four — one in each ward in the city. Other associations of like character were early formed in the settlements of the county, and improvement associations and literary societies had also been organized in several wards of Salt Lake City, and in other places previous to the general movement in 1875."— *Edward H. Anderson* (*The Past of Mutual Improvement, Improvement Era,* November, 1897).

The first of the Young Men's Mutual Improvement Associations was formally organized in Salt Lake City, June 10, 1875. In the following December two elders appointed to the task of organizing such associations in the various stakes entered upon their duties, which they performed so thoroughly that, within a year from that date, over 100 branches had been formed, representing a membership of more than 2,000. The ward branches, then formed, continued as separate organizations, with a general association holding regular meetings at stated times, until 1878, when the work was placed in the hands of the several stake authorities, and administered as stake organizations. Finally, in 1880, a general central board of direction was created, with a general superintendent and two assistants, who directed the work for the entire Church, assisted by a secretary, a treasurer, a music director and a board of thirty-four "aids." The stake and ward organizations are similarly presided over each by a superintendent and two assistants. The membership is about 34,000.

"The main function of the General Board is the supervision of all the Improvement associations throughout the world; to encourage and foster the study of the Scriptures; to recommend, publish and furnish other literature for the various associations; to formulate and arrange programs and outlines; to provide for the holding of conferences, conventions and other meetings; to establish and conduct missionary work among the young; to organize, in connection with local authorities, boards, committees, etc., in new stakes and in outlying territory; and to undertake and carry on many other things that tend to promote good citizenship and general welfare.

"Stake officers supervise the work of the local organizations. The ward presidents [superintendents] conduct the class work of their respective associations, look after the recreations and amusement in the wards, and labor with, and are helpful to, the young men in their several jurisdictions."—*Joseph B. Keeler* (*The Lesser Priesthood, etc.*, pp. 155–156.).

The subjects of study in the ward associations included theology, history, science and general literature, for which regular text books were provided and reference libraries selected. In 1891 the general authorities began the regular issuance of "manuals," pamphlets specially prepared for instruction along definite selected lines, and issued annually. These manuals have included some of the following practical and profitable subjects: "Spiritual Growth — Lessons on Practical Religion" (1908-1909); "The Making of the Man" (1909–1910); "The Making of a Citizen — Lessons in Economics" (1910–1911); "The Making of a Citizen — Problems in Economics, Agriculture and Public Finance" (1911–1912). In addition to these, regular manuals for the "junior classes" have been issued, including: "The Acts of the Apostles"— analysis and explanations (1907–1908); "The Development of Character — Lessons on Conduct" (1911–1912); "The Development of Character — Lessons on Success" (1911–1912), etc. In 1897 was begun the publication of the *Improvement Era,* the recognized organ of the Associations, a monthly magazine of literature and subjects of interest to the general reader. The regular work of the associations include also selected reading courses of literary, scientific and practical books. Among these may be mentioned the following selections: for 1906–1907, *John Halifax, Rasselas;* for 1907–1908, *Secret of Achievement, Great Truths, The Strength of Being Clean, Silas Marner;* for 1908–1909, *A Tale of Two Cities, Hypatia;* for 1909–1910, *Ancient America, Courage, The Crisis, Our Inland Sea;* for 1910–1911, *Brewer's Citizenship, Emerson's Essays,* "Friendship, Prudence, Heroism"; *Lorna Doone, Captain Bonneville;* for 1911–1912, *Dry Farming, Cities of the Sun, John Marvel, Assistant, The Young Man and the World.* Similarly well-selected lists have been prepared for the junior members, as follows: for 1906–1907, *True to His Home;* for 1907–1908, *Tom Brown's School Days, Wild Animals I Have Known;* for 1908–1909, *The Last of the Mohicans, Cortez;* for 1909–1910, Hapgood's *Life of Lincoln, John Stevens' Courtship, The Castle Builder;* for 1910–1911, *The Bishop's Shadow, Timothy Titcomb's Letters, Widow O'Callighan's Boys;* for 1911–1912, *Good Hunting, The Young Forester, Boy Wanted, Alfred the Great.*

The Young Ladies' Mutual Improvement Associations, while fulfilling the same function in the educational and social life of the young women of the Church, as does the Young Men's Association for the men, had an entirely separate origin. It began, in fact, not so much as an educational agency as one for promoting character and efficiency, coupled with firm religious conviction. The movement for the organization of this association was first launched by President Brigham Young, who formed the first Cooperative Retrenchment Association among the daughters of his own family. Having in mind the formation of an organization among the young women, "which should provide them with a training school, as it were, for their spiritual and intellectual development," he began the work by a direct appeal to the higher intelligence among them, which should rebel at the growing tendencies toward extravagance and frivolity. Accordingly, at a meeting held in his home on November 28, 1869, he made the following explanation of his position in these matters:

> "All Israel are looking to my family and watching the example set by my wives and children. For this reason I desire to organize my own family first into a society for the promotion of habits of order, thrift, industry, and charity; and, above all things, I desire them to retrench from their extravagance in dress, in eating and even in speech. The time has come when the sisters must agree to give up their follies of dress and cultivate a modest apparel, a meek deportment, and to set an example before the people of the world worthy of imitation. I am weary of the manner in which our women seek to outdo each other in all the foolish fashions of the world. For instance, if a sister invites her friends to visit her, she must have quite as many dishes as

her neighbor spread on a former occasion, and indeed she must have one or two more in order to show how much superior her table is to her neighbor's. This silly rivalry has induced a habit of extravagance in our food; it has involved fathers and husbands in debt, and it has made slaves of the mothers and daughters. It is not right. It is displeasing to the Lord, and the poor groan under the burden of trying to ape the customs of those who have more means. Then, again, our daughters are following the vain and foolish fashions of the world. I want you to set your own fashions. Let your apparel be neat and comely, and the workmanship of your own hands. . . . Make your garments plain, just to clear the ground in length, without ruffles or panniers or other foolish and useless trimmings and styles. I should like you to get up your own fashions, and set the style for all the rest of the world who desire sensible and comely fashions to follow. I want my daughters to learn to work and to do it. Not to spend their time for naught; for our time is all the capital God has given us, and if we waste that we are bankrupt indeed. . . . We are about to organize a Retrenchment Association, which I want you all to join, and I want you to vote to retrench in your dress, in your tables, in your speech, wherein you have been guilty of silly, extravagant speeches and light-mindedness of thought. Retrench in everything that is bad and worthless, and improve in everything that is good and beautiful. Not to make yourselves unhappy, but to live so that you may be truly happy in this life and the life to come."—*Susa Young Gates* (*History of the Young Ladies' Mutual Improvement Association, pp.* 8–10).

Following on this eloquent plea by their father, the young daughters of President Young adopted a set of resolutions, containing among other matters the following sentences:

"Resolved, that inasmuch as the Saints have been commanded to gather out from Babylon and not partake of her sins, that they may receive not of her plagues, we feel that we should not condescend to imitate the pride, folly and fashions of the world. And inasmuch as the Church of Jesus Christ is likened unto a city set on a hill, to be a beacon light to all nations, it is our duty to set examples for others, instead of seeking to pattern after them. . . .

"Resolved, inasmuch as cleanliness is a characteristic of a Saint, and an imperative duty, we shall discard the dragging skirts, and for decency's sake those disgustingly short ones extending no lower than the boot tops. We also regard 'panniers,' and whatever approximates in appearance toward the 'Grecian bend,' a burlesque on the natural beauty and dignity of the human female form, and will not disgrace our persons by wearing them. And also, as fast as it shall be expedient, we shall adopt the wearing of home-made articles, and exercise our united influence in rendering them fashionable."—*Ibid. pp.* 11–12.

Commenting on the work of the Associations founded in the excellent resolutions quoted above, Mrs. Gates gives the following fervent testimony:

"It is good for us to study the words and acts of those early days. The spirit of worldly pleasure and vain fashions was rapidly creeping into the ranks of the daughters of Zion. We women are no better than we should be to-day, nay, nor half as good; but can the mind picture where we should have been, if the training and check of these associations had not been given? No one will deny that the women of the Church have been magnificently disciplined by their various organizations, beginning with the Relief Society; and it would be a much easier thing for a great reform movement to sweep through our midst to-day than it was thirty-five years ago. All in all, there is much to encourage the sociologist in the steady improvement and progress of the women of the Church. It would be a blind if not an ungenerous historian who would not consider the cheering conditions which obtain among us to-day as the result of these early struggles."—*Ibid. pp.* 35–36.

Largely through the earnest efforts of Eliza R. Snow and Mary I. Horne, the society thus founded by President Young among the members of his own family was extended, first in Salt Lake City, and later among the further stakes of Zion. The branches organized by these ladies were divided, according to membership, into senior and junior departments, known, respectively, as the Ladies' Cooperative Retrenchment Association and the Young Ladies' Retrenchment Association. The spheres of usefulness of both were greatly widened, and the membership much increased, when, in 1880, all were united in the present organization, with a central presidency under the immediate direction of the general authorities of the Church. The organization is much the same as that of the Young Men's Association, having a general presidency controlling stake presidencies and these, in turn, directing work in the wards.

As at present organized, the work of the Young Ladies' Mutual Improvement Associations embraces the study of theology, domestic science, physiology and hygiene, literature and history. "Opportunity is also afforded members in the practice and management of deliberative assemblies, in the art of public speaking, and in work demanding self-effort along the channel of general culture." The membership is about 35,000.

The auxiliary organizations, or organizations separate from the quorums of the priesthood, are the Sunday School, the Primary Association, the General Church Board of Education and the Religion Class. All of these, while under the direction of the general authorities of the Church, have their own separate organization, usually formed along the lines indicated in the societies already described. Each one has a strong central authority, which works through stake and ward organizations, thus securing complete uniformity and efficiency in the work. The Sunday schools of the Mormon Church are graded for classes of various ages, whose instruction in religion varies accordingly. There are six grades, or "departments," as follows: (1) the Kindergarten; (2) the Primary, covering two years of instruction; (3) the First Intermediate, covering four years; (4) the Second Intermediate, covering four years; (5) the theological Department, for advanced pupils, also covering four years, and (6) the Parents' Department. The courses of instruction, which are regularly laid out by the General Board of the Sunday School Union, include graded and analyzed lessons in the Scriptures, noted events in Jewish and New Testament history, illustrated by stories and songs for the younger pupils, and by references to literature and recognized text books for the elder pupils. The Book of Mormon and the *Doctrine and Covenants* are included in these courses, as also the doctrines peculiar to the Mormon Church. The following article, prepared by the authorities of the Deseret Sunday School Union gives the essential facts:

"The Church of Jesus Christ of Latter-day Saints has from very early in its history made Sunday school service one of the very prominent features in its organization, although the work was not formally organized until the year 1849, in Salt Lake City, Utah, the Robert Raikes of Sunday school endeavor, in the Rocky Mountain West, being Richard Ballantyne, a lifelong worker in the service of the Master. From an extremely modest beginning—the first organized school having a membership of less than thirty—the Sunday schools of the Latter-day Saints have developed with remarkable rapidity until to-day the total enrollment of officers, teachers and members, according to the latest compiled statistics, is 179,254, with 1247 schools and an average attendance of members of 60 per cent, with all schools graded and otherwise fully equipped for the most successful training of the young and old in the ways of the Lord.

"In the third year of the occupancy of the Salt Lake valley by the Latter-day Saints, on Sunday, December 9th, 1849, the first Sunday school to be held in the Rocky Mountain region was organized by Richard Ballantyne in Salt Lake City, there being present about twenty of his neighbors, old and young. The house in which the school was held had been erected by Mr. Ballantyne's own hands, with some help from his friends. It was built of sundried brick, or adobes, and contained two rooms. For the first few years, the work of this school and of others, subsequently organized, was somewhat experimental, with the courses of study rather mixed, partaking of the dual nature of Sunday and day school, but with moral and religious training predominating. Later, regular plans for class work were formulated and the work throughout the Church was systematized and made universal. In 1866, under the editorship of George Q. Cannon, one of the Presidency of the Church, the publication of a Sunday school journal, called the *Juvenile Instructor,* was begun. This became the official organ of the Sunday schools of the Church and is still being published as such, now being in its forty-eighth volume. It is a magazine of eighty pages and is the medium through which general instructions and class-work outlines are disseminated.

"Among those prominently identified with the Sunday school work in its infancy, in addition to Richard Ballantyne, may be mentioned Brigham Young, Daniel H. Wells, George A. Smith, Wilford Woodruff, George Q. Cannon, William H. Sherman, Edward L. Sloan, George Goddard, Robert L. Campbell, David O. Calder, Brigham Young, Jr., Albert Carrington, John B. Maiben and John Morgan.

"By 1872, a total of 190 schools had been organized, located in twenty counties in Utah and two counties in Idaho, having a total membership of 14,781. About twenty-seven years later, there were 982 schools and the enrollment totaled 119,998, schools having been organized in practically every ecclesiastical district, or ward, of the Church at home and in many of the missions abroad. Wherever the Latter-day Saints located and commenced the reclamation of the desert, they organized Sunday and day schools. According to the latest official report, there were 1247 schools, with a total enrollment of practically 180,000. The average weekly attendance is 60 per cent of the enrollment. A rather remarkable showing and an indication of the interest taken in Sunday school work by the Latter-day Saints.

"The directing head and supreme authority, under the Presidency of the Church, of the Sunday school movement is the General Board of the Deseret Sunday School Union, composed at present of thirty-six representative men from almost every walk and avocation in life and including the President of the Church and his two counsellors, all of whom, in common with all other Sunday school workers, serve without financial compensation. The Union itself includes every Sunday school organization of the Church. Under the General Board, there are Stake organizations directing the work in their districts and these Stake boards supervise and direct the operation of the Ward organizations — the individual schools. The wards comprise small towns or divisions of large towns and cities, and the stakes correspond to counties or smaller divisions of thickly populated sections. The General Board is made up of a superintendent, first and second assistant superintendents, general secretary, general treasurer and associate members. The present general superintendent is Joseph Fielding Smith, President of the Church. The Stake organization is composed of a superintendent, first and second assistant superintendents, secretary and treasurer, assistant secretary and treasurer, chorister, organist, librarian, usher and department supervisors, there usually being at least twenty-two of the latter. The stake board conducts regular and frequent meetings of all workers within its jurisdiction for the purpose of instruction and lesson study, largely after the order of a teachers' institute.

"The Sunday schools themselves enroll all persons of 4 years of age and upwards who can be interested in the service. They are fully organized and graded and pursue a regular course of study, covering a period of sixteen years in the grades and an indefinite time in what is called the parents' department. The kindergarten department takes the beginner at 4 years of age, or even somewhat earlier, and the students pass successively through that department, the primary, first intermediate, second intermediate, junior theological, senior theological and into the parents' department. In some few schools, a normal or teachers' training department is maintained and quite a number have an advanced-theological department for those who do not care to identify themselves with the parents' class. The present course of study includes appropriate kindergarten work for that department; two years of Old and New Testament stories for the primary department; one year of Book of Mormon stories, two years of Old and New Testament stories and one year of Church history for the first intermediate department; two years of Book of Mormon history and two years of Old Testament history for the second intermediate department; one year of the subject, "Jesus the Christ," one year of the subject, "The Apostolic Age," one year of Church history and one year of doctrines of the Church for the theological department, while the parents' department considers all subjects vital to the home and family relations, interspersed with topics of general and special interest. The schools are officered by a superintendent and two assistants, secretaries, treasurers, librarians, choristers, organists and ushers, and every department of the school has a supervisor and one or more teachers. Local board meetings for consultation, instruction and lesson study, and made up of all school officers and teachers, are held weekly. The organization of the schools in the foreign missions is, where practicable, identical with that of those with the body of the Church. As an example of the work done each Sabbath day by the individual Sunday schools of the Church of Jesus Christ of Latter-day Saints, the following programme of a regular session is given:

9:30 A. M.— Prayer meeting of officers and teachers.
10 o'clock — School called to order, following five minutes of instrumental music.
Roll call.
Singing.
Prayer.
Abstract of minutes.
Singing — Sacramental.
Sacrament gem in concert.
Administration of Sacrament.
Sacrament thought by individual.
Concert recitation of Scriptural extracts.
Singing practice.
10:45 — Department work.
11:45 — Reassembly for closing exercises.
Remarks (if desired).
Singing.
Prayer.

"In addition to publishing the *Juvenile Instructor,* the Deseret Sunday School Union owns and operates a fully stocked book and stationery store at its headquarters in Salt Lake City, Utah. The book store is able to furnish everything in the way of supplies necessary for Sunday school workers and does a large volume of business. The finances of the Deseret Sunday School Union are managed by an executive committee. On the third Sunday in each September, every officer, teacher and member of every Sunday school in the Church is expected to contribute five cents each to the general fund. Of the total so contributed, twenty per cent goes to the support of the Stake organizations and the remainder to the general fund. This is the sole collection made for the general Sunday school cause. The individual schools provide for their own expenses, this work usually being in the hands of an amusement committee, which provides profit-making entertainments from time to time and thereby makes the school self-sustaining.

"At regular intervals, appropriate topics are considered in open assembly and in each department of every school in the Church, and certain days are designated for their consideration. Among these latter may be mentioned, 'Humane day,' 'Washington's birthday,' 'Lincoln's birthday,' 'Fourth of July,' 'Pioneer day,' 'Bird day,' 'Arbor day,' 'Thanksgiving' and 'Christmas.'"

Like all the other activities associated with the Mormon Church and people, the Sunday School organization is complete and efficient. Its usefulness has been greatly augmented, however, within recent years by the inauguration of the parents' class movement, which still further extends the sphere of religious instruction. The aims of the new department and the details of its organization are set forth in the following "Letter of the General (Sunday School) Superintendency," issued in 1906:

"The object of parents' classes is,— first, to aid parents in general culture; and secondly, to bring about a closer relationship between the home and the Sunday school, that parents may give more efficient aid in the general work of the Sunday school.

"Topics pertaining to the environment of the home, to the effect of one family's actions upon another's, to the influence of rewards and punishments as incentives to action, to the power of love as a disciplinary factor in the home — these and many kindred topics will aid the parents both as individuals and as heads of families.

"In the co-operation of the home and the Sabbath School, it is desired that parents will manifest an interest in getting children to be punctual, and to be regular in attendance; to take an active part in the singing, and in memory work; and above all, that parents will impress their children with the importance of preparing lessons. In this respect, it is one of the objects of parents' classes to aid the members to render practical assistance in the matter of home preparation. In brief, parents' classes aim to establish unity between the home and the Sunday school, in order to benefit the *parents,* the *children,* and the *school.*

"The parents' classes are primarily for the Latter-day Saints, though non-members of the Church are invited and should be made welcome. All parents attending the Sunday school, not connected with other classes, should be enrolled in the parents' class, unless they are officers or teachers, or have other duties in the school. A personal canvass of the ward should be made and an explanation of the objects of the classes given, to induce the parents to join.

"A suitable person should be selected as supervisor, who will direct and control the exercises and discussions in a wise way. In some places the Bishop of the ward or one of his counsellors is serving in this capacity with excellent results. One or more assistants may be chosen to aid the supervisor.

"The Stake Boards should also have one or more workers to look after this branch, and a department of the Union meeting should be established for it. In short: parents' classes should be considered as an integral department of the Sunday school and treated in the same respect as the other departments, except in the matter of statistics, as hereafter explained.

. . . .

"It is desirable that the parents' classes be held at no other time but during the Sunday school hour on Sunday. It is the purpose to imbue the parents as far as possible with a genuine Sunday school spirit, and this can only be acquired by attendance at the Sunday school and partaking of its influence; therefore parents should join the children in the opening and closing exercises of the school and participate in the spirit thereof. It is very desirable, where conditions are favorable, that a room be provided in the meeting house for the use of the class. Where this is not practicable, a room in a house adjacent to the place of meeting may be obtained.

"After the general opening exercises of the school, the parents' class should march to the room specially provided for its class work, where the following suggestive plan may be successfully followed:

"1. Roll call.

"2. Papers or addresses should be rendered on the topic before the class, by one or more persons, and then a full and free discussion should be entered into upon the subject presented. The discussion of the topic should not consume all the time; but a few minutes at the close of each recitation should be devoted to a summary of one or more important truths. These, the members of the class should determine to introduce into their home lives. Just how to do this will be prompted by the nature of the subject; it may be by improvement in personal habits, by improvement in home government, or by assisting the children in the lessons for the next Sunday.

"Perfect freedom should be encouraged in asking and answering questions pertaining to the subject in hand. The members who think and act are those who get most good out of the class work.

"Three lessons will be provided for each month. For Fast Day and an occasional fifth Sunday, the class supervisors may prepare special work. The Fast Day exercise may consist of testimonies on the effectiveness of the parents' class movement, as well as on the truthfulness of the Gospel."

The importance of the activities represented by the Sunday Schools of the Church of Jesus Christ of Latter-day Saints may be understood by the following figures, given for the year 1912. In that year the total number of schools in all the stakes and missions of the Church was 1,303, which represented a total enrolment of 181,152 persons, including officers, teachers and pupils. Of these the total number of officers and teachers was 20,656; the total number enrolled in the graded departments was 136,359, of which 113,081 were between the ages of 4 and 20 years. In the Kindergarten department were enrolled 29,695; in the Primary, 25,459; in the First Intermediate, 32,484; in the Second Intermediate, 22,325; in the Theological Department, 26,396, and in the Parents' Department, 23,290.

In addition to the Sunday school organization in the Deseret Sunday School Union, there is another organization having in charge the instruction of the young. This is known as the Primary Association, which is an organization of children officered by women. The Primary Association has a threefold object: (1) to promote spiritual development in the children; (2) to educate them in the ways of the Lord; (3) to encourage industrial occupations as an offset to idleness, street roaming and careless habits. The means employed for achieving these excellent ends include both class instruction in religious, literary and general topics and also such amusements as socials, concerts and dances. It is nearly the most admirable expression of the instinct for organization and mutual association, so conspicuous in all Mormon affairs. It serves to inculcate, not only the excellent principles for which it was founded, but also to instil into the growing mind the habit of association and the instinct of solidarity, which is the first step in real morality and valid religion, if the words of Christ are to be accepted as a guide in any real sense. The officers of the Primary Association, from the General Board to the smallest ward organization, are the "mothers and daughters of the Latter-day Saints communities," women who have a vital interest in the affairs of the organization, and whose children are being benefited by its influence.

According to authoritative figures compiled in 1912, the Primary Associations throughout the Church include a membership of 60,278, 24,849 boys and 35,429 girls, whose class instruction is divided into five distinct grades. There are also 9,726 officers of various degrees, from the General Presidency to the ward assistants. Over 3,000 children are enrolled whose parents, either one or both, are not members of the Mormon Church. The Primary Association conducts an excellent and well-edited children's magazine, *The Children's Friend.*

There are two other important organizations, controlled, like the others, by a general board, and extending their activities to the stakes. These are the Board of Education and the Religion Class. The former is concerned principally with the matter of general education, including religious instruction, which, in spite of the unfavorable reports constantly circulated, has always been a matter of prime importance among the Mormon people, from the earliest days to the present. Among the most famous sayings of the Prophet Joseph Smith are those to the effect that the "glory of God is intelligence," and that a "man is saved no faster than he gets knowledge," and these principles, constantly and persistently reiterated, are among the most firmly accepted beliefs of the people. The overdone charges of ignorance against Joseph Smith and his earliest associates by no means explain his own thirst for knowledge, as shown in the fact that he applied himself vigorously to the study of Hebrew, law and other learned branches, nor yet the enthusiasm for better education begotten in the minds of some of his most forceful, although little learned associates.

It is not strange, in view of these facts, to find that the general enthusiasm for knowledge, as exampled in the Mutual Improvement Associations, and others, should ultimately crystallize in the establishment of the Church Board of Education, which conducts and controls the operation of thirty-one distinct schools, including two of collegiate grade. The following outline of the educational system of the Church, since the settlement of Utah, was furnished by Mr. Horace H. Cummings, General Superintendent of Church Schools:

"On February 28, 1850, about two and a half years after the Pioneers arrived in Utah, the Legislature passed an act incorporating the "University of Deseret," now the Utah University. An appropriation of $5,000 a year was also made to maintain it. The curriculum provided for ancient and modern languages, astronomy, geology, chemistry, agriculture, engineering, and other branches of science. Elementary schools were also opened in Salt Lake City and all the principal settlements. . . .

"At first a tuition was charged students of the University as well as the pupils of the elementary schools, but as population and wealth increased they all became free. Thus a most excellent system of public schools was provided by the Mormons who gladly maintained and patronized them, and did all in their power to render them efficient.

"As religion was not taught in public schools the church continued the original practice of maintaining church schools. The Brigham Young Academy was founded at Provo, October 16, 1875 and the Brigham Young College at Logan in 1877, the latter being endowed by its founder, whose name it bears, with a valuable tract of land near Logan City. The deed of trust granting this endowment provided that besides the usual subjects then taught in colleges, the curriculum of this school should include instruction in what are now known as agriculture, manual training, or mechanic arts, domestic science, domestic art, etc., branches which were not taught in other institutions at that time, but which have since become so important.

"Under the wise direction of the General Church Board of Education, during the next decade, a system of church schools was established throughout the principal stakes of Zion. An Academy to do high school work was established in each of the most populous stakes, and seminaries for elementary work in the most wealthy wards.

"In all these schools, besides the branches taught in the public schools of like grade, theology was required, and the spirit and atmosphere of the schools made to conform to the ideals of the church as far as possible.

"The seminaries, however, did not continue many years because of the great expense to educate the vast number of children of elementary school age; but the academies still persist, though several discontinued during the financial depression of the early nineties.

"Dr. Karl G. Maeser, the first principal of the Brigham Young Academy, was also chosen as the first General Superintendent of the church schools, and under the guidance of the General Church Board of Education the peculiarities of the present school system were developed. He had great ability, both as a teacher and an organizer, and he originated many excellent features that are still peculiar to our church schools and have proved to be of the highest value. His labors came timely, for the growth of the church and the increased number of its schools demanded more perfect systemization and his peculiar ability had a unique field in which to operate.

"The problem of financing the church schools has always been a serious one, and in times of business panics or serious persecutions, it has several times become desperate. In many instances the devoted teachers have willingly given their services free, as missionaries, or for half pay, or whatever amount the people could give them, since the only sources of revenue are tithes and voluntary contributions.

"The Latter day Saints regret the present absence of religious training for the young. Public schools do not allow it; churches are not supplying it, and very little is given even in the home. While the intellect is now being trained, perhaps, as never before in the history of the race, the moral and religious instincts are correspondingly neglected. The chief aim of the church schools, therefore, is to make Latter day Saints of the young people — to put them into proper relations with their Heavenly Father and their fellow man.

"To accomplish this purpose they offer the usual courses in cultural and intellectual subjects, to which is added a goodly amount of industrial education and thorough courses in theology. Thus the head, the heart and the hand are trained together."

Distinct from the Board of Education, but largely supplementing its work, is the organization of the Religion Classes, first founded in 1890.

"The object as explained by the promoters of the organization was to furnish a means for the religious training of children of school age who do not regularly attend Church institutions of learning. It was created primarily to fill an educational need of the great mass of children of Latter-day Saint parentage. The practical training of the children in personal duties and requirements of the Gospel, as testimony bearing; prayer; the committing to memory of important passages of Scripture; learning sacred songs and hymns; drawing lessons from real life as found in biography; becoming acquainted with forms and ordinances of the Church, as well as Church government — these are some of the leading and concrete ideas that best express the character of the Religion Class. Two or three hours a week spent in the Sabbath Schools and like gatherings, so it was urged, was not sufficient time to devote to religious instruction as an offset to worldly and other detrimental influences. There was therefore room for the oranization; the field was extensive; the soil rich and deep; the fruitage ought to be abundant."—*J. B. Keeler* (*The Lesser Priesthood, etc., p.* 162).

The work of the Religion Class is conducted by an organization having general and stake boards, precisely as are all the other activities of the Church.

VI

TRUTH, JUSTICE AND MORMONISM

"Why has Mormonism been so much misunderstood? Simply because the Evangelical churches saw in its success their own downfall, and they dared not let their own followers know what Mormonism really was, lest they should embrace it."—Charles Ellis.

CHAPTER XXII

ANTI-MORMON ACCUSATIONS

DESPITE the beams in our own eyes, we have gallantly volunteered to remove the motes from the eyes of Mormons, and of the public generally. In this spirit, the late Rev. T. De Witt Talmage once shrieked from the United States artillery to "thunder the seventh commandment into the people of Utah." However, he never asked for any other arm of the service to thunder bayonet, sabre, or otherwise compel respect for the ninth commandment in any other element of the American public. Thus, he and many others of his profession have merrily, glibly and contemptuously borne unceasing false witness against the Mormon people; and it is high time that this fact should be brought to the attention of all.

The following passages and extracts have been selected as fair examples of "Christian," "American" and "righteous" utterances "evoked by Mormon misdoings." If they are the sort of things acceptable to decent, truth-respecting and justice-loving people, they are here conveniently at hand for any such who may wish to memorize and declaim them.

In 1882, the Rev. Dr. Talmage, as reported by several newspapers, gave vent to the following:

> "Mormonism will resist through the courts as long as possible, and then it will go into bloody encounter. I am more and more persuaded of the truth of what I said two years ago in this place, that polygamy will never be driven out of Utah except at the point of the bayonet. It is well to try peaceful legislation at first, but it is well enough to know that Mormonism is so thoroughly intrenched, so contemptuous of law, so infuriate against the United States Government that nothing that Congress has yet done will move the abomination the thousandth part of an inch. If President Buchanan had allowed Col. A. S. Johnston to go ahead with his army in 1857, after he had arrived in Utah, polygamy would have been dead a quarter of a century ago; but the over-married Mormons cut off three of our supply trains, and captured 800 oxen, and forthwith the United States Government went into treaty, the Mormons promising to behave well if the United States Government would fall back and let them alone. Our government fell back, and up to this hour the organized libertinism of Utah is master of the situation."

Of course, no one acquainted with this gentleman's type of mind and habits of thinking would expect to find him a consistent exponent of the "scientific method," but it is somewhat surprising to find how fully his zeal against the man of straw, which he has christened "Mormonism," blinds him to the real facts of history. Col. Johnston was not sent to Utah to extirpate polygamy, but to put down a rebellion falsely reported to exist there. President Buchanan, 2,800 miles away, and without telegraphic or railroad communications, did not forbid him to "go ahead with his army." Nor did the interference of individual bands of Mormon scouts and Indians with the army supply trains necessitate Johnston's failure to "smash the Mormons." If a preacher's "facts" are so distorted, what is to be said of the inferences he draws and the advice he gives?

The *Salt Lake Tribune* of January 24, 1882 contains the following:

> "New York, Jan. 23—Rev. Sheldon Jackson, for twenty-three years a missionary in Utah, Alaska and other parts of the North-west, preached last night in the Central Presbyterian Church on Mormonism. He said: Twenty-five years ago Mormonism, like a little cloud, appeared on the horizon of Utah. It has increased until to-day it covers that whole Territory, and holds controlling power in Utah, Idaho, Wyoming, Arizona, and New Mexico, and almost in the state of Colorado.
>
> "Nearly one-third of the United States is occupied by 150,000 Mormons, who, urged on by religious fanaticism, are determined soon to rebel and then fight to the death. We think that we make the laws which govern the territories, but the officials appointed to Utah by the President are mere figureheads. John Taylor is the governing power in Utah. . . . John Taylor says to Utah, to Arizona, or to Idaho: Send such a man as delegate to Congress, and the people dare not disobey him. In Colorado even he can dictate who shall not only be congressman, but also two senators from that State. Last summer when all Christendom was praying for the recovery of the beloved President (Garfield), all Mormondom was praying for his death, and Guiteau is now lauded to the skies by these people. Ever since the 27th of September Mormon bishops have been flaunting their prayer test in the face of the Gentiles. They are now securing arms and powder and drilling militia in the back part of Utah and preparing for a rebellion which is inevitable.
>
> "The only means of avoiding this is to educate the children. This work can be done by Christian women teachers. There are to-day 3,000 Mormon children in the day schools of Utah taught by missionaries who are exerting untold influence, not only among children, but also among Mormon women, and 500 more teachers are needed. In ten or fifteen years these children will be voters and citizens of Utah, and the seed now sown will solve the Mormon question without the aid of arms or law."

This is evidently a fragmentary newspaper report, and, likely enough, misquotes this speaker in several particulars—note, however, that people always complain of being "misquoted" when they read their silly sayings in print — but it is a typical anti-Mormon deliverance, and quite the kind of thing that has served to inflame the popular mind against Mormonism. It is probable, on any assumption, that this widely traveled gospeler repeated the groundless slander that all Mormons prayed for Garfield's death and lauded Guiteau, the assassin, to the skies. The same accusation has been made by others, quite as "honorable men," but it is utterly and absolutely mendacious. It seems to have been first made in a religious newspaper of Boston, but, although widely challenged, was neither substantiated or retracted. (It had probably become a "matter of faith.")

The present writer, with the intention of qualifying to speak honestly on Mormonism, carefully searched through the files of all leading Mormon and pro-Mormon newspapers and magazines, issued between the dates July 2d and Sept. 27, 1881, and failed to find one single remark, expressed or implied, that indicated the hope that Garfield would die; not one single remark derogatory to the eminent sufferer; not one single remark in any way favorable to Guiteau, or offering excuse or extenuation for his crime. The Mormon people received no very tangible benefits from Garfield's hands, and some — perhaps many — individuals among them may have expressed opinions similar to that mentioned above, as did many people, not Mormons, when McKinley was assassinated. But in neither case can all the people justly be blamed for the unwisdom of the few, who speak from prejudice, political or sectional.

Of course, although it was no missionary's business, it was scandalous that John Taylor alone, as alleged, should have controlled the votes and representatives of five states, when New York, Pennsylvania, and New England are divided among and with difficulty controlled by numerous corrupt political "rings" and "machines," but the honest historian would joyfully record, were it only possible, that all the venal and worthless creatures ever sent to Utah by the Federal Government had been mere "figureheads." Posterity would have gained a higher idea of our civilization and our people, even though back-biting missionaries had missed the opportunity they have so industriously exploited.

It is curious, however, when the Mormons are "determined soon to rebel and then [suicidally] fight to the death," and are "securing arms and powder and drilling militia in the back part of Utah," wherever that may be — it is not indicated on the map — that eastern backers of mission enterprises are urged to send five hundred women teachers to brave the terrors of this turbulent and immoral territory. The "arms and powder and drilling" would seem to indicate a more or less immediate intention to "resort to violence." In this event, the education of the children, "the only means of avoiding this," must needs be hurried amazingly, if it is to avail. (A "hurry call" to prospective contributors!)

Jackson's accusations are of a kind with those of numerous other missionaries in Utah. Thus, another Presbyterian missionary in the late "70s" is quoted as saying that his life was in constant danger in Sanpete County, and that he was obliged to preach with a Bible in one hand and a pistol in the other. (Excellent conditions for evoking spiritual and convincing discourses.) As a matter of fact, no more murderous assault had been attempted than verbal insults, probably accompanied by vague threats of violence by a gang of loiterers, and this gentleman is quoted as having acknowledged as much — privately. A Methodist missionary in the northern part of the territory had a similarly narrow and "miraculous" escape from death in the performance of his "duty" of abusing the Mormons' religion in the hope of inducing enthusiasm for his own sect. (He had been sent to Utah from the Northern New York conference, where, as stated, his pulpit methods were not wholly acceptable, on account of the violence and "uncouthness" of his expressions.) Both these gentlemen related their "sad experiences" to appreciative eastern audiences, and thereby gained high esteem as veritable Damiens, self-exiled among the "moral lepers" of the Rocky Mountains.

From the depths of sodden imbecility the abuse of Mormonism rushes to the shivering heights of barbarous truculence. What, pray, is the witchcraft in this system that so often transforms people, otherwise decent and righteous, into howling harpies or callous barbarians? The following passage, which the writer found quoted in a Utah newspaper of 1881, seemed so utterly impossible that he presents it only after verifying its presence in the files of the Presbyterian journal that first disgraced itself by printing it. In the *Interior* (Chicago) for April 28th, 1881, this occurs:

"Dr. Crosby says that Mormonism ought to be dynamited, and in so saying, he shows that he is a good practical engineer. Mormonism is lechery, covering itself in a garb of religion and indulging in a mixed dialect of cant and cursing. Like Hell-gate at the entrance of New York harbor (!), it has its foundations deep and strong, taking hold of the bottom rocks of depravity, and like that reef, it will never yield to anything but force. Crime never does. All the moral influences of society are expected to restrain the indurated characters and consciences of criminals in vain. They proceed to violence, and by violence alone can they be repelled. There are 500 bigamists in the penitentiaries of the various states, and yet fresh concubines are in process of shipment by the carload through Chicago for the supply of these leering beasts, who not only defy law, but are waging an open and avowed warfare for the possession of the surrounding territories. The people in the vicinity of Nauvoo, Illinois, rose in their righteous wrath, and gave the criminals a short alternative between hemp and a hegira. There is not a savage tribe in America so low down in the scale of decency as the Mormons — nor would they all be, if in paint and on the warpath, so dangerous to the peace and safety of the country as are the white savages of the Mountain Meadow (massacre). Let the lands and tenements of the Mormons be thrown open to original entry by civilized settlers. The United States army is not large — and it has enough to do without defending these outlaws. Let it be understood that the army will keep out of the way in Utah for four years, and that the use and occupation of Mormon property for a year is to give a pre-emption title. There are enough young men in the west and south, who are seeking homes, to finish up the pest, to fumigate the territory, and to establish themselves there in ninety days after the word 'go' is given. All the government needs to do is to let civilization have the same chance at the white savages that it has always given to settlers in dealing with the comparatively innocent red men."

It seems fairly evident that this trenchant editor of the *Interior* had neglected to emulate Rev. John Cotton's example and "sweeten his mouth," if only "with a morsel of Calvin," before he penned his intemperate and brutal tirade. Not only is he contemptuously oblivious to the fact that the federal courts, after a thorough threshing-out of the matter, had absolved the Mormon leaders from complicity in the Mountain Meadows massacre, and brought to justice the only men upon whom the crime could be fastened, but he openly and shamelessly advocates the commission of an enormity of even huger proportions. The Mormons, he tells us, are the worst savages in the land, and, as such, entitled to no rights which a "civilized man" should recognize. That seems to be the correct attitude toward savages, and has been indorsed by the august examples of Cortez, Pizarro, and other "pioneers of Christian civilization." It is a shame that such "savages" as the Mormons should be allowed to possess "lands and tenements," even though these have been created by their own industry and enterprise. Let us then take an arrow from the full quivers of the Spanish conquerors of America: they have created the precedents. Deprive the Mormons of their property "without due process of law"— change the Constitution, if necessary — and turn it over to the chaste and exemplary "young men in the west and south, who are seeking homes," and would not hesitate to steal them. (Does the crime of robbery find extenuation, when "savages" are despoiled?) The Government was more considerate than this, even with the red Indians, but that is no superlative indorsement of its policy. The British, in perpetrating the Acadian atrocity, merely transferred a population from one location to another one considered "more appropriate." But this Presbyterian editor wants all the Mormon people, even the "wronged women" and the jolly little children, driven from their homes into the alkali deserts to live or perish as predestined by "divine decrees." (And all this for the "glory of God"!)

When we read such a screed we are better able to understand how was perpetrated by clerical instigation the brutal massacre of Haun's Mill, in Missouri, when women and little boys were shot to death by an anti-Mormon mob, and which is never remembered by those who verbigerate about the Mountain Meadow; also, to measure the worth of a religious profession that can in any way justify the cowardly assaults on the people of Nauvoo.

The religious press, however, has not fought the "Mormon monster" single-handed. Even secular editors, who usually avoid issues of this kind, have now and then evinced anxiety to be "in at the death." Very generally, also, these "lay" attacks are as ill-judged as they are vulgar. A particularly aggravated example appeared in the New York *Herald* for September 15, 1855. The occasion is thus related by B. H. Roberts:

> "In August, 1854, Lieutenant-Colonel E. J. Steptoe arrived in Salt Lake, with a detachment of United States troops *en route* for California, but remained in Utah until the following spring. During their stay, it is said, that members of the command prostituted a number of squaws and also seduced a number of white women. The latter, having lost caste among their former associates, followed their betrayers to California!"

This incident, sadly characteristic of army camp life, is really significant in no particular whatever. Had it occurred elsewhere than in Utah, it would have escaped editorial comment, except, perhaps, in local newspapers. It furnished a good chance for anti-Mormon invective, however, and consequently, some editorial writer of the *Herald* embalmed it, as follows:

> "This is momentous news, and very significant, withal. It shows that the Mormon women are ripe for rebellion, and that a detachment of the regular army is a greater terror to the patriarchs of the Mormon Jerusalem than Indians or drouth or grass-hoppers. It indicates the way, too, for the abolishment of the peculiar institution of Utah. The astonishing results of the expedition of Col. Steptoe, in this view, do most distinctly suggest the future policy of the government, touching this nest of Mormons. It is to send out to the Great Salt Lake a fresh detachment of young, good-looking soldiers, and at the end of two or three months order them off to California and replace them by a new detachment at Salt Lake City, and so on until those Turks of the desert are reduced, by female desertions to the standard Christian regulation of one wife apiece. Unquestionably, if, with a taking detachment of the army in a new and showy uniform, the President were to send out to Utah at this crisis of impend-

ing famine, a corps of regular disciplined women's rights women, to lay down the law to their sisters among the Mormons, they would soon compel the patriarchal authorities of Salt Lake to an exodus to some other region beyond the reach of our gallant army, and our heroic warriors in petticoats who know their rights, and, knowing, dare maintain them. . . . We recommend, therefore, to the President and secretary of the Interior, the policy of detailing another detachment of troops for Great Salt Lake City with the auxiliary force of half a dozen regular women's rights women whatever the cost; and thus, even should the grasshoppers fail to conquer the territory in the expulsion of the Saints, the work may be done among the wives of the apostles."

The flippant style of this editorial might almost suggest that it was a labored effort at humor. How the downfall of a few unfortunate women could possibly prove that "the Mormon women are ripe for rebellion" is past the comprehension of any-one not a "Mormon-eater" or a humorist. One might as justly suppose that the all-too-frequent re-enactment of this sort of tragedy in every city and village in Christendom was a proof that "Christian women are ripe for rebellion." Probably, however, new and special canons of logic, as well as new standards of morals, must be adopted when dealing with such exceptional people as Mormons. The mention of "women's rights women," also, seems sadly out of place. This class of agitators have some serious failings, but the "humor" that makes them possible accessories to a proposed systematic debauchery of their "unawakened sisters" is dismal.

It is quite evident that, whether or not the writer of this filth was "only in fun," or whether he merely considered his style witty, there is here an undercurrent of earnestness that is a sad exhibition in any person having access to the columns of a great newspaper.

Sadder, also, is the fact that the same or similar suggestions have been made in dead earnest by a host of other anti-Mormon writers. These people, forgetting the divine principle, "provide things honest in the sight of all men. . . . Overcome evil with good," have deliberately advocated the introduction of immoral characters and practices into the comparatively unworldly settlements of Utah, in order that virtues irregularly derived may be neutralized, and thus remove a galling spectacle from the sight of evangelical believers, who find the propagation of virtue a much more serious business.

A choice example of this sort of thing appears in the Salt Lake *Tribune* of March 6, 1881. Under the caption, "What Utah Needs," some critic of Mormonism, who evidently considers his own a judicial type of mind, delivers himself thus:

"Apropos of the new and petty war recently started by the municipal government on the women of the town, the liquor dealers and the gambling fraternity, one of the enemy said to us the other day:

"'It may be a hard thing to say, and perhaps harder still to maintain, but I believe that billiard halls, saloons, and houses of ill-fame are more powerful reforming agencies here in Utah than churches and schools, or even the *Tribune.* What the young Mormons want is to be free. So long as they are slaves, it matters not much to what or to whom they are, and they can be nothing. . . . At all events, I rejoice when I see the young Mormon hoodlums playing billiards, getting drunk, running with bad women, anything to break the shackles they were born in, and that every so-called religious or virtuous influence only makes the stronger. Some of them will go quite to the bad, but it is better so, for they are made of poor stuff, and since there is no good reason why they were begun for, let them soon be done for, and the sooner the better. Most of them, however, will soon weary of vice and dissipation, and be all the stronger for the knowledge of it, and of its vanity. At the very least, they will be free, and it is of such vital consequence that a man should be free, that in my opinion his freedom is cheaply won at the cost of some familiarity with low life. And while it is not desirable in itself, it is to me tolerable, because it appears to offer the only inducement strong enough to entice men out of slavery into freedom.'

"Probably our friend was wrong, but it reminded us, to compare great things with small, of the roaring, flaming hell through which the French nation broke its chains. Nothing short of that unparalleled upheaval, which involved all forms of human slavery in one smoking bloody ruin, would have effected anything. The national convention spared nothing in Heaven or in earth, not even itself; in the fury of madness it dethroned God, beheaded the king, conquered Europe, and decimated itself time and time again; but within its brief term of three years it recovered itself, and from that memorable date France, after a century of revolutions required to perfect the work then begun, is at last the freest and most prosperous nation in Europe." [And so on *ad nauseam* for the remainder of the column.]

This editorial is noteworthy only because of its stupidity and its shameless advocacy of vice and immorality, which, so we are accustomed to assume, should be discouraged by all people laying claims to decency. If the several vices prescribed for Mormon youth, in order to cure them of their grave attack of slavery, are to be so effective in their cases, why not recommend that they be included in the "education" of all young men? It might help to develop the true American spirit of independence. Why the editor of the *Tribune* quoted this trash from "one of the enemy," if he did not entirely endorse it is not clear. It seems amazingly like the typical disowned child of one's own brain, which one modestly, although rather stupidly, fathers off upon some anonymous, and likely fictitious, "friend," probably because he is ashamed to acknowledge it himself. It shows merely to what desperate extremes the opponents of Mormonism had come.

The *Tribune* was the recognized organ of the anti-Mormon

party in Utah. It was read and quoted by all anti-Mormon missionaries. It printed full and appreciative reports of the conclaves and sermons of members of their several sects. It noticed Mormon meetings only in abusive and burlesque articles, including, for example, the preposterous remarks of "Elder Adam T. Ramp," and other silly satires. No protest from its clerical allies against any of its utterances ever reached the eyes or ears of the public. Some of them actually endorsed its shameless opinions, presumably holding that, in the case of the Mormons, at least, "the end justifies the means," and

> "That though men serve the devil and lust,
> They will with one accord,
> When tired and done with such sweet fun,
> Run panting to the Lord," *

and attend some evangelical conventicle.

Although in some moods the *Tribune* recognized that its "sacred cause" was so desperate that the Mormon youth must be seduced from their innocence by an introduction to "real life," other methods of attack were used occasionally. Thus, in an editorial printed in the issue of February 25, 1881, just nine days before the one just quoted, the following occurs:

> "One favorite defense of polygamy on the part of our church contemporaries is to charge almost universal licentiousness on the part of those not in polygamy, *as if one wrong justified another.*† . . . Superstition is invoked to weave its benumbing influence around a woman before she can be made to accept polygamy; that is, if she is a real woman. . . . The result upon the progeny of such women is thoroughly understood by scientists. It is in the children of these unnatural unions that nature works her revenges, and it is so apparent already in this city that a reformatory institution is called for. Mormons complain of the agitation of this subject by gentiles. We tell them in all sincerity, that could they have kept gentiles and gentile influences altogether away from Utah until this day, that pride, shame, respect for law, respect for women and for virtue would have been dead here now. . . . The system means the death of the soul, and when men seek to justify it on the ground that, in the other walks of life, men sometimes make brutes of themselves and women lose their womanhood, it only shows that the system has made such men dead to either a sense of justice or sense of shame."

People unfamiliar with life and conditions in Utah at this period would obtain a somewhat vague idea from reading newspaper editorials. In one week a reformatory is needed for Mormon juvenile delinquents; in the next, vices of several varieties are recommended to neutralize virtues rooted in slavery. In February, the editor thinks that, but for "gentile influence," the moral condition of the territory would have been hopeless; in March, "gentile" vices are declared to be the great desiderata

* "Poem on Universalism," by John Peck.
† Italics ours.

of its social and religious life. And this is the way in which "we tell them in all sincerity, that could they have kept gentiles and gentile influences altogether away from Utah, that pride, shame, respect for the opinions of men, respect for women and for virtue would have been dead!"

In criticizing the utterances of the *Tribune,* however, we must not forget that many of the "Gentiles" in Utah at that time were good and earnest men, honestly bent on achieving lasting benefits for the Mormon people, to the best of their lights. In their efforts to convert the Mormons from their "errors," however, they met with nearly insuperable discouragements. The reason for this is best explained in the words of one of their number writing in 1882:

> "The Mormons shrink from a civilization that introduces the brothel with its advance guard, fills our papers with unmentionable advertisements, and makes of every city a sink of iniquity; a civilization that converts women to prostitution faster than it does to Christian life, fills our ears with clerical scandals and our criminal courts with 'Christian' defaulters; that elevates Restellism into a social institution, and leads to a prevalence of fœticide and infanticide which, if its extent were known, might well fill us with horror and dismay."—*Utah and its People. By a Gentile.*

Probably such considerations as the foregoing were powerful in confirming the Mormons in preferring polygamy, even if only as the "lesser of two evils." They may have wished to "let bad enough alone."

But, while the Protestant clergy, and their recognized organs, were ceaselessly agitating what, in their minds, appeared probably the "cause of true religion and sound morals"—and such has ever been the slogan of persecutors—there is very respectable evidence for the contention that they were in reality being kept in a condition of chronic inflammation by persons having other, and very different, objects to achieve by the enactment of coercive and sumptuary legislation for Utah. That such persons were no others than those familiar American pests, the corrupt politician, the hungry "carpet-bagger," and the sufferer from insatiate greed, is suggested in the following passage:

> "The end and object of this whole system of hostile measures against Utah seems to be the destruction of popular rule in that territory. I may be wrong—for I can only reason from the fact that is known to the fact that is not known—but I do not think that the promoters of this legislation care a straw how much or how little the Mormons are married. It is not their wives, but their property; not beauty, but booty, they are after. I have not much faith in political piety, but I do most devoutly believe in the hunger of political adventurers for spoils of every kind. How else can you account for the struggles they are now making to get possession of all the local offices in the territory, including the treasurer, auditor, and all depositories of public money? If they do

not want to rob the people, why do they reach out their hands for such a grab as this?"—*Judge Jeremiah S. Black. Federal Jurisdiction in the Territories, p. 24.*

Whether Judge Black's suspicions were correct or not, the fact remains that "polygamy" was not the real and fundamental objection against Mormonism, nor the real occasion against the Mormons. It was merely a convenient word to be used much after the fashion in which the howling dervishes shout the Arabic name for God, "Allah! Allah! Allah!" until they actually induce a phrensy, which they seem to consider a very effective condition for glorifying God. Because the real occasion against the Mormons was precisely Mormonism itself, every convenient method of attack that promised any advantage against these people was worked to its full extent. The Salt Lake *Tribune,* as the leading anti-Mormon organ, ran the full chromatic gamut. Thus, under date Oct. 8, 1880, we find the following with caption, "The Real Object":

"Polygamy is not the worst curse of the Mormon church. The leaders cling to polygamy because it is a bait to catch and hold the gudgeons of their faith. As there was never a poor white in the South in the old days who did not dream of sometime being able to own at least one negro, so it is the dream of the poorest and most abject Mormon to sometime have a 'happy family' of two or three wives of his own. But the dream of the leaders is much more extensive in its range. As George Q. Cannon is now able to direct from his office in this city how every Mormon in Utah shall vote, so his dream is that before he dies he will have the casting of the decisive vote in not only Utah, but Idaho, Montana, Arizona, Colorado and New Mexico. His idea is by a balance of power to absolutely carry all this region — an empire in extent — beyond the control of the United States, and to bring it under the control of the Mormon church."

This is the "armed insurrection" scare again, an effort to fan the dying flames of prejudice. If Mr. Cannon, or any other leader in the Mormon church, really nurtured any such ambition, and the fact could be proved, it would seem a waste of space to abuse polygamy so often and at such length, while introducing this accusation of "disloyalty" only as a "filler," while waiting, apparently, for some new happy thought of sensational and slanderous character. The methods of this newspaper are the very best evidence of the utter futility of its charges.

Another healthy example of anti-Mormon utterances is the speech of Judge Jacob S. Boreman before a meeting of the Ladies Anti-polygamy Society in a Salt Lake Methodist chapel on the evening of Feb. 27, 1882.

Judge Boreman was one of the numerous "noted jurists" appointed by the Federal Government to "help the Mormons solve their problems." He is described as "a kindly and high-minded

Christian gentleman, and a member of the Methodist church." His deliverance before this virtuous conclave is reported in part in the Salt Lake *Tribune* of February 28th, as follows:

"Now when you compare Kansas with this territory [Utah], you can see what Americans can do for a place, and you can see what inspiration can do for it. Had Utah been settled by Americans these barren mountains would be now pouring forth their treasures of gold and silver. But now what a beggarly picture this — a lot of knaves and trembling widows and orphans, and the priests fattening at their expense. They have run the territory into the ground for forty years, and now, I think, it is time that they turned it over to Americans for a while, and let us see what we can do with it. We will knock the shackles from the wrists of the people of Utah and make something out of them.

"When Garfield was here the Mormons gave out that they had swallowed him. Now let's see how they did it. Walking down Main Street one day, he told me that while traveling in Utah men slipped up and whispered in his ear, 'For the Lord's sake help us. We are bound to the priests and want them broken up. We are afraid to say this openly. Don't believe a word the lying priests say.'

"Now they did not swallow Garfield, and I don't think they are getting Arthur down very fast. They won't want another Guiteau to crow over very soon. The twelve apostles and John Taylor are now running this country, and not the Mormons. It is the leaders who are getting all the good. When these white-headed old rascals get revelations the people have to bow. What blasphemy to say that these men are in league with God! We don't want a lot of sheep to be driven about as the leader dictates. We want a few men of common sense and honesty to run the country. We can't run it any longer on the European plan.

"When the [polygamy investigation] commission comes polygamy will be a thing of the past, and a few men will be playing checkers behind the bars of the penitentiary. The leaders will be disappointed, but the masses will find that the Commission, with 50,000,000 pairs of eyes looking at them, will be the best friends they ever had.

"Such a commission will do nothing blind or rash. They will thoroughly understand their position, and be careful to do the square thing all around. Then the children of the present generation will rise up and call it blessed."

Mr. Justice Boreman probably read this report in the *Tribune*, but, if he was misquoted in any particular, he never published any complaint. We may assume, therefore, that he fully consented to father the statements attributed to him. It is a sad exhibition of the way in which sectarian prejudice and the conceit of righteousness will aggravate the habitual depravity of our most "unruly member." The judge was evidently not "greater than he that taketh a city." As a man sufficiently informed and experienced to hold the office of a federal judge, even Utah territory, he was undoubtedly fully aware of the meaning and probable influence of all his utterances. And they do not rate him very high.

According to this jurist, the Mormons are not "Americans."

Although very many of their early leaders were of the "best blood of colonial New England," and the majority of them owned *legitimate* descent from revolutionary soldiers, things which usually constitute very good evidences of right to the title "American," the Mormons were something else. Evidently a profession of Mormonism acts as an "estoppel" to all claims in this direction. Had the Mormons been Americans, he is quoted as saying, "these barren mountains would be now pouring forth their treasures of gold and silver." The highest reach of true American effort, therefore, is "gold-digging." However, the Mormons, more interested in prophets than in profits, sought to found a secure community in the territory before opening the mines. In any other people similarly situated, we would have heard of the great wisdom of this course. But Brigham Young, who stated, in defense of his policy, that the "people can not eat gold and silver," could have spoken only from some "ulterior motive."

Judge Boreman has allowed his Methodist proclivities to lead him blindly into assisting the efforts of other Utah "gentiles," not peculiarly Methodist, whose zeal to deal with the Mormons, as the Israelites of old are said to have dealt with the Philistines, was largely spurred by the visions of a land "out of whose hills thou mayest dig brass." All this furnishes a very clear explanation of the kind of men who "slipped up" to President Garfield in various parts of Utah, and whispered pleas against "priestly domination." Garfield and Boreman seemed to have thought these whisperings a genuine "doleful sound" from "the tombs." They were almost as credulous as the editorial writer of the New York *Herald,* who gaily announced that "the Mormon women are ripe for rebellion." It is curious that, when both Mormon men and Mormon women are "ripe for rebellion" against the "priesthood," and all Mormons on the verge of precipitating an armed revolt against the Government, that the peace has always been kept fairly well in Utah. Is it evidence of some sinister influence of even graver import?

Quite in line with the other falsehoods circulated about the Mormons, is the amusing habit of the religious and sensational press of "discovering" that nearly every notorious criminal of national repute is an adherent of this faith. Guiteau, Garfield's assassin, was accused of Mormonism, or rather his alleged membership in the Mormon church was adduced as "explanation" of his crime. He, however, denied this "soft impeachment," and protested that he preferred to be called what he was, no very great loss to Mormonism, and no very great gain to his own repute. Even more recently, a certain preacher, who had confessed to the crime of murdering a young woman, under peculiarly atrocious circumstances, was similarly credited with being a "Mormon elder." His accuser explained that, "while it is not common, it is not unusual to find the more educated of the Mormon elders preaching in the pulpits of evangelical churches which baptize by immersion." The sole excuse for this absurd lie was that this person was reputed to have been in the course of his career, more or less closely associated with several young women. This fact to the clerical mind is proof positive that he was a "polygamist," hence, inevitably, a Mormon.

CHAPTER XXIII

THE ALLEGED POLITICAL ACTIVITIES OF THE MORMON AUTHORITIES

It seems fairly probable that Mormonism, either as a Church with an official head, or as a collection of individuals each having a vote, has a very definite political significance. It is proper to inquire, however, (a) whether this political significance is hostile to law, order, and well-being, and (b) whether it is distinctly un-American. The alleged fact that Mormons usually vote in a body — and it seems probable that they have so voted on several occasions — involves neither of these alternatives. Again, without seriously considering the futile slander that the real object of the Mormon authorities is to precipitate some sort of causeless, useless, and suicidal revolt against the government, such participation in politics as may justly be credited to them is explainable on two grounds:

1. Mormonism is essentially a social and colonizing system, involving normally a very real order of solidarity among its people, which is distinctly beneficial in many ways, as already explained. Thus, it is inevitable that their sense of common interest to a degree has political expression.

2. Considering the constant political agitation against these people, fostered by those who profess to decry any conjunction of church and state, it is scarcely remarkable that the leaders of their Church should occasionally appear as their leaders in politics.

No amazing turpitude appears to be involved in either of these conditions. As any candid mind will understand after reading all of the present volume, the much dreaded domination of the Mormon Church in any section of our country, if attended with the results moral and social, already found in the Mormon portions of Utah, would be, on the whole, a decided improvement over present conditions. On the other hand, if our chronic agitators wish to expel Mormonism from politics, why do they insist on making it a perpetual political issue? Reforming paranoids incapable of comprehending the wise methods of dealing with the liquor traffic, so effective in European countries, have forced the rum shop into politics, thus unspeakably corrupting the government of several of our large cities. If Mormonism has in any sense infiltrated an undesirable influence into local or national politics, its activities have been efficiently augmented in similar fashion by this same preposterous busybody element, which has trailed a contagion of corruption, violence and crime over the whole of the political history of our country. These people should be silenced first; then we can deal rationally and effectively with all other classes — including Mormons.

The political opposition to Mormonism first attained proportions in Illinois, at the period when the city of Nauvoo was under their domination. This episode is fully set forth by Governor Thomas Ford, himself an active participant in much of the history of the period. Says Governor Ford:

> "The great cause of popular fury was that the Mormons at several preceding elections, had cast their vote as a unit; thereby making the fact apparent that no one could aspire to the honors or offices of the country within the sphere of their influence, without their approbation and votes. It appears to be one of the principles by which they insist on being governed as a community, to act as a unit in matters of government and religion. They express themselves to be fearful that if division should be encouraged in politics, it would soon extend to their religion, and rend their church with schism and into sects."—*History of Illinois,* p. 329.

Governor Ford also relates how that the rivalry of the two parties, Whigs and Democrats, had effected the unanimous passage in the Legislature of the Nauvoo charter, so strongly objectionable to many of the people of Illinois, the rivalry of these contending parties being then obscured in the keen competition for the Mormon vote.

> "In a very short time after the two parties had their candidates in the field, Joe Smith published a proclamation to his followers in the Nauvoo papers, declaring Judge Douglass to be a master spirit, and exhorting them to vote for Mr. Snyder for governor. The Whigs had considerable hope of the Mormon support until the appearance of this proclamation. The Mormons had voted for the Whig candidate for Congress in August, 1841. But this proclamation left no doubt as to what they would do in the coming contest. It was plain that the Whigs could expect their support no longer, and that the Whig party in the Legislature had swallowed the odious charter without prospect of reward. . . .
>
> "A vast number of reports were circulated all over the country to the prejudice of the Mormons. They were charged with numerous thefts and robberies, and rogueries of all sorts; and it was believed by vast numbers of the people, that they entertained the treasonable design, when they got strong enough, of overturning the government, driving out the old population, and taking possession of the country, as The Children of Israel did in the Land of Canaan.
>
> "The Whigs seeing that they were out-generalled by the Democrats in securing the Mormon vote, became seriously alarmed, and sought

to repair their disaster by raising a kind of crusade against that people. The Whig newspapers teemed with accounts of the wonders and enormities of Nauvoo, and of the awful wickedness of a party which would consent to receive the support of such miscreants. Governor Duncan, who was really a brave, honest man,— took the stump on this subject in good earnest, and expected to be elected governor almost on this question alone." *Ibid,* pp. 268-269.

On a subsequent occasion, the Whig party believed that its candidate would receive Mormon support, and consequently adopted a policy of conciliation. However, Ford relates that Hyrum Smith, brother of the Prophet Joseph, issued a manifesto, declaring it to be the will of God that Hoge, the Democratic candidate, should be elected. On this theory he accounts for the fact that Hoge received 3,000 votes in Nauvoo.

"The result of the election struck the Whigs with perfect amazement. Whilst they fancied themselves secure of getting the Mormon vote for Mr. Walker, the Whig newspapers had entirely ceased their accustomed abuse of the Mormons. They now renewed their crusade against them, every paper was loaded with accounts of the wickedness, corruptions, and enormities of Nauvoo. The Whig orators groaned with complaints and denunciations of the Democrats, who would consent to receive Mormon support, and the Democratic officers of the State were violently charged and assaulted with using the influence of their offices to govern for the Mormons.

"From this time forth, the Whigs generally, and a part of the Democrats, determined upon driving the Mormons out of the State; and everything connected with the Mormons became political, and was considered almost entirely with reference to party."—*Ibid.* p. 319.

Governor Ford, it must be remembered, was no very strong friend of the Mormons. He plays, in fact, very much the part of Herod in their history. His statement of conditions, however, seems straightforward and unprejudiced, serving very well to show which lines of political behavior are properly to be classed as "American" and regular, and which, otherwise. He gives us good reasons, also, for asserting that the familiar accusation of political chicanery urged against the Mormons furnishes a close analogy to the fable of the sooty utensils which "called one another black." Nevertheless, the story is still told and re-told — it must be true, the assumption seems to be, because it is about Mormons,— and that newest and most undesirable type of sensational writer, the so-called "muck-raker," periodically serves it up in the popular magazines. This irresponsible fomenter of disorder and false opinion tells the same old lies with only slight variations in the way of embellishment, and displays the same contemptuous ignorance of the Mormon organization and its workings that has become a mere commonplace among us. Thus, as a good example at hand, a certain Barry, in *Pearson's Magazine* for September, 1910, discusses "The Political Menace of the Mormon Church" which, although presented as the very latest word on the subject consists principally of a tract issued by a certain Rev. Josiah Strong about 1898, interspersed with other matters evidently quite as ancient.

This dreadful "political menace" consists, however, in the alleged concordat between the Mormon Church and the leaders of the Republican Party, according to which the former agrees to deliver the votes of the Mormon states, as required, in exchange for protection. And, wherein does the Church seek protection? According to this unearther of wickedness, the sickening details are as follows:

> "The Church agreed to deliver to Roosevelt the electoral votes of Utah, Wyoming and Idaho, in exchange for three things; (1) a cessation of the movement and agitation within the Republican party for an amendment to the Federal Constitution giving Congress the power to legislate concerning polygamy and polygamous living; (2) a defense of Reed Smoot, apostle and representative of the Mormon hierarchy, as a senator of the United States, and a vote for his retention of his seat in the Senate; and (3) a disposition of federal patronage in Utah and the surrounding states in obedience to the wish of the Mormon hierarchy expressed to the federal administration through Apostle Reed Smoot."

This alleged agreement involves merely (a) the quashing of a hypocritical agitation, aimed not so much at polygamy as at the Mormon Church itself, (b) the reaffirmation of the right of a sovereign state to select and maintain its own representative in the national senate, and (c) the distribution of federal patronage to suit the desires of the dominant element in the population of several states. Mr. Barry, who evidently wishes the reader to believe that he has investigated the subject thoroughly, admits, however, the source of most of his "authority." Says he:

> "Concerning political deals I present information given me by men high in the counsels of the Republican party, Mormons of high standing and leading Gentiles of the Mormon section — men in whose integrity I believe; yet when you read these statements so fraught with meaning to him who loves a republican government, bear in mind that it is simply that which is called rumor, the stories of many men set together, but bear in mind also that it is the sort of rumor which emanates from men who do not play with truth, whose reputation would refute a charge of idle gossip."

It is sufficient, however, to reflect that these "men who do not play with truth," all modestly concealing their identities, do not appear to support the accuracy of any of their alleged statements, consequently, we need not consider these statements worthy to establish any contention whatsoever. Such hearsay allegations are not competent evidence in general affairs, any more than in a court of law.

Mr. Roosevelt, commenting on this alleged and *rumored* tripartite agreement, writes to a correspondent as follows:

"It is a little difficult to know how to deal with a story like this, which is not merely an outrageous lie, but one so infamous, so absolutely without the smallest particle of foundation, that it is utterly impossible that the men making the charge should be ignorant of the fact that they are lying. I never heard of this magazine article and do not know who wrote it. But whoever did knew perfectly well that he was lying— The accusation is not merely false, but so ludicrous that it is difficult to discuss it seriously. Of course it is always possible to find creatures vile enough to make accusations of this kind. The important thing to remember is that the men who give currency to the charge, whether editors of magazines or the presidents of colleges, show themselves in their turn unfit for association with decent men when they secure the repetition and encouragement of such scandals, scandals which they perfectly well know to be false.

"Not only was no such bargain made by me, but equally, of course, no such bargain was made by President Taft or by any one who could speak for any portion of the Republican national organization. No such bargain was ever in any way, directly or indirectly, suggested to or considered by me. It is not merely an atrocious falsehood, but it could by no possibility be anything but a falsehood. Neither the Church nor any one on behalf of the Church ever agreed to deliver me the votes of the States mentioned, nor to try to do so; nor was any allusion to the matter ever made to me. Neither Senator Smoot nor any other citizen of Utah, was, as far as I know, ever so much as consulted about the patronage in the States surrounding Utah, nor did the Mormon Hierarchy, through Senator Smoot or any one else, ever express a single wish in connection with that patronage. The appointments were made in Wyoming and Idaho precisely on the same system as they were made in New Jersey and Massachusetts, and no more attention was paid to any candidate's religious qualifications in one set of states than in another. Moreover, the same policy precisely was followed in Utah."
—*Collier's*, April 15, 1911.

Because, according to our "muck-raking" friend, the Mormons assert the belief that their President has as his "chief duty—to communicate the wishes of Deity to the children of men," all of them must vote precisely as directed. In fact, as he asserts, "Tammany Hall, an organization founded on men's selfish interests, is less a unit, and less uniformly successful in politics than the Mormon Church, which is founded on man's religious credulity." Such an argument as this, it is confidently assumed, should inspire any man "who loves a republican government" to assist in "smashing" Mormonism. "When such politico-ecclesiastical power is grasped by one man, as in the head of the Mormon Church, he becomes the most gigantic boss in America."

The comparison between the Mormon Church and Tammany Hall, although intended to be derogatory, is a very happy one, since, without pausing to inquire into the motives and characters of the leaders of either of the two organizations, it is evident that both owe the allegiance of the rank and file of their followers to the same fact, the systematic provision for their temporal needs and the ready sympathy of their officers in their troubles. The poor voter of New York City sees in the ward leader his friend and ready benefactor: every Mormon knows that, through his bishop, he may receive any needed benefits from the treasury of the Church. In both cases, whatever may be the ultimate motive, we have a very practical humanity. Consequently, the fact that dependent people give their allegiance and their votes to such organizations is in no sense remarkable.

What then is this dreadful "political menace of the Mormon Church?" Here is the climax:

> The Mormons now have as large a proportion of the population of Arizona as they have of Idaho, about 30 per cent. This is enough to constitute a balance of power. When you have 30 per cent. of any vote, which you can use absolutely as a unit, in any way you wish, things are bound to move your way. So, when Arizona was admitted to the Union, another Mormon State was added to the three already in. "In New Mexico, between 15 per cent. and 20 per cent. of the vote will be Mormon, and the Church will doubtless see to it that the state is colonized sufficiently to swing New Mexico as they wish, now that statehood is acquired. This makes five states, ten senatorial votes, fifteen electoral votes — almost a balance of power in this Republic. As fast as they see a chance in other states the Mormons will proceed to annex them. They have small percentages of the vote in Nevada, Colorado, Montana, Oregon and Washington. When they want one of these states they will get it. Because of the obedience of its members the power of the Mormon Church is entirely disproportionate to its numbers.
>
> "An order is issued by the authorities that a certain district shall furnish so many hundred colonizers for a given state or territory. The families are drafted, so many from a ward. Then each ward or district equips its own quota with wagons, animals, provisions, implements, etc. (Very villainous proceedings, indeed.)
>
> "Communities are then selected where the two great political parties are of nearly equal strength, and just enough Mormon families are planted there to hold the balance of power. Thus the Mormon leaders can mass their voters here and there with almost the same ease, and quite the same certainty of discipline, as that with which a general moves his troops."

These statements are marshalled quite in the same fashion as "a general moves his troops," with the deliberate intention of arguing to the "dangerous" and "un-American" activities of the Mormon authorities. But what do they amount to? If our republican principles and our republican government signify anything, precisely nothing. And this is true for two reasons:

(a) Political activities in America at the present day are, with characteristic uniformity, controlled by "organizations," "machines," "bosses," and parties. Why such an organization, controlled by "priests" or other leaders recognized in the chosen religion of a large percentage of voters in a given section, is materially worse than one maintained, as is too often the case, for the protection of law-breaking schemers of several varieties, "blackleg" politicians, gamblers, liquor sellers, and other corrupt characters, or for general self-interest, it is very difficult to see. Certainly one organization is quite as tolerable as the other, and no more of a menace to the country at large. Furthermore, it is difficult to see how that the one debases the free exercise of voting privileges in the rank and file of citizens any more than the other.

(b) Even if the extensive colonizing activities of the Mormon Church, which certainly involve great benefits for the people concerned, are primarily merely of political significance and all such colonizing is illegal, that excellent person, already referred to, "who loves a republican government," and feels obligated to oppose all things hostile thereto, will find himself extremely busy long before he reaches any of the doings of the Mormons. Such a person needs only to read a little in our country's history to know how very American this procedure is. What more frantic and determined efforts could the Mormons make to colonize and control any state whatsoever, than were made by both the pro-slavery and anti-slavery parties in their efforts to populate and gain control of the territory of Kansas? Representatives of both these elements would be anxious to justify this procedure in this case.

"The fertile soil of Kansas had been offered as a prize to be contended for by Free and Slave States, and both had accepted the contest. The slave-holders of Western Missouri, which shut off Kansas from the Free States, had crossed the border, pre-empted lands, and warned Free States imigrants not to pass through Missouri. The first election of a delegate took place November 29th, 1854, and was carried by organized bands of Missourians, who moved over the border on election day, voted, and returned at once to Missouri. The spring election of 1855, for a Territorial Legislature, was carried in the same fashion. In July, 1855, the Legislature, all Pro-Slavery, met at Pawnee, and adopted a State Constitution. To save trouble it adopted the laws of the State of Missouri entire, with a series of original statutes denouncing the penalty of death for nearly fifty offenses against slavery.

"All through the spring and summer of 1855 Kansas was the scene of almost continuous conflict, the Border Ruffians of Missouri endeavoring to drive out the Free State settlers by murder and arson and the Free Settlers retaliating. The cry of 'bleeding Kansas' went through the North. Emigration societies were formed in the Free States to aid, arm, equip and protect intending settlers. These, prevented from passing through Missouri, took a more northern route through Iowa and Nebraska, and moved into Kansas like an invading army. The Southern States also sent parties of intending settlers. But these were not generally slave-holders, but young men anxious for excitement. They did not go to Kansas, as their opponents did, to plow, sow, gather crops, and build up homes. Therefore, though their first rapid and violent movements were successful, their subsequent increase of resourçes and numbers was not equal to that of the Free State settlers. The territory soon became practically divided into a Pro-Slavery and Free State district."—*A. Johnston, "History of American Politics."*

We can readily imagine at this time the rage felt and expressed by adherents of either party at hearing of the advances made by their opponents in Kansas. When it comes to considering the accusations against the Mormons, therefore, we are expected to feel a similar displeasure over the alleged advantages gained by a political clique other than the one to which we may happen to be attached. The free exercise of citizenship is to be accorded only to those with whom we may agree politically. All others should be carefully controlled, since they cannot possibly be "loyal" to the Government.

Furthermore, the alleged activities of the Mormons, according to the ridiculous article quoted above, are no more and no less than fresh examples quite along the line of the time-honored procedure known as "gerrymandering." Whether this thing is right or wrong, it is altogether too old and too general a habit to constitute a valid condemnation of any party of our voting population now practicing it. It is thus explained by John Fiske:

"In the composition of the House of Representatives the state legislature plays a very important part. For the purpose of the election a state is divided into districts corresponding to the number of representatives the state is entitled to send to Congress. These electoral districts are marked out by the legislature, and the division is apt to be made by the preponderating party with an unfairness that is at once shameful and ridiculous. The aim, of course, is so to lay out the districts as to secure in the greatest possible number of them a majority for the party which conducts the operation. This is done sometimes by throwing the greatest possible number of hostile voters into a district which is anyhow certain to be hostile, sometimes by adding to a district where parties are equally divided some place in which the majority of friendly voters is sufficient to turn the scale. There is a district in Mississippi (the so called Shoe String District) 250 miles long by 30 broad, and another in Pennsylvania resembling a dumb-bell. . .

"In Missouri a district has been contrived longer, if measured along its windings, than the state itself, into which as large a number as possible of the negro voters have been thrown. The trick is called gerrymandering, from Elbridge Gerry, of Massachusetts, who was vice-president of the United States from 1813 to 1817. It seems to have been first devised in 1788 by the enemies of the Federal Constitution to the first Congress, and fortunately it was unsuccessful. It was introduced some years later into Massachusetts."—*Civil Government in the United States, pp.* 216-218

It must be clear, therefore, that, assuming the Barry-Strong charges as in any sense true, the Mormon organization would be doing no more and no less than other organizations and parties have been constantly doing in the history of the United States. It is quite probable, however, that most of the colonizing activities of the Church which Mr. Barry, Prof. Strong, and others, see fit to feature in the manner as quoted above, are carried on from motives quite other than political. This matter has been fully discussed in Chapter X.

In the "Address to the World," issued by the Mormon Church authorities in 1907, the following declarations occur:

"We declare that from principle and policy, we favor:

"The absolute separation of church and state;

"No domination of the state by the Church;

"No church interference with the functions of the state;

"No state interference with the functions of the church, or with the free exercise of religion;

"The absolute freedom of the individual from the domination of ecclesiastical authority in political affairs;

"The equality of all churches before the law.

"The reaffirmation of this doctrine and policy, however, is predicated upon the express understanding that politics in the states where our people reside, shall be conducted as in other parts of the Union; that there shall be no interference by the State with the Church, nor with the free exercise of religion. Should political parties make war upon the Church, or menace the civil, political, or religious rights of its members as such,—against a policy of that kind, by any political party or set of men whatsoever, we assert the inherent right of self-preservation for the Church, and her right and duty to call upon all her children, and upon all who love justice, and desire the perpetuation of religious liberty to come to her aid, to stand with her until the danger shall have passed. And this, openly submitting the justice of our cause to the enlightened judgment of our fellow men, should such an issue unhappily arise. We desire to live in peace and confidence with our fellow citizens of all political parties and of all religions."

Since, according to the terms of this Address, the Mormon Church is so constantly and so insidiously threatened with adverse legislation and judicial persecution, it considers itself justified in fortifying itself against such unjust and hypocritical procedures. This policy is perfectly just and perfectly American. If it is objectionable to any of our citizens, they have themselves alone to thank. That it is a menace to the country itself, or to the institutions of a republican government, is preposterous.

The writings of sectarian missionaries among the Mormons have generally complained feelingly that the "cause of Christ" is hampered by Mormon misdoings, and asked our people to petition for laws to remove these troublesome obstructions to upbuilding thriving congregations.

A conspicuous example of this is found in the manifesto of the Salt Lake Ministerial Association, circulated late in 1881, promulgated through the agency of Episcopal Bishop Tuttle and probably a potent influence in precipitating the oppression of the Mormons in the next few years. It reads as follows:

"SALT LAKE CITY, November, 1881.

"*To the Ministers of the —— Church in the United States.*

"DEAR BRETHREN: The undersigned ministers of the various Christian denominations in Salt Lake City hereby earnestly ask your attention to the following important statements concerning Mormonism:

"1. Out of a total population of 143,000 in Utah about 110,000 are adherents of Mormonism. Of the anti-Mormon minority only a small percent render us active aid in our endeavors to establish Christian homes in the place of the foul system of polygamy which prevails in Utah. Hence, we greatly feel the need of your sympathy, prayers and efforts.

"2. Mormonism is no longer confined to Utah, but already holds the balance of power in Idaho, and has gained a strong foothold in Wyoming, Arizona, and Southern Colorado.

"3. Although there has been a strict law against polygamy upon the United States statute book for more than eighteen years, only two persons have been convicted under it, and it is particularly a dead letter because of its defects.

"4. In this matter we believe you will give us valuable help. The anti-polygamy law of Congress, in order to accomplish its intended results, needs to be amended in the following respects:

"(1). So that the living together of the parties — the *cohabitation,* to use a legal term — shall be the proof of bigamy or polygamy, instead of the ceremony of marriage, because the latter is performed in the Endowment House, in the presence of faithful Mormons only, and no one of them will bear testimony to the fact.

"(2). So that polygamy shall be a continuous crime, instead of being allowed as now, to expire within three years by a statute of limitation.

"(3). So that the women shall be equally punishable with the men for this offense.

"(4). So that the accessories to the polygamous marriage shall be equally punishable with the principals.

"(5). So that the jury list may be increased to 400.

"(6). So that adultery, seduction, lewd and lascivious cohabitation, and kindred offenses may be punishable as in the States and other territories of the Union.

"Now, may we ask that you will help us by seeing that these facts and considerations are brought at once to the attention of the Members of Congress from the various districts in which you live, to the end that they may be interested in securing for us, *at the approaching session of Congress* such legislation as will at once and forever put a stop to the further spread of polygamy.

"Yours in behalf of Christian homes and American institutions."

DANIEL S. TUTTLE, Bishop of Utah.
R. M. KIRBY, Pastor, St. Mark's Episcopal Church.
L. SCANLAN,* Vicar-general of the Catholic Church in Utah.
S. J. MCMILLAN, Superintendent, Presbyterian Mission work in Utah.
G. D. B. MILLER, Head Master of St. Mark's School.
R. G. MCNIECE, Pastor, First Presbyterian Church.
LEWIS A. RUDISWILL, Pastor of Methodist Church.
D. L. LEONARD, Superintendent, Congregational Mission Work in Utah.
THEOPHILUS B. HILTON, President, Salt Lake Seminary.
C. M. ARMSTRONG, Pastor, St. Mark's Episcopal Church.

* It is stated on apparently reliable authority that Bishop Scanlan denied having signed this common petition, leaving the public to conclude that his name had been used without his authority. It does not seem probable that he would have participated with representatives of other bodies in this manner.

This is a modern rendition of the ancient summons, "Come over and help us," but it is no very conspicuous improvement on the original. What relation it bears to the work that missionaries are, supposedly, sent out to do is by no means clear. Plainly expressed, all these matters are none of a missionary's business.

Contributors to home missions may learn here, however, that some of their representatives, at least, consider themselves quite as truly, and even more conspicuously, advance agents for the "Christian homes and American Institutions" enterprise, as plain heralds and examplars of the "Gospel of Christ — the power of God unto Salvation." They come before "souls in error" as wielders of legislative and judicial terrors — as a part of government, in fact — rather than with the Pauline message, "the times of this ignorance God winked at, but now commands all men to repent and turn to Him." However, the world has progressed since Paul's day, and, so it happens, that missionaries now petition for "jury lists increased to 400"— a mystical number perhaps — and laws inculpating women, and "accessories," as well as the men, believing, likely, that imprisoning their bodies would effectually soften their hearts toward the "gospel of love." These heralds of salvation discover an amazing anxiety to inculpate women, holding, probably, that since their sects announce that females really have souls, they should be held sternly accountable for lapses from sectarian standards of righteousness.

To this humble and Christian prayer came, as answer, the Edmunds Law — no very distinct echo of the Declaration of Independence, and a rather doubtful successor to the Emancipation Proclamation and the Fourteenth Amendment — and the cruel "raid" of the middle and late "eighties" of the Nineteenth Century, which we purpose describing later. At the time of evangelically-precipitated raid, in furtherance of whose aims several long-established principles of law were most cavalierly set aside, not only were women found equally punishable with men — many of them in delicate condition being persecuted and brow-beaten by prosecuting officers and grand juries, also committed to jail for refusing to answer revolting and insulting questions — but even innocent children, some scarcely out of babyhood, were haled before these august bodies and questioned as to the "misdoings" of their parents.

If this is what may be expected from the influence of sectarian pulpiteers in politics, it is quite evident that their domination is in no very conspicuous sense superior to that of the much-hated Mormons. It might be well to keep them from "gerrymandering" any of our states.

Thus, however, were reaped into full garners the first fruits of missionary enterprise and "self-sacrifice" in Utah. And it is almost the only crop worth mentioning.

On the appearance of this missionary manifesto, the *Deseret News* thus commented on the current rant against the participation of religious bodies in politics:

> "There is a big noise over the alleged connection between Mormonism and Utah politics, while at the same time Methodism and other isms are interfering in national politics, and urging legislation with all the church influence they can command. It appears to be a heinous offense for Mormon Elders to have anything to do with secular affairs, but quite proper for Episcopal Bishops, Presbyterian priests or Methodist preachers to engage actively in political affairs, especially in bringing pressure to bear upon Congress antagonistic to the Latter-day Saints."

Apart from interests communal or sectional, which have occasionally determined the membership of the Mormon Church to vote as a virtual unit, and apart from their respect for the organized authorities of their Church, which they are entitled to observe quite as much as the Catholics — they also have been assailed by the same fanatical element that has always fomented anti-Mormon sentiment — there is positively no ground whatever for fear that the Mormon "hierarchy" may break down the institutions of a "free democracy," and substitute a theocratic government in this country. The charge is merely contemptible, not to say positively ludicrous. It is merely the old slogan of "Know-Nothingism," whose excesses disgraced our country half a century ago, and which still crops out in occasional agitation against Catholicism. The attempts, also, to justify the charges of disloyalty and superstition-led danger to the state, are competent in evidence to show the full futility of the charges.

Thus during the arguments upon the proposed amendments to the Edmunds law, in April, 1886, a certain R. N. Baskin of Salt Lake City, argued as follows before the Committee on Judiciary of the U. S. House of Representatives:

> "George Romney was one of the parties who was convicted, and when the court asked him if he would obey the law in the future, with a view to lightening the penalty, he refused to answer. The Salt Lake *Herald* of October 11, 1885, and of which my friend, the Hon, John T. Caine, is editor, came out with this statement:
>
> "'There is sorrow when a man like George Romney goes to the penitentiary; but when one does go his friends and acquaintances feel like taking off their hats to him, for they feel that a brave and honest man is suffering because of bravery and honesty which will not permit him to do otherwise."
>
> "That theocracy will not permit a man to obey the laws of the land in the future, notwithstanding it is stated to him by the court that if he would make a promise in that regard the penalty would be lightened.
>
> "Hiram B. Clawson was asked the same question, and answered:

"'To me there are only two courses: One is prison and Honor; the other is liberty and dishonor. Your honor, I have done.'

"Judge Zane, after hearing what Mr. Clawson said on the subject, proceeded in the course of the sentence to say:

"'As a man I have nothing to say whatever against you. I regret that you have not the courage and the manhood to stand up in defiance of a sect and say that you will obey the laws of your country, and that you will advise other men to abide by them. This timidity and cowardice is not becoming an American citizen. You seem to acknowledge that in your second reason, because you say that you would be ostracized and would become an outcast if you were to obey the laws of your country — if you were to promise to obey them — though many good men have died, not become ostracized, but died in their defense. That reason constituted no justification.'

"Judge Zane asked him, 'Are you prepared to say to me that you will obey the laws in the future?' His response was, 'I would become an outcast if I were to do so.' This shows what they do with their members for the purpose of preventing them from making such promises. Now, in connection with this, there is an address made by John Taylor and George Q. Cannon, to which I call your attention to show that these men have never for a moment yielded anything, but state that they intend to stand by polygamy:

"'Well meaning friends of ours have said that our refusal to renounce the principle of celestial marriage invites destruction. They warn us and implore us to yield.

"'They appeal to every human interest and adjure us to bow to a law which is admitted on all hands to have been framed expressly for the destruction of the principle which we are called upon to reject. . . . But they perceive not the hand of that Being who controls all storms, whose voice the tempest obeys, at whose fiat thrones and empires are thrown down — the Almighty God, Lord of Heaven and earth, who has made promises to us, and who has never failed to fulfil all his words. We do not reveal celestial marriage; we cannot withdraw or renounce it. God revealed it, and he has promised to maintain it and to bless those who obey it. Whatever fate, then, may threaten us, there is but one course for men of God to take; that is, to keep inviolate the holy covenants they have made in the presence of God and of angels.'

"Now, in the face of all the decisions of the courts, in the face of public sentiment, which they refer to here, they persist in the maintenance of an anti-American institution in our republic — a system of polygamy and theocracy. If these gentlemen will think of it for a moment, they will see that we would be recreant to our trust if we did not attempt to put a stop to this practice. Would it be right in the light of our history for us to sit idly by and to see established a system so anti-American as this system of polygamy, theocratic polygamy."—*Proposed Additional Legislation for Utah Territory* (1886) pp. 5–6.

The sharply defined issue between what Mr. Baskin chooses to designate "theocratic polygamy" and his own professed enthusiasm, "democratic monogamy," may be very well estimated from these utterances of an able and determined exponent of "what was known as the Gentile side of the question." Although, as here set forth, such men as the above-mentioned Clawson, and several others behaving similarly, are represented as quite contemptuous of law, for whose maintenance "many good men have died"— how heroic the death of him who battles against "theocratic polygamy," or "polygamic theocracy"! — the fact of the matter is that these men, as Mr. Baskin acknowledges at another place, were punished, not for polygamy, but for "unlawful cohabitation," as the law stated, "with more than one woman. Furthermore, as we shall see at another place, such "cohabitation" was most often found to be "constructive," merely, the courts convicting and condemning men, not for maintaining proved marital relations with several women, but for supporting the women and children involved in plural marriages entered into in good faith, even for maintaining friendly relations with them. Because these men refused to cast off their children and the mothers of these children, allowing them to shift for themselves, or, more terrible yet, be thrown upon the tender mercies of a democratic, monogamous and Christian community, they are haled before courts, convicted and sentenced, in order to allow the Gentile side of the question to derive a show of aggravated strength in the mouth of such an advocate as Baskin. Because, however, following the lead of Taylor, Cannon, and others, these accused chose to base their refusal to adjust their conduct to an unreasonable and brutal construction of the law — a construction directly calculated to recruit the "noble army" of vagabonds and social outcasts, who, like the poor, are "always with you"— on religious, rather than on moral, grounds, the natural duty of a man to protect his offspring and shield their mother, we hear this utterly disingenuous denunciation of "un-American theocracy." The simple truth of the matter is that these people, basing their social institutions upon religion, as they have received it, interpret moral obligations as religious duties; and this is, after all has been said, precisely what all religious sects attempt to express, often with far less success than does Mormonism. No set of people ever showed a greater ignorance of the genius of Mormonism than most of the federal judges sent to Utah to deal with alleged violations of the Edmunds law, unless it be the missionaries sent out to convert them, if possible.

It may be asserted, indeed, that the expressions above quoted from Presidents Taylor and Cannon were not so much a defiance of civil law as an assertion of the duty of observing the obligations involved in what is believed to be divine law. Nor, in other connections, have similar assertions been condemned as "distinctly seditious." It is well to remember that the Protestant sects, the busiest instigators of unjust legislation and oppressive constructions against Mormonism, owe their origin and existence to perfectly similar assertions of the superiority of divine commands, as they believed them to be, to the civil laws which forbade "heresy" and "non-conformity." The civil authorities which punished "heresy" with massacres, persecutions and inquisitions may be righteously condemned as cruel and wicked, but the "reformers" whose influence urged helpless persons to expose themselves to the fury of persecution have their part in the blame, also. It is reasonable, however, to assert that the Mormon "theocracy," even in the worst light which its enemies have thrown upon it, is eminently American in these alleged defiances of so-called "righteous laws." Indeed, in asserting the duty and obligation to follow the dictates of conscience and "to keep inviolate the holy covenants," they were but "harking back" to the very origin of American institutions. Our country was settled originally as a refuge for religious non-conformists, "heretics" and separatists. Thus, England, demanding conformity to her own national sect, drove out her Puritans, who settled in New England; allowed the Quakers to house themselves in Pennsylvania; granted a refuge to her Papists in Maryland, and distributed her poor debtors and other unappreciated elements in other sections. Strictly speaking, all of these classes maintained a firm defiance of the laws of their native land, the religious — also, perhaps, some of the debtors — on the grounds of conscience, as alleged. Furthermore, New England, especially the troublesome colony of Massachusetts Bay — like Utah, this was reputed a "turbulent territory" in its day — had a theocratic government of the most aggravated description. Non-conformity to law, theocracy and "loyalty to the dictates of conscience" are inseparably American institutions, whether found among Mormons, and condemned, or originated among Puritans, and embalmed in verse and song. We deem that man a heretic who refuses to recognize the finality and sufficiency of our conclusions. But heretics resemble lunatics in one particular: they are quick to discern in others the very disorders that afflict themselves. Thus it is that heretics, having "weathered the fury of persecution," and having established free institutions — free for them — turn persecutors themselves, and denounce others for the "heroic traits" of their own forebears.

Apart from the general tendency in religious circles to view non-conformity with displeasure, and to attribute to it all varieties of turpitude, even to misrepresent its motives and actions, it may be asserted with no serious danger of contradiction, that there exists in America no implacable antagonism to Mormonism. Such objections as exist in the mind of the average man rest entirely upon the misrepresentations of the system and its people, which certain classes of writer and speaker seem incapable of avoiding. Thus, the essence of the so-called theocracy menace is the supposed oppressive activity of the "priesthood," backed, supposedly by their faithful, and ever-ready "Danites," "Shanpips," or "destroying angels," who, as we are told, take vengeance on the "disobedient"; thus explaining "mysterious disappearances," etc. This allegation, even in the mouth of a judge-orator, like J. S. Boreman, as previously quoted, who was on the ground, and must have had the opportunity for knowing the absurdity of the charge, is made in spite of the fact that, according to received estimates, at least 90 per cent of the male population of Mormon territory hold the priesthood in some degree. Thus, with a total of 92,103 in the entire enrollment of quorums, of which 49,944 belong to the higher or Melchisedek priesthood, it would be a real service to the public to locate the seat of this alleged oppressive influence. It is evident, however, that the entire strength of the allegation, in the majority of cases, rests upon a play upon the word "priesthood"; using it in the sense of the total membership of all priestly quorums, rather than in the abstract sense of the "state of being a priest," the "essential dignity and office of a priest," which is the usual sense in Mormon writings. Thus the late Justin S. Morrill, when Congressman from a Vermont district, delivered a speech in the House of Representatives, February 24, 1857, which includes the following line of reasoning:

"This hierarchy is clearly repugnant to the Constitution of the United States, which guarantees to every State a republican form of government. The republican form of government in Utah is a dead letter, existing only *pro forma,* and only so much of the tattered remains are exhibited as will secure the largesses of the national Government; while the real *bona fide* government is that of the Mormon priesthood. The obligations of the Constitution cannot be held in abeyance or postponed, nor have the people of Utah the right to evade them. A republican form of government in substance, and not in shadow, is required at the hands of the United States at all hazards. How can this be complied with if we suffer our Territories, while in a state of pupilage, so to educate the people, mold their habits, fix their affections and their antipathies — so to control the rights of persons and property, as to make a republican form of government unprofitable, sinful, hated, and impossible.

. . . .

"The test which Brigham Young requires as the sole dispenser of the 'blessings of Abraham' is subserviency to the priesthood, as will be seen in one of his published discourses of February 27, 1853:

"'The elders of Israel frequently call upon me — "Brother Brigham, a word in private, if you please." "Bless me, this is no secret to me. I know what you want; it is to get a wife": "Yes, Brother Brigham, if you are willing."

"'I tell you here, now, in the presence of the *Almighty God,* it is not the privilege of any elder to have even *one wife* before he has *honored* his *priesthood,* before he has *magnified* his *calling.* If you *obtain one* it is by *mere permission,* to see *what* you will do, *how* you will *act,* whether you will *conduct yourself* in *righteousness* in that *holy estate.'*

"This power, held in the hands of one man, and that man Brigham Young, is one which may be wielded with tremendous effect."

As anyone acquainted with the history or organization of the Mormon Church must recognize beyond dispute, it is only Governor Morrill's evident ignorance of the subject that absolves him from the charge of deliberate misrepresentation. While, as seems well attested, quite as large a proportion of the male population held the priesthood in 1857 as at the present day, thus, providing that they voted as a unit, basing the "unrepublican government" of Utah upon the will of the majority in correct form, the quotation from President Young's discourse involves no such teaching as he attributes to it. In spite of Brigham Young's characteristic vigor of expression, which frequently lent itself to the hostile interpretations of his enemies, we must recognize that he is here asserting the duty of an "elder," or a man holding the priesthood of the higher order, to "honor his [own] priesthood," by suitable performances — to "magnify his calling," in other words — before seeking the privileges of which the President of the Church alone holds the "key." It is perfectly evident, in other words, that the word "priesthood," here indicates the state or dignity of a priest, more correctly of an "elder," and that, in this sense, it is made synonymous with the "calling," which each man is urged to "magnify." How a sentence worded, as is this one of President Young's, could thus be misinterpreted by so able a man as Morrill is mysterious indeed.

It is altogether certain that, whatever faults may be justly laid to the Mormons, or to Mormonism itself, the primary impetus for the traditional objections to and misrepresenation of both has been distinctly in the sectarian bodies opposed to them. Thus, from its earliest days, when its "priesthood" had as yet had no time to perfect its "repressive influence," when its alleged "disloyal intentions" could have been classed only as impotent railings against authority — if, indeed, there ever were any really disloyal intentions on the part of this organization or its people — the Mormons were persecuted and manhandled, as a regular part, apparently, of the routine duties of the neighborhoods which they inhabited. Also, the number of Protestant preachers, principally of the Methodist, Presbyterian and Baptist denominations, found participants in mobs attacking them, show the real origin of the persistent persecution of these people. It is perfectly reasonable to hold that people who persist in horse-stealing, and other forms of misdemeanor would be mobbed in the various places reached by them — and this explanation of Mormon persecutions is accepted by most people — but it is equally credible that the sectarian animosities, which had instigated mobs against them in one place, would communicate themselves to others, with the same results in all cases. The latter explanation is rather the preferable one, since the leading objectors to Mormons at the present day are the preachers of rival sects, who care nothing for horse-stealing or political chicanery in other parts of the country, but object very seriously to a system which, should it prevail, would actually abolish the clerical profession, with most of its attendant disadvantages to society and to the vitality of religion; and which, moreover, proclaims them apostates, one and all, devoid of authority to preach the Gospel of Christ or to administer in His name. This is the real Mormon "menace," and the real cause of the clerically conducted persecutions of these people. But for this no one would have discovered their "disloyalty" and "political significances"— unless indeed political "Carpet-baggers"— while, as for their polygamy, it would have passed to as venerable a stage of uninterrupted prosperity as "machine politics," or official betrayal of public trusts, which seem to argue some defects in the moral sentiments of our people, quite worthy to rank with even "immorality" of varieties sexual.

The conclusion that the "political menace of the Mormon Church" is a dream and a delusion has been repeatedly affirmed by really conscientious and capable observers of the system and people. Thus, Bishop F. S. Spalding of the Episcopal Church in Utah, writing in review of a recent violent and ill-informed anti-Mormon book, which he finds full of errors, states:

> "We have not commented on Dr. Kinney's references to the political power of the Mormons. We feel very strongly that the subject is chiefly a religious and theological one, and that Mission Study classes should treat it as such. Mr. Reed Smoot represents the Mormon business interests in the United States Senate in no different way than Senator Penrose represents the Pennsylvania Railroad, and Senator Aldrich the Morgan interests. Still, the inaccuracy of this book is increased by its acceptance of the absurdly exaggerated statistics, given in the *Cosmopolitan Magazine,* of the Mormon Church in other states than Utah and Idaho. To hint that the Mormons control Colorado, Oregon, Nevada and Washington is as absurd as to claim that the Prohibitionists control New York, Massachusetts and Connecticut."— *Spirit of Missions, Sept.* 1912, p. 688.

The situation in the present case, as in others where unreasoning prejudice reigns, may not be settled, probably, by referring to authoritative documents, even published statements of official assemblages. It is well, however, to quote such, and to insist that there is no evidence whatever that the Mormons have not always endeavored to the best of their abilities to live up to their professions of loyalty to the United States Constitution and the laws of the land. In the matter of polygamy, which, as we shall see later, was a religious tenet, their contention was that the laws made against it were unconstitutional, on the ground that the Constitution distinctly specified that "Congress shall make no law respecting an establishment of religion." Nor can there be a question that the objection admitted of legal argument. So, in the persistently repeated accusation that the Church authorities aimed to erect a "theocracy," whose rulings should be superior to those of the civil government, we are met at every point by plain statements that evidently show a sentiment contrary to any such designs. Furthermore, this is true of Mormon history from the days of Joseph Smith's domination in Nauvoo, as already shown, to the present. When, in February, 1883, the proposition to admit Utah as a state was argued before the Committee on Territories of the United States Senate, and violently opposed by certain persons professing to represent the "Gentile element," Representative John T. Caine made the following statements, whose accuracy may be verified by any historical student:

"Even admitting our good faith, the faction in Utah who oppose Utah's admission as a State of the Union would not be satisfied. They do not care anything about polygamy. They oppose Utah's admission with the Mormons in a voting majority. They raise the question of the union of church and state. If they would only be perfectly frank they would tell you that it is the Mormons' politics and not their religion or their practices that they object to.

"There is not, and never has been, an intention on the part of the Mormons to set up a church establishment or to countenance a union of church and state. They had an excellent opportunity to unite ecclesiastical and civil affairs when they settled in Salt Lake Valley before it had become a part of the territory of the United States; but they did nothing of the kind. On the contrary, when in 1849, they formulated a constitution for the State of Deseret and asked to be admitted to the Union, the preamble to the constitution adopted March 10, 1849, declared:

"'Whereas a large number of citizens of the United States, before and since the treaty of peace with the Republic of Mexico, emigrated to and settled in that portion of the territory of the United States lying west of the Rocky Mountains and in the Great Interior Basin of Upper California; and

"'Whereas by reason of said treaty all civil organization originating from the Republic of Mexico became abrogated; and

"'Whereas the Congress of the United States has failed to provide a form of Civil government for the territory so acquired or any portion thereof; and

"'Whereas it is a fundamental principle in all republican governments that all political power is inherent in the people, and governments instituted for their protection, security and benefit should emanate from the same:

"'Therefore, your committee beg leave to recommend the adoption of the following constitution until the Congress of the United States shall otherwise provide for the government of the territory herein after named and described.'

"Their declaration of rights contained the following:

"'All men (Shall) have a natural and inalienable right to worship God according to the dictates of their own consciences; and the general assembly shall make no law respecting an establishment of religion or prohibiting the free exercise thereof or disturb any person in his religious worship or sentiments; provided he does not disturb the public peace or obstruct others in their religious worship; and all persons, demeaning themselves peaceably as good members of the State, shall be equally under the protection of the laws; and no subordination or preference of any one sect or denomination to another shall ever be established by law, nor shall any religious test be ever required for any office of trust under this state.'

"Can you discover any theocratic tendencies in this declaration? Have the Mormons not been uniformly consistent?

"In 1849 they provided in their constitution for the State of Deseret that 'the general assembly shall make no law respecting an establishment of religion,' and forbade the 'Subordination or preference of any one sect or denomination to another.' In 1887 we provided that 'there shall be no union of church and state, nor shall any church dominate the state.'

"On the other hand, what do our opponents demand? They would have you, in spite of the prohibition of the Constitution of the United States, make a religious test so far as the Mormons are concerned. They have time and time again demanded that membership in the Mormon Church should *per se* disqualify a man for any office of public trust in the Territory of Utah.

"Realizing, finally, that you cannot disregard your solemn oaths, they demand that you shall do by indirection what you dare not do directly. They demand that every vestige of political power shall be taken from the people of Utah, and vested in a commission to be appointed by the President, by and with the advice of the Senate.

"In reply to our invitation to all citizens of Utah to participate in a movement for statehood, the little knot of zealots, who claim to speak for all non-Mormons of Utah, declared —

"'That we oppose placing governmental authority in Mormon hands, because we regard the system as one totally at war with all our recognized ideas of republican government, and incapable of being so reformed as to be made in any degree a depository of impartial governing power.'

"What is this but a declaration that Mormons ought not 'in any degree' be trusted with political power? The Mormons, because they are Mormons, ought to have no political rights if they are in the majority.

"That is the declaration of our opponents. It is a square religious test issue made by them. You can satisfy these malignant and ceaseless agitators in but one way — by giving them political control; by reversing the fundamental principles of American institutions and setting the minority to rule over the majority.

"You can only do that by making membership in the Mormon Church cause for disfranchisement. Before you can do that you will have to amend the Constitution, and destroy one of the strongest pillars of our Government — religious liberty — the right of every man to worship God according to the dictates of his own conscience." — *Admission of Utah (Pamphlet Report of a hearing before the Senate Committee on Territories, February* 18, 1888).

As must be evident to any candid reader, the "declaration of rights," above quoted, is similar in every respect to the edict of toleration, as it may be termed, which was passed by the Council of the City of Nauvoo, in the days of Joseph Smith himself. This document has already been quoted in the section discussing the history of Smith's activities "as lawgiver and executive."

It seems a remarkable fact that this "malignant and ceaseless" agitation against "un-American" influences, which had deceived so able a man as Justin Morrill into making the misstatements just quoted from his speech, should be so zealous against an influence that, in alleged un-American fashion, had supplanted the governing rights of the majority by the will and influence of a hypothetical clique, dubbed the "priesthood," as to reach its apogee in a movement to deprive the majority of its right to self-government. No one seems to have thought of running to earth the members of this oft-mentioned wicked clique of "priests," and depriving them of the rights to govern themselves or others. The whole people were discriminated against, when the "priests" seemed to vanish into the fastnesses of undiscoverable sequestration. The situation is precisely that outlined in a previous quotation from Judge Jeremiah S. Black, when he declared that "the end and object of this whole system of hostile measures against Utah seems to be the destruction of popular rule in that territory."

However completely sundry writers, blinded by their zeal for something quite other than accuracy of statement, may have distorted and misquoted the remarks of prominent Mormons into "disloyal expressions," it may be asserted, without fear of successful contradiction, that this "Mormon menace" bogie is merely a dream of bigotry and sectarian and sectional jealousy. Even in the worst light possible, the Mormon Church could not be any more of a menace to free institutions and other sacred rights of man than are sundry other influences at work in our midst, which receive little or no attention from our agitators. The entire accusation is merely the craven and cowardly spirit of "Know-Nothingism," which is, in itself, far more of a menace than Mormonism, Romanism, or any other object of its rage, has ever dreamed of being. The same statements have been made by persons eminently well acquainted with both Mormon and "Gentile" conditions in the Territory and State of Utah. Among such we may quote the late A. B. Carlton, formerly Chairman of the Utah Commission, and for seven years one of its members. He writes, under title "History Repeating Itself," the following characteristic comment:

"The advocacy of religious freedom is no new thing with the author of this volume. More than a third of a century ago, he defended the Catholic against the Know-Nothing crusade. He was not a Catholic and is a native of America, as were his ancestors for many generations; but a sense of justice and devotion to the Constitution, together with a natural disposition to take the side of the under dog in the fight, impelled him to take an active part in opposition to bigotry, intolerance and persecution. It is curious to observe that the same war cries and catch-words were invoked in the crusade against the Catholics as are now employed against the Mormons; for example, 'allegiance to a foreign power'; 'abject obedience to the commands of the head of the Church'; —'danger of the government being overthrown'; 'Americans must rule,' etc.

"In those days, too, similar means were employed to inflame the public mind. Books purporting to be written by apostate priests and escaped nuns, embellished with monstrous pictures, were circulated all over the country. This craze prevailed for one or two years, and finally met with an ignominious defeat in Virginia. In August, 1855, the spirit of persecution culminated in the murder of a large number of Catholics and foreigners, and the burning of churches and dwellings in Louisville, Ky. This tragic event and the spirit of the times which led up to it were commemorated by the author of this book in some stanzas, written in imitation of the 'Battle of Blenheim.'

"It should be explained that 'Sam' was a name assumed by the Know-Nothing-Party, 'Cheyennes' and 'Hindus' were epithets bestowed upon them by their opponents.

"THE BATTLE OF LOUISVILLE

"It was on an August evening; —
The Bloody work was done,
And 'Samuel' at his cottage door
Was sitting in the Sun;
And by him sitting on a stool
His little grandchild, William Poole.

"They saw the dead with ghastly wounds
And limbs burnt off, borne by; —
And then old Sam, he shook his head,
And with a holy sigh,
'*They're only Dutch and Irish,*' said he,
'*Who fell in the great victory.*'

"'Now, tell me what 'twas all about,'
Young William Poole he cries,
While looking in his grand-dad's face
With wonder-waiting eyes; —
'Now, tell me all about the war,
And what they killed the Irish for.'

"'They were Know-Nothings,' Samuel cried,
'Who put them all to rout;
But what they shot and burnt them for,
I could not well make out.
But Major Barker said,' quoth he,
'*That 'twas a glorious victory.*'

"'The Dutch and Irish lived in peace
Yon silvery stream hard by;

The Hindoos burnt their dwellings down,
And forced them all to fly;
So with their wives and children fled,
Nor had they where to rest their head.

"'With fire and guns the city round
Was wasted far and wide;
And many an Irish mother then,
And new-born baby died;
And things like that, you know *must be,*
At a Know-Nothing victory.

"'They say it was a shocking sight,
After the day was won; —
For twenty bloody corpses there
Lay rotting in the sun;
But things like these you know *must be*
After a Know-Nothing victory.'

"'Great glory George D. Prentice won,
And also Captain Stone'; —
'Why, 'twas a very wicked thing,'
Quoth Samuel's little son: —
'Nay, nay, my little boy,' said he,
'It was a famous victory.'

"'And Cheyennes said: Americans
America shall rule'; —
' But what good came of it at last?'
Quoth little William Poole; —
'Why, that I cannot tell,' said he.
'But 'twas a glorious victory.'"

— *Wonderlands of the Wild West,* pp. 344-345.

CHAPTER XXIV

HOW JUSTICE WAS DONE IN THE MORMON COUNTRY

THE previously-quoted statements made by Mormon women of character and intelligence upon the practical operation of the "order" of plural marriage are competent to evidence the fact that they did not consider themselves "down-trodden"; were not seeking or conniving at offers of sympathy and "assistance" from the outside, and show that they certainly were not "degraded." Whether, or not, the institution itself were wrong and unlawful, it is certain that by far the greater part of the opposition to it, with the resulting actual persecution and real injustice, was based upon prejudice that was unwilling, if not incapable, of "considering the matter from the other side." Thus, the Rev. J. P. Newman, after an absurd debate with Orson Pratt on the question "Does the Bible Sanction Polygamy?", in which he had by no means the best of the argument, retires to San Francisco and emits a statement to the effect that Washington was a Paradise of virtue as compared to Salt Lake City. Anyone acquainted with the morals of Washington, or of any other great city, might conclude that Salt Lake was a veritable "sink." The real meaning of his reported remark seems to be elucidated by the words of another preacher, the Rev. J. C. Talbot, an Episcopal bishop, who wrote of a visit to Salt Lake during the period of the Civil War:

> "Outwardly this is the most moral, orderly and quiet city I have ever seen. No saloon, gambling den or evil house exists in this community of 15,000 souls; yet the inner life is most shocking to the Christian sense."

It was not because these people did not achieve and preserve social order and decency; that they were not clean and upright in their lives; or, as their women testify, that they were not happy, as well as true to the "dictates of their consciences"—and these "dictates" have figured conspicuously in the history of our country—but, precisely, that they persisted in maintaining a social institution uncountenanced by traditional standards. We have seen already that, had the ideas of Joseph Smith, Ralph Waldo

Emerson, and other wise and sane leaders of thought, been more generally adopted, the institution of chattel slavery might have been abolished without the horrors of the cruel and expensive Civil War and all the injustices to the South. We may understand also, that, had the question of dealing with Mormon polygamy been placed wholly in the hands of intelligent and truly American statesmen, a closer approximation of real justice might have been achieved. In both cases hysterical and self-righteous elements were allowed to influence the judgment of men supposedly competent to make laws for civilized human beings, and with results that are by no means gratifying.

In addition to the various preachers who issued the appeal of November, 1881, to the American public, several worthy and well-meaning women seized upon the "polygamy issue" as an opportunity to make themselves conspicuous. One of these wrote a sensational book on the subject that was widely circulated in the East, also quoted extensively in tracts issued by several religious bodies. It is needless to remark, however, that very few of her dozens of horrible stories of "oppression and misery" contain any such definite specifications of names and places as would give the inquirer the ability to verify her statements. Some time after the appearance of this book, she contributed an article to an anti-Mormon newspaper in Salt Lake, deploring the prevalence of the "social evil" in that city, and making bold to assert that an overwhelming number of the abandoned women there found were of Mormon parentage and antecedents. The editor of the *Deseret Evening News* very reasonably inquired how it was that she could have had such intimate acquaintance with the life-histories of so many of these unfortunates. No answer to this query was ever vouchsafed: nor is this remarkable.

Several other ladies of recognized literary ability served the "cause" by lurid accounts of the "sad-faced" women to be met in every Mormon community, which constituted touching appeals to American womanhood to help break the chains of these "down-trodden" sisters. Nor did such appeals fail to excite the "compassion" of the "better element." It should be a sobering reflection to those "reformers" among us who assert that the vote in the hands of women will inevitably solve all the difficulties of society that the "oppression" of a large and representative body of women, who had exercised the voting privilege for years, had to be made the subject of a nation-wide agitation; furthermore, that, even then, these women could not be persuaded that they really were oppressed. One lady, a certain Mrs. Newman of Lincoln, Nebraska, evidently not a suffragist of the modern type, was particularly active in this "reforming" campaign. She attended the mass meeting of women in Salt Lake City, previously mentioned, and commented on it, as follows:

"Mrs. Hannah T. King, in her speech to-day in the theatre, says: 'I cannot refrain from asking, Am I in America?'

"Myself a New Englander by birth and education, reared in the atmosphere of loyalty, my own heart puts forth to-day the question, 'Am I in America?'

"I have traveled all over this fair land; I have sat in the councils of the women of the nation; I have participated in the discussions of the various organizations of women, both State and national; in benevolent, reformatory, in political action; and have to-day heard for the first time treasonable utterances from the lips of my own sex; for the first time a defiance of the laws which shelter womanhood. And I desire to state in your columns, as a representative of the loyal women of the states, that there is not a spot on this continent, outside of Utah, where the seditious sentiments expressed in the theatre to-day could have a hearing or receive a single personal endorsement from any woman of any race, color, or previous condition of servitude. Any woman in the States who should so insult the representatives of this great Republic would invite a fate more speedy and none the less terrible than that of J. Wilkes Booth.

"As a Christian wife and mother, I, in behalf of the Christian homes of this Republic, repudiate the oft-repeated charge of the speakers in the theatre, that the lasciviousness of the age is due to monogamous or Christian marriage." (Note: — No such charge was made by any speaker at this meeting, as must be insisted in all fairness. Mrs. Newman misunderstood.)

"'30,000' demi-monde of New York mentioned to-day are such in defiance of the laws of Christian homes over whose threshold they cannot pass. . . .

"The blessed Stars and Stripes which hung in mocking irony above the heads of disloyal women, to-day, are crimson with the blood of sons of loyal mothers. The stars have been set in that field of blue through the tears and toil and prayer to the God of battles, to the Christian's God (not Mormon god) to the God of Christian homes.

. . . .

"Treason is not to find shelter under the flag, and whatever of sympathy or protection the women of Utah expect from this Government is disclaimed in their present hostile attitude. They cut the cords which bind them to the world's heart when they thus blaspheme the nation's God, repudiate the nation's sovereignty and the Christian home.

"Liberty protected by law is the only liberty under the flag."—*Salt Lake Tribune, March* 9, 1886.

It is entirely unnecessary to comment on such a document as this, even though the editor of the *Tribune,* in the issue of the following day, characterized it as a "stinging card." The proceedings of the meeting referred to have been printed in a pamphlet, which may be found and read in the department devoted to Mormon literature in any large public library. The protest was against sumptuary legislation, which had entailed great hardships upon the women of Utah territory, violent arrests in several instances, as alleged, and badgering examinations in court by attorneys, whose zeal and self-importance often exceeded their humane sentiments. Protests against such doings as these, and against the laws basing them, are among the rights guaranteed to a "free people," who, in the words of the text books of two generations since, "choose their own rulers and make their own laws." To say that such protests are "seditious" or "treasonable" is absurd. One should read the Declaration of Independence for a fair example of precisely this kind of "treason." The mass meeting in question appointed a committee to prepare a memorial to Congress, and adopted resolutions, as follows:

Whereas, The rights and liberties of women are placed in jeopardy by the present cruel and inhuman proceedings in the Utah courts, and in the contemplated measure in Congress to deprive the women voters in Utah of the elective franchise; and,

Whereas, Womanhood is outraged by the compulsion used in the courts of Utah to force mothers on pain of imprisonment to disclose their personal condition and that of their friends in relation to anticipated maternity, and to give information as to the fathers of their children; and,

Whereas, These violations of decency have now reached the length of compelling legal wives to testify against their husbands without their consent, in violation both of written statutes and the provisions of the common law, therefore, be it

Resolved, By the women of Utah in mass meeting assembled, that the suffrage originally conferred upon us as a political privilege, has become a vested right by possession and usage for fifteen years, and that we protest against being deprived of that right without process of law, and for no other reason than that we do not vote to suit our political opponents.

Resolved, That as no wife of a polygamist, legal or plural, is permitted to vote under the laws of the United States, to deprive non-polygamous women of the suffrage is high-handed oppression for which no valid excuse can be offered.

Resolved, That the questions concerning their personal condition, the relationship they bear to men marked down as victims to special law, and the paternity of their born and unborn children, which have been put to women before grand juries and in open courts in Utah, are an insult to pure womanhood, an outrage upon the sensitive feelings of our sex and a disgrace to officers and judges who have propounded and enforced them.

. . . .

Resolved, That the action of the District Attorney and the Chief Justice of Utah, in compelling a lawful wife to testify for the prosecution in a criminal case involving the liberty of her husband and in face of her own earnest protest, is a violation of laws which those officials have sworn to uphold, is contrary to precedent and usage for many centuries, and is an invasion of family rights and of that union between husband and wife which both law and religion have held sacred from time immemorial.

Resolved, That we express our profound appreciation of the moral courage exhibited by Senators Call, Morgan, Teller, Brown and others, and also by Mrs. Belva H. Lockwood, who, in the face of almost overwhelming prejudice, have defended the rights of the people of Utah.

Resolved, That we extend our heartfelt thanks to the ladies of the

Woman Suffrage Association assembled in Boston, and unite in praying that God may speed the day when both men and women shall shake from their shoulders the yoke of tyranny.

Resolved, That we call upon the wives and mothers of the United States to come to our help in resisting these encroachments upon our liberties and these outrages upon our peaceful homes and family relations, and that a committee be appointed at this meeting to memorialize the President and Congress of the United States in relation to our wrongs, and to take all necessary measures to present our views and feelings to the country.

As may be recognized by any one having the remotest knowledge of the law, there was abundant excuse for protesting against the ruling by which a wife was compelled to testify against her husband in such proceedings as were then being instituted in the courts of Utah. The principle had long been accepted that a wife's testimony under such conditions is incompetent. That many women, some in delicate condition, were harshly treated by prosecuting attorneys cannot be denied. Yet the move to protest against these legal innovations and violations of personal rights is openly characterized by prejudiced writers and newspapers as an act of "treason."

The memorial to Congress, signed by a committee of twelve women, related the following causes of complaint:

"On the 22d of March, 1882, an act of Congress was passed which is now commonly known as the Edmunds law. It was generally understood to have been framed for the purpose of settling what is called the Utah question, by condoning plural marriages up to that date and preventing their occurrence in the future, and also to protect the home, maintain the integrity of the family and shield innocent women and children from the troubles that might arise from its enforcement. But instead of being administered and executed in this spirit, it has been made the means of inflicting upon the women of Utah immeasurable sorrow and unprecedented indignities, of disrupting families, of destroying homes, and of outraging the tenderest and finest feelings of human nature.

"The law has been so construed by the courts as to bring its penalties to bear upon the innocent. Men who had honestly arranged with their families so as to keep within the limits of the law have been punished with the greatest possible severity, and their wives and children have been forced before courts and grand juries, and compelled to disclose the most secret and private relations which in all civilized countries are held sacred to the parties. The meaning of the law has been changed so many times that no one can say definitely what is its signification. Those who have lived by the law, as interpreted in one case, find, as soon as they are entrapped, that a new rendering is constructed to make it applicable to their own. Under the latest ruling, a man who has contracted plural marriages, no matter at how remote a date, must not only repudiate his family and cease all connection with them, but if he is known to associate with them in the most distant manner, support them and show any regard whatever for their welfare, the offense of unlawful cohabitation is considered to have been fully established, and he is liable to exorbitant fines and imprisonment for an indefinite period, one district judge holding that a separate indictment may be found for each day of such association and recognition. In the case of Solomon Edwards, recently accused of this offense, it was proven by the evidence for the prosecution, that the defendant had lived with one wife only since the passage of the Edmunds act, but after having separated from his former plural wife, he called with his legal wife at the former's residence to obtain a child, an agreement having been made that each party should have one of the two children, and the Court ruled that this was unlawful cohabitation in the meaning of the law, and defendant was convicted.

"In the case of Lorenzo Snow, now on appeal to the Supreme Court of the United States, the evidence for the prosecution showed that the defendant had lived with only one wife since the passage of the Edmunds law, that he had not even visited other portions of his family except to call for a few moments to speak to one of his sons, but because he supported his wives and children and did not utterly and entirely cast them off, under instructions of Judge Orlando W. Powers, he was convicted three times for the alleged offense and sentenced in each case to the full penalties of the law, aggregating $900 fine, besides costs, and eighteen months' imprisonment, the judge stating in his instructions to the jury: 'It is not necessary that the evidence should show that the defendant and these women, or either of them, occupied the same bed, slept in the same room or *dwelt under the same roof.*' 'The offense of cohabitation is complete when a man, to all outward appearance, is living or *associating* with two or more women as his wives.'

"Thus women who are dependent upon the men whom they regard as their husbands, with whom they have lived, as they have regarded it, in honorable wedlock, must not only be separated from their society and protection, but must be treated as outcasts, and be driven forth with their children to shame and distress, for the bare 'association' of friendship is counted a crime and punished with all the severity inflicted upon those who have not in any way severed their plural family relations.

"In order to fasten the semblance of guilt upon men accused of this offense, women are arrested and forcibly taken before sixteen men and plied with questions that no decent women can hear without a blush. Little children are examined upon the secret relations of their parents, and wives in regard to their own condition and the doings of their husbands. If they decline to answer, they are imprisoned in the penitentiary as though they were criminals."—*Mormon Women's Protest, pp.* 82–84.

With all due allowance for the high and bitter feelings that doubtless inspired this document, it must be insisted that its allegations are perfectly correct, as evidenced by the authoritative reports on the cases then in course of prosecution. In accordance with the petition of November, 1881, professedly originated and signed by Episcopal Bishop Tuttle and other Protestant missionaries, but evidently concocted by political enemies of the Mormon system — they made these preachers mere tools of their spite — polygamy was not only construed as a "continuous crime," to be evidenced by the simple act of introducing a woman as one's wife, and to be evaded by no means other than complete repudiation of both wives and children, but, quite in accord with the "sense of justice" of these clerical busybodies, each such act of introducing, calling on, or otherwise acknowledging natural responsibilities — even those incurred against the letter of man-made civil law — was construed as a separate offense to be punished, if the court should so determine, by the extreme penalties prescribed by law. We then hear that protests against these astounding miscarriages of justice are "disloyal" and "treasonable." A brief review of some of the most notable cases in point will fully establish the justice of the protests made, and display the utter contempt for human rights possible under the influence of even American fanaticism. It is surprising also to find how strenuously the enemies of Mormonism — not merely the enemies of polygamy — labored to compel men to desert women and children, who, in any construction of morals, had a just right to expect support and assistance at their hands. Such procedures go far to argue that several of the grossest infamies of social life are accredited institutions of civilization; also, that they are so regarded by professed teachers of "righteousness."

This, in the case of the United States *vs.* Angus M. Cannon (reported in 4 Utah, pp. 122–152), the greatest fight made by defendant's counsel was in the effort to obtain a construction of the Edmunds Law of 1882, so as to define the term "unlawful cohabitation." The defense contended with some show of legal authority that sexual relationship was essential to the commission of this offense, and declared itself prepared to prove that this condition had not been fulfilled by the defendant during the period named in the indictment. The Supreme Court of Utah affirmed, however, as follows:

> "The offense of cohabiting with more than one woman is committed by a man who so associates with two women as to hold them out to the world as his wives, and it is not essential to the commission of such offense that he should have sexual intercourse with either of them."

An appeal to the Supreme Court of the United States a majority decision was rendered, affirming as follows:

> "A strong appeal was made in argument to this court, not to uphold the rulings of the trial court, because that would require a polygamous husband not only to cease living with his plural wives, but also to abandon the women themselves; and this court was asked to indicate what the conduct of the husband toward them must be in order to conform to the requirements of the law. It is sufficient to say that while what was done by the defendant in this case, after the passage of the Act of Congress, was not lawful, no court can say in advance what particular state of things will be lawful further than this: that he must not cohabit with more than one woman, in the sense of the word 'cohabit' as hereinbefore defined. While Congress has legitimated the issue of polygamous marriages, born before January 1, 1883, and thus

given to such issue claims upon their father which the law will recognize and enforce, it has made no enactment in respect to any right or status of a bigamous or polygamous wife. It leaves the conduct of the man toward her to be regulated by considerations which, outside of section 3, are not covered by the statute and which must be dealt with judicially, when properly presented."— 116 *U. S. Reports, p.* 80.

However, in this case, there is a dissenting opinion, signed by Justices Miller and Field, who declare expressly that legal precedents contain "no instance in which the word 'cohabitation' had been used to describe a criminal offense where it did not imply sexual intercourse."

The three cases of the United States *vs.* Lorenzo Snow contain further decisions upon the crime of "constructive cohabitation," which is made to consist in the mere act of introducing a polygamous wife as a wife, even without any further evidences of actual marital relations with her. Because of the fact that the defendant had a "legal wife" (first wife), although he had not lived with her for many years, his cohabitation with a plural wife was held to constitute the offense of "unlawful cohabitation with more than one woman," since the cohabitation with the "legal wife" (the term regularly used in these cases) was assumed conclusively to exist. Accordingly, by the principle of "segregation," then first introduced into criminal procedure, three separate instances of the offense alleged were erected into three separate crimes, calling for three separate indictments, tried in three separate cases (reported in 4 Utah, pp. 280–291, 295–312, 313–326), and each one requited by sentence to the extreme penalty of the law, six months' imprisonment and $300 fine. Such procedure, as is evident, would involve in many cases that men would be imprisoned for life and fined to the full extent of their resources — even beyond — for several repetitions of the heinous offense of introducing as his wife a woman, whom the law defines as no wife, to persons who perfectly understand his relations with her, also the legal limits set upon them. Whether or not, by an evident straining of law and contempt of precedent, as defined by Justices Miller and Field in the Cannon case, such acts constitute any intelligible evidence of "criminal conversation" or "unlawful cohabitation," it is quite certain that they were not the order of offenses which the laws of Congress sought to terminate. These laws condemned specific acts and relations; not opinions or statements. It is perfectly established that the law cannot justly take cognizance of a man's feelings and convictions, so long as he does not carry them, into a forbidden line of action, or attempt to so carry them. While, also, by the principles of Common Law, the introduction of a woman as one's wife has been held to constitute a valid form of marriage, involving enforceable rights and prerogatives, it is true, nevertheless, that such introduction of a woman, knowing her legal status in the premises, to persons also aware of that status, involves no enforceable rights whatsoever; since it is a mere form, whose legal significance is perfectly known to all parties. That a man, in such a transaction, is of the opinion that the woman is, morally or otherwise, entitled to be considered as his wife, or that the woman or other parties share such conviction, cannot be held to alter the legal status of the transaction. Properly speaking, its only valid legal significance would be as subsidiary evidence in an attempt to establish a suspicion or presumption of relations between the two, which the law forbids. When considered as the principal evidence in the attempt to establish "cohabitation" in any recognized sense, it cannot be denied that the mere alleged act of introducing a woman under the conditions mentioned is entirely inconclusive and incompetent to establish any allegation regarding their further relations "beyond reasonable doubt."

This very issue is raised in the appeal of the Lorenzo Snow cases to the Supreme Court of the United States. In the brief filed in the October term of 1885, it is claimed by the attorneys of the "plaintiff in error" that the Utah court had erred "in refusing instructions asked," as follows:

"Fourth Request. 'The defendant, though living with one wife, could lawfully visit another and her children at reasonable times and on lawful purposes, and the purposes of inquiring concerning the health and welfare of such other wife and his children by her, of providing for their support, and the education, employment, and business of the children would be lawful. He is not required to break off friendly relations with any of his wives and may attend friendly or social or religious meetings at their houses.'

"This request met every aspect of the evidence in the case and the defendant's claim of the purposes of his visits. If he can visit a plural wife at all, we submit that it should have been given.

"No equivalent instruction was given, but the jury was instructed as follows, and the plaintiff in error excepted:

"'Of course the defendant might visit his children by the various women, he may make direction regarding their welfare, he may meet the women on terms of social equality, but if he associates with them as a husband with his wife he is guilty. The Edmunds law says there must be an end to the relationship previously existing between polygamists; it says that relationship must cease.'

"The Fourth Request asked the Court to say that the plaintiff in error might visit his wives. There is no answer to this request in the charge. The jury were told that he might visit the *children* but there was no charge of cohabiting with them. They were also told that he may 'meet the women on terms of social equality.' This implies nothing more than that both may be guests at a friend's house or may meet on the street or in any public place, and the term 'meet' includes and would be understood to mean a casual meeting, and not an intentional one, while the term visit would mean an intentional going to see the very person visited; and it was to this view that the request was directed. What language could be more misleading and delusive than the expression: 'If he associates with them as a husband with his wife he is guilty'?"

Elsewhere in this same brief, the attorneys for the plaintiff in error, George Ticknor Curtis and Franklin S. Richards, claim error in the Utah Court's decisions, as follows:

"The court charged as follows and the plaintiff in error excepted:

. . . .

"'If the conduct of the defendant has been such as to lead to the belief that the parties were living as husband and wife live, then the defendant is guilty.'

. . . .

"*The issue was whether the plaintiff in error had in fact cohabited with more than one woman,* and this fact was to be found beyond a reasonable doubt. The defendant asked the court to say to the jury that the parties must have lived together. The court says if the jury find that some one may have been led to that belief it is enough, but it does not say who is to be led to that belief. If it be interpreted to mean that the jury must be led to the belief, it is still erroneous and would mean 'if you find you are led to this belief by the evidence the defendant is guilty.'"

Whatever may be one's prejudice against such an institution as polygamy, or against the people who have practiced it, it must seem ever a very nearly inexplicable fact that, in spite of constant and persistent effort on the part of able attorneys, several of them, like Judge Curtis, men of national reputation and standing, no authoritative construction could be obtained upon the term "cohabitation" that should precisely define the offense and put a stop to the miserable perversions of justice that were of daily occurrence in the Territory of Utah. It is remarkable, also, that, in the case of people so widely accused by venal politicians and other interested characters of contempt of law and essential viciousness, the searchers after infractions of a brand-new statute against an institution that had been virtually tolerated for over thirty years, should be obliged to indict men, because of verbal acknowledgments of their wives, because they dined with more than one of them, or because they had committed some other infraction of a precious fiction denominated "constructive cohabitation." The Mormons accused in these various proceedings asked merely for precise directions as to what they should do in regard to their plural wives, whether they should be allowed to retain them as "friends" and "acquaintances," or whether the law required that they cast them adrift, and, presumably, see to it that they did not drift back again. But to these questions the courts would vouchsafe no definitions whatever, and, as if the "crucify him" of the bigoted and disorderly elements could penetrate even to the shrine of justice, the people who professed themselves as desirous of conforming to the law were still left at the mercy of legalistic fictions.

These points are well enlarged upon in the argument of Judge Curtis before the Supreme Court of the United States on April 28, 1886. Enlarging upon the fact that, in the cases brought before that court on appeal, the evident sense of the proceedings in the lower courts was to punish a man for what he might have been assumed to think, or for what he was alleged to have said, regarding his relationship with given women, Curtis said:

"The first proposition to which I have to ask your attention is stated on the 22d page of my brief.

"The construction given by the court below to the third section of the act of March 22, 1882, and on which the plaintiff in error was thrice convicted, makes it violate the first amendment of the Constitution, because it makes the statute punish the profession of a religious belief, when, under that construction, it is applied to the evidence in the three cases now before the Court.

"In approaching the subject of religious liberty, there is of course a great deal of antecedent history to be taken into account. I do not propose to go over the whole of it, because most of us here are legal and historical scholars. You, Mr. Chief-Justice, in a recent case, Reynolds *vs.* United States, (98 U. S.,) had occasion to develop the subject somewhat. It is necessary for me, on this occasion, to supplement what you then said by a little further development of the subject; and, moreover, it is necessary for me to show what was the religious persecution on which history had set the seal of its condemnation before our Constitution was made. In all the modern ages of the world in which religious persecution has been carried on by governments, or in the name of public authority, the whole essence of the atrocious wrong has been this — power has said to the weak: 'Renounce your religious opinions, recant your religious beliefs, or die, or go to prison.' . . . This is what I am to show will be said by this Edmunds act to the Mormons of Utah, if it is to be construed and applied by the territorial judges. . . .

"The distinction between the case of Cannon *vs.* The United States (116 U. S., 55) and the three cases of Snow *vs.* The United States is broad and clear.

"Treating the three present cases as one, for the purposes of the argument, because, with reference to the constitutional question, all the evidence that needs to be considered was the same in all of them, I shall contend that the evidence on which Snow was convicted under an erroneous construction of the statute makes the conviction and sentence violate the free exercise of religion guaranteed by the 1st amendment of the Constitution.

"In Cannon's case unlawful cohabitation was held to consist in a man's living in the same house with two women, eating at their respective tables one-third of the time or thereabouts, and holding them out to the world, by his language or conduct, or both, as his wives, without occupying the same bed with either of them, or sleeping in the same room, . . . with either of them. No constitutional question arose in that case because there was no language proved to have been used by Cannon, in speaking of either of the two women as his wife, which required to be put to the jury to find whether he used the term 'wife' as indicating a spiritual and religious relation, or used it to signify a claim of right to continue a carnal relation with both of them notwithstanding the prohibition of the statute. But, in Snow's case, the only evidence of his language consisted in proof that he spoke of two women as his 'wives,' under circumstances which called for a distinct instruction to the jury to find in what sense and with what intent he used that language. If he spoke of the women as his 'wives,' meaning that by the religious law of his church he was bound to them in a spiritual and religious tie that did not necessarily signify the enjoyment of a carnal relation, but was a mere expression of his religious belief, he could not be convicted of unlawful cohabitation by his *language,* or by the use of his language as part of the evidence of guilt, without violating his rights of conscience. On the other hand, if he spoke of the women as his 'wives,' in a sense of a claim of right to maintain a carnal relation with them, or to dwell with both of them, notwithstanding the prohibition of the statute, the evidence of his language might go to the jury, along with the other facts proved, without violating his religious freedom; and if the whole evidence, taken together, had a reasonable tendency to show unlawful cohabitation, under a proper definition of that offence, he could have been convicted without a violation of his religious freedom. The imperative necessity, therefore, for a careful instruction to the jury to find in what sense and with what intent he used the word 'wife,' or 'wives,' which instruction was not given, and was refused, is perfectly apparent.

. . . .

"The sole proof of Mr. Snow's language consists in the fact that when under arrest, and in the marshal's office, he introduced *Harriet* and *Sarah* as his 'wives' to Mr. Peery, an acquaintance of his and a brother Mormon, just previous to the examination before the U. S. commissioner. His words were: 'Mr. Peery, or Brother Peery, this is my wife Harriet; Mr. Peery, or Brother Peery, this is my wife Sarah.' (Testimony of Franklin N. Snow, record in case No. 1278, p. 16.)

. . . .

"The whole evidence, taken together, consisted of the word 'wives,' as used by Mr. Snow, and the proof of his visits to the houses inhabited by some of them, besides Minnie, with whom he dwelt exclusively in a house which she and her children alone inhabited.

"In the case first tried, (Record 1278,) the conviction rested on this evidence, as applied to the case of *Sarah,* who was held by the appellate court to be the *lawful* wife. Cohabitation with *her* was held by the Chief-Justice of the court below, in his opinion, to be established by a presumption of *matrimonial* cohabitation, and by *inference* from the facts. As cohabitation in every sense with *Minnie* was admitted by the defendant, the general verdict of 'guilty as charged in the indictment' fixes the unlawful cohabitation in this case as cohabitation with *Sarah* and *Minnie.* In this all the judges below concurred.

"This covered the period from January 1, 1885, to December 1, 1885 — eleven months. There was evidence in this very case which should have admonished the trial judge of the nature of the relation of husband and wife claimed by these persons.

. . . .

"All this evidence gave to the trial judge the most pointed notice that here he was dealing with the term 'wife' or 'wives,' in a sense that might, when spoken by Mr. Snow, comprehend nothing but a religious doctrine and a religious belief.

. . . .

"The next case tried was that in Record 1279, the indictment covering the whole of the year 1884.

"Here the conviction rested on cohabitation with *Adeline* and *Minnie*.

"Here *Adeline* is taken as the *lawful* wife, and Minnie as the *unlawful* wife, in 1884, whereas *Sarah* was held to have been the lawful wife in the first trial, which related to eleven months of 1885.

. . . .

"*But* there is another aspect of his conduct. Standing here, as I do, on his absolute constitutional right to the free exercise of his religion, I ask you to see that his conduct consists of —

"1. A *declaration,* in which he used the word 'wife,' in speaking of *Harriet* and *Sarah*. He could have meant nothing but the spiritual and religious relation.

"2. Association and acts of a kind that could *not have* been dictated by anything but a religious obligation and duty.

"These acts were every one innocent and meritorious.

"They were not done in the assertion of any right of cohabitation.

"He had a perfect right to do them.

"They have not the smallest tendency to *prove cohabitation.*

"There was no cohabitation with either Sarah or Adeline.

"It is only by strained, distorted, and artificial construction of this word 'cohabitation,' that these acts can be preached and condemned.

"What were they?

"Visiting at rare intervals.

"Supporting.

"Driving out in a carriage with one or more of them.

"Attention to a sick child.

"A festivity on his birthday in the place of their public worship.

. . . .

"What 'flaunting in the face of the world of the ostentation and opportunities of a bigamous household' is there here?

"What did your honors mean by that language?

"Does it apply to these acts?

"What is a bigamous household?

"Do you mean that there is a household where the parties do not live in the same house?

"Do you mean that there is a household when they live one, five, ten miles apart?

"Remember, I pray you, that here, in one case, Sarah lives in one house and Minnie in another. That in another case Adeline lives in one house and Minnie in another; and the proof is incontrovertible that he never was seen in company with Adeline anywhere during the time covered by the indictment, and that he dwelt exclusively with Minnie.

"He had duties to discharge toward these women.

"These duties are natural; they spring from the law of nature.

"They are of moral obligation.

"They are of sacred obligation.

"They are duties, which, when we consider how and when they were assumed, and how they have become woven into the texture of his life, it would be barbaric to punish.

"The law says what? That he shall not 'cohabit' with more than one of them.

"Is that word to receive an interpretation that will require him to renounce *every duty,* to dishonor the dead, and agonize the living, and bring shame upon himself?

"Is it to receive an interpretation without any reference to the obligations or restraints resting on the sovereignty which enacted the law?

"Is it to be made to mean a constructive dwelling together, when there has been nothing but the discharge of duties of the highest obligation?

"This constructive cohabitation makes this single word the most elastic that was ever put into a statute.

"There is nothing that it will not reach. Let me enumerate.

"1. Cohabitation (with marital relations). This is of course within the statute.

"2. Cohabitation by dwelling under the same roof (without marital relations). That was Cannon's case. Now we come to the dividing line.

"3. Cohabitation by dwelling under different roofs, but occasionally seeing each other (and without marital relations).

"4. Cohabitation by dwelling in different towns, but writing to each other, sending supplies, delicacies, medicines, etc., in case of sickness.

"5. Cohabitation by living in different countries, but corresponding and speaking of each other as husband and wife.

"6. Cohabitation by acts of kindness and attention during a series of years, although not dwelling together; and then when the death-bed scene comes, and the husband stands there for a last farewell, and when all is over for this life, he follows her remains to the grave, and writes on the gravestone, *Harriet, wife* of Lorenzo Snow—that, too, is unlawful 'cohabitation'!

. . . .

"Now I must ask your honors' attention to the language of Judge Boreman, on page 25. This is what that judge says on the subject of polygamy in a written judicial opinion:

"'In the case under consideration we find a state of affairs which, by the facts developed in this class of cases, is coming to be well known to have a common existence in this Territory. The wife of a man's youth, and all the other women with whom he has lived as husband more or less of the time, and who have reared children to him, are, as they grow old, pushed off to lead a more lonely life, and the principal attention of the man is given to the youngest and most favored of his women. It is the natural result of a system founded on sensualism, and is the same here as in every other country where polygamy or any other system exists to shield the lust of men.'

"Oh, rare judicial consistency! These unfortunate Mormons are first charged with neglecting their elder wives, and pushing them off to lead lonely lives, and then such kindness and attention as they do show is used to convict them of unlawful cohabitation, by the aid of a legal presumption that they cohabit with the older ones, notwithstanding they have pushed them off! Can judicial folly go further than this?

. . . .

"Now let us see. It is simply impossible for the Court, in the cases before it, with the persons who assumed these relations under such circumstances (under religious sanction, and with a sense of religious duty), not to give any consideration to the public equities. If I am asked what the bearing of these facts and public equities should be in a court, I answer that they call for a construction of this one word 'cohabitation,' that will confine its meaning and operation so as not to require these men to renounce every possible duty to these women and force them to turn them and their children adrift upon the world. It is impossible for this Court not to give any consideration to the public equities, in construing and applying this statute to the cases before it, of persons who assumed their relations to each other under at least a tacit permission of the people and Government of the United States.

. . . .

"I do not ask you to go forward and give constructions and make provision for future cases. *I ask you to take this case,* and upon its plain facts to give a ruling and decision that will shut out these constructive 'cohabitations.'

"These people are a loyal and a law-abiding people. They have a code of political ethics, accepted as part of their religious creed. I have studied it. There is no better code of political morals for the ground that it covers, ever formulated by a human pen, that has fallen under my observation, and I have been somewhat of a student of that kind of literature. If your honors care to read it, you will find it in their book of *Doctrine and Covenants.*

"I here leave this case in your hands. But I cannot leave it without saying that the zealots who push this criminal law beyond the barriers of the Constitution are not the first, and perhaps they will not be the last, to seek to extend the kingdom of Christ by persecution, and to propagate a religion of love by the gospel of hate.

"Nor can I leave it without taking shame to myself that I have for so many years lived in ignorance of the condition of things in that devoted Territory. I have spent, on mere pecuniary interests, on lower politics, in the delight of letters and the pleasures of life, precious time that ought to have been given to the oppressed. If now my example, tardy as it is and feeble as it is, shall do something to arouse younger and more important men to a sense of their duty on this great problem, I shall have the consolation that I have done something to atone for my share in whatever blame rests upon this nation."—*Pleas for Religious Liberty and the Rights of Conscience* (*Pamphlet, Arguments before the U. S. Supreme Court,* 1886), pp. 4–5, 8–10, 16–17, 18–20, 21–22, 40–42.

The quotation from Judge Boreman reveals the kind of thing then allowed by governmental negligence in the Territories. Boreman, as will be remembered, was the author of the prejudiced and intemperate harangue before an anti-polygamy society in Salt Lake City, on the evening of February 27, 1882, which has been quoted in part in a previous chapter of the present volume. It would seem almost a miscarriage of justice that a man who could speak in the manner that he did on that occasion should be allowed to sit as judge in such cases as those against Lorenzo Snow. Nor does one need an exhaustive acquaintance with legal principles and precedents to understand that the construction placed on the term "cohabitation" in the cases tried before him and other judges in Utah, was, as Judge Curtis claimed, both strained and unwarranted, and as the minority opinion of the Supreme Court held in the Cannon case, devoid of authority in precedent. The action of Boreman and others was, in fact, but a repetition of the illegal methods of the notorious Judge McKean, who, in the prosecution of a "moral crusade," indicted Brigham Young for unlawful cohabitation, and then allowed a woman represented to be one of his "wives" to sue him for divorce, with heavy judgment for "alimony," a proceeding sufficiently illegal and preposterous to lead to his removal. It must have seemed no more than reasonable, therefore, that a construction should be given to terms used in a statute, in order that obvious injustice might be avoided, and judge-orators restrained in their enthusiasm for preconceived opinions on matters in litigation. This, however, for some mysterious reason, the Supreme Court refused to give. In its decision on the Cannon case, as already seen, it stated that such matters "must be dealt with judicially, when properly presented." In the cases of Lorenzo Snow, in which, evidently, distinct issues were "properly presented," the court decided on its own motion that it had no jurisdiction in the premises, and dismissed the writs of error.

As a consequence of this act of the Court, Mr. Snow was denied relief on his pleas, and after serving his first term of six months, and paying the fine imposed in the first case tried, he applied to the Chief Justice of the Supreme Court of Utah for a writ of habeas corpus. This writ was refused by the territorial court, but was granted by Justice Miller of the Supreme Court of the United States, on the decision then rendered that as unlawful cohabitation is a "continuous offense," the grand jury could find only one indictment, and the court impose only one sentence. (See 120 U. S., pp. 274–287.) This latter decision was a sad blow to the wanton injustice of fanatical judges, and put an effectual stop to one of the most high-handed methods of judicial oppression known in the history of the United States. The zealous ingenuity of the advocates of "true religion and undefiled," however, was equal to the situation, and although deprived of the valuable weapon of "segregation" of offenses within what had been repeatedly called a "continuous crime," the best available substitute was found in the practice of finding indictments for two separate offenses in the same set of facts, and consisting in the same essential acts. Thus, on September 27, 1888, a certain Hans Nielson was indicted for unlawful cohabitation, under Section 3 of the Edmunds Law of 1882, and on the same day by the same jury, of adultery, under Section 3 of the Act of March 3, 1887, otherwise known as the Edmunds-Tucker Act, the same period being covered in both cases. After serving a sentence of three months for the first named offense, and paying a fine of $100 and costs, he was placed on trial a second time under the second indictment, and, in spite of pleas of former conviction, and the claim that the same acts were essential to both indictments, he was sentenced to 125 days in the penitentiary. On appeal to the Supreme Court of the United States on a writ of habeas corpus, the second indictment was declared illegal, on the ground that its essential charges were included in the first. (See 131 U. S., pp. 176–191.) That the illegality of this proceeding would have been recognized under any circumstances, other than those existing in Utah at the time, and that without the assistance of the United States Supreme Court, need not be argued.

In answer, perhaps, to the repeated efforts of attorneys to obtain authoritative constructions on the terms above noted, the Edmunds-Tucker Act of 1887 changed the section on unlawful cohabitation—"if any male person . . . hereafter cohabits with more than one woman, he shall be deemed guilty of a misdemeanor"—to a prohibition of adultery. This, however, did not stop prosecutions under the old section, nor afford the asked-for definitions. Perversions of law were still continued, under the representation that, in no other manner could the guilty be reached and punished; since, as the Mormons "always stand together," there was no certainty that false testimony was not given to the courts. It would seem, however, that the majority of these people made an honest effort to live within the law, and that those who were the most anxious, oftentimes, were the very ones who were punished with the greatest severity. In the meantime, however, whether obedient or disobedient, the people were constantly under suspicion, owing to the monstrous lies constantly circulated about their social and domestic affairs, and always without attempts to verify them, or to discover the real basis of fact, if any. Nor can we doubt that the real objects in the minds of the originators of these falsehoods are set forth in previously-made quotations from Judge Jeremiah S. Black, and from passages from the *Salt Lake Tribune* of the period. As stated by a historian of the territory and state of Utah, the following conditions existed at this juncture:

> "The Edmunds Act, of March 22, 1882, was a disappointment to those who had taken upon themselves 'a mission for the social and political regeneration of Utah.' That law was not far-reaching enough to satisfy an element which, not content that pains and penalties should be visited upon the polygamous minority among the Mormons, desired something that would effect the destruction or emasculation of the entire Mormon system. 'We care nothing for your polygamy,' the Gentiles were wont to say in private, to individual Mormons. 'It's a good war-cry and serves our purpose by enlisting sympathy for our cause; but it's a mere bagatelle compared with other issues in the irrepressible conflict between our parties. What we most object to is your unity; your political and commercial solidarity; the obedience you render to your spiritual leaders in temporal affairs. We want you to throw off the yoke of the Priesthood, to do as we do, and be Americans

in deed as well as name.'"—*Orson F. Whitney, History of Utah, Vol. III., pp.* 547–548.

Accordingly, by the persistent repetition of this "good war-cry," Congress was constantly at work on some remodeling of the anti-polygamy statutes, and a great amount of oratory and debate was launched on both sides of the controversy. Finally, however, in spite of the strenuous stand for legal principles and human rights made by several senators, the crowning effort was completed, the notorious Edmunds-Tucker Act of February 15, 1887. This act was most inclusive, although nine out of its twenty-seven sections dealt with the marriage relation, its conditions, violations and limitations, and with offenses usually classed as "immoral." The following is a brief analysis:

Sec. 1. Making a legal husband or wife a competent witness in prosecutions for bigamy, etc., although not compelling such to testify without the permission of the other.

Sec. 2. Making it lawful to issue attachment for any witness in a trial for bigamy, etc., without issuance of previous subpœna.

Secs. 3 to 6. Defining penalties for adultery, incest, fornication, etc., and procedure in prosecution.

Secs. 7 and 8. Defining the duties and powers of U. S. commissioners and marshals, both exceptional.

Sec. 9. Of marriage ceremonies, certificates, etc.

Sec. 10. Of the proof of marriage.

Sec. 11. Declaring "illegitimate children" incapable of sharing in the inheritance of their father's property.

Sec. 12. Limiting the jurisdiction of the probate courts to matters connected with the estates of deceased persons and guardianship. (In the unsettled condition of the territory, these courts had often had a wider authority.)

Sec. 13. Appropriating all property escheated by the act of 1882 to the benefit of the common schools.

Sec. 14. Compelling all corporations and associations declared in violation of law to produce all books, records, etc., at the command of the courts.

Secs. 15–16. Decreeing the dissolution of the Perpetual Immigration Fund Company, and declaring its property escheated to the United States, to be expended for the benefit of the common schools of the territory.

Sec. 17. Decreeing the dissolution of the Corporation of the Church of Jesus Christ of Latter-day Saints, "in so far as it may now have, or pretend to have, any legal existence." (This was the provision for which the entire bill was enacted, but its relevance to the suppression of polygamy, or any other offense against the laws of the nation, is not perfectly apparent.)

Sec. 18. Defining a widow's right of dower.

Sec. 19. Providing that probate judges shall be appointed by the president.

Sec. 20. Abolishing female suffrage, which had been established in 1872, in the hope that it would act to terminate polygamy.

Sec. 21. Abolishing the secret ballot.

Sec. 22. Providing to re-district the territory.

Sec. 23. Providing to continue the Utah commission.

Sec. 24. Prescribing a test oath for all citizens, qualifying to vote, declaring that they will support the laws of the United States, particularly those forbidding polygamy, etc.

Sec. 25. Appointing a commissioner of schools, who should have power "to prohibit the use in any district school of any book of sectarian character or otherwise unsuitable."

Sec. 26. Enacting that churches may hold real property.

Sec. 27. Providing to reorganize the militia of the territory, but especially to declare annulled and of no effect the laws establishing the Nauvoo Legion.

This bill was vigorously attacked in both houses of Congress, but was passed by a safe majority, showing eminently well that wanton agitation had inflamed the credulous and bigoted elements among the people to such an extent that even its outrageous provisions were acceptable. It is well, however, to notice the kind of criticisms made upon it by the qualified lawmakers of the nation. Thus, on February 18th, Senator Vest spoke in part as follows:

"As a matter of course this bill will become a law, but I cannot vote for it. I am well aware what the public sentiment of the country is, but that makes no sort of impression on me, with my convictions as a legislator, nor will any amount of criticism on my action. I cannot vote for this bill because in my judgment it violates the fundamental principles of the Constitution of the United States. . . . It is naked, simple, bold confiscation and nothing else. . . . The whole spirit of this test-oath legislation is wrong; it is contrary to the principles and spirit of our republican institutions; and whenever the time comes in the Territories or States of this Union that test-oaths are necessary to preserve republican institutions, then republicanism is at an end."

The eleventh section of the bill, that relating to the incompetence of "illegitimate children"—meaning children born in polygamy—to inherit from their parents' estates, although distinctly specifying that its provisions did not apply to any children born within twelve months after the enactment of the bill, evoked the displeasure of Senator Wilkinson Call of Florida, who spoke as follows:

"What Christianity, what civilization, can justify this harsh and cruel provision? What has the poor child done that the Senator from Vermont should deprive it of subsistence, of the means of going through the world with credit to himself or herself? Why should it be persecuted with the terrors of this law, because the father and mother believed improperly; believed, if you please, barbarously, that a certain form of relation between the sexes was legitimate and of divine permission; believed a doctrine, if you please, pernicious to society, that by proper means, by free discussion, by moral suasion of the religion of Christ, should be eradicated and exterminated? What if they did, shall the poor child be the victim?

"Mr. President, the Spanish Inquisition . . . was not more cruel . . . than this provision of the bill, taking the poor illegitimate children whom Almighty God has permitted to come into the world, in fault, if you please, of their ancestors, but without fault of themselves, and branding them and depriving them of all subsistence and help and comfort.

"What should the father of an illegitimate child do in the theory of this bill? Abandon his offspring, and commit a thousand times fouler crime by abandoning his parental feelings, and leaving the offspring that he has begotten to starvation and misery; this is the wicked and cruel command of this bill; this is the morality it enjoins. Let the child born of innocent purposes, and under a form of religious belief, be an outcast from human sympathy, because we deny the right of the Divine Ruler of the Universe to establish an order of nature, which allows children to enter the world otherwise than as we think proper, and, notwithstanding the fault of their parents, endows them with the faculties which command success.

"The Divine Law-giver said 'Let little children come unto me,' and He blessed them, and His followers have established charities for them, and even the 'foundlings' have their guardians and their friends in the gentle hearts of Christian men and women. But the insane fanaticism of this bill seeks to place a curse and a stigma on them, and deprive them of their natural protectors, and of natural love and affection.

"Sir, the bill is barbarous and inhuman in every light. Be as strong anti-polygamist as you please, you can not be a follower of the divine religion of Christ and maintain a doctrine, a principle, a provision of law, that has this effect. It is an insult to Christ's precepts and religion, and a deadly assault on all the beautiful charities and humanities that have grown up under it. As false to human nature and the conditions of life, as it is to the divine economy that governs the world."

CHAPTER XXV

A SHELTER FOR THE "ERRING AND OPPRESSED"

UNFORTUNATELY no comments by a "Christian wife and mother," such as heard and reported on the mass meeting of Mormon women in Salt Lake City, were ever published on the utterances of United States senators on the provisions of the several anti-polygamy bills bearing the family name of Edmunds. The public cannot judge, therefore, whether the expressions used in the Senate were distinctly "disloyal" and "treasonable," or not. As a matter of fact, the denunciations of the Senators were much more impassioned and severe than anything heard at the meeting of the women, so widely commented on by bigoted critics. Nor, in either case was there a word that could justly be condemned as "treasonable" or "disloyal."

Many supposedly well-meaning people at this time seem to have been, as at present, readily victimized by habitual purveyors of absurd falsehoods. Thus, Mrs. Newman, who had come, apparently, from Lincoln, Nebraska, to help the people of Utah, addressed several memorials to Congress, embodying sad tales of misery, degradation and neglect. Among these, she stated, on the professed authority of a certain unnamed "lady missionary," horrible conditions alleged to exist in the Utah penitentiary. The report states:

> "I found in one cell, 10 x 13½, without a floor, six women, three of whom had babies under six months of age, who were incarcerated for contempt of court in refusing to acknowledge the paternity of their children. When I plead with them to answer the court and be released, they said, 'If we do, there are many wives and children to suffer the loss of a father.'
>
> "In another cell were two girls, one fourteen, one sixteen, each married to her own father, both with babes."

On the publication of these statements, which were sent forth to help prejudice the mind of the public against Mormonism — particularly the monstrous story about two young girls married to their own fathers, a thing as utterly foreign to the teachings and practices of Mormonism as to those of any other civilized society — investigations were at once started by several persons.

Thus was elicited from U. S. Marshal Frank H. Dyer, then in charge of the Penitentiary, the following statement:

"With regard to there being seven women confined in the penitentiary at that time, I desire to say that it is correct. Two were being held for contempt of court in refusing to answer certain questions put to them by the court touching their polygamous marriage relations; one, [name here given omitted], twenty-three years of age, with babe, on the charge of fornication; another for robbery, another for selling liquor without a license, and two for adultery. The statement as to the size of the room, in which these persons are kept, is about correct, being so small as for it to be almost inhuman to keep female prisoners in such a place; but it is the only place we have for the purpose. There is a floor in it, however, which is always kept neat and clean.

"The last item to which you call my attention is this: 'In another cell were two girls, one fourteen and one sixteen, who were married to their own father, both with babes.' This is wholly incorrect, and I cannot understand how anybody could have been so misled. Somebody must have made malicious misrepresentations to Mrs. Newman on this subject, as we have never had any girls of this age confined in the penitentiary since I have been marshal.

"These facts are taken from the records at the penitentiary and I personally know them to be correct."—*From letter addressed to H. N. Clawson, under date, October* 9, 1888.

The false stories eagerly accepted by Mrs. Newman and other agitators, utterly without attempts at verification, as seems clear, were used as "exhibits" in the movement to persuade Congress to appropriate sufficient funds to enable the erection and maintenance of a "Christian home" in Salt Lake City, especially for the dependent and indigent women and children victims of polygamy. So strongly was the need of such an institution urged upon Congress that $40,000 were appropriated, and the "noble work" begun. In the meantime, however, protests against the need of such a home were made by some of the very persons supposed to be among the prospective beneficiaries. Thus, Mrs. Emmeline B. Wells and three other Mormon women vigorously protested, in part, as follows:

"As we are the representatives of the Mormon women, we do, in their name, most emphatically protest against any such pretext being used for obtaining a share of the public funds. No Mormon woman, old or young, is compelled to marry at all; still less to enter into polygamy. . . .

"Mrs. Newman has no right to insult the noble band of Mormon matrons and maidens by asking public alms for their benefit, while she is industriously circulating the malignant falsehoods by which bitter prejudice has already been created against them and their religion.

"We most positively assert that there is not a Mormon wife, whether plural or otherwise, who would accept charity at the hands of those who have procured, and are still demanding the passage of, laws whose enforcement has brought sorrow and desolation into their once happy homes."

This protest is incorporated, with other historical material, in the annual reports of the "home," together with Mrs. Newman's "stinging reply":

"The appropriation is not asked for in behalf of the aristocracy of the Mormon Church, whose very luxury is the holocaust of 'others' woes.' These women by their treasonable political attitude, and their avowed hostility to Christian marriage, have cut the cords which bind them to the world's heart. The 'insult' should not be misappropriated."—*The Industrial Christian Home Association, of Utah.* (*Report,* 1893) *p.* 15.

However, on Mrs. Newman's return to the scene of her chosen labors for humanity, a reception was tendered her, at which Governor Caleb W. West made a speech, lauding her labors and congratulating her on the results, as follows:

"The laws of the country will and must be enforced, but the enforcement of the laws always brings suffering to the innocent wives and children of the offenders. Nothing so appeals to the human heart as a suffering woman or a suffering child. We recognize the situation and we appreciate the noble efforts of her who has striven to alleviate the suffering of the women and children of Utah, who are left upon the cold charity of the world by the enforcement of these laws, and for such there should be a wide, great home in which they could be taught the branches of education and industry, that they may enjoy the comforts of life. That object will receive the approval of the One who set the great example in all such work, the Great Lord of the Universe, who became a man that He might visit the lowly; that He might comfort the distressed; that He might help the helpless; and it seems to me that this noble lady must have found the greatest joy and comfort in this thought, that she was following in the footsteps of our Savior. It is wonderful, indeed, that this lady could do so much alone; but yet not alone, because she had the presence of the One who inspired her to the sacrifice she was making; she had back of her here in Utah the prayers of all the helpless women and innocent children; and, with resolute purpose and strong arm, she pushed forward and has returned more than victorious; and the highest compliment that can be paid her is, that the Christian people, by their prayers and efforts and labors, shall, when the institution is completed, try to find an inmate for it—some poor woman or suffering child."—*Ibid, p.* 15.

There is no need to criticize the motives back of the "Christian home," or enlarge upon the futility of the entire enterprise. Under the then existing conditions, when by judicial persecutions the Federal Government had broken up many family connections, and, presumably, thrown many women and children upon their own resources, the establishment of some sort of refuge for the helpless among such would seem to have been no more than a just attempt to right wrongs and compensate for injuries done, although such injuries may have been "necessary." The entire trouble with the project from the start was that it was based upon deliberate misrepresentations by some one or other—such person or persons being usually quoted anonymously—of the social and moral conditions in the territory of Utah, and was carried to completion in a spirit of utter ignorance of the genius and character of Mormonism. As was remarked by Hon. John T. Caine, Utah delegate in Congress, during the discussion of the proposition:

> "An 'industrial home' which would confine itself to instructing women and children in the arts of refined domestic pursuits, while affording them maintenance, would indeed be a great boon to any people. But when a charity is coupled with the condition that it is attainable only by abandoning their faith, 'the better element of Mormon society' will indeed spurn it. So far as 'the pauper element' is concerned, Mormonism eradicates rather than produces it. It is no idle boast of ours that in exclusively Mormon communities there are no alms houses and no need of them. But we have the poor, the sick, the needy who require, and not in vain, at our hands, relief. 'The poor ye always have with ye,' said our Savior. Charity no Mormon believes a thing to be spurned. They know that 'to give is better than to receive,' but they know, also, that 'to receive' is often a necessity."

In anticipation, doubtless, of doing a great work in the relief of the hypothetical "distressed victims of polygamy," an imposing building was erected in Salt Lake City, containing a total of 60 finished living rooms, 43 of which were sleeping rooms, with space for about a dozen more in the unfinished portions of the third story and in the attic. Such provisions must seem to have been wholly inadequate to accommodate the "hundreds of cases of distress" supposedly existing in Utah. But very few, if any, of the class for whom the home was erected ever applied for relief. Mormon writers assert that no Mormon women in good standing were ever sheltered there. Thus:

> "The 'home' was opened November 27, 1886, in rented quarters, but in June, 1889, moved into a new building of its own, erected at Salt Lake City with additional means provided by Congress. Its object, as stated by Congressmen, was to provide homes and employment for 'homeless and destitute' polygamous wives and their children. The project was a complete and costly failure; there being no 'homeless and destitute' characters of that kind for the Government to support. The new building was finally converted into offices for the Utah Commission, etc. The main promoter of the Industrial home was Mrs. Angie F. Newman, who denied, to the writer, that the main object of its establishment was the one above mentioned."—*Orson F. Whitney, History of Utah, Vol.* III, *pp.* 550–551 *note.*

Although as Mrs. Newman represented to Bishop Whitney, and as the managers of the home repeatedly suggested, the "original object" was to provide relief for all distressed women and children of worthy character in the territory, a "strict construction of the law" was made, confining its activities solely to the relief of "victims of polygamy." Thus:

> "To provide employment and means of self-support for the dependent women who renounce polygamy, and the children of such women, of tender age, in said Territory, with a view to aid in the suppression of

polygamy therein."—*Quoted from Act of Congress and circulated in Utah.*

Nevertheless, under date December, 1886, the Board of Control of the home, headed by Governor West, issued a letter, from which the following passages are quoted:

"A permanently established Industrial Home is now prepared to receive such occupants as conform to the provisions of the act, and who may have been left destitute by abandonment or neglect, or by the results of the enforcement of the United States Law against the criminal practices peculiar to this Territory.

"It is the sceptre of justice in one hand and the olive branch of mercy in the other, extended in sympathy and tenderness to the suffering, to the erring, and to the repentant.

"The prayers and supplications of forsaken women for themselves and their children are now abundantly answered.

"An American Christian Home, under the care and supervision of Christian women, and the fostering support of the United States government, through its official Board of Control, opens its doors and welcomes under its roof all who may worthily seek this refuge.

"Encouragement, hope, sympathy, instruction and love extend their arms to welcome you and provide for you!

"The wife, deceived, not honored, disowned, neglected, for herself and her little children, may here find comforting strength and a new blessedness opening out before her, care and instruction leading them to successive steps to a way of usefulness and a self-reliant support."—*Industrial Christian Home Association* (*Pamphlet*), *p.* 17.

At the end of the first year, according to the figures published in the above-mentioned pamphlet, a total of 154 women and children had applied for relief at the home, and of these only 33 could be received "under the letter of the law." Of this total of 33 eligibles, as given at another place, 11 were women, 15 boys and 7 girls; 12 of the children being "of tender age." In spite of this meagre showing, however, the report states that in the first ten months of operation the inmates had made, in the sewing room, 415 articles; mended 259 articles; darned 310 pairs of stockings; and "cut and fitted" 159 garments, giving a total of 1,143 pieces of work done in the sewing room. These darnings, mendings, cuttings and fittings, together with other work about the place, netted the inmates a grand total of $212.82 "for their own benefit" in the same period, or about $19.35 per adult inmate. Nor was there ever a greater number of inmates in the home, according to the reports of the president.

The defective success of the institution, due, undoubtedly, to the fact that its object was to relieve a class that either did not need, or would not accept, such relief, was attributed by the managers, in part, to the "direct vilification of the management by Mormons to inmates and through the public press." Nevertheless, deploring the fact that the original "broad plan" of the institution had been "narrowed," the president, Mrs. J. H.

Ferry, remarks, "It is a pain to send from these open doors a needy woman or a motherless boy because such applicant is not a Mormon." (*Ibid.* p. 78.) She also urged constantly that the scope of the institution be broadened, so as to accept other classes, such as "legal wives," who, as she still seemed to suppose, would eagerly avail themselves of the proffered shelter.

In spite of the few inmates, who rightfully, or not, had obtained admission, under the "strict construction of the law," there were numerous applicants at all times, very many of them of the same class, apparently, as the ladies found by Mrs. Newman's anonymous female missionary, "in one cell, . . . without a floor." In spite of the fervid rhetoric of his public utterances, Governor West seems to have been unwilling to extend assistance to most of these persons "without visible means of support." Some such cases are mentioned in the pamphlet above quoted as competent to "uphold those favorable to a liberal construction of the statute with a view to its usefulness." Thus:

"Mrs. David May; five children: Mr. May was employed in the silk factories of Glasgow, Scotland; was induced by missionaries of the Latter Day to come to Zion; arriving in Salt Lake, found things at variance with the representations which had been made by the missionaries; was urged to go into polygamy; then resolved to leave the Territory.

"The wife secured employment at the Continental hotel, Salt Lake City; husband started east on foot by the Denver and Rio Grande railway; the wife's health failed; took her five children and went to Provo for lighter work; found none; applied to the Mormon Church for help; was refused; appealed to Judge Henderson, exclaiming; 'Must I starve, and my little ones, in this land of liberty?' Judge Henderson attempted to find the bishop of Provo; the bishop took the under-ground, lest the woman had given information concerning his plural relations; Judge Henderson then made application to the Industrial Home for the woman and her five children; case rejected by Governor West."—*Pamphlet, pp.* 19–20.

This case, possibly a real example of distress, due to simple abandonment, which is no exclusive specialty of Mormons, is here elaborated and exaggerated, as is perfectly evident, in order to create further feeling against the Mormons and their institutions. That a man, so indigent as to be obliged to walk east on the railway tracks should be "urged to go into polygamy" by people who already had their own troubles on this score, or that the "Bishop of Provo" should "take the underground," fearing "lest the woman had given information," etc., are evident additions made for the purpose of qualifying this unfortunate woman to appear as a "victim of polygamy." Why must benevolently-minded people be ever thus credulous?

Another "sad case" was that of two girls, then in the hands of a lady Presbyterian school teacher, who is quoted as writing:

"I sent Emma away with the weight of her soul resting upon me, but I could not keep her longer; I still have the sister; the mother of these girls was left an orphan in her infancy; was brought up by the bishop, a polygamist, who made her marry a sixty-year-old polygamist when she was twelve years old; she now has four husbands."—*Ibid. p.* 20.

This case also was rejected by Governor West, who, adhering to the "strict construction of the law," doubtless saw that these girls were the victims of "polyandry," rather than of "polygamy," and probably disagreed with the Presbyterian lady, who seems to have thought that this "practice" also was a "Mormon institution."

But the depths of infamy — or should we say the "heights of absurdity"— are attained by another "case" mentioned. Thus:

"Case: Second wife, sixty-three years of age, helpless in bed; no one to bring her a drink of water; no Liberal has dared to help her but me, for they dread the attacks of the Mormons.

"I am a widow, living alone with two daughters, and I am seriously threatened for the service I have rendered her. The Mormons have cut down my wood and drawn it away; they have fenced out the public road so that I could not go to town to get supplies — all because I have given help to this Mormon woman. I know three or four other Mormon women for whom my heart is weeping. I wish the Governor would send a detachment of soldiers to help them away. My home should shelter them. Ask the Governor to assist me now and send commissioners to open the road.

"This letter was taken to the Governor and he declined to have anything to do about it, and rejected the cases."—*Ibid. p.* 20.

It is scarcely remarkable that an institution, whose managers persisted in circulating wretched stories of this description, should have been very largely avoided by the very classes for whose benefit it was intended. Nor is there any need to assume "direct vilification" by Mormons or other persons. On any basis, the failure of the institution would seem to constitute an additional argument for the oft-asserted contention that the Mormon women were not seeking sympathy, and did not desire it. Whatever may have been the basis in fact for any of the tales of suffering and "oppression," so widely circulated at this period, it is evident that the Church and the people provided in some satisfactory manner for all such women and children, "victims of polygamy"— and "law enforcement"— as were in need. In view of the fact that scarcely a dozen "eligible" women were ever in the care of this institution at any one time, there seems to be a sad element of satire in the reported remark of Governor West, as above quoted:

"The highest compliment that can be paid to her (Mrs. Newman) is, that the Christian people, by their prayers and efforts and labors, shall, when the institution is completed, try to find an inmate for it."

As early as 1888, Mrs. Ferry, the president of the Association, contributed a statement to the annual report of the Utah Commission, in which she stated:

"The board of this association do not propose to close the doors of this home so long as our government gives them the means to provide a home. True, there are disheartened and discouraged members of the association — tired of giving time and toil where it is unappreciated, but most of those who began the work are as true to-day, and if this effort for good fails, it will not be their fault."

The Congressional appropriation was withdrawn in 1896, when Utah was admitted to statehood, and the work of the home association ceased automatically. There was a movement to locate the Federal offices, post office, etc., in the building, but it also failed. After several years' use as a private residence, the building was sold at public auction, Sept. 7, 1899.

On the announcement that the building and property of the Association were to be disposed of by auction, the following comments were published in a local newspaper:

"The Women's Industrial Home is at last no more. The building and premises on Fifth East street will now be sold to the highest responsible bidder. This Utopian dream of Utah philanthropists has had many a rude awakening, but none quite so harsh and realistic as the present prosaic announcement that the place is to be knocked down under the hammer, as it were, as so much old junk, for which the government has no use.

"By the way, as a mere matter of fact, the government never did have any real use for the place. It was used to provide certain zealous men and women of good intentions but faulty judgment, with fairly good offices for a while, but that was the only good purpose it ever served."—*Deseret Evening News, July 29, 1899.*

A POLYGAMIST'S PRAYER

The following verses are from a poem written by a Mormon, who was suffering imprisonment for unlawful cohabitation under the Edmunds Law. It is interesting as an exhibit of the state of mind of many of these offenders and "constructive" offenders against a law, under which their enemies had ample opportunity to catch them on all kinds of technicalities.

"I WILL PRAY FOR YOU TO-NIGHT

"Dear Family; When last we met
In truth my heart did ache.
I murmured low, ''Tis sad to go
To prison for conscience' sake,
To part with friends and family dear
For the Gospel truth and light.'
I dashed aside the silent tear,
Resolved with God to fight,
That God may bless all in distress
I'll pray for you to-night.

. . . .

"Through wicked men and unjust laws
Into prison we are cast,
For daring defend the word of God,
As were His saints in ages past.
But while we remain upon the earth
And enjoy true Gospel light,
We'll sing His praise in these latter days,
Though in prison we are to-night.

"Dear Family; Cheer up; Fresh courage take.
Our love will again entwine,
And pervade our family circle:
Yes, we'll keep God's law divine,
For time and all eternity
Heavenly vows did us unite.
No mortal device can rend those ties.
I thank God for this to-night.

"Dear Family; Trials we must pass through
If we expect to gain
The blest reward of the faithful saints
Who with Jesus Christ shall reign;
As kings and queens mid heavenly scenes
We'll be crowned in power and might.
That we may endure, and the prize secure
Is my humble prayer to-night."

BX 8635.2
.M3
Robert Rodcolff Mullen

BX 8635.W44
1975
Robert C Webb
Real Mormonism

ords, but all records shall be

11-MARC records conforming to the

and matching the Library's

RC-format records found in the

2

VII

ANTI-MORMON EXPLANATIONS

"Vain babblings and oppositions of science."—I Timothy vi. 20.

CHAPTER XXVI

WAS JOSEPH SMITH AN EPILEPTIC?

THE traditional hypothesis — that of Smith's entire duplicity and "imposture"— involves altogether too many absurd and self-contradictory assumptions, when we come to a careful examination. Nowhere is this essential absurdity more fully apparent than in the elaboration of the theory of the Spaulding authorship of the Book of Mormon, as will be seen at a later place. According to any of these explanations, Smith certainly deserves credit as nearly the most ingenious and able of all men promulgating a system of belief, popularly classed as "untrue." The astuteness and positive executive ability, presumably shown by him in these matters, is not explained by the unworthy origin and evil youth, as vehemently asserted by these same critics. Nor do we find more "promising material" in any of his early associates, except, possibly, the Pratt brothers, who, able as they doubtless were, showed no signs of such colossal genius as we are asked to assume resided in, or near, Joseph Smith. It takes genius to accomplish great results, even though these be rated "evil"; nor, as already suggested, is a "bad will" the only equipment needed for success in such matters.

Later theorizers, aware doubtless of the defects in earlier methods of treating Smith's career and teachings, have attempted to apply the principles of psychology and pathology to an explanation of his case. Thus, we have the now popular theory that Smith, although honest, so far as his own conscience was concerned, was a victim of some such serious derangement as epilepsy. The authorized accounts of his several visions are taken as the primary evidences of this allegation, together with certain data on ancestral and parental disease and eccentricity, as predetermining causes. His own alleged bad habits are credited with effect as "aggravating conditions." The sufficiency of this theory may be judged by citations from one of its earliest promulgators, and its real value, apart from its interest as an academic discussion, may be found by an examination of his allegations. Of course, as the adherents of this theory confess, there is a lack of data sufficient to positively establish their contentions, or, as a matter of fact, to establish any other proposed explanation of the reported experiences of Smith's visions. It would seem far more satisfactory to report merely his claims and beliefs in the matter, and proceed to a discussion of his other claims and teachings. However, we must be reconciled, in the present connection, to the fact that the numerous confident solutions of the "riddle of Joseph Smith," all of them by persons more or less incapable of handling such matters satisfactorily, must be considered before we can be allowed to proceed to anything like a just estimate of his career and personality. Nor can we complain because these numerous critics render unfavorable opinions in regard to him. Like the testimonies of his "old neighbors," so often quoted, they are embarrassing very largely because they allege with competent proof so little that is worthy consideration, so little that constitutes a finality in way of explanation. Nor is this any the less true of the alleged scientific analysis which professes to find Smith an epileptic and mental degenerate.

The earliest, and best known, exponent of the epileptic theory is a certain Woodbridge Riley, formerly instructor in English in the New York University, who, having taken up the study of psychology, presented as a thesis for his doctor's degree at Yale University the book subsequently published under the title, *The Founder of Mormonism.* In his preface this author states:

> "Sectarians and phrenologists, spiritualists and mesmerists have variously interpreted his [Smith's] more or less abnormal performances — It now remains for the psychologist to have a try at them."

As candid investigators of the case of Mr. Smith, it must be confessed at the start that Mr. Riley has made out the weakest kind of a case for his thesis that Smith was an epileptic. In the character of the "psychologist" mentioned in his preface, he is very much like the dentist who will attribute all the ills of a patient to defective teeth, or the oculist who will blame poor eyes for the same symptoms. He makes Mr. Smith not only some vague variety of epileptic, but also a most interesting psychological study, a veritable magazine of about all the obscure and remarkable psychological and "psychic" symptoms recognized by modern writers. Thus, Smith was a "hypnotist" who could persuade the eleven witnesses of the Book of Mormon that they had actually seen the golden plates; as an "automatic writer" he produces the Book of Mormon; he is a "faith healer," occultist and exorcist, who, in spite of a personality and manners, which Mr. Riley finds were distinctly repulsive in several particulars, and, in spite of real derangement of several probable varieties, is able to accomplish, or at the least to lay the foundation of a work that has worried sensitive souls very sorely during the past eighty years. Riley's claims may be true, but his proffered "proofs" are inconclusive; partly because he evidently has no clinical or professional knowledge of the symptoms of epileptic affections, and partly because that, according to him, Mr. Smith displayed such a profusion of rare and doubtful symptoms that one must regret that such a case should have missed observation. Just as many medical students are said to begin finding the symptoms of the diseases they read about in themselves, so Riley seems to suspect that Smith "had them all." In spite of these defects, his work has been accepted as a genuine contribution to the literature of the subject, and his explanation has been endorsed by repetition in well-known works of reference.

Aware of the fact that such a disease as epilepsy must be explained by definite conditions or occurrences in the history of the patient, or in the experiences of his parents or ancestors, Riley offers an analysis of the family history of the Smiths, which seeks to account for the prophet's experiences and his mental peculiarities by his ancestors' "illiteracy, their restlessness and their credulity," matters in which, however, they were in no sense unique. In addition to their belief in dreams and other spiritual manifestations, certain traits common to both lines are adduced as evidence that the descendant must have been in some way of unstable mentality. Thus, his maternal grandfather, Solomon Mack, in addition to alcoholic addiction in early life, suffered an accident shortly before the birth of Smith's mother, the limb of a tree falling on his head and inducing "fits." He also had hallucinations in old age. (pp. 346–347.) Smith's paternal grandfather, Asael Smith, "nicknamed 'crook-necked' Smith, at the age of eighty six, is spoken of as 'just recovering from a severe fit' and of 'weak mind.' There is nothing more to be made of this than mental failure due to senility." (p. 348.) His maternal grandmother, Lydia Gates Mack, is credited with a "severe fit of sickness" at the age of forty-seven, although she was "alive in 1815, aged eighty." (p. 348.) However, "it is noticeable that the collaterals on the male side were uniformly healthy." (p. 348.) Much is made of the "hallucinations" of Smith's mother, the dreaming habit of his father, and the religious excitability of both, but, as the author evidently recognizes, no conclusive predisposition to disease is to be found in these facts.

Among the "predisposing causes" in the case of Smith himself are mentioned "an infectious fever and an ulceration";

and among "exciting causes," "nervous instability, consequent on protracted religious excitement" and "fright," the latter occurring when a "gun was fired across his pathway." (p. 351.) Riley then proceeds to account for the visions of the prophet, as follows:

"Now the first vision may be explained as a migraine, but the recurrence of this psychic aura, in a more or less stereotyped form, along with otherwise inexplicable injuries and contusions, is to be laid to a real epilepsy. Here alcoholism was first in the list of provocative causes. Joseph's confession as to the 'weakness of youth, foolish errors, divers temptations and gratifications of appetites offensive in the sight of God,' is to be coupled with the confessions of his adherents that he sometimes drank too much liquor. The frequency of his intoxication cannot be determined; along with Joseph, senior, he was charged by his enemies with public drunkenness; the Mormons themselves acknowledge at least two of the counts. . . . That alcoholism did but little to debilitate Joseph is proved by his general good health after thirty. It was, however, a provocative agent of his second attack at eighteen, for only the slightest stimulation was necessary to bring about a repetition of the first attack.

"The two earliest seizures may be now examined in conjunction. As already suggested, the theophanic portion of the visions may be largely explained as an ophthalmic migraine. Whether this is to be associated with a partial sensorial epilepsy, is determinable, in one case, by what precedes, in the other by what follows. Collecting the terms there are the following expressions: 'A pillar of light exactly over my head, above the brightness of the sun, which descended gradually until it fell upon me.' In the second vision the details are fuller and more exact: 'On a sudden, a light like that of day, only of a far purer and more glorious appearance and brightness burst into the room; indeed the first sight was as though the house was filled with a consuming fire. . . . I saw the light in the room begin to gather immediately around the person of him who had been speaking to me, and it continued to do so, until the room was again left dark, except just around him, when instantly I saw, as it were, a conduit open right up into heaven, and he ascended up till he entirely disappeared, and the room was left as it had been before this heavenly light had made its appearance.' This manifestation was repeated twice that night, once on the following day, and also throughout the series. As usual the apparent objective manifestations were actually subjective symptoms. Their similarity is due to the fact that in ophthalmic migraine periodical attacks tend to be similar in the same patient. The visual disturbance is ushered in by a dimness or blindness, then a scintillating scotoma occupies the outer portions of the visual field. Patients experiencing this symptom for the first time cannot give an exact account of it, more than that it is a dazzling comparable to that observed in looking at the sun. But with repetition there comes a more accurate envisagement, as in the second vision of Joseph. 'The luminous ball of fire enlarges; its center becomes obscure; gradually it passes beyond the limits of the visual field above and below, and the patient sees only a portion of it, in the form of a broken luminous line, which continues to vibrate until it has entirely disappeared. Then follows a phase of exhaustion and sometimes somnolence.'

"These sequelæ appear in the second vision, but to turn to the prodromata of the first. Joseph says that in this time of great excitement his mind was in a state of 'great uneasiness,' his feelings 'deep and pungent,' and he 'kept himself aloof.' These are the remote premonitory symptoms of an attack, when the patient labors under a singular oppression two or three days beforehand and is irritable, sad and secretive. The real seizure does not follow, unless there are immediate premonitory symptoms. These are not lacking in Joseph's case; the 'think darkness' may be explained as a migrainous scotoma, but fuller explanation is needed of Joseph's additional statements: 'I was seized upon by some power as to bind my tongue; I was ready to sink into despair, until I found myself delivered from the enemy; I saw two personages, whose brightness and glory defy all description, one of whom spake unto me.' Taken in order and with proper terminology these phenomena appear to constitute the real epileptic aura. After the gradually increasing melancholic depression, the patient manifests: first, a sudden terror; second, violent palpitations of the heart, accompanied by a difficulty in breathing and a constriction of the larynx; third, along with these symptoms are complex visual and auditory hallucinations of corporeal figures, such as of fantastic personages who carry on a conversation or deliver a message. More marked, psychic, sensitive and sensory prodromata are manifest in the second vision. Whether this first psychic paroxysm was followed by a real seizure, is undeterminable. It is not, at any rate, the classic major attack. There is loss of consciousness — 'when I came to myself' — but nothing from which general convulsions can be inferred. Nevertheless the sensorial migraine is an equivalent for convulsive paroxysms. Again, in the major attacks, there is often lacking the initial cry, tongue biting, and evacuations. . . . Turning to the second seizure, it represents the more essential features of mental and motor disturbance, — a verbal deafness and feebleness of the limbs, followed by exhaustion and somnolence. The vision proper took place the night before the real seizure. As there was no apparent loss of consciousness, it may be considered merely as the immediate premonition. Moreover, this vision, like the first, was preceded by anxiety and disquietude — 'I often felt condemned for my weakness and imperfections.' As an immediate prodroma, it is marked by more exact details. The parallel account gives these extra data. The celestial messenger's appearance was like 'fire,' and 'produced a shock which affected the whole body.' These may be explained as the sensory aura of red color (rothen flammenschein) and the sensitive aura of numbness (engourdissement). — *I. W. Riley* (*The Founder of Mormonism, pp.* 352–356).

While there can be no doubt that in the foregoing analysis Mr. Riley has mentioned and, apparently, identified several of the leading symptoms of epileptic seizures, it is, nevertheless, true that he has also assumed as proven several other things that are by no means obvious, if we are to form a diagnosis of this case on the basis of principles advanced by some of the most careful authorities. Thus, while it will be agreed that very many epileptic patients are affected with "sensory auræ," which take the form of apparent visual and auditory perceptions — causing the patient to believe to be properly objective certain effects arising from internal derangements of the centres of sight and hearing — it is equally true that cases in which are found perfectly definite sense experiences, such as Smith describes, are certainly rare, if not extremely doubtful. Thus, although some authorities assert that all the vivid visions recorded in the past are only so many evidences of epileptic, or epileptoid, affection, there can be no doubt that the average sensory experience of this character in the patients examined by competent physicians, are vague, inchoate and indefinite. We find mention, for example, of "flashes of light," "flashes of various colors," "wavelike motions in the air," "balls of fire in rapid vibratory motion," "zigzag lines and figures resembling an electric spark"; occasionally, also, figures of people or animals, usually in motion; frequently a delusion of magnification of visible objects. Among the commoner auditory auræ, which are sometimes associated with the visual, we find mention of "roaring and buzzing," "roaring and voices," "sounds like sea waves." Anything like the definite visual and auditory experiences recorded in the case of Joseph Smith is absent in the reports of the more careful investigators of the recognized epileptic and epileptiform affections. That this should be the case may be readily understood, when we consider that the physical cause of the symptom known as "migraine"—this word is cognate with "megrim," and means primarily "headache"—is some localized oppression of the brain centre involved. Such condition is likely to result in the orders of sensory phenomena mentioned above, far oftener than in anything of a clean-cut and definite character.

There seems to be considerable uncertainty among authorities touching the exact relation between migraine and epilepsy. This may be understood from the following:

"The relationship between these affections (migraines) and epilepsy has long been in dispute. I believe it is associated with the disease, especially in women, who more frequently show a periodicity in convulsive phenomena than men. Unquestionably some of the lighter forms of epilepsy pass for periodic sick headaches. It is the rule for psychic seizures to be followed by an intense, protracted pain in the head, that may persist for several days. . . . Before we can understand the relationship between periodic migraine and some of the lighter epileptic states or equivalents, we must have a thorough understanding of the scope, character, and causes of such states and equivalents."—*William P. Spratling, M. D., (Epilepsy and Its Treatment, pp.* 180–181).

"Sir Lauder Brunton discusses at length the possible relationship between migraine and epilepsy, saying in part: 'If the terminal branches of the temporosphenoidal artery become contracted like a bit of piano wire, as the one which runs up my forehead does during a headache, the nutrition for the center of sight in the brain must necessarily be impaired, and if the spasm should extend further down the artery, the centers of hearing, taste, and smell will also suffer. I think it probable that such impairment is the cause of the indistinct vision in hemianopsia, *i.e.*, blindness to all objects on one side of the body, either to right or left, even of complete blindness and of zigzags which occur either before or during an attack of migraine.'

"This distinguished author says, moreover, that, while the idea to some may be far-fetched, he inclines to believe that the fairies which many people declare they see are nothing more than the colored zigzags of migraine modified by imagination, and in some cases occasioned by an abnormal condition of one or the other eye.

"Hallucinations of sight during epileptic attacks in which there is mental disturbance are not uncommon, but, in my experience, *such ocular manifestations as those described by Fere and alluded to by Brunton, in which this condition is the only indication of an attack of epilepsy, are exceedingly rare,* while the very fact that visual auræ are so common before ordinary attacks, and often so complicated in their formation, constitutes additional reasons for the existence of partial epileptic attacks that find the eye in ophthalmic migraine the center of disturbance. In such conditions the pupils are usually contracted, while in ordinary epilepsy they are the reverse."—*Ibid. pp.* 185–186.

While it must be extremely difficult to analyze the conditions of epileptic and epileptoid affections, and to say definitely which of the minor symptoms are characteristic of a true seizure of any variety, and which not, it seems to be fairly well accepted among authorities that the sensory hallucinations incident on migraines, and other affections of the brain and circulation, are by no means indicative of an epileptic condition. Such experiences, as the consequence of fevers and general disorders of the brain and nervous system, are by no means uncommon. Nor is there any one definite assignable cause that may be cited in the case of the reported visions of Joseph Smith, or any other person. The identification of these visions with "ophthalmic migraine" by the author quoted above consists merely in the use a term habitually associated with epilepsy, but which does not certainly cover the involved experiences. To identify them with prodromic symptoms of epileptic attacks is thoroughly gratuitous, unless they be accepted as highly embellished accounts based on the simple phenomena of the ordinary sensory aura. The authority just quoted illustrates this contention, as follows:

"Sensory auræ are vastly more common than all the rest and partake of the greatest imaginable range in character. . . Visual auræ greatly predominate, occurring as often as those of taste, hearing and smell combined. They usually take the form of flashes of light, the colors of the rainbow passing in rapid succession across the field of vision. In other instances they appear in the nature of optical illusions, people, dogs, cats, and wild animals of various kinds being engrafted on the visual field; while it still more rarely happens that temporary blindness immediately precedes the attack."—*Ibid. pp.* 225–226.

Judging from the testimony of experts, it is probable that definite ideas are occasionally derived from sensory illusions, when experienced in combination with aura more definitely "psychic." Thus "Gowers mentions a woman who saw London in ruins, the Thames emptied to receive them, and herself the lonely survivor. This he calls a manifest 'psycho-sensory warning.'" The application for all this to the discussion of the case in hand is evident, when we come to a study of the leading symptoms of the disorders mentioned, and see how far they apply to the case of Joseph Smith.

As defined by several authorities, epilepsy is a "group of symptoms, due to different pathological conditions," which is characterized by a loss of consciousness, short or long in duration, frequently associated with chronic recurrent paroxysms, popularly known as "fits." On the varying nature and extent of these paroxysms authorities have found a basis for classification of several types of epileptic affection. Thus (1) *Grand Mal,* which includes a complete loss of consciousness and of motor coordination, accompanied by a violent fall to the ground and severe convulsions; (2) *Petit Mal,* in which there need not be a complete loss of consciousness or motor control, nor, as a rule, a violent falling to the ground, the muscular convulsions being also less violent; (3) *Partial Seizure,* called by some authorities "Jacksonian Epilepsy," which consists essentially in convulsive movements of some one limb or group of muscles, although not involving loss of consciousness — this seems to be the "transitional" form mentioned by other authorities; (4) *Psychic Epilepsy,* which is merely a "temporary blank in the field of consciousness . . . rarely accompanied by muscular disturbance of any kind," although sometimes characterized by visual phenomena. There are, in addition, various milder forms of seizure, which are either the early stages of some definite type of the general malady, or, because of symptomatic resemblances, are classed as "epileptoid" or "epileptiform."

In discussing Smith's case, Mr. Riley claims as evidences of real seizures several facts mentioned by either Smith himself or his mother. Among these are his several losses of consciousness; the several cases of great exhaustion and fright; the fact that, on one occasion, as related, he had dislocated his thumb — a result of inflexion on the palm of the hand, as the first movement in a progressive and violent series of muscular convulsions; and that, on at least one occasion —"when returning home with the golden plates"— he was found to have been severely bruised, either as the result of an assault by highwaymen, as he stated, or of the injuries resulting from a true *"grand mal"* attack, as Riley claims. However, in spite of these data, Mr. Riley concludes, as follows:

"The evidence in Joseph's case is now in. It remains, if possible, to locate it among the various forms of epilepsy: — 1. *grand mal; 2. petit mal;* 3. transitional; 4. irregular; 5. epileptoid and epileptiform (Northnagel). . . . Joseph's case is not in the first category, *grand mal,* for 'the major convulsive attack, with loss of consciousness, presents this constant characteristic,—that it leaves no trace in the memory of the patient.' This amnesia varies in duration. 'Many patients remember the remote premonitory phenomena and even the sensations of the aura. Some retain the memory of the first convulsive movements' (Fere). . . . There is no single experience of Joseph's which completely fulfils the classic formula:—premonitory symptoms remote and immediate, with both mental and motor disturbances; the attack proper, with its two periods of tonic and clonic convulsions; the after-stage of gradual return to consciousness, with abnormally deep sleep; and the sequelæ—of wounds, bruises, excoriations.

"If Joseph's case is not *grand mal,* it is also not *petit mal.* He had in the first half of the series premonitions, and in the last half spasms. Again, to anticipate, the depth of his exhaustion and of his unnerved and bruised state militate against the penultimate class,—the so-called irregular forms, in which the epileptic delirium is mild; and in greater degree against the first class,—the epileptoid and epileptiform seizures. These are slight and incomplete and do not comprise violent acts of ambulatory automatism in which the patient senselessly wounds himself. Possibly Joseph's last recorded seizure, with the long flight from home, may be one of those irregular forms, in which convulsions are replaced by running. On the whole, out of the five given varieties, the third, from its inclusive character, best describes Joseph's case."—*The Founder of Mormonism, pp.* 361–362.

It is disappointing to find a professed scientific discussion of an interesting case ending in such a manner, although, to one investigating the matter from an unprejudiced point of view, it would be difficult to see exactly how it could be otherwise. As a matter of fact, no one of the alleged "symptoms" mentioned by Riley, nor all of them together, can certainly establish the suspicion that Smith was afflicted in any such manner as is claimed. Some of these "symptoms" seem to indicate the graver forms of epileptic attack, while others, mentioned in close association with them, suggest merely the minor forms of the affection, or, even some of the numerous orders of malady classed as "epileptiform" or "epileptoid." We must conclude, therefore, that either the accounts of the experiences, as recorded by Smith and his mother, are inaccurate as to detail, several experiences being confused and massed together, or else that their true nature and explanation have not as yet been found. Thus the alleged "prodromata," discerned in the recorded "great uneasiness" and the feelings "deep and pungent" ("poignant"), as well as the "keeping aloof," appear in Smith's narration, above quoted,* as chronic and constant states of mind, rather than the forerunners of any attacks whatever. His religious anxieties and perturbations, as was quite characteristic at the time, seem to be described in the first two expressions, while, as regards the third, as seen in the

* See page 16.

quotation from his journal given above, he distinctly states that "I kept aloof from all these parties (religious denominations), though I attended their several meetings as often as occasion would permit." It is quite unlikely that a person laboring under a "delusion of persecution" and who is "irritable, sad and secretive," should, "as occasion would permit," put himself into the company of those supposed to be the cause of his misfortunes, and the subjects of his diseased aversion.

A very similar judgment may be recorded on the attempted explanation of Smith's account of his several cases of exhaustion. Such exhaustion follows, of course, from epileptic attacks, but its presence does not involve such causes by any necessary conditions, particularly in a person of active habits. Furthermore, it is probable that such effects, when noticeably present, would indicate far more serious complications, also much severer paroxysms than can be alleged in the case of Smith, by Riley's own acknowledgment. Unless such "symptoms" be very much overstated, it seems safer to say that they would indicate some order of "exhaustive paralysis" than any mere fatigue of ordinary type. This may be illustrated in the following quotation from the authority above cited:

"Exhaustion-paralysis, or a more or less complete but temporary loss of function of some part of the body, may follow certain types of epileptic seizures. This condition of transient paralysis is epilepsy was first carefully observed by Bravais in 1824, as mentioned in his work on hemiplegic epilepsy. . . . Some degree of paralysis, exhaustive in nature, is not rare after Jacksonian or partial epilepsy, and may be easily demonstrated in which consciousness is retained during the fit; it probably occurs in some degree after every attack in this form of epilepsy. The fewer the muscles affected by the fit, the greater will be the subsequent weakness, inasmuch as it is a result of a local and complete discharge of one particular motor area. . . . The motor weakness more or less rapidly disappears after single fits, but when it results after serial or status periods in which the fits are partial in type and range, the paralysis may be fully as complete as that seen after an apoplectic stroke, and it may remain more or less marked for days and weeks. In rare cases of idiopathic epilepsy the paralysis has been known to persist as an anomalous type of hemiplegia. . . . The paralysis is always most marked in those parts which are engaged most in the convulsion. It is, therefore, an exhaustion of the cortical elements; in other words, it is a problem in fatigue of cortical elements and not of muscles alone. It is quite probable that the general exhaustion which follows general fits and which is covered by coma may be analogous to the local weakness here described.—*W. P. Spratling, Op. cit., pp.* 252–254.

"The most serious clinical phase of the cortical pathology is due to the ultimate disappearance of the cortical cells; their destruction explains many of the permanent symptoms of the disease, especially the slowness, awkwardness, and incoordination of muscle movements, and the progressive mental failure (dementia) which is seen in so many epileptics. The disorder of motility in chronic cases amounts to a *paralysis* in many instances. The local and general exhaustion present after local or general fits (especially seen in those parts which participate most in the convulsion), are true exhaustion-paralyses in type, congeners of paralyses from destructive lesions of motor cells and tracts, but the sluggish, awkward, and incoordinate movements present in chronic epilepsy are really consequent upon cell destruction."—*Ibid. p.* 332.

Among the other physical symptoms mentioned by Riley are "running," which is often an "equivalent" of paroxysms; lapses of consciousness, which are characteristic of the graver forms of seizure; and the fact that on one occasion, as recorded by his mother, Smith dislocated his thumb. He also mentions the several recorded fallings-down, although carefully refraining from discussion of the statement, "When I came to myself again, I found myself lying on my back." This might seem to suggest a graver case of seizure than Riley can establish from his "symptoms." On the whole, the dislocation of the thumb is the best evidence adduced in this connection, as above suggested. It is remarkable, however, that the equally characteristic dislocation of the shoulder is nowhere mentioned (although this is a symptom of *grand mal*), nor yet the familiar bitten tongue. Such matters if present would probably have been mentioned, either by Smith or his mother, whose ignorance of the characteristic marks of the epileptic need not have been urged to their discredit. As for the bruises and contusions, mentioned by Riley (p. 360) as evidences of a seizure, it must be insisted that their value is largely discounted, in view of the absence of the other "marks" that should reasonably have been expected as the results of convulsions of violence sufficient to result in physical injury.

On the whole, this attempt to diagnose a case of epileptic affection from a few scattered symptoms cannot be other than abortive and unsatisfactory. Smith may have had epileptic symptoms — may have been an epileptic of some variety all his life, just as were sundry other great and conspicuous men, according to the findings of our pathologists — but we have not seen it proved. If any better evidence is needed than that already advanced, we may quote the words of an authority, who is still recognized among specialists in this kind of malady, as follows:

"Epilepsy, like paralysis, is not a morbid entity existing by itself, but a manifestation of manifold derangements disturbing the nervous system and giving rise to definite inseparate conditions — immediate cause of the convulsive paroxysm — that remain the same whatever be the occasional origin of the epilepsy.

"No other malady exhibits a wider range in its etiology. *There is scarcely a disease deranging the human frame in which epileptiform convulsions might not happen as an accident or essential phenomenon,* and it may be safely set down as a truth of great importance that the numerous conditions capable of inducting epilepsy give to each of its species a characteristic impression that will ever prevent conforming their individual symptoms to any typical case, or finding any specific cure for every instance of the disease. To establish the peculiar morbid conditions influencing its development, to discriminate the general from the local circumstances, in order to arrive at a rational and successful treatment, is the fundamental question in the study of epilepsy." —*Echeverria* (*Epilepsy, p.* 10).

On the other hand, the supposition that Smith's recorded experiences may have been in some sense actual occurrences might yield an explanation of very many of the physical and mental effects recorded by him. Without wishing to incur the charge of being over-credulous, even in these days of "rationalism," when all sorts of absurdities are eagerly accepted, when labeled "scientific," we may state that a vision of God, or of any other supernal beings, for that matter, could, imaginably, occasion the symptoms of fear, or some similar strong emotion, many of which closely suggest some of the leading effects described and discussed above. Thus, the physical symptoms of fear, for example, as described by several authorities, show many of the elements already noted and described as characteristic of pathological seizures. This fact may be illustrated in the following quotation:

"Fear is often preceded by astonishment, and is so far akin to it, that both lead to the senses of sight and hearing being instantly aroused. In both cases the eyes and mouth are widely opened, and the eyebrows raised. The frightened man at first *stands like a statue, motionless and breathless,* or crouches down as if instinctively to escape observation.

"*The heart beats quickly and violently,* so that it palpitates or knocks against the ribs; but it is very doubtful whether it then works more efficiently than usual, so as to send a greater supply of blood to all parts of the body; for the skin instantly becomes pale as during incipient faintness. . . . In connection with the disturbed action of the heart, the breathing is hurried. The salivary glands act imperfectly; the mouth becomes dry, and is often open and shut. . . . One of the best-marked symptoms is the trembling of all the muscles of the body; and this is often first seen in the lips. From this cause, and from the dryness of the mouth, the *voice becomes husky or indistinct or may altogether fail.* . . . As fear increased into an agony of terror, we behold, as under all violent emotions, diversified results. The heart beats wildly or must fail to act and faintness ensue; there is a deathlike pallor; the breathing is labored; the wings of the nostrils are widely dilated; 'there is a gasping and convulsive motion of the lips, a tremor on the hollow cheek, *a gulping and* catching of the throat.' . . . *All the muscles of the body may become rigid, or may be thrown into convulsive movements.—Charles Darwin* (*Expression of the Emotions, pp.* 289–292).

However, in commenting on the reflex effects brought about by the emotions, Prof. William James remarks:

"Were we to go through the whole list of emotions which have been named by men, and study their organic manifestations, we should but ring the changes on the elements which these three typical cases (sorrow, fear and hatred) involve. Rigidity of this muscle, relaxation of that, constriction of arteries here, dilatation there, breathing of this sort or of that, pulse slowing or quickening, this gland secreting and that one dry, etc., etc. We should, moreover, find that our descriptions had no absolute truth; that they only applied to the average man; that every one of us, almost, has some personal idiosyncrasy of expression. . . . Now the moment the genesis of an emotion is accounted for, as the arousal by an object of a lot of reflex acts which are forthwith felt, we immediately see why there is no limit to the number of possible different emotions which may exist, and why the emotions of different individuals may vary indefinitely, both as to their constitution and as to objects which call them forth. For there is nothing sacramental or eternally fixed in reflex action. Any sort of reflex effect is possible, and reflexes actually vary indefinitely, as we know."—*Principles of Psychology, Vol.* II., *pp.* 447–448; 454.

In view of the principles and data set forth in the above quotation, it may be asked if any strong emotion-reflexes, produced by some exceptional experience, as an exciting cause, could be called upon to account for such symptoms as are described in the words used by Joseph Smith in narrating the occurrences before and during his first vision. It is interesting, at any rate, to compare some such explanation as this with that given in the words of Mr. Riley, as quoted above. Nor is it out of place to remind the reader that the expression of emotion in normal individuals under exceptional stimuli, may approximate many symptoms of pathological disorders. Thus, for example, we hear of cases described with perfect accuracy, so far as the apparent symptoms are concerned, in which people have been "paralyzed with horror" or "terrified into a fit." Other "grave symptoms" are common in such cases.

In view of the facts just mentioned, we must acknowledge that, even on the theory that Smith's reported experiences are part and parcel of a wholly fictitious narrative, the details are well worked out—the author of any such fictitious narrative must have experienced deep and unusual emotions at some periods in his career. Again, as we shall see later, these accounts agree in detail with the effects recorded in connection with the several theophanous visions of the Old and New Testaments. His accounts, if fictitious, are very well conceived as to details.

From still another point of view we may judge of the pathological significance of the events recorded by Smith. Since he records with sufficient accuracy to attract the attention of Mr. Riley and other psychologists, the symptoms attributed to pathological seizure of some kind, it is reasonable to assert that he must have been unaware that they could indicate any such conditions as these theorizers assert. Since, therefore, other striking symptoms must have been present in a case of epilepsy, it is surprising that we find no mention of them as a part of the emotions liable to be excited by theophanous and angelic visions or visitations. As indicated by Riley, a case involving such vivid recollections of sensory phenomena could not have involved a complete loss of consciousness; consequently other events should have impressed the memory with similar vividness. Further, a case of epilepsy involving, at times, paroxysms severe enough to produce "injuries and contusions," also thumb dislocations, would probably have involved convulsions severe enough to be remembered with the other recorded symptoms, along with the visual phenomena. In other words, the narrator would probably have considered them essential parts of his story. Not only does he record no such "twitchings and writhings," however, but, at a later period, he distinctly states that such things are no part of the experiences of a true prophet of God. Thus:

> "One great evil is, that men are ignorant of the nature of spirits; their power, laws, government, intelligence, etc., and imagine that when there is anything like power, revelation, or vision manifested, that it must be of God. Hence the Methodists, Presbyterians, and others frequently possess a spirit that will cause them to lie down, and during its operation, animation is frequently entirely suspended; they consider it to be the power of God, and a glorious manifestation from God — a manifestation of what? Is there any intelligence communicated? Are the curtains of heaven withdrawn, or the purposes of God developed? Have they seen and conversed with an angel — or have the glories of futurity burst upon their view? No! but their body has been inanimate, the operation of their spirit suspended, and all the intelligence that can be obtained from them when they arise, is a shout of 'glory' or 'hallelujah,' or some incoherent expression; but they have had 'the power.' . . .
>
> "The 'French Prophets' were possessed of a spirit that deceived; they existed in Vivaris and Dauphiny, in great numbers in the year 1688; there were many boys and girls from seven to twenty-five; they had strange fits, as in tremblings and faintings, which made them stretch out their legs and arms, as in a swoon; they remained awhile in trances, and coming out of them, uttered all that came in their mouths.
>
> "Now God never had any prophets that acted in this way; there was nothing indecorous in the proceeding of the Lord's prophets in any age; neither had the apostles, nor prophets in the apostles' day anything of this kind. Paul says, 'Ye may all prophesy, one by one; and if anything be revealed to another let the first hold his peace, for the spirit of the prophets is subject to the prophets'; but here we find that the prophets are subject to the spirit, and, falling down, have twitchings, tumblings, and faintings through the influence of that spirit, being entirely under its control. Paul says, 'Let everything be done decently and in order,' but here we find the greatest disorder and indecency in the conduct of both men and women, as above described. The same rule would apply to the fallings, twitchings, swoonings, shaking, and trances of many of our modern revivalists.—*History of the Church, Vol.* IV. *pp.* 572, 576.

It is noticeable that the speaker admits the validity of "suspended animation" in true spiritual manifestations, provided, apparently, that it lead to "intelligence communicated," etc. As regards the "twitchings, tumblings, and faintings," however, he makes no such proviso. Of course, in any such case, it is easy to say that a man may falsify in suppressing the details not mentioned, but why, then, should we accept any of his statements as perfectly accurate?

However, Mr. Riley's "case" of epilepsy, which he himself finds must have been of a very "inclusive character," and actually so vague and indeterminate that he attempts no further definition of its symptoms, beyond suggesting that it was principally "psychic," is of importance to the student of Joseph Smith's career merely because it contains, professedly, an explanation of Smith's recorded visions. These, as already seen, he states "may be *largely explained* as an ophthalmic migraine" (p. 352). However, in referring to a later experience, he states:

> "Whether these visitations are to be identified with epileptic seizures is immaterial; the point here is that, as regards mental manifestations, 'it is undoubtedly possible for an absolutely healthy state of mind to co-exist with epilepsy.' Historical tradition tells of numerous highly gifted men who suffer from epilepsy, and whose deeds do not allow the recognition of any mental deterioration."—*Op. cit., pp.* 365–366.

The real question is, then not whether Smith suffered in youth from an epileptiform malady,—and such afflictions are much more common than one might wish to think—but as to whether it explains the visions which he claims to have experienced. To this latter question credible authorities on epilepsy, as well as Mr. Riley himself, furnish a rather conclusive negative. We find no reported visual experiences that more than partially parallel those described by Joseph Smith, in vividness and definiteness, and, as is fair to suppose, Mr. Riley has also found none; otherwise, presumably, he would have quoted them.

However, as in other points, curiously enough, the question refers less to the judgment to be passed on Joseph Smith's case than to that which we are to apply to a far more general situation. It is briefly this, as to whether the foundations of religion itself are not laid in occurrences that may be interpreted, with the skill and information present, as in some very real sense pathological. In other words, since the general characteristics of Smith's reported visions are the same as those of other and more ancient theophanists, is it admissible to claim, with Lombroso and others, that they also were afflicted with grave maladies? While many modern theologians may be willing to admit such a conclusion, it must be insisted that its assertion is a distinct presumption on the all-sufficiency of our present knowledge of matters psychic and pathological; hence not to be reasonably considered.

In order to illustrate the ease with which certain writers have made out an apparently strong case, we may quote Lombroso, who in the course of argument in support of his theory of the "epileptoid nature of genius," quotes Renan on the case of St. Paul, as follows:

"St. Paul was of low stature, but stoutly made. His health was always poor, on account of a strange infirmity which he calls 'a thorn in the flesh,' and which was probably a serious neurosis.

"His moral character was anomalous; naturally kind and courteous, he became ferocious when excited by passion. In the school of Gamaliel, a moderate Pharisee, he did not learn moderation; as the enthusiastic leader of the younger Pharisees, he was among the fiercest persecutors of the Christians. . . . Hearing that there was a certain number of disciples at Damascus, he demanded of the high priest a warrant for arresting them, and left Jerusalem in a disturbed state of mind. On approaching the plain of Damascus at noon, he had a seizure, evidently of an epileptic nature, in which he fell to the ground unconscious. Soon after this, he experienced an hallucination, and saw Jesus himself, who said to him in Hebrew, 'Paul, Paul, why persecutest thou me?' For three days, seized with fever, he neither ate nor drank, and saw the phantom of Ananias, whom, as head of the Christian community, he had come to arrest, making signs to him. The latter was summoned to his bed, and calm immediately returned to the spirit of Paul, who from that day forward became one of the most fervid Christians. Without desiring any more special instruction — as having received a direct revelation from Christ himself — he regarded himself as one of the apostles, and acted as such, to the enormous advantage of the Christians. The immense dangers occasioned by his haughty and arrogant spirit were compensated a thousand times over by his boldness and originality, which would not allow the Christian idea to remain within the bounds of a small association of people 'poor in spirit,' who would have let it die out like Hellenism, but, so to speak, steered boldly out to sea with it. At Antioch he had an hallucination similar to that of Mahomet at a later period; he felt himself rapt into the third heaven, where he heard unspeakable words, which it is not lawful for a man to utter."— *The Man of Genius, pp.* 347-348.

Lombroso, who quotes Renan in the above passage, evidently with complete approval, does not hesitate to attempt an explanation of Christ's career on precisely similar principles. Thus, as they tell us, must science shatter the opinions of the past — the "superstitions," presumably. It is a sad satire on the sufficiency of the canons of the "science" followed by such men, that Lombroso, in his old age, became a doting dupe of the crudest kind of "spiritistic" swindle, and found his "faith in immortality" renewed by tipping tables and levitated coal scuttles. Why the "supernatural" becomes any the more believable under such conditions than under others is a question that should invite an answer from some competent mind.

In view of the professed experiences of Joseph Smith, as described above, and the symptoms and auræ of epileptic affections, as outlined in quotations, also given, it seems interesting to note that the correspondences mentioned by Riley and others apply with equal force to far more ancient personages. Thus,

Abraham, in the course of a theophany, experiences "a horror of great darkness" (Gen. xv, 12); Moses has a vision of God in the midst of flames, in which "the bush was not consumed" (Exod. iii, 2); Elijah experiences a divine manifestation, which includes a "great and strong wind," presumably attended with noise, and "a fire," succeeded by a "still small voice" (I Kings xix, 9–18); Ezekiel, on four distinct occasions, in the course of prolonged visions of God and heavenly beings, records, "I fell upon my face" (Ezek. i, 28; iii, 23; xliii, 3; xliv, 4), although whether in obeisance or as one overcome is not stated; John the Revelator records, "I fell at his feet as (one) dead" (Rev. i, 17); Daniel also fell upon his face at the approach of Gabriel (Dan. viii, 17); Jacob, "left alone," has an experience—a wrestling with an angel—which results in the dislocation of his thigh. It is notable, also, that in all the greater visions recorded in the Bible the elements of light and color are prominent; also, that the details are most numerous and complex. In the matter of color perceptions in these visions and theophanies, it is interesting to notice that an intense white is not unfamiliar. Thus, for example, in the account of the transfiguration of Christ (Matt. xvii, 2; Mark ix, 3), we find mention of garments "white as the light" and exceeding white as snow; so as no fuller on earth can white them." Of course, such data will move many theorizers to assert that the real basis was some kind of pathologic seizure in each case; but it is not too much to say that such statement is a mere presumption on the sufficiency of our present knowledge in every instance. It is also perfectly certain that we know nothing whatever about the conditions and experiences described; nor can we assert with proof that they are impossible; hence we cannot undertake to classify them. It is interesting, however, to note that the recorded experiences, criticized in certain quotations already given, agree in general "symptoms" with those always accepted as of exceptional and divine origin. It is certain that the details are correctly "worked out."

While considering the epilepsy theory, as set forth by Riley and others to explain the case of Joseph Smith, it must not be forgotten that it explains by no means all the facts alleged by Smith, his family and his personal associates. This is true because, while some pathologic seizure may be assumed, in order to explain such visions, when occurring to a person by himself, they are worthless when others in his company testify that they have seen the same things themselves, and, further, persist in their representations to this effect until the day of their death. Thus, as recorded in the history of Joseph Smith and of the

Church founded by him, there were several distinct visions of angelic and divine personages experienced by Smith, in company with others. Of such character were the reported experiences of the "three witnesses to the Book of Mormon," who, as they testify, and never denied, saw an angel, and a glorious light, and were shown the plates of the Book of Mormon; the experiences of Oliver Cowdery, who testifies that he saw the glorified personages, "John the Baptist" and the apostles, "Peter, James and John"; finally, the other visions in the Kirtland Temple, shared by this same person and by Sidney Rigdon.

The only excuse for considering the epileptic theory at such length is that it has been adopted as a convenient explanation of Smith and Mormonism by several writers and works of reference that have the attention of the public. Apart from this fact, the theory is worthless, both because its original promulgator knows little or nothing of the conditions and facts of epileptic and epileptoid affections, also because, in these same affections, there is such a wide range of uncertainty and misunderstanding, both as regards symptoms and as regards conclusive diagnosis. Indeed, it may be safely said, no careful physician would venture to label a given case epileptic until he had had opportunity to observe the patient. Although the theory of genius and epilepsy, advocated by Lombroso and others, is regarded with interest in some quarters, it is universally agreed, apparently, that works of real worth produced by persons, supposed to have been affected, were not produced in the epileptic condition, but rather in spite of it. Nor would there be serious opposition to the statement that a stage of such a disease sufficiently advanced to have definite serious symptoms would preclude the production of great and lasting works of any description. In this connection we may compare the fatuity of a paranoid, such as Rienzi, with the achievements of Joseph Smith: clever writers and theorizers are still trying to explain Joseph Smith. The following statements from Dr. Charles L. Dana, a noted alienist, are of interest:

> "True epilepsy is not compatible with extraordinary intellectual endowments. Cæsar, Napoleon, Peter the Great, and other geniuses may have had some symptomatic fits, but not idiopathic epilepsy."—*Text Book of Nervous Diseases, 3d edition, p.* 408.

Joseph Smith's works were all well-reasoned, persistent and able, worthy the serious attention, as we have seen, of informed minds. They are as incompatible with the theory that he was deranged as they are with the equally unjustified theory that he was an habitual drunkard. Judging him by the writings, orations and practical works of organization and thought which he has left us, he was evidently neither the one nor the other.

Whatever may be the actual truth about any of the matters recorded by Joseph Smith and his associates, the fact remains that, in the insufficient state of human knowledge regarding all things divorced from the sphere of verifiable experience, it is the duty of any critic professing to be fair and intelligent to give careful and respectful attention to any professed experiences of people, not evidently insane, and to refrain from confident assertions that such experiences are completely explained on "rationalistic" grounds, so called, until something more than the vague theories of psychological experimenters can be invoked in support of our conclusions. (And do not our psychologists do this very thing in the case of spiritistic "mediums"?) Although, as is familiar, the average feeble brain of the present day supinely accepts the assurances of our rationalistic dreamers that there is certainly no possibility of a supernatural superstratum in the universe, it remains true, nevertheless, that the belief in such is sufficiently fundamental and persistent in human history and experience to be classed, very nearly, among the instincts, or "innate ideas" of the mind. Without the element of the supernatural, no valid system of religion has ever been founded, and even where the supernatural traditions have been discountenanced, we find that the "most active minds" eagerly seek consolation in the newer forms of "spiritual philosophy," in travestied Buddhism and Brahmanism, as well as in spiritistic "assurances of a future life." How else shall we explain the large number of prominent experimental scientists — physicists, astronomers, zoologists, and others — who have openly declared their allegiance to the "doctrine of spirit-return"? On the other hand, many persons, still firmly favorable to inherited traditions, will assert that all claims to visions, theophanies, miraculous gifts, and the like, made at the present day, must be fallacious; such things belonging wholly to the past, and not to be tolerated as possibilities now. While, as rational and honest beings, we cannot deny the possibility of the supernatural, we must insist that a belief in its manifestations involves no necessary time limits; nor are we possessed of any sure rules for discriminating the true from the false manifestation, nor stating that, as applied to the cases of certain persons, such things cannot be assumed, even tentatively, as an explanation.

CHAPTER XXVII

DID SOLOMON SPAULDING WRITE THE BOOK OF MORMON?

THE Spaulding authorship theory, briefly stated, involves that the Book of Mormon was written *in toto,* with the probable exception, as stated, of the "religious portions," by a certain Rev. Solomon Spaulding, who had at one time been a Presbyterian minister, but later was engaged in business of several descriptions, first in New York state, later in Ohio. As related, his several business ventures were by no means successful, and he made an effort, desperate as it must seem, to retrieve his fortunes and pay his numerous debts, by writing novels. At least one such story has been attributed to him, bearing the title, *The Manuscript Found,* in which, on the basis of the alleged translation of a parchment manuscript, discovered, professedly, by the author of the book, the reader is given an account of certain prehistoric nations of the western hemisphere. The alleged identifications of this production — or some other — of Spaulding's with the Book of Mormon is based upon the same line of poorly-conceived "testimony" as that which supposedly establishes the worthless character of Smith's family and of himself. We have seen, already, how inconclusive and irrelevant are these latter "evidences." We shall see how extremely inconclusive are the former also.

According to accepted accounts, Spaulding died in 1816, fourteen years before the publication of the Book of Mormon, without having published any of his writings. It is evident, therefore, that he was not so conspicuous a figure in literature that the Book of Mormon, or any other production, could be properly identified as his, by comparison of literary style, diction or other marks recognized as evidences of authorship. Furthermore, in order to establish a "line of descent" for this theory, by which its sufficiency and credibility may be established, it is only fair to say that it was first promulgated by a certain E. D. Howe, in his book *Mormonism Unveiled,* in which he enlarges on every possible presumption of "evidence" and allegation that may be urged against the system attacked. In this effort, he presents a lot of affidavits, alleged to have been made by numerous old neighbors, relatives and former associates of Mr. Spaulding, evidently considering them competent to establish the contention that the Book of Mormon was Spaulding's *Manuscript Found,* which had been lost for nearly twenty years. Other anti-Mormon writers have reproduced Howe's documents with sundry additions, and they still form the basis of the popular attacks on Mormonism. The story, as given by the alleged "testimonies" of these numerous witnesses, is as follows:

Sometime in 1834 a Mormon missionary was conducting a meeting at Conneaut, Ohio, the former home of Solomon Spaulding, and, in the course of his exercise, read some portions of the Book of Mormon. As it happened, a brother of Solomon Spaulding, by name John Spaulding, was present, and, according to the story, "recognized perfectly the work of his brother . . . was annoyed and afflicted, that it should have been perverted to so wicked a purpose," and "his grief found vent in a flood of tears." Forthwith, this gentleman, blessed with a singularly retentive memory and keen sensibilities, "arose on the spot and expressed to the meeting his sorrow and regret that the writings of his deceased brother should be used for a purpose so vile and shocking." As a sequel to this dramatic occurrence, as alleged, a meeting of citizens was held, both to voice their indignation and to set right the memory of the late Mr. Spaulding, with the result that a certain Dr. Philastus Hurlburt was deputed to visit the widow of Spaulding, then remarried to a Mr. Davidson, and obtain the "original manuscript" of the book, in order that it might be printed, together with the usual host of affidavits, to prove Solomon Spaulding its true author.

Now, as the reader may note in this account, there are two elements of the exceptional, to say the least: first, that the memories of John Spaulding and other neighbors, could be so retentive as to "recognize perfectly" extracts read to them from a manuscript book over twenty years before, and, second, that they should also remember, with equal perfection, that Mr. Spaulding had made two manuscripts of his book. That Hurlburt actually visited Mrs. Davidson seems to be an admitted fact, but that he was deputed by a mass meeting of indignant citizens is not so clear. He was himself a former believer in Smith's teachings, and, like all apostate Mormons, a victim of monumental bitterness against his former associates and co-religionists. Furthermore, it has been claimed that he was himself the author of *Mormonism Unveiled,* for the production of which he used the name of his printer, E. D. Howe. That he did not obtain the "duplicate" of Spaulding's manuscript, as he expected, seems now to be an established fact, as we shall see later. Nevertheless, the book written by himself, or Howe, asserts with the greatest confidence that such a "duplicate" must have existed, and that Spaulding must have written the Book of Mormon.

The evidence for this confidently-urged contention is embodied in affidavits from numerous people, to the following general effects: John Spaulding testifies that his brother had written "a historical romance of the first settlers of America, and endeavored to show that the American Indians are the descendants of the Jews, or the Ten Lost Tribes." Mrs. John Spaulding is similarly quoted as saying that she had heard her brother-in-law read from his manuscript story in 1810, and that "He was then writing a historical novel founded on the first settlers of America. . . . He had for many years contended that the aborigines of America were the descendants of some of the lost tribes of Israel; and this idea he carried out in the book in question." Mrs. Spaulding then continues:

> "The lapse of time which has intervened prevents my recollecting but few of the leading incidents of his writings; but the names Lehi and Nephi are yet fresh in my memory as being the principal heroes of his tale. They were officers of the company which first came off from Jerusalem. He gave a particular account of their journey by land and by sea, till they arrived in America, after which disputes arose between the chiefs, which caused them to separate into bands, one of which was called Lamanites, the other Nephites. Between these were recounted tremendous battles, which frequently covered the ground with slain and these being buried in large heaps, was the cause of the many mounds in the country. Some of these people he represents as being very large."

To very similar effect is the affidavit attributed to a certain Henry Lake, a "business partner" of Spaulding's:

> "Solomon Spaulding frequently read to me from a manuscript which he was writing, which he entitled the *Manuscript Found,* and which he represented as having found in this town (Conneaut, Ohio). I spent many hours in hearing him read said writings, and became well acquainted with their contents. The book represented the American Indians as being the descendants of the Lost Tribes of Israel, and gave an account of their having left Jerusalem, and of their contentions and wars, which were many and great. I remember telling Mr. Spaulding that so frequent use of the words: 'And it came to pass,' 'Now it came to pass,' rendered the book ridiculous."

Affidavits are also given of persons named Aaron Wright, Oliver Smith, Artemus Cunningham and John N. Miller, who testify that Spaulding had been writing a romance based on the ideas that the inhabitants of America were descended from certain emigrants from Jerusalem. Two of them relate also that they distinctly remembered the names Nephi and Lehi, which seem to be the only ones of all the peculiar Book of Mormon names that are recollected by most of the witnesses quoted. There are others, much more striking and unusual, which might reasonably have been remembered by some of those who had heard the entire book read, if, indeed, it was the Book of Mormon that they heard.

Other friends of Mr. Spaulding are similarly quoted in affidavits, as, for example, a certain Joseph Miller of Amity, Pennsylvania, who is quoted as saying:

> "Some time ago I heard most of the Book of Mormon read. On hearing read the account of the battle between the Amlicites (Alma, Chap. ii), in which the soldiers of one army placed a red mark on their foreheads, to distinguish them from their enemies, it seemed to reproduce in my mind not only the narrative but the very words, as they had been imprinted on my mind by reading Spaulding's manuscript."

Similarly, another friend of Spaulding's, a certain Ruddick McKee of Washington, D. C., states:

> "I have an indistinct recollection of the passage referred to by Mr. Miller, about the Amlicites making a cross with red paint in their foreheads to distinguish them from their enemies in the confusion of battle."

Among the other most highly esteemed "testimonies" are alleged affidavits from Spaulding's daughter Martha, later Mrs. McKinstry. She is made to state:

> "My father read the manuscript I had seen him writing to the neighbors and to a clergyman, a friend of his, who came to visit him. Some of the names he mentioned while reading to the people I have never forgotten. They are as fresh in my memory as though I had heard them but yesterday. They are Mormon, Moroni, Lamanite and Nephi, etc., etc."

Similarly, a certain Abner Johnson of Canton, Ohio, relates as follows:

> "Spaulding frequently read his manuscript to the neighbors and commented on it as he progressed. He wrote it in Bible style. 'And it came to pass' occurred so often that some called him 'Old Come-to-pass.' The names Mormon, Moroni, Nephi, Nephite, Laman, Lamanite, etc., were in it. The closing scene was at Cumorah, where all the righteous were slain."

As will be noticed, there is a "singular unanimity" among these witnesses, which is usually relied upon as complete evidence of their truthfulness. In such a case, however, this very "unanimity" is a distinctly suspicious circumstance. As the reader will notice, several of these alleged affidavits seem to have been prepared by one person, and while most of them reiterate the recollection of the names of Lehi, Nephi, Lamanite, etc., and no others whatever, precisely as if their affirmations had been given in answer to direct questions as to whether such names occurred to their memories, four of them, alleged to have been given by relatives and close friends of Spaulding (to wit, John Spaulding, his wife, Henry Lake and Aaron Wright), state that the aborigines of America were represented by Spaulding as descendants of "some of the Lost Tribes of Israel," "the Ten Lost Tribes," etc., which is a matter utterly foreign to anything taught or expressed in the Book of Mormon, from beginning to end. Such statement, however, forms the substance of a theory of the origin of these people, which is upheld by several writers, notable among them a certain James Adair, a trader among the Indians and observer of their habits, who in 1775 issued his book *History of the American Indians,* basing his theory on alleged resemblances in language, customs, etc., between the Indians and the Jews. It would be difficult indeed to argue that anyone, making such an erroneous statement as this about the contents of a book under discussion, could be credited with a memory of names sufficiently vivid to constitute a complete identification. Several others of these "witnesses," also, testify that Spaulding's professed object was to account for the great mounds and other aboriginal works found in various parts of America. Thus, from several of these "affidavits" we have the following statements:

"They buried their dead in large heaps which caused the mounds so common in this country. Their arts, sciences and civilization were all brought into view, in order to account for all the curious antiquities found in various parts of Northern and Southern America." (John Spaulding); "He told me his object was to account for the fortifications, etc., that were to be found in this country, and said that in time, it would be fully believed by all except learned men and historians." (Aaron Wright); "He said he intended to . . . give an account of their arts, sciences, civilization, laws, and contentions. In this way he would give a satisfactory account of all the old mounds, so common in this country." (Oliver Smith); "In conversation with Solomon Spaulding I expressed my surprise that we had no account of the people once in this country, who erected the old forts, mounds, etc. He told me that he was writing a history of that people." (Nahum Howard).

If, as these and others have alleged, Spaulding wrote a book with the object of accounting for the mounds, forts, etc., to be found in various parts of the United States, as, for example, in Ohio, it is quite certain that some book other than the Book of Mormon, in its present form, at least, is intended by them, or else that the author became so interested in the development of his narrative that this main "object" entirely slipped his attention. No such "object" is in any sense apparent in the Book of Mormon, as may be discovered readily by any investigator.

In another point do the alleged "affidavits" purporting to connect Mr. Spaulding with the Book of Mormon seem to fail of their object. This is in the statement that the "historical portions" of the book are by Spaulding, while the "religious portions" have evidently been added by another hand. Thus we have such alleged statements of old friends of Spaulding to the following effects:

> "I have examined the Book of Mormon and have no hesitation in saying that the historical part of it is principally, if not wholly, taken from the *Manuscript Found*" (Henry Lake); "I have examined the Book of Mormon, and I find in it the writings of Solomon Spaulding from beginning to end, but mixed up with Scripture and other religious matter, which I did not meet in the *Manuscript Found*" (J. N. Miller); "I have read the Book of Mormon and believe it to be the same as Spaulding wrote, except the religious part" (Nahum Howard); "I have examined the Mormon Bible and am fully of the opinion that Solomon Spaulding had written its outlines before leaving Conneaut" (Artemus Cunningham).

One need be suspected of no over-powering partiality for Mormonism, or for Joseph Smith or any of his claims, to insist that such statements as the above are certainly "inspired." It is curious to what lengths of falsehood and downright imbecility people will go in the effort to ruin or discredit, if possible, someone whom they happen to dislike. As if in evidence of the essential unrighteousness of such an attitude, however, we find usually that such persons will over-reach themselves, to the discrediting of their claims. Never has this fact been better exemplified than in the present instance. If, as seems now an established fact, Solomon Spaulding actually wrote a romance of ancient America — several, as some tell us — it is very certain that neither Sidney Rigdon, nor anyone else worked that novel over into an alleged revelation from God, by the addition of a "religious element," not present in Spaulding's story, as these witnesses are made to state. Nor is there any possibility that such a statement can be contradicted, since a mere casual reading of the Book of Mormon will convince any capable editor that the religious portions are as much a part of the whole, as are similar parts and passages in the Old Testament. There is scarcely a page in the entire book that does not contain passages and references of a distinctly and consistently religious character. Indeed, to assume that these are to be omitted to bring the book to the form in which it left the hands of its "author" means to emasculate every episode and to change the story into something so utterly different that even the "old neighbors" and lachrymose relatives of the Rev. Solomon Spaulding must claim as great skill in literary criticism as we are asked to believe was possessed by Sidney Rigdon in the capacity of editor.

As a matter of fact, as seems evident on this analysis of the "testimony" of these various persons, the real facts in the case seem to be that, with the publication of the Book of Mormon, and the disputes and antagonisms that followed it, numerous people in the neighborhood of Conneaut, Ohio, and elsewhere, former friends of Mr. Spaulding, remarked that he had once written a romance of ancient America. It is not improbable, also, that several of them might have suggested that the Book of Mormon was merely this manuscript in print at last. Such a rumor coming to the ears of such men as Hurlburt, who had been dismissed from the Mormon Church, for alleged "immoral conduct," and E. D. Howe, who was, as we are informed, annoyed because his wife and daughter had joined this church, constituted a temptation far too strong to be resisted that the story should be elaborated and given definite shape, as a real weapon for opposing, and, if possible, destroying Mormonism. Thus, although they could find many who could remember Spaulding and his book, they undoubtedly put into their mouths many things that had nothing to do with either the *Manuscript Found,* or the Book of Mormon. Among these, as we have seen, were the allegations relating to the "Lost Ten Tribes." The names, Nephi, Lehi, Mormon, etc., were evidently suggested to these "witnesses," and then "remembered" by them, as seems fairly evident when we consider that these few, and no others, are mentioned by and among the witnesses "testifying." In this matter of names it certainly seems strange that none of these people seem to have remembered that Nephi, whom they recall so distinctly, had a brother called Sam, whose name has attracted the notice and excited the ridicule of such critics as the Rev. Mr. Lamb, and several others professing a knowledge of Hebrew and Biblical names. This "English nickname," as Mr. Lamb calls it, was certainly quite as startling a feature as the phrase "It came to pass."

In addition to all these matters, it is nothing short of absurd to allege that so many people as are quoted on this point could have had a sufficiently distinct recollection of a book that had been read to them at a time twenty or twenty-five years before the giving of their "testimony" to be able positively to identify it, when seen in print. Seeming to realize some such difficulty, one bitter and determined opponent of Mormonism, a certain Rev. C. Braden, resorts to the time-worn "character test," in an attempt to justify the "testimony" of these witnesses. He says:

"Let us view the evidence we have presented, and settle several questions. I. Are the witnesses competent? II. Are they worthy of belief? III. What is established by their testimony? In determining the first and second queries there are several points to be weighed. I. Is the point at issue one that can be settled by testimony? No question is susceptible of clearer proof. The facts to be determined are: I. Did Solomon Spaulding write a certain MS? What were its contents? II. Did they have adequate means of knowing these facts? No witnesses ever had better. Mr. Spaulding was a preacher in poor health and out of employment, the very man who would attract company, and of the highest character and intelligence. There was much excitement and curiosity over certain mounds that had been opened. Spaulding had taken great interest in the matter. He was writing an unusual book concerning this exciting topic. He was very fond of reading his productions to all who would listen to him. All this would secure him a circle of intelligent hearers. The singularity of his theme would cause his hearers to remember what they heard. To such hearers Spaulding read large portions of his MS. III. Were they competent in intelligence? No one can read their testimony and fail to see that they were persons of unusual intelligence — the very class of persons that such a man as Spaulding would attract around him — that would be interested in his theme — the very ones to whom he would read his work — and who would talk with him. IV. Were they persons of good character for truth and veracity? Their character cannot be excelled. Compare them with the gang of loafing, money-hunting knaves and dupes, upon whose testimony the Book of Mormon stands. Their intelligence is infinitely above that gang of ignorant, superstitious, illiterate ignoramuses. . . . Never were witnesses more independent and individual in their testimony. Each tells his story in his own way — is careful to tell no more — is careful where not certain to say so. Had they fabricated their testimony they would have stated more than they did."— *The Braden and Kelley Debate, p.* 65.

In order to exalt still more the character of these witnesses, who, as the chosen friends of "a preacher, in poor health and out of employment," must not be allowed to tarry under any cloud of suspicion, Mr. Braden makes the following sharp antithesis:

"Contrast their evidence with that of the eight witnesses to the Book of Mormon. These witnesses do not testify separately, but sign a statement prepared for them. . . . They testified to what they did not know, and could not know. There is every evidence of collusion and perjury. The three witnesses are worse, for they testify to what an angel told them." [This is undoubtedly a most serious breach of good manners!] "The character of the entire twelve has been impeached. They had every motive to induce them to lie. They had concocted a fraud to make money and lied to carry it out. Our witnesses are absolutely free from all such fatal defects as those that utterly destroy the evidence of the witnesses to the Book of Mormon."— *Ibid.*

While it is highly unnecessary to attempt to blacken the character of "Mr. Braden's witnesses," about whom neither he nor any of the rest of us knows anything more than that some of them probably existed somewhere, and at some period, it is only necessary to reiterate that they were evidently laboring under several serious misapprehensions, as already indicated, and that even their impeccable characters and the friendship of a "preacher, in poor health" can not suffice to guarantee the evidence based on recollections, evidently so faulty in several particulars. As a matter of fact, the phrase, "And it came to pass," is the only element in the collective testimony of these people that possesses any semblance of presumption that they might have heard or read the Book of Mormon previous to its publication. This seems rather meagre evidence upon which to rear the fabric of the Spaulding authorship of this book. Taken with the other things alleged by them, it is worthless.

Allowing, however, that there is any basis in fact or allegation for the Spaulding theory, there is still a difficulty in explaining the process by which this manuscript came into the hands of Joseph Smith, and as to what was the real motive behind the publication of it as a new revelation. There is, to be sure, a theory on the subject, which has been industriously elaborated by numerous anti-Mormon writers, and confidently presented by them as an established fact. It is a "weird tale," however, and, if related as explanation of any matter in which common sense had ever had an opportunity to shape opinions, it would be classed, without hesitation, among the "things that do not happen."

According to the first version of this story, the manuscript of Spaulding's *Manuscript Found* had been left with a Pittsburg printer by the name of Patterson, who, as related, had consented to print it, "as soon as Mr. Spaulding wrote a title page and preface." While waiting for these essential elements of a real book, which seem to have been beyond the ingenuity of this "preacher in poor health," the manuscript was allowed to lie nakedly and accessibly around the office, in such convenient places that an "utterly unscrupulous person," such as Sidney Rigdon, then slightly over twenty years of age, and already filled, seemingly, with high hopes and great ambitions, could easily find, read, become interested in, copy, or purloin it, and thus supply himself with the indispensable and pre-ordained instrument for "setting the whole world by the ears." At first Rigdon was confidently declared to have been an apprentice of Patterson's; later, on disproof of this statement, an apprentice in a neighboring tannery, who spent so much of his employer's time "loafing about Patterson's printery"— there seems to have been a prodigious amount of "loafing", done in the course of founding Mormonism — that there were serious complaints uttered. It is supposed, moreover confidently asserted, that in the course of these "loafing expeditions," Rigdon either copied or stole the priceless manuscript, thus robbing the unfortunate Spaulding of the fruits of his years of toil, and really contributing to his untimely death, at the age of fifty-five. All this shows, of course, the exceptional "heartlessness" and "selfish indifference to human rights" that are at the base of the Mormon movement. It proves too much, however, as do all the "evidences" in this matter; since it is exceptional, to say the least, that an unlettered youth of about twenty years of age should so highly esteem a manuscript story that he would copy or steal and preserve it either for rereading, or on the theory, apparently, that it might be useful — later.

This entire story seems to have been founded on a statement published in the *Boston Recorder* in May, 1839, over the name of Mrs. Davidson (formerly Spaulding's widow), but subsequently traced to a certain Rev. D. R. Austin. It is another example of confident overstatement, quite worthy to rank with the other "affidavits," so familiar in the Mormon "controversy," as may be understood by any candid mind, not blinded by this absurd anti-Mormon prejudice. It is partly as follows:

> "Mr. Spaulding found a friend and acquaintance in the person of Mr. Patterson, who was very much pleased with it (the manuscript), and borrowed it for perusal. He retained it for a long time, and informed Mr. Spaulding that, if he would make out a title page and preface, he would publish it, as it might be a source of profit. This Mr. Spaulding refused to do. Sidney Rigdon, who has figured so largely in the history of the Mormons, was at that time connected with the printing office of Mr. Patterson, as is well known in that region, and, as Rigdon himself had frequently stated, became acquainted with Mr. Spaulding's manuscript and copied it. It was a matter of notoriety and interest to all connected with the printing establishment. At length the manuscript was returned to its author, and soon after he removed to Amity, where Mr. Spaulding died in 1816. The manuscript then fell into my hands, and was carefully preserved."

As is scarcely remarkable, Mrs. Davidson immediately denied having written this "affidavit," and discredited many of its statements. Mr. Rigdon also addressed a letter to this newspaper, denying all knowledge of Spaulding, and stating that there was no printer named Patterson in Pittsburg, during his residence there. He also repeatedly denied the allegations of this story, asserting his firm belief in the "divine authenticity" of the Book of Mormon until the very day of his death. Nevertheless, as with all the persons connected with early Mormon history, Rigdon's alleged activities can be explained only by the theory of a superlatively bad character. He must have been a thief, they say, since the theory demands it; therefore, he must have been a liar also. Of course, a man who could conceive and carry out so preposterous a plot as is ascribed to him could be expected to do or say almost anything. Thus, in the development of the Spaulding manuscript romance, we are faced with the usual line of gossiping affidavits from a horde of utterly unknown, but, as we are assured, entirely impeccable personages, who seem to have had unusually numerous opportunities to spy upon the secretive Sidney, and find out precisely what he was intending to do years before it was ever done. Among such, a certain Rev. John Winter, M.D., is quoted as stating that Rigdon had shown him a manuscript "history of the American Indians" in 1822 or 1823, stating that it had been written by "one Spaulding, a Presbyterian preacher whose health had failed," and that he (Rigdon) "had borrowed it from the printer as a curiosity."

Another alleged affidavit, which is presented by Braden in the above-quoted debate with E. L. Kelley, is even more amusingly absurd, both in its anachronisms and local inconsistencies. Thus a certain James Jeffries, who was, of course, "an old and highly respected citizen" of Churchville, Hartford County, Maryland, is said to have uttered an affidavit in January, 1884, deposing as follows:

> "Forty years ago I was in business in St. Louis. The Mormons then had their temple in Nauvoo, Illinois. I had business transactions with them. I knew Sidney Rigdon. He acted as general manager of the business of the Mormons (with me). Rigdon told me several times in his conversation with me, that there was in the printing office with which he was connected in Ohio, a MS. of the Rev. Spaulding, tracing the origin of the Indians from the lost tribes of Israel. This MS. was in the office for several years. He was familiar with it. Spaulding wanted it published but had not the means to pay for printing. He (Rigdon) and Joe Smith used to look over the MS. and read it on Sundays. Rigdon said Smith took the MS. and said 'I'll print it,' and went off to Palmyra, New York."

In spite of the strong presumption evident in this writing that this "old and highly respected citizen" had, in the course of years, confused his conversations with Rigdon with the numerous reports circulated about him and his doings — thus he transfers the "printing office" from Pittsburg to Ohio — Mr. Braden comments as follows:

> "'Forty years ago' would be in the fall of 1844, just after Rigdon had been driven out of Nauvoo. The *Times and Seasons* assailed him bitterly, that fall and winter, for exposing Mormonism. On his way from Nauvoo to Pittsburg, he called on his old acquaintance, Mr. Jeffries, in St. Louis, and, in his anger at the Mormons, he let out the secrets of Mormonism, just as he told the Mormons he would, if they did not make him their leader."— *B. and K. Debate, p.* 42.

Although it is unnecessary to repeat many of these alleged testimonies, quoted in support of Rigdon's complicity in the assumed purloining and revamping of a manuscript by Solomon Spaulding, it is really astounding to observe the lengths and depths of improbability and absurdity to which the enemies of Mormonism will go, in their effort to uphold a theory which is essentially absurd and inconsistent. Thus, a certain Mrs. A. Dunlap of

Warren, Ohio, as quoted by Braden, "deposeth and saith" that she was a niece of Rigdon, and while visiting at his house:

"That in her presence her uncle went into his bedroom and took from a trunk which he kept carefully locked a manuscript, and came back, seated himself by the fire, and began to read. His wife came into the room and exclaimed: 'What, you are studying that thing again? I mean to burn that paper.' Rigdon replied: 'No indeed you will not. This will be a great thing some day.' When he was reading this manuscript he was so completely occupied that he seemed entirely unconscious of anything around him."—*Ibid. p.* 45.

Of course, no other manuscript than that by Spaulding could possibly interest Mr. Rigdon to the extent described, but the public does not know that, and can hardly be expected to accept it, without competent demonstration. Similarly inconclusive are the testimonies of some of his former associates, clerical and otherwise, among them Alexander Campbell, A. Bently, a certain Z. Rudolph and his brother John, a certain Almon Green, and others, that for several years previous to the publication of the Book of Mormon he had been preaching Millennarianism, Christian communism, and other "advanced ideas," and had even mentioned that primitive pure Christianity should soon be restored. All these matters were then in course of agitation, particularly the "restored primitive Christianity," which was the leading inspiration of the Campbellite sect. The additional fact that certain of these persons "distinctly remember" that Rigdon had also mingled with his teachings on these matters certain remarks about "gold plates" and "ancient records" may be attributed to precisely such a confusion of event and rumor as is seen in the "testimony" of Mr. Jeffries, above quoted, and which is more or less inevitable in all attempts, even of honest persons, to recall happenings and conversations many years in the past. The fact is that merely incidental occurrences and conversations, as they must have seemed at the time, positively cannot be recalled by anyone with complete accuracy, after a long lapse of years. To claim that it has been done by certain persons, because of their "undoubted veracity," is merely to perpetrate still further absurdities, as we have seen already.

Furthermore, as would be expected, we are not without good presumptive evidence that the most ordinary remarks, displaying mere interest in passing questions or issues, have been, in some cases, constructed into all kinds of "complete confessions" of a plot to hoax the public into a vital faith in religion. Thus, as confidently quoted by the same trenchant debater above named, we have the following "testimony" from another person whose word had "never been impeached." This is a certain Darwin

Atwater, said to have resided in Mantua, Ohio, who testifies thus:

> "Sidney Rigdon preached for us when the Mormon defection came on us, and notwithstanding his extraordinary wild freaks, he was held in high repute by many. For a few months before his pretended conversion to Mormonism, it was noted that his wild extravagant propensities had been more marked. That he knew beforehand of the coming of the Book of Mormon is to me certain, from what he had said during the first of his visits to my father's some years before (in 1826). He gave a wonderful description of the mounds and other antiquities found in some parts of America, and said that they must have been made by the aborigines. He said that there was a book to be published containing an account of these things. He spoke of them in his eloquent, enthusiastic style, as being a thing most extraordinary. Though a youth I took him to task for expending so much enthusiasm on such a subject, instead of the things of the Gospel. In all my intercourse with him afterwards he never spoke of the antiquities or of the wonderful book that should give an account of them, till the Book of Mormon was really published. He must have thought that I was not the man to reveal to."—*Ibid. p.* 45.

Very probably the principal difference between this gentleman and the others quoted with such confidence by the Spauldingites is that, as it seems, he had a clearer and better memory of precisely what occurred. However, as was once said of another, and far more famous, gentleman bearing the name of Darwin, he is a "poor logician," as is shown, apparently, by his confident conclusion that Rigdon's enthusiasm about American antiquities revealed his knowledge of the Book of Mormon, previous to its publication. No one interested to reason fairly on the matter would consider such "testimony" competent to prove anything of the kind. Taken in connection with other statements, however, it may be held to suggest strongly that Rigdon was at this period much interested in antiquities, and in speculations on the identity of the people whose existence they evidence. Any such interest argues no knowledge of Mr. Spaulding or his ultra-famous manuscript, since the subject was then, as now, a live one, and had been discussed by numerous writers. It is not impossible, also, that, following the lead of Adair, and several others before and after his day, he inclined to the belief that the Indians were actually the descendants of Jewish ancestors, the "Ten Lost Tribes," for example. Any such interest would move him to give the reported immediate attention to the Book of Mormon, when presented to him, as recorded, by Parley P. Pratt. Nor would his conversion be at all improbable under these very conditions. However, his mention of a "book to be published containing an account of these things" is no very evident reference to the Book of Mormon, which contains no such account, except in the most general and incidental fashion.

The assumption that Rigdon, like many other intelligent men of his section at the time, was interested in the antiquities, so common around them, and in the fashion prevalent in the early years of the nineteenth century, explains perfectly his reported conversation with Alexander Campbell and A. Bently, his brother-in-law. As given by the gentleman quoted above, this "testimony" is to the following effect:

> "The conversation alluded to in Brother Bently's letter [Millenial Harbinger, 1844, p. 39] was in my presence, as well as his. My recollection of it led me, some two or three years ago, to interrogate Bro. Bently concerning his recollections of it. They accorded with mine in every particular, except in regard to the year in which it occurred. He placed it in the summer of 1827. I placed it in the summer of 1826. Rigdon, at the same time, observed that on the plates dug up in New York, there was an account, not only of the aborigines of this continent, but it was stated also that the Christian religion had been preached, during the first century, just as we were then preaching it on the Western Reserve."—*Ibid. p.* 45.

Even if we admit, however, that Rigdon's knowledge of the Spaulding manuscript is established, and that he may have edited it into the form now known as the Book of Mormon, the difficulties are by no means exhausted. The method of publication alleged to have been adopted by him is about as idiotic and preposterous as could be imagined by a sane man. Nor is there the slightest intelligible reason for supposing that any such line of conduct was followed; nor would any intelligent person think of crediting the "evidence" upon which it is based, were it not for the popular sentiment that "it must be true; therefore is true."

Briefly stated, the situation is about as follows: Mr. Rigdon, an ambitious, impetuous, irascible, and, otherwise violent man, filled with high thoughts and big ambitions, a subject of enthusiasms, as suggested by the remarks of sundry friends, as quoted above, becomes possessed by some means, fair or foul, of a manuscript purporting to deal with the history of pre-Columbian America, and asserting that the aborigines of this continent are descendants of the Hebrew race. To this manuscript he adds certain "religious matter," with the intention of eventually foisting it upon the public as an inspired record. With such a man as Rigdon is represented to have been, previous to his identification with the Mormon Church, there is no just reason for assuming that his alleged intention of publishing any such book as the one in question was other than to give currency to the teachings embodied in it. If he was really its editor and reviser, it is perfectly evident that he conceived and executed the "religious portions" with a very fair show of conviction as to their sufficient truth. Had his intention been merely "to make money," he could not have been ignorant of the fact that the ordinary methods of publication provide far better promise of good profits than any such eccentric and unprecedented scheme as he is supposed to have adopted. Evidently his enemies are not satisfied with making him out a scoundrel: they must also prove him to have been a fool. The theory that Rigdon, in his feverish desire to "get the book published somehow," turned the precious manuscript over to an unknown and unlettered youth of bad reputation, as alleged, who resided in a back-woods hamlet some two hundred miles away from his own home, and allowed him to print and publish it with credit as "author and proprietor," is precisely the sort of thing that would be labeled "ridiculous," if proposed as explanation in any other connection whatsoever.

The situation is ably expressed in the words of Prof. Nelson, as above quoted. In commenting on the lame and prejudiced theory advanced by William A. Linn, in his attempted revamping of the Spaulding hypothesis, he writes:

"Mr. Rigdon must, moreover, be supplied with a motive for stealing it [the Spaulding manuscript]: This motive Mr. Linn finds in a deep-laid plot by Rigdon to start a new religion, in order to get revenge on the 'Campbells,' who got all the glory for founding the Disciple or Campbellite Church — a glory which Rigdon should have shared.

"Rigdon must next have been attracted — somehow — to Joseph Smith as the very man to become the prophet of the new dispensation. Accordingly he makes Rigdon prepare the copy of the Book of Mormon by injecting into the 'other' Spaulding's manuscript [there are supposed to have been several, as will be explained later] the religious dogmas of the Campbellites, and then makes him take it by installments to Joseph Smith; who, hid behind a screen, dictates it to a scribe, quite according to the verified account of its coming forth. Rigdon thereby becomes the 'mysterious visitor,' seen entering and leaving Joseph's house occasionally, in the early accounts by the Prophet's neighbors.

"But now come two difficulties. The first is that Rigdon, whose motive for theft and forgery was to get even with the Campbells for robbing him of glory, consents nevertheless to play second fiddle to Joseph Smith and to be 'snubbed and ill-treated' by the very tool of his successful villainy. Mr. Linn sees in the latter fact some deep mysterious power which the younger man exercised over the older,— quite in the dime-novel fashion. The other difficulty is the very consistent, logical, undeviating account by Joseph Smith of each successive event in the coming forth of the Book of Mormon. But this narrative, Mr. Linn points out, was not written till 1838, ten years after the translation of the Book of Mormon, and seven years after Sidney Rigdon joined the Church — time enough for the arch-plotter Rigdon to make the invention smooth and plausible!"— *The Mormon Point of View, pp.* 160–162.

Although, as would be amply acknowledged in any other connection, there is not even "circumstantial evidence" that Rigdon ever saw or read any manuscript book of Solomon Spaulding, much less purloined such — even if possessed of prophetic foresight of his "row" with the Campbells twelve or fourteen years later — for he must have stolen the manuscript previous to 1816, if at all — there is no reason whatever for assuming that he ever saw or heard of Joseph Smith, previous to the publication of the Book of Mormon and the organization of the Mormon Church. We have only gossiping and evidently "inspired" statements of utterly unknown people for assuming the main acts alleged in either case. If he really stole this famous screed, how did he happen to do it, and why? If he turned it over to Joseph Smith for publication and exploitation, how did he happen to do it, and why? If he had happened to have approached Prof. Anthon, for example, with a proposition to "go into the scheme," and been "indignantly repulsed," it might have been said that he had "aimed too high," but when he chooses as his confederate a man whose conditions of life would scarcely have marked him as a "likely" accomplice, he seems to have come dangerously near to risking the safety of his entire alleged project. To be sure, it has been stated by various ingenious persons that Parley P. Pratt, an early friend of Rigdon's and the agent of his conversion to Mormonism, according to accepted accounts, had made the acquaintance of Smith, during some of his wanderings over New York state, and had mentioned him to the "arch-conspirator" as a possible accomplice. This solution of the "difficulty" may be correct, although there is not a shred of proof to support it, but the question naturally occurs as to why, supposing that Pratt was entirely in Rigdon's confidence, he did not himself essay the rôle of "prophet." His personality and educational equipment were certainly competent to the task, and his subsequent services to Mormonism, ending in his murder — this was in "revenge" for a crime of which a jury had already acquitted him — suggest that, if "in the plot," he would have carried out the character to the end.

However, because, by the Spaulding theory, Rigdon, Smith, Pratt, and all their associates, must be made out a gang of criminal lunatics, not to say imbeciles, Rigdon is represented as doing everything precisely contrary to reason and common sense. Thus, in the carrying-out of his absurd plot, he is represented as having exposed himself repeatedly to the spying eyes of neighborhood gossips, all of whom, so it seems, were perfectly familiar with his appearance, name and reputation. His indiscretion in this particular is embalmed in another series of "affidavits," which profess to identify him with a certain "mysterious stranger" often seen around Smith's residence — although in this instance, at least, these deponents fail to specify the "loafing," characteristic, apparently, of all of Smith's other associates. Thus, as though no one living in a country town can be allowed to have visitors unknown to his idle-minded neighbors, anti-Mormon writers habitually insult the intelligence of the public by serving up a line of alleged affidavits, embodying nothing whatever but vile and gratuitous rural gossip. Nor is this to be said because one objects to considering real evidence against Mormonism, Smith, Rigdon, or anything or any person whatsoever, beside, but because the usual line of anti-Mormon accusation involves such nonsense, lies, slanders, and downright indecency, that, without the popular prejudice against this Church and people, one naturally concludes that we have to deal with simple "false witness," and nothing else. Thus, we may quote passages from one of the most abusive of anti-Mormon books:

> "A mysterious stranger now appears at Smith's residence and holds private interviews with the far-famed money-digger. For a considerable length of time no intimation of the name or purpose of this personage transpired to the public, nor even to Smith's nearest neighbors. It was observed by some of them that his visits were frequently repeated. The sequel of these private interviews between the stranger and the money-digger will sufficiently appear hereafter. . . . The reappearance of the mysterious stranger at Smith's was again the subject of inquiry and conjecture by observers, from whom was withheld all explanation of his identity or purpose. . . . Up to this time Sidney Rigdon had played his part in the background, and his occasional visits at Smith's residence had been noticed by uninitiated observers as those of the mysterious stranger. It had been his policy to remain in concealment until all things should be in readiness for blowing the trumpet of the new gospel."—*Pomeroy Tucker (The Origin, Rise and Progress of Mormonism), pp.* 28, 46, 75–76.

The allegations included in these passages make a very "good story," but it is not so certain that they are worthy the consideration that has been accorded them hitherto. The Smith family may have entertained a "mysterious stranger" at frequent intervals — indeed, for all that can be said to the contrary, dozens of "mysterious strangers"— and they may have declined to gratify the vulgar curiosity of their neighbors, who inquired as to his identity. It is unnecessary, however, to make their refusal of this request appear as contumacy, in declining to answer "perfectly reasonable questions." Nevertheless, the public is still assured that the acquaintance between Smith and Rigdon, previous to the appearance of the Book of Mormon, is an established fact of history. Upon such "testimonies" as the following, however, is this contention presumably established. Thus, as quoted by Braden and others, we learn that a certain Mrs. Eaton, "wife of Horace Eaton, D.D., for thirty-two years a resident of Palmyra," deposed as follows:

> "Early in the summer of 1827 a mysterious stranger seeks admission to Joe Smith's cabin. The conferences of the two are most private. This person whose coming immediately preceded a new departure in

the faith was Sidney Rigdon, a backslidden clergyman, then a Campbellite preacher in Mentor, Ohio."

Whether or not, as the wording of this document might suggest, the calling of a "Campbellite preacher" is a suitable occupation for a "backslidden clergyman," it seems fairly evident that her husband's degree of D.D. so far establishes the presumption of this lady's veracity that no one has ever considered it necessary to ask how it was that she knew this "mysterious stranger" to have been Sidney Rigdon, any more than how she knew that "this person" held "most private" conferences with Smith. There is altogether too much of the atmosphere of gossip about this statement to allow it any evidential value. Nor was Sidney Rigdon in any sense so striking a man in appearance that he could readily be picked out of a crowd, and identified as the very "mysterious stranger," about whose identity all the neighborhood gossips about Palmyra had been worrying their brains for several years. Rigdon was, if his portrait correctly represents him, a rather "ordinary-looking" person, who wore the familiar chin and cheek whiskers, with the lip shaven, as was the popular style among Americans during the early and middle decades of the nineteenth century. In default of information as to the way in which Rigdon was finally identified with Smith's visitor, we have no reason beyond this lady's advertised reputation for honesty and probity, to convince us that she was not mistaken. Certainly this is not evidence, either on Mormon matters, or anything beside.

But Smith's old neighbors come forward as confidently in this Rigdon matter, as in revealing his bad and depraved character, as already mentioned. Thus a certain Abel Chase is quoted as saying: "I saw Rigdon at Smith's at different times with considerable intervals between them"; and a certain Lorenzo Saunders assures us that, "I saw Rigdon at Smith's several times, and the first visit was more than two years before the Book (of Mormon) appeared." There are a few others of similar import, but none of them rise to the dignity of conclusive evidence to any candid mind, in the simple fact that they fail to give information as to how Rigdon was identified.

If, however, such "testimonies" as these suffice to establish a presumption in favor of the Spaulding romance, it is not improper to adduce testimony, which is, at least, as conclusive on the other side of the "controversy." As given by Prof. Nelson, as quoted above, we have the following, which can doubtless be investigated, even at the present day, and, if possible, discredited:

"As final disproof of Rigdon's authorship of the Book of Mormon, I present herewith passages from a manuscript *Life of Sidney*

Rigdon, written by his son, John W. Rigdon, and quoted by Roberts in his new History of the Church. The reader should first be informed that Rigdon, failing in his ambition to be President of the Church after the Prophet's death, withdrew from the body of the Saints on their exodus to the Rocky Mountains, tried to build up the church anew in Pittsburg, and, failing, retired to Friendship, Alleghany County, New York, where he died in 1876.

"John W. Rigdon visited Utah in 1863 with a view to studying Mormonism. He was not favorably impressed, and among other things, came to the conclusion that the Book of Mormon itself was a fraud. Accordingly, he determined, on returning home, to sift thoroughly his father's alleged part in getting it up.

"'You have been charged with writing that book and giving it to Joseph Smith to introduce to the world. You have always told me one story. . . . Is this true? If so, all right, if not, you owe it to me and to your family to tell it. You are an old man and will soon pass away, and I wish to know if Joseph Smith in your intimacy with him for fourteen years, has not said something to you to lead you to believe that, he obtained that book in some other way than what he had told you. . . . My father looked at me a moment, raised his hand above his head and slowly said, with tears glistening in his eyes: 'My son, I can swear before high heaven, that what I have told you about the origin of that book is true. Your mother and sister, Mrs. Athalia Robinson, were present when that book was handed to me in Mentor, Ohio, and all I ever knew about that book was what Parley P. Pratt, Oliver Cowdery, Joseph Smith and the witnesses told me; and in all my intimacy with Joseph Smith, he never told me but the one story . . . and I have never, to you or to any one else, told but the one story, and that I repeat to you.' I believed him, and still believe he told me the truth.'

"Mr. Rigdon also gives testimony from his mother, just previous to her death, corroborating that of his father, and an affidavit of his sister, Mrs. Athalia Robinson, who was ten years old at the time Rigdon joined the Church, and who testifies to the visit of the elders and of Parley P. Pratt's handing her father a copy of the Book of Mormon, saying it was a revelation from God. There seems to be really no grounds whatever for connecting Rigdon with the Book of Mormon, save the desperate need of anti-Mormons to account for it somehow in consonance with a fixed notion that Mormonism is a false religion. Needless to say, they are doomed to failure by the Rigdon hypothesis. In the meanwhile, the Book of Mormon is still here, and the field is open for new romancers to try their hand."—*The Mormon Point of View, pp.* 183–185.

Certain Spauldingite theorists, realizing evidently the weakness of the arguments for Rigdon's complicity in the production of the Book of Mormon, have qualified their statements of the theory by admitting that "some other scoundrel" might have acted as editor, instead of this "backslidden clergyman." Their cause now demands the identification of an "original author," rather than a mere editor or reviser, since, by the recovery of the original autograph copy of Spaulding's *Manuscript Found,* the only book that he is known to have written, the Spaulding authorship of the Book of Mormon is effectually disproved to any competent literary critic or judge of characteristics of style. The evident weakness and inconclusiveness, also, of the several alleged "affidavits" given by Howe and others, which, as any intelligent reader can see, describe the Book of Mormon only very imperfectly, if at all, early gave rise to the theory that Spaulding had written several distinct romances of ancient America, two of which, at least — the Nephite and the Jaredite "portions"— had been combined by some editor as integral parts of the Book. This theory served a double use; accounting at once for the deficiencies of the Howe affidavits, which, as acknowledged by the critics, "refer only to the Nephite portion"— we may allow them the use of this comforting supposition — and also for the fact that the manuscript obtained by Hurlburt from Mrs. Davidson's trunk, as related, bore no resemblance to the Book of Mormon, and was useless for the purpose to which they had hoped to apply it. But, with the formulation of the theory of several manuscripts, new depths of "infamy," "rascality," and imbecility are discovered and explored. Never, in the whole history of literature, had such crimes been committed, and such absurdities perpetrated — or alleged. Thus, the Rev. C. Braden, although a person of "iron conviction" and an abusive debater, evidently regarding his opponents with lofty disdain, does not hesitate to use such a line of argument as the following, as a bolster for his contentions:

"In their conferences Imposter Joe told Rigdon of the existence of the other Spaulding manuscripts, then at Hardwicke, New York, in the house of Mrs. Davidson, formerly Spaulding's wife and widow. [Evidently some of Smith's inquiring and veracious neighbors also owned 'peepstones' or had learned the secrets of wireless telephone 'out of due time,' thus enabling them to overhear and report on conferences held in a manner 'most private.'] The two concocted a scheme to steal them and thus destroy all likelihood of detection of the theft of the Spaulding manuscript, and exposure of the fraud. Smith was loafing at Hardwicke, in the summer and early fall of 1827, superintending a gang of men, who were trying to find a silver mine, on the farm of Mr. Stowell. He dug some wells in the town also, one for Stowell. September 21–22, 1827, Smith succeeded in stealing some of the Mormon manuscripts of Solomon Spaulding, perhaps Mormon manuscript No. 1, the one Miss Martha Spaulding had read a few years before at her uncle's when the trunk was in her care, and the first one Spaulding wrote, the one he read to most of the witnesses who lived in Conneaut, also Mormon manuscript No. 2, the one he told Smith he was writing before he left Conneaut, the one of which he read a portion to J. N. Miller — the one to which he added the Zarahemla portion. The theft of the manuscripts is the true interpretation of Smith's wonderful visions of September 21–22, 1827. Smith's neighbors say that he never mentioned his visions of 1820 and 1823 while in the state of New York, and his visions of September 1827, as first told, have no resemblance to his final version. He dressed up his hearing of the existence of the Spaulding manuscripts into his second vision of September, 1823."—*Braden and Kelley Debate, p.* 55.

It would be highly unnecessary to quote such utterly unsupported nonsense as this, were it not for the fact that the story of Smith's supposed theft of these suppositious manuscripts has been mentioned by other anti-Mormon writers with similar confidence and elaboration. But there is not even a gossiping "affidavit" to uphold it. Nor does it explain why, with so favorable an opportunity, Smith did not steal all of Spaulding's remaining manuscripts, and thus effectually forestall all possibility of "detection" to the end of time. This could not be, however, since Hurlburt is reported to have obtained at least one other, which he is acknowledged to have given to Howe, who retained it, in spite of Mrs. Davidson's repeated requests for its return. But anti-Mormonism has learned many new "tricks" in course of "unraveling" the tortuous plottings and "loafings" of Smith, Rigdon, and others, and is fully equal to the emergency. Thus it is that Mr. Braden is able to out-Rigdon even Rigdon himself, and expose the full villainy of the plot. The following will show the depth of downright absurdity sounded by some of these people:

"There can be no doubt that he [Spaulding] wrote it for the sole purpose of publishing it, and that he expected to make money by publishing it. There is nothing wrong about this. But that his motives, he knew, were some of them wrong, is evident from the fact that he kept them from his wife and daughter [very evident], and also lied to them in regard to his object in writing the manuscript. Some of his expressions show that his motives were very questionable. He intended to assert that his book was copied from a manuscript dug out of the earth, or found in a cave. He expected to deceive the world except the learned few, and cause them to believe this falsehood that he intended to palm off on them; and also to induce all, but the learned few, to believe his book to be veritable history as much so as any history. So he declared to Miller of Conneaut, Wright, Cunningham and others. No wonder he concealed his purpose from his wife and daughter. Howe says on page 289 of his history, that he has a letter in his possession that proves that Spaulding was sceptical in his last days. If so we can understand his caricaturing the Bible in the way he did, in his romance. . . .

"Mrs. Davidson declares that Hurlburt wrote to her from Hardwicke that he found the manuscript and would return it to her when through with it. He came to Howe with a lie and told him he only found a portion of an entirely different manuscript. He sold the manuscript to Rigdon and Smith, took the money and went to Western Ohio and bought a farm, and Mrs. Davidson and her daughter, Mrs. McKinstry, could never get a word of reply from him, although they sent several letters to parties who wrote; they gave the letters to Hurlburt. This answers the Mormon "Why did they not publish the Spaulding 'Manuscript Found'?" Because Mormons had gotten it into their possession by bribing Hurlburt."—*Ibid. pp.* 64–65.

It is interesting to note that neither Braden nor any other writer of his "school" has ever attempted to offer justification for the assertions here made, although they have been variously repeated. That Hurlburt might have been "bribed," as suggested, is not impossible, but the question is, where did he get the manuscript which he sold to "Rigdon and Smith"? Why had Smith not stolen it on his alleged "loafing" descent upon Hardwicke? The testimony of Mrs. Martha McKinstry, Spaulding's daughter, has already been quoted to the effect that she knew of a manuscript by her father "about one inch thick." This one Howe received, as will be shown later. How thick was the manuscript sold by Hurlburt? In spite of these difficulties, Mr. Braden sums the "facts established," as he alleges, under twenty-three heads of features peculiar only to the Book of Mormon and the *Manuscript Found*. They are as follows:

"I. The plot and matter of Spaulding's 'Manuscript Found.' They (the affidaviting 'witnesses') describe it clearly and definitely. It is precisely the plot and matter of two books and only two of all books that have ever been written. (This assertion is made in spite of the definite mention by several of these witnesses of the 'Lost ten tribes of Israel,' which is a feature utterly foreign to anything expressed or suggested in the Book of Mormon.)

"II. That it purported to be a real truthful history of the aborigines — the first settlers of America.

"III. An attempt to account for the antiquities of America by giving a real history of their construction.

"IV. It assumed that the Israelites were the aborigines of America.

"V. That they left Jerusalem.

"VI. Journeyed by land and by sea.

"VII. Their leaders were Nephi and Lehi.

"VIII. They quarrelled and divided into two parties called Nephites and Lamanites.

"IX. There were terrible wars between the Nephites and Lamanites, and between the parties into which these nations divided.

"X. They buried their dead after the awful slaughter in their wars, which were unprecedented, in great heaps, which caused the mounds.

"XI. The end of their wars in two instances was the total annihilation in battle of all but one, who escaped to make the record of the catastrophe.

"XII. It gives a historical account of the civilization, arts, sciences, laws and customs of the aborigines of America.

"XIII. These people were the ancestors of our American Indians.

"XIV. The names, Lehi, Nephi, Lamanite, Nephite, Moroni, Mormon, Zarahemla, Laban.

"XV. These in every instance are the names of the same persons or places or things, and have the same characteristics and history, etc.

"XVI. Written in Scriptural style.

"XVII. Absurd repetition of 'And it came to pass,' 'And now it came to pass.'

"XVIII. One party left Jerusalem to escape judgments about to overtake the Israelites.

"XIX. History was written and buried by one of the lost people.

"XX. The book was obtained from the earth.

"XXI. One party of emigrants landed near the Isthmus of Darien, which they called Zarahemla, and migrated across the continent in a northeast direction.

"XXII. In a battle the Amlicites marked their foreheads with a red cross, so that they could distinguish themselves (one another?) from their enemies.

"XXIII. The book could be used as an addition to the Bible by an imposter, as an addition coming from America."—*Ibid. pp.* 65–66.

As we have already read several of the most definite "affidavits" upon which these large claims are founded, and have discussed the probability of so many people "distinctly remembering" such names and incidents after twenty years, and more, it is necessary only to add, therefore, that these twenty-three statements, so confidently given, have positively not been established by the "testimonies" quoted by Mr. Braden, or by any others. The mention of the "Ten Lost Tribes" and of a book written to "account for" the mounds, and other American antiquities, should go very far toward discrediting the "testimonies" offered by Howe and others, in the minds of any persons who have read the Book of Mormon.

The Braden and Kelley debate was held in Kirtland, Ohio, during the four weeks between February 12th and March 8th, 1884. All that was said, therefore, about the Spaulding manuscript or its alleged contents was anterior to the recovery of the manuscript book, bearing the title *Manuscript Found,* and in the handwriting of Solomon Spaulding, which occurred later in the same year. This incident may be described in the words of President James H. Fairchild of Oberlin College, as follows:

"The theory of the origin of the Book of Mormon in the traditional manuscript of Solomon Spaulding will probably have to be relinquished. The manuscript is doubtless now in the possession of Mr. L. L. Rice, of Honolulu, Hawaiian Islands, formerly an anti-slavery editor in Ohio, and for many years state printer at Columbus. During a recent visit to Honolulu, I suggested to Mr. Rice that he might have some valuable anti-slavery documents in his possession, which he might be willing to contribute to the rich collection already in the Oberlin College library. In pursuance of this suggestion Mr. Rice began looking over his old pamphlets and papers, and at length came upon an old, worn, and faded manuscript of about 175 pages, small quarto, purporting to be a history of the migrations and conflicts of the ancient Indian tribes which occupied the territory now belonging to the states of New York, Ohio, and Kentucky. On the last page of his manuscript is a certificate and signature giving the names of several persons known to the signer, who have assured him that, to their personal knowledge, the manuscript was the writing of Solomon Spaulding. Mr. Rice has no recollection of how or when this manuscript came into his possession. It was enveloped in a coarse piece of wrapping paper and endorsed in Mr. Rice's handwriting 'A Manuscript Story.' . . . It is unlikely that anyone who wrote so elaborate a work as the Mormon Bible would spend his time getting up so shallow a story as this. There seems no reason to doubt that this is the long-lost story. Mr. Rice, myself, and others compared it with the Book of Mormon, and could detect no resemblance between the two, in general or in detail. There seems to be no name or incident common to the two."—*Bibliotheca Sacra, Jan.* 1885.

That the manuscript is thoroughly identified as the famous *Manuscript Found* of Solomon Spaulding seems assured. On the fly-leaf is written the title, *The Manuscript Found,* and below it, as a sort of sub-title *Manuscript Story.* On the last page of the manuscript is an endorsement in the handwriting of Hurlburt, as follows:

"The writings of Sollomon Spaulding proved by Aaron Wright Oliver Smith John Miller and others The testimonies of the above Gentlemen are now in my possession D. P. Hurlburt."

Commenting on this fact, Prof. Nelson remarks:

"The reader will call to mind that Hurlburt (alias Howe) prints affidavits . . . representing two of these men, John Miller and Aaron Wright, as saying that they immediately recognized Spaulding's story in the Book of Mormon by the similarity of names, and the recurrence of the phrase. 'It came to pass.' Wright is represented as exclaiming: 'Old "come to pass" has come to life again!' Yet here is Hurlburt's certificate of the fact that these men were acquainted with the real manuscript (that is to say the one found by Mr. Rice), in which none of these expressions occur at all. . . . Nevertheless . . . Mr. Linn proceeds to build up his hypothesis of another manuscript, and of Rigdon's theft and forgery; bolstering it by the affidavits of such men as John N. Miller and Aaron Wright, above quoted—men who are demonstrated to have sworn to lies. Linn's subterfuge is, however, unworthy of credence for following reasons: (1) Spaulding never claimed anywhere or to anyone to have written more than one story about ancient America. (2) His wife refers constantly to only one—the 'Manuscript Found.' (3) His daughter, whose testimony has already been quoted, mentions no other, though she often went through his papers in the old trunk and handled this manuscript, which, she says, 'was about an inch thick and closely written.' (4) Hurlburt got permission to open this trunk, and found but one story—'The Manuscript Found'—which he turned over to E. D. Howe."—*The Mormon Point of View, pp.* 100, 164–165.

In addition to the facts mentioned by Nelson, it is significant to notice that none of the Howe "affidavits," which are supposed to have been freely given by the "deponents," and in their own words, mention that there was a manuscript by Spaulding having the character of the one discovered in Honolulu. While it may be answered that it was unnecessary that any of them should mention it, it remans true, nevertheless, that a confusion between some of the incidents of this story, and of the other one, which they are represented as stating that they had heard read, must have occurred in the minds of some of them, if there really were two manuscripts. That they should have remembered this one more vividly than the other, which they are made to state that he wrote, seems reasonable, in view of the fact that it possesses a distinct "local color," as representing that the parchment manuscript containing the narration was found near Conneaut Creek. We might reasonably have expected that either Wright, Miller, or Oliver Smith, who, by Hurlburt's attestation, as already seen, had identified the Honolulu-Oberlin manuscript as Spaulding's writing, would state definitely that it was not the one referred to. They do not appear to have done anything of the kind.

In comparing the *Manuscript Found* with the Book of Mormon, the sole task before the critic is to determine whether or not the same author can be assumed to have written both; for it is evident, even on a most casual reading, that the latter book positively is in no sense whatever an elaboration of the former. Nor is it necessary to make too severe a criticism of this established production of Mr. Spaulding, although, in the opinion of President Fairchild, as quoted above, it is justly said that, "It is unlikely that anyone who wrote so elaborate a work as the Mormon Bible would spend his time getting up so shallow a story as this." Spaulding's manuscript shows nothing more clearly than the work of a confirmed amateur in literature. Although, as must be admitted, the author had undoubted talents as a story teller, and some elements of good imagination, he is evidently "working at another man's trade," and has succeeded in producing a composition singularly free from real literary merit. His episodes are of the simplest order, and his descriptions, either defective or overdrawn. Thus, while his plot is one susceptible of great developments, if attempted by such a writer as H. Rider Haggard, for example, he seems utterly incapable of producing anything but the most commonplace situations. His dialogues, orations — if they can be so called — and remarks show no talent for elaboration, nor are his characters at all interesting.

In all these particulars, the Book of Mormon is the direct antithesis of Spaulding's story; being a very elaborate work, abounding in situations, some of which are well worthy to be called "dramatic" in the best sense, and supported by well-conceived narrations, dialogues and several orations showing both profound thought and real human interest. Whatever may have been its origin, it is certainly not to be compared with the only proved production of Mr. Spaulding. No competent critic would decide that the two had been written by one hand. On the basis of far smaller "variations" of style do our "higher critics" conclude that the books of the Bible are "composite productions," and cut them up into "documents," supposed to have been written by various hands. In another point, also, do these two books differ radically, and this is in the fact that they represent wholly different classes of composition. Spaulding's story is a simple narrative of travel and adventure, and a rather feeble one at that: the Book of Mormon professes to be an historical record, and carries out its character consistently throughout, as is shown in the "year-by-year" accounts in the Book of Helamon. Thus, whether or not we can agree with Prof. Nelson that this story "is no more like the Book of Mormon than the coarse yarns of a horse-jockey resemble the Sermon on the Mount," (p. 100), it is highly probable that if the labor and energy evidently necessary to produce so elaborate a work as the Book of Mormon had been expended on it, we might have had a story worth reading. Nor is it likely, assuming the Spaulding authorship of the Book of Mormon, that it was the book "heard read repeatedly," as is testified in effect of Spaulding's story, by any persons, "friends" or otherwise, unless they believed it to be a sacred record, or unless they were suitably remunerated for their time. Like all narratives in historic form, the Old Testament books among them, the source of interest is in what they are believed to involve, rather than in their immediate interest as literature. Thus:

> "Men who never read the Book of Mormon tell us that it was a novel, that a book received by hundreds of thousands as God's word was originally written as a romance, and yet not one of them reading it as a romance would ever read it half through. I should as soon expect to see Swedenborg's works published in serial form to compete for fame with the *Haut-Boy's Revenge.—Utah and its People by a Gentile (D. D. Lum)*.

Apart from the evident wide differences of style between the two books, which, in any other connection, would be held to establish diversity of authorship, there is reasonably good presumption that the *Manuscript Found* was Spaulding's sole literary effort. (1) It was evidently written at some period between 1809 and 1814, since in the former year he is said to have come to Conneaut, Ohio, in whose neighborhood the parchment manuscript, in "an elegant hand with Roman Letters and in the Latin Language," is supposed to have been found. (2) It may be held to have been, for this reason, the manuscript read to some of Spaulding's neighbors, as related, about 1810. (3) It accords with their descriptions to the extent of giving "an account of their (the aborigines') arts, sciences, civilization, laws and contentions," since six of its fourteen chapters (5, 6, 7, 8, 9, 10) go into these very matters at great length. (4) It is of convenient size to be read repeatedly to complacent neighbors, as testified, containing only 175 pages of "foolscap" paper, and being "about one inch thick."

If it is not Spaulding's only manuscript story, it is certainly his first, as may be judged from the evident crudities of its style. The author of this story is not a trained writer, nor even one of experience in producing "copy." But, if this work was produced after 1809, when Spaulding was 48 years of age, there is very small chance that his talents so improved in the remaining seven years of his life that he would have developed ability to produce so highly elaborated a work as the Book of Mormon. His first book shows no traces of such talents, and it was rather late in life to develop them; also, there was very little time left to him. He must have worked night and day. Small wonder he "failed in business," also that he died at the comparatively early age of fifty-five!

Another fact may be urged as strong presumptive evidence that Spaulding did not write the Book of Mormon. This is that, instead of being, as Braden supposes, "a preacher, in poor health and out of employment," he turns out to be a rank "unbeliever." As if his *Manuscript Found* were his sole literary output, he files with it a statement of belief, as published copies show, in which he definitely renounces Christianity. In it he says of the Christian religion:

> "It is in my view a mass of contradictions and an heterogeneous mixture of wisdom and folly — nor can I find any clear and incontrovertible evidence of its being a revelation from an infinite, benevolent and wise God. . . . I disavow any belief in the divinity of the Bible and consider it a mere human production designed to enrich and aggrandize its authors and to enable them to manage the multitude."

To be sure, there have been several men who have essayed to write books as "substitutes for the Bible," but judging from the temper of the "infidels" of Spaulding's time, and from his own state of mind, as revealed in this wholly irrelevant renunciation of his formerly professed beliefs — and he is usually mentioned as the "Reverend Mr. Spaulding"— he would undoubtedly have attempted no such "substitute" as the Book of Mormon, which is replete with piety of the most unmistakable description from start to finish. Also, as any capable critic can see, this element was positively not "added" by any reviser whatsoever, unless wc allow that he might have amplified a few of the longer discourses and orations which are found in every section of the Book. We may, therefore, dismiss the Spaulding hypothesis with the traditional Scotch verdict, "not proven."

CHAPTER XXVIII

WAS THE BOOK OF MORMON PRODUCED BY "AUTOMATIC WRITING"?

A LATER theory of the origin of the Book of Mormon holds that it was an original production of Joseph Smith, howbeit transcribed by what is known to psychological theorists as "automatic writing." It would be scarcely worth the while of any investigator of the subject to give this theory more than a passing notice, were it not for the fact that it has received the attention and endorsement of numerous persons, who, while devoid of psychological or scientific knowledge of any particular variety, still have the ear of the public, and can form opinion. The theory was first promulgated by the same Mr. Riley, who, as previously noted, also advanced the theory that Smith's recorded visions are to be explained as some kind of "ophthalmic migraines" or "visual aura of epilepsy," although himself innocent of any exhaustive or clinical knowledge of the varieties of the affliction on which he writes so confidently. It is needless to say, that, if Mr. Riley's "proofs" are to be accepted as evidence that Smith originated the Book of Mormon, there is no reason for invoking the rare and doubtful phase of "automatic writing." Because, however, he was at work upon a thesis to explain Smith's performances on psychological grounds, he must needs invoke epilepsy to explain visions and experiences, which any "rationalist" might, otherwise, have attributed to a fervid imagination or a habit of dreaming vividly, and assume "unconscious mental activity" to explain the literary output of an undoubtedly active mind backed by an "adhesive memory." Of course, in the formulation of this theory, which, by its terms, must absolve Smith from the charge of conscious and willful "imposture," no account is made of any such states of mind — not necessarily diseased, in spite of the theories of various pathologists — as afforded to even so learned a man as Swedenborg the elaborate dreams and visions recorded in his voluminous writings.

Reduced to plain English, the "automatic" theory is merely

a return to the one strongly suggested in the writings of several early critics of Mormonism, notably Alexander Campbell, that the " materials " for the Book of Mormon are only such as could be readily gleaned from the surroundings of the youthful Smith, as well as from the experiences and reflections of Sidney Rigdon. That is to say that it combines current theories of the origin, beliefs, etc., of the American Indians, with the " live questions " of the times — temperance, Free Masonry, baptism, anti-slavery, government, etc.— and a firsthand exposition of the Scriptures. Thus, from Campbell:

"He decides all the great controversies: infant baptism, ordination, the Trinity, regeneration, repentance, justification, the fall of man, the atonement, transubstantiation, fasting, penance, church government, religious experience, the call to the ministry, the general resurrection, eternal punishment, who may baptize, and even the question of Free Masonry, republican government, and the rights of man."—*Delusions: an Analysis of the Book of Mormon, p.* 13.

Although, as is perfectly possible, most of the subjects here listed are quite as properly matters of interest throughout Christian centuries, presumably also in the earliest statements of Christ's teachings, it is perfectly evident to a reader of the Book of Mormon that the assertions touching Free Masonry and temperance are rather overdrawn. As compared with the text of the book in question, it seems perfectly evident that the temperance and anti-Masonic movements of the early part of the nineteenth century are duplicated only in so far as they represent protests against the evils of secret combines of supposed unrighteous men and assertions of the superior virtues of abstinence. As properly could we conclude that the descendants of Jonadab the son of Rechab, who neither drank wine, nor dwelt in houses, were merely the Mohammedan Arabs of the present, who are credited with similar professions, transferred to antiquity by some imaginative author. Such comparisons are made only by persons who have a settled conviction that the book under discussion is and must be a " fraud," and that any argument based on resemblance, is competent to demonstrate.

By similarly inconclusive and forced arguments and statements, does Mr. Riley attempt to assert that the representation of the Lamanites (aborigines) in the Book of Mormon is entirely derived from current knowledge and opinions on the Indians. Thus, he asserts with confidence, on the authority of Francis Parkman, " that the primitive red man had no idea of a great spirit, and that the observations of early writers were made upon savages who had been for generations in contact with the doctrines of Christianity "— although some such " contact " is postulated for the Lamanites in the Book of Mormon. His pretended criticisms of the representations of this book on the doings of the Lamanites may be judged from the following:

> "In Joseph's lucubrations the mounds which the Indians regarded with great reverence, and of which they had lost the tradition [*foot note*, "D. G. Brinton claimed that tradition among the Indians is untrustworthy after three generations. Lectures at Yale University, 1898"], were built by Moroni as defenses of his people against the Lamanites; while the caches of arms were due to the penitent Lamanites burying their weapons rather than commit sin."—*The Founder of Mormonism, p.* 131.

The accuracy of investigation involved in this remark may be judged by reference to the passages in the Book of Mormon cited by him. Thus, on page 305 (383?), Alma xxiii. 13, "these are they that laid down the weapons of their rebellion, yea, all their weapons of war"; also on page 308, Alma xxiv. 25, "And it came to pass that they threw down their weapons of war, and they would not take them again, for they were stung for the murders which they had committed; and they came down even as their brethren, relying upon the mercies of those whose arms were lifted to slay them." As may be seen, the reference to "caches of arms" is very indistinct.

Similarly, Riley states that Smith must have derived the ideas found in the Book of Mormon from some of the various authors who wrote on the Indian problem at and near his time. He attempts to uphold some such contention by a comparison with Josiah Priest's *American Antiquities,* as follows:

> "Moreover the contents of this book resembles that of the plates of Nephi. The chapter on the course of the lost ten tribes is suggestive of the wanderings of the Nephites. In 1841 the Prophet, reviewing a volume of Mormon evidences, noted four parallel passages drawn between Priest's work and the Book of Mormon. The fact that the Mormon book was subsequently called in by Brigham Young, would excite a suspicion of Joseph's original plagiarism from Priest's *American Antiquities,* except that the latter appeared in 1833. However, Smith frequently printed in his newspaper curious notices of the current works on American archæology, and pointed with triumph to various 'ancient records,' as they were dug up from time to time."—*Ibid. p.* 127.

Why a candidate for a scientific degree in Yale University, or elsewhere, should include such suggestions as this in his book is not evident. Similarly inconclusive is his allegation that "the advocate of a prehistoric deism . . . quotes opaquely from the *Age of Reason* (by Thomas Paine) and for his hardness of heart is punished" (p. 155). The attempted demonstration of this assertion by the parallel column method reveals the exceeding "opaqueness" of the quotation; the two passages (Alma xxx. 15, 16, 17, 18, 25, 23, 27, 28 and selected passages from Part I of Paine's work) consist of fragments of sentences distributed over three pages in the Book of Mormon, being literally torn from their context to example this alleged parallelism of thought, and of a lengthy section from the other book, consisting, however, for the most part, of sentences entire.

When, however, Mr. Riley comes to his attempt to trace the sources of the theology of the Book of Mormon, which he describes as "a hodgepodge of heterodoxy" (p. 134), he does nothing more effectually than to demonstrate himself the veriest amateur in theological literature. Thus, his elaborate flounderings through the mazes of "Calvinism," "Arminianism" and "Hopkinsianism," fortified with parallel passages, demonstrates nothing in particular about the Book of Mormon, since he does not undertake a serious and exhaustive analysis, which is the only thing that could demonstrate his proposition. In one case he attempts a parallelism between a compound of passages from I Nephi (xv. 31, 29, 35, 32, 33, 35) and another from the Westminster Confession (Chapters 32-33), which is evidently the same kind of "hodge-podge" as the other effort just noted. Such evidences are not conclusive, particularly when they reveal nothing more distinctly than that their author knows little, or nothing, of the department of thought with which he is attempting to deal. Nevertheless, he apparently sums his estimate of the "theology of the Book of Mormon" in the follow passage:

> "On the whole, the influence here exerted was more practical than theoretical; one cause of the rapid spread of Mormonism was its partial adaptation of the ways and means of Methodism. Out of the latter's marvelous organization of local and itinerant clergy, with their various conferences, societies and circuits, the founder of the church of the Latter-day Saints extracted a dislocated hierarchy with unprecedented functions. What were the offices and duties of Mormon apostles and elders, evangelists and bishops, priests and teachers and deacons, may be obscurely seen in the last of the fourteen books. Judging from a parallel revelation given in June, 1830 (?), this little book of Mormon is essentially a book of discipline and has presumably (!) been added as an afterthought.
>
> "Without entering the penumbra of minor creeds, some idea has been gained of 'the confusion and strife among the different denominations,' in Joseph's fifteenth year. It is now ten years later and he has done little to reconcile the differences; instead he has but transferred to paper his own obfustication (slang!); his ancient record, like an old-fashioned mirror, gives back images vague and ill defined."—*Ibid. pp.* 147–148.

The attempt to derive the Mormon organization from the model of Methodism is merely silly. There is no resemblance between the two that does not hold for any two well-conceived organizations, such as the Society of Jesus and the German army, both of which have been compared to the organization of the Mormon Church, and in none too appreciative a spirit.

In his effort to prove that the Book of Mormon is really the mental history of Joseph Smith, a "cross-section of his brain," in fact, the best evidence adduced is undoubtedly the close parallel between the dream of Lehi, as recorded in the Book of Mormon (I. Nephi viii. 2–27) and a dream of his father, Joseph Smith, Sr., as described in a work entitled *Biographical Sketches* (pp. 58–59). These resemblances Mr. Riley explains in the following manner: "This quotation implies and reverts to ancestry; even more does it disclose environment." All this may be true, but it is also quite as reasonable that the elder Smith, in setting about to recount one of his vivid dreams, unconsciously borrowed many ideas from the account found in the Book of Mormon. A borrowing is assumed in either case, and there is no evidence that supports the one rather than the other.

Mr. Riley also undertakes to identify the famous "transcript," labeled *Caractors,* as an example of genuine "automatic writing," as follows:

> "As will be seen, the paper bears marks of being written under the influence of veritable crystal gazing. In that self-induced, trancelike state Joseph's involuntary scratchings would appear to him occult, mysterious, true revelations from heaven. For a scientific explanation of the matter there is no need to call in the activities of a 'second personality,' but merely those of the subconscious self. The scrawl is analogous to the scribblings of the undeveloped automatically-writing hand, such as is found even among the uncivilized. If the ultimate solution of this document is a problem for abnormal psychology, its make up is no great mystery. As the contents of the Book of Mormon can be traced to indigenous sources—the ideas which Joseph picked up in the Indian country where he lived—so it is with these characters. The more elaborate resemble the picture writing of the aborigines, such as would interest a boy. It is going too far to hunt for Greek and Hebrew letters, for the tables of foreign alphabets had not yet appeared in current dictionaries. [*Foot note,* "Noah Webster's Dictionary of this date has only tables of moneys, weights and measures. Thus the pound sterling sign occurs in the top line of the 'caractors.'"] The job is home-made: if Joseph had not taken the matter so seriously, this might be considered an amusing burlesquè on a farmer's almanac, for he has only half concealed the signs of the Zodiac, and those cabalistic aspects and nodes which may go with the planting of potatoes.
>
> "That which betrays the puerility, and, at the same time, the genuineness of the document, is the curious fact that the youth's own name appears twice in a sort of cryptogram. . . . As is elsewhere shown, Joseph's condition, under the influence of his 'Urim and Thummim,' was semi-hypnotic. Now it is a commonplace of experiment that while in this state, which is hardly more than reverie, the subject often writes back-handed, or backwards, or even left-handed with the right hand. Now if the transcription be turned over and read through from the back there may be deciphered towards the right end of the third line, below 'Caractors,' first, the letters JOE, backhand and rather indistinct; and, second, the letters SOJ, more upright and better formed. In other words, the youth, without knowing it, wrote his nickname entire and half of his given name in reverse."—*Ibid. pp.* 84–87.

In spite of Riley's confidence in his solution of the situation involved in the discussion of this "transcript," it is desirable to notice that there is no evidence adduced, that it is certainly an example of "automatically-writing hand." One could as reasonably claim that it is evidently copied from some original by a person unaccustomed to copying hieroglyphics of any kind, or to do any very neat or exact work with a pen. For this suggestion one might offer the evidence that, assuming the actual writing was begun at the upper left hand end, as with all modern scripts, there is evidence that the writing was started with large figures and careful attention to details, while, as the work progresses, the figures become smaller and less carefully formed, until, as one might assume, the last three lines are copied, not only smaller, but also much more rapidly, as though the writer had "got his speed."

There are some other interesting situations involved in this document: For example, although evidently written from left to right, and from the top line down, there seems to be a suggestion that the text copied, or intended to be represented, was written from right to left. We might gather this from the presence of the three black squares, in the second, sixth, and seventh lines, which seem to suggest some kind of stops, as between periods or paragraphs. The last one is on the left end of the seventh line. Similarly, several of the characters closely suggest forms familiar in the hieratic Egyptian, as, for example, the fifth figure from the right hand of the first line. This is probably the one referred to by Riley as the "pound sterling sign," but is far closer to the hieratic sign for "S." Similarly ill-judged is the remark that we see here the "signs of the Zodiac," which are "only half concealed." "Only half" must be equivalent to "very effectually," since careful search will enable one to recognize very few Zodiacal suggestions in this document. The first figure on the top line might be the sign for Pisces, were it not that the right hand curve is turned the wrong way. The fourth sign in this same line might be called Sagittarius by anyone in search of resemblances. Similarly, the fourth sign from the left end of line four might be held to represent the planet Mars, badly drawn, were it not for the fact that it shows a semi-circle, instead of a circle, and is thus a figure frequently seen in both Hieratic and demotic Egyptian scripts. The fifth sign from the left end of the last line might be held to represent the astronomical sign for the moon's nodes, or for an opposition of planets, but this figure, contrary to our friend's supposition, does not appear in "farmers' almanacs," hence must be from some other source. None of these signs seem to have

Caractors

Copy of the professed transcript from the "golden plates" of the Book of Mormon, now in the possession of Joseph Smith's grandson. Whatever may have been the origin of this document, two things are evident in regard to it: (1) It seems to be a studied transcript or combination of characters, not a mere haphazard product composed of any shapes or combinations that may have come to the writer's hand. (2) It is evidently the work of an unskilled penman, one unaccustomed to exact copying of figures, hence liable to distort, or miscopy, many of them. This may be judged from the second figure from the left on the top line, resembling a script capital "H," which seems to be repeated several times in the other lines, always varied. The whole inscription is, it is claimed, written in "reformed Egyptian," by which may be understood some form of Egyptian writing other than Hieroglyphic. Admitting the writer's evident inexperience as a copyist, it is possible to discover several close resemblances to some of the several forms of Hieratic. Thus, the "capital H" contains all the essential lines and strokes of the crouching lioness, the symbol for "L," a familiar figure, and might be held to be an attempt to represent it, without the knowledge of its original nature. Near the right hand end of the first line is a character resembling a script capital "L," which closely suggests the Hieratic character for "S." Immediately following it is another closely suggesting that for "M." Both seem to be repeated several times. Also, suggestions of the characters for "F," "Z," "P," "Kh," etc., seem to be present, also several others to be met with in various forms of Hieratic and Demotic writing.

much concern with the "planting of potatoes." The contention that this document is copied from some Egyptian original, instead of being automatically written might be argued from a number of resemblances, more or less obvious. Not to delay with this view, however, it might be urged in opposition to Lamb's criticism of the "capital letter H," the second sign on the first line (also five times repeated), might be held to represent an amateurish effort to represent the essential lines of the hieratic figure of the crouching lioness, the symbol of "L." The other figures mentioned by Lamb, notably those held to resemble English numerals, even the sign for ½, the ninth from the left of line six, are not foreign in appearance to some signs to be seen in hieratic manuscripts. Riley's "JOe" and "SoJ" are, as he remarks, "rather indistinct," and are nearly the only real presumption that he presents in favor of considering this document an example of "automatic writing," or simple fabrication. Such casual resemblances, of which many could be found in odd and foreign texts, need not be considered as over-significant.

As a matter of fact, however, when, for the sake of argument, we begin to explain Smith's activities by the hypothesis of automatism, we are immediately brought face-to-face with a system of phenomena by no means definitely hostile to the claims made by and for him. This is true, because, while there are numerous theories to account for the phenomena observed under this condition, there is no clue to an explanation that shall cover all its phases. There are also various kinds of automatism, including perfectly unconscious activities of the several muscles and senses, as well as the writing habit. In the automatism often occurring with psychic epilepsy, for example, the acts performed consist sometimes of mere repetitions, as when the patient writes the same name and address several times in succession; sometimes of ordinary acts done apart from the conscious participation of the will, as in somnambulism. In automatic writing and automatic speaking there seems to be very often some apparent "alter ego," a real doubling of the personality, which furnishes, apparently, the excuse for the spiritistic explanation of a disembodied "control," or some kind of "telepathic" communication with other intelligences. In default of exact knowledge of the causes and conditions of this phenomenon, many eminent psychologists have strongly inclined to the theory of a real "control," apart from the person apparently active. Scientific examination of the phenomena inclines, of course, to explanations involving only the individual self in question, as by the theory of two or more separate states of consciousness, really distinct from one another, as if appropriating various sets of cells or special areas of the brain. In discussing this matter, Prof. William James writes as follows:

"In 'mediumships' or 'possessions' the invasion and the passing away of the secondary state are both relatively abrupt, and the duration of the state is usually short — i.e., from a few minutes to a few hours. Whenever the secondary state is well developed no memory for aught that happened during it remains after the primary consciousness comes back. The subject during the secondary consciousness speaks, writes, or acts as if animated by a foreign person, and often names this foreign person and gives his history. In old times the foreign 'control' was usually a demon, and is so now in communities which favor that belief. With us (Americans) he gives himself out at the worst for an Indian or other grotesquely speaking but harmless personage. Usually he purports to be the spirit of a dead person known or unknown to those present, and the subject is then what we call a 'medium.' Mediumistic possession in all its grades seems to form a perfectly natural special type of alternate personality, and the susceptibility to it in some form is by no means an uncommon gift, in persons who have no other obvious nervous anomaly. The phenomena are very intricate, and are only just beginning to be studied in a proper scientific way. The lowest phase of mediumship is automatic writing, and the lowest grade of that is where the subject knows what words are coming, but feels impelled to write them as if from without. . . . Inspirational speaking, playing on musical instruments, etc., also belong to the relatively lower phases of possession, in which the normal self is not excluded from conscious participation in the performance, though their initiative seems to come from elsewhere. . . . One curious thing about trance-utterances is their generic similarity in different individuals. . . . If he (the control) ventures on higher intellectual flights, he abounds in a curiously vague optimistic philosophy-and-water, in which phrases about spirit, harmony, beauty, law, progression, development, etc., keep recurring. It seems exactly as if one author composed more than half of the trance-messages, no matter by whom they are uttered. Whether all subconscious selves are peculiarly susceptible to a certain stratum of the *Zeitgeist,* and get their inspiration from it, I know not; but this is obviously the case with the secondary selves which become 'developed' in spiritualist circles. There the beginnings of the medium trance are indistinguishable from effects of hypnotic suggestion. The subject assumes the rôle of a medium simply because opinion expects it of him under the conditions which are present. . . . But the odd thing is that persons unexposed to spiritualist traditions will so often act in the same way when they become entranced, speak in the name of the departed, go through the motions of their several death agonies, send messages about their happy home in the summer-land, and describe the ailments of those present. I have no theory to publish of these cases, several of which I have personally seen."—*Principles of Psychology, Vol.* I. *pp.* 393–394.

It is interesting to read such a resume of this "very intricate" phase of mental activity from the pen of so careful and tireless an investigator as Prof. James, and to find that there are very many phenomena that do not admit, apparently, classification under a theory of "secondary consciousness." It is perfectly well known that Prof. James was strongly inclined to accept certain phases of the spiritistic theory, which involves, in effect, that he was willing to admit that some phenomena could possibly be explained by assuming the activity of some person or entity apart from that of the "medium" himself. This explanation, indeed, is a part of human tradition, as already suggested, and has been invoked to account for the alleged influences of angels, demons, divine personages, even of the spirits of the departed, long before the rise of modern spiritism. The theory of an extra-personal "control" of some order seems to occur strongly in cases wherein the "subject" or "medium" speaks or acts on a basis of knowledge quite foreign to his normal or conscious equipment, as when he becomes a good musician "under control," although the reverse in normal conditions, or, when he speaks as if seeing or hearing things and persons at a distance, particularly when he reports correctly, as occasionally happens, if the accounts of investigators are to be accepted. It is thus possible to say that the very theory of control by an external personality, as assumed by Prof. Nelson, as quoted above, to explain the activities of Joseph Smith, may be justified, apparently, in great measure, by independent psychological investigation. Prof. James, in the work above quoted, describes at length a case of "automatic writing" which is singularly analogous to the one under discussion. He writes:

"As an example of the automatic writing performances I will quote from an account of his own case kindly furnished me by Mr. Sidney Dean of Warren, R. I., member of Congress from Connecticut from 1855 to 1859, who has been all his life a robust and active journalist, author, and man of affairs. He has for many years been a writing subject, and has a large collection of manuscript automatically produced.

"'Some of it,' he writes, 'is in hieroglyph, or strange compounded arbitrary characters, each series possessing a seeming unity in general design or character, followed by what purports to be a translation or rendering into mother English. I never attempted the seemingly impossible feat of copying the characters. They were cut with the precision of a graver's tool, and generally with a single rapid stroke of the pencil. Many languages, some obsolete and passed from history, are professedly given. To see them would satisfy you that no one could copy them except by tracing.

"'These, however, are but a small part of the phenomena. The "automatic" has given place to the *impressional,* and when the work is in progress I am in the normal condition, and seemingly two minds, intelligences, persons, are practically engaged. The writing is in my own hand but the dictation not of my own mind and will, but that of another, upon subjects of which I can have no knowledge and hardly a theory; and I, myself, consciously criticize the thought, fact, mode of expressing it, etc., while the hand is recording the subject-matter and even the words impressed to be written. If *I* refuse to write the sentence, or even the word, the impression instantly ceases, and my willingness must be mentally expressed before the work is resumed, and it is resumed at the point of cessation, even if it should be the middle of a sentence. Sentences are commenced without knowledge of mine as to their subject or ending. In fact, I have never known in advance the subject of disquisition.

"'There is in progress now, at uncertain times, not subject to my will, a series of twenty-four chapters upon the scientific features of life, moral, spiritual, eternal. . . . Each chapter is signed by the name of some person who has lived on earth,—some with whom I have been personally acquainted, others known in history. . . . I know nothing of the alleged authorship of any chapter until it is completed and the name impressed and appended. . . . I am interested not only in the reputed authorship,—of which I have nothing corroborative,—but in the philosophy taught, of which I was in ignorance until these chapters appeared. From my standpoint of life—which has been that of Biblical orthodoxy—the philosophy is new, seems to be reasonable, and is logically put. I confess to an inability to successfully controvert it to my own satisfaction.

"'It is an intelligent *ego* who writes, or else the influence assumes individuality, which practically makes of the influence a personality. It is *not* myself; of that I am conscious at every step of the process. I have also traversed the whole field of the claims of "unconscious cerebration," so called, so far as I am competent to critically examine it, and it fails, as a theory, in numberless points, when applied to this strange work through me. . . . The easiest and most natural solution to me is to admit the claim made, i.e., that it is a decarnated intelligence who writes. But *who?* that is the question. The names of scholars and thinkers who once lived are affixed to the most ungrammatical and weakest of bosh. . . .

"'It seems reasonable to me—upon the hypothesis that it is a person using another's mind or brain—that there must be more or less of that other's style or tone incorporated in the message, and that to the unseen personality, i.e., the power which impresses, the thought, the fact, or the philosophy, and not the style or tone, belongs. For instance, while the influence is impressing my brain with the greatest force and rapidity, so that my pencil fairly flies over the paper to record the thoughts, I am conscious that, in many cases, the vehicle of the thought, i.e., the language, is very naturally and familiar to me, as if, somehow, *my* personality as a writer was getting mixed up with the message. And, again, the style, language, everything, is entirely foreign to my own style.'"—*Ibid. pp.* 394–396.

This description and partial analysis of an unusual condition by a person, evidently intelligent and capable, gives the reader a very good idea of the conditions occasionally present in automatic mental action of several varieties. The phase mentioned, wherein foreign ideas are expressed in what this "subject" states are his own words and forms, is certainly significant in the present connection. Of course, in admitting that "possession" or "mediumship" may be something quite other than some merely unusual and obscure phase of brain activity, we do no more than admit that the traditional explanation of the involved phenomena may be correct. This might involve the theory that all people have a certain "spiritual" or "psychic" sense or susceptibility—whatever one may call it—by which impressions may be received of any intelligences or influences, embodied or disembodied, that may be capable of affecting it. Such may range in dignity from the stupidest among the departed, or the meanest of "evil spirits," to angels or divine personages. On this point Prof. James remarks:

"I am myself persuaded by abundant acquaintance with the trances of one medium that the 'control' may be altogether different from any *possible* waking self of the person. In the case I have in mind, it professes to be a certain departed French doctor; and is, I am convinced, acquainted with facts about the circumstances, and the living and dead relatives and acquaintances, of numberless sitters whom the medium never met before, and of whom she has never heard the names. . . . Many persons have found evidence conclusive to their minds that in some cases the control is really the departed spirit whom it pretends to be. The phenomena shade off so gradually into cases where this is obviously absurd, that the presumption (quite apart from *a priori* 'scientific' prejudice) is great against its being true."—*Ibid.* *p.* 396.

In the last paragraph, of course, Prof. James bases his judgment on the assumption that all phenomena of similar character, and occurring under similar conditions, are to be explained on one theory. The facts mentioned may be held to represent merely a series of gradations in the "vividness" of the impressions originated in and received from a common source or environment. Thus, admitting on his authority, as, apparently, we must, that the "French doctor" has the reported ability to discover facts unknown to the "medium" in her waking state, it is evident that there is no one theory that can be invoked to explain everything.

As already suggested, the Book of Mormon, considered as a literary production, *might* have originated in any one of several different ways—even by the assumed action of an invisible or distant personage upon the mind of its writer or "author and proprietor"—and have, possibly, the same character and contents. However, the real object of any study should be to discover, as far as possible, the significance of the book to the movement supposedly based on its teachings, rather than to guess, merely whence it may have come, or how it happened to be written. Whatever may have been the part played by Joseph Smith in this connection, it is altogether certain that he was sincerely convinced of the truth of its teachings, and consistently adherent to them in all his published utterances. It is asking a little too much of popular credulity to expect belief in the statement that an "unlettered youth," such as he is represented to have been, should be able to take a work written by some other hand, and so thoroughly assimilate its teachings that he could become their faithful exponent. It is also nothing less than a deliberate insult to public intelligence to ask belief in the hypothesis that a youth, not only ignorant, but depraved, as they tell us, could have originated any such book, let alone devote his life to publishing its teachings. Similarly beneath contempt are the familiar stories, dating from Howe and Tucker, to the effect that Smith, having found some white sand, or a brick, covered it with a napkin or other rag, and on persuading his family that it was a "gold bible," such as was reported to have been found in Canada, remarked to a friend — a certain loquacious Ingersoll —" I've got the d——d fools fixed, and will carry out the fun." Nevertheless, on the recognized theory that any argument is good when used against the Mormons, it is confidently served up by the latest critics of Mormonism, as if historically established. If Smith was a man possessed of ability sufficient to stir up all the antagonism, clerical and otherwise, that still persists, we may be logical in expecting him to be able to perform even more surprising things.

Of course, as must be evident to any candid and unprejudiced student of the history of Joseph Smith and of Mormonism, the origin of all the bitter opposition and persecution, which has disgraced our history, lay in the mere fact that he, a man outside of the clerical profession — nor even officially connected with any of even the most insignificant of Protestant sects — actually had the "presumption" to claim divine revelation and guidance, in the work of founding a church and promulgating a gospel at variance with, and in condemnation of, all other bodies whatever. It was for this reason that the numerous persecutions of this man and his adherents were usually, if not always, led by ordained Protestant preachers, or launched by their direct instigation. Apart from this "breach of proprieties"— for his persecutors did not have the specious excuse of "polygamy" until some of their most brutal persecutions had been years in history — Joseph Smith holds precisely the same relation to the Church founded by him as has been ascribed, in effect, to all other "reformers" and founders of religious bodies. Some of these, like George Fox and Emmanuel Swedenborg — both out of the clerical profession, hence both severely abused, criticized, and misrepresented, in the same manner as Joseph Smith — have made direct claims to divine revelation and guidance. Others, such as Luther, Calvin, Wesley, and numerous "reformers" of smaller importance, while making no such claim on their own behalf, have been credited with an authority and understanding of religious truths, which are not classed as of direct divine impartation merely because no such term has been applied to explain their activities. It remains, nevertheless, that, until within a very few years, before the disintegration of Protestantism began, these men have been regarded by their respective followers as the true, authorized and sufficient guides to an understanding of the truths of God. They have had ascribed to them all the functions of prophets and apostles, except the right to be so called. Indeed, in view of the varied deportment of Calvin, and numerous other "Christian" lights, the charges of "ignorance" and "rascality" might seem to lie, not altogether on one side. If, then, the teachings of the Book of Mormon, of Smith, and of the Church of Jesus Christ of Latter-day Saints, are not proved to be hostile to Scripture and sound reason, they are entitled to the same respectful consideration and attention as are those of our Luthers, Wesleys, Calvins and other "prophets." If, as would not be difficult to prove, they are of a far more "practical" nature, and even better calculated to meet the needs of the world, morally and sociologically, if no otherwise, the inference is that, in these respects, at least, they come nearer to the ideal of truth. But, as the truth of what a man teaches is not to be judged on the basis of knowledge regarding his personality, history or local reputation,— be these the best or the worst possible — so a book is not to be judged as a "divine revelation," because of its "elegant diction" and "lofty flights"; nor rejected in this same character, because of defects in these same particulars. "Ripe scholars," and other varieties of fault-finders, are now busily picking flaws in the Bible itself, and gaining adherents, even among professing Christians — and many of these absurdly argue that the "higher criticism," so called, is laying the foundations of a "deeper and more vital faith." It is possible to find faults with any book, and condemn its literary and other qualities, just as the "higher critics" mangle the Bible. It is no argument. Obviously, an excellent method of settling such a dispute, and finding out the real truth of the claim of divine authority, supposed to be back of a book, is to apply the test prescribed in the Book of Mormon itself:

> "Behold I would exhort you that when ye shall read these things, if it be wisdom in God that ye should read them . . . that ye would ask God, the eternal Father, in the name of Christ, if these things are not true; and if ye shall ask with a sincere heart, with real intent, having faith in Christ, he will manifest the truth of it unto you, by the power of the Holy Ghost; and by the power of the Holy Ghost ye may know the truth of all things."—*Moroni,* x. 3–5.

No anti-Mormon has ever stated that he has followed this advice, and received no "testimony." This may be, however, because anti-Mormons are afraid that they might learn "something disagreeable."

NOTE I.—DANITES OR DESTROYING ANGELS.

The stories persistently circulated about a murderous order among the Mormons, known as "Danites," or "Destroying angels," deserve some kind of brief notice in a book like this. As a matter of fact, in spite of the repetition of this story by all anti-Mormon writers, all on the same allegations at the start, there is no respectable evidence that any such order or society was ever prominent in Mormon affairs, or that it ever committed the atrocities charged by enemies. The sole excuse for the tale in the beginning was the "affidavit" uttered by Thomas B. Marsh, and affirmed by Orson Hyde (page 102), which, however, was negatived by their subsequent return to the Church. The following account of the matter appears in the journal of Joseph Smith, among entries made sometime in the latter part of 1838:

"While the evil spirits were raging up and down in the state (Missouri) to raise mobs against the 'Mormons,' Satan himself was no less busy in striving to stir up mischief in the camp of the Saints: and among the most conspicuous of his willing devotees was one Doctor Sampson Avard, who had been in the Church but a short time, and who, although he had generally behaved with a tolerable degree of external decorum, was secretly aspiring to be the greatest of the great, and become the leader of the people. This was his pride and his folly, but as he had no hopes of accomplishing it by gaining the hearts of the people openly he watched his opportunity with the brethren—at a time when mobs oppressed, robbed, whipped, burned, plundered and slew, till forbearance seemed no longer a virtue, and nothing but the grace of God without measure could support men under such trials—to form a secret combination by which he might rise a mighty conqueror, at the *expense and the overthrow of the Church.* This he tried to accomplish by his smooth, flattering, and winning speeches, which he frequently made to his associates, while his room was well guarded by some of his followers, ready to give him the signal on the approach of anyone who would not approve of his measures.

"In these proceedings he stated that he had the sanction of the heads of the Church for what he was about to do; and by his smiles and flattery, persuaded them to believe it, and proceeded to administer to the few under his control, an oath, binding them to everlasting secrecy to everything which should be communicated to them by himself. Thus Avard initiated members into his band, firmly binding them, by all that was sacred, in the protection of each other in all things that were lawful; and was careful to picture out a great glory that was then hovering over the Church, and would soon burst upon the Saints as a cloud by day, and a pillar of fire by night, and would soon unveil the slumbering mysteries of heaven, which would gladden the hearts and arouse the stupid spirits of the Saints of the latter day, and fill their hearts with that love which is unspeakable and full of glory, and arm them with power, that the gates of hell could not prevail against them; and would often affirm to his company that the principal men of the Church had put him forward as a spokesman, and a leader of this band, which he named *Danites.*

"Thus he duped many, which gave him the opportunity of figuring as a person of importance. He held his meetings daily, and carried on his crafty work in great haste, to prevent mature reflection upon the matter by his followers, until he had them bound under the penalties of death to keep the secrets and certain signs of the organization by which they were to know each other by day or night.

"After these performances, he held meetings to organize his men into companies of tens and fifties, appointing a captain over each company. After completing this organization, he went on to teach the members of it their duty under the orders of their captains; he then called his captains together and taught them in a secluded place, as follows:

"'My brethren, as you have been chosen to be our leading men, our captains to rule over this last kingdom of Jesus Christ—and you have been organized after the ancient order—I have called upon you here to-day to teach you, and instruct you in the things that pertain to your duty, and to show you what your privileges are, and what they soon will be. Knew ye not, brethren, that it soon will be your privilege to take your respective companies and go out on a scout on the borders of the settlements, and take to yourselves spoils of the goods of the ungodly Gentiles? for it is written, the riches of the Gentiles shall be consecrated to my people, the house of Israel; and thus you will waste away the Gentiles by robbing and plundering them of their property; and in this way we will build up the kingdom of God, and roll forth the little stone that Daniel saw cut out of the mountain without hands, and roll forth until it filled the whole earth. For this is the very way that God destines to build up His kingdom in the last days. If any of us should be recognized, who can harm us? for we will stand by each other and defend one another in all things. If our enemies swear against us, we can swear also. (The captains were confounded this, but Avard continued). Why do you startle at this, brethren? As the Lord liveth, I would swear to a lie to clear any of you; and if this would not do, I would put them or him under the sand as Moses did the Egyptian; and in this way we will consecrate much unto the Lord, and build up His kingdom; and who can stand against us? And if any of us transgress, we will deal with him amongst ourselves. And if any one of this Danite society reveals any of these things, I will put him where the dogs cannot bite him.'

"At this lecture all of the officers revolted, and said it would not do, they would not go into any such measures, and it would not do to name any such thing; 'such proceedings would be in open violation of the laws of our country, would be robbing our fellow-citizens of their rights, and are not according to the language and doctrine of Christ, or of the Church of Latter-day Saints.'

"Avard replied, and said there were no laws that were executed in justice, and he cared not for them, this being a different dispensation, a dispensation of the fullness of times; in this dispensation he learned from the Scriptures that the kingdom of God was to put down all other kingdoms, and the Lord Himself was to reign, and His laws alone were the laws that would exist.

"Avard's teachings were still manfully rejected by all. Avard then said that they had better drop the subject, although he had received his authority from Sidney Rigdon the evening before. The meeting then broke up; the eyes of those present were opened, Avard's craft was no longer in the dark, and but very little confidence was placed in him, even by the warmest of the members of his Danite scheme.

"When the knowledge of Avard's rascality came to the Presidency of the Church, he was cut off from the Church, and every means proper used to destroy his influence, at which he was highly incensed, and went about whispering his evil insinuations, but finding every effort unavailing, he again turned conspirator, and sought to make friends with the mob.

"And here let it be distinctly understood, that these companies of tens and fifties got up by Avard, were altogether separate from those companies of tens and fifties organized by the brethren for self-defense, in case of an attack from the mob. This latter organization was called into existence more particularly that in this time of alarm no family or person might be neglected; therefore, one company would be engaged in drawing wood, another in cutting it, another in gathering corn, another in grinding, another in butchering, another in distributing meat, etc., etc., so that all should be employed in turn, and no one lack the necessaries of life. Therefore, let no one hereafter, by mistake or design, confound this organization of the Church for good and righteous purposes, with the organization of the 'Danites' of the apostate Avard, which died almost before it existed."—*History of the Church, Vol.* III, *pp.* 178–182.

NOTE II.—POLYGAMY AND THE LAW AS INTERPRETED BY CHRIST.

On page 217 of the present volume the remark occurs that the institution of polygamy, or plural marriage, as recognized, or allowed, by the Mosaic Law, was recognized by Christ Himself, and not repudiated. The evidence for this statement is to be found in such analysis of Christ's teachings on marriage and divorce, as are given in the little volume, "The Scriptural Doctrine of Divorce," by Edward Williams, A.M. This author adopts the thesis that the dicta of Jesus upon the subject of divorce are all framed in perfect harmony with the precedent principles of Jewish law, and are to be understood only in their relation to them. Commenting on the teachings involved in Christ's divorce dicta (Matt. v. 32; xix. 9; Luke xvi. 18; Mark x. 11–12), he says:

"In every one of Jesus' dicta on marriage and divorce He is as surely combating an existing evil as enunciating a vital principle. Dr. Scott, a thoroughly conservative, and highly scholarly commentator, says (*in loc.* Deut. xxiv: 1) 'In the days of Christ the Jewish teachers, having construed this permission into a commandment, extended it to the most frivolous matters: so that a licentious mind could not desire more allowance. Hence, divorces prevailed to the disuse of polygamy and to the still greater hardship of the women who were sent away, one after another, under color of this law, on various pretexts, to make way for a new object of the roving affections.'

"In support of the accuracy of this statement another commentator remarks, 'Josephus saith, "The law runs thus, He that will be disjoined from his wife for any cause whatsoever, as many such cases there are, let him give her a bill of divorce," and he confesseth that he himself put away his wife after she had borne him three children, because he was not pleased with her behavior.' Rabbi Hillel's interpretation of the Law seems to amount to an almost unlimited freedom in the repudiation of wives, and the familiar quotation from some unnamed rabbi, to the effect that, 'if a man sees a woman, whom he loves better than his wife, let him divorce his wife and marry her,' may be considered a fair sample of the opinions current in Jesus' time.

"It may be readily seen that Jesus' objection to such a practice as this is on perfectly Mosaic grounds; for, in the first place, contrary to Mosaic Law, the woman is faultless, hence not divorceable; secondly, she is repudiated in order to make room for another wife, which is impiously contrary to the provisions of Exod. xxi. 10, which specifies: 'If he take him another wife; her food, her raiment and her duty of marriage shall he not diminish.' We can see, therefore, with how great consistency this practice of 'covering violence as with a garment' and 'dealing treacherously' with a wife, operating, as it certainly did in Jesus' time, not only to iniquitously dissolve many marriage contracts, but also, and particularly, to practically annihilate the very institution of matrimony can be described by no gentler term than adultery.

. . . .

"In divorcing a *legally* faultless wife, in order that he may marry another, a man is declared guilty, not because of either the divorcing or the remarrying — divorce, remarriage and polygamy are all allowed by the Mosaic statutes — but solely and entirely because the motive and object of divorce is the remarriage. For this reason the repudiating husband who does not immediately remarry is not accused of direct offence; his only fault being that in the act of divorcing a wife, apart from grave and sufficient reason, he causes her thereby to adulterate (Matt. v. 32), probably in the event of her taking a second husband. The consistency of this dictum with legal principles is readily perceived when we consider that a woman illegally divorced is, in reality, still in coverture; and that in contracting a union with another man, she is not married, but, technically and morally, adulterous.

. . . .

"To sum up, then, the occasions of the crime of adultery, as we have thus far discovered them, we find, on lines strictly Mosaic, that:

"(1) A husband is guilty in marrying one woman after groundlessly divorcing another, in order to make room for that second woman.

"(2) A wife so divorced is guilty in taking a second husband when not legally free herself.

"(3) The second husband is guilty in marrying a woman, who, strictly speaking, is still another's wife.

"If, however, as some hold, the Lord, in His dicta on divorce, is only advocating the original and essential 'indissolubleness' of all ratified marriages, with reference to no law or practice whatsoever, it were difficult, indeed, to understand how it is that He makes adulterous a man marrying a repudiated wife — and his motives for so doing may have been of the noblest and most Mosaic character, to provide her a home and protection, also quite in harmony with modern laws on the subject, since he is marrying the 'aggrieved party' — while the woman married by the repudiating husband is accused in no regard. To be sure, Mark (x. 11–12) incriminates neither the second wife of the *repudiating* husband, nor the second husband of the *repudiating* wife, when a woman has thus usurped the man's prerogative, but, if, by comparison of his version with those of Matthew and Luke, we are to assume that those persons marrying the *guilty* and *adulterous* parties in such invalid divorce transactions are innocent of all offense, while those persons marrying the *innocent* and *violenced* parties are accused of adultery, we have a very remarkable pronouncement indeed, and one also utterly at variance with all ancient or modern principles of law.

"But what light can the Mosaic Law throw upon this apparently 'contradictory' situation? Here the matter is only too simple, for we readily perceive that the second wife of the *repudiating* husband is *technically* guiltless, because that according to the Jewish Law polygamy was lawful, a fact which Jesus evidently recognizes, consistently preferring a plurality of wives to monogamy maintained by a series of legally invalid and iniquitous repudiations. The *repudiated* woman's second husband is guilty of offense because, upon the strict grounds of interpretation that Jesus adopts he has taken to wife a woman still rightfully in bonds to another — and this by the old law was a capital crime." — *Scriptural Doctrine of Divorce*, pp. 38–39, 45–46, 47.

It is well to remind the reader that the method of divorcing recognized by the Mosaic Law, and mentioned by Christ in the passages relating to divorce, consisted merely in the giving of a "bill of divorce" to the wife, in accord with the provisions of Deut. xxiv. 1–2. It was, therefore, an act of repudiation, rather than of divorce in the modern judicial sense. The above analysis, which has strong claim to being accurate, establishes the fact that polygamy is recognized as an essential feature of Jewish law and custom.

SELECTIONS FROM THE BOOK OF MORMON
THE VISION OF NEPHI

I Nephi, Chapter II., 14–36.

And it came to pass that I saw the heavens open; and an angel came down and stood before me; and he said unto me, Nephi, what beholdest thou?

And I said unto him, a virgin, most beautiful and fair above all other virgins.

And he said unto me, Knowest thou the condescension of God?

And I said unto him, I know that he loveth his children; nevertheless, I do not know the meaning of all things.

And he said unto me, Behold the virgin whom thou seest, is the mother of the Son of God, after the manner of the flesh.

And it came to pass that I beheld that she was carried away in the Spirit; and after she had been carried away in the Spirit for the space of a time, the angel spake unto me, saying, Look!

And I looked and beheld the virgin again, bearing a child in her arms.

And the angel said unto me, Behold the Lamb of God, yea, even the Son of the Eternal Father! Knowest thou the meaning of the tree which thy father saw?

And I answered him saying, Yea, it is the love of God, which sheddeth itself abroad in the hearts of the children of men; wherefore, it is the most desirable above all things.

And he spake unto me saying, Yea, and the most joyous to the soul.

And after he had said these words, he said unto me, Look! and I looked, and I beheld the Son of God going forth among the children of men; and I saw many fall down at his feet and worship him.

And it came to pass that I beheld that the rod of iron which my father had seen, was the word of God, which led to the fountain of living waters, or to the tree of life; which waters are a representation of the love of God; and I also beheld that the tree of life was a representation of the love of God.

And the angel said unto me again, Look and behold the condescension of God!

And I looked and beheld the Redeemer of the world, of whom my father had spoken; and I also beheld the prophet, who should prepare the way before him. And the Lamb of God went forth and was baptized of him; and after he was baptized, I beheld the heavens open, and the Holy Ghost come down out of heaven and abode upon him in the form of a dove.

And I beheld that he went forth ministering unto the people, in power and great glory; and the multitudes were gathered together to hear him; and I beheld that they cast him out from among them.

And I also beheld twelve others following him. And it came to pass that they were carried away in the Spirit, from before my face, and I saw them not.

And it came to pass that the angel spake unto me again, saying, Look! And I looked, and I beheld the heavens open again, and I saw angels descending upon the children of men; and they did minister unto them.

And he spake unto me again, saying, Look! And I looked, and I beheld the Lamb of God going forth among the children of men. And I beheld multitudes of people who were sick, and who were afflicted with all manner of diseases, and with devils, and unclean spirits; and the angel spake and showed all these things unto me. And they were healed by the power of the Lamb of God; and the devils and the unclean spirits were cast out.

And it came to pass that the angel spake unto me again, saying, Look! And I looked and beheld the Lamb of God, that he was taken by the people; yea, the Son of the everlasting God was judged of the world; and I saw and bear record.

And I, Nephi, saw that he was lifted up upon the cross, and slain for the sins of the world.

And after he was slain I saw the multitudes of the earth, that they were gathered together to fight against the apostles of the Lamb; for thus were the twelve called by the angel of the Lord.

And the multitude of the earth was gathered together; and I beheld that they were in a large and spacious building, like unto the building which my father saw! And the angel of the Lord spake unto me again, saying, Behold the world and the wisdom thereof; yea, behold the house of Israel hath gathered together, to fight against the twelve apostles of the Lamb.

And it came to pass that I saw and bear record, that the great and spacious building was the pride of the world: and it fell; and the fall thereof was exceeding great. And the angel of the Lord spake unto me again, saying, Thus shall be the destruction of all nations, kindreds, tongues, and people, that shall fight against the twelve apostles of the Lamb.

Mosiah, Chapter III, 5–27.

For behold, the time cometh, and is not far distant, that with power, the Lord Omnipotent who reigneth, who was, and is from all eternity to all eternity, shall come down from heaven, among the children of men, and shall dwell in a tabernacle of clay, and shall go forth amongst men, working mighty miracles, such as healing the sick, raising the dead, causing the lame to walk, the blind to receive their sight, and the deaf to hear, and curing all manner of diseases;

And he shall cast out devils, or the evil spirits which dwell in the hearts of the children of men.

And lo, he shall suffer temptations, and pain of body, hunger, thirst, and fatigue, even more than man can suffer, except it be unto death; for behold, blood cometh from every pore, so great shall be his anguish for the wickedness and the abominations of his people.

And he shall be called Jesus Christ, the Son of God the Father of heaven and earth, the Creator of all things, from the beginning; and his mother shall be called Mary.

And lo, he cometh unto his own, that salvation might come unto the children of men, even through faith on his name; and even after all this, they shall consider him a man, and say that he hath a devil, and shall scourge him, and shall crucify him.

And he shall rise the third day from the dead; and behold, he standeth to judge the world; and behold, all these things are done, that a righteous judgment might come upon the children of men.

For behold, and also his blood atoneth for the sins of those who have fallen by the transgression of Adam, who have died, not knowing the will of God concerning them, or who have ignorantly sinned.

But wo, wo unto him who knoweth that he rebelleth against God; for salvation cometh to none such, except it be through repentance and faith on the Lord Jesus Christ.

And the Lord God hath sent his holy prophets among all the children of men, to declare these things to every kindred, nation, and tongue, that thereby whosoever should believe that Christ should come, the same might receive remission of their sins, and rejoice with exceeding great joy, even as though he had already come among them.

Yet the Lord God saw that his people were a stiff-necked people, and he appointed unto them a law, even the law of Moses.

And many signs, and wonders, and types, and shadows shewed he unto them, concerning his coming; and also holy prophets spake unto them concerning his coming; and yet they hardened their hearts, and understood not that the law of Moses availeth nothing, except it were through the atonement of his blood;

And even if it were possible that little children could sin, they could not be saved; but I say unto you they are blessed; for behold, as in Adam, or by nature they fall, even so the blood of Christ atoneth for their sins.

And moreover, I say unto you, that there shall be no other name given, nor any other way nor means whereby salvation can come unto the children of men, only in and through the name of Christ, the Lord Omnipotent.

For behold he judgeth, and his judgment is just; and the infant perisheth not that dieth in his infancy; but men drink damnation to their own souls, except they humble themselves and become as little children, and believe that salvation was, and is, and is to come, in and through the atoning blood of Christ, the Lord Omnipotent;

For the natural man is an enemy to God, and has been from the fall of Adam, and will be, for ever and ever; but if he yields to the enticings of the Holy Spirit, and putteth off the natural man, and becometh a saint, through the atonement of Christ the Lord, and becometh as a child, submissive, meek, humble, patient, full of love, willing to submit to all things which the Lord seeth fit to inflict upon him, even as a child doth submit to his father.

And moreover, I say unto you, that the time shall come, when the knowledge of a Saviour shall spread throughout every nation, kindred, tongue, and people.

And behold, when that time cometh, none shall be found blameless before God, except it be little children, only through repentance and faith on the name of the Lord God Omnipotent;

And even at this time, when thou shalt have taught thy people the things which the Lord thy God hath commanded thee, even then are they found no more blameless in the sight of God, only according to the words which I have spoken unto thee.

THE DREAM OF LEHI

I Nephi, Chap. VIII, 5–38

And it came to pass that I saw a man, and he was dressed in a white robe: and he came and stood before me.

And it came to pass that he spake unto me, and bade me follow him.

And it came to pass that as I followed him, I beheld myself that I was in a dark and dreary waste.

And after I had travelled for the space of many hours in darkness, I began to pray unto the Lord that he would have mercy on me, according to the multitude of his tender mercies.

And it came to pass after I had prayed unto the Lord, I beheld a large and spacious field.

And it came to pass that I beheld a tree, whose fruit was desirable to make one happy.

And it came to pass that I did go forth, and partake of the fruit thereof; and I beheld that it was most sweet, above all that I ever before tasted. Yea, and I beheld that the fruit thereof was white, to exceed all the whiteness that I had ever seen.

And as I partook of the fruit thereof, it filled my soul with exceeding great joy; wherefore, I began to be desirous that my family should partake of it also; for I knew that it was desirable above all other fruit.

And as I cast my eyes round about, that perhaps I might discover my family also, I beheld a river of water; and it ran along, and it was near the tree of which I was partaking the fruit.

And I looked to behold from whence it came; and I saw the head thereof a little way off; and at the head thereof, I beheld your mother Sariah, and Sam, and Nephi; and they stood as if they knew not whither they should go.

And it came to pass that I beckoned unto them; and I also did say unto them with a loud voice, That they should come unto me, and partake of the fruit, which was desirable above all other fruit.

And it came to pass that they did come unto me, and partake of the fruit also.

And it came to pass that I was desirous that Laman and Lemuel should come and partake of the fruit also; wherefore, I cast mine eyes towards the head of the river, that perhaps I might see them.

And it came to pass that I saw them, but they would not come unto me.

And I beheld a rod of iron, and it extended along the bank of the river, and led to the tree by which I stood.

And I also beheld a straight and narrow path, which came along by the rod of iron, even to the tree by which I stood; and it also led by the head of the fountain, unto a large and spacious field, as if it had been a world;

And I saw numberless concourses of people; many of whom were pressing forward, that they might obtain the path which led unto the tree by which I stood.

And it came to pass that they did come forth, and commence in the path which led to the tree.

And it came to pass that there arose a mist of darkness; yea, even an exceeding great mist of darkness, insomuch that they who had commenced in the path, did lose their way, that they wandered off and were lost.

And it came to pass that I beheld others pressing forward, and they came forth and caught hold of the end of the rod of iron; and they did press forward through the mist of darkness, clinging to the rod of iron, even until they did come forth and partake of the fruit of the tree.

And after they had partaken of the fruit of the tree, they did cast their eyes about as if they were ashamed.

And I also cast my eyes round about, and beheld, on the other side of the river of water, a great and spacious building; and it stood as it were in the air, high above the earth;

And it was filled with people, both old and young, both male and female; and their manner of dress was exceeding fine; and they were in the attitude of mocking and pointing their fingers towards those who had come at, and were partaking of the fruit.

And after they had tasted of the fruit they were ashamed, because of those that were scoffing at them; and they fell away into forbidden paths and were lost.

And now I, Nephi, do not speak all the words of my father.

But, to be short in writing, behold, he saw other multitudes pressing forward; and they came and caught hold of the end of the rod of iron; and they did press their way forward, continually holding fast to the rod of iron, until they came forth and fell down and partook of the fruit of the tree.

And he also saw other multitudes feeling their way towards that great and spacious building.

And it came to pass that many were drowned in the depths of the fountain; and many were lost from his view, wandering in strange roads.

And great was the multitude that did enter into that strange building. And after they did enter into that building, they did point the finger of scorn at me, and those that were partaking of the fruit also; but we heeded them not.

These are the words of my father: For as many as heeded them, had fallen away.

And Laman and Lemuel partook not of the fruit, said my father.

And it came to pass after my father had spoken all the words of his dream or vision, which were many, he said unto us, because of these things which he saw in a vision, he exceedingly feared for Laman and Lemuel; yea, he feared lest they should be cast off from the presence of the Lord:

And he did exhort them then with all the feeling of a tender parent, that they would hearken to his words that, perhaps the Lord would be merciful to them, and not cast them off; yea, my father did preach unto them.

And after he had preached unto them, and also prophesied unto them of many things, he bade them to keep the commandments of the Lord; and he did cease speaking unto them.

THE FRAILTIES, AND THE FOOLISHNESS OF MEN.

II Nephi ix. 28–38

O that cunning plan of the evil one! O the vainness, and the frailties, and the foolishness of men! When they are learned, they think they are wise, and they hearken not unto the counsel of God, for they set it aside, supposing they know of themselves,—wherefore, their wisdom is foolishness, and it profiteth them not. And they shall perish.

But to be learned is good, if they hearken unto the counsels of God.

But wo unto the rich, who are rich as to the things of the world. For because they are rich, they despise the poor, and they persecute the meek, and their hearts are upon their treasures; wherefore their treasure is their God. And behold, their treasure shall perish with them also.

And wo unto the deaf, that will not hear; for they shall perish.

Wo unto the blind, that will not see; for they shall perish also.

Wo unto the uncircumcised of heart; for a knowledge of their iniquities shall smite them at the last day.

Wo unto the liar; for he shall be thrust down to hell.

Wo unto the murderer, who deliberately killeth; for he shall die.

Wo unto them who commit whoredoms; for they shall be thrust down to hell.

Yea, wo unto those that worship idols; for the devil of all devils delighteth in them.

And, in fine, wo unto all those who die in their sins; for they shall return to God. and behold his face and remain in their sins.

O, THAT I WERE AN ANGEL!

Alma xxix. 1–9

O that I were an angel, and could have the wish of mine heart, that I might go forth and speak with the trump of God, with a voice to shake the earth, and cry repentance unto every people;

Yea, I would declare unto every soul, as with the voice of thunder, repentance, and the plan of redemption, that they should repent and come unto our God, that there might not be more sorrow upon all the face of the earth.

But behold I am a man, and do sin in my wish; for I ought to be content with the things which the Lord hath allotted unto me.

I ought not to harrow up in my desires, the firm decree of a just God, for I know that he granteth unto men according to their desire, whether it be unto death or unto life; yea, I know that he allotteth unto men, according to their will; whether they be unto salvation or unto destruction.

Yea, and I know that good and evil have come before all men; or he that knoweth not good from evil is blameless; but he that knoweth good and evil, to him it is given according to his desires; whether he desireth good or evil, life or death, joy or remorse of conscience.

Now seeing that I know these things, why should I desire more than to perform the work to which I have been called?

Why should I desire that I was an angel, that I could speak unto all the ends of the earth?

For behold, the Lord doth grant unto all nations, of their own nation and tongue, to teach his word; yea, in wisdom, all that he seeth fit that they should have; therefore we see that the Lord doth counsel in wisdom, according to that which is just and true.

I know that which the Lord hath commanded me, and I glory in it: I do not glory of myself, but I glory in that which the Lord hath commanded me; yea, and this is my glory, that perhaps I may be an instrument in the hands of God, to bring some soul to repentance; and this is my joy.

INDEX